YEARBOOK OF AMERICAN & CANADIAN CHURCHES 1999

Previous Issues

Sixty-Seventh Issue   Annual

YEARBOOK OF AMERICAN & CANADIAN CHURCHES 1999

Edited by Eileen W. Lindner

Prepared and edited for the
National Council of the Churches of Christ in the U.S.A.
475 Riverside Drive, New York, NY 10115-0050

Published and Distributed
by Abingdon Press
Nashville

YEARBOOK OF AMERICAN & CANADIAN CHURCHES
1999

Telephone: (212) 870-2031

Fax: (212) 870-2817

E-mail: yearbook@ncccusa.org

Printed in the United States of America
ISBN 0-687-07474-6
ISSN 0195-9034
Library of Congress catalog card number
16-5762

Preparation of this Yearbook is an annual project of the National Council of the Churches of Christ in the United States of America.

This is the sixty-seventh edition of a yearbook that was first published in 1916. Previous editions have been entitled: Federal Council Yearbook (1916-1917), Yearbook of the Churches (1918-1925), The Handbook of the Churches (1927), The New Handbook of the Churches (1928), Yearbook of American Churches (1933-1972), and Yearbook of American and Canadian Churches (1973-1999).

Roger L. Burgess	*Project Director*
Joan Brown Campbell	*Publisher*
Eileen W. Lindner	*Editor*
Noah C. Migel	*Assistant Editor*
Derek J. Lander	*Assistant Editor*

Editor's Preface

A Word of Thanks

As in previous years, the 1999 Yearbook of American & Canadian Churches represents the striving of hundreds of individuals who gather, analyze and report data and of hundreds more who carefully review proofsheets for the Yearbook's directories. Only through such a concerted effort can an annual publication like the *Yearbook* hope to achieve a degree of comprehensiveness and accuracy. We are grateful to all who contribute in both great and small ways to this effort. After two years as assistant editor, Noah C. Migel will return to his pursuit of graduate studies. He departs with our continued admiration and good wishes.

Features of the 1999 Yearbook

With the twentieth century rapidly drawing to a close we have provided Table 1 in the "Trends and Development" chapter to permit a backward glance at church growth over the past one hundred years. While this table tells the tale of church membership, it cannot fully reflect the growth in diversity of U.S. church life in this century. That story is better recounted in chapter 6, "Religious Bodies in the United States," which this year reports 213 religious bodies, a record number. The Trends chapter likewise reflects a continued stability in rates of growth and decline and reveals a modest apparent increase in benevolence giving.

Making sense of trends in American life involves more, of course, than statistical reports. In this sixty-seventh edition of the *Yearbook*, Gustav Niebuhr, Senior Religion Correspondent at the *New York Times*, reflects on "America's Religion at the Millenium's End," giving attention to the megachurch as one contemporary expression of church life.

The place of religion in American life has frequently been the focus of attempts to understand the culture of the United States. By century's end a host of both general and specialized centers for research related to religious life have been established. A new feature of the *Yearbook* is "Sources in Religion-Related Research," chapter 3, which lists selected centers of research and study. Both practitioners and scholars will find here new sources of data and analysis on topics as diverse as financial giving and mission personnel.

In the 1998 *Yearbook* we initiated a chapter on the "Electronic Church." Greatly expanded for the 1999 edition, this chapter was compiled with the assistance of Ric Justice of Wylie, Texas. For those seeking information about religious organizations via the Internet, this chapter provides an unparalleled guide.

One of the most highly used directories within the *Yearbook* is "United States Regional and Local Ecumenical Bodies." This year we have introduced a special program index for chapter 9, offering a compilation of agencies that provide programs in five key areas including: Interfaith Dialogue, Hunger/Food Programs, Youth Activities, Faith and Order, Homelessness/Shelter Ministries.

Chapter 12, "Church Archives and Historical Records Collections," has been entirely revamped with the assistance of Mark Duffey, Episcopal Church Archivist. This effort reflects significant improvement in contact information for the bulk of the nation's religion related archives.

Finally, the calendar for 1999-2002 has again been compiled from various sources but with special assistance from Father Will Krieger of Ecumenical Books, San Antonio, Texas.

As we move toward the new century and millennium, aided by new technologies, the student of American religious life can hope to secure the data necessary to analyze more deeply and more comprehensively that life. Guided by such reliable data and analysis we may move forward in ever-greater assurance of our understanding of the past. Those who have compiled data in the past, as well as those who have assisted in this year's edition of the *Yearbook*, deserve our thanks.

Eileen W. Lindner
Editor

v

Contents

I

COMMENTARY

Trends & Developments

The century which began in the United States as a much heralded "Christian Century" appears at its conclusion to have been the "Century of Religious Pluralism". To be sure, the growth in religious pluralism was more characteristic of the last third of the century than of the first two-thirds.

The twentieth century in the United States opened with a vast expansion of population from immigration and of geographical territory by the addition of 15 states between 1850–1912. The religious affiliations of new arrivals as well as the character and culture of the frontier itself were generative of shifts in the relative size of American denominations. Exactly a century ago the celebrated revival preacher Dwight L. Moody died. That date has become an enduring symbol of the close of the great revival period.

In the new century, the vigor of voluntary evangelical Christianity, already fractured by sectional rivalries and schisms in the Civil War era, found fresh areas of conflict within and among religious traditions. Theological tensions between fundamentalists and proponents of the liberal synthesis of Christian faith and modern thought, along with the rise of Pentecostal churches, set the stage for protracted struggles and growing diversity within American Christianity. Through two world wars, the postwar boom in population and church affiliation, and the "Death of God" controversy of the 1960s, the various strands of Christian tradition have made their way, sometimes in comfortable complacency with regard to the culture around them and sometimes in sharp conflict with it. While church historians work at the analysis of the century now winding to a close, the church statistician can contribute a numerical snapshot of religious affiliation, which despite periodic boom and bust cycles, remains among the highest in the industrial world (see Table 1).

Later in the century and into the contemporary period, the cultural hegemony of classical Protestant churches has been challenged by aging and declining membership, new prominence of "younger" churches, especially Evangelical and Pentecostal, and growing religious pluralism. In the late 1970s and 1980s much literature addressed the data that demonstrated the sharp decline of the old "mainline" churches and the rapid ascendance of newer churches. Often characterized as a prolonged expression of liberal and conservative thought split along both theological and socio-political lines, the trend continued through the mid-1990s. For the last four years, the *Yearbook of American & Canadian Churches* has noted a flattening of the rate of change for both those churches with increasing membership as well as those with declining membership. (See Table 2).

While two of the nine bodies considered in Table 2 did not have current data available at publication, the extant data permit a cautious confirmation of the trend of slower rates both of decline among churches perceived as liberal and of increase among the churches perceived as conservative. The Church of Jesus Christ of Latter Day Saints stands as something of an exception in that it is generally perceived as conservative yet is experiencing an accelerating growth rate. The theological distinctions of the Mormon faith perhaps exclude it from consideration within these categories of study.

In the area of financial statistics, overall giving totals remain fairly constant for the year reported. A very modest increase in per capita giving is nearly offset by the overall decline in membership (see Table 3).

A larger number of churches reported data in this edition of the *Yearbook* than in the past; yet a change in publication date made it impossible to publish current data from two large bodies (The United Methodist Church and The American Baptist Churches). With that caution in mind, a trend toward the return to higher benevolence giving can be identified. (See Table 3)

Despite the fact that inclusive membership has slipped just below 50 million in the past year, the total benevolence giving has continued to rise steadily. Further, although total contributions have also continued to rise, benevolences constitute a greater proportion of the total contributions than they did last year, an increase of three percentage points. That is, benevolences show an increase both in relation to membership and as a percentage of total giving.

This pattern of rising benevolence giving will bear close scrutiny in the years ahead. The strong performance of the U.S. economy has likely contributed to this increase, although such an influence is not reflected in a commensurate increase in total giving. Other factors such as widespread news coverage of natural disasters and of others in need may have occurred simultaneously with a declining priority in maintaining denominational structures and programs to yield greater assignment of income to benevolence causes. Whatever the factors contributing to this trend, it must be emphasized that the increase, though statistically significant, is modest (from $67.68 to $84.80 per capita for confirmed members). Benevolence giving as a function of total giving rises from 12% (reported in 1998) to 15%. This recovery from the 1998 low of 12% still leaves benevolence giving below the 17-21% patterns reported for 1994–1997.

While data for an additional year will eventually be considered within the corpus of church statistics for the twentieth century, there is little doubt that the highly diversified patterns of affiliation will continue to be the hallmark of the century. At century's close as at its opening, vigorous voluntary religion continues to be a pervasive aspect of American culture.

Trends Table 1
INCLUSIVE MEMBERSHIP

Year	Membership	Source	Year	Membership	Source
1890	41,699,342	CRB	1964	123,307,499	YBAC
1906	35,068,058	CRB	1965	124,682,422	YBAC
1916	41,926,852	CRB	1966	125,778,656	YBAC
1926	54,576,346	CRB	1967	126,556,110	YBAC
1931	59,268,764	CH	1968	128,469,636	YBAC
1932	60,157,392	CH	1969	128,505,084	YBAC
1933	60,812,624	CH	1970	131,045,053	YBAC
1934	62,007,376	CH	1971	131,389,642	YBAC
1935	62,678,177	CH	1972	131,424,564	YBAC
1936	55,807,366	CRB	1973	131,245,139	YBAC
1936	63,221,996	CH	1974	131,871,743	YBACC
1937	63,848,094	CH	1975	131,012,953	YBACC
1938	64,156,895	YBAC	1976	131,897,539	YBACC
1940	64,501,594	YBAC	1977	131,812,470	YBACC
1942	68,501,186	YBAC	1978	133,388,776	YBACC
1944	72,492,699	YBAC	1979	133,469,690	YBACC
1945	71,700,142	CH	1980	134,816,943	YBACC
1946	73,673,182	CH	1981	138,452,614	YBACC
1947	77,386,188	CH	1982	139,603,059	YBACC
1948	19,435,605	CH	1983	140,816,385	YBACC
1949	81,862,328	CH	1984	142,926,363	YBACC
1950	86,830,490	YBAC	1985	142,926,363	YBACC
1951	88,673,005	YBAC	1986	142,799,662	YBACC
1952	92,277,129	YBAC	1987	143,830,806	YBACC
1953	94,842,845	YBAC	1988	145,383,739	YBACC
1954	97,482,611	YBAC	1989	147,607,394	YBACC
1955	100,162,529	YBAC	1990	156,331,704	YBACC
1956	103,224,954	YBAC	1991	156,629,918	YBACC
1957	104,189,678	YBAC	1992	156,557,746	YBACC
1958	109,557,741	YBAC	1993	153,127,045	YBACC
1959	112,226,905	YBAC	1994	158,218,427	YBACC
1960	114,449,217	YBAC	1995	157,984,194	YBACC
1961	116,109,929	YBAC	1996	159,471,758	YBACC
1962	117,946,002	YBAC	1997	157,503,033	YBACC
1963	120,965,238	YBAC			

CRB—Census of Religious Bodies, Bureau of the Census, Washington CH—*The Christian Herald,* New York
YBAC—*Yearbook of American Churches,* New York
YBACC—*Yearbook of American & Canadian Churches,* New York

As a general record of the trends in church membership since 1890, the above table is very useful since it presents the results of sixty-nine compilations made by statisticians. It is the only record existing on church membership. Although the table follows a logical progression upward over time, it is by no means without faults.

There are certain qualifications relating to the above data that should be kept in mind. First of all, aggregate data on inclusive membership, while accounting for the bulk of church membership, is always incomplete. A small number of religious bodies do not have membership statistics. Further, some smaller religious groups are excluded from these totals by virtue of the definitions used for a "religious body" by the various compilers of these data.

Second, because not all religious bodies gather and report statistics every year, and because different bodies update their statistics at different points throughout the yearly cycle, for the sake of completeness the totals reported here combine both current and non-current data.

Third, definitions of inclusive membership vary from one religious body to another. Some count only full members and exclude children, and those nominally related, while other religious bodies include this wider grouping. Occasionally a religious body will shift from the more restrictive to the more inclusive definition over time. A third category of religious bodies has no actual statistical records and only makes estimates of inclusive membership which roughly parallel the ethnic and cultural community to which they relate.

Last, these compilations were made by three different organizations from data derived from the religious bodies themselves; the U.S. Bureau of the Census made five compilations, The *Christian Herald* made twelve, and the *Yearbook of American & Canadian Churches* (formally *Yearbook of American Churches*) made fifty-two. Criteria for defining inclusive membership has not been completely standard over the 98-year period of these compilations.

Trends Table 2

US Membership Changes Denomination	1996 Edition Membership Change	Percentage Change	1997 Edition Membership Change	Percentage Change	1998 Edition Membership Change	Percentage Change	1999 Edition Membership Change	Percentage Change
The Roman Catholic Church	332,563	0.56	89,849	0.15	927,460	1.54	355,855	0.578
Southern Baptist Convention	215,418	1.40	49,236	0.32	28,668	0.18	199,550	1.25
The United Methodist Church	-62,470	-0.72	-45,463	-0.53	-43,284	-0.51	*	*
Evangelical Lutheran Church in America	-13,737	-0.26	-4,629	-0.12	-9,579	-0.18	4,145	0.07994
The Church of Jesus Christ of Latter-Day Saints	93,000	2.06	98,400	2.39	88,500	1.88	123,100	2.5
Presbyterian Church (U.S.A.)	-98,630	-2.60	-32,986	-1.22	-32,114	-0.88	-26,622	-0.737
The Lutheran Church—Missouri Synod	-2,008	-0.08	-1,624	-0.08	6,589	0.25	1,892	0.07268
Assemblies of God	52,897	2.33	22,983	1.70	79,606	3.33	26,986	1.08
American Baptist Churches in the U.S.A.	-8,571	-0.57	9,466	0.63	-14,133	-0.93	*	*

Trends Table 3
US FINANCIAL SUMMARIES FOR 1994-1999 EDITIONS

Edition Year	Number Reporting	Full or Confirmed Members	Inclusive Members	Total Contributions	Per Capita Full or Confirmed Members	Per Capita Inclusive Members	Total Congregational Contributions	Benevolences as a Percentage of Total Contributions
1994	44	39,521,497	43,191,444	$16,647,464,955	$421.43	$385.43	$13,656,854,125	19%
1995	52	41,842,642	46,667,687	$19,631,560,798	$469.18	$420.67	$16,152,245,431	18%
1996	47	40,997,058	44,886,207	$15,308,625,032	$373.41	$341.05	$15,308,625,032	21%
1997	55	43,104,555	48,115,704	$21,433,517,908	$497.24	$445.46	$17,743,597,668	17%
1998	55	43,321,039	50,047,599	$24,170,133,464	$557.93	$482.94	$20,417,988,771	12%
1999	58	44,724,732	49,980,841	$24,913,914,465	$557.05	$498.47	$21,124,174,647	15%

Edition Year	Per Capita Full or Confirmed Members	Per Capita Inclusive Members	Total Benevolences	Per Capita Full or Confirmed Members	Per Capita Inclusive Members
1994	$343.25	$314.09	$3,081,610,830	$77.97	$71.35
1995	$386.02	$346.11	$3,481,455,047	$83.20	$74.60
1996	$373.41	$341.05	$3,259,090,326	$79.50	$72.61
1997	$411.64	$368.77	$3,689,920,239	$85.60	$76.69
1998	$471.32	$407.97	$2,939,584,874	$67.86	$58.74
1999	$472.32	$422.65	$3,792,486,358	$84.80	$75.88

11

American Religion at the Millennium's End*

As the century and the millennium draw to a close, an occasion is provided for reflection on both the changes and constancy of religious life. The twentieth century saw both expansion and topographical alteration to America's religious landscape. One hundred years ago a smaller diversity of Christian churches populated this land with fewer urban parishes at hand to address the burgeoning pastoral needs of the industrial revolution. Throughout the early years of the century, congregations would adapt to meet modern needs seeking to harmonize contemporary realities with venerable truths: The congregation, always a highly adaptable social organization, again shows signs of responding and renewing itself at the dawn of a new age. Gustav Niebuhr, Senior Religion Correspondent at the New York Times offers one thoughtful analysis on the degree and likely direction of some of those changes.

—Editor

Among the smaller-scale wonders of New York City these days you may see a ... commercial billboard with an illuminated panel that counts down not only the days, but also the hours, the minutes, and even the seconds remaining until the year 2000.

On the one hand, the clock serves to remind us that the present century is rushing to a close. If you have something you would still like to accomplish before the new one arrives—mastering a foreign language, for example, or learning how to ice-skate—well then, here's exactly how much time you have left. But the clock also reflects a public fascination with the prospect of having three zeros come up on the chronological odometer. As someone who writes about religion in the United States as a news story, I have found it both interesting and also important to my job, to be aware that many people attach a cosmic significance to the millennium's approach. Visit a Christian bookstore, and you will not have to look hard to find ample evidence of a flourishing genre of fiction, the end-of-the-world novel, in which armaggedon and the second coming are experienced through the lives of middle-class people living in contemporary America. These books, I have been assured, sell very well. . . .

. . . This is a fundamentally religious nation. The United States, over the last 30 years, has not followed the trajectory of many western European countries toward an intrinsically secular society in which religious belief and behavior is marginalized. The theological proposition that God was absent or dead never took root here. Geographically large as America is, and culturally diverse, it has never provided a fertile soil for atheism. If one accepts the results of nationwide polls, then the basic religious outlook of Americans is unchanged since the mid-1960s, despite the intervening years of social upheaval and traumatic political events. Surveys by Gallup and other organizations report that about 19 of 20 people profess a belief in God, a statistic considerably above the findings for other developed nations. Furthermore, large majorities of Americans claim to pray daily; about two of five people say they attend church or synagogue on a weekly basis.

When the *New York Times* ran the results of a nationwide survey on religious belief and practice last year, one of the more interesting findings was that 60 percent of people claimed to say grace at meal time. That was exactly the same percentage that answered that question affirmatively in 1967. Perhaps this should not seem so unusual in a nation where the Reverend Billy Graham and the late Mother Teresa have been consistently ranked as among the most admired people. But without being cynical, one can reasonably ask how much these statistics tell us beyond the constancy of the public in its basic religious outlook. Such poll results, after all, tell us almost nothing about the depth of people's religious understanding or their religious commitments beyond an elemental personal piety.

The Fate of Religious Institutions

The poll numbers tell us that the will to believe is alive. But they offer no evidence that religious institutions have the same degree of influence over people's lives that they exercised 30 years ago, or that many people have kept up an attachment to the denominational bodies that served to organize and guide religious life throughout much of this century. A problem for national church organizations these days is that we live in a time suspicious of institutions and their authority. Anyone old enough to remember the Vietnam War remembers, too, how hatred of that conflict became fused for many people with a deep distrust of the so-called establishment. The war's end did not exorcise that suspicion. Instead, it has lingered and even spread.

Unfortunately for religious institutions (and I might add for the news media as well), this attitude is

*Excerpted from Gustav Niebuhr, "American Religion at the Millennium's End," The 1997–98 *Word & World* Lecture, *Word & World* 18, 1 (Winter 1998) 5-13. Copyright © 1998 *Word & World,* Luther Seminary. Reprinted by permission.

not directed simply at the various agencies of government, but exists as a more general distrust of or alienation from sources of authority. This attitude, too, coexists with a heightened sense of spiritual individualism among Americans, one that places the satisfaction of personal needs above maintaining traditional loyalties. Herein lies a major challenge for the churches.

Not long ago, a Roman Catholic priest who had tracked donations from the pew by American Catholics said that he believed giving had fallen over the years because people distrusted "headquarters," regardless of whether that headquarters was in Washington, D.C. or in Rome. It is common these days to hear church dissidents threatening to hold back on giving to register some protest or other. Recent cutbacks in staff and programs at the national level of the major protestant churches show, too, that financial shortfalls can have severe consequences.

However, people may simply redirect their priorities in a more gradual way, as their vision of what they want to be doing shifts. A couple of years ago, an Episcopal bishop said to me that he felt that the members of his diocese were increasingly likely to focus their loyalties on their local parish at the expense of the regional or the national church. That posed a problem, he said, when it came time to raise money for projects run by the denomination, such as hunger relief or missionary work. Many of the Episcopalians he encountered, he said, much preferred to give to causes where they could see their money at work, going to help rehabilitate the parish's buildings or to run its soup kitchen.

This focus on the local portends serious negative consequences for the work and influence of the national church bodies. It also opens the door to a certain religious entrepreneurism. The last few years of this century have seen the rise of a new institution, the megachurch, whose focus is decidedly local, in that such churches are typically oriented toward the interests and desires of middle-class, suburban America.

Megachurches—the term itself is a new one, used by some to describe churches that draw a minimum of 2,000 worshipers each week—have sprouted up all over the country, mainly in the south, the midwest, and the west, and often in suburban areas within an easy drive of an interstate exit. They tend to be independent, non-denominational churches or churches whose denominational ties are lightly held. These institutions are either fascinating or a bit off-putting (or perhaps both), depending on your point of view. In the last few years, I have visited several, including one where the many parking lots that surrounded the main sanctuary were identified by the names of biblical cities.... In addition to convenient parking, megachurches tend to offer amenities with a personal or local focus: a wide range of activities for children, volunteer opportunities for adults, sermons geared more to responding to practical issues than to theological reflection. In the more upscale of these institutions you can find gymnasiums, cafeterias, even in-house cinemas—it is the church as your local mall.

Megachurches have become an important and influential feature of American religious life in the last ten or so years. If nothing else, they have identified—and many of them have oriented themselves toward—the spiritually-inclined but denominationally-detached individual, the "seeker," as he or she is called. To attract these people, the pastors and staffs of megachurches have felt free to experiment with the forms and the surroundings of worship. Thus, you can find a band with electric guitars playing pop music sounds with religious lyrics in place of the organ and hymnals. The sanctuary itself may be so devoid of Christian ornamentation that it resembles a secular auditorium. The emphasis is on packaging the essentials of the sacred in culturally familiar forms.

One of the most successful and influential of the megachurches is the Willow Creek Community Church in suburban Chicago, whose building was designed to blend in with a surrounding secular landscape of corporate headquarters, thereby providing a familiar environment to coax the unaffiliated to come to the Christian life. From its start 20 years ago, it now draws around 14,000 people a week. It has provided a model for pastors starting new congregations and for those looking for a way to make older ones seem vital again. What has happened is that a new institution has been created to accommodate a social phenomenon, the heightened individualism and detachment from traditional institutions.

Megachurch pastors say what they are doing is evangelism in that it provides a Christian harbor for people who might otherwise be a adrift. But there are plenty of skeptics, who might wonder just how much spiritual nurture the average person is likely to find in such places, particularly if they do not find their way into some sort of small group within the larger body....

Yet the spiritual seeking that makes the megachurch possible is also felt outside the walls of those institutions, evident in the increasing porousness of the boundaries that separate the denominationally affiliated churches. During the various national church meetings I attended this past summer, I heard one Episcopal laywoman describe the churchgoing habits of people in her part of the midwest. They "slide around" from church to church, she said, a telling description of the state of denominational ties of many protestants. Ministers in many churches I have visited as a reporter seem increasingly to say, when asked, that many, perhaps most, of their congregants began in another denomination than the one to which that particular church is linked. In such situations, it is clear that the primary identity of the church in the minds of its members is something other than its denominational identity. Instead, what draws people to the church is, to borrow a term from one church consultant, its non-denominational "niche" appeal—its location, its particular type of social activism or, perhaps more likely, the breadth of its religious education.

These days, that may sound unremarkable, but it does make for some interesting experiences in visiting churches. A year ago, for example, I visited a historic church…which stood not far from the very spot where its original congregation had been founded early in the seventeenth century. The building itself was more recent,…but one could…read the church's original statement of faith, written by the Puritans and printed in the bulletin each Sunday. Yet in more than a dozen interviews there, I do not recall meeting anyone born into the…denomination with which that congregation was affiliated. I did meet former Presbyterians, Lutherans, and Roman Catholics, and they all seemed quite enthusiastic about the various local projects of that particular congregation.

If one encounters such attitudes at the level of the pews, should it be at all surprising that there is considerable support for the broad types of ecumenical agreements that the Evangelical Lutheran Church in America faced at its churchwide assembly last summer? As you know, the delegates there produced a mixed verdict on just how closely the ELCA should embrace the cause of protestant unity: delegates voted for full communion with three Reformed denominations, the Presbyterian Church (U.S.A.), the United Church of Christ, and the Reformed Church in America; but the delegates also rejected—by the narrowest of margins—a similar agreement with the Episcopal Church.

Supporters of the agreements had made an appeal to practicality, saying that full communion between the denominations would allow small congregations, now separated by denominational lines, to share a clergyperson, the sort of arrangement that one could easily imagine could keep a marginal church alive. What was impressive was the earnestness and seriousness that both supporters and opponents of the proposals brought to the debate at the assembly. Here were searching discussions of what it meant to belong to a particular church, to believe its distinctive teachings, and what common ground existed with other protestant groups. It was obvious, too, that many delegates had invested considerable emotion in these discussions, when, after the *Concordat* with the Episcopalians was defeated, many of its supporters wept in each other's arms.

Yet it is also very difficult to believe that finding common ground is not important these days, especially among people who share so much theologically and historically as those protestant churches involved in the agreements. In the absence of attempts at a greater unity, one might ask how else are protestants to make their voice heard these days?

At the end of the twentieth century, it is possible to look back on a time, one not too distant, when the mainline protestant churches dominated the religious life of this country. In some regions, the upper midwest, for example, that condition may still prevail and may even continue for some time. But it is unlikely to recur within the nation as a whole.

Religious Pluralism

Over the last three decades, the nation has experienced an extraordinary growth in religious and cultural pluralism. Just as there has arisen a large, spiritually-inclined group called seekers, so too there have emerged important religious minorities whose mosques and temples are increasingly visible. Members of those communities, immigrants and the children of immigrants, tend to be middle-class; they are building their houses of worship in urban, suburban, and even rural areas. No major American city is without its Islamic center now, a fact that is as true of the Bible belt as it is of the coasts. In northern Indiana, for example, a mosque can be seen rising against the background of a cornfield, a visual conjunction that speaks to the emergence of an American Islam.

Hindu temples, too, may be found throughout the country, in the suburbs of Chicago, in the hill country of south Texas near Austin, and in Ashland, Massachusetts, where the Boston marathon starts. In New York, one of the most important temples can be found in Queens, just down the street from a synagogue and a couple of ethnic protestant churches, one Chinese, the other Korean. In some cases, where immigrant groups have recently become organized, their religious presence is not easily discerned from the street level. But they are there.…

Many of these congregations will become more visible as their members are better established economically and socially, and build new sanctuaries to proclaim their permanence in the United States. But already, in some cases, their representatives have begun applying for admission to the local council of churches or the council of churches and synagogues. One result has been the initiation of Jewish-Christian-Muslim dialogues, the descendants of Abraham meeting to find what they share. In a few places, too, the circle has been occasionally broadened to include other groups: Hindus, Sikhs, Jains, and Buddhists. The presence of a multitude of faith groups will no doubt make for some interesting theological discussions. But more importantly, it will force some decisions on what it is that religious people in a diverse America truly share. At the least, perhaps the basis for agreement would be a rock-solid commitment to protecting the constitutional guarantees of religious freedom and also to proclaiming a conviction that faith matters, and that believers have an important role in sharing their principles in any discussion of public issues.

What happens next will help shape the sort of public presence of American religion in the twenty-first century. The search for common ground, especially among the groups that are theologically close to one another, will be vital to preserving the sort of strong religious voice that can contribute to public life in American society.

14

Sources in Religion-Related Research

The editorial office of the *Yearbook of American & Canadian Churches* receives innumerable requests for data about churches, religious organizations, attendance patterns, and comparative religion concerns. Sometimes we are able to furnish the requested data, but more often we refer the inquirer to other research colleagues in the field. We are always interested in and aided by such requests, and we find ourselves informed by each question.

As a new feature in this edition of the *Yearbook of American & Canadian Churches*, we have identified some of the organizations that conduct religion related research. In each instance, contact information and a brief summary of the organization's specialized area of interest is listed. Our colleagues Carol Fouke and Wendy McDowell at the National Council of the Churches of Christ in the USA and Ian Evison of the Alban Institute assisted in the compiling of entries that follow. We are grateful for this effort. Numerous research centers in the area of American religious life, each with specific areas of concern, conduct timely and significant research. We hope that researchers at such centers will contact us for inclusion in subsequent editions of the *Yearbook*. We trust that readers will find utility in this listing and invite them to identify additional sources by email: yearbook@ncccusa.org or Fax: (212)870-2817.

Yearbook of American and Canadian Churches
475 Riverside Dr., Room 812
New York, NY 10115
http://www. ncccusa.org
yearbook@ncccusa
Phone: 212-870-2031
Fax: 212-870-2817

The office of the *Yearbook of American & Canadian Churches* annually collects statistical information on membership and finances from those churches listed in its publication. When churches are unable to update statistics, the *Yearbook* publishes the most recent information available for that edition. In addition, the *Yearbook* office has an abbreviated number of membership statistics dating back to the beginning of their collection and publication (1951-Present). The directories within the Yearbook provide extensive contact information for denominational headquarters, seminaries, archives, theological schools, and local and regional ecumenical bodies. A chapter on the Electronic church provides an extensive list of Internet locations for church related organizations.

The Public Religion Project
919 N. Michigan Ave., Suite 540
Chicago, IL 60611-1601
http://www.publicreligionproj.org
prp-info@publicreligionproj.org
Database Staff: Phone 773-702-9565 Fax 9099
Other Staff: 312-397-6400 Fax 6401

The Public Religion Project maintains a comprehensive database of internationally recognized scholars, experts and spokespersons who can address questions about religion and the role in plays in public life. Its role is to provide access to experts; it does not do original research.

American Religion Data Archive
Department of Sociology and Anthropology
Purdue University
1365 Stone Hall
West Lafayette, IN 47907-1365
http://www.arda.tm
archive@sri.soc.purdue.edu
Phone: 765-494-0081 Fax 765-496-1476
Director: Roger Finke
Phone: 765-497-9827 Fax 765-496-1476

The American Religion Data Archive is an Internet-based archive for the study of American religion. It includes dozens of leading studies on American religion, with more studies being added periodically. Users may search across data files to quickly locate topics of interest, then view, print, or download file descriptions and codebooks. Users may conduct basic analysis on-line or download the data files for analysis.

Barna Research Group, Ltd.
5528 Everglades St.
Ventura, CA 93003
http://www.barna.org
Phone: (805) 658-8885 Fax 7298
Barna Research Group, Ltd. is a full-service marketing research company located in Ventura, California. Barna Research has been providing information and analysis regarding cultural trends and the Christian church since 1984.

Independent Sector
1828 L Street, NW
Washington, DC 20036
http://www.indepsec.org
info@indepsec.org
Phone: 202-223-8100 Fax: 202-416-0580
Publications Orders: 888-860-8118
Documents on Request: 800-575-2666
Independent Sector is a national leadership forum, working to encourage philanthropy, volunteering, not-for-profit initiative, and citizen action to better serve people and communities. IS provides information on non-governmental organizational statistics, especially trends in charitable giving, the contribution of non-governmental organizations financially to the nation, etc.

The Pluralism Project
Harvard Divinity School
Ellie Pierce, Project Manager
pluralsm@fas.harvard.edu
http://www.fas.harvard.edu/~pluralsm/
Phone: 617-496-2482
The Pluralism Project offers information on interfaith trends and statistics and, most importantly, places them in perspective. It also refers people to representatives of the different faiths. The Project has developed a CD-ROM that makes its findings available to teachers, students, researchers, and religious leaders.

National Opinion Research Center
Main Office:
1155 East 60th Street
Chicago, IL 60637
http://www.norc.uchicago.edu
norcinfo@norcmail.uchicago.edu
(773) 753-7500
The National Opinion Research Center is a non-profit corporation affiliated with the University of Chicago that conducts survey research in the public interest for government agencies, educational institutions, private foundations, non-profit organizations, and private corporations. NORC collects data to help policy makers, researchers, educators, and others address the crucial issues facing the government, organizations, and the public. NORC puts out a general social survey every year which gets information about church attendance and social attitudes (e.g., about infidelity and race relations). The survey sample is not large enough to have information about groups other than Christians and Jews.

Princeton Religion Research Center
47 Hulfish Street
PO Box 389
Princeton, NJ 08542
Phone: 609-921-8112 Fax: 609-683-9040
http://www.prrc.com
prrc1977@aol.com
The purpose of the PRRC is to gain a better understanding of the nature and depth of religious commitment in the United States and abroad and to explore the factors behind spiritual growth or decline. The information provided by the PPRC, much of it unavailable elsewhere, offers an in-depth profile of America's religious beliefs and practices, as well as survey findings that can be put to immediate practical use. Publications include *Emerging Trends, Religion in America,* and *The Religious Life of Young Americans: Five Years Later.*

16

Institute for the Study of American Religion
P. O. Box 90709
Santa Barbara, CA 93190-0709
Phone: 805-967-7721 Fax: 805-683-4876
http://www.americanreligion.org
　　The Institute for the Study of American Religion was founded in 1969 in Evanston, Illinois as a religious studies research facility with a particular focus upon the smaller religions of the United States. The groups it has concentrated upon have been known under a variety of labels including sect, cult, minority religion, alternative religion, non-conventional religion, spiritual movement, and new religious movement. In 1985, the ISAR moved to its present location in Santa Barbara, California.

Association of Theological Schools in the U.S. and Canada
10 Summit Park Drive
Pittsburgh, PA 15275-1103
412-788-6505
fax: 412-788-6510
email: ats@ats.edu
http://www.ats.edu
　　The Association of Theological Schools in the U.S. and Canada is the accrediting body for Christian theological schools. It compiles information on theological education from its member institutions and publishes an annual yearbook.

Hartford Seminary
Center for Social and Religious Research
Phone: 860-509-9546 Fax 9551
csrr@hartsem.edu
http://www.hartsem.edu/csrr/
　　The CSRR pursues research on American religious institutions and provides data on congregational studies, conservative religion, church use of computers and the Web, congregational ministries, social ministries, women in ministry, spiritually vital parishes, Christian-Muslim relations, and many other topics.

The Alban Institute
4550 Montgomery Avenue, Suite 433N
Bethesda, MD 20814-3341
Phone: 301-718-4407 / 800-486-1318 Fax: 301-718-1958
Contact: Ian Evison - ievison@alban.org - 301-718-4407 x 246
　　The Alban Institute works to encourage congregations to be vigorous and faithful so that they equip the people of God to minister within their faith communities and in the world. To assist those who lead or care for congregations, the Institute gathers, generates and shares practical knowledge across denominational lines through action research, consulting, publications, and education programs. Research is completed on all areas related to congregational life.

J.W. Dawson Institute of Church-State Studies at Baylor University
Dr. Derrick H. Davis, Director
P.O. Box 96308
Waco, TX 76798-7308
Phone: 254-710-1510 Fax: 1571
http://www.baylor.edu/~Church_State/
derek_davis@baylor.edu
　　The Institute carries out research in church-state relations and offers Master's and doctoral level degrees. It publishes the quarterly *Journal of Church and State* and monographs on church-state studies. The focus is more thematic than statistical.

Glenmary Research Center
235 E. Ponce De Leon Ave., Ste. 226
Decatur, GA 30030
Phone: (404)377-7010
Media Contact: Ursula Durden
　　The Research Center is a department of the Glenmary Home Missioners, a Catholic society of priests and brothers. The Center was established in 1966 to serve the rural research needs of the Catholic Church in the United States. Its research has led it to serve ecumenically a wide variety of church bodies. Local case studies as well as quantitative research is done to understand better the

diversity of contexts in the rural sections of the country. The Center's statistical profiles of the nation's counties cover both urban and rural counties.

The Empty Tomb, Inc.
Champaign, Ill.
Contact: John and Sylvia Ronsvalle
217-356-2262 or 9519
http://www.emptytomb.org
    Empty Tomb, Inc. is a Christian research and service organization based in Champaign, Illinois. The research component focuses on national church giving trends, analyzing both data and dynamics affecting the giving patterns.

Selected Bibliography

Below are reference works which offer a wide range of religion related data. Most titles are broadly available.

Concise Dictionary of Christianity in America
    Edited by Daniel G. Reid, Robert D. Linder, Bruce L. Shelley, Harry S. Stout, Craig A. Noll. Downers Grove, IL: InterVarsity Press, 1955

Dictionary of Pentecostal and Charismatic Movements
    Edited by Stanley M. Burgess and Gary B. McGee. Grand Rapids, MI: Zondervan, 1988.

The Encyclopedia of American Religions
    Edited by J. Gordon Melton. Detroit, MI: Gale Research.

Encyclopedic Handbook of Cults in America
    J. Gordon Melton. New York, NY: Garland Publishing, Inc., 1992.

Handbook of Denominations in the United States
    Frank S. Mead. Revised by Samuel S. Hill. Nashville, TN: Abingdon Press, 1995

The HarperCollins Dictionary of Religion
    Edited by Jonathan Z. Smith. New York: HarperCollins, 1995. A project of the American Academy of Religion.

The HarperCollins Encyclopedia of Catholicism
    Edited by Richard P. McBrien. New York: HarperCollins, 1995.

The Penguin Dictionary of Religions
    Edited by John R. Hinnells. New York, NY: Penguin Books, 1984.

World Religions in America: An Introduction
    Edited by Jacob Neusner, Louisville, KY: Westminster/John Knox Press, 1994.

Yearbook of American & Canadian Churches
    Edited by Rev. Dr. Eileen W. Lindner. Nashville, TN, Abingdon Press.

SOURCES

II

DIRECTORIES

1. United States Cooperative Organizations, National

The organizations listed in this section are cooperative religious organizations that are national in scope.

Alban Institute, Inc.

Founded in 1974, the Alban Institute, Inc. is a non-profit, non-denominational membership organization. Its mission is to work to encourage local congregations to be vigorous and faithful so that they may equip the people of God to minister within their faith communities and in the world. Through its publications, education programs, consulting and training services and research, the Alban Institute provides resources and services to congregations and judicatories of all denominations and their lay and ordained leaders.

The Institute has long been a pioneer in identifying, researching and publishing information about key issues in the religious world such as conflict management, clergy transition, and involuntary termination of clergy and lay leadership. The Institute's resources include over 100 book titles, over 40 courses offered nationally each year, and a staff of senior consultants located across the country ready to assist local congregations. Individuals, congregations, and institutions may support Alban's work as well as maintain their cutting-edge skills for ministry through membership in The Institute.

Headquarters

7315 Wisconsin Ave., Ste. 1250 W., Bethesda, MD 20814-3211 Tel. (800)486-1318
Email: pwalker@alban.org
Website: http://www. alban.org
Media Contact, Marketing and Communications Director, Holly Hemphill

Officers

Pres., The Rev. James P. Wind, Ph.D.
Exec. Vice-Pres., Leslie L. Buhler

American Bible Society

In 1816, pastors and laymen representing a variety of Christian denominations gathered in New York City to establish an organization "to disseminate the Gospel of Christ throughout the habitable world." Since that time the American Bible Society (ABS) has continued to provide God's Word, without doctrinal note or comment, wherever it is needed and in the language and format the reader can most easily use and understand. The ABS is the servant of the denominations and local churches. It provides Scriptures at exceptionally low costs in various attractive formats for their use in outreach ministries here in the United States and all across the world.

Today the ABS serves more than 100 denominations and agencies, and its board of trustees is composed of distinguished laity and clergy drawn from these Christian groups.

Fifty years ago the American Bible Society played a leading role in the founding of the United Bible Societies, a federation of 138 national Bible Societies around the world that enables global cooperation in Scripture translation, publication and distribution in more than 200 countries and territories. The ABS contributes approximately 45 percent of the support provided by the UBS to those national Bible Societies which request support to meet the total Scripture needs of people in their countries.

The work of the ABS is supported through gifts from individuals, local churches, denominations and cooperating agencies. Their generosity helped make the distribution of 287.2 million copies of the Scriptures during 1994, out of a total of 608 millon copies of the Scriptures distributed by all member societies of the UBS.

Headquarters

National Service Center, 1865 Broadway, New York, NY 10023 Tel. (212)408-1200
Media Contact, Dir. Public Rel., Mike Maus, Tel. (212)408-1419 Fax (212)408-1456
E-mail: mmaus@americanbible.org
Website: http://www.americanbible.org

Officers

Chpsn., Sally Shoemaker Robinson
Vice-Chpsn., Harold Bennett
Pres., Dr. Eugene B. Habecker
Exec. Vice-Pres., Peter Bradley
Vice-Pres. for Scripture Publications, Maria I. Martinez
Vice-Pres. for Dev., Arthur Caccese
Vice-Pres. for Admin./CFO, Patrick English

19

Acting Vice-Pres. for Marketing, John Cruz Departmental Heads: Church Relations & ABS Chaplain, Asst. to Pres., Rev. Fred A. Allen; Scripture Publications, Assoc. Vice-Pres., Rev. Dr. David G. Burke; Volunteer Activities & Field Services, Dir., Dr. Haviland C. Houston; National Program Promotions, Dir., Jeanette Russo; Human Resources, Dir., Robert P. Fichtel; Public Relations, Dir., Mike Maus; Scripture Production Services, Dir., Gary R. Ruth

American Council of Christian Churches

The American Council of Christian Churches is a Fundamentalist multidenominational organization whose purposes are to provide information, encouragement, and assistance to Bible-believing churches, fellowships, and individuals; to preserve our Christian heritage through exposure of, opposition to, and separation from doctrinal impurity and compromise in current religious trends and movements; to protect churches from religious and political restrictions, subtle or obvious, that would hinder their ministries for Christ; and to promote obedience to the inerrant Word of God.

Founded in 1941, The American Council of Christian Churches (ACCC) is a multi-denominational agency for fellowship and cooperation among Bible-believing churches in various denominations/ fellowships: Bible Presbyterian Church, Evangelical Methodist Church, Fellowship of Fundamental Bible Churches (formerly Bible Protestant), Free Presbyterian Church of North America, Fundamental Methodist Church, General Association of Regular Baptist Churches, Independent Baptist Fellowship of North America, Independent Churches Affiliated, along with hundreds of independent churches. The total membership nears 2 million. Each denomination retains its identity and full autonomy, but cannot be associated with the World Council of Churches, National Council of Churches or National Association of Evangelicals.

Headquarters
P.O. Box 5455, Bethlehem, PA 18015 Tel. (610)865-3009 Fax (610)865-3033
E-mail: accc@juno.com
Website: http://www.amcouncilc.org
Media Contact, Exec. Dir., Dr. Ralph Colas

Officers
Pres., Dr. Richard A. Harris
Vice-Pres., Rev. Mark Franklin
Exec. Sec., Dr. Ralph Colas
Sec., Rev. Ron Fieker
Treas., William H. Worrilow, Jr.
Commissions: Chaplaincy; Education; Laymen; Literature; Missions; Radio & Audio Visual; Relief; Youth

American Friends Service Committee

Founded: 1917, Regional Groups: 9, Non-membership. Founded by and related to the Religious Society of Friends (Quakers) but supported and staffed by individuals sharing basic values regardless of religious affiliation. Attempts to relieve human suffering and find new approaches to world peace and social justice through nonviolence. Work in 22 countries includes development and refugee relief, peace education, and community organizing. Sponsors off-the-record seminars around the world to build better international understanding. Conducts programs with U.S. communities on the problems of minority groups such as housing, employment, and denial of legal rights. Maintains Washington, D.C. office to present AFSC experience and perspectives to policymakers. Seeks to build informed public resistance to militarism and the military-industrial complex. A co-recipient of the Noble Peace Prize. Programs are multiracial, non-denominational, and international.

Divisions: Community Relations, International, Peace Education.

Headquarters
1501 Cherry St., Philadelphia, PA 19102 Tel. (215)241-7000 Fax (215)864-0104
E-mail: afscinfo@afsc.org
Website: http://www.afsc.org
Dir. of Media Relations, Carl Mangeri

Officers
Chpsn., Donald Gann
Treas., Kate Nicklin
Exec. Dir., Kara Newell

The American Theological Library Association, Inc.

The American Theological Library Association, Inc. (ATLA) is a library association that works to improve theological and religious libraries and librarianship by providing continuing education, developing standards, promoting research and experimental projects, encouraging cooperative programs and publishing and disseminating research tools and aids. Founded in 1946, ATLA currently has a membership of over 200 institutions and 600 individuals.

Headquarters
820 Church St., Ste. 400, Evanston, IL 60201
Tel. (847)869-7788 Fax (847)869-8513
Email: Alta@alta.com
Website: http://atla.library.vanderbilt.edu/alta/home.html
Media Contact, Dir. of Member Services

Offlicers
Pres., Milton J. (Joe) Coalter, Louisville Presbyterian Theological Seminary, 1646 Cowling Ave., Louisville, KY 40205-1370
Vice-Pres., Dorothy G. Thomason, Union Theological Seminary in Virginia, 3401 Brook Rd., Richmond, VA 23227

Sec., Christopher P. Brennan, Colgate Rochester Divinity School, Crozer Theological Seminary, 1100 S. Goodman St., Rochester, NY 14620
Exec. Dir. & CEO, Dennis A. Norlin, 820 Church St., Ste. 400, Evanston, IL 60201

American Tract Society

The American Tract Society is a nonprofit, interdenominational organization, instituted in 1825 through the merger of most of the then-existing tract societies. As one of the earliest religious publishing bodies in the United States, ATS has pioneered in the publishing of Christian books, booklets and leaflets. The volume of distribution has risen to 25-30 million pieces of literature annually. For free samples or a free catalog contact 1-800-54-TRACT.

Headquarters
P.O. Box 462008, Garland, TX 75046 Tel. (972)276-9408 Fax (972)272-9642
Email: —
Website:—
Media Contact, Vice-Pres. Marketing, Tom Friday

Officer
Chpsn., John A. Mawhinney

The American Waldensian Society

The American Waldensian Society (AWS) promotes ministry linkages, broadly ecumenical, between U.S. churches and Waldensian (Reformed)-Methodist constituencies in Italy and Waldensian constituencies in Argentina-Uruguay. Founded in 1906, AWS aims to enlarge mission discovery and partnership among overseas Waldensian-Methodist forces and denominational forces in the U.S.

AWS is governed by a national ecumenical board, although it consults and collaborates closely with the three overseas Waldensian-Methodist boards.

The Waldensian experience is the earliest continuing Protestant experience.

Headquarters
475 Riverside Dr., Rm. 1850, New York, NY 10115 Tel. (212)870-2671 Fax (212)870-2499
Email: —
Website:—
Media Contact, Exec. Dir., Rev. Frank G. Gibson, Jr.

Officers
Pres., Rev. Laura R. Jervis
Vice-Pres., Rev. James O'Dell
Sec., Rev. Kent Jackson
Treas., Lon Haines
Exec. Dir., Rev. Frank G. Gibson, Jr.

Appalachian Ministries Educational Resource Center (AMERC)

The Appalachian Ministries Educational Resource Center (AMERC) is the largest ecumenical consortial effort in the history of theological education in the U.S. Forty-nine seminaries comprise the consortium with 39 other theological institutions sending their students for AMERC training programs. Forty-nine denominations are represented in its students.

The goal of AMERC is to train persons for the Christian ministry in small towns and rural communities in Appalachia and beyond. In order to fulfill this goal, AMERC has the following objectives: (1) to provide participants with the highest quality of training in relating to Christian Theology and ministry to the people, cultures and political economies of Appalachia; (2) to provide direct experiences of Appalachian life both religious and secular and to help participants reflect theologically these experiences; (3) to recruit, support and encourage persons considering ministry in Appalachia and similar settings; (4) to provide and promote research of Appalachia and its churches; (5) to cooperate with religious bodies in the region in planning and implementing educational programs; (6) to provide training for theological faculty and denominational leaders; and (7) to seek and find spiritual, personal, financial, and administrative resources to suppport AMERC programs.

Headquarters
300 Harrison Rd., Berea, KY 40403 Tel. (606) 986-8789 Fax (606)986-2576
Email: —
Website:—
Media Contact, Devel. Coord., Kathy Williams

Officers
Co-Exec. Dir., Rev. Dr. Mary Lee Daugherty
Co-Exec. Dir., Rev. Dr. J. Stephen Rhodes
Chpsn. of Board, Dr. Douglass Lewis

The Associated Church Press

The Associated Church Press was organized in 1916. Its member publications include major Protestant, Catholic, and Orthodox groups in the U.S. and Canada. Some major ecumenical journals are also members. It is a professional Christian journalistic association seeking to promote excellence among editors and writers, recognize achievements, and represent the interests of the religious press. It sponsors seminars, conventions, awards programs, and workshops for editors, staff people, and business managers. It is active in postal rates and regulations on behalf of the religious press.

Headquarters
Media Contact, Exec. Dir., Dr. John Stapert, P.O. Box 30215, Phoenix, AZ 85046-0215 Tel. (602)569-6371 Fax (602)569-6180
E-mail: john_stapert@ecunet.org
Website:—

Officers
Pres.,Roger Kahle, 8765 West Higgins Rd., Chicago , Il. 60631

Exec. Dir., Dr. John Stapert, P.O. Box 30215, Phoenix, AZ 85046-0215 Tel. (602)569-6371 Treas., Nena Asquith, P.O. Box 1245, Bethlehem, PA 18016-1245

The Associated Gospel Churches

Organized in 1939, The Associated Gospel Churches (AGC) endorses chaplains primarily for Fundamental Independent Baptist and Bible Churches to the U.S. Armed Forces. The AGC has been recognized by the U.S. Department of Defense for 57 years as an Endorsing Agency, and it supports a strong national defense. The AGC also endorses VA chaplains, police, correctional system and civil air patrol chaplains.

The AGC provides support for its associated constituent churches, (Fundamental Independent Churches), seminaries, Bible colleges and missionaries.

The AGC believes in the sovereignty of the local church, the historic doctrines of the Christian faith and the infallibility of the Bible.

The AGC is a member of the National Conference on Ministry to the Armed Forces (NCMAF).

Headquarters

Media Contact, Pres., George W. Baugham, D.D., National Hdqt., P.O. Box 733, Taylors, SC 29687 Tel. (864)268-9617 Fax (864)268-0166
Email: —
Website:—

Officers

Commission on Chaplains, Pres. and Chmn., George W. Baugham, D.D.
Vice-Pres., Rev. Chuck Flesher
Sec.-Treas., Eva Baugham
Natl. Field Sec., Rev. Bob Ellis

ADRIS/Association for the Development of Religious Information Services

The Association for the Development of Religious Information Services was established in 1971 to facilitate coordination and cooperation among information services that pertain to religion. Its goal is a worldwide network that is interdisciplinary, inter-faith and interdenominational to serve both administrative and research applications. ADRIS publishes a newsletter and provides internet consulting services toward these goals.

Headquarters

ADRIS Newsletter Office, P.O. Box 210735, Nashville, TN 37221-0735 Tel. (615)662-5189 Fax (615)662-5251
E-mail: adris@firestormcom.com
Website: http://www.firestormcom.com/adris
Media Contact, Newsletter Ed., Edward W. Dodds, P.O. Box 210735, Nashville, TN 37221-0735 Tel. (615)662-5189 Fax (615)662-5251

Association of Catholic Diocesan Archivists

The Association of Catholic Diocesan Archivists, which began in 1979, has been committed to the active promotion of professionalism in the management of diocesan archives. The Association meets annually: in the even years it has its own summer conference, in the odd years it meets in conjunction with the Society of American Archivists. Publications include Standards for Diocesan Archives, Access Policy for Diocesan Archives and the quarterly Bulletin.

Headquarters

Archives & Records Center, 711 West Monroe, Chicago, IL 60661 Tel. (312)831-0711 Fax (312)736-0488
Email: —
Website:—
Media Contact, Ms. Nancy Sandleback

Officers

Episcopal Mod., —
Pres., Msgr. Francis J. Weber, 15151 San Fernando Mission Blvd., Mission Hills, CA 91345 Tel. (818)365-1501
Vice-Pres., Dr. Charles Nolan, 1100 Chartres St., New Orleans, LA 70116 Tel. (504)529-2651 Fax (504)529-2001
Sec.-Treas., Sr. Catherine Louise LaCoste, C.S.J., 10291/2 Hayes Ave., San Diego, CA 92103 Tel. (619)298-6608
Bd. Members: Kinga Perzynska, P.O. Box 13124, Capital Station, Austin, TX 78711 Tel. (512)476-6296 Fax (512)476-3715; Timothy Cary, P.O. Box 07912, Milwaukee, WI 19807 Tel. (414)769-3407 Fax (414)769-3408; Lisa May, P.O. Box 907, 1700 San Jacinto, Houston, TX 77001 Tel. (713)659-5461 Fax (713)759-9151; John J. Treanor, 711 W. Monroe, Chicago, IL 60661 Tel. (312)736-5150 Fax (312)736-0488; Bernice Mooney, 27 C St., Salt Lake City, UT 84103-2397 Tel. (801)328-8641 Fax (801)328-9680
Newsletter Editor, Nancy Sandleback

Association of Statisticians of American Religious Bodies

This Association was organized in 1934 and grew out of personal consultations held by representatives from *The Yearbook of American Churches, The National* (now *Official*) *Catholic Directory,* the Jewish Statistical Bureau, The Methodist (now The United Methodist), the Lutheran and the Presbyterian churches.

ASARB has a variety of purposes: to bring together those officially and professionally responsible for gathering, compiling, and publishing denominational statistics; to provide a forum for the exchange of ideas and sharing of problems in statistical methods and procedure; and to seek such standardization as may be possible in religious statistical data.

Headquarters

c\o Greta Lauria, Presbyterian Church (U.S.A.), 100 Witherspoon St., Rm. 4625, Louisville, KY 40202 Tel. (502)569-5412 Fax (502)569-8005
Email: —
Website:—
Media Contact, Sec./Treas., Greta Lauria

Officers (Executive Board)

Pres., Richard H. Taylor, United Church of Christ, 292 Bellview, Benton Harbor, MI 49022 Tel. (616)925-0695 Fax (616)925-5514
1st Vice-Pres., Cliff Tharp, Southern Baptist Convention, 127 Ninth Ave. N., Nashville, TN 37220 Tel. (615)251-2517 Fax (615)251-5636
2nd Vice-Pres., Rich Houseal, Church of the Nazarene, 6401 The Paseo, Kansas City, MO 64131 Tel. (816)333-7000 Fax (816)361-5202
Sec./Treas., Greta Lauria, Presbyterian Church (U.S.A.), 100 Witherspoon St., Rm. 4625, Louisville, KY 40202 Tel. (502)569-5412 Fax (502)569-8005

Members-at-Large

Clifford Grammich, Glenmary Research Center, 414 S. Warwick Ave., Westmont, IL 60559-2063 Tel. (630)769-0958 Fax (219)844-7566
James Schwartz, UJA Federations of N.A., 111 Eighth Ave., Suite 11E, New York, NY 10011-5201 Tel. (212)284-6729 Fax (212)284-6805

The Association of Theological Schools in the United States and Canada

The Association of Theological Schools is the accrediting and program agency for graduate theological education in North America. Its member schools offer graduate professional and academic degrees for church-related professions. For information about enrollment in member schools see "Trends in Seminary Education" in the statistical section of this book beginning on page 326.

Headquarters

10 Summit Park Drive, Pittsburgh, PA 15275-1103 Tel. (412)788-6505 Fax (412)788-6510
E-mail: ats@ats.edu
Website: http://www.ats.edu
Media Contact, Dir. Of Comm., Nancy Merrill, Tel. (412)788-6505

Officers

Pres., Luder G. Whitlock, Jr., Reformed Theological Seminary, Jackson, MS
Vice-Pres., Martha J. Horne, Protestant Episcopal Theological Seminary in Virginia, Alexandria, VA
Secretary, M. William Howard, New York Theological Seminary, New York, NY
Treasurer, Thomas E. Fahey, Ernst & Young, New York, NY
STAFF
Executive Director, Daniel O. Aleshire

Blanton-Peale Institute

Blanton-Peale Institute is dedicated to helping people overcome emotional obstacles by joining mental health expertise with religious faith and values. The Blanton-Peale Graduate Institute provides advanced training in marriage and family therapy, psychotherapy and pastoral care for ministers, rabbis, sisters, priests and other counselors. The Blanton-Peale Counseling Centers provide counseling for individuals, couples, families and groups. Blanton-Peale also offers a nationwide telephone support service for clergy, social service agencies, and other employers and promotes interdisciplinary communication among theology, medicine and the behavioral sciences. Blanton-Peale was founded in 1937 by Dr. Norman Vincent Peale and psychiatrist Smiley Blanton, M.D.

Headquarters

3 W. 29th St., New York, NY 10001 Tel. (212)725-7850 Fax (212)689-3212
Email: —
Website:—
Media Contact, —

Officers

Chpsn., John Allen
Vice-Chpsn., Arthur Caliandro
Sec., Janet E. Hunt
Treas., Mary McNamara
Pres. & CEO, —

Bread For The World

Bread for the World is a non-profit, nondenominational Christian citizen's movement of 45,000 members that advocates specific hunger policy changes and seeks justice for hungry people at home and abroad. Founded in 1974, Bread for the World is supported by more than 45 Protestant, Catholic and Evangelical denominations and church agencies. Rooted in the gospel of God's love in Jesus Christ, its 45,000 members write, call and visit their members of Congress to win specific legislative changes that help hungry people, and place the issue of hunger on the nation's policy agenda.

Bread for the World works closely with Bread for the World Institute. The Institute seeks to inform, educate, nurture and motivate concerned citizens for action on policies that affect hungry people.

Headquarters

1100 Wayne Ave., Suite 1000, Silver Spring, MD 20910 Tel. (301)608-2400 Fax (301)608-2401
E-mail: bread@bread.org
Website: http://www.bread.org
Media Contact, Andrea Jeyaveeran, 1100 Wayne Ave., Suite 1000, Silver Spring, MD 20910 Tel. (301)608-2400 Fax (301)608-2401

Officers

Pres., Rev. David Beckmann
Bd. Chpsn., Patricia Ayers

23

Bd. Vice-Chpsn., Fr. Clarence Williams, CPPS

Campus Crusade for Christ International

Campus Crusade for Christ International is an interdenominational, evangelistic and discipleship ministry dedicated to helping fulfill the Great Commission through the multiplication strategy of "win-build-send." Formed in 1951 on the campus of UCLA, the organization now includes 50 plus separate ministries reaching out to almost every segment of society. There are more than 16,700 staff members and 199,134 trained volunteers in 172 countries, with the numbers expanding almost daily. The NewLife 2000 strategy helps to give every person on earth an opportunity to say "yes" to Jesus Christ by the year 2000.

Headquarters

100 Sunport Ln., Orlando, FL 32809 Tel. (407) 826-2000 Fax (407)826-2120
E-mail: ofcom@ccci.org
Website: http://www.ccci.org
Media Contact, Sid Wright

Officers

Pres., William R. Bright
Exec. Vice-Pres., Stephen B. Douglass
Vice-Pres. of Admn. & Chief Fin. Officer, Kenneth P. Heckmann
Vice-Pres. of Intl. Ministries, Bailey E. Marks

CARA-Center for Applied Research in the Apostolate

CARA-the Center for Applied Research in the Apostolate is a not-for-profit research organization of the Roman Catholic Church. It operates on the premise that not only theological principles but also the findings ofthe social sciences must be the basis for pastoral care.

CARA's mission since its founding in 1964 has been "To discover, promote, and apply modern techniques and scientific informational resources for practical use in a coordinated and effective approach to the Church's social and religious mission in the modern world, at home and overseas."

CARA performs a wide range of studies and services including church management, church personnel, and needs assessments of parishioners or religious order members. Since its roots are Roman Catholic, many of its studies are done for dioceses, religious orders, parishes, and the National Conference of U.S. Catholic Bishops. Interdenominational studies are also performed. Publishes The CARA Report, a research newsletter on Catholic Church related topics, four times a year and The Catholic Ministry Formation Directory, a guide and statistical compilation of enrollments for Catholic seminaries, diaonate formation programs, and lay ministry formation programs.

Headquarters

Georgetown University, Washington, DC 20057 Tel. (202)687-8080 Fax (202)687-8083
E-mail: cara@gunet.georgetown.edu
Website: http://www.georgetown.edu/research/cara/index.html
Media Contact, Executive Director, Dr. Bryan Froehle

Periodical

The CARA Report

Center for Parish Development

The Center for Parish Development is an ecumenical, non-profit research and development agency whose mission is to help church bodies learn to become faithful expressions of God's mission in today's post-modern, post-Christendom world. Founded in 1968, the Center brings to its client-partners a strong theological orientation, a missional ecclesial paradigm with a focus on faithful Christian communities as the locus of mission, research-based theory and practice of major change, a systems approach, and years of experience working with national, regional, and local church bodies.

The Center staff provides research, consulting and training support for church organizations engaging in major change. The Center is governed by a 12-member Board of Directors.

Headquarters

5407 S. University Ave., Chicago, IL 60615 Tel. (773)752-1596
Email: —
Website:—
Media Contact, Exec. Dir., Paul M. Dietterich

Officers

Chpsn., Eugene L. Delves, 9142 S. Winchester Ave., Chicago, IL 60620
Vice-Chpsn., Pastor Gordon Nusz, United Methodist Church, 111 E. Ridge St., Marquette, MI 49855
Sec., Delton Krueger, 10616 Penn Ave. South, Bloomington, MN 55431
Exec. Dir., Paul M. Dietterich

Chaplaincy of Full Gospel Churches

The Chaplaincy of Full Gospel Churches (CFGC) is a unique coalition of 129 nondenominational churches and networks of churches united for the purpose of being represented in military and civilian chaplaincies. Since its inception in 1984, CFGC has grown rapidly-recently representing over 6.5 million American Christians.

Churches, fellowships and networks of churches which affirm the CFGC statement of faith that "Jesus is Savior, Lord and Baptizer in the Holy Spirit today, with signs, wonders and gifts following" may join the endorsing agency. CFGC represents its 120 member-networks of churches and over 1200 independent churches before the Pentagon's Armed Forces Chaplains

Board, the National Conference of Ministry to the Armed Forces, Endorsers Conference for Veterans Affairs Chaplaincy, Federal Bureau of Prisons, College of Chaplains, and other groups requiring professional chaplaincy endorsement. The organization also ecclesiastically credentials professional counselors.

Headquarters

2721 Whitewood Dr., Dallas, TX 75233-2713 Tel. (214)331-4373 Fax (214)333-4401
Email: cfgc@fastlane.net
Website:—
Media Contact, Rev. Dr. E. H. Jim Ammerman

Officers

Pres. & Dir., Rev. Dr. E. H. Jim Ammerman
Deputy Dir., Rev. Dr. Charlene Ammerman
Vice-Pres., Ed Leach

Christian Endeavor International

Christian Endeavor International is a Christ-centered, youth-oriented ministry which assists local churches in reaching young people with the gospel of Jesus Christ, discipling them in the Christian faith, and equipping them for Christian ministry and service in their local church, community and world.It trains youth leasers for effective ministry and provides opportunities for Christian inspiration, spiritual growth, fellowship, and service. Christian Endevor International reaches across denominational, cultural, racial and geographical boundaries.

Headquarters

1221 East Broad St., P.O. Box 2106, Columbus, OH 43216-2106 Tel. (614)258-3947 Fax (614) 258-4950
Email: —
Website: —
Media Contact, Exec. Dir., Rev. David G. Jackson

Officers

Pres., Dr. Kent D. Maxwell
Exec. Dir., Rev. David G. Jackson

Christian Holiness Partnership

The Partnership is a coordinating agency of those religious bodies that hold the Wesleyan-Arminian theological view. It was organized in 1867.

Headquarters

CHP Office & Media Contact, Marlin Hotle, 263 Buffalo Rd., Clinton, TN 37716 Tel. (423)457-5978 Fax (423)463-7280
E-mail: bbpa28a@prodigy.com
Website: http://www.holiness.org

Officers

Pres., Dr. Jack Stone
Exec. Dir., Marlin Hotle

AFFILIATED ORGANIZATIONS

The American Rescue Workers

Association of Evangelical Churches
Association of Independent Methodists
Bible Holiness Movement
Brethren in Christ Church
Church of God, Anderson, IN
The Church of the Nazarene
Churches of Christ in Christian Union
Congregrational Methodist Church
Evangelical Christian Church
Evangelical Church of North America
Evangelical Friends Alliance
Evangelical Methodist Church
Free Methodist Church in North America
Japan Immanuel Church
Missionary Church (North Central Dist.)
OMS, International, Inc.
The Salvation Army
The Salvation Army in Canada
United Brethren in Christ Church (Sandusky Conference)
The Wesleyan Church
World Gospel Mission

Christian Management Association

Christian Management Association provides management training and leadership resources for Christian organizations and larger churches. It's membership represents CEOs/executive directors, pastors, church administrators, finance officers and other managers from more than 1,600 organizations in the United States. CMA publishes a bi-monthly magazine, *Christian Management Report,* a monthly newsletter, an annual *Who's Who in Christian Management* Membership directory, and other resources. CMA also provide comprehensive training and strategic networking opportunities through CMA's annual leadership and management conference for Christian organizations (the next conference is CMA Colorado Springs 99, Feb. 15-18, 1999), CEO Dialogues one-day roundtables, the all new, School of Management (multiple sites), local chapter meetings, management books and audiotapes. Annual membership is open to Christian Organizations and individuals. Companies that provide products or services to Christian organizations and churches may apply for Business Membership. Contact CMA for a **FREE** membership information packet and sample publications.

Headquarters

P.O. Box 4638, Diamond Bar, CA 91765 Tel. (909)861-8861 Fax (909)860-8247
John Pearson, CEO
Media Contact, Director of Membership Development, Jackie Tsujimoto
E-mail: CMA@CMAonline.org
Website: http://www. CMAonline.org

Officers

Chairman, Mark G. Holbrook, President/CEO, Evangelical Christian Credit Union
Vice-Chairman, Frank Sommerville, Attorney, Weycer, Kaplan, Pulaski & Zuber, P.C.

25

Secretary, Robert Peterson, Retired Chief Financial Officer, Evangelical Free Church of America

Treas., James A. Canning, Vice-President Finance & Administration, World Vision International

CEO, John Pearson

A Christian Ministry in the National Parks

This ministry is recognized by over 40 Christian denominations and extends the ministry of Christ to the millions of people who live, work and vacation in our National Parks. Staff ministers conduct services of worship in the park. Secular employment and housing is coordinated with the ministry staff and park concessionaires.

Headquarters
45 School Street, Boston, MA 02108 Tel. (617)720-5655 Fax (617)720-7899

E-mail: acmnp@juno.com

Website: http://www.coolworks.com/showme /acmnp/

Media Contact, The Rev. Richard P. Camp, Jr.

Officer
Dir., The Rev. Richard P. Camp, Jr.

Church Growth Center

The Church Growth Center is an interfaith, nonprofit, professional organization which exists to bring transformational change of the Christian church toward the effective implementation of the Lord's Great Commission, to make disciples of all people. This effort is done through consultations, resources, and educational events.

Founded in 1978 by Kent R. Hunter, president and chairman of the board, the Church Growth Center offers several services including church consultations by experienced consultants under the Creative Consultation Services arm, cutting edge resources through our bookstore, The Church Doctor(tm) Resource Center, and by providing educational events at churches and organizations in the way of providing speakers and resources at seminars, workshops, and conferences.

Other ministries under the arm of the Church Growth Center include Mission Teams International (taking teams overseas to train pastors to be more effective in their churches), The Church Doctor(tm) daily radio program (which is practical direction and helps for the lay person in the church), Nehemiah Guest House (where short-term missionaries may stay while learning church growth and working at the Center), and *Strategies for Today's Leader* (a quarterly magazine with timely thematic issues geared for pastors and leaders).

Headquarters
1230 U. S. Highway Six, P.O. Box 145, Corunna, IN 46730 Tel. (219)281-2452 Fax (219)281-2167

E-mail: churchgrowth@juno.com

Website: —

Media Contact, Office Mgr. and Assistant to Pres., Cheryl A. Kroemer

Officers
Pres., Dr. Kent R. Hunter, DMin STD

Vice-Pres., Rev. Paul Griebel, 312 S. Oak St., Kendallville, IN 46755

Sec.-Treas., Roger Miller, 1060 Park Dr., Turkey Lake, LaGrange, IN 46761

Church Women United in the U.S.A.

Church Women United in the U.S.A. is a grassroots ecumenical movement of one-half million Protestant, Orthodox, Roman Catholic and other Christian women, organized into more than 1,300 local and state units throughout the United States and Puerto Rico. Founded in 1941, CWU works in coalition with religious and secular groups on issues of peace and justice. A major program emphasis in the 1996 - 2000 Quadrenium is "Making the World Safer for Women and Children."

Headquarters
NATIONAL OFFICE
475 Riverside Dr., Ste. 500, New York, NY 10115 Tel. (800) CWU-5551 OR (212)870-2347 Fax (212)870-2338

E-mail: cwu@churchwomen.org

Website: http://www.churchwomen.org

Media Contact,Rev. Martha M. Cruz, Tel. (212)870-2344

LEGISLATIVE OFFICE
CWU Washington Ofc., 110 Maryland Ave. NE, Rm. 108, Washington, DC 20002 Tel. (202)544-8747, Fax (202)544-9133

E-mail: cwu-dc@churchwomen.org

Dir., Wash. Ofc., Ann Delory

Legislative Asst., Wash. Ofc., Tiffany L. Heath

UNITED NATIONS OFFICE
475 Riverside Dr., Ste. 500, New York, NY 10115 Tel. (212)661-3856

UN Ofc., Staff Liaison, Rev. Martha M. Cruz

UN Ofc., Intern, Christina M. Casado

ADMINISTRATION
General Director, Dr. Kathleen S. Hurty

Deputy Dir. for Admin. and Director of Comm., Rev. Martha M. Cruz, Tel. (212)870-2344

Email: mmcruz@churchwomen.org

Dir. of Finance, Lorraine M. Parker

Officers
Pres., Susan Shank Mix, New York, NY

1st Vice-Pres., Dr. Thelma Adair, New York, NY

2nd Vice-Pres., Rev. Jerrye Champion, Scottsdale, AZ

Sec.-Treas., Joan K. Regal, Maplewood, MN

PROGRAM DIRECTORS
Ecumenical Celebrations, Dir., Rev. Mary Cline Detrick

Ecumenical Development, Dir., Jeannie H. Lee

Ascension Day, Leadership Development

Regional Coordinators: Central, Ednabelle Madushaw, Pewaukee, WI; East Central, Catherine Childs, Columbus, OH; Mid-Atlantic, (Vacant); Northeast, Debbie B. Kaynor, West Hartford, CT; Northwest, Louise Smith-Woods, Seattle, WA; South Central, Kitty Polk; Southeast, Morene Williams, Athens, GA; Southwest, Winifred Hardy, Bailey, CO

Consultation on Church Union

Officially constituted in 1962, the Consultation on Church Union is a venture in reconciliation of nine American communions. It has been authorized to explore the formation of a uniting church, truly catholic, truly evangelical and truly reformed. In 1992 the participating churches were African Methodist Episcopal Church, African Methodist Episcopal Zion Church, Christian Church (Disciples of Christ), Christian Methodist Episcopal Church, The Episcopal Church, International Council of Community Churches, Presbyterian Church (U.S.A.), United Church of Christ and The United Methodist Church. Eight of nine communions have approved one covenantal agreement.

The Plenary Assembly is composed of 10 delegates and 10 associate delegates from each of the participating churches. Included also are observer-consultants from more than 20 other churches, other union negotiations and conciliar bodies. The Executive Committee has set the date of the 1998 Plenary as December 9-13, 1998; the location will be the Hyatt Regency Hotel in St. Louis. The Executive Committee will recommend to the Plenary that the Inaugural Liturgy for the Church of Christ Uniting take place on the First Sunday in Advent (December 3), in 2000. Location will be St. Louis.

The Executive Committee is composed of the president, two representatives from each of the participating communions and the secretariat. The secretariat consists of the full-time executive staff of the Consultation, all of whom are based at the national office in Princeton, N.J. Various task groups are convened to fulfill certain assignments. In 1990 there were four task groups: Communications; Unity & Justice; Theology and Special Gifts. In addition there was an Editorial Board for the annual Lenten Booklet of devotional meditations called *Liberation and Unity*.

Headquarters

151 Wall St., Princeton, NJ 08540 Tel. (609)921-7866 Fax (609)921-0471
Email: —
Website: —
Media Contact, Interim Gen. Sec., Lewis H. Lancaster, Jr.

Officers

Interim Gen. Sec., Lewis H. Lancaster, Jr.
Treas./Bus. Mgr., Christine V. Bilarczyk
Pres., Dr. Vivian U. Robinson, 125 Hernlen St., Augusta, GA 30901

Vice-Pres.: Bishop Vinton R. Anderson, P.O. Box 6416, St. Louis, MO 63108
Sec., Abraham Wright, 1912-3 Rosemary Hills Dr., Silver Springs, MD 20910

Rep. from Participating Churches

African Methodist Episcopal Church: Bishop Vinton R. Anderson, 4144 Lindell Blvd., Ste. 222, St. Louis, MO 63108; Bishop McKinley Young, 1656 Adams Dr., Atlanta, GA 30311
African Methodist Episcopal Zion Church: Bishop Marshall H. Strickland, 2000 Cedar Circle Dr., Baltimore, MD 21228; Bishop Cecil Bishop, 2663 Oakmeade Dr., Charlotte, NC 28270
Christian Church (Disciples of Christ): Rev. Dr. Paul A. Crow, Jr., P.O. Box 1986, Indianapolis, IN 46206; Rev. Mildred Slack, Five Church Assoc., 2149 South Grand, St. Louis, MO 63104
Christian Methodist Episcopal Church: Bishop Marshall Gilmore, 2323 W. Illinois Ave., Dallas, TX 75224; Dr. Vivian U. Robinson, 8th Episcopal Dist. Hdqt., 1256 Hernlen St., Augusta, GA 30901
The Episcopal Church: Rt. Rev. William G. Burrill, 935 East Ave., Rochester, NY 14607; Rev. Dr. Rena Karefa-Smart, 4601 North Park Ave., Chevy Chase, MD 20815
Intl. Council of Community Churches: Rev. Dr. Jeffrey R. Newhall, 19715 S. LaGrange Rd. Ste. C, Mokena, IL 60448; Abraham Wright, 1612-3 Rosemary Hills Dr., Silver Springs, MD 20910
Presbyterian Church (U.S.A.): Rev. Michael E. Livingston, CN-821, Princeton, NJ 08542; Dorothy G. Barnard, 2410 Fairoyal Dr., St. Louis, MO 63131
United Church of Christ: Rev. Dr. Thomas E. Dipko, Exec. V.P. 1st. Christian Church, 700 Prospect Ave., Cleveland, OH 44115; Rev. Diane C. Kessler, Mass. Council of Churches, 14 Beacon St., Boston, MA 02108
The United Methodist Church: Bishop William B. Grove, 234 Lark St., Albany, NY 12210

Ecumenical Development Cooperative Society (EDCS)

Based in the Netherlands, EDCS is often called "the churches' bank for the poor." EDCS borrows funds from churches, religious communities and concerned individuals and re-lends the funds to enterprises operated by low-income communities. Launched in 1975 through an initiative of the World Council of Churches, EDCS is organized as a cooperative of religious institutions and is governed by annual membership meetings and an elected board of religious leaders and development and financial professionals.

An international network of 15 EDCS Regional Managers is responsible for lending funds to cooperative enterprises and microcredit institutions. At the present time over $50 million

27

is at work in coffee shops, fishing enterprises, handicraft production, truck farming, and many other commercial ventures owned and operated by poor people.

EDCS is represented in the United States by the Ecumenical Development Corporation- USA (EDC-USA), a 501(c)3 non-profit corporation. American individuals and congregations can invest in EDCS by purchasing five year notes paying 2% interest that are issued by EDC-USA.

U.S. Headquarters
475 Riverside Dr., 16th Floor, New York, NY 10115 Tel. (212)870-2725 Fax (212)870-2722 E-mail: edcusa@erols.com Media Contact, Regional Manager for North America, The Rev. Louis L. Knowles

Officers, EDC-USA
Chpsn., The Rev. Dr. DarEll Weist
Vice-Chpsn., Thomas Dowdell
Treas., Bruce Foresman
Sec., Suzanne Sattler, IHM

Evangelical Council for Financial Accountability
Founded in 1979, the Evangelical Council for Financial Accountability has the purpose of helping Christ-centered, evangelical, nonprofit organizations earn the public's trust through their ethical practices and financial accountability. ECFA assists its nearly 900 member organizations in making appropriate public disclosure of their financial practices and accomplishments, thus materially enhancing their credibility and support potential among present and prospective donors.

Headquarters
P.O. Box 17456, Washington, DC 20041-7456 Tel. (703)713-1414 Fax (703)713-1133 Email: webmaster@ecfa.org Website: www.ecfa.org Media Contact, Pres., Paul D. Nelson

Officers
Pres., Paul D. Nelson
Vice-Pres., Donor & Member Services, Daniel D. Busby
Dir. of Member Review & Compliance, Lucinda Repass
V.P. Member Review & Compliance, Bill Altman

Evangelical Press Association
The Evangelical Press Association is an organization of editors and publishers of Christian periodicals which seeks to promote the cause of Evangelical Christianity and enhance the influence of Christian journalism.

Headquarters
314 Dover Rd., Charlottesville, VA 22901 Tel. (804)973-5941 Fax (804)973-2710 Email: 74463,272@compuserve.com Website: http://www. epassoc.org Media Contact, Exec. Dir., Ronald Wilson

Officers
Pres., David Neff, *Christianity Today*, 465 Gundersen Dr., Carol Stream, IL, 60188
Pres-Elect, Terry White, *Inside Journal*, PO Box 17429, Washington, DC 20041-0429
Treas., Lamar Keener, *Christian Times*, PO Box 2606, El Cajon, CA 92021
Sec., Jeanette Thomason, *Aspire*, 107 Kenner Ave., Nashville, TN 37205
Advisor, Dean Ridings, *Christian Camp & Conference Journal*, PO Box 62189, Colorado Springs, CO 80962-2189
Advisor, Brian Peterson, *New Man*, 600 Rinehart Rd., Lake Mary, FL 32746
Exec. Dir., Ronald Wilson

Fellowship of Reconciliation
The Fellowship of Reconciliation is an interfaith pacifist organization that has been working for peace and justice since 1915. The FOR has programs in the areas of international peace, nuclear disarmament, racial and economic justice, and nonviolence education in an effort to respond creatively and compassionately to issues of violence and injustice.

Headquarters
Box 271, Nyack, NY 10960 Tel. (914)358-4601 Fax (914)358-4924 E-mail: fornatl@igc.apc.org Website: http://www.nonviolence.org/~nvweb/For Media Contact, Ed. and Communications Dir., Richard Deats

Officers
Chpsn., Natl. Council, Rev. James Lawson, Holman United Methodist Church, 3320 W. Adams Blvd., Los Angeles, CA 90018
Vice-Chpsn., Natl. Council, Lou Ann Ha'aheo Guanson, P.O. Box 62305, Honolulu, HI 96839-2305
Exec. Dir., Rev. John Dear

PEACE FELLOWSHIPS & RELATED GROUPS
Baptist Peace Fellowship
Brethren Peace Fellowship
Buddhist Peace Fellowship
Catholic Peace Fellowship
Church of God Peace Fellowship
Disciples Peace Fellowship
Episcopal Peace Fellowship
Jewish Peace Fellowship
Lutheran Peace Fellowship
Mennonite Board of Cong. Ministries Peace & Soc. Justice Concerns
Methodist Peace Fellowship
Muslem Peace Fellowship
New Call to Peacemaking
NISBCO
Orthodox Peace Fellowship
Pax Christi
Presbyterian Peace Fellowship
Sojourners Peace Ministries

Unitarian Universalist Peace Fellowship
United Church of Christ FOR
United Methodist Peace Fellowship
World Peacemakers

Friends World Committee for Consultation (Section of the Americas)

The Friends World Committee for Consultation (FWCC) was formed in 1937. There has been an American Section as well as a European Section from the early days and an African Section was organized in 1971. In 1974 the name, Section of the Americas, was adopted by that part of the FWCC with constituency in North, Central, and South America and in the Caribbean area. In 1985 the Asia-West Pacific Section was organized. The purposes of FWCC are summarized as follows: To facilitate loving understanding of diversities among Friends while discovering together, with God's help, a common spiritual ground; and to facilitate full expression of Friends' testimonies in the world.

Headquarters

Section of the Americas Headquarters
1506 Race St., Philadelphia, PA 19102 Tel. (215)241-7250 Fax (215)241-7285
E-mail: Americas@FWCC.Quaker.org
Media Contact, Exec. Sec., Clide Grover

Offices

Right Sharing of World Resources, 3630 Winding Way, Cincinnati, OH 45229-1250 Tel. (513)281-4401
E-mail: Rswr@earthlink.net
Western Field Office, PO Box 4157, Salem, OR 97302-9998
Midwest Field Office, 315 Market St., Carlisle, IA 50047
Latin American Office, Guerrero 223 Pte., Zona Centro, Cd. Mante, TAM 89800 Mexico

Glenmary Research Center

The Research Center is a department of the Glenmary Home Missioners, a Catholic society of priests and brothers. The Center was established in 1966 to serve the rural research needs of the Catholic Church in the United States. Its research has led it to serve ecumenically a wide variety of church bodies. Local case studies as well as quantitative research is done to understand better the diversity of contexts in the rural sections of the country. The Center's statistical profiles of the nation's counties cover both urban and rural counties.

Headquarters

1312 Fifth Ave. North, Nashville, TN 37208 Tel. (615)256-1905 Fax (615)256-1902
Email: —
Website: —
Media Contact, —

Officers

Pres., Rev. Gerald Dorn, P.O. Box 465618, Cincinnati, OH 45246-5618

1st Vice-Pres., Rev. Wilfred Steinbacher, P.O. Box 465618, Cincinnati, OH 45246-5618
2nd Vice-Pres., Bro. Jack Henn, P.O. Box 465618, Cincinnati, OH 45246-5618
Treas., Robert Knueven, P.O. Box 465618, Cincinnati, OH 45246-5618
Dir., Kenneth M. Sanchagrin, Ph.D.
E-mail: ksanchagrin@mhc.edu

Graymoor Ecumenical & Interreligious Institute (GEII)

Graymoor Ecumenical & Interreligious Institute has its roots in the Graymoor Ecumenical Institute which was founded in 1967 by the Franciscan Friars of the Atonement, to respond to the Friars' historical concern for Christian Unity in light of the theological and ecumenical developments arising from the Second Vatican Council.

In 1991, in response to developments in both the Institute and the wider ecumenical scene, the Graymoor Ecumenical Institute was expanded into an information and service organization with a mission of Christian Unity and interreligious dialogue. Today, the Graymoor Ecumenical & Interreligious Institute employs several means to acomplish this goal. Among these are specialization desks for African-American Churches; Evangelical and Free Churches; Lutheran, Anglican, Roman Catholic Affairs; Interreligious Dialogue; and Social Ecumenism. Another is the annual Week of Prayer of Christian Unity—a world-wide observance initiated in 1908 by the Rev. Paul Wattson, co-founder of the Society of the Atonement—the theme and text of which are now chosen and prepared by the Pontifical Council for Promoting Christian Unity and representatives of the World Council of Churches. The Institute publishes the monthly journal *Ecumenical Trends*—to keep clergy and laity abrest of developments in the ecumenical and interreligious movements; provides membership in, and collaboration with, national and local ecumenical and interreligious organizations and agencies; and cooperates with individuals engaged in ecumenical and interreligious work.

Over the years, the Graymoor Ecumenical & Interreligious Institute has sponsored and co-sponsored meetings, colloquia, and workshops in areas of ecumenical and interreligious dialogue. These have been as diverse as colloquia between African-American and Hispanic Pentecostal scholars; Christians, Muslims, and Jews; state Councils of Churches; and interfaith training workshops for Christian leaders.

Headquarters

475 Riverside Dr., Rm. 1960, New York, NY 10115-1999 Tel. (212)870-2330 Fax (212)870-2001
E-mail: 104075,2312@compuserv.com
Media Contact: Walter Gagne, SA, Graymoor, Route 9, PO Box 300, Garrison, NY 10524-

29

0300 Tel. (914)424-3671ext. 3540 Fax (914)424-3433

STAFF
Interreligious Affairs Desk, Dir., Elias D. Mallon, SA, Ph.D.
Lutheran, Anglican, Roman Catholic Affairs Research Desk, Assoc. Dir., Lorelei F. Fuchs, SA, MA, STL, Katholieke Universiteit Leuven, Groot Begijnhof 12/2, 3000 Leuven, Belgium Tel./Fax 011(3216)20.78.05
E-mail: 100772,372@compuserv.com
African American Churches, Assoc. Dir., Pual Teresa Hennessee, SA, MA
Evangelical & Free Churches, Assoc. Dir., Elizabeth H. Mellen, M.Div.
Ecumenical Trends, Editor, Assoc. Dir., Keven McMorrow, SA, STD, Graymoor, Route 9, PO Box 300, Garrison, NY 10524-0300 Tel. (914)424-3671 ext. 3120
Social Ecumenism/National Public Policy Ministries, Paul Ojibway, SA, MA, GEII/Washington Office: 110 Maryland Ave. NE, Washington, DC 20002 Tel. (202)543-2800 Fax (202)547-8107
E-mail: briefing@voicesforjustice.org
Website: http://www.voicesforjustice.org
Business Manager, Betty Fedro, Graymoor, Route 9, PO Box 300, Garrison, NY 10524-0300 Tel. (914)424-3458 Fax (914)424-3473

Interfaith Impact for Justice and Peace

Interfaith Impact for Justice and Peace is the religious community's united voice in Washington. It helps Protestant, Jewish, Muslim and Catholic national organizations have clout on Capitol Hill and brings grassroots groups and individual and congregational members to Washington and shows them how to turn their values into votes for justice and peace.

Interfaith Impact for Justice and Peace has established the following Advocacy Networks to advance the cause of justice and peace: Justice for Women; Health Care; Hunger and Poverty; International Justice and Peace; Civil and Human Rights. The Interfaith Impact Foundation provides an annual Legislative Briefing for their members.

Members receive the periodic Action alerts on initiatives, voting records, etc., and a free subscription to the Advocacy Networks of their choice.

Headquarters
100 Maryland Ave. N.E., Ste. 200, Washington, DC 20002 Tel. (202)543-2800 Fax (202)547-8107
Email: —
Website: —
Media Contact, Jane Hull Harvey

Officers
Chpsn. of Bd., Jane Hull Harvey, United Methodist Church

MEMBERS
African Methodist Episcopal Church
African Methodist Episcopal Zion Church
Alliance of Baptists
American Baptist Churches, USA: Washington Office; World Relief Office
American Ethical Union
American Muslim Council
Center of Concern
Christian Methodist Episcopal (CME) Church
Christian Church (Disciples of Christ)
Church of the Brethren
Church Women United
Commission on Religion in Appalachia
Episcopal Church
Episcopal Urban Caucus
Evangelical Lutheran Church in America
Federation of Southern Cooperatives/LAF
Federation for Rural Empowerment
Graymoor Ecumenical and Interreligious Institute
Jesuit Social Ministries
Maryknoll Fathers and Brothers
Moravian Church in America
National Council of Churches of Christ: Church World Service; Washington Office
National Council of Jewish Women

NETWORK
Peoria Citizens Committee
Presbyterian Church (USA)
Progressive National Baptist Convention
Presbyterian Hunger Fund
Reformed Church in America
Rural Advancement Fund
Society of African Missions
Southwest Organizing Project
Southwest Voter Registration/Education Project
Toledo Metropolitan Ministries
Union of American Hebrew Congregations
Unitarian Universalist Association
Unitarian Universalist Service Committee
United Church of Christ: Bd. for Homeland Ministries; Bd. for World Ministries; Hunger Action Ofc.; Ofc. of Church in Society
United Methodist Church: Gen. Bd. of Church & Society; Gen. Bd. of Global Ministries Natl. Div.; Gen. Bd. of Global Ministries Women's Div.; Gen. Bd. of Global Ministries World Div.
Virginia Council of Churches
Western Organization of Resource Councils

International Union of Gospel Missions

The International Union of Gospel Missions (IUGM) is an association of 250 rescue missions and other ministries that serve more than 7 million homeless and needy people in the inner cities of the U.S., Canada and overseas each year. Since 1913, IUGM member ministries have offered emergency food and shelter, evangelical outreach, Christian counsel, youth and family services, prison and jail outreach, rehabilitation and specialized programs for the mentally ill, the elderly, the urban poor and street youth.

Headquarters

1045 Swift, N. Kansas City, MO 64116-4127 Tel. (816)471-8020 Fax (816)471-3718
E-mail: iugm@igum.org
Website: http://www.iugm.org
Media Contact, Exec. Dir., Rev. Stephen E. Burger or Phil Rydman

Officers

Exec. Dir., Rev. Stephen E. Burger
Pres., Richard McMillen, 10 S. Prince St., Lancaster, PA 17603 Tel. (717)393-7709 Fax (717)393-4966
Vice-Pres., Dr. Malcolm C. Lee, P.O. Box 1112, Richmond, CA 94802 Tel. (510)215-4888 Fax (510)215-0178
Sec.-Treas., Lorraine Minor, 5409 W. 79th St.,Prairie Village, KS 66208 Tel. (816)474-9380 Fax (816)231-7597

NATIONAL PROGRAM UNITS AND STAFF

Education, Rev. Michael Liimatta
Membership Services, Debbie McClendon
Newsletter and Magazine: Stephen E. Burger; Debra Palmer
Convention, Stephen E. Burger
Business Admn., Len Conner
Historian, Delores Burger
Exec. Sec., Madeleine Wooley
Communications & Development, Phillip Rydman
Resource Clerk, Dru Gray
Expansion, Philip Rydman

Interreligious Foundation for Community Organization (IFCO)

IFCO is a national ecumenical agency created in 1966 by several Protestant, Roman Catholic and Jewish organizations, to be an interreligious, interracial agency for support of community organization and education in pursuit of social justice. Through IFCO, national and regional religious bodies collaborate in development of social justice strategies and provide financial support and technical assistance to local, national and international social-justice projects.

IFCO serves as a bridge between the churches and communities and acts as a resource for ministers and congregations wishing to better understand and do more to advance the struggles of the poor and oppressed. IFCO conducts workshops for community organizers and uses its national and international network of organizers, clergy and other professionals to act in the interest of justice.

Headquarters

402 W. 145th St., New York, NY 10031 Tel. (212)926-5757 Fax (212)926-5842
Email: IFCO@igc.apc.org
Website: http://www. IFCOnews.org
Media Contact, Dir. of Communications, Gail Walker

Officer

Pres. Natl. Min., Rev. Schuyler Rhodes, Washington Sq. United Methodist Church

Inter-Varsity Christian Fellowship of the U.S.A.

Inter-Varsity Christian Fellowship is a non-profit, interdenominational student movement that ministers to college and university students and faculty in the United States. Inter-Varsity began in the United States when students at the University of Michigan invited C. Stacey Woods, then General Secretary of the Canadian movement, to help establish an Inter-Varsity chapter on their campus. Inter-Varsity Christian Fellowship-USA was incorporated two years later, in 1941.

Inter-Varsity's uniqueness as a campus ministry lies in the fact that it is student-initiated and student-led. Inter-Varsity strives to build collegiate fellowships that engage their campus with the gospel of Jesus Christ and develop disciples who live out biblical values. Inter-Varsity students and faculty are encouraged in evangelism, spiritual discipleship, serving the church, human relationships, righteousness, vocational stewardship and world evangelization. A triennial missions conference held in Urbana, Illinois, jointly sponsored with Inter-Varsity-Canada, has long been a launching point for missionary service.

Headquarters

6400 Schroeder Rd., P.O. Box 7895, Madison, WI 53707 Tel. (608)274-9001 Fax (608)274-7882
Email: —
Website: —
Media Contact, Dir. of Development Services, Carole Sharkey, P.O. Box 7895, Madison, WI 53707 Tel. (608)274-9001 Fax (608)274-7882

Officers

Pres. & CEO, Stephen A. Hayner
Vice-Pres.: C. Barney Ford; Robert A. Fryling; Samuel Barkat; Ralph Thomas; Jim Malliet
Bd. Chpsn., Virginia Viola
Bd. Vice-Chpsn., E. Kenneth Nielson

The Liturgical Conference

Founded in 1940 by a group of Benedictines, the Liturgical Conference is an independent, ecumenical, international association of persons concerned about liturgical renewal and meaningful worship. The Liturgical Conference is known chiefly for its periodicals, books, materials and sponsorship of regional and local workshops on worship-related concerns in cooperation with various church groups.

Headquarters

8750 Georgia Ave., Ste. 123, Silver Spring, MD 20910-3621 Tel. (301)495-0885
E-mail: litconf@aol.com
Website: —
Media Contact, Exec. Dir., Robert Brancatelli

Pres., Eleanor Bernstein
Vice-Pres., Samuel Torvend
Sec., Robert Rimbo
Treas., Victor Cinson

The Lord's Day Alliance of the United States

The Lord's Day Alliance of the United States, founded in 1888 in Washington, D.C., is the only national organization whose sole purpose is the preservation and cultivation of Sunday, the Lord's Day, as a day of rest and worship. The Alliance also seeks to safeguard a Day of Common Rest for all people regardless of their faith. Its Board of Managers is composed of representatives from 25 denominations.

It serves as an information bureau, publishes a magazine, *Sunday*, and furnishes speakers and a variety of materials such as pamphlets, a book, *The Lord's Day*, videos, posters, radio spot announcements, decals, cassettes, news releases, articles for magazines and television programs.

Headquarters

2930 Flowers Rd. S., Ste. 16, Atlanta, GA 30341 Tel. (770)936-5376 Fax (770)452-6582
Media Contact, Exec. Dir. & Ed., Dr. Jack P. Lowndes
E-mail: dlowndes@georgiabaptist.org
Website: http://www.gabaptist.org

Officers

Exec. Dir. & Ed., Dr. Jack P. Lowndes
Pres., Dr. Paul Craven, Jr.
Vice-Pres.: Charles Holland; Roger A. Kvam; Timothy E. Bird; John H. Schaal; William B. Shea; W. David Sapp
Sec., Rev. Donald Pepper
Treas., E. Larry Eidson

Lutheran World Relief

Lutheran World Relief (LWR) is an overseas development and relief agency based in New York City which responds quickly to natural and man-made disasters and supports more than 160 long-range development projects in countries throughout Africa, Asia, the Middle East and Latin America.

Founded in 1945 to act on behalf of Lutherans in the United States, LWR has as its mission "to support the poor and oppressed overseas in their efforts to meet basic human needs and participate with dignity and equity in the life of their communities; and to alleviate human suffering resulting from natural disaster, war, social conflict or poverty."

Headquarters

390 Park Ave. S., New York, NY 10016 Tel. (212)532-6350 Fax (212)213-6081
E-mail: lwr@lwr.org
Website: http://www.lwr.org/
Media Contact, Jonathan C. Frerichs

Pres., Kathryn F. Wolford

The Mennonite Central Committee

The Mennonite Central Committee is the relief and service agency of North American Mennonite and Brethren in Christ Churches. Representatives from Mennonite and Brethren in Christ groups make up the MCC, which meets annually in February to review its program and to approve policies and budget. Founded in 1920, MCC administers and participates in programs of agricultural and economic development, education, health, self-help, relief, peace and disaster service. MCC has about 875 workers serving in 50 countries in Africa, Asia, Europe, Middle East and South, Central and North America.

MCC has service programs in North America that focus both on urban and rural poverty areas. There are also North American programs focusing on such diverse matters as community conciliation, employment creation and criminal justice issues. These programs are administered by two national bodies-MCC U.S. and MCC Canada.

Contributions from North American Mennonite and Brethren in Christ churches provide the largest part of MCC's support. Other sources of financial support include the contributed earnings of volunteers, grants from private and government agencies and contributions from Mennonite churches abroad. The total income in 1997, including material aid contributions, amounted to $48.9 million.

MCC tries to strengthen local communities by working in cooperation with local churches or other community groups. Many personnel are placed with other agencies, including missions. Programs are planned with sensitivity to locally felt needs.

Headquarters

Box 500, 21 S. 12th St., Akron, PA 17501 Tel. (717)859-1151 Fax (717)859-2171
Canadian Office, 134 Plaza Dr., Winnipeg, MB R3T 5K9 Tel. (204)261-6381 Fax (204)269-9875
Email: mailbox@mcc.org
Website: http://www. mennonitecc.ca/mcc/
Media Contact, Exec. Dir., Ronald J.R. Mathies, P.O. Box 500, Akron, PA 17501 Tel. (717)859-1151 Fax (717)859-2171

Officers

Exec. Secs.: Intl., Ronald J.R. Mathies; Canada, Marv Frey; U.S.A., Stephen Penner

National Association of Ecumenical and Interreligious Staff

This is the successor organization to the Association of Council Secretaries which was founded in 1940. The name change was made in 1971.

NAES is an association of professional staff in

ecumenical and interreligious work. It was established to provide creative relationships among them and to encourage mutual support and personal and professional growth. This is accomplished through training programs, through exchange and discussion of common concerns at conferences, and through the publication of the Corletter, in collaboration with NCCC Ecumenical Networks.

Headquarters

c/o National Council of Churches, 475 Riverside Dr., New York, NY 10115-0050 Tel. (212)870-2155 Fax (212)870-2690
Email: —
Website: —
Media Contact, Barbara George, Dir., Ecumenical Networks Office, NCCC USA

Officers

Past Pres., Rev. David T. Alger, Assoc. Min. of Tacoma/Pierce Co., 1224 South I St., Tacoma, WA 98405-5021 Tel. (206)383-3056 Fax (206) 383-2672
Pres., Arthur Lee, Emergency Feeding Program, Church Council of Greater Seattle, PO Box 18145, Seattle, WA 98118-0145 Tel. (206)723-0647
Sec., Rev. David P. Baak, Grand Rapids Area Ctr. for Ecumenism, 38 Fulton W., Grand Rapids, MI 49503 Tel. (616)774-2042 Fax (616)774-2883
Treas., James Robinson, Tulsa Metropolitan Ministry, 221 S. Nogales Ave., Tulsa, OK 74127 Tel. (918)582-3147 Fax (918)582-3159
Registrar, Rev. N. J. L'Heureux, Queens Fed. of Churches, 86-17 105th St., Richmond Hill, NY 11418 Tel. (718)847-6764 Fax (718)847-7392

The National Association of Evangelicals

The National Association of Evangelicals (NAE) is a voluntary fellowship of evangelical denominations, churches, organizations and individuals demonstrating unity in the body of Christ by standing for biblical truth, speaking with a representative voice, and serving the evangelical community through united action, cooperative ministry and strategic planning.

The association is comprised of approximately 43,000 congregations nationwide from 49 member denominations and fellowships, as well as several hundred independent churches. The membership of the association includes over 250 parachurch ministries and educational institutions. Through the cooperative ministry of these members, NAE directly and indirectly benefits over 27 million people. These ministries represent a broad range of theological traditions, but all subscribe to the distinctly evangelical NAE Statement of Faith. The association is a nationally recognized entity by the public sector with a reputation for integrity and effective service.

The cooperative ministries of the National Association of Evangelicals demonstrate the association's intentional desire to promote cooperation without compromise.

Headquarters

450 Gundersen Dr., Carol Stream, IL 60188 Tel. (630)665-0500 Fax (630)665-8575
Office for Govt. Affairs, 1023 15th St. N.W., Ste. 500, Washington, DC 20005 Tel. (202)789-1011 Fax (202)842-0392
Email: NAE@nae.net
Website: http://www. nae.net
Media Contact, Vice Pres., David L. Melvin, P.O. Box 28, Wheaton, IL 60189 Tel. (630)665-0500 Fax (630)665-8575

Officers

Chair, Dr. R. Lamar Vest, P.O. Box 2430, Cleveland, TN 37320-2430
1st Vice-Chairman, Dr. Edward L. Foggs, 1303 E. 5th St., P.O. Box 2420, Anderson, IN 46018-2420
2nd Vice Chairman, Dr. L. Edward Davis, 29140 Buckingham Ave. #5, Livonia, MI 48154-4572
Sec., Bishop Ray A. Seilhamer, 302 Lake St., Huntington, IN 46750
Treas., Mr. Donald Duff, 1824 Old Lantern Trail, Ft. Wayne, IN 46825

Staff

President, —
Vice-Pres., Director of Operations, Rev. David L. Melvin
Finance & Management: Vice-Pres., Darrell L. Fulton
Office for Govt. Affairs, Vice-Pres-at-large ., Dr. Robert P. Dugan, Jr.
Policy Analyst, Rev. Richard Cizik
Counsel, Forest Montgomery
Special Representative, Timothy D. Crater
Vice-Pres.-At-Large, Dr. Billy A. Melvin

MEMBER DENOMINATIONS

Advent Christian General Conference
Assemblies of God
Baptist General Conference
Brethren Church, The (Ashland, Ohio)
Brethren in Christ Church
Christian & Missionary Alliance
Christian Catholic Church(Evan. Protestant)
Christian Church of North America
Christian Reformed Church in Noth America
Christian Union
Church of God, Cleveland, TN
Church of God, Mountain Assembly
Church of the Nazarene
Church of the United Brethren in Christ
Churches of Christ in Christian Union
Congregational Holiness Church
Conservative Baptist Assoc. of America
Conservative Congregational Christian Conf.
Conservative Lutheran Association
Elim Fellowship
Evangelical Church of North America
Evangelical Congregational Church

Evangelical Free Church of America
Evangelical Friends Intl./North America
Evangelical Mennonite Church
Evangelical Methodist Church
Evangelical Presbyterian Church
Evangelistic Missionary Fellowship
Fellowship of Evangelical Bible Churches
Fire-Baptized Holiness Church of God of the Americas
Free Methodist Church of North America
General Association of General Baptists
Intl. Church of the Foursquare Gospel
Intl. Pentecostal Church of Christ
Intl. Pentecostal Holiness Church
Mennonite Brethren Churches, USA
Midwest Congregational Christian Fellowship
Missionary Church
Open Bible Standard Churches
Pentecostal Church of God
Pentecostal Free Will Baptist Church
Presbyterian Church in America
Primitive Methodist Church, USA
Reformed Episcopal Church
Reformed Presbyterian Church of N.A.
Salvation Army
Synod of Mid-America (Reformed Church in America)
Wesleyan Church
Worldwide Church of God

National Bible Association

The National Bible Association is an autonomous, interfaith organization of lay people who advocate regular Bible reading and sponsors National Bible Week (Thanksgiving week) each November. Program activities include public service advertising, distribution of nonsectarian literature and thousands of local Bible Week observances by secular and religious organizations. The Association also urges constitutionally acceptable use of the Bible in public school classrooms. All support comes from individuals, corporations and foundations.

Founded in 1940 by a group of business and professional people, the Association publishes a quarterly newsletter and has the IRS nonprofit status of a 501(c)(3) educational association.

Headquarters

1865 Broadway, New York, NY 10023 Tel. (212)408-1390 Fax (212)408-1448
E-mail: biblenet@usa.net
Website: http://www.biblenet.org
Media Contact, Pres., Thomas R. May

Officers

Chpsn., Stewart S. Furlong
Vice-Chpsn., Robert Cavalero
Pres., Thomas R. May
Treas., Philip Clements
Sec., Max Chopnick, Esq.

The National Conference

The National Conference, founded in 1927 as the National Conference of Christians and Jews is a human relations organization dedicated to fighting bias, bigotry and racism in America. The National Conference promotes understanding and respect among all races, religions and cultures through advocacy, conflict resolution and education.

Primary program areas include interfaith and interracial dialogue, youth intercultural communications, training for the administration of justice and the building of community coalitions. The NCCJ has 61 regional offices staffed by approximately 240 people. Nearly 200 members comprise the National Board of Trustees and members from that group form the 22-member Executive Board. Each regional office has its own local board of trustees with a total of about 2,800. The National Board of Trustees meets once annually, the Executive Board at least three times annually.

Headquarters

71 Fifth Ave., New York, NY 10003 Tel. (212) 206-0006 Fax (212)255-6177
Email: —
Website: —
Media Contact, Dir. of Communications, Joyce Dubensky

Officer

Pres. & CEO, Sanford Cloud, Jr.

National Conference on Ministry to the Armed Forces

The Conference is an incorporated civilian agency. Representation in the Conference with all privileges of the same is open to all endorsing or certifying agencies or groups authorized to provide chaplains for any branch of the Armed Forces.

The purpose of this organization is to provide a means of dialogue to discuss concerns and objectives and, when agreed upon, to take action with the appropriate authority to support the spiritual ministry to and the moral welfare of Armed Forces personnel.

Headquarters

4141 N. Henderson Rd., Ste. 13, Arlington, VA 22203 Tel. (703)276-7905 Fax (703)276-7906
Email: jackw@erols.com
Website: —
Media Contact, Jack Williamson

Staff

Coord., Jack Williamson
Admn. Asst., Maureen Francis

Officers

Chpsn., Richard O. Stenbakken
Chpsn.-elect, Rodger Venzke
Sec., Theodore Hepner
Treas., Jacob Heerema
Committee Members: Catholic Rep., Msgr. John J. Glynn; Protestant Rep., Jeannette Flynn;

Jewish Rep., Rabbi David Lapp; Orthodox Rep., Ted Boback; Member-at-Large, —

National Council of the Churches of Christ in the U.S.A.

The National Council of the Churches of Christ in the U.S.A. is the preeminent expression in the United States of the movement toward Christian unity. The NCC's 35 member communions, including Protestant, Orthodox and Anglican church bodies, work together on a wide range of activities that further Christian unity, that witness to the faith, that promote peace and justice and that serve people throughout the world. Approximately 52 million U.S. Christians belong to churches that hold Council membership. The Council was formed in 1950 in Cleveland, Ohio, by the action of representatives of the member churches and by the merger of 12 previously existing ecumenical agencies, each of which had a different program focus. The roots of some of these agencies go back to the 19th century.

Headquarters

475 Riverside Dr., New York, NY 10115. Tel. (212)870-2

Media Contact, Dir. of News Services, Carol J. Fouke, 475 Riverside Dr., Rm. 850, New York, NY 10115, Tel. (212)870-2252, Fax (212)870-2030

Website: http://www.ncccusa.org

General Officers

Pres., Rt. Rev. Craig Anderson
Gen. Sec., Rev. Dr. Joan B. Campbell
Pres.-Elect, The Hon. Andrew Young
Immediate Past Pres., Bishop Melvin G. Talbert
Sec., Bishop Cecil Bishop
Treas., Rev. Dr. Margaret J. Thomas
Vice-Pres., Church World Service and Witness: Rev. Dr. Will L. Herzfeld
Vice-Pres., National Ministries, Rev. Elenora Giddings Ivory
Vice Pres. at Large: Archbishop Khajag Barsamian; Ms Rebecca Cruz; Dr. Sylvia M. Faulk

THE GENERAL SECRETARIAT

Tel. (212)870-2141 Fax (212)870-2817
Gen. Sec., Rev. Dr. Joan B. Campbell
Christian Unity
Assoc. Gen. Sec. for Christian Unity, Rev. Dr. Eileen W. Lindner
Inter-Faith Relations Commission
Co-directors: Rev. Dr. Bert Breiner. Tel. (212)870-2156 and Dr. Jay T. Rock, Tel. (212)870-2560
Faith and Order Commission
Dir., Rev. William G. Rusch. Tel. (212)870-2569
Yearbook of American and Canadian Churches
Editor, Rev. Dr. Eileen W. Lindner
Assistant Editor, Mr. Derek J. Lander, Tel. (212)870-2031 Fax (212)870-2817

Inclusiveness and Justice
Assoc. Gen. Sec. for Inclusiveness and Justice, Nell B. Gibson
Ecumenical Networks
Interim Director, Barbara J. George
Communication Commission
Tel. (212)870-2574 Fax (212)870-2030
Assoc. Gen. Sec. for Communication and Interpretation, Rev. Randolph Naylor
Dir., News Services, Carol J. Fouke
Dir., Electronic Media, Rev. David W. Pomeroy
Dir., Interpretation Resources, Sarah Vilankulu
Assoc. Dir., Electronic Media, Rev. Roy T. Lloyd
Friendship Press
Dir., Roger Burgess
Art Production, Manager, Sean Grandits
Washington Office
110 Maryland Ave. NE Washington, D.C. 20002. Tel. (202)544-2350. Fax (202)543-1297.
Dir., Dr. Albert M. Pennybacker
Assoc. Dir., Mary Anderson Cooper

CHURCH WORLD SERVICE AND WITNESS

Tel. (212)870-2061 Fax (212)870-3523
Unit Dir./Deputy Gen. Sec., Rev. Dr. Rodney I. Page
Dir. of Programs and Operations, Linda Hartke
Dir., Constituency Information and Development, —
Dir., Agricultural Missions, Rev.Eva Jensen
Dir., World Community, —
Dir., Global Educ., Loretta Whalen, 2115 N. Charles St., Baltimore, MD 21218. Tel. (410)727-6106 Fax (410)727-6108
Dir., Office on Development Policy CWS/LWR, Carol Capps, 110 Maryland Ave., NE, Suite 108, Washington, DC 20002. Tel. (202)543-6336 Fax (202)543-1297
Interim Dir., Emergency Response, Donna Derr
Dir., Immigration and Refugee Program, —
Dir., Leadership Development, John W. Backer
Manager, Overseas Program Administration, —
Dir., Intl. Congregations, Rev. Arthur O. Bauer
Dir., Africa, Willis H. Logan
Dir., Caribbean and Latin America, Rev. Oscar Bolioli Fax: (212)870-3220
Dir., East Asia and the Pacific, Rev. Victor W. C. Hsu
Dir., Japan North America Commission (JNAC), Patricia Patterson
Dir., Europe, Rev. Paul Wilson
Dir., Middle East, David Weaver
Dir., Southern Asia, Rev. Larry Tankersley
Dir., Community Education and Fund Raising, Rev. Mel H. Luetchens, P.O. Box 968, Elkhart, IN 46515 Tel. (219)264-3102 Fax (219)262-0966

NATIONAL MINISTRIES UNIT

Tel. (212)870-2491 Fax (212)870-2265
Deputy Gen. Sec. / Unit Dir., Rev. Dr. Staccato Powell
Director, Environmental Justice, Rev. Richard Killmer

35

Dir., Bible Translation and Utilization, Dr. David J. Lull
Dir./Education for Mission, Roger Burgess
Dir., Evangelization, Rev. George Handley
Dir., Justice for Women, Karen Hessel
Dir., Ministries in Christian Education, —
Assoc. Dir., Ministries in Christian Education, Dr. Joe Leonard
Staff Assoc. for Professional Church Leadership, Karen Hessel
Assoc. Dir., Racial Justice and Reconciliation, Sammy Toineeta
Managing Director, Ecumenical Programs for Urban Service, Rev. Doran Porter
Director, EPRUS/AmeriCorps Special Projects, Rev. Janet Schrock
Director, Black Church EPRUS/AmeriCorps, Ms. Gloria White
Director, Hispanic Church EPRUS/AmeriCorps, Rev. Eddie Lopez
Director, CRVA EPRUS/AmeriCorps, Fred Gilbert
Related Movements
Interfaith Center for Corporate Responsibility, Timothy Smith. Tel. (212)870-2293
Natl. Farm Worker Ministry, Executive Director, Rev. David Crump. Tel. (312)829-6436

ADMINISTRATION AND FINANCE
Tel. (212)870-2088 Fax (212)870-3112
Chief Financial Officer, —
Financial Services
Dir. of Finance, Horace Nelson
Dept. of Business Services
Dir., Melrose B. Corley
Dept. of Information Technology
Dir., Rev. Nelson R. Murphy
Office of Human Resources
Director, ———
Manager, Rev. Evelyn Miller-Suber

CONSTITUENT BODIES OF THE NATIONAL COUNCIL
(with membership dates)
African Methodist Episcopal Church (1950)
African Methodist Episcopal Zion Church (1950)
American Baptist Churches in the U.S.A. (1950)
The Antiochian Orthodox Christian Archdiocese of North America (1966)
Armenian Apostolic Church of America, Diocese of the (1957)
Christian Church (Disciples of Christ) (1950)
Christian Methodist Episcopal Church (1950)
Church of the Brethren (1950)
Coptic Orthodox Church (1978)
The Episcopal Church (1950)
Evangelical Lutheran Church in America (1950)
Friends United Meeting (1950)
Greek Orthodox Archdiocese of America (1952)
Hungarian Reformed Church in America (1957)
Intl. Council of Community Churches (1977)
Korean Presbyterian Church in America, Gen. Assembly of the (1986)
Malankara Orthodox Syrian Church (1998)

Mar Thoma Church (1997)
Moravian Church in America, Northern Province, Southern Province (1950)
National Baptist Convention of America, Inc. (1950)
National Baptist Convention, U.S.A., Inc. (1950)
National Missionary Baptist Convention of America (1995)
Orthodox Church in America (1950)
Philadelphia Yearly Meeting of the Religious Society of Friends (1950)
Polish Natl. Catholic Church of America (1957)
Presbyterian Church (U.S.A.) (1950)
Progressive Natl. Baptist Convention, Inc. (1966)
Reformed Church in America (1950)
Russian Orthodox Church in the U.S.A., Patriarchal Parishes of the (1966)
Serbian Orthodox Church in the U.S.A. & Canada (1957)
The Swedenborgian Church (1966)
Syrian Orthodox Church of Antioch(Archdiocese of the U.S. and Canada) (1960)
Ukrainian Orthodox Church in America (1950)
United Church of Christ (1950)
The United Methodist Church (1950)

National Institute of Business and Industrial Chaplains
NIBIC is the professional organization for industrial chaplains, that includes members from a wide variety of denominations and work settings, including corporations, manufacturing plants, air and sea ports, labor unions and pastoral counseling centers. NIBIC has six membership categories, including Clinical, Professional, Affiliates and Organizational.

NIBIC works to establish professional standards for education and practice; promotes and conducts training programs; provides mentoring, networking and chaplaincy information; encourages research and public information dissemination; communicates with business leaders and conducts professional meetings. NIBIC publishes a quarterly newsletter and co-sponsors *The Journal of Pastoral Care*. A public membership meeting and training conference is held annually.

Headquarters
7100 Regency Square Blvd., Ste. 210, Houston, TX 77036-3202 Tel. (713)266-2456 Fax (713)266-0845.
E-mail: nibic@aol.com
Website: http://www. nibic.com
Media Contact, Rev. Diana C. Dale, 7100 Regency Square Blvd., Ste. 210, Houston, TX 77036-3202 Tel. (713)266-2456 Fax (713)266-0845

Officers
Pres., Rev. Diana C. Dale, D.Min.
Vice-Pres., Rev. Stephen Holden
Treas., Rev. Timothy Bancroft, D.Min.
Sec., Rev. Gregory Edwards

National Interfaith Cable Coalition, Inc.

The National Interfaith Cable Coalition, Inc. (NICC) was formed as a not-for-profit 501 (c) (3) corporation, in December 1987 and is currently comprised of nearly 70 Protestant, Catholic, Jewish and Eastern Orthodox faith groups and evangelical traditions. NICC's mission is to make faith visible on television.

NICC is the parent organization of Odyssey, a cable channel presenting a mix of religious, moral/ethical, values-based and family-oriented programming.

Odyssey was launched in September 1988 as VISN (Vision Interfaith Satellite Network). The channel's name was changed in October 1992 to VISN/ACTS, in 1994 to the Faith & Values Channel, and in 1996 to Odyssey.

As of July 1995, Odyssey is jointly owned by VISN Management Corp., a wholly owned subsidiary of NICC, and Vision Group Inc., a wholly owned subsidiary of Liberty Media Corp. ACTS (American Christian Television System) is a major provider of programming on the channel.

Headquarters
74 Trinity Place, Ste. 1602, New York, NY 10006 Tel. (212)406-4121 Fax (212)406-4105
Media Contact, Beverly Judge
E-mail: bjudge1@ix.netcom.com
Website: —

Officers
Chair, Dr. Daniel Paul Matthews
Vice Chair, Ralph Hardy Jr., Esq.
Secretary, Rabbi Paul J. Menitoff
Treasurer, Betty Elam

Staff
Admn. Dir., Beverly Judge

National Interfaith Coalition on Aging

The National Interfaith Coalition on Aging (NICA), a constituent unit of the National Council on Aging, is composed of Protestant, Roman Catholic, Jewish and Orthodox national and regional organizations and individuals concerned about the needs of older people and the religious community's response to problems facing the aging population in the United States. NICA was organized in 1972 to address spiritual concerns of older adults through religious sector action.

Mission Statement: The National Interfaith Coalition on Aging (NICA), affiliated with the National Council on the Aging (NCOA), is a diverse network of religious and other related organizations and individual members which promotes the spiritual well being of older adults and the preparation of persons of all ages for the spiritual tasks of aging. NICA serves as a catalyst for new and effective research, networking opportunities, resource development, service provision, and dissemination of information.

Headquarters
c/o NCOA, 409 Third St., SW, 2nd Floor, Washington, DC 20024 Tel. (202)479-6689 Fax (202)479-0735
Email: —
Website: —
Media Contact, NCOA Dir. of Communications, Michael Reinmer

Officers
Chpsn., Josselyn Bennett
Chpsn.-Elect, Richard Gentzler
Past Chpsn., Elaine Titler
Sec., Jan McGitliard
Dir., Barbara P. Clemons

National Interfaith Committee for Worker Justice

The National Interfaith Committee for Worker Justice (NICWJ) is a network of forty interfaith groups and people of faith who educate and mobilize the U.S. religious community on issues and campaigns to improve wages, benefits and working conditions for workers, especially low-wage workers. The organization rebuilds relationships between the religious community and organized labor.

The organization supports and organizes local interfaith worker justice groups around the country, publishes *Faith Works* six times a year providing congregations resources and updates on religion-labor work, coordinates the Poultry Justice project to improve conditions for poultry workers, and promotes healthy dialogue between management and unions in religious owned or sponsored health care facilities.

Headquarters
1020 West Bryn Mawr, 4th floor, Chicago, IL 60660-4627. Tel. (773)728-8400 Fax (773)728-8409
E-mail: nicwj@igc.org
Website: http://www.igc.org/nicwj
Media Contact: Ms. Jill Cashen

Officers
President, Bishop Jesse DeWitt (retired United Methodist Bishop)
Vice President, Bishop Howard Hubbard (Bishop of the Catholic Diocese of Albany)
Secretary-Treasurer, Rev. Jim Sessions (Highland Research and Education Center)
Chair of Action & Issues Committee, Rev. Michael Rouse (Pastor, St. Catherine African Methodist Episcopal Zion Church)
Chair of Education Committee, Rabbi Robert Marx (Congregation Hakafa)
Chair of Board Development Committee, Ms. Evely Laser Shlensky (Committee on Social Action of Reform Judaism)

Staff
Executive Director, Ms. Kim Bobo
Education & Outreach Coordinator, Ms. Regina Botterill

Poultry Justice Coordinator, Ms. Miltoria Bey
North Carolina Poultry Justice Coordinator, Dr. Jerry Taylor
Religious Employers Project Coordinator, Sr. Barbara Pfarr
Communications Coordinator, Ms. Jill Cashen
Office Manager, Ms. Kathy Kline

NETWORK AFFILIATES

ARIZONA
Phoenix Interfaith Committee for Worker Justice, 4302 N. 87th Pl., Scottsdale, AZ 85251; Tel. (602)946-5843; Contact: Mrs. Margaret Grannis

ARKANSAS
Forth Smith Religion and Labor Committee of Jobs With Justice, PO Box 2354, Alma, AK 72921; Tel. (501)783-1149; Fax (501)783-0512; Contact: Matt Joyce
Little Rock Religion and Labor Committee of Jobs with Justice, PO Box 477, Hampton, AK 71744; Tel. (840)783-1149; Fax (840)783-0512; Contact Matt Joyce

CALIFORNIA
Los Angeles Clergy and Laity United for Economic Justice, 548 S. Spring St., Suite 630, Los Angeles, CA 90013-2313; Tel. (213)486-9880 x103; Fax (213)486-9886; Contact Ms. Linda Lotz
San Jose Interfaith Council on Race, Religion, Economic & Social Justice, 2102 Almaden Rd., #107, Santa Clara, CA 95125; Tel. (408)269-7872; E-mail: tic@atwork.org
Coordinator: Poncho Guevara

DELAWARE
Delmarva Poultry Justice Alliance, c/o La Esperanza, 319 Race St., Georgetown, DE 19947; Tel. (302)854-9264; Fax (302)854-9277 Contact: Ms. Andrea Lukowsky

FLORIDA
Immokalee - Religious Leaders Concerned, 3619 Woodlake Drive, Bonita Springs, FL 34134; Tel. (941)495-1679; Fax (941)495-6595; Contact: Rhea Gray.
South Florida Interfaith Committee for Worker Justice, 6801 NW 15th Ave., Miami, FL 33147; Tel. (305)835-9808; Fax (305)835-7227; Contact: Rev. Richard Bennett

ILLINOIS
Chicago Interfaith Committee on Worker Issues, 1020 West Bryn Mawr, Chicago, IL 60660-4627; Tel. (773)728-8400; Fax (773)728-8409; Contact: Rev. Richard Bundy or Ms. Kristi Sanford

INDIANA
Northwest Indiana - Calumet Project, 7128 Arizona Ave., Hammond, IN 46323-2223; Tel. (219)845-5008; Fax (219)845-5032; Contact: Mr. Steven Ashby
Central Indiana - St. Joseph Valley Project, 2015 W. Western, #209, South Bend, IN 46629; Tel. (219)287-3834; Fax (219)233-5543; Coordinator: Mr. Dan Lane

Indianapolis - Interfaith Committee for Worker Justice, c/o East Tenth United Methodist Church, 2327 East 10th St., Indianapolis, IN 46220-0530; Tel. (317)636-9017; Fax (317)633-8368; Contact: Rev. Darren Cushman-Wood

KENTUCKY
Worker Rights Outreach & Kentucky Jobs with Justice, 1815 Fernwood Avenue, Louisville, KY 40205; Tel. (502)568-5600; Fax (502)581-1437; Contact: Mr. Chris Sanders

MASSACHUSETTS
Massachusetts Interfaith Committee for Worker Justice, 33 Harrison Ave., 4th floor, Boston, MA 02111; Tel. (617)574-9296; Fax (617)426-7684; E-mail: inalliance@aol.com; Contact: Dr. Jonathan Fine
Religion & Labor Committee, c/o Labor Guild of Boston, 883 Hancock St., Quincy, MA 02170; Tel. (617)786-1822; Fax (617)472-2486; Contact: Father Edward Boyle
Holy Cross Student Labor Action Committee, PO Box 840, College of the Holy Cross, Worcester, MA 01610; E-mail: mldorosa@holycross.edu

MICHIGAN
Detroit Interfaith Committee on Worker Issues, 1641 Webb, Detroit, MI 48206; Tel. (313)869-1632; Fax (313)869-8266; Contact: Ms. Barbara Hunt

MISSOURI
Kansas City Religion and Labor Coalition, PO Box 240595, Kansas City, MO 64124; Tel. (816)861-0073; Fax (816)861-0071; Contact: Mr. Jerry Meszaros
Labor & Religion Committee of the Human Rights Commission, 3519 N. 14th St., St. Louis, MO 63107; Tel. (314)241-9165; Fax (314)436-9291; Contact Rev. Rich Creason

NEVADA
Las Vegas Interfaith Council for Worker Justice, 1630 S. Commerce St., Las Vegas, NV 89102; Tel. (702)386-5258; Fax (702)384-0845; Contact: Ms. Paula Tusiani

NEW HAMPSHIRE
Interfaith Committee for Worker Justice, PO Box 292, Goffstown, NH 03045; Tel. (603)497-5167; Contact: Fred Robinson

NEW YORK
Albany Capitol District Labor Religion Coalition, 159 Wolf Road, Albany, NY 12205; Tel. (518)459-5400; Fax (518)454-6411; Contact: Ms. Margaret Shirk
Buffalo Coalition for Economic Justice, 2123 Bailey Ave., Buffalo, NY 14211; Tel. (716)894-2013; Contact: Ms. Joan Malone
New York City Labor-Religion Coalition, 40 Fulton St., 22nd Floor, New York, NY 10038; Tel. (212)406-2156, ext. 237; Fax (212)406-2296; Contact: Rabbi Michael Feinberg
New York City Staten Island Religion Labor Coalition, 32D Franklin Lane, Staten Island, NY 10306; Tel. (212)406-2156; Fax (212)406-2296; Contact: Ms. Lilly Gioia

New York State Labor-Religion Coalition, 159 Wolf Road, Albany, NY 12205; Tel. (518)459-5400; Contact: Mr. Brian O'Shaughnessy
Syracuse Central New York Labor Religion Coalition, 614 James St., Syracuse, NY 13201; Tel. (315)445-1690; Fax (315)445-1690; Contact: Ms. Mary Hannick

NORTH CAROLINA
North Carolina Poultry Justice Alliance, 417 Arlington St., Greensboro, NC 27406; Tel. (336)271-4070; E-mail: jtaylor54@juno.com; Contact: Dr. Jerry Taylor
Pulpit Forum, 1310 MLK Dr., Greensboro, NC 27406; Tel. (336)272-8441; Fax (336)378-1165; Contact: Rev. W.F. Wright

OHIO
Central Ohio Religion-Labor Network, Office of Social Action, Diocese of Columbus, Columbus, OH 42315; Tel. (614)241-2541; Contact: Mr. Mark Huddy
Cincinnati Interfaith Committee on Worker Justice, c/o Social Action Office, 100 E. 8th St., Cincinnati, OH 45212; Tel. (513)421-3131; Fax (513)421-1582; Contact: Mr. Thomas Choquette
Cleveland Jobs with Justice, 20525 Center Ridge Rd., Rocky River, OH 44116; Tel. (440)333-6363; Fax (440)333-1491; Contact: Mr. Steve Cagan

OKLAHOMA
Labor-Religion Council of Oklahoma, PO Box 2009, Tulsa, OK 74101-2009; Tel. (918)587-3115; Fax (918)587-6692; Contact: Rev. Donald Brooks

OREGON
Eugene-Springfield Solidarity Network, 4355 Pinecrest Dr., Eugene, OR 97405; Tel. (541)345-3253; Fax (541)346-2790; Contact: Mr. Charles Spencer

PENNSYVANIA
Area Religious Task Force on the Economy, 5125 Tenn. Ave., Pittsburgh, PA 15224; Tel. (412)361-3022; Contact: Rev. Ted Erickson

TENNESSEE
Nashville Middle Tennessee Jobs with Justice, 516 Riverwood Circle, Nashville, TN 37216; Tel. (615)226-9420; Fax (615)227-3185; Contact: Ms. Laurie Bullock
Knoxville Religious Outreach Committee, Jobs with Justice, 1259 Highlander Way, New Market, TN 37820; Tel. (423)933-3443; Fax (423)933-3424; Contact: Rev. Jim Sessions

TEXAS
Brazor Valley Interfaith Alliance for Worker Justice, St. Mary's Catholic Church, 603 Church St., College Station, TX 77840; Tel. (409)846-5717; Contact: Ms. Maureen Murray
Dallas Jobs with Justice, c/o Camp Wisdom UMC, 1300 W. Camp Wisdom Rd., Dallas, TX 75232; Tel. (972)224-4556; Fax (972)228-9434; Contact: Rev Charles Stovall
Houston Interfaith Committee for Worker Justice, c/o Worklife Ministries, 7100 Regency Sq., Suite 210, Houston, TX 77036; Tel. (713)266-2456; Fax (713)266-0845; Contact: Rev. Diana Dale

WASHINGTON
Washington Religious Labor Partnership, c/o Wash. Association of Churches, 419 Occidental Ave., South, #201, Seattle, WA 98104; Tel. (206)625-9790 Fax (206)625-9791; Contact: Rev. John Boonstra

WISCONSIN
Faith Community for Worker Justice, 2128 N. 73rd St., Wauwatosa, WI 53213; Tel. (414)771-7250; Fax (414)771-0509; Contact: Mr. Bill Lange

National Interfaith Hospitality Network

The National Interfaith Hospitality Network is a non-profit organization which works with congregations to form Networks which provide shelter, meals and assistance to homeless families. The program mobilizes existing community resources: churches and synagogues for overnight lodging, congregations for volunteers, social service agencies for referrals and day programs. The Network also employs a director who provides assistance and advocacy to Network families as they seek housing and jobs.

NIHN provides technical assistance as well as videotapes, guides and manuals for successful programs.

Headquarters
120 Morris Ave., Summit, NJ 07901 Tel. (908) 273-1100
E-mail: nihnnj@aol.com
Website: http://www. nihn.org
Media Contact, Pres., Karen Olson

National Interreligious Service Board for Conscientious Objectors

NISBCO, formed in 1940, is a nonprofit service organization supported by individual contributions and relating to more than thirty religious organizations. Its purpose is to defend and extend the rights of conscientious objectors to war and organized violence. NISBCO provides information on how to register for the draft and to document one's convictions and qualify as a conscientious objector, how to cope with penalties if one does not cooperate, and how to qualify as a conscientious objector while in the Armed Forces. It also provides more general information and training for counselors and the public about conscientious objection, military service and the operation of the draft and possible programs for national service. It operates an international advocacy program for conscientious objectors focusing on Latin America.

As a national resource center it also assists research in its area of interest including the peace witness of religious bodies. Its staff provides referral to local counselors and attorneys and professional support for them. Through publications and speaking, NISBCO encourages people to decide for themselves what they believe about participation in war and to act on the basis of the dictates of their own informed consciences.

Headquarters
1830 Connecticut Ave. NW, Washington, DC 20009-5732 Tel. (202)483-2220 Fax (202)483-1246
Email: nisbco@igc.apc.org
Website: http://www. nisbco.org
Media Contact, Exec. Dir., Shazia N. Anwar

Officers
Exec. Dir., Shazia N. Anwar
Chpsn., David Radcliff
Vice-Chpsn., Jonathan Ogle
Sec., William Galvin
Treas., John Michael Sophos

National Religious Broadcasters

National Religious Broadcasters is an association of more than 1,000 organizations which produce religious programs for radio and television and other forms of electronic mass media or operate stations carrying predominately religious programs. NRB member organizations are responsible for more than 75 percent of all religious radio and television in the United States, reaching an average weekly audience of millions by radio, television, and other broadcast media.

Dedicated to the communication of the Gospel, NRB was founded in 1944 to safeguard free and complete access to the broadcast media. By encouraging the development of Christian programs and stations, NRB helps make it possible for millions to hear the good news of Jesus Christ through the electronic media.

Headquarters
7839 Ashton Ave., Manassas, VA 20109 Tel. (703)330-7000 Fax (703)330-7100
E-mail: info@nrb.org
Website: http://www.nrb.org
Media Contact, Pres., Brandt Gustavson; Vice-Pres., Michael Glenn

Officers
Chmn., David W. Clark, Family Net, Ft. Worth, TX
1st Vice Chmn., Thomas Rogeberg, In Touch Min., Atlanta, GA.
2nd Vice Chmn., Glenn Plummer, Christian Television Network, Detroit, MI
Sec., Wayne Pederson, Skylight Network, Minneapolis, MN
Treas., John Corts, Billy Graham Evan. Assoc., Minneapolis, MN

National Woman's Christian Temperance Union

The National WCTU is a not-for-profit, non-partisan, interdenominational organization dedicated to the education of our nation's citizens, especially children and teens, on the harmful effects of alcoholic beverages, other drugs and tobacco on the human body and the society in which we live. The WCTU believes in a strong family unit and, through legislation, education and prayer, works to strengthen the home and family.

WCTU, which began in 1874 with the motto, "For God and Home and Every Land," is organized in 58 countries.

Headquarters
1730 Chicago Ave., Evanston, IL 60201 Tel. (708)864-1396
Website: http://www.wctu.org
Media Contact, Michael C. Vitucci, Tel. (813) 394-1343

Officers
Pres., Sarah F. Ward, 33 N. Franklin, Knightstown, IN 46148
E-mail: sarah@wctu.org
Vice-Pres., Rita Wert, 2250 Creek Hill Rd., Lancaster, PA 17601
Promotion Dir., Nancy Zabel, 1730 Chicago Ave., Evanston, IL 60201-4585
Treas., Faye Pohl, P.O. Box 739, Meade, KS 67864
Rec. Sec., Mildred Burks, 3924 Penniman Ave., Oakland, CA 94619

MEMBER ORGANIZATIONS
Loyal Temperance Legion (LTL), for boys and girls ages 6-12
Youth Temperance Council (YTC), for teens through college age

North American Baptist Fellowship

Organized in 1964, the North American Baptist Fellowship is a voluntary organization of Baptist Conventions in Canada and the United States, functioning as a regional body within the Baptist World Alliance. Its objectives are: (a) to promote fellowship and cooperation among Baptists in North America and (b) to further the aims and objectives of the Baptist World Alliance so far as these affect the life of the Baptist churches in North America. Its membership, however, is not identical with the North American membership of the Baptist World Alliance.

Church membership of the Fellowship bodies is more than 28 million.

The NABF assembles representatives of the member bodies once a year for exchange of information and views in such fields as evangelism and education, missions, stewardship promotion, lay activities and theological education. It conducts occasional consultations for denominational leaders on such subjects as church extension. It encourages cooperation at the city and county level where churches of more than one member group are located.

Headquarters
Baptist World Alliance Bldg., 6733 Curran St., McLean, VA 22101

E-mail: nabf@bwanet.org
Website: http://www. bwanet.org
Media Contact, Dr. Denton Lotz

Officers
Pres., Dr. Morris M. Chapman, 901 Commerce St., Nashville, TN 37203
Vice-Pres., Dr. Robert Ricker, 2002 S. Arlington Heights Rd., Arlington Heights, IL 60005
Vice-Pres., Dr. Tyronne Pitts, 601 50th St., NE, Washington, DC 20019
Vice-Pres., Dr. Robert Wilkins, 7185 Millcreek Dr. Mississauga, ON I5N 5R4, Canada

MEMBER BODIES
American Baptist Churches in the USA
Baptist General Conference
Canadian Baptist Federation
General Association of General Baptists
National Baptist Convention of America
National Baptist Convention, USA, Inc.
Progressive National Baptist Convention, Inc.
Seventh Day Baptist General Conference
North American Baptist Conference
Southern Baptist Convention

North American Broadcast Section, World Association for Christian Communication

This group was created in 1970 to bring together those persons in Canada and the United States who have an interest in broadcasting from a Christian perspective.

An annual Faith & Media Conference is held during the week after Thanksgiving in the United States that draws over 150 persons from over 20 communions.

Headquarters
21440 Lathrup St., Southfield, MI 48075 Tel. (248)569-1751 Fax (248)559-6184
E-mail: nabswacc@aol.com
Website: http://www.united.edu/nabs/nabs1.htm

Officer
Bus. Mgr., Rev. Edward Willingham

Parish Resource Center, Inc.

Parish Resource Center, Inc. promotes, establishes, nurtures and accredits local Affiliate Parish Resource Centers. Affiliate centers educate, equip and strengthen subscribing congregations of all faiths by providing professional consultants, resource materials and workshops. The Parish Resource Center was founded in 1976. In 1997, there were six free-standing affiliates located in Lancaster, PA; Long Island, NY; South Bend, IN.; Denver, CO.; Dayton, OH and New York City. These centers serve congregations from 49 faith traditions.

Headquarters
633 Community Way, Lancaster, PA 17603 Tel. (717)299-2223 Fax (717)299-7229
E-mail: prcinc@redrose.net

Website: —
Media Contact, Pres., Dr. D. Douglas Whiting

Officers
Chair, Richard J. Ashby, Jr.
Vice-Chair, Margaret M. Obrecht
Sec., Dr. Robert Webber
Treas., Stephen C. Eyre
Pres., Dr. D. Douglas Whiting

Pentecostal/Charismatic Churches of North America

The Pentecostal/Charismatic Churches of North America (PCCNA) was organized October 19, 1994, in Memphis TN. This organizational meeting came the day after the Pentecostal Fellowship of North America (PFNA) voted itself out of existence in order to make way for the new fellowship.

The PFNA had been formed in October 1948 in Des Moines, IA. It was composed of white-led Pentecostal denominations. The move to develop a multiracial fellowship began when the PFNA Board of Administration initiated a series of discussions with African-American Pentecostal leaders. The first meeting was held July 10-11, 1992, in Dallas, TX. A second meeting convened in Phoenix, AZ, January 4-5, 1993. On January 10-11, 1994, 20 representatives from each of the two groups met in Memphis to make final plans for a Dialogue which was held in Memphis, October 1994.

This racial reconciliation meeting has been called "The Memphis Miracle." During this meeting the PFNA was disbanded, and the PCCNA was organized. The new organization quickly adopted the "Racial Reconciliation Manifesto."

Forty thousand copies of the PCCNA- sponsored magazine's inaugural issue of Reconciliation were published in June, 1998 and distributed to pastors in PCCNA- member churches. Dr. Harold D. Hunter and Dr. Cecil M. Robeck, Jr., are co-editors of this publication issued twice a year. The magazine is available online at http://www. pctii.org/pccna/index.html

Headquarters
1910 W. Sunset Blvd. Ste. 200, Los Angeles, CA 90026-0176 Tel. (213)484-2400, ext. 309 Fax (213)413-3824
Email: comm@foursquare.org
Website: http://www. iphc.org/pccna/index.html
Media Contact, Dr. Ronald Williams

Executive Committee
Co-Chpsn., Bishop Gilbert E. Patterson, 240 E. Raines Rd., Memphis, TN 38109
Co-Chpsn., Rev. Thomas Trask, 1445 Boonville Ave., Springfield, MO 65802
1st. Vice-Chpsn., Bishop Barbara Amos, 1010 East 26th St., Norfolk, VA 23504
2nd Vice-Chpsn., Rev. Rev. Billy Joe Daugherty, 7700 S. Lewis, Tulsa, OK 74136-6600

Sec., Rev. Oswill Williams, 3720 N Keith Street, Cleveland, TN 37320

Treas., Dr. Ronald Williams, P.O. Box 26902, Los Angeles, CA 90026

Co-Editors of *Reconciliation*: Dr. Harold D. Hunter, PO Box 12609, Oklahoma City, OK 73157; Dr. Cecil M. Robeck, Jr., 135 North Oakland Ave., Pasadena, CA 91182

Members: Bishop Ithiel Clemmons, 221 Kingston Ave., Brooklyn, NY 11213; Rev. Bishop Rodderick Ceasar, 110-25 Buy Brewer Blvd., Jamaica Queens, NY 11433; Bishop George D. McKinney, 5825 Imperial Ave., San Diego, CA 92114; Bishop James Leggett, P.O. Box 12609, Oklahoma City, OK 73157; Dr. Paul Walker, 2055 Mount Paran Rd., NW, Atlanta, GA 30327; Rev. Ann Gimenez, 640 Kempsville Rd., Virginia Beach, VA 23464

Advisors: Bishop B.E. Underwood, 172 Tanglewood South, Royston, GA 30662; Rev. Perry Gillum, 3720 N. Keith St., Cleveland, TN 37320; Dr. Vinson Synan, Regent University, P.O.Box 1056, Chesapeake, VA 23327; Dr. Ray Hughes, P.O.Box 2430, Cleveland, TN 37320

Project Equality, Inc.

Project Equality is a non-profit national interfaith program for affirmative action and equal employment opportunity.

Project Equality serves as a central agency to receive and validate the equal employment commitment of suppliers of goods and services to sponsoring organizations and participating institutions, congregations and individuals. Employers filing an accepted Annual Participation Report are included in the Project Equality "Buyer's Guide."

Workshops, training events and consultant services in affirmative action, diversity, and equal employment practices in recruitment, selection, placement, transfer, promotion, discipline and discharge are also available to sponsors and participants.

Headquarters

Pres., 6301 Rockhill Rd., Ste. 315, Kansas City, MO 64131 Tel. (816)361-9222 or toll free 1877-PE-IS-EEO Fax (816)361-8997

E-mail: KirkP@projectequality.org

Website: http://www.projectequality.org

Media Contact, Pres., Rev. Kirk P. Perucca

Officers

Chpsn., Donald Hayashi

Vice-Chpsn., Cheryl Hammond-Hopewell

Sec., Rev. Ronald Bonner, Sr.

Treas., Joan Green

Pres., Rev. Kirk P. Perucca

SPONSORS/ENDORSING ORGANIZATIONS

American Baptist Churches in the U.S.A.

American Friends Service Committee

American Jewish Committee

Assoc. Of Junior Leagues, Intl.

Central Conference of American Rabbis

Church of the Brethren

Church Women United

Consultation on Church Union

The Episcopal Church

Evangelical Lutheran Church in America

Nat. Assoc.of Church Personnel Administrators

National Council of Churches of Christ in the U.S.A.

National Education Association

Presbyterian Church (USA)

Reformed Church in America

Reorganized Church of Jesus Christ of Latter-Day Saints

Roman Catholic Dioceses & Religious Orders

The United Methodist Church

Unitarian Universalist Association

Union of American Hebrew Congregations

United Church of Christ

United Methodist Assoc. of Health & Welfare Ministries

YWCA of the USA

Protestant Radio and Television Center, Inc.

The Protestant Radio and Television Center, Inc. (PRTVC) is an interdenominational organization dedicated to the purpose of creating, producing, marketing and distributing audio-visual products for the non-profit sector. Its primary constituency is religious, educational and service-oriented groups. The "Flagship" production is the weekly radio show "The Protestant Hour."

Chartered in 1949, PRTVC provides a state-of-the-art studio facility, professional staff and a talent pool for radio, TV, cassettes and other forms of media production.

Affiliate members include the Episcopal Radio & TV Foundation, Evangelical Lutheran Church in America, Presbyterian Church (U.S.A.), United Methodist Communications, Agnes Scott College, Candler School of Theology, Emory University and Columbia Theological Seminary.

Headquarters

1727 Clifton Rd., NE, Atlanta, GA 30329 Tel. (404)634-3324 Fax (404)634-3326

Email: —

Website: —

Media Contact, Sandra Rogers

Officers

Bd. Chpsn., Dr. Gerald Troutman

Vice-Chpsn., Dale VanCantfort

Pres., J. Paul Howard

Treas., William W. Horlock

Sec., Betty Chilton

The Religion Communicators Council, Inc.

RCC is an international, interfaith, interdisciplinary association of professional communicators who work for religious groups and causes. It was founded in 1929 and is the oldest non-profit professional public relations organization in the world. RCC's 600 members include those who work in communications and related fields for church-related institutions, denominational agencies, non-and interdenominational organizations and communications firms who primarily serve religious organizations.

Members represent a wide range of faiths, including Presbyterian, Baptist, Methodist, Lutheran, Episcopalian, Mennonite, Roman Catholic, Seventh-day Adventist, Jewish, Salvation Army, Brethren, Bah†'°, Disciples, Latter-Day Saints and others.

On the national level, RCC sponsors an annual three-day convention, and has published five editions of a Religious Public Relations Handbook for churches and church organizations (6th Edition to be published in 1999), and a videostrip, The Church at Jackrabbit Junction. Members receive a quarterly newsletter (Counselor). RCC also co-sponsors an annual national satellite teleconference. There are 11 regional chapters.

RCC administers the annual Wilbur Awards competition to recognize high quality coverage of religious values and issues in the public media. Wilbur winners include producers, reporters, editors and broadcasters nationwide. To recognize communications excellence within church communities, RCC also sponsors the annual DeRose-Hinkhouse Awards for its own members.

In 1970, 1980 and 1990, RCC initiated a global Religious Communications Congress bringing together thousands of persons from western, eastern and third-world nations who are involved in communicating religious faith. Another Congress is planned for 2000 in Chicago, IL. March 29-April 1, 2000, Chicago Marriott Downtown Hotel.

Headquarters
475 Riverside Dr., Rm. 1948A, New York, NY 10115-1948 Tel. (212)870-2985 Fax (212)870-3578
Email: —
Website: http://www.rprc.org

Officers
Pres., Thomas R. May, National Bible Association, 1865 Broadway, New York, NY 10023 Tel. (212)408-1432
Vice-Pres., Richard Duerksen, Director, Spiritual Devlopment, Florida Hospital, 601 East Rollins St., Orlando, FL 32803 Tel. (407)895-7782

Religion In American Life, Inc.
Religion In American Life (RIAL) is a unique cooperative program of some 50 major national religious groups (Catholic, Eastern Orthodox, Jewish, Protestant, Muslim, etc.). It provides ser-

vices for denominationally-supported, congregation-based outreach and growth projects such as the current *Invite a Friend* program. These projects are promoted through national advertising campaigns reaching the American public by the use of all media. The ad campaigns are produced by a volunteer agency with production/distribution and administration costs funded by denominations and business groups, as well as by individuals.

Since 1949, RIAL ad campaign projects have been among the much coveted major campaigns of The Advertising Council. This results in as much as $30 million worth of time and space in a single year, contributed by media as a public service. Through RIAL, religious groups demonstrate respect for other traditions and the value of religious freedom. The RIAL program also includes seminars and symposia, research and leadership awards.

Headquarters
2 Queenston Pl., Rm. 200, Princeton, NJ 08540 Tel. (609)921-3639 Fax (609)921-0551
Email: —
Website: —
Media Contact, Manager, Sharon E. Lloyd, Tel. (609)921-3639

Executive Committee
Natl. Chpsn., Thomas S. Johnson, Chairman & CEO, Greenpoint Bank, NY
Chpsn. of Bd., Rev. Dr. Edwin G. Mulder
Vice-Chpsns.: Bishop Khajag Barsamian, Primate (Armenian Church of America);The Rev. Dr. M. William Howard, (President, New York Theological Seminary); Most Rev. William Cardinal Keeler, (Archbishop of Baltimore); Rabbi Ronald B. Sobel, (Cong. Emanu-El of the City of N.Y.)
Sec.,Sonia Francis, (The Episcopal Church)
Treas., Robertson H. Bennett

Staff
Pres., Dr. Nicholas B. Van Dyck
Manager, Sharon E. Lloyd

Religion News Service
Religion News Service (RNS) has provided news and information to the media for more than 60 years. Owned by the Newhouse News Service, it is staffed by veteran jounalists who cover stories on all of the world religions as well as trends in ethics, morality and spirituality.

RNS provides a daily news service, a weekly news report, and photo and graphic services. The daily service is available via the AP Data Features wire, fax, Ecunet, or e-mail. The weekly report is available electronically or by mail. Photos and graphics are supplied electronically.

Headquarters
1101 Connecticut Ave. NW, Ste. 350, Washington, DC 20036 Tel. (202)463-8777 Fax (202) 463-0033
Email: info@religionnews.com

Website: http://www. religionnews.com
Media Contact, Dale Hanson Bourke

Officers

Publisher, Dale Hanson Bourke
Editor, David Anderson

Religion Newswriters Association

Founded in 1949, the RNA is a professional association of religion news editors and reporters on secular daily and weekly newspapers, news services, news magazines, radio and television stations. It sponsors five annual contests for excellence in religion news coverage in the secular press. Annual meetings are held anytimefrom late spring to early fall..

Headquarters

88 West Plum St., Westerville, OH 43081 Tel. (614)891-9001
E-mail: rnastuff@aol.com
Website: http://www.rna.org
Media Contact, Exec. Dir., Debra Mason

Officers

Pres., Gayle White, Journal Constitution, Atlanta, GA
1st Vice-Pres., David Briggs, Associated Press
2nd Vice-Pres., —
Treas., Sandy Dolbee, San Diego Union Tribune, San Diego, CA
Sec., —

Religious Conference Management Association, Inc.

The Religious Conference Management Association, Inc. (RCMA) is an interfaith, nonprofit, professional organization of men and women who have responsibility for planning and/or managing meetings, seminars, conferences, conventions, assemblies or other gatherings for religious organizations.

Founded in 1972, RCMA is dedicated to promoting the highest professional performance by its members and associate members through the mutual exchange of ideas, techniques and methods.

Today RCMA has more than 3,000 members and associate members.

The association conducts an annual conference and exposition which provides a forum for its membership to gain increased knowledge in the arts and sciences of religious meeting planning and management.

Headquarters

One RCA Dome, Ste. 120, Indianapolis, IN 46225 Tel. (317)632-1888 Fax (317)632-7909
Email: —
Website: http://www.aip.com
Media Contact, Exec. Dir., Dr. DeWayne S. Woodring

Officers

Pres., Rudy Becton, United Pentecostal Church International, 3737 Red Hawk Ct., Bridgton,

MO 63044
Vice-Pres., Dr. Jack Stone, Church of the Nazarene, 6401 The Paseo, Kansas City, MO 64131
Sec.-Treas., Dr. Melvin Worthington, Natl. Assoc. of Free Will Baptists, P.O. Box 5002, Antioch, TN 37011-5002
Exec. Dir., Dr. DeWayne S. Woodring

Standing Conference of Canonical Orthodox Bishops in the Americas (SCOBA)

The Standing Conference of Canonical Orthodox Bishops in the Americas (SCOBA), established in 1960 with Archbishop Iakovos as Chairman, brings together the canonical hierarchs of the Orthodox Jurisdictions in America. The purpose of the Conference is to make the ties of unity among the canonical Orthodox Churches and their administrations stronger and more visible. The hierarchs meet twice annually for discussions and decisions on matters of common concern. Various commissions and committees have been established to implement the decisions of SCOBA. Among these are: the Orthodox Christian Education Commission (OCEC); International Orthodox Christian Charities (IOCC); the Orthodox Christian Mission Center (OCMC); the Military Chaplaincy Commission; the Study and Planning Commission; the Scouting Commission; and the Liturgical Commission.

Headquarters

10 East 79th St., New York, NY 10021 Tel. (212)570-3593 Fax (212)774-0202
Email: scoba@goarch.org
Website: —
Media Conatct, Ecumenical Officer, Bishop Dimitrios Conchell

Officers

Chmn., Archbishop Spyridon
Vice-Chmn., Metropolitan Philip
Sec., Metropolitan Joseph
Recording Sec., V. Rev. Paul Schneirla
Treas., Metropolitan Nicholas
Inter-Orthodox Relations, Bishop Dimitrios

T.H.E.O.S. International Foundation, Inc.

T.H.E.O.S. is a nonprofit, nondenominational self-help support network of men and women who provide emotional assistance to the widowed. Established in 1962, T.H.E.O.S. chapters hold monthly group meetings so that bereaved people can help themselves and others through the process of grieving. THEOS provides services that offer emotional, psychological, educational, and spiritual support. The spiritual component of healing grief flows freely from the heart of those in the support group, as well as from the publications and workshops offered by the T.H.E.O.S. International Foundation, Inc. The organization also publishes a magazine called *Survivor's Outreach* and the brochure "Grief is not a sign of weakness." In addition, T.H.E.O.S. hosts an international annual conference.

T.H.E.O.S. is comprised of more than 500 volunteers throughout the United States and Canada. There are 70 T.H.E.O.S. chapters in United States, Canada, and Africa.

Headquarters
322 Boulevard of the Allies, Ste. 105, Pittsburgh, PA 15222-1919 Tel. (412)471-7779 Fax (412) 471-7782
Email: —
Website: —
Media Contact, Manager, John F. Webber

United Ministries in Higher Education

United Ministries in Higher Education is a cooperative effort to provide religious programs and services on campuses of higher education.

Headquarters
7407 Steele Creek Rd., Charlotte, NC 28217 Tel. (704)588-2182 Fax (704)588-3652
Media Contact, Res. Sec., Linda Danby Freeman
E-mail: linda_freeman@ecunet.org
Website: —

Officers
Treas., Linda Danby Freeman
Personnel Service, Kathy Carson, 11780 Borman Dr., Ste. 100, St.Louis, MO 63146 Tel. (314)991-3000 Fax (314)993-9018
Resource Center, Linda Danby Freeman
PARTICIPATING DENOMINATIONS
Christian Church (Disciples of Christ)
Church of the Brethren
Moravian Church (Northern Province)
Presbyterian Church (U.S.A.)
United Church of Christ

Vellore Christian Medical College Board (USA), Inc.

The Vellore Christian Medical College Board has been linked since 1900 to the vision of the young
American medical doctor, Ida S. Scudder. Dr. Ida's dream initially was to ensure quality health care for women and children in India.
American women and men representing several church denominations wanted to be a part of Dr. Ida's dream and in 1916 recommended Vellore as the site for the proposed Missionary Medical College for Women. Since 1947 the Christian Medical College has admitted women and men. The hospital has a commitment to serve all regardless of ability to pay. The partnership between Vellore India and Vellore USA has continued uninterrupted to the present time.

Headquarters
475 Riverside Dr., Rm. 243, New York, NY 10115 Tel. (212)870-2640 Fax (212)870-2173

E-mail: usaboard@vellorecmc.org
Website: http://www.vellorecmc.org
Media Contact, President, Rev. William Salmond
E-mail: wsalmond@vellorecmc.org

Officers
Chair., Alfred E. Berthold, 2452 Club Rd., Columbus, OH 43221
Vice-Chair., Miriam Ballert, 7104 Olde Oak Ct., Prospect, KY 40059
Sec., Patricia Gass, 468 Riverside Dr., Apt. #2, New York, NY 10027
Treas., Anish Mathai, 235 W. 56th St., Apt. 25M, New York, NY 10119

The World Conference on Religion and Peace (WCRP/USA)

The World Conference on Religion and Peace in the United States (WCRP/USA) provides a forum for the nation's religious bodies based upon respect for religious differences. In today's world cooperation among religions offers an important opportunity to mobilize and coordinate the great moral and sociological capacities for constructive action inherent in religious communities.

WCRP/USA provides American religious bodies with opportunities for the following: to clarify their respective orientation to both national and international social concerns; to coordinate their efforts with other religious groups on behalf of widely-shared concerns; to design, undertake and evaluate joint action projects; and to communicate and collaborate with similar national religious forums organized by WCRP around the world.

Headquarters
WCRP/USA OFFICE, 777 United Nations Plaza, New York, NY 10017 Tel. (212)687-2163 Fax (212)983-0566
E-mail: info@wcrp.org
Website:—
Media Contact, Sec. Gen., Dr. William F. Vendley

Officer
Sec. Gen., Dr. William F. Vendley

World Council of Churches, United States Office

The United States Conference of the World Council of Churches was formed in 1938 when the WCC itself was still in the "Process of Formation." Henry Smith Leiper, an American with many national and international connections, was given the title of "Associate General Secretary" of the WCC and asked to carry out WCC work in the U.S. After the World Council of Churches was officially born in 1948 in Amsterdam, Netherlands, Leiper raised millions of dollars for WCC programs.

Today the U.S. Conference of the WCC is composed of representatives of U.S. member churches of the worldwide body. The U.S. Office of the WCC works to develop relationships among the churches, advance the work of WCC and interpret the council in the United States.

Headquarters
475 Riverside Dr., Rm. 915, New York, NY 10115 Tel. (212)870-2533 Fax (212)870-2528
E-mail: worldcoun@mail.wcc-coe.org
Website: http://www.wcc-coe.org
Media Contact, Philip E. Jenks

Officers
Moderator, Bishop Vinton R. Anderson, African Methodist Episcopal Church
Vice-Moderator, The Rev. Leonid Kishkovsky, Orthodox Church in America
Secretary, Kristine Thompson, Presbyterian Church (USA)

Staff
Exec. Dir., Jean S. Stromberg, Tel. (212)870-2522
Comm. & Publ. Officer, Philip E. Jenks, Tel. (212)870-3193
Office Admn., Sonia P. Omulepu, (212)870-2470
Young Adult Intern, Mary Christine Lohr, Tel. (212)870-3340

World Day of Prayer
World Day of Prayer is an ecumenical movement initiated and carried out by Christian women in 170 countries who conduct a common day of prayer on the first Friday of March to which all people are welcome. There is an annual theme for the order of worship which, has been prepared by women in a different country each year. For 1999 the women of Venezuela have prepared a worship service on the theme, "God's Tender Touch." The WDP motto is informed prayer and prayful action. The offering at this service is gathered by the WDP National Committee and given to help people who are in need.

Headquarters
World Day of Prayer International Comm., 475 Riverside Dr., Rm. 560, New York, NY 10115 Tel. (212)870-3049 Fax (212)870-3587
Email: —
Website: —
Media Contact, Exec. Dir., Eileen King

World Methodist Council- North American Section
The World Methodist Council, one of the 30 or so "Christian World Communions," shares a general tradition which is common to all Christians.

The world organization of Methodists and related United Churches is comprised of 73 churches with roots in the Methodist tradition. These churches found in 108 countries have a membership of more than 33 million.

The Council's North American Section, comprised of nine Methodist and United Church denominations, provides a regional focus for the

Council in Canada, the United States and Mexico. The North American Section meets at the time of the quinquennial World Conference and Council, and separately as Section between world meetings. The Section met in Rio de Janeiro, Brazil in August 1996 during the 17th World Methodist Conference to elect its officers for the 1997-2001 quinquennium.

North American Churches related to the World Methodist Council have a membership of approximately 15 million and a church community of more than 29 million.

Headquarters
P.O. Box 518, Lake Junaluska, NC 28745 Tel. (828)456-9432 Fax (828)456-9433
E-mail: wmc6@juno.com
Website: —
Media Contact, Gen. Sec., Joe Hale

Officers
Section Pres., Bishop Neil L. Irons, 900 S. Arlington Ave., Rm. 214, Harrisburg, PA 17109-5086 Tel. (717)652-6705 Fax (717)652-5109
First Vice-Pres., Bishop Thomas L. Hoyt, CME Church
Vice-Pres.: Bishop John R. Bryant, AME Church; Bishop Cecil Bishop, AMEZ Church; Bishop Richard D. Snyder, Free Methodist Church; Bishop Gracela Alverez, Methodist Church in Mexico; Bishop Keith Elford, Free Methodist Church of Canada; Dr. Brian D. Thorpe, United Church of Canada; Dr. Earle L. Wilson, The Wesleyan Church
Treas., Dr. James W. Holsinger, Jr.
Asst. Treas., Edna Alsdurf
General Sec., Dr. Joe Hale
World Officers from North America: Dr. Frances M. Alguire; Dr. Maxie D. Dunnam; Bishop Donald Ming

YMCA of the USA
The YMCA is one of the largest private voluntary organizations in the world, serving about 30 million people in more than 100 countries. In the United States, more than 2,000 local branches, units, camps and centers annually serve more than 14 million people of all ages, races and abilities. About half of those served are female. No one is turned away because of an inability to pay.

The Y teaches youngsters to swim, organizes youth basketball games and offers adult aerobics. But the Y represents more than fitness-it works to strengthen families and help people develop values and behavior that are consistent with Christian principles.

The Y offers hundreds of programs including day camp for children, child care, exercise for people with disabilities, teen clubs, environmental programs, substance abuse prevention, family nights, job training and many more programs from infant mortality prevention to overnight camping for seniors.

The kind of programs offered at a YMCA will vary; each is controlled by volunteer board members who make their own program, policy, and financial decisions based on the special needs of their community. In its own way, every Y works to build strong kids, strong families, and strong communities.

The YMCA was founded in London, England, in 1844 by George Williams and friends who lived and worked together as clerks. Their goal was to save other live-in clerks from the wicked life of the London streets. The first members were evangelical Protestants who prayed and studied the Bible as an alternative to vice. The Y has always been nonsectarian and today accepts those of all faiths at all levels of the organization.

Headquarters
101 N. Wacker Dr., Chicago, IL 60606 Tel. (312)977-0031 Fax (312)977-9063
Email: —
Website: http://www.ymca.net
Media Contact, Media Relations Manager, Arnie Collins

Officers
Board Chpsn., Daniel E. Emerson
Exec. Dir., David R. Mercer
(Int.) Public Relations Assoc., Mary Pyke Gover

Young Women's Christian Association of the United States

The YWCA of the U.S.A. is comprised of 364 affiliates in communities and on college campuses across the United States. It serves one million members and program participants. It seeks to empower women and girls to enable them, coming together across lines of age, race, religious belief, economic and occupational status to make a significant contribution to the elimination of racism and the achievement of peace, justice, freedom and dignity for all people. Its leadership is vested in a National Board, whose functions are to unite into an effective continuing organization the autonomous member Associations for furthering the purposes of the National Association and to participate in the work of the World YWCA.

Headquarters
Empire State Building,350 fifth Ave., Ste. 301 New York, NY 10118 Tel. (212)273-7800 Fax (212)465-2281
E-mail: HN2062@handsnet.org
Website: http://www.ywca.org
Media Contact, Chief of Staff, Cynthia Sutliff

Officers
National Pres., Alexine Clement Jackson
Sec., Tina Maree Herrera
Cheif Exec. Officer, Prema Mathai-Davis

Youth for Christ/USA

Founded in 1944, as part of the body of Christ, our vision is to see every young person in every people group in every nation have the opportunity to make an informed decision to be a follower of Jesus Christ and become a part of a local church.

There are 231 locally controlled YFC programs serving in cities and metropolitan areas of the United States.

YFC's Campus Life Club program involves teens who attend approximately 1,557 high schools in the United States. YFC's staff now numbers approximately 1,000. In addition, nearly 21,000 part-time and volunteer staff supplement the full-time staff. Youth Guidance, a ministry for nonschool-oriented youth includes group homes, court referrals, institutional services and neighborhood ministries. The year-round conference and camping program involves approximately 200,000 young people each year. A family-oriented ministry designed to enrich individuals and church family education programs is carried on through Family Forum, a daily five-minute radio program on more than 300 stations. Independent, indigenous YFC organizations also work in 127 countries overseas.

Headquarters
U.S. Headquarters, P.O. Box 228822, Denver, CO 80222 Tel. (303)843-9000 Fax (303)843-9002
Canadian Organization, 1212-31 Avenue NE, #540, Calgary, AB T2E 7S8
Email: —
Website: http://www. yfc.org
Media Contact, Pres., Roger Cross

Officers
United States, president, Roger Cross
Canada, Pres., Randy L. Steinwand
Intl. Organization: Pres., Sam Sherrard

2. Canadian Cooperative Organizations, National

In most cases the organizations listed here work on a national level and cooperate across denominational lines. Regional cooperative organizations in Canada are listed in the Directory for Canadian Regional and Local Ecumenical Bodies.

Aboriginal Rights Coalition (Project North)

ARC is a coalition for education and action on issues of Aboriginal justice in Canada. It works in partnership with native organizations and local network groups. The major focus is on the just settlement of Aboriginal land rights, impacts of major resource development, self-determination, and related military and environmental concerns.

Headquarters

153 Laurier Ave. East, 2nd Floor, Ottawa, ON K1N 6N8 Tel. (613)235-9956 Fax (613)235-1302 E-mail: arc@istar.ca

Media Contact, Natl. Coord., Ed Bianchi

Officers

Chpsn.: Joe Gunn

Natl. Coord., Ed Bianchi

MEMBER ORGANIZATIONS

Anglican Church of Canada
Canadian Conference of Catholic Bishops
Canadian Religious Conference
Council of Christian Reformed Churches in Canada
Evangelical Lutheran Church in Canada
Mennonite Central Committee
Oblate Conference in Canada
Presbyterian Church of Canada
Religious Society of Friends (Quakers)
Society of Jesus (Jesuits)
Canadian Unitarian Council
United Church of Canada

Alliance For Life-Alliance Pour La Vie

Alliance For Life was incorporated in 1972 to promote the right to life from conception to natural death. A registered charity for the purpose of education, Alliance conducts research on all life issues: abortion, infanticide, euthanasia and more. Alliance publishes materials to disseminate the information gained through that research. Alliance has prepared a one-hour documentary on untimely pregnancy and maintains a toll-free line to counsel women with inconveniently timed pregnancies and to help others suffering from post-abortion syndrome.

Alliance is the umbrella organization for 245 pro-life organizations in Canada. Governed by a Board of Directors composed of representatives from all provinces, it holds annual conferences in alternating provinces. Conferences are open to the public.

In 1992, Alliance For Life was split to permit the establishment of Alliance Action, Inc., a non-profit, non-charitable entity which is mandated to do advocacy work which Alliance For Life cannot do as a charity. It is located at the same address and publishes *Pro Life News* magazine 10 times annually.

Headquarters

B1-90 Garry St., Winnipeg, MB R3C 4H1 Tel. (204)942-4772 Fax (204)943-9283

Media Contact, Exec. Dir., Anna M. Desilets

ALLIANCE FOR LIFE OFFICERS

Pres., Chuck Smith
1st Vice-Pres., Rachel Murray
Treas., Jim Arsenault
Sec., Keith McCormick

ALLIANCE ACTION OFFICERS

Pres., Rachel Murray
Media Contact, Exec. Dir., Ingrid Krueger, Tel. (204)943-5273 Fax (204)943-9283
1st Vice-Pres., Chuck Smith
Treas., Jim Arsenault
Sec., Keith McCormick
Medical Advisor, Dr. J. L. Reynolds

Association of Canadian Bible Colleges

The Association brings into cooperative association Bible colleges in Canada that are evangelical in doctrine and whose objectives are similar. Services are provided to improve the quality of Bible college education in Canada and to further the interests of the Association by means of conferences, seminars, cooperative undertakings, information services, research, publications and other projects.

Headquarters

Box 4000, Three Hills, AB T0M 2N0 Tel. (403) 443-5511 Fax (403)443-5540

Media Contact, Sec./Treas., Peter Doell

Officers

Pres., Larry J. McKinney, Tel. (204)433-7488 Fax (204)433-7158
Vice-Pres., James Cianca, Tel. (519)434-6801 Fax (519)434-4998
Sec./Treas., Peter Doell, Tel. (403)443-5511 Fax (403)443-5540
Members-at-Large: Virginia Sherman, Tel. (403)284-5100 Fax (403)220-9567; David Boyd, Tel. (705)748-9111 Fax (705)748-3931; Walter Unger, Tel. (604)853-3358 Fax (604) 853-3063

Canadian Bible Society

As early as 1804, the British and Foreign Bible Society was at work in Canada. The oldest Bible Society branch is at Truro, Nova Scotia, and has been functioning continually since 1810. In 1904, the various auxiliaries of the British and Foreign Bible Society joined to form the Canadian Bible Society.

The Canadian Bible Society has 16 district offices across Canada, each managed by a District Secretary. The Society holds an annual meeting consisting of one representative from each district, plus an Executive Committee whose members are appointed by the General Board.

Each year contributions, bequests and annuity income of $11 million come from Canadian supporters. Through the Canadian Bible Society's membership in the United Bible Societies' fellowship, over 74 million Bibles, Testaments and Portions were distributed globally in 1994. At least one book of the Bible is now available in over 2090 languages.

The Canadian Bible Society is nondenominational. Its mandate is to translate, publish and distribute the Scriptures, without doctrinal note or comment, in languages that can be easily read and understood.

Headquarters

10 Carnforth Rd., Toronto, ON M4A 2S4 Tel. (416)757-4171 Fax (416)757-3376
Media Contact, Dir., Ministry Funding, Barbara Walkden

Officer

Gen. Sec., Dr. Floyd C. Babcock

Canadian Centre for Ecumenism

The Centre has facilitated understanding and cooperation among believers of various Christian traditions and world religions since 1963. An active interdenominational Board of Directors meets annually.
Outreach:
ECUMENISM, a quarterly publication, develops central themes such as Rites of Passage, Sacred Space, Interfaith Marriages, Care of the Earth, etc. through contributions from writers of various churches and religions in addition to its regular ecumenical news summaries, book reviews and resources.
A specialized LIBRARY is open to the public for consultation in the areas of religion, dialogue, evangelism, ethics, spirituality, etc.
CONFERENCES and SESSIONS are offered on themes such as Ecumenism and Pastoral Work, Pluralism, World Religions, Prayer and Unity.

Headquarters

2065 Sherbrooke St. W. Montreal, QC H3H 1G6 Tel. (514)937-9176 Fax (514)937-2684
Media Contact, Bernice Baranowski
Directors: Emmanuel Lapierre, O.F.; Diane Willey, N.D.S.

The Canadian Council of Churches

The Canadian Council of Churches was organized in 1944. Its basic purpose is to provide the churches with an agency for conference and consultation and for such common planning and common action as they desire to undertake. It encourages ecumenical understanding and action throughout Canada through local councils of churches. It also relates to the World Council of Churches and other agencies serving the worldwide ecumenical movement.

The Council has a Governing Board which meets semiannually and an Executive Committee. Program is administered through two commissions-Faith and Witness, Justice and Peace.

Headquarters

3250 Bloor St. West, 2nd Floor, Toronto, ON M8X 2Y4 Tel. (416)232-6070 Fax (416)236-4532
Media Contact, General Secretary
E-mail: ccchurch@web.net
Website: http://www.web.net/~ccchurch

Officers and Staff

Pres., Most Rev. Barry Curtis
Vice-Pres.: Dr. Dorcas Gordon; Rev. Robert Hankinson; Most Rev. Brendan O'Brien
Treas., John Hart
Gen. Secretary., Janet Somerville, ext. 2027
Faith & Witness, Dr. Eileen Scully, ext. 2022

AFFILIATED INSTITUTION

Aboriginal Rights Coalition: Ed Bianchi, 153 Larier Ave. E., Ottawa, ON K1N 6N8 Tel. (613) 235-9956 Fax (613)235-1302
E-mail: arc@istar.ca
Canada-Asia Working Group: Daisy Francis, 947 Queen St. E., Toronto, ON M5S 1K5 Tel. (416)465-8826 Fax (416)463-5569
E-mail: cawg@web.net
Canadian Churches' Forum for Global Min.: Dir. Robert Faris; 230 St. Clair Ave. W., Toronto, ON M4V 1R5 Tel. (416)924-9351 Fax (416)924-5356
E-mail: ccforum@web.net
Ecumenical Coalition for Economic Justice: John Dillon, 947 Queen St. E., Toronto, ON M5S 1K5 Tel. (416)462-1613 Fax (416)463-5569
E-mail: gattfly@web.net and ecej@acessv.com
Interchurch Coalition on Human Rights in Latin America: Bill Fairbairn, 129 St. Clair Ave. W., Toronto, ON M4V 1N5 Tel. (416)921-0801 Fax (416)921-3843
E-mail: icchrla@web.net
Interchurch Committee on Refugees: Tom Clark, 129 St. Clair Ave., W., Toronto, ON M4V 1N5 Tel. (416)921-9967 (416)921-3843
E-mail: iccr@web.net
Interchurch Coalition on Africa: Gary Kenny, 129 St. Clair Ave., W., Toronto, ON M4V 1N5 Tel. (416)927-1124 Fax (416)927-7554
E-mail: iccaf@web.net

Interchurch Action for Development, Relief and Justice: Dale Hildebrand, 947 Queen St. E., Toronto, ON M5S 1K5 Tel. (416)463-3634 Fax (416)463-5569
E-mail: icact@web.net
P.L.U.R.A.: Paulette Brown, 15 Candlewood Cres., Downsview, ON M3J 1G7 Tel. (416)663-3281 Fax (416)638-5654
Project Ploughshares: Ernie Regehr, Conrad Grebel College, Waterloo, ON N2L 3G6 Tel. (519)888-6541 Fax (519)885-0806
E-mail: plough@web.net
Taskforce on Churches and Corporate Responsibility: Daniel Gennarelli, 129 St. Clair Ave., W., Toronto, ON M4V 1N5 Tel. (416)923-1758 Fax (416)927-7554
E-mail: tccr@web.net
Interchurch Committee on Ecology: Daniel Gennarelli, 129 St. Clair Ave., W., Toronto, ON M4V 1N5 Tel. (416)923-1758 Fax (416)927-7554
E-mail: tccr@web.net
Ten Days for Global Justice: Dennis Howlett, 947 Queen St., E., Toronto, ON M5S 1K5 Tel. (416)463-5312 Fax (416)463-5569
E-mail: tendays@web.net

MEMBERS
The Anglican Church of Canada
The Armenian Orthodox Church-Diocese of Canada
Baptist Convention of Ontario and Quebec
British Methodist Episcopal Church*
Canadian Conference of Catholic Bishops
Christian Church (Disciples of Christ)
Coptic Orthodox Church of Canada
Christian Reformed Church in North America-Canadian Ministries
Ethiopian Orthodox Church in Canada
Evangelical Lutheran Church in Canada
Greek Orthodox Metropolis of Toronto, Canada
Orthodox Church in America, Diocese of Canada
Polish National Catholic Church
Presbyterian Church in Canada
Reformed Church in Canada
Religious Society of Friends-Canada Yearly Meeting
Salvation Army-Canada and Bermuda
The Ukrainian Orthodox Church
The United Church of Canada
*Associate Member

Canadian Evangelical Theological Association
In May 1990, about 60 scholars, pastors and other interested persons met together in Toronto to form a new theological society. Arising out of the Canadian chapter of the Evangelical Theological Society, the new association established itself as a distinctly Canadian group with a new name. It sponsored its first conference as CETA in Kingston, Ontario, in May 1991.

CETA provides a forum for scholarly contributions to the renewal of theology and church in Canada. CETA seeks to promote theological work which is loyal to Christ and his Gospel, faithful to the primacy and authority of Scripture and responsive to the guiding force of the historic creeds and Protestant confessions of the Christian Church. In its newsletters and conferences, CETA seeks presentations that will speak to a general theologically-educated audience, rather than to specialists.

CETA has special interest in evangelical points of view upon and contributions to the wider conversations regarding religious studies and church life. Members therefore include pastors, students and other interested persons as well as professional academicians. CETA currently includes about 100 members, many of whom attend its annual conference in the early summer. It publishes the Canadian Evangelical Review and supports an active internet discussion group, which may be accessed through *listserv@listserv.uottawa.ca.*

Headquarters
c/o Gordon Smith, Canadian Theo. Seminary, 4400 4th Ave., Regina, SK S4T 0H8 Tel. (306)545-1515 Fax (306)545-0210
Media Contact, Dr. Gordon Smith

Officers
Pres., Dr. Gordon Smith
Sec./Treas., Dr. David Priestley
Publications Coord., Dr. John G. Stackhouse, Jr.
CETA-List Coord., Alan Bulley
Executive Members: Dr. Edith Humphrey; Dr. Stanley Grenz

Canadian Society of Biblical Studies/Société Canadienne des Études Bibliques
The object of the Society shall be to stimulate the critical investigation of the classical biblical literatures, together with other related literature, by the exchange of scholarly research both in published form and in public forum.

Headquarters
Dept. of Religion and Culture, Wilfrid Laurier University, Waterloo, ON N2L 3C5 Tel. (519)884-0710, ext.3323 Fax (519)884-8854
E-mail: mdesjard@mach1.wlu.ca
Media Contact, Exec. Sec., Dr. Michel Desjardins

Officers
President ('98-'99), Daniel Fraikin, Queen's Theological College, Kingston, ON K7L 3N6 Tel. (613)545-2110, E-mail: fraikind@post.queensu.ca
Vice-Pres. ('98-'99), John Van Seters, Department of Religious Studies, University of North Carolina, 101 Saunders Hall, CB3225, Chapel Hill, NC 27599 Tel. (919)962-3929
E-mail: jvanset@email.unc. edu

Exec. Secretary. ('97-'02), Dr. Michel Desjardins, Dept. of Religion and Culture, Wilfrid Laurier University, Waterloo, ON N2L 3C5 Tel. (519)884-0710, ext.3323
E-mail: mdesjard@mach1.wlu.ca
Treas. ('97-'02), William Morrow, Queen's Theological College, Kingston, ON K7L 3N6 Tel. (613)545-2110
E-mail: morroww@post. queensu.ca
Publications Officer ('96-'99), Steven N. Mason,York University, 219 Vanier College, North York, ON M3J 1P3 Tel. (416)736-2110, ext.66987
E-mail: smason@yorku.ca
Programme Coord. ('98-'01), Edith Humphrey, 42 Belmont, Aylmer, QC J9H 2M7 Tel. (819)682-9257
E-mail: ehumphre@ccs.carleton.ca
Student Member-at-Large ('98-'99), Jane Webster, 233 Lock St. West, Dunnville, ON N1A 1V3 Tel.(905)774-4489
E-mail: webster@linetap.com

Canadian Tract Society

The Canadian Tract Society was organized in 1970 as an independent distributor of Gospel leaflets to provide Canadian churches and individual Christians with quality materials proclaiming the Gospel through the printed page. It is affiliated with the American Tract Society, which encouraged its formation and assisted in its founding, and for whom it serves as an exclusive Canadian distributor. The CTS is a nonprofit international service ministry.

Headquarters
26 Hale Rd., P.O. Box 2156, Brampton, ON L6T 3S4 Tel. (905)457-4559 Fax (905)457-4559
Media Contact, Mgr., Donna Croft

Officers
Director/Sec., Robert J. Burns
Director, John Neufeld

The Church Army in Canada

The Church Army in Canada has been involved in evangelism and Christian social service since 1929.

Headquarters
397 Brunswick Ave., Toronto, ON M5R 2Z2 Tel. (416)924-9279 Fax (416)924-2931
Media Contact, National Dir., Capt. Walter W. Marshall

Officers
National Dir., Capt. R. Bruce Smith
Dir. of Training, Capt. Roy E. Dickson
Field Sec., Capt. Reed S. Fleming
Bd. Chmn., Ivor S. Joshua, C.A.

The Churches' Council on Theological Education in Canada: An Ecumenical Foundation

The Churches' Council (CCTE:EF) maintains an overview of theological education in Canada on behalf of its constituent churches and functions as a bridge between the schools of theology and the churches which they serve.

Founded in 1970 with a national and ecumenical mandate, the CCTE:EF provides resources for research into matters pertaining to theological education, opportunities for consultation and cooperation and a limited amount of funding in the form of grants for the furtherance of ecumenical theological education.

Headquarters
60 St. Clair Avenue E, Ste. 302, Toronto, ON M4T 1N5 Tel. (416)928-3223 Fax (416)928-3563
Media Contact, Exec. Dir., Dr. Thomas Harding
E-mail: ccte@web.net
Website: www.web.net/~ccte

Officers
Bd. of Dir., Chpsn., Dr. Richard C. Crossman, Waterloo Lutheran Seminary, 75 University Ave. W., Waterloo, ON N2L 3C5
Bd. of Dir., Vice-Chpsn., Sr. Ellen Leonard, CSJ, Univ. of St. Michaels's College, 81 St. Mary St., Toronto, ON M5S 1J4
Interim Treas., John Wevers, 60 Southport St. Ut.# 6, Toronto, ON M6S 3N4
Exec. Dir., Dr. Thomas Harding

MEMBER ORGANIZATIONS
The General Synod of the Anglican Church of Canada
Canadian Baptist Ministries
The Evangelical Lutheran Church in Canada
The Presbyterian Church in Canada
The Canadian Conference of Catholic Bishops
The United Church of Canada

Concerns, Canada: a corporate division of Alcohol & Drug Concerns, Inc.

Concerns, Canada is a registered, non-profit, charitable organization that has been closely associated with the Christian Church throughout its long history. The organization's mandate is "to promote and encourage a positive lifestyle free from dependence upon alcohol, tobacco and other drugs."

The organization was granted a national charter in 1987, moving from an Ontario charter dating back to 1934. Among its services are: Toc Alpha (its youth wing for 14-to-24 year olds; PLUS (Positive Life-style Skills), a teacher curriculum for grades 4 to 8; two Institutes on Addiction Studies; courses for clients of the Ontario Ministry of Corrections; and educational materials for target groups.

Headquarters
4500 Sheppard Ave. E, Ste. 112H, Agincourt, ON M1S 3R6 Tel. (416)293-3400
Media Contact, CEO, Rev. Karl N. Burden

Officers
Pres., Rev. Larry Gillians, 11 Dundas St. West, Napanee, ON K7R 1Z3

Vice-Pres.: Scot Lougheed, 97 Dean Ave., Guelph, ON N1G 1L7
Treas., Jean Desgagne, Union Bank of Switzerland, 154 Univeristy Ave., Toronto, ON M5H 3Z4
CEO, Rev. Karl N. Burden

Ecumenical Coalition for Economic Justice (ECEJ)

The Ecumenical Coalition for Economic Justice (ECEJ) enables member churches to have a more effective public voice in advocating for a just, moral and sustainable economy. ECEJ undertakes research, education and advocacy to promote economic policy alternatives that are grounded in a Christian perspective. Sponsoring denominations include: the Anglican Church of Canada, the Canadian Catholic Bishops Conference, the Evangelical Lutheran Church in Canada, the Presbyterian Church in Canada and the United Church of Canada. ECEJ also acts as a link to social movements and coalitions to bring a collective church presence to them and to inform our own analysis.

The program focus of the next three years will be to advance alternative economic policies which support our vision of an "economy of hope". This includes proposing different ways to assess economic prosperity, challenging the growth model, envisioning a new model for social programs in global economy, and presenting alternative fiscal and monetary policies.

ECEJ publishes a quarterly briefing paper on current issues, the Economic Justice Report, as well as education and action resources.

An Administrative Committee oversees ECEJ and is made up of representatives from the sponsoring denominations as well as participating members which currently include: the School Sisters of Notre Dame, the Scarboro Foreign Mission, and the Religious Society of Friends (Quaker).

Headquarters
77 Charles St. W, Ste. 402, Toronto, ON M5S 1K5 Tel. (416)921-4615 Fax (416)922-1419
Media Contact, Educ. & Communications, Jennifer Henry
E-mail:gattfly@web.net

Officers
Co-Chpsn., Doryne Kirby
Co-Chpsn., Jim Marshall

Staff
Research, John Dillon
Women & Economic Justice Programme, Kathryn Robertson
Education/Communication, Jennifer Henry
Administration/Finance, Diana Gibbs

Evangelical Fellowship of Canada

The Fellowship was formed in 1964. There are 31 denominations, 124 organizations, 1,200 local churches and 11,000 individual members.

Its purposes are: "Fellowship in the gospel" (Phil. 1:5), "the defence and confirmation of the gospel" (Phil. 1:7) and "the furtherance of the gospel" (Phil. 1:12). The Fellowship believes the Holy Scriptures, as originally given, are infallible and that salvation through the Lord Jesus Christ is by faith apart from works.

In national and regional conventions the Fellowship urges Christians to live exemplary lives and to openly challenge the evils and injustices of society. It encourages cooperation with various agencies in Canada and overseas that are sensitive to social and spiritual needs.

Headquarters
Office: 600 Alden Rd. Ste. 300, Markham, ON L3R 0E7 Tel. (905)479-5885 Fax (905)479-4742
Mailing Address: M.I.P. Box 3745, Markham, ON L3R 0Y4
Media Contact, Pres., Dr. Gary Walsh, 600 Alden Rd., Ste. 300, Markham, ON L3R 0E7 Tel. (905)479-5885 Fax (905)479-4742
E-mail: efc@efc-canada.com

Officers
Pres., Dr. Gary Walsh
Chair, Rev. Ken Birch
Vice-Chair, Dr. Rick Penner
Sec., Marjorie Osborne
Treas., Lt. Col. Ralph Stanley
Past Pres., Dr. Donald Jost

COMMITTEE: MEMBERS-AT-LARGE
Dr. Arnold Cook; Rev. Grover Crosby; Rev. Abe Funk; Rev. Gillis Killam; Dr. Paul Magnus; Mr. Donald Simmonds; Rev. Harmony Thiesser, Rev. Winston Thurton
Task Force on Evangelism, Chpsns., Mr. Ross Rains, Dr. John Hull, Mrs. Marjorie Osborne
Social Action Commission, Chpsn., Dr. James Read
Education Commission, Chpsn., Dr. Glenn Smith
Women in Ministry Task Force, Chpsn., Rev. Eileen Stewart-Rhude
Aboriginal Task Force, Co-Chairs, Wally McKay; Wendy Peterson
Religious Liberties Commission, Chpsn., Dr. Paul Marshall
Task Force on Global Mission, Chpsn., Dr. Geoff Tunnicliffe

Interchurch Communications

Interchurch Communications is made up of the communication units of the Anglican Church of Canada, the Evangelical Lutheran Church in Canada, the Presbyterian Church in Canada, the Canadian Conference of Catholic Bishops (English Sector), and the United Church of Canada. ICC members collaborate on occasional video or print coproductions and on addressing public policy issues affecting religious communications.

Headquarters
3250 Bloor St. W., Etobicoke, ON M8X 2Y4

Media Contact, Chpsn., Douglas Tindal, Anglican Church of Canada, 600 Jarvis St., Toronto, ON M4Y 2J6 Tel. (416)924-9199 Fax (416)968-7983
E-mail: doug_tindal@national.anglican.ca

MEMBERS

Ms. Helga Dyck, Evangelical Lutheran Church in Canada, 302-393 Portage Ave., Winnipeg, MB R3B 3H6 Tel. (204)984-9166 Fax (204)984-9185

Rev. Glenn Cooper, Presbyterian Church in Canada, 50 Wynford Dr., Don Mills, ON M3C 1J7 Tel. (902)485-1561 Fax (902)485-1562
Email: gcooper@atcon.com

Rev. Rod Booth, Religious Television Associates, 3250 Bloor St. W., Etobicoke, ON M8X 2Y4 Tel. (416)231-7680 Fax (416)232-6004
E-mail: rbooth@uccon.org

Mr. Douglas Tindal, Anglican Church of Canada, 600 Jarvis St., Toronto, ON M4Y 2J6 Tel. (416)924-9199 ext.286 Fax (416)968-7983
E-mail: doug_tindal@ecunet.org

Ms. Linda E. Slough, United Church of Canada, 3250 Bloor St. W., Etobicoke, ON M8X 2Y4 Tel. (416)231-7680 ext.4011 Fax (416)232-6004
E-mail: lslough@uccon.org

Mr. William Kokesch, Canadian Conference of Catholic Bishops, 90 Parent Ave., Ottawa, ON K1N 7B1 Tel. (613)241-9461 Fax (613)241-8117
E-mail: kokesch@cccb.ca

Inter-Varsity Christian Fellowship of Canada

Inter-Varsity Christian Fellowship is a non-profit, interdenominational student movement centering on the witness to Jesus Christ in campus communities, universities, colleges and high schools and through a Canada-wide Pioneer Camping program. It also ministers to professionals and teachers through Nurses and Teacher Christian Fellowship.

IVCF was officially formed in 1928-29 by the late Dr. Howard Guinness, whose arrival from Britain challenged students to follow the example of the British Inter-Varsity Fellowship by organizing themselves into prayer and Bible study fellowship groups. Inter-Varsity has always been a student-initiated movement emphasizing and developing leadership in the campus to call Christians to outreach, challenging other students to a personal faith in Jesus Christ and studying the Bible as God's revealed truth within a fellowship of believers. A strong stress has been placed on missionary activity, and the triennial conference held at Urbana, IL. (jointly sponsored by U.S. and Canadian IVCF) has been a means of challenging many young people to service in Christian vocations. Inter-Varsity works closely with and is a strong believer in the work of local and national churches.

Headquarters

Unit 17, 40 Vogell Rd., Richmond Hill, ON L4B 3N6 Tel. (905)884-6880 Fax (905)884-6550
Media Contact, Gen. Dir., Rob Regier

Officer

Gen. Dir., Rob Regier

John Howard Society of Ontario

The John Howard Society of Ontario is a registered non-profit charitable organization providing services to individuals, families and groups at all stages in the youth and criminal justice system. The Society also provides community education on critical issues in the justice system and advocacy for reform of the justice system. The mandate of the Society is the prevention of crime through service, community education, advocacy and reform.

Founded in 1929, the Society has grown from a one-office service in Toronto to 17 local branches providing direct services in the major cities of Ontario and a provincial office providing justice policy analysis, advocacy for reform and support to branches.

Headquarters

6 Jackson Pl., Toronto, ON M6P 1T6 Tel. (416) 604-8412 Fax (416)604-8948
Media Contact, Exec. Dir., Graham Stewart

Officers

Pres., Susan Reid-MacNevin, Dept. of Sociology, Univ. Of Guelph, Guelph, ON N1G 2W1
Vice-Pres., Richard Beaupe, 4165 Fernand St., Hamner, ON B3A 1X4
Treas., Jack Battler, Waterloo, ON
Sec., Peter Angeline, OISE, 252 Bloor St. W., Toronto, ON
Exec. Dir., Graham Stewart

LOCAL SOCIETIES

Collins Bay
Hamilton
Kingston
Lindsay
London
Niagara
Oshawa
Ottawa
Peel
Peterborough
Sarnia
Sault Ste. Marie
Sudbury
Thunder Bay
Toronto
Waterloo
Windsor

John Milton Society for the Blind in Canada

The John Milton Society for the Blind in Canada is an interdenominational Christian charity whose mandate is producing Christian publications for Canadian adults or young people who are visually impaired or blind. As such, it produces *Insight*, a large-print magazine, *Insound*, a cassette magazine and *In Touch*, a braille magazine. The John Milton Society also features an audio cassette library called the *Library in Sound*, which contains Christian music, sermons, seasonal materials and workshops.

Founded in 1970, the Society is committed to seeing that visually-impaired people receive accessible Christian materials by mail.

Headquarters
40 St. Clair Ave. E., Ste. 202, Toronto, ON M4T 1M9 Tel. (416)960-3953
Media Contact, David Brinton

Officers
Pres., James MacMillan, 24 Kenridge Ave., Etobicoke, ON M8Y 2E3
Exec. Dir., David Brinton, 40 St. Clair Ave. E., Ste. 202, Toronto, ON M4T 1M9

Lutheran Council in Canada
The Lutheran Council in Canada was organized in 1967 and is a cooperative agency of the Evangelical Lutheran Church in Canada and Lutheran Church-Canada.

The Council's activities include communications, coordinative service and national liaison in social ministry, chaplaincy and scout activity.

Headquarters
302-393 Portage Ave., Winnipeg, MB R3B 3H6 Tel. (204)984-9150 Fax (204)984-9185
Media Contact, Pres., Bishop Telmor G. Sartison
E-Mail: sartison@elcic.ca

Officers
Pres., Rev. Telmor G. Sartison
Treas., Stephen Klinck

Mennonite Central Committee Canada (MCCC)
Mennonite Central Committee Canada was organized in 1964 to continue the work which several regional Canadian inter-Mennonite agencies had been doing in relief, service, immigration and peace. All but a few of the smaller Mennonite groups in Canada belong to MCC Canada.

MCCC is part of the bi-national Mennonite Central Committee (MCC) which has its headquarters in Akron, Pa. from where most of the overseas development and relief projects are administered. In 1996-97 MCCC's income was $22 million, about 36 percent of the total MCC income. There were 347 Canadians out of a total of 867 MCC workers serving in North America and abroad during the same time period.

The MCC office in Winnipeg administers projects located in Canada. Domestic programs of Voluntary Service, Native Concerns, Peace and Social Concerns, Food Program, Employment Concerns, Ottawa Office, Victim/Offender

Ministries, Mental Health and immigration are all part of MCC's Canadian ministry. Whenever it undertakes a project, MCCC attempts to relate to the church or churches in the area.

Headquarters
134 Plaza Dr., Winnipeg, MB R3T 5K9 Tel. (204)261-6381 Fax (204)269-9875
Communications, Rick Fast, 134 Plaza Dr., Winnipeg, MT R3T 5K9 Tel. (204)261-6381 Fax (204)269-9875

Officer
Exec. Dir., Marvin Frey

Project Ploughshares
The founding of Project Ploughshares in 1976 was premised on the biblical vision of transforming the material and human wealth consumed by military preparations into resources for human development. An internationally recognized Canadian peace and justice organization, the Project undertakes research, education, advocacy programs on common security, demilitarization, security alternatives, arms transfer controls, demobilization and peace building. Project Ploughshares is a project of the Canadian Council of Churches and is supported by national churches, civic agencies, affiliated community groups and more than 10,000 individuals.

Publications: the Ploughshares Monitor (quarterly), the Armed Conflicts Report(annual), Briefings and Working Papers(occasional).

Headquarters
Institute of Peace and Conflict Studies, Conrad Grebel College, Waterloo, ON N2L 3G6 Tel. (519)888-6541 Fax (519)885-0806
Media Contact, Policy & Public Affairs Dir., Ernie Regehr
E-mail: plough@watserv1.uwaterloo.ca
Website: http://www.ploughshares.ca

Officers
Chpsn., Walter Pitman
Treas., Philip Creighton

SPONSORING ORGANIZATIONS
Anglican Church of Canada
Canadian Catholic Organization for Development & Peace
Canadian Friends Service Committee
Conrad Grebel College
Evangelical Lutheran Church in Canada
Mennonite Central Committee Canada
Presbyterian Church in Canada
United Church of Canada
Voice of Women

Religious Television Associates
Religious Television Associates was formed in the early 1960s for the production units of the Anglican, Baptist, Presbyterian, Roman Catholic Churches and the United Church of Canada. In the intervening years, the Baptists have with-

drawn and the Lutherans have come in. RTA provides an ecumenical umbrella for joint productions in broadcasting and development education. The directors are the heads of the Communications Departments participating in Interchurch Communications.

Headquarters
3250 Bloor St. W., Etobicoke, ON M8X 2Y4 Tel. (416)231-7680 ext. 4051 Fax (416)232-6004
Media Contact, Exec. Dir., Rod Booth
E-mail:rbooth@uccan.org

MEMBER ORGANIZATIONS
The Anglican Church of Canada
Canadian Conference of Catholic Bishops
The Canadian Council of Churches
The Evangelical Lutheran Church in Canada
The Presbyterian Church in Canada
The United Church of Canada

Scripture Union

Scripture Union is an international interdenominational missionary movement working in 120 countries.

Scripture Union aims to work with the churches to make God's Good News known to children, young people and families and to encourage people of all ages to meet God daily through the Bible and prayer.

In Canada, a range of daily Bible guides are offered to individuals, churches, and bookstores from age four through adult. Sunday School curriculum and various evangelism and discipling materials are also offered for sale.

A program of youth and family evangelism, including beach missions and community-based evangelistic holiday clubs, is also undertaken.

Headquarters
1885 Clements Rd., Unit 226, Pickering, ON L1W 3V4 Tel. (905)427-4947 Fax (905)427-0334
E-mail: sucan@istar.ca
Website: http://home.istar.ca/~sucan
Media Contact, Gen. Dir., John Irwin

DIRECTORS
Harold Murray, 216 McKinnon Pl. NE, Calgary, AB T2E 7B9

Student Christian Movement of Canada

The Student Christian Movement of Canada was formed in 1921 from the student arm of the YMCA. It has its roots in the Social Gospel movements of the late 19th and early 20th centuries. Throughout its intellectual history, the SCM in Canada has sought to relate the Christian faith to the living realities of the social and political context of each student generation.

The present priorities are built around the need to form more and stronger critical Christian communities on Canadian campuses within which individuals may develop their social and political

analyses, experience spiritual growth and fellowship and bring Christian ecumenical witness to the university.

The Student Christian Movement of Canada is affiliated with the World Student Christian Federation.

Headquarters
310 Danforth Ave., Ste. C3, Toronto, ON M4K 1N6 Tel. (416)463-4312 Fax (416)466-6854
E-mail: scmcan@web.net
Website: http://www.web.net/~scmcan/
Media Contact, Natl. Coord., Rick Garland

Officer
Natl. Coord., Rick Garland

Taskforce on the Churches and Corporate Responsibility

The Taskforce on the Churches and Corporate Responsibility is a national ecumenical coalition of the major churches in Canada. Official representatives from the General Synod of the Anglican Church of Canada, the Canadian Conference of Catholic Bishops, the Evangelical Lutheran Church in Canada, the Presbyterian Church in Canada, the Religious Society of Friends (Quakers), the United Church of Canada, CUSO, the YWCA, and a number of religious orders of women and men, serve as links between the Taskforce and the decision-making structures of the members. The Taskforce assists the members in implementing policies adopted by the churches in the areas of corporate responsibility. Among the policies and issues placed on the agenda of the Taskforce by the participating churches are: principles for global corporate responsibility and bench marks for measuring business performance; corporate operating practices and codes of operation conduct; environmental reporting; human rights and Aboriginal land rights in relation to corporate conduct; social and environmental issues relative to corporate global citizenship; corporate governance issues; responsible investing issues.

Headquarters
129 St. Clair Ave., W., Toronto, ON M4V 1N5 Tel. (416)923-1758 Fax (416)927-7554
E-mail: tccr@web.net
Media Contact, Coord., Daniel Gennarelli, Tel. (416)923-1758 Fax (416)927-7554

Officers
Coord., Daniel Gennarelli
Bd. Co-Chpsns.: Norah Murphy; Tim Ryan
Treas., Doug Peter
Chpsn., Corp. Governance Comm., Richard Soo
Chpsn. Inter-Church Comm. on Ecology, Joy Kennedy

MEMBERS
Anglican Church of Canada
Basilians
Baptist Convention Ontario/Quebec

Canadian Conference of Catholic Bishops
Canadian University Service Overseas
Christian Reformed Church in Canada
Congregation of Notre Dame
Evangelical Lutheran Church in Canada
Grey Sisters of the Immaculate Conception
Jesuit Fathers of Upper Canada
Les Soeurs de Sainte-Anne
Oblate Conference of Canada
Presbyterian Church in Canada
Redemptorist Fathers
Religious Hospitallers of St. Joseph
School Sisters of Notre Dame
Scarboro Foreign Mission Society
Sisterhood of St. John the Divine
Sisters of Charity-Mount St. Vincent
Sisters of Charity of the Immaculate Conception
Sisters of Mercy Generalate
Sisters of St. Joseph-Diocese of London
Sisters of Service of Canada
Sisters of St. Joseph-Sault Ste. Marie
Sisters of St. Joseph-Toronto
Sisters of the Holy Names of Jesus & Mary Windsor, ON
Sisters of Holy Names of Jesus and Mary, Longueil, P.Q.
Sisters of Providence of St. Vincent dePaul
Sisters of St. Martha
United Church of Canada
Ursulines of Chatham Union
Young Women's Christian Association

Ten Days for Global Justice

Supported by five of Canada's major Christian denominations. Ten Days is dedicated to helping people discover, examine and reflect on the ways global and domestic structures and policies promote and perpetuate poverty and injustice for the majority of the world's people. Ten Days is an education and action program that attempts to influence the policies and practice of Canadian churches, government, business, labour, education and the media.

Headquarters
77 Charles St. W. Ste. 401, Toronto, ON M5S 1K5 Tel. (416)922-0591 Fax (416)922-1419
E-mail: tendays@web.net
Website: http://www.web.net/~tendays
Media Contact, Natl. Coord., Dennis Howlett

Staff
Natl. Coord., Dennis Howlett
Coord. for Leadership Dev. & Regional Communication, David Reid
Resource Coord., Julie Graham
Admn. Asst., Ramya Hemachandra

MEMBER ORGANIZATIONS
Anglican Church of Canada
Canadian Cath. Orgn. for Dev. & Peace
Evangelical Lutheran Church in Canada
Presbyterian Church in Canada
United Church of Canada

Women's Interchurch Council of Canada

Women's Inter-Church Council of Canada is a national Christian women's council that encourages women to grow in ecumenism, to share their spirituality and prayer and to engage in dialogue about women's concerns. The Council calls women to respond to national and international issues affecting women and to take action together for justice. WICC sponsors the World Day of Prayer and Fellowship of the Least Coin in Canada. Human rights projects are supported and a quarterly newsletter distributed.

Headquarters
60 St. Clair Ave., E. Ste. 602, Toronto, ON M4T 1N5 Tel. (416)929-5184 Fax (416)929-4064
Media Contact, Exec. Dir., Karen Hincke

Officers
Pres., Ann Austin Cardwell
Exec. Dir., Karen Hincke

World Vision Canada

World Vision Canada is a Christian humanitarian relief and development organization. Although its main international commitment is to translate child sponsorship into holistic, sustainable community development, World Vision also allocates resources to help Canada's poor and complement the mission of the church.

World Vision's Reception Centre assists government-sponsored refugees entering Canada. The NeighbourLink program mobilizes church volunteers to respond locally to people's needs. A quarterly publication, Context, provides data on the Canadian family to help churches effectively reach their communities. The development education program provides resources on development issues. During the annual 30-Hour Famine, people fast for 30 hours while discussing poverty and raising funds to support aid programs.

Headquarters
6630 Turner Valley Rd., Mississauga, ON L5N 2S4 Tel. (905)821-3030 Fax (905)821-1356
E-mail:info@worldvision.ca
Website: http://www.worldvision.capar
Address Para = Media Contact, Senior Information Officer, Philip Maher, Tel. (905)567-2726

Officers
Pres., Dave Toycen
Vice-Pres.: Intl. & Govt. Relations, Linda Tripp; Natl. Programs, Don Posterski; Fin. & Admin., Charlie Fluit; Donor Development Group, Brian Tizzard

s
Young Men's Christian Association in Canada

The YMCA began as a Christian association to help young men find healthy recreation and meditation, as well as opportunities for education, in the industrial slums of 19th century England. It came to Canada in 1851 with the same mission in mind for young men working in camps and on the railways.

Today, the YMCA maintains its original mission, helping individuals to grow and develop in spirit, mind and body, but attends to those needs for men and women of all ages and religious beliefs. The YMCA registers almost 1 million participants and 300,000 annual members in 64 autonomous associations representative of their communities.

The program of each association differs according to the needs of the community, but most offer one or more programs in each of the following categories: community support, housing and shelters, guidance and counselling, camping and outdoor education, leadership development, refugee and immigrant services, international development and education.

The YMCA encourages people of all ages, races, abilities, income and beliefs to mix in an environment which promotes balance in life, breaking down barriers and helping to create healthier communities.

Headquarters
42 Charles St. E., 6th Floor., Toronto, ON M4Y 1T4 Tel. (416)967-9622 Fax (416)967-9618
Media Contact, Dir., Communications, Pat Thompson

Officers
Chpsn., E. G. (Ted) Robinson
CEO, Sol Kasimer

Young Women's Christian Association of/du Canada

The YWCA of/du Canada is a national voluntary organization serving 44 YWCAs and YM-YWCAs across Canada. Dedicated to the development and improved status of women and their families, the YWCA is committed to service delivery and to being a source of public education on women's issues and an advocate of social change. Services provided by YWCAs and YM-YWCAs include adult education programs, residences and shelters, child care, fitness activities, wellness programs and international development education. As a member of the World YWCA, the YWCA of/du Canada is part of the largest women's organization in the world.

Headquarters
80 Gerrard St. E., Toronto, ON M5B 1G6 Tel. (416)593-9886 Fax (416)971-8084
Media Contact, Int. CEO, Margaret MacKenzie

Officer
Pres., Ann Mowatt

Youth for Christ/Canada

Youth For Christ is an interdenominational organization founded in 1944 by Torrey Johnson. Under the leadership of YFC's 11 national board of directors, Youth For Christ/Canada cooperates with churches and serves as a mission agency reaching out to young people and their families through a variety of ministries.

YFC seeks to have maximum influence in a world of youth through high-interest activities and personal involvement. Individual attention is given to each teenager through small group involvement and counselling. These activities and relationships become vehicles for communicating the message of the Gospel.

Headquarters
822-167 Lombard Ave., Winnipeg, MB R3B 0V3 Tel. (204)989-0056 Fax (204)989-0067

Officer
Natl. Dir., Randy L. Steinwand

3. Religious Bodies in the United States

The following lists were supplied by the denominations. They are printed in alphabetical order by the official name of the organization. A list of religious bodies by family group is found at the end of this section.

Information found in other places in this yearbook is not repeated. The denominational listing points you to additional information. Specifically, addresses and editor's names for periodicals are found in the listing of United States Periodicals. Statistical information is found in the statistical section, and several church websites are listed in Chapter 5 of the Directories section.

When an organization supplied a headquarters address it is listed immediately following the description of the organization. This address, telephone number and fax number is not reprinted for entries that have exactly the same address and numbers. An address or telephone number is only printed when it is known to be different from the headquarters'. Individuals listed without an address can be contacted through the headquarters.

Denominations were asked to provide the name of a media contact. Many responded with a specific person that newspaper or other reporters can contact for official information. These people are listed with the headquarters address.

The organizations listed here represent the denominations to which the vast majority of church members in the United States belong. It does not include all religious bodies functioning in the United States. The Encyclopedia of American Religions (Gale Research Inc., P.O. Box 33477, Detroit MI 48232—5477) contains names and addresses of additional religious bodies.

Advent Christian Church

The Advent Christian Church is a conservative, evangelical denomination which grew out of the Millerite movement of the 1830s and 1840s. The members stress the authority of Scripture, justification by faith in Jesus Christ alone, the importance of evangelism and world missions and the soon visible return of Jesus Christ.

Organized in 1860, the Advent Christian Church maintains headquarters in Charlotte, N.C., with regional offices in Rochester, N. H., Princeton, N.C., Ellisville, MO., Lewiston, Idaho, and Lenoir, N.C. Missions are maintained in India, Nigeria, Ghana, Japan, Liberia, Croatia, New Zealand, Malaysia, the Philippines, Mexico, South Africa, Honduras and Memphis, Tenn.

The Advent Christian Church maintains doctrinal distinctives in three areas: conditional immortality, the sleep of the dead until the return of Christ and belief that the kingdom of God will be established on earth made new by Jesus Christ.

Headquarters

P.O. Box 23152, Charlotte, NC 28227 Tel. (704) 545-6161 Fax (704)573-0712
Media Contact, Exec. Director, David E. Ross
E-mail: acpub@adventchristian.org

Officers

Pres., Rev. Glennon Balser
Exec. Dir., David E. Ross
Sec., Rev. John Gallagher, P.O. Box 551, Presque Isle, ME 04769
Appalachian Vice-Pres., Rev. James Lee, 1338 Delwood Dr. SW, Lenoir, NC 28645
Central Vice-Pres., Rev. Glenn Fell, 1525 Plainfield Rd., LaGrange, IL 60525
Eastern Vice-Pres., Rev. Glenn Rice, 130 Leighton St., Bangor, ME 04401

Southern Vice-Pres., Rev. Brent Ross, 3635 Andrea Lee Ct., Snellville, GA 30278-4941
Western Vice-Pres., Brad Neil, 4035 S. 275th Pl., Auburn, WA 98001
The Woman's Home & Foreign Mission Soc., Pres., Hazel Blackstone, 2141 Broadway, Bangor, ME 04901

Periodicals

Advent Christian News; The Advent Christian Witness; Insight; Maranatha; Henceforth...; Coast to Coast on Campus; Leadership Letter

African Methodist Episcopal Church

This church began in 1787 in Philadelphia when persons in St. George's Methodist Episcopal Church withdrew as a protest against color segregation. In 1816 the denomination was started, led by Rev. Richard Allen who had been ordained deacon by Bishop Francis Asbury and was subsequently ordained elder and elected and consecrated bishop.

Headquarters

1134 11th St., NW, Washington, DC 20001 Tel. (202)371-8700

Officers

Senior Bishop, Bishop John H. Adams, 3700 Forest Dr., Ste. 402, Columbia, SC 29204 Tel. (803)691-0771

Periodicals

The Christian Recorder; A.M.E. Review; Journal of Christian Education; Secret Chamber; Women's Missionary Magazine

African Methodist Episcopal Zion Church

The A.M.E. Zion Church is an independent body, having withdrawn from the John Street

Methodist Church of New York City in 1796. The first bishop was James Varick.

Headquarters

Dept. of Records & Research, P.O. Box 32843, Charlotte, NC 28232 Tel. (704)332-3851 Fax (704)333-1769
Media Contact, Gen. Sec.-Aud., Dr. W. Robert Johnson, III

BOARD OF BISHOPS
Officers

*President, Bishop Nathaniel Jarrett, Jr., 7322 South Clyde Ave., Chicago, IL 60649 Tel. (773)684-8098 Fax (773)684-0810
Secretary., Bishop Marshall H. Strickland I, 2000 Cedar Circle Dr., Baltimore, MD 21215 Tel. (410)744-7330 Fax (410)788-5510
Asst. Sec., Bishop Clarence Carr, 2600 Normandy Dr., Greendale, MO 63121, Tel. (314)727-2931 Fax (314)727-0663
Treas., Bishop George Washington Carver Walker, Sr., 137 Talcott Notch Rd., Farmington, CT 06032 Tel.(860)676-8414 Fax (860)676-8424
*Note: Presidency rotates every six months according to seniority.

MEMBERS
ACTIVE

Battle, Jr. George Edward, 8403 Dembridge Ln., Davidson, NC 28036 Tel. (704)332-7600 Office Tel. (704)332-7600 Fax (704)343-3745
Bishop, Cecil, 2663 Oakmeade Dr., Charlotte, NC 28270 Tel. (704)846-9370 Fax (704)846-9371
Brown, Warren Matthew, 22 Crowley Dr., Randolph, MA 02368 Tel. (781)961-2434 Fax (781)961-2939
Carr, Clarence, 2600 Normandy Dr., Greendale, MO 63121, Tel. (314)727-2931 Fax (314)727-0663
Ekeman, Sr., Samuel Chuka, 98 Okigwe Rd., PO Box 1149, Owerri, Nigeria West Africa Tel. (011)234-83-232271
Jarrett, Jr., Nathaniel, 7322 South Clyde Ave., Chicago, IL 60649 Tel. (773)684-8098 Fax (773)684-0810
Johnson, Joseph, 320 Walnut Point Dr., PO Box 608 Matthews, NC 28106 Tel. (704)849-0521 Fax (704)849-0571
Rochester, Enoch Benjamin, Office: Hwy. 130 South, Suite 2A, Cinnaminson, NJ 08077 Tel. (609)786-2555 Fax (609) 786-8568; Home: 129 Sagebush Dr., Belleville, IL 62221 Tel (618)257-8481
Strickland I, Marshall Hayward, 2000 Cedar Circle Dr., Baltimore, MD 21215 Tel. (410)744-7330 Fax (410)788-5510
Thompson, Richard Keith, 1420 Missouri Ave., N.W., Washington, DC 20011, Mailing Address: PO Box 55458, Washington, DC, 20040 Tel (202)723-8993 Fax (202)722-1840
Walker, Sr., George Washington Carver, 137 Talcott Notch Rd., Farmington, CT 06032 Tel.(860)676-8414 Fax (860)676-8424
Williams, Milton Alexander, 12904 Canoe Court, Fort Washington, MD 20744 Tel. (301)292-0002 Fax (301)292-6655; Office: 2001 Ninth St., N.W., Suite 306, Box 322, Washington, DC 20001 Tel. (202)265-9590 Fax (202)265-9593

RETIRED

Foggie, Charles H., 1200 Windermere Dr., Pittsburgh, PA 15218 Tel. (412)242-5842
Hilliard , William Alexander, 690 Chicago Blvd., Detroit, MI 48202
Hoggard, James Clinton, 4515 Willard Ave., Apt, 2203, South Chevy Chase, MD 20815 Tel. (301)652-9010; Office: Howard University School of Divinity, 1400 Shepherd St., N.E., Suite 189/191, Washington, DC 20017 Tel. (202)635-6201
Miller, Sr., John Henry, Springdale Estates, 8605 Caswell Ct., Raleigh, NC 27612 Tel. (919)848-6915
Speaks, Ruben Lee, P.O. Box 986, Salisbury, NC 28145 Tel. (704)637-6018 Fax (704) 639-0059

EPISCOPAL ASSIGNMENTS

Piedmont Episcopal District: Blue Ridge, West Central North Carolina, Western North Carolina, and Jamaica Conferences: Bishop Cecil Bishop
North Eastern Episcopal District: New England, New York, Western New York, and Bahamas Islands Conferences: Bishop George W. Walker, Sr.
Mid-Atlantic II Episcopal District: East Tennessee-Virginia, India, London-Birmingham, Manchester-Midland, Philadelphia- Baltimore, and Virginia Conferences: Bishop Milton A. Williams
Eastern West Africa Episcopal District: Central Nigeria, Lagos- West Nigeria, Nigeria, Northern Nigeria, and Rivers Conferences: Bishop S. Chuka Ekemam, Sr.
Eastern North Carolina Episcopal District: Albemarle, Cape Fear, Central North Carolina, North Carolina, and Virgin Islands Conferences: Bishop George E. Battle, Jr.
South Atlantic Episcopal District: Georgia, Palmetto, Pee Dee, South Carolina, and South Georgia Conferences: Bishop Joseph Johnson
Alabama-Florida Episcopal District: Alabama, Cahaba, Central Alabama, North Alabama, South Alabama, West Alabama, Florida, and South Florida Conferences: Bishop Richard K. Thompson
Mid-West Episcopal District: Indiana, Kentucky, Michigan, Missouri, Tennessee, and South Africa Conferences: Bishop Enoch B. Rochester
Mid-Atlantic I Episcopal District: Allegheny, New Jersey, Ohio, Guyana, Trinidad-Tobago,

and Barbados Conferences: Bishop Marshall Haywood Strickland I

Western Episcopal District: Alaska, Arizona, California, Oregon-Washington, Southwest Rocky Mountain, and Colorado Conferences: Bishop Clarence Carr

Southwestern Delta: Arkansas, Louisiana, Oklahoma, South Mississippi, West Tennessee-Mississippi, and Texas Conferences: Bishop Nathaniel Jarrett

Western West Africa: Cote D'Ivore, East Ghana, Liberia, Mid-Ghana, and West Ghana Conferences: Bishop Warren Matthew Brown

General Officers and Departments

Dept. of Records & Research, Gen. Sec.-Aud., Dr. W. Robert Johnson, III, 401 E. Second St., Ste. 108, Charlotte, NC 28202 Tel. (704)332-3851 Fax (704)333-1769; Mailing Address: P.O. Box 32843, Charlotte, NC 28232

Dept. of Finance, Chief Financial Officer, Dr. Madie Simpson, 401 E. Second St., Ste. 101, Charlotte, NC 28202 Tel. (704)333-4847 Fax (704)333-6517; Mailing Address: P.O. Box 31005, Charlotte, NC 28231

Star of Zion, Morgan W. Tann, Editor, 401 E. Second St., Suite 106, Charlotte, NC 28202 Tel. (704)377-4329 Fax (704)377-4329 Fax (704)377-2809; E-mail: starozion@juno.com Mailing Address: PO Box 31005, Charlotte, NC 28231

A.M.E. Zion Quarterly Review and Historical Society: James D. Armstong, Sec.-Ed., 401 E. Second St., Suite 103, Charlotte, NC 28202 Tel. (704)334-0728 Fax (704)333-1769 Mailing Address: PO Box 33247, Charlotte, NC 28231

Dept. of Overseas Missions and Missionary Seer: Sec.-Ed., Dr. Kermit J. DeGraffenreidt, 475 Riverside Dr., Rm. 1935, New York, NY 10115 Tel. (212)870-2952 Fax (212)870-2808

Dept. Brotherhood Pensions & Min. Relief: Sec.-Treas., Dr. David Miller, 401 E. Second St., Suite 209, Charlotte, NC 28202 Tel. (704)333-3779 or 1-800-762-5106 Fax (704)333-3867P.O. Box 34454, Charlotte, NC 28234-4454

Christian Education Dept.: Gen. Sec., Rev. Raymon Hunt, 401 E. Second St., Suite 207, Charlotte, NC 28202 Tel. (704)332-9323 Fax (704)332-9332 E-mail: ced1amez@juno.com Mailing Address: P.O. Box 32305, Charlotte, NC 28232-2305

Dept. of Church School Literature: Ed., Dr. Mary A. Love, 401 E. Second St., Suite 208, Charlotte, NC 28202 Tel. (704)332-1034 Fax (704)333-1769 Mailing Address: P.O. Box 31005, Charlotte, NC 28231

Dept. of Church Extension & Home Mission: Sec-Treas., Dr. Lem Long, Jr., 401 E. Second St., Suite 104, Charlotte, NC 28202 Tel. (704)334-2519 Fax (704)334-3806 Mailing Address: P.O. Box 31005, Charlotte, NC 28231

Bureau of Evangelism: Dir., Rev. Darryl B. Starnes, Sr., 401 E. Second St., Suite 111, Charlotte, NC 28202 Tel. (704)342-3070 Fax (704)342-2389 Mailing Address: P.O. Box 33623, Charlotte, NC 28233-3623

Public Affairs and Convention Manager: Dir., Rev. George E. McKain, II, 943 West 1st North St., Summerville, SC 29483 Tel. (803)873-2475

Dept. of Health & Social Concerns: Dir., Dr. Bernard H. Sullivan, P.O. Box 972, Gastonia, NC 28053 Tel. (704)866-0325 or (704)864-1791 Fax (704)864-7641

A.M.E. Zion Publishing House: Int. Gen. Mgr., Dr. David Miller, 401 E. Second St., Suite 106, Charlotte, NC 28202 Tel. (704)334-9596 Fax (704)334-9592; 1-800-343-9835 Mailing Address: PO Box 30714, Charlotte, NC 28230

JUDICIAL COUNCIL

Pres., Judge Adele M. Riley, 625 Ellsworth Dr., Dayton, OH 45426

Vice-Pres., Robert E. Richardson, Esq., 1511 K St. NW, Ste. 438, Washington, DC 20005

Clk., Dr. Mozella G. Mitchell, P.O. Box 1855, Brandon, FL 33509

MEMBERS

Rev. Monica H. Royce, Esq., 1330 Kingston Ave., Alexandria, VA 22302

Alean Rush, 22 Parkview Dr., Rochester, NY 14625

Dr. E. Alex Brower, Esq., 604 Second St., Mamaroneck, NY 10543

Rev. Medis Cheek, 4072 Sloop Trail, Chesapeake, VA 23323

Dr. George L. Blackwell, 220 N. Elm St., Williamston, NC 27892

Neville Tucker, Esq., 865 S. Figueroa, Ste. 2640, Los Angeles, CA 90017

CONNECTIONAL LAY COUNCIL

Pres., Mrs. Lula K. Howard, 4009 Landside Dr., Louisville, KY 40220-3080 Tel. (502) 499-7842

1st. Vice-Pres., ., ., Mr. Jasper McCormick, 9510 Ave "N", Brooklyn, NY 11236 Tel. (718) 531-1436

2nd Vice-Pres., Linda F. Starnes, 505 Starnes Ct., Gastonia, NC 28052 Tel. (704)865-1763

Sec., Frances J. Glenn, 221 Emmett St., Rock Hill, SC 29730 Tel. (803)329-2271

Treas., Ervin D. Reid, 5309 Dayan Dr., Charlotte, NC 28216-2156 Tel. (704)596-7330

Chaplain, Mrs. Annie M. Williams, 2416 Heyward Brockington Rd., Columbia, SC 29203-9681 Tel. (803) 754-8561

Editor, "The laity Speaks", Theodore Shaw, 7529 South Rhodes Ave., Chicago, IL 60619 Tel. (312)488-0057

Pres. Emeritus, Arthur Brooks, 778 Hobart Pl. N.W., Washington, DC 20001 Tel. (202)462-3159

Address: P.O. Box 31005, Charlotte, NC 28231

**General Officers of
The Womans Home & Overseas
Missionary Society**

Pres., Dr. Adlise Ivey Porter, 1991 Thornhill Pl., Detroit, MI 48207 Tel. (313)393-0601 Fax (313)393-0590 E-mail: aporter@edcen.ehhs.cmich.edu

1st Vice-Pres., Lillian T. Shelborne, P.O. Box 185, Hickory Grove, SC 29717 Tel. (803)925-2617 [Deceased]

2nd Vice-Pres., Essie Curnell, 3510 Rosewood Ave., Houston, TX 77004-5512 Tel. (713)522-2034

Exec. Sec., Alice Steele-Robinson, 3510 Rock Hill Church Rd., Concord, NC 28027 Tel. (704)795-1506 Fax (704)795-3925; Office: 401 E. Second St., Suite 113, Charlotte, NC 28202 Tel. (704)344-9085

Recording Sec., Dr. Betty V. Stith, Carrington Arms, Apt, 10-L, 33 Lincoln Ave., New Rochelle, NY 10810 Tel. (910)235-3596

General Treas., Elease W. Johnson, P.O. Box 25582, Charlotte, NC 28229 Tel. (704)535-3193 Office: 401 E. Second St., Suite 113, Charlotte, NC 28202 Tel. (704)344-9085

Gen. Coord. of YAMS, JoAnn Holmes, 6527 Heatherbrook Dr., Charlotte, NC 28213 Tel. (704)596-3515

Sec. of Young Women, Millicent D. Thomas, 1312 North 55th St., Philadelphia, PA 19131 Tel. (215) 477-3226

Supt. of Buds of Promise, Mary Hicklin, 818 Rockdale St., Rock Hill, SC 29730 Tel. (803) 327-1571

Sec., Bureau of Supplies, Annette E. Whitted, P.O. Box 994, Salisbury, NC 28145 Tel. (704)633-0278 Fax (704)639-1433

Chmn., Life Members Council, Gladys M. Felton, 6958 S. Vernon St., Chicago, IL 60637 Tel. (312)651-4028

Editor, Woman's Section, Missionary Seer, Mattie W. Taylor, 650 Grassmere Terrace, Far Rockaway, NY 11691 Tel. (718)471-4636

Periodicals

Star of Zion; Quarterly Review; Church School Herald, Missionary Seer, and Vision Focus

Albanian Orthodox Archdiocese in America

The Albanian Orthodox Church in America traces its origins to the groups of Albanian immigrants which first arrived in the United States in 1886, seeking religious, cultural and economic freedoms denied them in the homeland.

In 1908 in Boston, the Rev. Fan Stylian Noli (later Archbishop) served the first liturgy in the Albanian language in 500 years, to which Orthodox Albanians rallied, forming their own diocese in 1919. Parishes began to spring up throughout New England and the Mid-Atlantic and Great Lakes states. In 1922, clergy from the United States traveled to Albania to proclaim the self-governance of the Orthodox Church in the homeland at the Congress of Berat.

In 1971 the Albanian Archdiocese sought and gained union with the Orthodox Church in America, expressing the desire to expand the Orthodox witness to America at large, giving it an indigenous character. The Albanian Archdiocese remains vigilant for its brothers and sisters in the homeland and serves as an important resource for human rights issues and Albanian affairs, in addition to its programs for youth, theological education, vocational interest programs and retreats for young adults and women.

Headquarters

523 E. Broadway, S. Boston, MA 02127
Media Contact, Sec., Dorothy Adams, Tel. (617) 268-1275 Fax (617)268-3184

Officers

Metropolitan Theodosius, Tel. (617)268-1275

Chancellor, V. Rev. Arthur E. Liolin, 60 Antwerp St., East Milton, MA 02186 Tel. (617)698-3366

Lay Chpsn., Gregory Costa, 727 Righters Mill Rd., Narberth, PA 19103 Tel. (610)664-8550

Treas., Ronald Nasson, 26 Enfield St., Jamaica Plains, MA 02130 Tel. (617)522-7715

Albanian Orthodox Diocese of America

This Diocese was organized in 1950 as a canonical body administering to the Albanian faithful. It is under the ecclesiastical jurisdiction of the Ecumenical Patriarchate of Constantinople (Istanbul).

Headquarters

6455 Silver Dawn Lane, Las Vegas, NV 89118 Tel. (702)221-8245 Fax (702)221-9167
Media Contact, Rev. Ik. Ilia Katre

Officer

Vicar General, Rev. Ik. Ilia Katre

Allegheny Wesleyan Methodist Connection (Original Allegheny Conference)

This body was formed in 1968 by members of the Allegheny Conference (located in eastern Ohio and western Pennsylvania) of the Wesleyan Methodist Church, which merged in 1966 with the Pilgrim Holiness Church to form The Wesleyan Church.

The Allegheny Wesleyan Methodist Connection is composed of persons "having the form and seeking the power of godliness, united in order to pray together, to receive the word of exhortation, and to watch over one another in love, that they may help each other to work out their salvation." There is a strong commitment to congregational government and to holiness of heart and life. There is a strong thrust in church extension within the United States and in missions worldwide.

Headquarters

P.O. Box 357, Salem, OH 44460 Tel. (330)337-9376

Media Contact, Pres., Rev. Michael Marshall
E-mail: awmc@juno.com

Officers

Pres., Rev. Michael Marshall, P.O. Box 357, Salem, OH 44460

Vice-Pres., Rev. William Cope, 1827 Allen Drive, Salem, OH 44460

Sec., Rev. Ray Satterfield, Rt. 1, Box N-12, Wolf Summit, WV 26462

Treas., James Kunselman, 2161 Woodsdale Rd., Salem, OH 44460

Periodical

The Allegheny Wesleyan Methodist

The American Association of Lutheran Churches

This church body was constituted on Nov. 7, 1987. The AALC was formed by laity and pastors of the former American Lutheran Church in America who held to a high view of Scripture (inerrancy and infallibility). This church body also emphasizes the primacy of evangelism and world missions and the authority and autonomy of the local congregation.

Congregations of the AALC are distributed throughout the continental United States from Long Island, N.Y., to Los Angeles. The primary decision-making body is the General Convention, to which each congregation has proportionate representation.

Headquarters

The AALC National Office, 10800 Lyndale Ave. S., Ste. 210, Minneapolis, MN 55420-5614 Tel. (612)884-7784 Fax (612)884-7894

The AALC Regional Office, 2211 Maynard St., Waterloo, IA 50701 Tel. (319)232-3971 Fax (319)232-1523

Media Contact, Admn. Coord., Rev. Charles D. Eidum, 10800 Lyndale Ave. So., # 210 Minneapolis, MN 55420-5614, Tel. (612) 884-7784 FAX (612) 884-7894

Officers

Presiding Pastor, Dr. Duane R. Lindberg, P.O. Box 416, Waterloo, IA 50701 Tel. (319)232-3971

Asst. Presiding Pastor, Rev. John A. Anderson, 310 Seventh St., Ames, IA 50010 Tel. (515)232-3815

Sec., Rev. Dick Hueter, N9945 Highway 180, Wausaukee, WI 54177 Tel. (715)732-0327

Treas., Rev. Dale Zastrow, 700 Second Ave. NE, Minot, ND 58703 Tel. (701)839-7474

The American Baptist Association

The American Baptist Association (ABA) is an international fellowship of independent Baptist churches voluntarily cooperating in missionary, evangelistic, benevolent and Christian education activities throughout the world. Its beginnings can be traced to the landmark movement of the 1850s. Led by James R. Graves and J.M. Pendleton, a significant number of Baptist churches in the South, claiming a New Testament heritage, rejected as extrascriptural the policies of the newly formed Southern Baptist Convention (SBC). Because they strongly advocated church equality, many of these churches continued doing mission and benevolent work apart from the SBC, electing to work through local associations. Meeting in Texarkana, TX, in 1924, messengers from the various churches effectively merged two of these major associations, the Baptist Missionary Association of Texas and the General Association, forming the American Baptist Association.

Since 1924, mission efforts have been supported in Australia, Africa, Asia, Canada, Central America, Europe, India, Israel, Japan, Korea, Mexico, New Zealand, South America and the South Pacific. An even more successful domestic mission effort has changed the ABA from a predominantly rural southern organization to one with churches in 48 states.

Through its publishing arm in Texarkana, the ABA publishes literature and books numbering into the thousand. Major seminaries include the Missionary Baptist Seminary, founded by Dr. Ben M. Bogard in Little Rock, AR; Texas Baptist Seminary, Henderson, TX; Oklahoma Oxford Baptist Institute, Oxford, MS; and Florida Baptist Schools in Lakeland, FL.

While no person may speak for the churches of the ABA, all accept the bible as the inerrant Word of God. They believe Christ was the virgin-born Son of God, that God is a triune God, that the only church is the local congregation of scripturally baptized believers and that the work of the church is to spread the gospel.

Headquarters

4605 N State Line Ave. Texarkana, TX 75503 Tel. (903) 792-2783

Media Contact: Jim Jones, Public Relations Director

E-mail: bssc@abaptist.org

Officers

President: David Robinson, 15716 Marlene, Little Rock, AR 72206

Vice Presidents: G.F. Crumley, 9 Paul, Texarkana, TX 75503; John Owen, P.O. Box 142, Bryant, AR 72089; George Raley, 9890 Hwy 15, Rison, AR 71665

Recording Clerks: Larry Clements, 270 Tracy Dr., Monticello, AR 71655; Gene Smith, 5602 Deer Creek Dr., Texarkana, TX 75503

Publications: Editor in Chief, Bill Johnson; Bus. Mgr., Tom Sannes, 4605 N. State Line Ave., Texarkana, TX 75503

Meeting Arrangements Director: Edgar N. Sutton, P.O. Box 240, Alexander, AR 72002

Sec.-Treas. of Missions: Randy Cloud, P.O. Box 1050 Texarkana, TX 75504

American Baptist Churches in the U.S.A

Originally known as the Northern Baptist Convention, this body of Baptist churches changed the name to American Baptist Convention in 1950 with a commitment to "hold the name in trust for all Christians of like faith and mind who desire to bear witness to the historical Baptist convictions in a framework of cooperative Protestantism."

In 1972 American Baptist Churches in the U.S.A. was adopted as the new name. Although national missionary organizational developments began in 1814 with the establishment of the American Baptist Foreign Mission Society and continued with the organization of the American Baptist Publication Society in 1824 and the American Baptist Home Mission Society in 1832, the general denominational body was not formed until 1907. American Baptist work at the local level dates back to the organization by Roger Williams of the First Baptist Church in Providence, R. I. in 1638.

Headquarters
American Baptist Churches Mission Center
P.O. Box 851, Valley Forge, PA 19482-0851 Tel. (610)768-2000 Fax (610)768-2320
Media Contact, Dir., Office of Comm., Richard W. Schramm, Tel. (610)768-2077 Fax (610) 768-2320
E-mail: richard.schramm@abc-usa.org
Website: http://www.abc-usa.org

Officers
Pres., James B. Johnson
Vice-Pres., Trinette V. McCray
Budget Review Officer, Kenneth Hines
Gen. Sec., Daniel E. Weiss
Assoc. Gen. Sec.-Treas., Cheryl H. Wade

REGIONAL ORGANIZATIONS
Central Region, ABC of, Fred A. Ansell, 5833 SW 29th St., Topeka, KS 66614-2499
Chicago, ABC of Metro, Millie A. Myren, 28 E. Jackson Blvd., Ste. 210, Chicago, IL 60604-2207
Cleveland Baptist Assoc., Dennis E. Norris, 1836 Euclid Ave., Ste. 603, Cleveland, OH 44115-2234
Connecticut, ABC of, Lowell H. Fewster, 100 Bloomfield Ave., Hartford, CT 06105-1097
Dakotas, ABC of, Ronald E. Cowles, 1524 S. Summit Ave., Sioux Falls, SD 57105-1697
District of Columbia Bapt. Conv., W. Jere Allen, 1628 16th St., NW, Washington, DC 20009-3099
Great Rivers Region, J. Dwight Stinnett, ABC of the, P.O. Box 3786, Springfield, IL 62708-3786
Indiana, ABC of, Larry Mason, 1350 N. Delaware St., Indianapolis, IN 46202-2493
Indianapolis, ABC of Greater, Larry D. Sayre, 1350 N. Delaware St., Indianapolis, IN 46202-2493

Los Angeles, ABC of, Samuel S. Chetti, 605 W. Olympia Blvd., Ste. 700, Los Angeles, CA 90015
Maine, ABC of, Gary G. Johnson, P.O. Box 667, Augusta, ME 04332-0667
Massachusetts, ABC of, Linda C. Spoolstra, 20 Milton St., Dedham, MA 02026-2967
Metropolitan New York, ABC of, James D. Stallings, 475 Riverside Dr., Rm. 432, New York, NY 10115-0432
Michigan, ABC of, Robert E. Shaw, 4578 S. Hagadorn Rd., East Lansing, MI 48823-5396
Mid-American Baptist Churches, Gary L. Grogan, Ste. 15, 2400 86th St., Des Moines, IA 50322-4380
Nebraska, ABC of, J. David Mallgren, 6404 Maple St., Omaha, NE 68104-4079
New Jersey, ABC of, A. Roy Medley, 3752 Nottingham Way, Ste. 101, Trenton, NJ 08690-3802
New York State, ABC of, William A. Carlson, 5842 Heritage Landing Dr., East Syracuse, NY 13057-9359
Northwest, ABC of, Paul D. Aita, 409 Third Ave. South, Suite A, Kent, WA 98032-5843
Ohio, ABC of, C. Jeff Woods, P.O. Box 376, Granville, OH 43023-0376
Oregon, ABC of, W. Wayne Brown, 0245 SW Bancroft St., Ste. G, Portland, OR 97201-4270
Pacific Southwest, ABC of the, Dale V. Salico, 970 Village Oaks Dr., Covina, CA 91724-3679
Pennsylvania & Delaware, ABC of, Clayton R. Woodbury, P.O. Box 851, Valley Forge, PA 19482-0851
Philadelphia Baptist Assoc., Larry K. Waltz, 100 N. 17th St., Philadelphia, PA 19103-2736
Pittsburgh Baptist Assoc., Larry Swain, 429 Forbes Ave., #1620, Pittsburgh, PA 15219-1627
Puerto Rico, Baptist Churches of, E. Yamina, Mayaguez #21, Hato Rey, PR 00917
Rhode Island, ABC of, Donald R. Rasmussen, 734 Hope St., Providence, RI 02906-3549
Rochester-Genesee Region, ABC of, W. Kenneth Williams, 151 Brooks Ave., Rochester, NY 14619-2454
Rocky Mountains, ABC of, Louise B. Barger, 3900 Wadsworth Blvd. Suite 365, Lakewood, CO 80235
South, ABC of the, Walter L. Parrish, II, 5124 Greenwich Ave., Baltimore, MD 21229-2393
Vermont/New Hampshire, ABC of, Louis A. George, P.O. Box 2403, Concord, NH 03302-0796
West, ABC of the, Conrad Lowe, P.O. Box 23204, Oakland, CA 94610
West Virginia Baptist Convention, Lloyd D. Hamblin, Jr., P.O. Box 1019, Parkersburg, WV 26102-1019
Wisconsin, ABC of, George E. Daniels, 15330 W. Watertown Plank Rd., Elm Grove, WI 53122-2391

BOARDS

Bd. of Educational Ministries: Exec. Dir., Jean B. Kim; Pres., Scott Moore

American Baptist Assembly: Green Lake, WI 54941; Pres., Kenneth P. Giacoletto; Chpsn., Patricia Kern

American Baptist Historical Society: 1106 S. Goodman St., Rochester, NY 14620; or P.O. Box 851, Valley Forge, PA 19482-0851; Admn./Archivist, Deborah B. VanBroekhoven; Pres., Loyd M. Starrett

American Baptist Men: Exec. Dir., Z. Allen Abbott, Jr.; Pres., David Gnirk

American Baptist Women's Ministries: Exec. Dir., Carol Franklin Sutton; Pres., Thelma Schaller

Ministerial Leadership Commission: Int. Exec. Dir., Brenda Egolf-Fox

Bd. of Intl. Ministries: Exec. Dir., John A. Sundquist; Pres., Judith Dean

Bd. of Natl. Ministries: Exec. Dir., Aidsand F. Wright-Riggins; Pres., Danny Cortes

Ministers & Missionaries Benefit Bd.: Exec. Dir., Sumner M. Grant; Pres., Mary H. Purcell, 475 Riverside Dr., New York, NY 10115

Minister Council: Dir., Carole (Kate) H. Harvey; Pres., G. Daniel Jones

Periodicals

Tomorrow Magazine; Baptist Leader; The Secret Place; American Baptist Quarterly; American Baptists In Mission

The American Carpatho-Russian Orthodox Greek Catholic Church

The American Carpatho-Russian Orthodox Greek Catholic Church is a self-governing diocese that is in communion with the Ecumenical Patriarchate of Constantinople. The late Patriarch Benjamin I, in an official Patriarchal Document dated Sept. 19, 1938, canonized the Diocese in the name of the Orthodox Church of Christ.

Headquarters

312 Garfield St., Johnstown, PA 15906 Tel. (814)539-4207

Media Contact, Chancellor, V. Rev. Msgr. Frank P. Miloro, Tel. (814)539-8086 Fax (814)536-4699

Officers

Bishop, Metropolitan Nicholas Smisko

Vicar General, V. Rev. Msgr. John Yurcisin, 249 Butler Ave., Johnstown, PA 15906

Chancellor, V. Rev. Msgr. Frank P. Miloro, 127 Chandler Ave., Johnstown, PA 15906

Treas., V. Rev. Msgr. Ronald A. Hazuda, 115 East Ave., Erie, PA 16503

American Catholic Church

The American Catholic Church was founded in 1988, and incorporated in 1989, as an alternative to the oppressive structures and strictures of the Roman Catholic Church, yet without denying basic catholic beliefs of faith and love, spirituality and community, prayer and sacramentality. The American Catholic Church is a federation of independent churches offering a progressive alternative in the Catholic tradition. It is a newly formed rite, as in the tradition of the Orthodox churches of the Catholic tradition and the Old Catholic Church of Utrecht. It remains a *Catholic Church*, and its priests are considered Catholic priests.

Headquarters

Good Shepherd Rectory, P.O. Box 725, Hampton Bays, NY 11946 Tel. (516)723-2012, Fax (516)723-0348

Media Contact, Archbishop, Most Rev. Robert J. Allmen, D.D.

Officers

Archbishop, Most Rev. Robert J. Allmen, D.D.

American Evangelical Christian Churches

Founded in 1944, the AECC is composed of individual ministers and churches who are united in accepting "Seven Articles of Faith." These seven articles are: the Bible as the written word of God; the Virgin birth; the deity of Jesus Christ; Salvation through the atonement; guidance of our life through prayer; the return of the Saviour; the establishment of the Millennial Kingdom.

The American Evangelical Christian Churches offers the following credentials: Certified Christian Worker, Commission to Preach, Licensed Minister and Ordained Minister to those who accept the Seven Articles of Faith, who put unity in Christ first and are approved by AECC.

A.E.C.C. seeks to promote the gospel through its ministers, churches and missionary activities. Churches operate independently with all decisions concerning local government left to the individual churches.

The organization also has ministers in Canada, England, Bolivia, Philippines Thailand, Brazil and South America.

Headquarters

P.O. Box 47312, Indianapolis, IN 46227 Tel. (941)314-9370 Fax (941)314-9570

E-mail: alpha@strato.net

Website: —

Media Contact, International Mod., Dr. Otis O. Osborne, 1421 Roseland Ave., Sebring, FL 33870 Tel. (941)314-9370

INTERNATIONAL Officers

Mod., Dr. Otis O. Osborne, 1421 Roseland Ave., Sebring, FL 33870 Tel. (941)314-9370

Sec., Dr. Charles Wasielewski, Box 51, Barton, NY 13734 Tel. (607)565-4074

Treas., Dr. S. Omar Overly, 2481 Red Rock Blvd., Grove City, OH 43123-1154 Tel. (614) 871-0710

REGIONAL MODERATORS

Northwest Region: Rev. Alvin House, PO Box 393, Darby MT 59829 Tel.(406)821-3141
Central-West Region: Rev. Charles Clark, Box 314, Rockport, IL 62370 Tel.(217)437-2507
Central Region: Dr. S. Omar Overly, 2481 Red Rock Blvd., Grove City, OH 43123-1154 Tel.(614)871-0710
Northeast Region: Rev. John Merrill, PO Box 183, East Smithfield, PA 18817 Tel.(717)596-4598
East Region: Rev. Larry Walker, PO Box 1165, Lillington, NC 27546 Tel.(919)893-9529
Southeast Region: Rev. James Fullwood, 207 5th Avenue, N.E., Lutz, FL 33549

STATE MODERATORS

Rev. James Brown:	Maryland
Rev. John W. Coats:	Delaware
Rev. James H. Day:	Ohio
Rev. Linda Felice:	New York
Dr. Berton G. Heleine:	Illinois
Rev. R. Eugene Hill:	New Jersey
Rev. Emma W. Layton:	West Virginia
Rev. Kenneth Pope:	Washington
Rev. Timothy Waldrop:	South Carolina
Rev. Art Mirek:	Michigan
Rev. Charles Jennings:	Pennsylvania
Rev. Jerry Myers:	Indiana

FOREIGN OUTREACH MINISTRIES

Philippine Evangelical Christian Churches Director, Rev. Alan A. Olubalang, PO Box 540, Cotabato City, Philippines 9600
F.A.I.T.H. Ministries
Director, Oseas Andres, PO Box 17, Valenzuela, Metro Manila, Philippines

American Rescue Workers

Major Thomas E. Moore was National Commander of Booth's Salvation Army when a dispute flared between Booth and Moore. Moore resigned from Booth's Army and due to the fact that Booth's Army was not incorporated at the time, Moore was able to incorporate under said name. The name was changed in 1890 to American Salvation Army. In 1913 the current name American Rescue Workers was adopted.

It is a national religious social service agency which operates on a quasimilitary basis. Membership includes officers (clergy), soldiers/adherents (laity), members of various activity groups and volunteers who serve as advisors, associates and committed participants in ARW service functions.

The motivation of the organization is the love of God. Its message is based on the Bible. This is expressed by its spiritual Ministry, the purposes of which are to preach the gospel of Jesus Christ and to meet human needs in his name without discrimination. It is a branch of the Christian Church...A Church with a Mission.

Headquarters

Operational Headquarters: 643 Elmira St., Williamsport, PA 17701 Tel. (717)323-8401
National Field Office, 1209 Hamilton Blvd., Hagerstown, MD 21742 Tel. (301)797-0061
Media Contact, Natl. Communication Sec., Col. Robert N. Coles, Rev., Natl. Field Ofc., Fax (301) 797-1480

Officers

Commander-In-Chief & Pres. Of Corp., General Claude S. Astin, Jr. Rev
Chief of Staff, Col. Larry D. Martin
Natl. Bd. Pres., Col. George B. Gossett, Rev.
Ordination Committee, Chpsn., Gen. Paul E. Martin, (Emeritus) Rev.
Natl. Chief Sec., Major Dawn R. Astin, NQ-643 Elmira St., Williamsport, PA 17701

PERIODICAL

The Rescue Herald
Editor in Cheif- Col. Robert N. Cole, Rev.

The Anglican Orthodox Church

This body, formed in 1963, is composed of clergy and parishes that are traditionally Anglican in practice and historically orthodox in doctrine. Congregations include both traditional Anglican parishes and Orthodox parishes using a Western liturgy. The church is a member of the worldwide Orthodox Anglican Communion, other branches being located in South Africa, Kenya, Liberia, Congo, Central African Republic, Madagascar, Pakistan, South India, the Philippines, Fiji, Japan, and Columbia.

In 1998, the Missionary Diocese of the United States was formed under the direction of the Presiding Bishop, specifically to foster new parish formation and to encourage an expanded ministry of worker-priests throughout the country. The Mission Statement of the new Diocese seeks to identify the unique role this body plays in the greater Church. It is "to incarnate Christ specifically to those who understand the Bible as the Word of God and who sense their need for sacramental worship and ministy, as well as to those who seek a spiritual experience of God."

The church operates the School of Divinity of the Anglican Theological Seminary International, a distance-learning educational consortium composed of Cranmer Seminary, in North Carolina, and the Theological College of Southern Africa, located in Johnnesburg, South Africa.

Headquarters

The Chancery of the Archdiocese
2558 Hickory Tree Road, Winston-Salem, NC 27127 Tel. (336)775-9866 Fax (336)775-9867
Media Contact, The Rev. Scott McLaughlin
E-mail: aocbishop@aol.com
Website:http://www. netministries.org/churches/ch01051

Officer

Presiding Bishop, Most Rev. Dr. Robert J. Godfrey, The Chancery of the Archdiocese, 2558 Hickory Tree Road, Winston-Salem, NC 27127 Tel. (336)775-9866 Fax (336)775-9867

Periodical

The AOC Encounter

The Antiochian Orthodox Christian Archdiocese of North America

The spiritual needs of Antiochian faithful in North America were first served through the Syro-Arabian Mission of the Russian Orthodox Church in 1895. In 1895, the Syrian Orthodox Benevolent Society was organized by Antiochian immigrants in New York City. Raphael Hawaweeny, a young Damascene clergyman serving as professor of Arabic language at the Orthodox theological academy in Kazan, Russia, came to New York to organize the first Arabic-language parish in North America in 1895, after being canonically received under the omophorion of the head of the Russian Church in North America. Saint Nicholas Cathedral, now located at 355 State St. in Brooklyn, is considered the "mother parish" of the Archdiocese.

On March 12, 1904, Hawaweeny became the first Orthodox bishop to be consecrated in North America. He traveled throughout the continent and established new parishes. The unity of Orthodoxy in the New World, including the Syrian Greek Orthodox community, was ruptured after the death of Bishop Raphael in 1915 and by the Bolshevik revolution in Russia and the First World War. Unity returned in 1975 when Metropolitan Philip Saliba, of the Antiochian Archdiocese of New York, and Metropolitan Michael Shaheen of the Antiochian Archdiocese of Toledo, Ohio, signed the Articles of Reunification, ratified by the Holy Synod of the Patriarchate. Saliba was recognized as the Metropolitan Primate and Shaheen as Auxiliary Archbishop. A second auxiliary to the Metropolitan, Bishop Antoun Khouri, was consecrated at Brooklyn's Saint Nicholas Cathedral, in 1983. A third auxiliary, Bishop Basil Essey was consecrated at Wichita's St. George Cathedral in 1992. Two additional bishops were added in 1994: Bishop Joseph Zehlaoui and Bishop Demetri Khoury.

The Archdiocesan Board of Trustees (consisting of 60 elected and appointed clergy and lay members) and the Metropolitan's Advisory Council (consisting of clergy and lay representatives from each parish and mission) meet regularly to assist the Primate in the administration of the Archdiocese.

Headquarters

358 Mountain Rd., Englewood, NJ 07631 Tel. (201)871-1355 Fax (201)871-7954

Media Contact, Father Thomas Zain, 52 78th St., Brooklyn, NY 11209 Tel. (718)748-7940 Fax (718)855-3608

Officers

Primate, Metropolitan Philip Saliba
Auxiliary, Bishop Antoun Khouri
Auxiliary, Bishop Joseph Zehlaoui
Auxiliary, Bishop Basil Essey
Auxiliary, Bishop Demetri Khoury

Periodicals

The Word; Credo; Again Magazine

Apostolic Catholic Assyrian Church of the East, North American Dioceses

The Holy Apostolic Catholic Assyrian Church of the East is the ancient Christian church that developed within the Persian Empire from the day of Pentecost. The Apostolic traditions testify that the Church of the East was established by Sts. Peter, Thomas, Thaddaeus and Bartholomew from among the Twelve and by the labors of Mar Mari and Aggai of the Seventy. The Church grew and developed carrying the Christian gospel into the whole of Asia and islands of the Pacific. Prior to the Great Persecution at the hands of Tamer'leng the Mongol, it is said to have been the largest Christian church in the world.

The doctrinal identity of the church is that of the Apostles. The church stresses two natures and two Qnume in the One person, Perfect God-Perfect man. The church gives witness to the original Nicene Creed, the Ecumenical Councils of Nicea and Constantinople and the church fathers of that era. Since God is revealed as Trinity, the appellation "Mother of God" is rejected for the "Ever Virgin Blessed Mary Mother of Christ," we declare that she is Mother of Emmanuel, God with us!

The church has maintained a line of Catholicos Patriarchs from the time of the Holy Apostles until this present time. Today the present occupant of the Apostolic Throne is His Holiness Mar Dinkha IV, 120th successor to the See of Selucia Ctestiphon.

Headquarters

Catholicos Patriarch, His Holiness Mar Dinkha, IV, Metropolitanate Residence, The Assyrian Church of the East, Baghdad, Iraq

Media Contact, Rev. Chancellor C. H. Klutz, 7201 N. Ashland, Chicago, IL 60626 Tel. (773)465-4777 Fax (773)465-0776

BISHOPS- NORTH AMERICA

Diocese Eastern USA: His Grace Bishop Mar Aprim Khamis, 8908 Birch Ave., Morton Grove, IL 60053 Tel. (847)966-0617 Fax (847) 966-0012; Chancellor to the Bishop, Rev. Chancellor C. H. Klutz, 7201 N. Ashland, Chicago, IL 60626 Tel. (773)465-4777 Fax (773)465-0776

Diocese Western USA: ——, St. Joseph Cathedral, 680 Minnesota Ave., San Jose, CA 95125 Tel. (408)286-7377 Fax (408)286-1236

Diocese of Canada: His Grace Bishop Mar Emmanuel Joseph, St. Mary Cathedral, 57

Apted Ave., Weston, ON M9L 2P2 Tel.
(416)744-9311

Comm. on Inter-Church & Religious Ed.: His
Grace Bishop Mar Bawai, Diocese of Seattle
in WA, 165 NW 65th, Seattle, WA 98117 Tel.
(206)789-1843

Periodical

Qala min M'Dinkha (Voice from the East)

Apostolic Christian Church (Nazarene)

This body was formed in America by an immigration from various European nations, from a movement begun by Rev. S. H. Froehlich, a Swiss pastor, whose followers are still found in Switzerland and Central Europe.

Headquarters

Apostolic Christian Church Foundation, 1135
Sholey Rd., Richmond, VA 23231 Tel. (804)
222-1943 Fax (804)236-0642

Media Contact, Exec. Dir., James Hodges

Officers

Exec. Dir., James Hodges

Apostolic Christian Churches of America

The Apostolic Christian Church of America was founded in the early 1830s in Switzerland by Samuel Froehlich, a young divinity student who had experienced a religious conversion based on the pattern found in the New Testament. The church, known then as Evangelical Baptist, spread to surrounding countries. A Froehlich associate, Elder Benedict Weyeneth, established the church's first American congregation in 1847 in upstate New York. In America, where the highest concentration today is in the Midwest farm belt, the church became known as Apostolic Christian.

Church doctrine is based on a literal interpretation of the Bible, the infallible Word of God. The church believes that a true faith in Christ's redemptive work at Calvary is manifested by a sincere repentance and conversion. Members strive for sanctification and separation from worldliness as a consequence of salvation, not as a means to obtain it. Security in Christ is believed to be conditional based on faithfulness. Uniform observance of scriptural standards of holiness are stressed. Holy Communion is confined to members of the church. Male members are willing to serve in the military, but do not bear arms. The holy kiss is practiced and women wear head coverings during prayer and worship.

Doctrinal authority rests with a council of elders, each of whom serves as a local elder (bishop). Both elders and ministers are chosen from local congregations, do not attend seminary and serve without compensation. Sermons are delivered extemporaneously as led by the Holy Spirit, using the Bible as a text.

Headquarters

3420 N. Sheridan Rd., Peoria, IL 61604

Media Contact, secretary., William R. Schlatter,
14834 Campbell Rd., Defiance, OH 43512
Tel. (419) 393-2621

Officers

Sec., Elder (Bishop) William R. Schlatter, 14834
Campbell Rd., Defiance, OH 43512 Tel. (419)
393-2621

Periodical

The Silver Lining

Apostolic Episcopal Church

Apostolic Episcopal Church was founded in 1925 by a former priest of the Episcopal Church in USA, Rev. Arthur W. Brooks. The orientation of the new church was definitely New Age and New Thought with an emphasis on healing and charismatic teachings. When Bishop Brooks passed to his eternal reward, his successor as Bishop of the Province of the East was Dr. Harold Jarvis, Mar Haroldus, who established the visiting Church Missions. The purpose of the visiting Church Missions was to visit daily in homes, hospitals, prisons, and places of business. The sick, shut-ins, discouraged, imprisoned and those in need of pastoral counseling. Free of charge each person received prayer of healing or consolation or literature as required. This is still the Church's main goal and work.

In 1978 upon the retirement of Dr. Jarvis, the Rev. Francis C. Spataro, Founder & President of the Vilatte Guild, became both Preist-in-Charge and Administrator of the Province of the East. Fr. Francis had been ordained preist on 12/26/76 by Archbishop Uladyslau at the American College & Seminary. After 14 years as Administrator, Fr. Francis was elected & consecrated the Bishop on 10/31/92 in London at Christ the King Cathedral by Archbishop Bertil Persson assisted by Bishops George Boyer and Eric Eades. On Setember 13, 1995, Bishop Spataro also succeeded the deceased Dr. Paul Schultz as Rector Pro Provincial of the U.S. Council of the Order of Corporate Re-union.

The Order of Corporate Re-union, founded in 1874, is dedicated to the restoration of unity in the Holy Catholic Church, Eastern & Western. In the U.S.A. it publishes the Tover of St. Cassian and hosts ecumenical gatherings in various churches; it works closely with the Temple of Understanding, a global interfaith forum as well as with the World Peace Prayer Society. On June 12, 1994, it donated a Peace Pole to the Church of St. Joseph of Arimathea, Preston Hollow, N.Y. Present for the dedication ceremony in front of the Church were: Archbishop Bertil Persson, Mother Lucia L. Grosch, Bishop Francis C. Spataro and all the parishioners.

On August 21, 1993, Bishop Spataro assisted His Eminence Macario Ga, Obispo Maximo of the Iglesia Filipina Independiente to consecrate the new presiding archbishop of the continuing Aglican Church in the USA, M. Rev. H. Edwin Caudill in New York City at Holy Cross PNC Church in the East Village. Present were the heads of several independent Catholic & Orthodox Churches in New York City.

Headquarters

Order of Corporate Reunion, 80-46 234 Street, Queens, NY 11427-2116 Tel. (718)740-4134

Media contact, Rt. Rev. Francis Spataro, Box 192B-1, Preston Hollow, NY 12469

Office of *The Tower of St. Cassian*, 80-46 234 St., RR 1, Queens NY 11427-2116

Periodical

The Tower of St. Cassian

Apostolic Faith Mission Church of God

The Apostolic Faith Mission Church of God was founded and organized July 10, 1906, by Bishop F. W. Williams in Mobile, Ala.

Bishop Williams was saved and filled with the Holy Ghost at a revival in Los Angeles under Elder W. J. Seymour of The Divine Apostolic Faith Movement. After being called into the ministry, Bishop Williams went out to preach the gospel in Mississippi, then moved on to Mobile.

On Oct. 9, 1915, the Apostolic Faith Mission Church of God was incorporated in Mobile under Bishop Williams, who was also the general overseer of this church.

Headquarters

Ward's Temple, 806 Muscogee Rd., Cantonment, FL 32533

Media Contact, Natl. Sunday School Supt., Elder Thomas Brooks, 3298 Toney Dr., Decatur, GA 30032 Tel. (404)284-7596

Officers

Bd. of Bishops: Presiding Bishop, Donice Brown, 2265 Welcome Cir., Cantonement, FL 32535 Tel. (904)968-5225; Billy Carter; J. L. Smiley; T. L. Frye; T. C. Tolbert; James Truss

NATIONAL DEPARTMENTS

Missionary Dept., Pres., Sarah Ward, Cantonment, FL

Youth Dept., Pres., Johnny Kennedy, Birmingham, AL

Sunday School Dept., Supt., Thomas Brooks, Decatur, GA

Mother Dept., Pres., Mother Juanita Phillips, Birmingham, AL

INTERNATIONAL DEPARTMENTS

Morobia, Liberia, Bishop Beter T. Nelson, Box 3646, Bush Rhode Islane, Morobia, Liberia

Apostolic Faith Mission of Portland, Oregon

The Apostolic Faith Mission of Portland, Oregon, was founded in 1907. It had its beginning in the Latter Rain outpouring on Azusa Street in Los Angeles in 1906.

Some of the main doctrines are justification by faith which is a spiritual new birth, as Jesus told Nicodemus and as Martin Luther proclaimed in the Great Reformation; sanctification, a second definite work of grace; the Wesleyan teaching of holiness; the baptism of the Holy Ghost as experienced on the Day of Pentecost and again poured out at the beginning of the Latter Rain revival in Los Angeles.

Mrs. Florence L. Crawford, who had received the baptism of the Holy Ghost in Los Angeles, brought this Latter Rain message to Portland on Christmas Day 1906. It has spread to the world by means of literature which is still published and mailed everywhere without a subscription price. Collections are never taken in the meetings and the public is not asked for money.

Camp meetings have been held annually in Portland, Ore., since 1907, with delegations coming from around the world.

Missionaries from the Portland headquarters have established churches in Korea, Japan, the Philippines and many countries in Africa.

Headquarters

6615 SE 52nd Ave., Portland, OR 97206 Tel. (503)777-1741 Fax (503)777-1743

Media Contact, Superintendent General, Dwight L. Baltzell

Website:http:// www.apostolicfaith.org

Officer

President, Rev. Dwight L. Baltzell

Periodical

Higher Way

Apostolic Lutheran Church of America

Organized in 1872 as the Solomon Korteniemi Lutheran Society, this Finnish body was incorporated in 1929 as the Finnish Apostolic Lutheran Church in America and changed its name to Apostolic Lutheran Church of America in 1962.

This body stresses preaching the Word of God. There is an absence of liturgy and formalism in worship. A seminary education is not required of pastors. Being called by God to preach the Word is the chief requirement for clergy and laity. The church stresses personal absolution and forgiveness of sins, as practiced by Martin Luther, and the importance of bringing converts into God's kingdom.

OFFICE OF THE SECRETARY

332 Mt. Washington Way, Clayton, CA 94517-1546 Tel. (925)672-3320 Fax (925)673-0965

Media Contact, Secretary, Ivan M. Seppala

Officers

Pres., Earl Kaurala, 119 Penny Way, Marquette, MI 49855

Treas., Ben Johnson, Rt. 2, Box 566, Astoria, OR 97103

Periodical

Christian Monthly

Apostolic Orthodox Catholic Church

The Apostolic Orthodox Catholic Church's North American history began in September 1794, when Russian Orthodox missionaries from Valaam Monastery established the very first Orthodox Christian mission, then church (Holy Resurrection-Kodiak), on North American soil in present-day Alaska. Their missionary efforts continued down the Pacific coast, beginning at Fort Ross, California, in 1824, then across the continent. Being North America's canonical founder of Orthodox Christianity, for over 100 years the Russian Orthodox Church maintained and presided over all Orthodox missions and churches throughout North America without question or challenge. Due to the Russian Bolshevik-Communist Revolution of 1917 and rising destructive ethnic and old-country nationalist turbulence causing division among Orthodox Christians in America, the Russian Mother church through its Patriarch, Sergius Stragordsky, approved Archbishop Aftimios Ofiesh to found and lead North America's first, very own and rightful autocephalous (self-governing) church in 1927- English-speaking, and not dominated or constrained by ethnicity or old-country nationalism or other Orthodox Church hierarchy. Full and complete independence was established by declaration for this North American Orthodox Catholic Church on July 25, 1929. The Apostolic Orthodox Catholic Church, as it is known by today, is a remnant continuation of North America's first-born autocephalous-independent Orthodox Christian Church founded by Archbishop Aftimios Ofiesh of Blessed Memory.

Headquarters

AOCC Office of Comm. & Policy: P.O. Box 1834, Glendora, CA 91740-1834 Tel. (626)857-7640 Fax (626)857-7642
Media Contact, AOCC Ecumenical Relations Officer, Archpriest Fr. Bartimaeus, 1206 E. Third St., Anaconda, MT 59711-2704 Tel. (406)563-5426 Fax (406)563-5426

Officers

Presiding Archbishop, Most Rev. GORAZD, Bishop of the Diocese of Los Angeles & Greater Pacific, P.O. Box 1834, Glendora, CA 91740-1834 Tel. (626)857-7640 FAX(626) 857-7642; Rectory (626)335-7369
Second-Presiding Archbishop, Most Rev. ANGELO, Bishop of the Diocese of the Eastern United States, 37 Shippee School House Rd., Foster, RI 02825 Tel. (401)647-2867
Secretary Archbishop, Most Rev. AFTIMIOS, Bishop of the Diocese of the Rocky Mountains & Midwest,
3512 South Hillcrest Drive, Denver, CO 80237 Tel. (303)753-1945 E-mail: Baftimii@aol.com

SEMINARY

Holy Trinity Apostolic Orthodox Catholic Seminary, PO Box 1834, Glendora, CA 91740-1834

Apostolic Overcoming Holy Church of God, Inc.

The Right Reverend William Thomas Phillips (1893-1973) was thoroughly convinced in 1912 that Holiness was a system through which God wanted him to serve. In 1916 he was led to Mobile, Alabama, where he organized the Ethiopian Overcoming Holy Church of God. In April 1941 the church was incorporated in Alabama under its present title.

Each congregation manages its own affairs, united under districts governed by overseers and diocesan bishops and assisted by an executive board comprised of bishops, ministers, laymen and the National Secretary. The General Assembly convenes annually.

The church's chief objective is to enlighten people of God's holy Word and to be a blessing to every nation. The main purpose of this church is to ordain elders, appoint pastors and send out divinely called missionaries and teachers. This church enforces all ordinances enacted by Jesus Christ. The church believes in water baptism (Acts 2:38, 8:12, and 10:47), administers the Lord's Supper, observes the washing of feet (John 13:4-7), believes that Jesus Christ shed his blood to sanctify the people and cleanse them from all sin and believes in the resurrection of the dead and the second coming of Christ.

Headquarters

1120 N. 24th St., Birmingham, AL 35234
Media Contact, Natl. Exec. Sec., Juanita R. Arrington, Tel. (205)324-2202

Officers

Senior Bishop & Exec. Head, Rt. Rev. Jasper Roby
National Treas., Elder W. T. Parker
Exec. Sec., Juanita R. Arrington

Periodical

The People's Mouthpiece

Armenian Apostolic Church of America

Widespread movement of the Armenian people over the centuries caused the development of two seats of religious jurisdiction of the Armenian Apostolic Church in the World: the See of Etchmiadzin, in Armenia, and the See of Cilicia, in Lebanon.

In America, the Armenian Church functioned under the jurisdiction of the Etchmiadzin See from 1887 to 1933, when a division occurred within the American diocese over the condition of the church in Soviet Armenia. One group chose to remain independent until 1957, when the Holy See of Cilicia agreed to accept them under its jurisdiction.

Despite the existence of two dioceses in North

69

America, the Armenian Church has always functioned as one church in dogma and liturgy.

Headquarters
Eastern Prelacy, 138 E. 39th St., New York, NY 10016 Tel. (212)689-7810 Fax (212)689-7168
Western Prelacy, 4401 Russel Ave., Los Angeles, CA 90027 Tel. (213)663-8273 Fax (213)663-0438
Media Contact, Vasken Ghougassian

Officers
Eastern Prelacy, Prelate, Bishop Oshagan Choloyan
Eastern Prelacy, Chpsn., Jack Mardoian
Western Prelacy, Prelate, Bishop Moushegh Mardirossian
Western Prelacy, Chpsn., Vatche Madenlian

DEPARTMENTS
AREC, Armenian Religious Educ. Council, Exec. Coord., Deacon Shant Kazanjian
ANEC, Armenian Natl. Educ. Council, Exec. Coord., Gilda Kupelian

Periodical
Outreach

Assemblies of God

From a few hundred delegates at its founding convention in 1914 at Hot Springs, Ark., the Assemblies of God has become one of the largest church groups in the modern Pentecostal movement worldwide. Throughout its existence it has emphasized the power of the Holy Spirit to change lives and the participation of all members in the work of the church.

The revival that led to the formation of the Assemblies of God and numerous other church groups early in the 20th century began during times of intense prayer and Bible study. Believers in the United States and around the world received spiritual experiences like those described in the Book of Acts. Accompanied by baptism in the Holy Spirit and its initial physical evidence of "speaking in tongues," or a language unknown to the person, their experiences were associated with the coming of the Holy Spirit at Pentecost (Acts 2), so participants were called Pentecostals.

The church also believes that the Bible is God's infallible Word to man, that salvation is available only through Jesus Christ, that divine healing is made possible through Christ's suffering and that Christ will return again for those who love him. In recent years, this Pentecostal revival has spilled over into almost every denomination in a new wave of revival sometimes called the charismatic renewal.

Assemblies of God leaders credit their church's rapid and continuing growth to its acceptance of the New Testament as a model for the present-day church. Aggressive evangelism and missionary zeal at home and abroad characterize the denomination.

Assemblies of God believers observe two ordinances-water baptism by immersion and the Lord's Supper, or Holy Communion. The church is trinitarian, holding that God exists in three persons: Father, Son and Holy Spirit.

Headquarters
1445 Boonville Ave., Springfield, MO 65802 Tel. (417)862-2781 Fax (417)862-8558
Media Contact, Dir. of Public Relations, Juleen Turnage, Fax (417)862-5554

EXECUTIVE PRESBYTERY
Gen. Supt., Thomas E. Trask
Asst. Supt., Charles T. Crabtree
Gen. Sec., George O. Wood
Gen. Treas., James E. Bridges
Foreign Missions, Exec. Dir., John Bueno
Home Missions, Exec. Dir., Charles Hackett
Great Lakes, M. Wayne Benson, 2100 44th St. SW, Grand Rapids, MI 49509
Gulf, Gene Jackson, PO Box 358, Madison, TN 37116
North Central, David Argue, 1111 Old Cheney Rd., Lincoln, NE 68512
Northeast, Almon Bartholomew, 13 Cedarwood Dr., Queensbury, NY 12804
Northwest, R. L. Brandt, 1601 Judd Circle, Billings, MT 59102
South Central, Armon Newburn, P.O. Box 13179, Oklahoma City, OK 73113
Southeast, Dan Betzer, 4701 Summerlin Rd., Ft. Myers, FL 33919
Southwest, Richard Dresselhaus, 8404 Phyllis Pl., San Diego, CA 92123
Language Area, Jesse Miranda, 3527 Thaxton, Hacienda Heights, CA 91745

International Headquarters
Division of the Treasury, Gen. Treas., James E. Bridges
Division of Christian Education, Natl. Dir., LeRoy Bartel
Division of Church Ministries, Natl. Dir., —
Division of Foreign Missions, Exec Dir., John Bueno
Division of Home Missions, Exec. Dir., Charles Hackett
Div. of Publication, Gospel Publishing House, Natl. Dir., Arlyn Pember

Periodicals
Enrichment: A Journal for Pentecostal Ministry; At Ease; Caring; High Adventure; Club Connection; Mountain Movers; Pentecostal Evangel; Christian Education Counselor; Woman's Touch; Heritage; On Course

Assemblies of God International Fellowship (Independent/Not affiliated)

April 9, 1906 is the date commonly accepted by Pentecostals as the 20th-century outpouring of God's spirit in America, which began in a humble gospel mission at 312 Azusa Street in Los Angeles.

This spirit movement spread across the United States and gave birth to the Independent Assemblies of God (Scandinavian). Early pioneers instrumental in guiding and shaping the fellowship of ministers and churches into a nucleus of independent churches included Pastor B. M. Johnson, founder of Lakeview Gospel Church in 1911; Rev. A. A. Holmgren, a Baptist minister who received his baptism of the Holy Spirit in the early Chicago outpourings, was publisher of Sanningens Vittne, a voice of the Scandinavian Independent Assemblies of God and also served as secretary of the fellowship for many years; Gunnar Wingren, missionary pioneer in Brazil; and Arthur F. Johnson, who served for many years as chairman of the Scandinavian Assemblies.

In 1935, the Scandinavian group dissolved its incorporation and united with the Independent Assemblies of God of the U.S. and Canada which by majority vote of members formed a new corporation in 1986, Assemblies of God International Fellowship (Independent/Not Affiliated).

Headquarters

5284 Eastgate Mall, San Diego, CA 92121 Tel. (619)677-9701 Fax (619)677-0038
Media Contact, Exec. Dir. & Ed., Rev. T. A. Lanes
E-mial:agifellowship.org

Officers

Exec. Dir., Rev. T. A. Lanes
Sec., Rev. George E. Ekeroth
Treas., Dr. Joseph Bohac
Canada, Sec., Harry Nunn, Sr., 15 White Crest Ct., St. Catherines, ON 62N 6Y1

Periodical

The Fellowship Magazine

Associate Reformed Presbyterian Church (General Synod)

The Associate Reformed Presbyterian Church (General Synod) stems from the 1782 merger of Associate Presbyterians and Reformed Presbyterians. In 1822, the Synod of the Carolinas broke with the Associate Reformed Church (which eventually became part of the United Presbyterian Church of North America).

The story of the Synod of the Carolinas began with the Seceder Church, formed in Scotland in 1733 and representing a break from the established Church of Scotland. Seceders, in America called Associate Presbyterians, settled in South Carolina following the Revolutionary War. They were joined by a few Covenanter congregations which, along with the Seceders, had protested Scotland's established church. The Covenanters took their name from the Solemn League and Covenant of 1643, the guiding document of Scotch Presbyterians. In 1790, some Seceders and Covenanters formed the Presbytery of the

Carolinas and Georgia at Long Cane, S.C. Thomas Clark and John Boyse led in the formation of this presbytery, a unit within the Associate Reformed Presbyterian Church. The presbytery represented the southern segment of that church. In 1822 the southern church became independent of the northern Associate Reformed Presbyterian Church and formed the Associate Reformed Presbyterian Church of the South. "Of the South" was dropped in 1858 when the northern group joined the United Presbyterian Church and "General Synod" was added in 1935. The General Synod is the denomination's highest court; it is composed of all the teaching elders and at least one ruling elder from each congregation.

Doctrinally, the church holds to the Westminster Confession of Faith. Liturgically, the synod has been distinguished by its exclusive use of psalmody; in 1946 this practice became optional.

Headquarters

Associate Reformed Presbyterian Center, One Cleveland St., Greenville, SC 29601-3696 Tel. (864)232-8297 Fax (864)271-3729
Media Contact, Principal Clk., Rev. C. Ronald Beard, D.D., 3132 Grace Hill Rd., Columbia, SC 29204 Tel. (803)787-6370.
Moderator: Mr. James M. Dickson, 106 Marietta St., Clover, SC 29710 Tel. (803) 222-9079
Moderator-Elect: Rev. Dwight L. Pearson, D.D., PO Box 174, Chester, SC 29706-0174 Tel.(803)385-2228

AGENCIES AND INSTITUTIONS

Admn. Ser. Dir., Ed Hogan
Christian Education, Dir., Dr. David Vickery
Church Extension, Dir., Rev. James T. Corbitt, D.D.
Publications, Editor, E. Benton Johnston
Treasurer, Guy H. Smith, III
World Witness, Bd. of Foreign Missions, Exec. Sec., John E. Mariner
Bonclarken Assembly, Dir., James T. Brice, 500 Pine St., Flat Rock, NC 28731 Tel. (704)692-2223
Erskine College, Pres., Rev. John L. Carson, Ph.D., Due West, SC 29639 Tel. (864)379-8759
Erskine Theological Seminary, Dean, Ralph J. Gore, Jr., Ph.D., Due West, SC 26939 Tel. (864) 379-8885

Periodicals

The Associate Reformed Presbyterian; The Adult Quarterly

The Association of Free Lutheran Congregations

The Association of Free Lutheran Congregations, rooted in the Scandinavian revival movements, was organized in 1962 by a Lutheran Free Church remnant which rejected

71

merger with The American Lutheran Church. The original 42 congregations were joined by other like-minded conservative Lutherans, especially from the former Evangelical Lutheran Church and the Suomi Synod. There has been more than a fivefold increase in the number of congregations. Congregations subscribe to the Apostles', Nicene and Athanasian creeds; Luther's Small Catechism; and the Unaltered Augsburg Confession. The Fundamental Principles and Rules for Work (1897) declare that the local congregation is the right form of the kingdom of God on earth, subject to no authority but the Word and the Spirit of God.

Distinctive emphases are: (1) the infallibility and inerrancy of Holy Scriptures as the Word of God; (2) congregational polity; (3) the spiritual unity of all believers, resulting in fellowship and cooperation transcending denominational lines; (4) evangelical outreach, calling all to enter a personal relationship with Jesus Christ; (5) a wholesome Lutheran pietism that proclaims the Lordship of Jesus Christ in all areas of life and results in believers becoming the salt and light in their communities; (6) a conservative stance on current social issues.

A two-year Bible school and a theological seminary are in suburban Minneapolis. Support is channeled to churches in Brazil, Mexico, Canada and India.

Headquarters
3110 E. Medicine Lake Blvd., Minneapolis, MN 55441 Tel. (612)545-5631 Fax (612)545-0079
Media Contact, Pres., Rev. Robert L. Lee

Officers
Pres., Rev. Robert L. Lee
Vice-Pres., Rev. Elden K. Nelson, 1633 Co. Rd. 8 SE, Kandiyohi, MN 56251
Sec., Rev. Brian Davidson, 908 W. Third St., Weslaco, TX 78596

Periodical
The Lutheran Ambassador

Baptist Bible Fellowship International
Organized on May 24, 1950 in Fort Worth, Tex., the Baptist Bible Fellowship was founded by about 100 pastors and lay people who had grown disenchanted with the policies and leadership of the World Fundamental Baptist Missionary Fellowship, an outgrowth of the Baptist Bible Union formed in Kansas City in 1923 by fundamentalist leaders from the Southern Baptist, Northern Baptist and Canadian Baptist Conventions. The BBF elected W. E. Dowell as its first president and established offices and a three-year (now four-year with a graduate school) Baptist Bible College.

The BBF statement of faith was essentially that of the Baptist Bible Union, adopted in 1923, a variation of the New Hampshire Confession of Faith. It presents an infallible Bible, belief in the substitutionary death of Christ, his physical resurrection and his premillennial return to earth. It advocates local church autonomy and strong pastoral leadership and maintains that the fundamental basis of fellowship is a missionary outreach. The BBF vigorously stresses evangelism and the international missions office reports 858 adult missionaries working on 107 fields throughout the world in 1996.

There are BBF-related churches in every state of the United States, with special strength in the upper South, the Great Lakes region, southern states west of the Mississippi, Kansas and California. There are six related colleges and one graduate school or seminary.

A Committee of Forty-Five, elected by pastors and churches within the states, sits as a representative body, meeting in three subcommittees, each chaired by one of the principal officers: an administration committee chaired by the president, a missions committee chaired by a vice-president and an education committee chaired by a vice-president.

Headquarters
Baptist Bible Fellowship Missions Bldg., 720 E. Kearney St., Springfield, MO 65803 Tel. (417) 862-5001 Fax (417)865-0794
Mailing Address, P.O. Box 191, Springfield, MO 65801
Media Contact, Mission Dir., Dr. Bob Baird, P.O. Box 191, Springfield, MO 65801

Officers
Pres., Sam Davison, Southwest Baptist Church, 1300 SW 544th St., Oklahoma City, OK 73119
First Vice-Pres., Rev. Dave Hardy, Eastland Baptist Church, 1835 S. 129th E. Ave., Tulsa, OK 74108
Second Vice-Pres., David Brown, Yakima Bible Baptist Church, P.O. Box 167, Yakima, WA 98907
Sec., K. B. Murray, Millington Street Baptist Church, Box 524, Winfield, KS 67156
Treas., Ken Adrian, Thomas Rd. Baptist Church, 5735 W. Thomas Rd., Phoenix, AZ 85031
Mission Dir., Dr. Bob Baird, P.O. Box 191, Springfield, MO 65801

Periodicals
The Baptist Bible Tribune; The Preacher; Global Partners

Baptist General Conference
The Baptist General Conference, rooted in the pietistic movement of Sweden during the 19th century, traces its history to Aug. 13, 1852. On that day a small group of believers at Rock Island, Illinois, under the leadership of Gustaf Palmquist, organized the first Swedish Baptist Church in America. Swedish Baptist churches flourished in the upper Midwest and Northeast, and by 1879, when the first annual meeting was held in Village Creek, Iowa, 65 churches had

been organized, stretching from Maine to the Dakotas and south to Kansas and Missouri.

By 1871, John Alexis Edgren, an immigrant sea captain and pastor in Chicago, had begun the first publication and a theological seminary. The Conference grew to 324 churches and nearly 26,000 members by 1902. There were 40,000 members in 1945 and 135,000 in 1993.

Many churches began as Sunday schools. The seminary evolved into Bethel, a four-year liberal arts college with 1,800 students, and theological seminaries in Arden Hills, Minn. and San Diego, California.

Missions and the planting of churches have been main objectives both in America and overseas. Today churches have been established in the United States, Canada and Mexico, as well as a dozen countries overseas. In 1985 the churches of Canada founded an autonomous denomination, The Baptist General Conference of Canada. The Baptist General Conference is a member of the Baptist World Alliance, the Baptist Joint Committee on Public Affairs and the National Association of Evangelicals. It is characterized by the balancing of a conservative doctrine with an irenic and cooperative spirit. Its basic objective is to seek the fulfillment of the Great Commission and the Great Commandment.

Headquarters

2002 S. Arlington Heights Rd., Arlington Heights, IL 60005 Tel. (847)228-0200 Fax (847)228-5376
Media Contact, Pres., Dr. Robert S. Ricker
E-mail: gmbgcstd@aol.com
Website: http://www.bgc.bethel.edu

Officers

Pres. & Chief Exec. Officer, Dr. Robert Ricker
Exec, Vice-Pres., Ray Swatkowski
Vice-Pres. of Development, Dennis Smith
Vice-Pres. of Finance, Stephen R. Schultz
Vice Pres. of Church Enrichment, Dr. John C. Dickau
Vice-Pres. of Church Planting, Rev. Ronald Larson

OTHER ORGANIZATIONS

Bd. of Trustees: Bethel College & Seminary, Pres., Dr. George K. Brushaber, 3900 Bethel Dr., St. Paul, MN 55112

Periodical

The Standard

Baptist Missionary Association of America

A group of regular Baptist churches organized in associational capacity in May, 1950, in Little Rock, Ark., as the North American Baptist Association. The name changed in 1969 to Baptist Missionary Association of America. There are several state and numerous local associations of cooperating churches. In theology, these churches are evangelical, missionary, fundamental and for the most part premillennial.

Headquarters

9219 Sibly Hole Rd., Little Rock, AR Tel. (501) 455-4977 Fax (501)455-3636
Mailing Address, P.O. Box 193920, Little Rock, AR 72219-3920
Media Contact, Dir. of Baptist News Service, James C. Blaylock, P.O. Box 97, Jacksonville, TX 75766 Tel. (903)586-2501 Fax (903)586-0378

Officers

Pres., Ronald Morgan, 14717 Heartside Pl., Dallas, TX 75234
Vice-Pres.: Leon J. Carmical, 85 Midway Church Rd., Sumrall, MS 39428; David T. Watkins, 1 Pineridge St., Magnolia, AR 71753
Rec. Sec.: Rev. Ralph Cottrell, P.O. Box 1203, Van, TX 75790; Don J. Brown, P.O. Box 8181, Laruel, MS 39441; James Ray Raines, 5609 N. Locust, N. Little Rock, AR 72116

DEPARTMENTS

Missions: Gen. Sec., Rev. F. Donald Collins, P.O. Box 193920, Little Rock, AR 72219-3920
Publications: Ed.-in-Chief, Rev. James L. Silvey, 311 Main St., P.O. Box 7270, Texarkana, TX 75505
Christian Education: Bapt. Missionary Assoc. Theological Sem., Pres., Dr. Philip R. Bryan, Seminary Heights, 1530 E. Pine St., Jacksonville, TX 75766
Baptist News Service: Dir., Rev. James C. Blaylock, P.O. Box 97, Jacksonville, TX 75766
Life Word Broadcast Ministries: Dir., Rev. George Reddin, P.O. Box 6, Conway, AR 72032
Armed Forces Chaplaincy: Exec. Dir., Bobby C. Thornton, P.O. Box 240, Flint, TX 75762
BMAA Dept. of Church Ministries: Donny Parish, P.O. Box 10356, Conway, AR 72033
Daniel Springs Encampment: James Speer, P.O. Box 310, Gary, TX 75643
Ministers Resource Services: Craig Branham, 4001 Jefferson St., Texarkana, AR 75501

OTHER ORGANIZATIONS

Baptist Missionary Assoc. Brotherhood: Pres., Bill Looney, 107 Bearskin Dr., Sherwood, AR 72120
National Women's Missionary Auxiliary: Pres., Mrs. Bill Skinner, 819 Carrell St., Tomball, TX 77375

Periodical

The Gleaner

Beachy Amish Mennonite Churches

The Beachy Amish Mennonite Church was established in 1927 in Somerset County, Pa. following a division in the Amish Mennonite Church in that area. As congregations in other locations joined the movement, they were identified by the same name. There are currently 97 churches in the United States, 9 in Canada and 34 in other countries. Membership in the United States is 7,059, according to the 1996 Mennonite Yearbook.

Beachy Churches believe in one God eternally existent in three persons (Father, Son and Holy Spirit); that Jesus Christ is the one and only way to salvation; that the Bible is God's infallible Word to us, by which all will be judged; that heaven is the eternal abode of the redeemed in Christ; and that the wicked and unbelieving will endure hell eternally.

Evangelical mission boards sponsor missions in Central and South America, Ireland, and in Kenya, Africa.

The Mission Interests Committee, founded in 1953 for evangelism and other Christian services, sponsors homes for handicapped youth and elderly people, mission outreaches among the North American Indians in Canada and a mission outreach in Europe.

Headquarters
Media Contact, David L. Miller, 3015 Partridge Rd., Partridge, KS 67566 Te. (316)567-2376

ORGANIZATIONS
Amish Mennonite Aid: Sec.-Treas., Vernon Miller, 2675 U.S. 42 NE, London, OH 43140 Tel. (614)879-8616

Mission Interests Committee: Sec.-Treas., Melvin Gingerich, 42555 900W, Topeka, IN 46571 Tel. (219)593-9090

Choice Books of Northern Virginia: Supervisor, Simon Schrock, 4614 Holly Ave., Fairfax, VA 22030 Tel. (703)830-2800

Calvary Bible School: HC 61, Box 202, Calico Rock, AR 72519 Tel. (501)297-8658; Sec.-Treas., Elmer Gingerich, HC 74, Box 282, Mountain View, AR 72560 Tel. (501)296-8764

Penn Valley Christian Retreat, Bd. Chmn., Wayne Schrock, RR 2, Box 165, McVeytown, PA 17015 Tel. (717)529-2935

Periodical
The Calvary Messenger

Berean Fundamental Church
Founded 1932 in North Platte, Nebraska. this body emphasizes conservative Protestant doctrines.

Headquarters
Box 6103, Lincoln, NE 68506 Tel. (402)489-8056 Fax (402)489-8056
Media Contact, Pres., Pastor Doug Shada

Officers
Pres., Doug Shada
Vice-Pres., Richard Crocker, 419 Lafayette Blvd., Cheyenne, WY 82009 Tel. (307)635-5914
Sec., Roger Daum, 1510 O Street, Cozad, NE 69130 Tel. (308)784-3675
Treas., Virgil Wiebe, P.O. Box 6103, Lincoln, NE 68506

Exec. Advisor, Curt Lehman, Tel. (402)483-4840
Exec. Advisor, Carl M. Goltz, P.O. Box 397, North Platte, NE 69103 Tel. (308)532-6723

The Bible Church of Christ, Inc.
The Bible Church of Christ was founded on March 1, 1961 by Bishop Roy Bryant, Sr. Since that time, the Church has grown to include congregations in the United States, Africa and India. The church is trinitarian and accepts the Bible as the divinely inspired Word of God. Its doctrine includes miracles of healing, deliverance and the baptism of the Holy Ghost.

Headquarters
1358 Morris Ave., Bronx, NY 10456 Tel. (718) 588-2284 FAX (718) 992-5597
Media Contact, Pres., Bishop Roy Bryant, Sr

Officers
Pres., Bishop Roy Bryant, Sr.
V. Pres., Asst. Bishop Derek G. Owens
Sec., Sissieretta Bryant, Treas., Elder Artie Burney
Exec. Admn., Sr. Autholene Smith

EXECUTIVE TRUSTEE BOARD
Chpsns.: Elder Alberto L. Hope, 1358 Morris Ave., Bronx, NY 10456, Tel. (718)588-2284; Bishop Derek G. Owens, 100 W. 2nd St., Mount Vernon, NY 10550 Tel. (914)664-4602

OTHER ORGANIZATIONS
Bookstore: Mgr., Evangelist Beryl C. Foster, Tel. (718)293-1928
Evangelism: Intl. Pres., Evangelist Gloria Gray
Foreign Missions: Pres., Sr. Autholene Smith
Food Pantry: Dir., Evangelist Susie Jones
Home Missions: Pres., Evangelist Eleanor Samuel
Minister of Music: Ray Brown
Prison Ministry Team: Pres., Evangelist Marvin Lowe
Public Relations: Deacon Abraham Jones
Publications: Dir., Deaconess Betty Hamilton
Sunday Schools: Gen. Supt., Elder A. M. Jones
Theological Institute: Pres., Dr. Roy Bryant, Sr.; Dean, Elder A. M. Jones
Women's Committee: Natl. Chpsn., Sissieretta Bryant
Youth: Pres., Deacon Tommy Robinson, Presiding Elders: Delaware, Elder Edward Cannon, R R Box 70-B5, Diamond Acre, Dagsboro, DE 19939 Tel. (302)732-3351; Virginia, Elder Jesse Alston, 221 Keith Rd., Newport News, VA 23606 Tel. (804)930-2445; Monticello, 104 Waverly Ave., Monticello, NY 12701; Mount Vernon, Elder Artie Burney, 100 W. 2nd St., Mount Vernon, NY 10550; Bronx, Elder Anita Robinson, 1358 Morris Ave., Bronx, NY 10456, Tel. (718)588-2284; Annex, Elder Reginald Gullette, 1069 Morris Ave., Bronx, NY 10456 Tel. (718)992-4653; Albany, New York: Minister Monica Hope; India, Dr. B. Veeraswamy, 46-7-34, Danavaya Peta,

Rajahmunry, India, 533103; Haiti, Antoine Polycarpe, P.O. Box 197, Port-au-Prince, Haiti; St. Croix, Elder Floyd Thomas, 1-J Diamond Ruby, P.O. Box 5183, Sunny Isles, Christiansted, St. Croix Tel. (809)778-1002

Periodicals
The Voice; The Gospel Light; The Challenge

Bible Fellowship Church

The Bible Fellowship Church grew out of divisions in the Mennonite community in Pennsylvania in the 1850s. Traditional church leadership resisted the freedom of expression and prayer meetings initiated by several preachers and church leaders. These evangelical Mennonites formed the Evangelical Mennonite Society. Over the next two decades various like minded groups in Canada, Ohio and Pennsylvania joined the Society.

In 1959 the Conference became the Bible Fellowship Church and a new articles of faith were ratified. They now hold a unique combination of Reformed doctrines with insistence on "Believer Baptism" and Premillennialism.

Headquarters
Bible Fellowship Church, 3000 Fellowship Dr., Whitehall, PA 18052
Media Contact, David J. Watkins, Greater Bible Fellowship Church, 693 Church Rd., Graterford, PA 19426 Tel. (610)489-9389

Officers
Chmn., James A. Beil
Vice-Chmn., Carl C. Cassel
Sec., Randall A. Grossman
Asst Sec., Robert W. Smock

BOARDS AND COMMITTEES
Bd. of Dir., Bible Fellowship Church
Bd. of Christian Education
Board of Extension
Bible Fellowship Church Homes, Inc.
Board of Pensions
Board of Pinebrook Bible Conference
Board of Missions
Board of Publication and Printing
Bd. of Victory Valley Camp
Board of Higher Education

Periodical
Fellowship News

Bible Holiness Church

This church came into being about 1890 as the result of definite preaching on the doctrine of holiness in some Methodist churches in south-eastern Kansas. It became known as The Southeast Kansas Fire Baptized Holiness Association. The name was changed in 1945 to The Fire Baptized Holiness Church and in 1995 to Bible Holiness Church. It is entirely Wesleyan in doctrine, episcopal in church organization and intensive in evangelistic zeal.

Headquarters
600 College Ave., Independence, KS 67301 Tel. (316)331-3049
Media Contact, Gen. Supt, Leroy Newport

Officers
Gen. Supt., Leroy Newport
Gen. Sec., Wayne Knipmeyer, Box 457, South Pekin, IL 61564
Gen. Treas., Dale Cauthon, R.R. 1, Box 8B, Independence, KS 67301

Periodicals
The Flaming Sword; John Three Sixteen

Bible Way Church of Our Lord Jesus Christ World Wide, Inc.

This body was organized in 1957 in the Pentecostal tradition for the purpose of accelerating evangelistic and foreign missionary commitment and to effect a greater degree of collective leadership than leaders found in the body in which they had previously participated.

The doctrine is the same as that of the Church of Our Lord Jesus Christ of the Apostolic Faith, Inc., of which some of the churches and clergy were formerly members.

This organization has churches and missions in Africa, England, Guyana, Trinidad and Jamaica, and churches in 25 states in America. The Bible Way Church is involved in humanitarian as well as evangelical outreach with concerns for urban housing, education and economic development.

Headquarters
4949 Two-Notch Rd., Columbia, SC 29204 Tel. (800)432-5612 Fax (803)691-0583
Media Contact, Chief Apostle, Presiding Bishop Huie Rogers

Officers
Presiding Bishop, Bishop Huie Rogers, 4949 Two Notch Rd., Columbia, SC 29204 Tel. (800)432-5612 Fax (803)691-0583
Gen. Sec., Bishop Edward Williams, 5118 Clarendon Rd., Brooklyn, NY 11226 Tel. (718)451-1238

Brethren Church (Ashland, Ohio)

The Brethren Church (Ashland, Ohio) was organized by progressive-minded German Baptist Brethren in 1883. They reaffirmed the teaching of the original founder of the Brethren movement, Alexander Mack, and returned to congregational government.

Headquarters
524 College Ave., Ashland, OH 44805 Tel. (419) 289-1708 Fax (419)281-0450
Media Contact, Editor of Publications, Richard C. Winfield
E-mail: brethren@bright.net
Website:http:// www.apollotrust.com/~brethren

GENERAL ORGANIZATION
Executive Dir., Dr. Emanuel W. Sandberg

Dir. of Missionary Ministries, Rev. Reilly Smith
Dir. of Congregational Ministries, Rev. David West
Dir. of Pastoral Ministries, Rev. David Cooksey
Director of Publications, Rev. Richard C. Winfield

Periodical
The Brethren Evangelist

Brethren in Christ Church

The Brethren in Christ Church was founded in Lancaster County, Pa. in about the year 1778 and was an outgrowth of the religious awakening which occurred in that area during the latter part of the 18th century. This group became known as "River Brethren" because of their original location near the Susquehanna River. The name "Brethren in Christ" was officially adopted in 1863. In theology they have accents of the Pietist, Anabaptist, Wesleyan and Evangelical movements.

Headquarters
General Church Office, P.O. Box 290, Grantham, PA 17027-0290 Tel. (717)697-2634 Fax (717)697-7714
Media Contact, Mod., Dr. Warren L. Hoffman, Tel. (717)697-2634 Fax (717)697-7714

Officers
Mod., Dr. Warren L. Hoffman, P.O. Box 290, Grantham, PA 17027 Tel. (717)697-2634 Fax (717)697-7714
Gen. Sec., Rev. Kenneth O. Hoke
Tresurer, Allen Carr

OTHER ORGANIZATIONS
General Conference Board: Chpsn., Mark Garis, 504 Swartley Rd., Hatfield, PA 19440
Bd. for Media Ministries: Chpsn., —, P.O. Box 189, Nappanee, IN 46550
Bd. for World Missions: Chpsn., Lowell D. Mann, 8 W. Bainbridge St., Elizabethtown, PA 17022 Fax 1; Exec. Dir., Rev. Jack McClane, P.O. Box 390, Grantham, PA 17027-0390
Jacob Engle Foundation Bd. of Dir.: CEO, Dr. Donald R. Zook
Pension Fund Trustees: Chpsn., Donald R. Zook
Bd. for Stewardship Services: Chpsn., Donald J. Winters, 1727 Lincoln Hwy. East, Lancaster, PA 17602; Exec. Dir., Rev. Phil Keefer, Box 290, Grantham, PA 17027-0290
Publishing House: Exec. Dir., Roger Williams, Evangel Press, P.O. Box 189, Nappanee, IN 46550

Periodical
Evangelical Visitor: Editor, Glen Pierce, P.O. Box 166, Nappanee, IN 46550

Christ Catholic Church

The church is a catholic communion established in 1968 to minister to the growing number of people who seek an experiential relationship with God and who desire to make a total commitment of their lives to God. The church is catholic in faith and tradition and its orders are recognized as valid by catholics of every tradition. Participating cathedrals, churches and missions are located in several states.

Headquarters
405 Kentling Rd., Highlandville, MO 65669 Tel. (417)443-3951
Media Contact, Archbishop, Most Rev. Karl Pruter

Officers
Archbishop, Most Rev. Karl Pruter, P.O. Box 98, Highlandville, MO 65669 Tel. (417)443-3951

Periodical
St. Willibrord Journal

Christ Community Church (Evangelical-Protestant)

This church was founded by the Rev. John Alexander Dowie on Feb. 22, 1896 at Chicago, Ill. In 1901 the church founded the city of Zion, IL and moved their headquarters there. Theologically, the church is rooted in evangelical orthodoxy. The Scriptures are accepted as the rule of faith and practice. Other doctrines call for belief in the necessity of repentance for sin and personal trust in Christ for salvation. The church is Calvinistic in its approach to the scriptures and pre-millennial in its approach to prophecy.

The Christ Community Church is a denominational member of The National Association of Evangelicals. It has work in six other nations in addition to the United States. Branch ministries are found in Tonalea, Ariz. and Lindenhurst, Ill.

Headquarters
2500 Dowie Memorial Dr., Zion, IL 60099 Tel. (847)746-1411 Fax (847)746-1452

Officer
Senior Pastor, Ken Langley

Christadelphians

The Christadelphians are a body of people who believe the Bible to be the divinely inspired word of God, written by "Holy men who spoke as they were moved by the Holy Spirit" (II Peter 1:21). They also believe in the return of Christ to earth to establish the Kingdom of God; in the resurrection of those dead, at the return of Christ, who come into relation with Christ in conformity with his instructions, to be judged as to worthiness for eternal life; in opposition to war; in spiritual rebirth requiring belief and immersion in the name of Jesus; and in a godly walk in this life.

The denomination was organized in 1844 by a medical doctor, John Thomas, who came to the United States from England in 1832, having survived a near shipwreck in a violent storm. This experience affected him profoundly, and he vowed to devote his life to a search for the truth of God and a future hope from the Bible.

Headquarters

Media Contact, Trustee, Norman D. Zilmer, Christadelphian Action Society, 1000 Mohawk Dr., Elgin, IL 60120-3148 Tel. (847)741-5253

Email: nz-cas@juno OR nfadelle@juno.com OR nzilmer@aol.com

Website: Http://www.christadelphia.org

Leaders

Co-Ministers: Norman Fadelle, 815 Chippewa Dr., Elgin, IL 60120 Norman D. Zilmer, 1000 Mohawk Dr., Elgin, IL 60120-3148

Periodicals

Christadelphian Tidings; Christadelphian Watchman; Christadelphian Advocate

The Christian and Missionary Alliance

The Christian and Missionary Alliance was formed in 1897 by the merger of two organizations begun in 1887 by Dr. Albert B. Simpson, The Christian Alliance and the Evangelical Missionary Alliance. The Christian and Missionary Alliance is an evangelical church which stresses the sufficiency of Jesus-Savior, Sanctifier, Healer and Coming King-and has earned a worldwide reputation for its missionary accomplishments. The Canadian districts became autonomous in 1981 and formed The Christian and Missionary Alliance in Canada.

Headquarters

P.O. Box 35000, Colorado Springs, CO 80935-3500 Tel. (719)599-5999 Fax (719)593-8692

Media Contact, Rev. Robert L. Niklaus

Officers

Pres., Rev. Peter N. Nanfelt, D.D.

Corp. Vice-Pres., Rev. Donald A. Wiggins, D.Min.

Sec., Rev. David L. Goodin

Vice-Pres. for Operations/Treas., Mr. Duane A. Wheeland, CPA

Vice-Pres. for National Church Ministries, Rev. P. David Klinsing

Vice-Pres. for International Ministries, Rev. Robert L. Fetherlin, D.Min.

Vice-Pres. for Advancement, Rev. Francis W. Grubbs, Ph.D.

BOARD OF MANAGERS

Chpsn., Rev. Richard W. Bailey, DD

Vice-Chpsn., Rev. Robert L. Thune

DISTRICT SUPERINTENDENTS

Central: Rev. Howard D. Bower, 1218 High St., Wadsworth, OH 44281 Tel. (330)336-2911 Fax (330)334-3702

Central Pacific: Rev. Edward A. Cline, 3824 Buell St., Ste. A, Oakland, CA 94619 Tel. (510)530-5410 Fax (510)530-1369

Eastern Pennsylvania: Rev. Randall B. Corbin, DMin., 1200 Spring Garden Dr., Middletown, PA 17057 Tel. (717)985-9240 Fax (717)985-9246

Great Lakes: Rev. Donald A. Wiggins, 2250 Huron Pkwy, Ann Arbor, MI 48104 Tel. (313) 677-8555 Fax (313)677-0087

Metropolitan: Rev. John F. Soper, 349 Watchung Ave., N. Plainfield, NJ 07060 Tel. (908)668-8421 Fax (908)757-6299

MidAmerica: Rev. Fred G. King, 1301 S. 119th St., Omaha, NE 68144 Tel. (402)330-1888 Fax (402)330-7213

Mid-Atlantic: Rev. John E. Zuch, Jr., 7100 Roslyn Ave., Rockville, MD 20855 Tel. (301) 258-0035 Fax (301)258-1021

Midwest: Rev. Gerald R. Mapstone, 260 Glen Ellyn Rd., Bloomingdale, IL 60108 Tel. (630) 893-1355 Fax (630)893-1027

New England: Rev. Cornelius W. Clarke, P.O. Box 288, S. Easton, MA 02375 Tel. (508)238-3820 Fax (508)238-4454

Northeastern: Rev. David J. Phillips, Jr., 6275 Pillmore Dr., Rome, NY 13440 Tel. (315)336-4720 Fax (315)336-0347

Northwestern: Rev. Gary M. Benedict, 1813 Lexington Ave. N., Roseville, MN 55113-6127 Tel. (612)489-1391 Fax (612)489-8535

Ohio Valley: Rev. David F. Presher, 4050 Executive Park Dr., Ste. 402, Cincinnati, OH 45241 Tel. (513)733-4833 Fax (513)733-4877

Pacific Northwest: Rev. Richard W. Colenso, DD, P.O. Box 1030, Canby, OR 97013 Tel. (503)226-2238 Fax (503)263-8052

Puerto Rico: Rev. Julio Aponte, P.O. Box 51394, Levittown, PR 00950 Tel. (787)261-0101 Fax (787)261-0107

Rocky Mountain: Rev. Harvey A. Town, 2545 Saint Johns Ave., Billings, MT 59102 Tel. (406)656-4233 Fax (406)656-5502

South Atlantic: Rev. Gordon G. Copeland, 10801 Johnston Rd., Ste. 125, Charlotte, NC 28226 Tel. (704)543-0470 Fax (704)543-0215

South Pacific: Rev. Bill J. Vaughn, 4130 Adams St., Ste. A, Riverside, CA 92504 Tel. (909)351-0111 Fax (909)351-0146

Southeastern: Rev. Mark T. O'Farrell, P.O. Box 720430, Orlando, FL 32872-0430 Tel. (407) 823-9662 Fax (407)823-9668

Southern: Rev. A. Eugene Hall, 8420 Division Ave., Birmingham, AL 35206 Tel. (205)836-7048 Fax (205)836-7168

Southwestern: Rev. Daniel R. Wetzel, 5600 E. Loop 820 S., Fort Worth, TX 76119 Tel. (817)561-0879 Fax (817)572-4131

Western Great Lakes: Rev. John W. Fogal, W6107 Aerotech Dr., Appleton, WI 54915 Tel. (414) 734-1123 Fax (414)734-1143

Western Pennsylvania: Rev. D. Paul McGarvey, P.O. Box 429, Punxsutawney, PA 15767 Tel. (814)938-6920 Fax (814)938-7528

INTERCULTURAL MINISTRIES DISTRICTS

Cambodian: Supt., Rev. Joseph S. Kong, 1616 S. Palmetto Ave., Ontario, CA 91762 Tel. (909) 988-9434 Fax (909)395-0572

Haitian South: Rev. Brave Laverdure, 1300 Gwinnett Station Cr #1323, Tucker, GA 30084 Tel. (770)908-0782

Haitian North: Dir., Sainvilus Point DuJour, 22 S. Main St., Spring Valley, NY 10977 Tel. (914)426-1394 Fax (914)358-1682

Hmong: Supt., —, P.O. Box 219, Brighton, CO 80601 Tel. (303)659-1538 Fax (303)659-2171

Korean: Supt., Rev. Gil Kim, 713 W. Commonwealth Blvd., Ste. 2C, Fullerton, CA 92832 Tel. (714)879-5201 Fax (714)879-5202

Laotian: Dir., Rev. Bouathong Vangsoulatda, 724 S. Layton Blvd., Milwaukee, WI 53215 Tel. (414)645-2629 Fax (414)645-2657

Native American: Dir., John C. Cranford, 1610 NW 19th St., Gresham, OR 97030 Tel. (503) 666-7685

Spanish Central: Supt., Rev. Kenneth N. Brisco, 260 Glen Ellyn Rd., Bloomingdale, IL 60108 Tel. (630)924-7171 Fax (630)924-7186

Spanish Eastern: Supt., Rev. Marcelo Realpe, 410 23rd St., Union, NJ 07087 Tel. (201)866-6676 Fax (201)866-6636

Spanish Western: Dir., Rev. Douglas M. Domier, P.O. Box 3805, Dana Point, CA 92629 Tel. (619)489-3816

Vietnamese: Supt., Rev. Tai Anh Nguyen, 2275 W. Lincoln Ave., Anaheim, CA 92801 Tel. (714)491-8912

NATIONAL ASSOCIATIONS

African American Pastors Assoc.: Pres., Rev. Gus H. Brown, 445 Briarwood Dr., Akron, OH 44320 Tel. (330)376-4654

Chinese Association of the C&MA: Pres., Rev. Philip Teng, 517 Floyd St., Englewood Cliffs, NJ 07632 Tel. (201)894-5192

Filipino Association of the C&MA: Pres., Rev. Asterio J. Wee, 14900 Central Ave., Baldwin Park, CA 91706 Tel. (818)962-2080

ETHNIC/CULTURAL MINISTRIES

Arab: Rev. Norman P. Camp, 2 S. 175 Burning Trail, Wheaton, IL 60187 Tel. (708)668-2669

Asian Indian: Rev. David R. Peace, 124-13 23rd Ave., College Point, NY 11356 Tel. (718)353-2745

Dega: c/o Intercultural Ministries, P.O. Box 35000, Colorado Springs, CO 80935

Jewish: Missionary, Rev. Abraham Sandler, 9820 Woodfern Rd., Philadelphia, PA 19115 Tel. (215)676-5122 Fax (215)676-4593

Periodical

Alliance Life

Christian Brethren (also known as Plymouth Brethren)

The Christian Brethren began in the 1820s as an orthodox and evangelical movement in the British Isles and is now worldwide. The name Plymouth Brethren was given by others because the group in Plymouth, England, was a large and influential congregation. In recent years the term Christian Brethren has replaced Plymouth Brethren for the "open" branch of the movement in Canada and British Commonwealth countries and to some extent in the United States.

The unwillingness to establish a denominational structure makes the autonomy of local congregations an important feature of the movement. Other features are weekly observance of the Lord's Supper and adherence to the doctrinal position of conservative, evangelical Christianity.

In the 1840s the movement divided. The "exclusive" branch, led by John Nelson Darby, stressed the interdependency of congregations. Since disciplinary decisions were held to be binding on all assemblies, exclusives had subdivided into seven or eight main groups by the end of the century. Since 1925 a trend toward reunification has reduced that number to three or four.

The "open" branch of the movement was led by George M.ller of orphanage fame. It stressed evangelism and foreign missions. Now the larger of the two branches, it has never experienced world-wide division.

CORRESPONDENT

James A. Stahr, 327 W. Prairie Ave., Wheaton, Il 60187-3408 Tel. (630)665-3757

RELATED ORGANIZATIONS

Interest Ministries, P.O. Box 190, Wheaton, Il. 60189

Christian Missions in Many Lands, Box 13, Spring Lake, NJ 07762

Stewards Foundation, 14275 Midway Rd., Ste. 285, Dallas, TX 75244

International Teams, Box 203, Prospect Heights, IL 60070

Emmaus Bible College, 2570 Asbury Rd., Dubuque, IA 52001

Stewards Ministries, 18-3 E. Dundee Rd., Ste. 100, Barrington, IL 60010

Christian Church (Disciples of Christ)

Born on the American frontier in the early 1800s as a movement to unify Christians, this body drew its major inspiration from Thomas and Alexander Campbell in western Pennsylvania and Barton W. Stone in Kentucky. Developing separately, the "Disciples," under Alexander Campbell, and the "Christians," led by Stone, united in 1832 in Lexington, Ky.

The Christian Church (Disciples of Christ) is marked by informality, openness, individualism and diversity. The Disciples claim no official doctrine or dogma. Membership is granted after a simple statement of belief in Jesus Christ and baptism by immersion-although most congregations accept transfers baptized by other forms in other denominations. The Lord's Supper-generally called Communion-is open to Christians of all persuasions. The practice is weekly Communion, although no church law insists upon it.

Thoroughly ecumenical, the Disciples helped organize the National and World Councils of Churches. The church is a member of the Consultation on Church Union. The Disciples and the United Church of Christ have declared themselves to be in "full communion" through the General Assembly and General Synod of the two churches. Official theological conversations have been going on since 1967 directly with the Roman Catholic Church, and since 1987 with the Russian Orthodox Church.

Disciples have vigorously supported world and national programs of education, agricultural assistance, urban reconciliation, care of persons with retardation, family planning and aid to victims of war and calamity. Operating ecumenically, Disciples' personnel or funds work in more than 100 countries outside North America.

Three manifestations or expressions of the church (general, regional and congregational) operate as equals, with strong but voluntary covenantal ties to one another. Entities in each manifestation manage their own finances, own their own property, and conduct their own programs. A General Assembly meets every two years and has voting representation from each congregation.

Headquarters
130 E. Washington St., P.O. Box 1986, Indianapolis, IN 46206-1986 Tel. (317)635-3100 Fax (317)635-3700
Media Contact, Dir. of News & Information, Cliff Willis
E-mail: cmiller@oc.disciples.org OR cwillis@oc.disciples.org
Website: http://www.disciples.org

Officers
Gen. Minister & Pres., Richard L. Hamm
Mod., Michael W. Mooty, Central Christian Church, 205 E. Short St., Lexingotn, KY 40591-1459
1st Vice-Mod., Zola M. Walker, Jarvis Christian College, PO Box 1470, Hawkins, TX 75765

General Officers
Gen. Minister & Pres., Richard L. Hamm
Assoc. Gen. Min. for Admn., Donald B. Manworren

ADMINISTRATIVE UNITS
Bd. of Church Extension: Pres., James L. Powell, 130 E. Washington St., P.O. Box 7030, Indianapolis, IN 46207-7030 Tel. (317)635-6500 Fax (317)635-6534
Christian Bd. of Publ. (Chalice Press): Pres., Cyrus N. White, 1316 Convention Plaza Dr., P.O. Box 179, St. Louis, MO 63166-0179 Tel. (314)231-8500 Fax (314)231-8524
Christian Church Foundation, Inc.: Pres., James P. Johnson, Fax (317)635-1991
Church Finance Council, Inc.: Pres., —
Council on Christian Unity, Inc.: Pres., Robert K. Welsh

Disciples of Christ Historical Society: Pres., Peter M. Morgan, 1101 19th Ave. S., Nashville, TN 37212-2196 Tel. (615)327-1444 Fax (615)327-1445
Division of Higher Education: Int. Pres., Dennis L. Landon, 11780 Borman Dr., Ste. 100, St. Louis, MO 63146-4159 Tel. (314)991-3000 Fax (314)991-2957
Division of Homeland Ministries: Pres., Ann Updegraff Spleth, Fax (317)635-4426
Division of Overseas Ministries: Pres., Patricia Tucker Spier, Fax (317)635-4323
National Benevolent Association: Pres., Cindy Dougherty, 11780 Borman Dr., Ste. 200, St. Louis, MO 63146-4157 Tel. (314)993-9000 Fax (314)993-9018
Pension Fund: Pres., Arthur A. Hanna, 130 E. Washington St., Indianapolis, IN 46204-3645 Tel. (317)634-4504 Fax (317)634-4071

REGIONAL UNITS OF THE CHURCH
Alabama-Northwest Florida: Regional Minister, John P. Mobley, 1336 Montgomery Hwy. S., Birmingham, AL 35216-2799 Tel. (205)823-5647 Fax (205)823-5673
Arizona: Regional Minister, Gail F. Davis, 4423 N. 24th St., Ste 700, Phoenix, AZ 85016-5544 Tel. (602)468-3815 Fax (602)468-3816
Arkansas: Regional Min./Pres., Barbara E. Jones, 6100 Queensboro Dr., P.O. Box 191057, Little Rock, AR 72219-1057 Tel. (501)562-6053 Fax (501)562-7089
California North-Nevada: Int. Regional Min./Pres., Charles R. Blaisdell, 9260 Alcosta Blvd., C-18, San Ramon, CA 94583-4143 Tel. (510)556-9900 Fax (510)556-9904
Canada: Exec. Director, Stan Litke, 128 Woolwich St., Ste. 202, P.O. Box 64, Guelph, ON N1H 6J6 Tel. (519)823-5190 Fax (519)823-5766
Capital Area: Regional Minister, Wm. Chris Hobgood, 8901 Connecticut Ave., Chevy Chase, MD 20815-6700 Tel. (301)654-7794 Fax (301)654-8372
Central Rocky Mountain Region: Exec. Regional Minister, William E. Crowl, 4325 W. 29th Ave., P.O. Box 12186, Denver, CO 80212 Tel. (303)561-1790 Fax (303)561-1795
Florida: Regional Minister, Jimmie L. Gentle, 924 N. Magnolia, Ste. 200, Orlando, FL 32803 Tel. (407)843-4652 Fax (407)246-0019
Georgia: Regional Minister, David L. Alexander, 2370 Vineville Ave., Macon, GA 31204-3163 Tel. (912)743-8649 Fax (912)741-1508
Idaho-South: Regional Minister, Larry Crist, 4900 N. Five Mile Rd., Boise, ID 83713-1826 Tel. (208)322-0538 Fax (208)375-5442
Illinois-Wisconsin: Regional Minister/Pres., Nathan S. Smith, 1011 N. Main St., Bloomington, IL 61701-1797 Tel. (309)828-6293 Fax (309)829-4612
Indiana: Regional Minister, C. Edward Weisheimer, 1100 W. 42nd St., Indianapolis,

IN 46208-3375 Tel. (317)926-6051 Fax (317)931-2034

Kansas: Regional Minister/Pres., Patsie Sweeden, 2914 S.W. MacVicar Ave., Topeka, KS 66611-1787 Tel. (913)266-2914 Fax (913)266-0174

Kansas City,Greater: Int. Regional Min./Pres., Paul J. Diehl, Jr., 5700 Broadmoor, Ste. 205, Mission, KS 66202-2405 Tel. (913)432-1414 Fax (913)432-3598

Kentucky: Gen. Minister, A. Guy Waldrop, 1125 Red Mile Rd., Lexington, KY 40504-2660 Tel. (606)233-1391 Fax (606)233-2079

Louisiana: Regional Minister, Bill R. Boswell, 3524 Holloway Prairie Rd., Pineville, LA 71360-5816 Tel. (318)443-0304 Fax (318)449-1367

Michigan: Regional Minister, Morris Finch, Jr., 2820 Covington Ct., Lansing, MI 48912-4830 Tel. (517)372-3220 Fax (517)372-2705

Mid-America Region: Regional Minister, Stephen V. Cranford, Hwy. 54 W., P. O. Box 104298, Jefferson City, MO 65110-4298 Tel. (573)636-8149 Fax (573)636-2889

Mississippi: Regional Minister, William E. McKnight, 1619 N. West St., P.O. Box 4832, Jackson, MS 39296-4832 Tel. (601)352-6774 Fax (601)355-1221

Montana: Regional Minister, Karen Frank-Plumlee, 1019 Central Ave., Great Falls, MT 59401-3784 Tel. (406)452-7404

Nebraska: Interim Regional Ministers, John and Dawn Stemple, 1268 S. 20th St., Lincoln, NE 68502-1699 Tel. (402)476-0359 Fax (402)476-0350

North Carolina: Regional Minister, Rexford L. Horne, 509 N.E. Lee St., P.O. Box 1568, Wilson, NC 27894 Tel. (919)291-4047 Fax (919)291-3338

Northeastern Region: Regional Minister, Charles F. Lamb, 1272 Delaware Ave., Buffalo, NY 14209-1531 Tel. (716)882-3735 Fax (716)882-7671

Northwest Region: Regional Minister/Pres., Jack Sullivan, Jr., 6558-35th Ave. SW, Seattle, WA 98126-2899 Tel. (206)938-1008 Fax (206)933-1163

Ohio: Regional Pastor/Pres., Howard M. Ratcliff, 38007 Butternut Ridge Rd., P.O. Box 299, Elyria, OH 44036-0299 Tel. (216)458-5112 Fax (216)458-5114

Oklahoma: Regional Pastor, Thomas R. Jewell, 301 N.W. 36th St., Oklahoma City, OK 73118-8661 Tel. (405)528-3577 Fax (405)528-3584

Oregon: Regional Minister, Mark K. Reid, 0245 S.W. Bancroft St., Ste. F, Portland, OR 97201-4267 Tel. (503)226-7648 Fax (503)228-6983

Pacific Southwest Region: Regional Minister/Pres., Don W. Shelton, 2401 N. Lake Ave., Altadena, CA 91001-2418 Tel. (818)296-0385 Fax (818)296-1280

Pennsylvania: Regional Minister, W. Darwin Collins, 670 Rodi Rd., Pittsburgh, PA 15235-4524 Tel. (412)731-7000 Fax (412)731-4515

South Carolina: Interim Regional Minister, Carl R. Flock, 1098 E. Montague Ave., North Charleston, SC 29405-4837 Tel. (803)554-6886 Fax (803)554-6886

Southwest Region: Regional Minister, Ralph Glenn, 3209 S. University Dr., Fort Worth, TX 76109-2239 Tel. (817)926-4687 Fax (817) 926-5121

Tennessee: Regional Minister/Pres., Glen J. Stewart, 3700 Richland Ave., Nashville, TN 37205-2499 Tel. (615)269-3409 Fax (615)269-3400

Upper Midwest Region: Regional Minister/Pres., Richard L. Guentert, 3300 University Ave., P.O. Box 1024, Des Moines, IA 50311-1024 Tel. (515)255-3168 Fax (515)255-2625

Virginia: Regional Minister, Lee Parker, 518 Brevard St., Lynchburg, VA 24501 Tel. (804)846-3400 Fax (804)528-4919

West Virginia: Regional Minister, William B. Allen, Rt. 5, Box 167, Parkersburg, WV 26101-9576 Tel. (304)428-1681 Fax (304)428-1684

Periodicals

The Disciple; Vanguard; Mid-Stream: An Ecumenical Journal

Christian Church of North America, General Council

Originally known as the Italian Christian Church, its first General Council was held in 1927 at Niagara Falls, N.Y. This body was incorporated in 1948 at Pittsburgh, Pa., and is described as Pentecostal but does not engage in the "the excesses tolerated or practiced among some churches using the same name."

The movement recognizes two ordinances-baptism and the Lord's Supper. Its moral code is conservative and its teaching is orthodox. Members are exhorted to pursue a life of personal holiness, setting an example to others. A conservative position is held in regard to marriage and divorce. The governmental form is, by and large, congregational. District and National officiaries, however, are referred to as Presbyteries led by Overseers.

The group functions in cooperative fellowship with the Italian Pentecostal Church of Canada and the Evangelical Christian Churches-Assemblies of God in Italy. It is an affiliate member of the Pentecostal Fellowship of North America and of the National Association of Evangelicals.

Headquarters

1294 Rutledge Rd., Transfer, PA 16154-9005 Tel. (412)962-3501 Fax (412)962-1766

Media Contact, Exec. Sec., Lynn Brest

Officers

Executive Bd., Gen. Overseer, Rev. John DelTurco, P.O. Box 1198, Hermitage, PA 16148

Exec. Vice-Pres., Rev. Andrew Farina, 3 Alhambra Pl., Greenville, PA 16125

Asst. Gen. Overseers: Rev. James Demola, P.O. Box 157, Mullica Hill, NJ 08062; Rev. Vincent Prestigiacomo, 21 Tyler Hill Rd., Jaffrey, NH 03452; Rev. Charles Gay, 26 Delafield Dr., Albany, NY 12205; Rev. Michael Trotta, 224 W. Winter Ave., New Castle, PA 16101; Rev. William Nash, 8 Belleview Blvd. #402, Clearwater, FL 34616

DEPARTMENTS

Benevolence, Rev. Eugene DeMarco, 155 Scott St., New Brighton, PA 15066

Church Growth & Media Ministries, Rev. John Ferguson, 78C Kaphank Ave., Yaphank, NY 11980

Faith, Order & Credentials, Rev. Andrew Farina, 3 Alhambra Pl., Greenville, PA 16125

Missions, Rev. David Verzilli, 1100 Boardman Canfield Rd., Apt. A-17, Youngstown, OH 44512

Publications & Promotion, Rev. John Tedesco, 1188 Heron Rd., Cherry Hill, NJ 08003

Youth, Education & Sunday School, Rev. Lours Fortunato, Jr., 248 Curry Pl., Youngstown, OH 44504

Periodical

Vista

Christian Churches and Churches of Christ

The fellowship, whose churches were always strictly congregational in polity, has its origin in the American movement to "restore the New Testament church in doctrine, ordinances and life" initiated by Thomas and Alexander Campbell, Walter Scott and Barton W. Stone in the early 19th century.

Headquarters

Media Contact, No. American Christian Convention Dir., Rod Huron, 4210 Bridgetown Rd., Box 11326, Cincinnati, OH 45211 Tel. (513) 598-6222 Fax (513)598-6471

CONVENTIONS

North American Christian Convention: Dir., Rod Huron, 4210 Bridgetown Rd., Box 11326, Cincinnati, OH 45211 Tel. (513)598-6222; NACC Mailing Address, Box 39456, Cincinnati, OH 45239

National Missionary Convention, Coord., Walter Birney, Box 11, Copeland, KS 67837 Tel. (316)668-5250

Eastern Christian Convention, Kenneth Meade, 5300 Norbeck Rd., Rockville, MD 20853 Tel. (301)460-3550

Periodicals

Christian Standard; Restoration Herald; Horizons; The Lookout

The Christian Congregation, Inc.

The Christian Congregation is a denominational evangelistic association that originated in 1787 and was active on the frontier in areas adjacent to the Ohio River. The church was an unincorporated organization until 1887. At that time a group of ministers who desired closer cooperation formally constituted the church. The charter was revised in 1898 and again in 1970.

Governmental polity basically is congregational. Local units are semi-autonomous. Doctrinal positions, strongly biblical, are essentially universalist in the sense that ethical principles, which motivate us to creative activism, transcend national boundaries and racial barriers. A central tenet, John 13:34-35, translates to such respect for sanctity of life that abortions on demand, capital punishment and all warfare are vigorously opposed. All wars are considered unjust and obsolete as a means of resolving disputes.

Early leaders were John Chapman, John L. Puckett and Isaac V. Smith. Bishop O. J. Read was chief administrative and ecclesiastic officer for 40 years until 1961. Rev. Dr. Ora Wilbert Eads has been general Superintendent since 1961. Ministerial affiliation for independent clergymen is provided.

Headquarters

804 W. Hemlock St., LaFollette, TN 37766

Media Contact, Gen. Supt., Rev. Ora W. Eads, D.D., Tel. (423)562-8511

Officer

Gen. Supt., Rev. Ora W. Eads, D.D.

Christian Methodist Episcopal Church

In 1870 the General Conference of the Methodist Episcopal Church, South, approved the request of its colored membership for the formation of their conferences into a separate ecclesiastical body, which became the Colored Methodist Episcopal Church.

At its General Conference in Memphis, Tenn., May 1954, it was overwhelmingly voted to change the name of the Colored Methodist Episcopal Church to the Christian Methodist Episcopal Church. This became the official name on Jan. 3, 1956.

Headquarters

First Memphis Plaza, 4466 Elvis Presley Blvd., Memphis, TN 38116

Media Contact, Exec. Sec., Dr. W. Clyde Williams, 201 Ashby St., N.W., Ste. 212, Atlanta, GA 30314 Tel. (404)522-2736 Fax (404)522-2736

Officers

Exec. Sec., Dr. W. Clyde Williams, 201 Ashby St., NW, Suite 212, Atlanta, GA 30314 Tel. (404)522-2736

Sec. Gen. Conf., Rev. John Gilmore, Mt. Olive CME Church, 538 Linden Ave., Memphis, TN 38126

81

OTHER ORGANIZATIONS

Christian Education: Gen. Sec., Dr. Ronald M. Cunningham, 4466 Elvis Presley Blvd., Ste. 214, Box 193, Memphis, TN 38116-7100 Tel. (901)345-0580

Lay Ministry: Gen. Sec., Dr. I. Carlton Faulk, 1222 Rose St., Berkeley, CA 94702 Tel. (415) 655-4106

Evangelism, Missions & Human Concerns: Gen. Sec., Rev. Raymond F. Williams, 14244 Avenida Munoz, Riverside, CA 92508 Tel. (909)656-9716

Finance: Sec., Joseph C. Neal, Jr., P.O. Box 75085, Los Angeles, CA 90075 Tel. (213)233-5050

Publications: Gen. Sec., Rev. William George, 4466 Elvis Presley Blvd., Memphis, TN 38116 Tel. (901)345-0580

Personnel Services: Gen. Sec., Dr. N. Charles Thomas, P.O. Box 9, Memphis, TN 38101 Tel. (901)345-0580

Women's Missionary Council: Pres., Judith E. Grant, 723 E. Upsal St., Philadelphia, PA 19119 Tel. (215)843-7742

BISHOPS

First District: Bishop William H. Graves, 4466 Elvis Presley Blvd., Ste. 222, Memphis, TN 38116 Tel. (901)345-0580

Second District: Bishop Nathaniel L. Linsey, 6322 Elwynne Dr., Cincinnati, OH 45236 Tel. (513) 861-0655

Third District: Bishop Dotcy I. Isom, Jr., 5925 W. Florissant Ave., St. Louis, MO 63136 Tel. (314)381-3111

Fourth District: Bishop Thomas L. Hoyt, Jr., 109 Holcomb Dr., Shreveport, LA 71103 Tel. (318) 222-6284

Fifth District: Bishop Richard O. Bass, 310 18th St. N., Ste. 400, Birmingham, AL 35203 Tel. (205)252-2587

Sixth District: Bishop Othal H. Lakey, 2001 M.L. King, Jr. Dr. SW, Ste. 423, Atlanta, GA 30310 Tel. (404)752-7800

Seventh District: Bishop Oree Broomfield, Sr., 6524 16th St., N.W., Washington, DC 20012 Tel. (202)829-8070

Eighth District: Bishop Marshall Gilmore, Sr., 1616 E. Illinois, Dallas, TX 75216 Tel. (214) 372-9073

Ninth District: Bishop E. Lynn Brown, 3844 W. Slauson Ave., Ste. 1, Los Angeles, CA 90043 Tel. (213)294-3830

Tenth District: Bishop Charles Helton, 5937 Ruth Dr., Charlotte, NC 28215 Tel. (704)567-6092

Retired: Bishop Henry C. Bunton, 853 East Dempster Ave., Memphis, TN 38106; Bishop Chester A. Kirkendoll, 10 Hurtland, Jackson, TN 38305; Bishop C. D. Coleman, Sr., 1000 Longmeadow Ln., DeSoto, TX 75115; Bishop Joseph C. Coles, Jr., P.O. Box 172, South Boston, VA 24592

Periodicals

The Christian Index; The Missionary Messenger

Christian Reformed Church in North America

The Christian Reformed Church represents the historic faith of Protestantism. Founded in the United States in 1857 and active in Canada since 1908, it asserts its belief in the Bible as the inspired Word of God, and is creedally united in the Belgic Confession (1561), the Heidelberg Catechism (1563), and the Canons of Dort (1618-19).

Headquarters

2850 Kalamazoo Ave., SE, Grand Rapids, MI 49560 Tel. (616)224-0744 Fax (616)224-5895 Media Contact, Gen. Sec., Dr. David H. Engelhard; website: http://www.crcna.org

Officers

Gen. Sec., Dr. David H. Engelhard

Exec. Dir. of Ministries, Dr. Peter Borgdorff

Canadian Ministries Director, Raymond Elgersma, 3475 Mainway, PO Box 5070 STN LCR 1, Burlington, ON L7R 3Y8

Director of Finance and Administration, Kenneth Horjus

OTHER ORGANIZATIONS

The Back to God Hour: Dir. of Ministries, Dr. Calvin L. Bremer, International Headquarters, 6555 W. College Dr., Palos Heights, IL 60463

Christian Reformed Home Missions: Dir., Rev. John A. Rozeboom

Christian Reformed World Missions, US: Dir., Rev. Merle Den Bleyker

Christian Ref. World Missions, Canada: Dir., Albert Karsten, 3475 Mainway, P.O. Box 5070 STN LCR 1, Burlington, ON L7R 3Y8

Christian Reformed World Relief, US: Dir., Andrew Ryskamp

Christian Reformed World Relief, Canada: Dir., H. Wayne deJong, 3475 Mainway, P.O. Box 5070 STN LCR 1, Burlington, ON L7R 3Y8

CRC Publications: Dir., Gary Mulder

Ministers' Pension Fund: Admn., Kenneth Horjus

CRC Pastoral Ministries, Adm. Dir., —

Periodical

The Banner

Christian Union

Organized in 1864 in Columbus, Ohio, the Christian Union stresses the oneness of the Church with Christ as its only head. The Bible is the only rule of faith and practice and good fruits the only condition of fellowship. Each local church governs itself.

Headquarters

c/o Christian Union Bible College, P.O. Box 27, Greenfield, OH 45123 Tel. (513)981-2897 Media Contact, Pres., Dr. Joseph Harr, 3025

Converse-Roselm Rd., Grover Hill, OH 45849
Tel. (419)587-3226

Officers
Pres., Dr. Joseph Harr
Vice-Pres., Rev. Harold McElwee, P.O. Box 132, Milo, IA 50166 Tel. (419)822-4261
Sec., Rev. Joseph Cunningham, 1005 N. 5th St., Greenfield, OH 45123 Tel. (513)981-3476
Asst. Sec., Rev. Earl Mitchell, 17500 Hidden Valley Rd., Independence, MO 64057 Tel. (816)373-3416
Treas., Rev. Lawrence Rhoads, 902 N.E. Main St., West Union, OH 45693 Tel. (513)544-2950

Church of Christ
Joseph Smith and five others organized the Church of Christ on April 6, 1830 at Fayette, New York In 1864 this body was directed by revelation through Granville Hedrick to return in 1867 to Independence, Missouri to the "consecrated land" dedicated by Joseph Smith. They did so and purchased the temple lot dedicated in 1831.

Headquarters
Temple Lot, 200 S. River St., P.O. Box 472, Independence, MO 64051 Tel. (816)833-3995
Media Contact, Gen. Church Rep., William A. Sheldon, P.O. Box 472, Independence, MO 64051 Tel. (816)833-3995

Officers
Council of Apostles, Secy., Apostle Smith N. Brickhouse, P.O. Box 472, Independence, MO 64051
Gen. Bus. Mgr., Bishop Alvin Harris, P.O. Box 472, Independence, MO 64051

Periodical
Zion's Advocate

The Church of Christ (Holiness) U.S.A.
The Church of Christ (Holiness) U.S.A., has a Divine commission to propagate the gospel throughout the world, to seek the conversion of sinners, to reclaim backsliders, to encourage the sanctification of believers, to support divine healing, and to advance the truth for the return of our Lord and Savior Jesus Christ. This must be done through proper organization.

The fundamental principles of Christ's Church have remained the same. The laws founded upon these principles are to remain unchanged. The Church o Christ (Holiness) U.S.A. is representative in form of government; therefore, the final authority in defining the organizational responsibilities rests with the national convention. The bishops of the church are delegated special powers to act in behalf of or speak for the church. The pastors are ordained ministers, who under the call of God and His people, have divine oversight of local churches. However, the representative form of government gives ministry and laity equal authority in all deliberate bodies. With the leadership of the Holy Spirit, Respect, Loyalty and Love will greatly increase.

Headquarters
329 East Monument Street, P.O. Box 3622, Jackson, MS 39207 Tel. (601)353-0222 Fax (601)353-4002
Media Contact, Maurice D. Bingham, Ed. D., Senior Bishop

BOARD OF BISHOPS
Senior Bishop, Maurice D. Bingham, Ed. D.
Eastern Diocese, Bishop Lindsay E. Jones
North Central Diocese, Elder Bennett Wolfe
Northern Diocese, Bishop Ernery Lindsay
Pacific Northwest Diocese, Bishop Robert Winn
South Central Diocese, Bishop Joseph Campbell
Southeastern Diocese, Bishop Victor P. Smith
Southwestern Diocese, Bishop Vernon Kennebrew
Western Diocese, Bishop Robert Winn
Board Member, Bishop James K. Mitchell

Church of Christ, Scientist
The Church of Christ, Scientist, was founded by New England religious leader Mary Baker Eddy in 1879 "to commemorate the word and works of our Master (Christ Jesus), which should reinstate primitive Christianity and its lost element of healing." In 1892 the church was reorganized and established as The First Church of Christ, Scientist, in Boston, Massachusetts, also called The Mother Church, with local branch churches around the world, of which there are approximately 2200 in 70 countries today.

The church is administered by a five-member board of directors in Boston. Local churches govern themselves democratically. Since the church has no clergy, services are conducted by lay persons elected to serve as Readers. There are also several thousand Christian Science practitioners who devote their full time to healing through prayer.

Organizations within the church include the Board of Education, the Board of Lectureship, the Committee on Publication and the Christian Science Publishing Society.

Headquarters
The First Church of Christ, Scientist, 175 Huntington Ave., Boston, MA 02115
Media Contact, Mgr., Comm. on Publication, Gary A. Jones, Tel. (617)450-3301 Fax (617)450-3325
E-mail: —
Website: http://www. tfccs.com

Officers
Bd. of Directors: Virginia S. Harris; Walter D. Jones; Olga M. Chaffee, J. Anthony Periton; John Lewis Selover
President, Jon G. Harder
Treas., Walter D. Jones
Clk., Olga M. Chaffee

83

First Reader, J. Thomas Black
Second Reader, Patricia Tupper Hyatt

Periodicals
The Christian Science Monitor (website: http://www. csmonitor.com); *The Christian Science Journal; Christian Science Sentinel; The Herald of Christian Science* (2 languages); *Christian Science Quarterly Bible Lessons*

Church of God (Anderson, Indiana)

The Church of God (Anderson, Indiana) began in 1881 when Daniel S. Warner and several associates felt constrained to forsake all denominational hierarchies and formal creeds, trusting solely in the Holy Spirit as their statement of belief. These people saw themselves at the forefront of a movement to restore unity and holiness to the church, not to establish another denomination, but to promote primary allegiance to Jesus Christ so as to transcend denominational loyalties.

Deeply influenced by Wesleyan theology and Pietism, the Church of God has emphasized conversion, holiness and attention to the Bible. Worship services tend to be informal, accentuating expository preaching and robust singing.

There is no formal membership. Persons are assumed to be members on the basis of witness to a conversion experience and evidence that supports such witness. The absence of formal membership is also consistent with the church's understanding of how Christian unity is to be achieved- that is, by preferring the label Christian before all others.

The Church of God is congregational in its government. Each local congregation is autonomous and may call any recognized Church of God minister to be its pastor and may retain him or her as long as is mutually pleasing. Ministers are ordained and disciplined by state or provincial assemblies made up predominantly of ministers. National program boards serve the church through coordinated ministries and resource materials.

There are Church of God congregations in 89 foreign countries, most of which are resourced by one or more missionaries. There are slightly more Church of God adherents overseas than in North America. The heaviest concentration is in the nation of Kenya.

GENERAL OFFICES
Box 2420, Anderson, IN 46018-2420 Tel. (765)642-0258 Fax (765)648-2180
Media Contact, Gen. Sec., Leadership Council, Edward L. Foggs
E-mail: elfsr@juno.com
Website: http://www. chog.org

LEADERSHIP COUNCIL
Gen. Sec., Edward L. Foggs

MINISTRIES COUNCIL
Gen. Dir., Robert W. Pearson, Box 2420,

Anderson, IN 46018-2420 Tel. (765)642-0256 Fax (765) 648-2184
Includes Congregational Ministries, Resource & Linking Ministries and Outreach Ministries

OTHER ORGANIZATIONS
Bd. of Church Extension, Pres., J. Perry Grubbs, Box 2069, Anderson, IN 46018
Women of the Church of God, Natl. Coord., Linda J. Mason, Box 2328, Anderson, IN 46018
Bd. of Pensions, Exec. Sec.-Treas., Jeffrey A. Jenness, Box 2299, Anderson, IN 46018

Periodicals
Inform; Church of God Missions; The Shining Light

Church of God by Faith, Inc.

Founded 1914, in Jacksonville Heights, Fla., by Elder John Bright, this church believes the word of God as interpreted by Jesus Christ to be the only hope of salvation and Jesus Christ the only mediator for people.

Headquarters
3220 Haines St., P.O. Box 3746, Jacksonville, FL 32206 Tel. (904)353-5111 Fax (904)355-8582
Media Contact, Ofc. Mgr., Sarah E. Lundy

Officers
Presiding Bishop, James E. McKnight, P.O. Box 121, Gainesville, FL 32601
Treas., Elder Theodore Brown, 93 Girard Pl., Newark, NJ 07108
Ruling Elders: Elder John Robinson, 300 Essex Dr., Ft. Pierce, FL 33450; Elder D. C. Rourk, 207 Chestnut Hill Dr., Rochester, NY 14617
Exec. Sec., Elder George Matthews, 8834 Camphor Dr., Jacksonville, FL 32208

Church of God (Cleveland, Tenn.)

America's oldest Pentecostal Church began in 1886 as an outgrowth of the holiness revival under the name Christian Union. Reorganized in 1902 as the Holiness Church, in 1907 the church adopted the name Church of God. Its doctrine is fundamental and Pentecostal; it maintains a centralized form of government and an evangelistic and missionary program.

Headquarters
P.O. Box 2430, Cleveland, TN 37320 Tel. (423) 472-3361 Fax (423)478-7066
Media Contact, Dir. of Publ. Relations, Michael L. Baker, Tel. (423)478-7112 Fax (423)478-7066

EXECUTIVES
Gen. Overseer, Paul L. Walker
Asst. Gen. Overseers: R. Lamar Vest; G. Dennis McGuire; T. L. Lowery
Gen. Sec.-Treas., Bill F. Sheeks

DEPARTMENTS
Benefits Board, CEO, O. Wayne Chambers

Benevolence, Dir., John D. Nichols
Black Evangelism, Dir., Joseph E. Jackson
Business & Records, Dir., Julian B. Robinson
Chaplains Commission, Dir., Robert D. Crick
Computer Services, Dir., Timothy D. O'Neal
Cross-Cultural Min., Dir., Billy J. Rayburn
East Coast Bible College, Pres., T. David Sustar
European Bible Seminary, Dir., John Sims
Evangelism & Home Missions, Dir., Junus C. Fulbright
Hispanic Institute of Ministry, Dir., Isaias Robles
Hispanic Ministry, Dir., Esdras Betancourt
International Bible College, Pres., Alex Allan
Ladies Ministries, Dir., Rebecca J. Jenkins
Lay Ministries, Dir., Leonard Albert
Lee College, Pres., C. Paul Conn
Legal Services, Dir., Dennis W. Watkins
Media Ministries, Dir., —
Men/Women of Action, Dir., Robert D. Pace
Ministerial Care, Dir., Robert E. Fisher
Ministerial Development, Dir., Larry G. Hess
Ministry to Israel, Dir., J. Michael Utterback
Ministry to the Military, Dir., G. Dennis McGuire
Music Ministries, Dir., Delton Alford
Native American Ministries, Dir., Douglas M. Cline
Publications, Dir., Kenneth T. Harvell
Public Relations, Dir., Michael L. Baker
Puerto Rico Bible School, Dir., Ismael Lopez
Stewardship, Dir., Al Taylor
Western School of Christian Ministry, Dir., W. A. Davis
World Missions, Dir., Gene D. Rice
Youth & Christian Education, Dir., David M. Griffis

Periodicals
Church of God Evangel; Unique

Church of God General Conference (Oregon, IL and Morrow, GA)

This church is the outgrowth of several independent local groups of similar faith. Some were in existence as early as 1800, and others date their beginnings to the arrival of British immigrants around 1847. Many local churches carried the name Church of God of the Abrahamic Faith. State and district conferences of these groups were formed as an expression of mutual cooperation. A national organization was instituted at Philadelphia in 1888. Because of strong convictions on the questions of congregational rights and authority, however, it ceased to function until 1921, when the present General Conference was formed at Waterloo, Iowa.

The Bible is accepted as the supreme standard of faith. Adventist in viewpoint, the second (premillenial) coming of Christ is strongly emphasized. The church teaches that the kingdom of God will be literal, beginning in Jerusalem at the time of the return of Christ and extending to all nations. Emphasis is placed on the oneness of God and the Sonship of Christ, that Jesus did not pre-exist prior to his birth in Bethlehem and that the Holy Spirit is the power and influence of God. Membership is dependent on faith, repentance and baptism by immersion.

The work of the General Conference is carried on under the direction of the board of directors. With a congregational church government, the General Conference exists primarily as a means of mutual cooperation and for the development of yearly projects and enterprises.

The headquarters and Bible College were moved to Morrow, Ga. in 1991.

Headquarters
P.O. Box 100,000, Morrow, GA 30260 Tel. (404)362-0052 Fax (404)362-9307
Media Contact, Pres., David Krogh
E-mail: atlbc@mindspring.com
Website: http://www.abc-coggc.org

Officers
Chpsn., Joe E. James, 100 Buck Dr., Piedmont, SC 29673
Vice-Chpsn., Pastor Dale Swartz, 6375 S. Kessler-Frederick Rd., Tipp City, OH 45371
Pres., David Krogh, Georgia Ofc.
Sec., Pastor David Cheatwood, 3035 17th Street, Rockford, IL 61109
Treas., Robert Huddlestun, 16460 Fairfield Ln., Granger, IN 46530

OTHER ORGANIZATIONS
Bus. Admn., Controller, Gary Burnham, Georgia Ofc.
Atlanta Bible College, Pres., David Krogh, Georgia Ofc.

Periodicals
The Restitution Herald; A Journal From the Radical Reformation; Church of God Progress Journal

The Church Of God In Christ

The Church of God in Christ was founded in 1907 in Memphis, Tennessee, and was organized by Bishop Charles Harrison Mason, a former Baptist minister who pioneered the embryonic stages of the Holiness movement beginning in 1895 in Mississippi.

Its founder organized four major departments between 1910-1916: the Women's Department, the Sunday School, Young Peoples Willing Workers and Home and Foreign Mission.

The Church is trinitarian and teaches the infallibility of scripture, the need for regeneration and subsequent baptism of the Holy Ghost. It emphasizes holiness as God's standard for Christian conduct. It recognizes as ordinances Holy Communion, Water Baptism and Feet Washing. Its governmental structure is basically episcopal with the General Assembly being the Legislative body.

Headquarters
Mason Temple, 939 Mason St., Memphis, TN 38126

85

World Headquarters, 272 S. Main St., Memphis, TN 38103 Tel. (901)578-3800
Mailing Address, P.O. Box 320, Memphis, TN 38101
Temple Church Of God In Christ, 672 S. Lauderdale St., Memphis, TN 38126 Tel. (901)527-9202

GENERAL OFFICES

Office of the Presiding Bishop: Presiding Bishop, Bishop Chandler D. Owens, Tel. (901)578-3838; Exec. Sec., Elder A. Z. Hall, Jr.
Office of the General Secretary: Gen. Sec., Bishop W. W. Hamilton, (901)578-3858
Office of the Financial Secretary: Sec., Bishop Frank O. White, Tel. (901)578-3810
Office of the Board of Trustees: Chmn., Elder Dwight Green
Office of the Clergy Bureau: Dir., Bishop W. W. Hamilton, Tel. (901)578-3855
Office of Supt. of National Properties: Supt., Bishop W. L. Porter, Tel. (901)774-0710
Board of Publications: Chmn., Bishop Norman Quick, Tel. (901)578-3841
Publishing House: Mgr., Mr. Hughea Terry, Tel. (901)578-3842
Dept. of Missions: Pres., Bishop Carlis L. Moody, Tel. (901)578-3876; Exec. Sec., Elder Jesse W. Denny
Dept. of Women: Pres.-Gen. Supervisor, Mother Emma Crouch, Tel. (901)578-3834; Exec. Sec., Elizabeth C. Moore
Dept. of Evangelism: Pres., Dr. Edward L. Battles, 4310 Steeplechase Trail, Arlington, TX 76016 Tel. (817)429-7166
Dept. of Music: Pres., Lavonia Whitty, Chicago, IL
Dept. of Youth (Youth Congress): Pres., Bishop C. H. Brewer, 260 Roydon Rd., New Haven, CT 06511
Dept. of Sunday Schools: Gen. Supt., Elder Jerry Macklin, 1027 W. Tennyson Rd., Hayward, CA 94544
World Headquarters, C.O.O., Bishop G. E. Pattersen, 438 Mason, Memphis, TN 38126
Church of God in Christ Book Store: Mgr., Geraldine Miller, 272 S. Main St., Memphis, TN 38103 Tel. (901)578-3803
Charles Harrison Mason Foundation: Exec. Dir., 272 S. Main St., Memphis, TN 38103 Tel. (901)578-3803; Bd. of Dir., Chmn., Bishop P. A. Brooks
Dept. of Finance: Chief Financial Officer, Sylvia H. Law
Fine Arts Dept.: Dir., Sara J. Powell

BISHOPS IN THE U.S.A.

Alabama: First, Chester A. Ashworth, 2901 Snavely Ave., Birmingham, AL 35211; Second, W. S. Harris, 3005 Melrose Pl., N.W., Huntsville, AL 35810
Alaska: Charles D. Williams, 2212 Vanderbilt Cir., Anchorage, AK 99504

Arizona: Felton King, P.O. Box 3791, Phoenix, AZ 84030
Arkansas: First, L. T. Walker, 2315 Chester St., Little Rock, AR 72206; Second, D. L. Lindsey, 401 W. 23rd St., North Little Rock, AR 72114
California: North-Central, 815 Calmar Ave., Oakland, CA 94610; Northern, B. R. Stewart, 734 12th Ave., San Francisco, CA 94118; Northeast, L. B. Johnson, 3121 Patridge Ave., Oakland, CA 94605; Evangel, 31313 Braeburn Ct., Haywood, CA 96045; Northwest, Bishop W. W. Hamilton, 14145 Mountain Quail Rd., Salinas, CA 93906; Southern #1, C. E. Blake, 1731 Wellington Rd., Los Angeles, CA 90019; Southern #2, George McKinney, 5848 Arboles, San Diego, CA 92120; Southern Metropolitan, 12418 Gain St., Pacoima, CA 91331; Southwest, B. R. Benbow, 504 Rexford Dr., Beverly Hills, CA 90210; Valley, Warren S. Wilson, 1435 Modoc St., Fresno, CA 93706
Colorado: Colorado, Frank Johnson, 12231 E. Arkansas Pl., Aurora, CO 80014
Connecticut: First, Charles H. Brewer, Jr., 180 Osborne St., New Haven, CT 06515; Second, H. Bordeaux, 135 Westwood Rd., New Haven, CT 06511
Delaware: Lieutenant T. Blackshear, Sr., 17 S. Booth Dr., Penn Acres, New Castle, DE 19720
District of Columbia: Bishop W. Crudup, 5101 Martin Dr., Oxon Hill, MD 20745
Florida: Central, Calvin D. Kensey, 9462 August Dr., Jacksonville, FL 32208; Eastern, Jacob Cohen, 3120 N. W. 48th Terr., Miami, FL 33142; Southwestern, W. E. Davis, 2008 33rd Ave., Tampa, FL 33610; Western, P.O. Box 5472, Orlando, FL 32805
Georgia: Central & Southeast, P.O. Box 824, Atlanta, GA 30301; Southeast, Andrew Hunter, Rt. 4, Box 328, St. Simons Island, GA 31502; Northern, 1717 Havilon Dr., S.W., Atlanta, GA 30311; Southern, C. J. Hicks, 1894 Madden Ave., Macon, GA 31204
Hawaii: First, 1223 W. 80th St., Los Angeles, CA 90044
Idaho: Nathaniel Jones, 630 Chateau, Barstow, CA 92311
Illinois: Sixth, W. Haven Bonner, 1039 Bonner Ave., Aurora, IL 60505; Central, T. T. Rose, 1000 Dr. Taylor Rose Sq., Springfield, IL 62703; Northern, Cody Marshall, 8836 Blackstone, Chicago, IL 60637; Southeast, L. E. Moore, 7840 Contour Dr., St. Louis, MO 63121; Southern, J. Cobb, 323-30th St., Cairo, IL 62914
Indiana: First, Milton L. Hall, 1404 Delphos, Kokomo, IN 46901; Indiana Northern, J. T. Dupree, 1231 Hayden St., Fort Wayne, IN 40806
Iowa: Hurley Bassett, 1730 4th Ave., S.E., Cedar Rapids, IA 52403
Kansas: Central, I. B. Brown, 1635 Hudson Blvd., Topeka, KS 66607; East, William H.

McDonald, 1627 N. 78th St., Kansas City, KS 66112; Southwest, J. L. Gilkey, 2403 Shadybrook, Wichita, KS 67214

Kentucky: First, Bishop M. Sykes, P.O. Box 682, Union City, TN 38621

Louisiana: Eastern, #1, Bishop J. E. Gordon, 6610 Chenault Dr., Marrero, LA 70072; Eastern #2, Bishop J. A. Thompson, 2180 Holiday, New Orleans, LA 70114; Eastern #3, Bishop H. E. Quillen, 1913 Lasley St., Bogalusa, LA 70427; Western, Roy L. H. Winbush, 235 Diamond Dr., Lafayette, LA 70501

Maine: Bishop D. W. Grayson, 1237 Eastern Pkwy., Brooklyn, NY 11213

Maryland: Central, S. L. Butts, P.O. Box 4504, Upper Marboro, MD 20775; Eastern Shore, James L. Eure, 635 West Main St., Salisbury, MD 21801; Greater, David Spann, 5023 Gwynn Oak Ave., Baltimore, MD 21207

Massachusetts: First, L. C. Young, 19 Almont St., Mattanpan, MA 02126; Second & New Hampshire, C. W. Williams, 270 Division St., Derby, CT 06418; West, Bryant Robinson, Sr., 1424 Plumtree Rd., Springfield, MA 01119

Michigan: Great Lakes, C. L. Anderson, 20485 Mendota, Detroit, MI 48221; North Central, Herbert J. Williams, 1600 Cedar St., Saginaw, MI 48601; Northeast, P. A. Brooks, II, 30945 Wendbrook Lane, Birmingham, MI 48010; Southwest, First, W. L. Harris, 1834 Outer Dr., Detroit, MI 48234; Second, Earl J. Wright, 18655 Autumn La., Southfield, MI 48076; Third, Rodger L. Jones, 1118 River Forest, Flint, MI 48594; Fourth, N. W. Wells, 530 Sue Lane, Muskegon, MI 49442

Minnesota: Bishop S. N. Frazier, 4309 Park Ave. So., Minneapolis, MN 55409

Mississippi: Northern, T. T. Scott, 1066 Barnes Ave., Clarksdale, MS 38614; Southern #1, Theodore Roosevelt Davis, 1704 Topp Ave., Jackson, MS 39204; Southern #2, Bishop R. Nance, 803 Fayard St., Biloxi, MS 39503

Missouri: Eastern #1, R. J. Ward, 4724 Palm Ave., St. Louis, MO 63115; Eastern #2, W. W. Sanders, 8167 Garner La., Berkeley, MO 63134; Western, E. Harris Moore, 405 E. 64th Terr., Kansas City, MO 64131

Montana: Bishop Carlis L. Moody, 2413 Lee St., Evanston, IL 60202

Nebraska: Eastern, Monte J. Bradford, 3901 Ramelle Dr., Council Bluff, IA 51501; Northeastern, B. T. McDaniels, 1106 N. 31st St., Omaha, NE 68103

Nevada: E. N. Webb, 1941 Goldhill, Las Vegas, NV 89106

New Jersey: First, Esau Courtney, 12 Clover Hill Cir., Trenton, NJ 08538; Third, Bishop William Cahoon, 14 Van Velsor Pl., Newark, NJ 07112

New Mexico: W. C. Griffin, 3322 Montclaire, Albuquerque, NM 87110

New York: Eastern #1, Bishop Ithiel Clemmons, 190-08 104th Ave., Hollis, NY 11412; Eastern #2, Bishop Frank O. White, 67 The Boulevard, Amityville, NY 11701; Eastern #3, Bishop D. W. Grayson, 1233 Eastern Pkwy., Brooklyn, NY 11213; Eastern #4, Bishop C. L. Sexton, 153 McDougal St., Brooklyn, NY 11233; Western #1, LeRoy R. Anderson, 265 Ranch Trail, W., Amherst, NY 14221; Western #2, Charles H. McCoy, 168 Brunswick Blvd., Buffalo, NY 14208

North Carolina: Greater, L. B. Davenport, P.O. Box 156, Plymouth, NC 28803; Second, J. Howard Sherman, Sr., P.O. Box 329, Charlotte, NC 28201

North Dakota: Mission Dept., Bishop Carlis L. Moody, 272 S. Main St., Memphis, TN 38103

Ohio: Northern, Bishop William James, 3758 Chippendale Ct., Toledo, OH 44320; Robert S. Fields, 419 Crandell Ave., Youngstown, OH 44504; Northwest, Robert L. Chapman, 3194 E. 18th St., Cleveland, OH 44120; Northern, Bishop Warren Miller, 3618 Beacon Dr., Cleveland, OH 44122; Southern, Floyde E. Perry, Jr., 3716 Rolliston Rd., Shaker Hts., OH 44120

Oklahoma: Northwest, J. A. Young, P.O. Box 844, Lawton, OK 73501; Southeast, Bishop F. D. Lawson, P.O. Box 581, Stillwater, OK 74076

Oregon: First, Bishop A. R. Hopkins, 1705 N.E. Dekum, Portland, OR 97211; Second, J. C. Foster, 2716 N.E. 9th Ave., Portland, OR 97212

Pennsylvania: Commonwealth, O. T. Jones, Jr., 363 N. 60th St., Philadelphia, PA 19139; Eastern, DeWitt A. Burton, 1400 Wistar Dr., Wyncote, PA 19095; Western, Gordon E. Vaughn, 6437 Stanton Ave., Pittsburgh, PA 15206

Rhode Island: Norman Quick, 1031 E. 215th St., Brooklyn, NY 11221

South Carolina: Johnnie Johnson, 679 Liberty Hall Rd., Goose Creek, SC 29445

South Dakota: Bishop Carlis L. Moody, 2413 Lee St., Evanston, IL 60202

Tennessee: Headquarters, Bishop J. O. Paterson, Jr., 229 Danny Thomas Blvd., Memphis, TN 38126; Second, H. Jenkins Bell, P.O. Box 6118, Knoxville, TN 37914; Central, W. L. Porter, 1235 East Parkway, S., Memphis, TN 38114

Texas: Eastern, J. E. Lee, 742 Calcutta Dr., Dallas, TX 75241; Northeast, J. Neauell Haynes, Watson, W. H, 15622 Rockhouse Rd., Houston, TX 77060; Southeast #1, Robert E. Woodard, , Sr., 2614 Wichita, Houston, TX 77004; Southeast #2, A. LaDell Thomas, 4401 McArthur Dr., Waco, TX 76708; Southeast, R. E. Ranger, 325 Terrell Rd., San Antonio, TX 78209

Utah: Nathaniel Jones, c/o Mission Dept., 630 Chateau Rd., Barstow, CA 92311

Vermont:Virginia: First, Sr., 4145 Sunkist Rd.,

Chesapeake, VA 23321; Second, Samuel L. Green, Jr., 2416 Orcutt Ave., Newport News, VA 23607; Third, Levi E. Willis, Levi E., 5110 Nichal Ct., Norfolk, VA 23508

Washington: T. L. Westbrook, 1256 176th St., Spanaway, WA 98402

West Virginia: Northern, Bishop G. F. Walker, P.O. Box 1467, Princeton, VA 24740; Southern, St. Claire Y. Burnett, P.O. Box 245, Altamonte Springs, FL 32715

Wisconsin: First, Dennis Flakes, 3420 N. 1st St., Milwaukee, WI 53212; Third, J. C. Williams, 4232 N. 24th Pl., Milwaukee, WI 53209

Wyoming: A. W. Martin, 2453 N. Fountain St., Wichita, KS 67220

Periodical
Whole Truth

Church of God in Christ, International

The Church of God in Christ, International was organized in 1969 in Kansas City, Mo., by 14 bishops of the Church of God in Christ of Memphis, Tenn. The doctrine is the same, but the separation came because of disagreement over polity and governmental authority. The Church is Wesleyan in theology (two works of grace) but stresses the experience of full baptism of the Holy Ghost with the initial evidence of speaking with other tongues as the Spirit gives utterance.

Headquarters
170 Adelphi St., Brooklyn, NY 11205 Tel. (718) 625-9175
Media Contact, Natl. Sec., Rev. Sis. Sharon R. Dunn

Officers
Presiding Bishop, Most Rev. Carl E. Williams, Sr.
Vice-Presiding Bishop, Rt. Rev. J. P. Lucas, 90 Holland St., Newark, NJ 07103
Sec.-Gen., Deacon Dennis Duke, 360 Colorado Ave., Bridgeport, CT 06605
Exec. Admn., Horace K. Williams, Word of God Center, Newark, NJ
Women's Dept., Natl. Supervisor, Evangelist Elvonia Williams
Youth Dept., Pres., Dr. Joyce Taylor, 137-17 135th Ave., S., Ozone Park, NY 11420
Music Dept., Pres., Isaiah Heyward
Bd. of Bishops, Chpsn., Bishop J. C. White, 360 Colorado Ave., Bridgeport, CT 06605

Church of God in Christ, Mennonite

The Church of God in Christ, Mennonite was organized in Ohio in 1859 by the evangelist-reformer John Holdeman. The church unites with the faith of the Waldenses, Anabaptists and other such groups. Emphasis is placed on obedience to the teachings of the Bible, including the doctrine of the new birth and spiritual life, noninvolvement in government or the military, head-coverings for the women, beards for the men and separation

from the world shown by simplicity in clothing, homes, possessions and life-style. The church has a worldwide membership of about 17,000, most of them in the United States and Canada.

Headquarters
P.O. Box 313, 420 N. Wedel Ave., Moundridge, KS 67107 Tel. (316)345-2532 Fax (316)345-2582
Media Contact, Dale Koehn, P.O. Box 230, Moundridge, KS 67107 Tel. (316)345-2532 Fax (316)345-2582

Periodical
Messenger of Truth

Church of God, Mountain Assembly, Inc.

The church was formed in 1895 and organized in 1906 by J. H. Parks, S. N. Bryant, Tom Moses and William Douglas.

Headquarters
164 N. Florence Ave., P.O. Box 157, Jellico, TN 37762 Tel. (423)784-8260 Fax (423)784-3258
Media Contact, Gen. Sec.-Treas., Rev. Alfred Newton, Jr.

Officers
Gen. Overseer, Rev. Cecil Johnson
Asst. Gen. Overseer/World Missions Dir., Rev. Lonnie Lyke
Gen. Sec.-Treas., Rev. Alfred Newton, Jr.
Youth Ministries & Camp Dir., Rev. Ken Ellis

Periodical
The Gospel Herald

Church of God of Prophecy

The Church of God of Prophecy is one of the churches that grew out of the work of A. J. Tomlinson in the first half of the twentieth century. Historically it shares a common heritage with the Church of God (Cleveland Tennessee) and is in the mainstream of the classical Pentecostal-holiness tradition.

At the death of A. J. Tomlinson in 1943, M. A. Tomlinson was named General Overseer and served until retirement in 1990. He emphasized unity and fellowship unlimited by racial, social or political differences. The present general overseer, Billy D. Murray, Sr., is committed to promoting Christian unity world evangelization.

From its beginnings, the Church has based its beliefs on "the whole Bible, rightly divided," and has accepted the Bible as God's Holy Word, inspired, inerrant and infallible. The church is firm in its commitment to orthodox Christian belief. The Church affirms that there is one God, eternally existing in three persons: Father, Son and Holy Spirit. It believes in the deity of Christ, His virgin birth, His sinless life, the physical miracles He performed, His atoning death on the cross, His bodily resurrection, His ascension to the right hand of the Father and his Second coming. The church professes that salvation results from grace alone through faith in Christ, that regeneration by the Holy Spirit is essential for the salvation of sinful men, and that sanctification by the blood of Christ makes possible personal holiness. It affirms the present ministry of the Holy Spirit by Whose indwelling believers are able to live godly lives and have power for service. The church believes in, and promotes, the ultimate unity of believers as prayed for by Christ in John 17. The church stresses the sanctity of human life and is committed to the sanctity of the marriage bond and the importance of strong, loving Christian families.

Other official teachings include Holy Spirit baptism with tongues as initial evidence; manifestation of the spiritual gifts; divine healing; premillenial second-coming of Christ; total abstinence from the use of tobacco, alcohol and narcotics; water baptism by immersion; the Lord's supper and washing of the saints' feet; and a concern for moderation and holiness in all dimensions of lifestyle.

The Church is racially integrated on all levels, including top leadership. Women play a prominent role in church affairs, serving in pastoral roles and other leadership positions. The church presbytery has recently adopted plurality of leadership in the selection of a General Oversight Group. This group consists of three bishops who, along with the General Overseer, are responsible for inspirational leadership and vision casting for the church body. This group is presently composed of General Overseer Murray and Bishops Perry Gillum, JosÈ Reyes, and Larry Wilson.

The Church has local congregations in all 50 states and more than 100 nations worldwide. Organizationally there is a strong emphasis on international missions, evangelism, youth and children's ministries, women's and men's ministries, stewardship, communications, publishing, leadership development and discipleship.

INTERNATIONAL OFFICES

P.O. Box 2910, Cleveland, TN 37320-2910
Media Contact, Larry Wilson, Tel. (423)559-5125 Fax (423)559-5108
E-mail: wilson@wingnet.net
Website: http://www.cogop.org

Officers

General Oversight Group: Gen. Overseer, Bishop Billy D. Murray, Sr.; General Presbyters: Perry Gillum, JosÈ Reyes, and Larry Wilson
International Offices Ministries Dirs.: Admin. Services, Vernon Van Deventer; Communications/Publishing, John Pace; Global Outreach, Randy Howard; Leadership Development, Oswill Williams; Specialized Ministries, Larry Wilson

Periodicals

White Wing Messenger; Victory (Youth Magazine/ Sunday School Curriculum); *The Happy Harvester; Sunday School Info*

The Church of God (Seventh Day), Denver, Colo

The Church of God (Seventh Day) began in southwestern Michigan in 1858, when a group of Sabbath-keepers led by Gilbert Cranmer refused to give endorsement to the visions and writings of Ellen G. White, a principal in the formation of the Seventh-Day Adventist Church. Another branch of Sabbath-keepers, which developed near Cedar Rapids, Iowa, in 1860, joined the Michigan church in 1863 to publish a paper called The Hope of Israel, the predecessor to the Bible Advocate, the church's present publication. As membership grew and spread into Missouri and Nebraska, it organized the General Conference of the Church of God in 1884. The words "Seventh Day" were added to its name in 1923. The headquarters of the church was in Stanberry, Mo., from 1888 until 1950, when it moved to Denver.

The church observes the seventh day as the Sabbath. It believes in the imminent, personal and visible return of Jesus; that the dead are in an unconscious state awaiting to be resurrected, the righteous to immortality and the wicked to extinction by fire; and that the earth will be the eternal abode of the righteous. It observes two ordinances: baptism by immersion and an annual Communion service accompanied by foot washing.

Headquarters

330 W. 152nd Ave., P.O. Box 33677, Denver, CO 80233 Tel. (303)452-7973 Fax (303)452-0657
Media Contact, Pres., Whaid Rose
E-mail: cofgsd@denver.net
http://www.denver.net/~cofgsd

Officers

Board Chpsn., Loren Stacy
Conference Pres., Whaid Rose
Dir. of Admin., John Crisp
Spring Vale Academy, Dir., John Tivald
Youth Agency, Dir., Kurt Lang
Bible Advocate Press, Dir., John Crisp
Women's Assoc., Pres., Emogene Coulter
Missions Abroad, Dir., Victor Burford
Summit School of Theology, Dir., Jerry Griffin

Periodical

The Bible Advocate

The Church of Illumination

The Church of Illumination was organized in 1908 for the express purpose of establishing congregations at large, offering a spiritual, esoteric, philosophic interpretation of the vital biblical teachings, thereby satisfying the inner spiritual needs of those seeking spiritual truth, yet permitting them to remain in, or return to, their former church membership.

Headquarters

Beverly Hall, 5966 Clymer Rd., Quakertown, PA 18951 Tel. (800)779-3796

Media Contact, Dir. General, Gerald E. Poesnecker, P.O. Box 220, Quakertown, PA 18951 Tel. (215)536-7048 Fax (215) 536-7058 E-mail: bevhall@comcat.com Website: http://www.soul.org

Officers

Dir.-General, Gerald E. Poesnecker, P.O. Box 220, Quakertown, PA 18951

The Church of Jesus Christ (Bickertonites)

This church was organized in 1862 at Green Oak, Pa., by William Bickerton, who obeyed the Restored Gospel under Sidney Rigdon's following in 1845.

Headquarters

Sixth & Lincoln Sts., Monongahela, PA 15063 Tel. (412)258-3066
Media Contact, Exec. Sec., John Manes, 2007 Cutter Dr., McKees Rocks, PA 15136 Tel. (412)771-4513

Officers

Pres., Dominic Thomas, 6010 Barrie, Dearborn, MI 48126
First Counselor, Paul Palmieri, 319 Pine Dr., Aliquippa, PA 15001 Tel. (412)378-4264
Second Counselor, Robert Watson, Star Rt. 5, Box 36, Gallup, NM 87301
Exec. Sec., John Manes, 2007 Cutter Dr., McKees Rocks, PA 15136 Tel. (412)771-4513

Periodical

The Gospel News

The Church of Jesus Christ of Latter-day Saints

This church was organized April 6, 1830, at Fayette, N.Y., by Joseph Smith. Members believe Joseph Smith was divinely called to restore the gospel to the earth, and that through him the keys to the Aaronic and Melchizedek priesthoods and temple work also were restored. Members believe that both the Bible and the Book of Mormon (a record of the Lord's dealings with His people on the American continent 600 B.C. - 421 A.D.) are scripture. Membership is over ten million.

In addition to the First Presidency, the governing bodies of the church include the Quorum of the Twelve Apostles, the Presidency of the Seventy, the Quorums of the Seventy and the Presiding Bishopric.

Headquarters

47 East South Temple St., Salt Lake City, UT 84150 Tel. (801)240-1000 Fax (801)240-1167
Media Contact, Dir., Media Relations, Michael Otterson, Tel. (801)240-4378 Fax (801)240-1167
Website: http://www.lds.org

Officers

Pres., Gordon B. Hinckley
1st Counselor, Thomas S. Monson
2nd Counselor, James E. Faust

Council of the Twelve Apostles: Pres., Boyd K. Packer; L. Tom Perry; David B. Haight; Neal A. Maxwell; Russell M. Nelson; Dallin H. Oaks; M. Russell Ballard; Joseph B. Wirthlin; Richard G. Scott; Robert D. Hales; Jeffrey R. Holland; Henry B. Eyring

AUXILIARY ORGANIZATIONS

Sunday Schools, Gen. Pres., Harold G. Hillam
Relief Society, Gen. Pres., Mary Ellen Smoot
Young Women, Gen. Pres.,Margaret Nadauld
Young Men, Gen. Pres., Jack H. Goaslind
Primary, Gen. Pres., Patricia P. Pinegar

Periodicals

The Ensign; Liahona; The New Era; Friend Magazine

Church of Our Lord Jesus Christ of the Apostolic Faith, Inc.

This church body was founded by Bishop R.C. Lawson in Columbus, Ohio, and moved to New York City in 1919. It is founded upon the teachings of the apostles and prophets, Jesus Christ being its chief cornerstone.

Headquarters

2081 Adam Clayton Powell Jr. Blvd., New York, NY 10027 Tel. (212)866-1700
Media Contact, Exec. Sec., Bishop T. E. Woolfolk, P.O. Box 119, Oxford, NC 27565 Tel. (919)693-9449 Fax (919)693-6115

Officers

Board of Apostles: Chief Apostle, Bishop William L. Bonner; Presiding Apostle, Bishop Gentle L. Groover; Bishop Frank S. Solomon; Bishop Henry A. Ross, Sr.; Bishop Matthew A. Norwood; Bishop James I. Clark, Jr.; Bishop Wilbur L. Jones; Bishop J. P. Steadman
Bd. of Bishops, Chmn., Bishop Henry A. Moultrie II
Bd. of Presbyters, Pres., Elder Michael A. Dixon
Exec. Sec., Bishop T. E. Woolfolk
Natl. Rec. Sec., Bishop Fred Rubin, Sr.
Natl. Fin. Sec., Bishop Clarence Groover
Natl. Corr. Sec., Bishop Raymond J. Keith, Jr.
Natl Treas., Elder Richard D. Williams

Church of the Brethren

German pietists-anabaptists founded the Church of the Brethren in 1708 under Alexander Mack in Schwarzenau, Germany. They entered the colonies in 1719 and settled at Germantown, Pa. They have no other creed than the New Testament, hold to principles of nonviolence, temperance and volunteerism and emphasize religion in daily life.

Headquarters

Church of the Brethren General Offices, 1451 Dundee Ave., Elgin, IL 60120 Tel. (847)742-5100 Fax (847)742-6103
New Windsor Service Center, 500 Main Street, P.O. Box 188, New Windsor, MD 21776-0188 Tel. (410)635-6464 Fax (410)635-8789

Washington Office, 337 N. Carolina Ave. SE, Washington, DC 20003 Tel. (202)546-3202 Fax (202)544-5852
Media Contact, Staff for Interpretation, Howard Royer, Elgin Ofc.

Officers
Mod., Lowell A. Flory
Mod.-Elect, Emily M. Mumma
Sec., Cathy Huffman

GENERAL BOARD STAFF
Ofc. of Ex. Dir.: Ex. Dir., Judy Mills Reimer; Assistant to Ex. Dir., Sue Snyder; Coordinator of Human; Resources, Elsie Holderread

LEADERSHIP TEAM
Exec. Director, Judy Mills Reimer
Treas. & Director of Centralized Resources, Judy E. Keyser
Director & Publisher of Brethren Press, Wendy McFadden
Director of Brethren Witness, David Radcliff
Director of Congregational Life Ministries, Glenn F. Timmons
Director of Funding, Kenneth E. Neher
Director of Global Mission Partnerships, Mervin Keeney
Director of Ministry, Allen T. Hansell
Director of Volunteer Service Ministries, Dan McFadden

Periodical
Messenger

Church of the Living God (Motto: Christian Workers for Fellowship)

The Church of the Living God was founded by William Christian in April 1889 at Caine Creek, Ark. It was the first black church in America without Anglo-Saxon roots and not begun by white missionaries.

Christian was born a slave in Mississippi on Nov. 10, 1856 and grew up uneducated. In 1875 he united with the Missionary Baptist Church and began to preach. In 1888 he left the Baptist Church and began what was known as Christian Friendship Work. Believing himself to have been inspired by the Spirit of God through divine revelation and close study of the Scriptures, he was led to the truth that the Bible refers to the church as The Church of the Living God (I Tim. 3:15).

The church believes in the infallibility of the Scriptures, is Trinitarian and believes there are three sacraments ordained by Christ: baptism (by immersion), the Lord's Supper (unleavened bread and water) and foot washing.

The Church of the Living God, C.W.F.F., believes in holiness as a gift of God subsequent to the New Birth and manifested only by a changed life acceptable to the Lord.

Headquarters
430 Forest Ave., Cincinnati, OH 45229 Tel. (513)569-5660
Media Contact, Chief Bishop, W. E. Crumes

EXECUTIVE BOARD
Chief Bishop, W. E. Crumes
Vice-Chief Bishop, Robert D. Tyler, 3802 Bedford, Omaha, NE 68110
Exec. Sec., Bishop C. A. Lewis, 1360 N. Boston, Tulsa, OK 73111
Gen. Sec., Gwendolyn Robinson, 8611 S. University, Chicago, IL 60619
Gen. Treas., Elder Harry Hendricks, 11935 Cimarron Ave., Hawthorne, CA 90250
Bishop E. L. Bowie, 2037 N.E. 18th St., Oklahoma City, OK 73111
Chaplain, Bishop E. A. Morgan, 735 S. Oakland Dr., Decatur, IL 65525;
Bishop Alonza Ponder, 5609 N. Terry, Oklahoma City, OK 73111
Bishop Luke C. Nichols, Louisville, KY
Bishop Jeff Ruffin, Phoenix, AZ
Bishop R. S. Morgan, 12100 Greystone,Terr., Oklahoma City, OK 73120
Bishop S. E. Shannon, 1034 S. King Hwy., St. Louis, MO 63110
Bishop J. C. Hawkins, 3804 N. Temple, Indianapolis, IN 46205
Overseer, Elbert Jones, 4522 Melwood, Memphis, TN 38109

NATIONAL DEPARTMENTS
Convention Planning Committee
Young People's Progressive Union
Christian Education Dept.
Sunday School Dept.
Natl. Evangelist Bd.
Natl. Nurses Guild
Natl. Women's Work Dept.
Natl. Music Dept.
Gen. Sec. Ofc.

Periodical
The Gospel Truth

Church of the Lutheran Brethren of America

The Church of the Lutheran Brethren of America was organized in December 1900. Five independent Lutheran congregations met together in Milwaukee, Wisconsin, and adopted a constitution patterned very closely on that of the Lutheran Free Church of Norway.

The spiritual awakening in the Midwest during the 1890s crystallized into convictions that led to the formation of a new church body. Chief among the concerns were church membership practices, observance of Holy Communion, confirmation practices and local church government.

The Church of the Lutheran Brethren practices a simple order of worship with the sermon as the primary part of the worship service. It believes that personal profession of faith is the primary criterion for membership in the congregation. The Communion service is reserved for those who profess faith in Christ as savior. Each congregation is autonomous and the synod serves the congregations in advisory and cooperative capacities.

The synod supports a world mission program in Cameroon, Chad, Japan and Taiwan. Approximately 40 percent of the synodical budget is earmarked for world missions. A growing home mission ministry is planting new congregations in the United States and Canada. Affiliate organizations operate several retirement/nursing homes, conference and retreat centers.

Headquarters

1020 Alcott Ave., W., Box 655, Fergus Falls, MN 56538 Tel. (218)739-3336 Fax (218)739-5514
Media Contact, Pres., Rev. Robert M. Overgaard

Officers

Pres., Rev. Robert M. Overgaard, Sr.
Vice-Pres., Rev. David Rinden
Sec., Rev. Richard Vettrus, 707 Crestview Dr., West Union, IA 52175
Exec. Dir. of Finance, Bradley Martinson
Lutheran Brethren Schools, Pres., Rev. Joel Egge, Lutheran Brethren Schools, Box 317, Fergus Falls, MN 56538
World Missions, Exec. Dir., Rev. Matthew Rogness
Home Missions, Exec. Dir., Rev. Armin Jahr
Church Services, Exec. Dir., Rev. David Rinden
Youth Ministries, Exec. Dir., Nathan Lee

Periodical

Faith & Fellowship

Church of the Lutheran Confession

The Church of the Lutheran Confession held its constituting convention in Watertown, S.D., in August of 1960. The Church of the Lutheran Confession was begun by people and congregations who withdrew from church bodies that made up what was then known as the Synodical Conference over the issue of unionism. Following such passages as I Corinthians 1:10 and Romans 16:17-18, the Church of the Lutheran Confession holds the conviction that mutual agreement with the doctrines of Scripture is essential and necessary before exercise of church fellowship is appropriate.

Members of the Church of the Lutheran Confession uncompromisingly believe the Holy Scriptures to be divinely inspired and therefore inerrant. They subscribe to the historic Lutheran Confessions as found in the Book of Concord of 1580 because they are a correct exposition of Scripture.

The Church of the Lutheran Confession exists to proclaim, preserve and spread the saving truth of the gospel of Jesus Christ, so that the redeemed of God may learn to know Jesus Christ as their Lord and Savior and follow him through this life to the life to come.

Headquarters

501 Grover Rd., Eau Claire, WI 54701 Tel. (715)836-6622
Media Contact, Pres., Daniel Fleischer Tel.(512)241-5147

E-mail: JohnHLau@juno.com
Website: http://www.primenet.com/~mpkelly/clc/clc.html

Officers

Pres., Rev. Daniel Fleischer, 201 Princess Dr., Corpus Christi, TX 78410-1615
Vice-Pres., Rev. Elton Hallauer, 608 1st St., Hancock, MN 56244
Mod., Prof. Ronald Roehl, 515 Ingram Dr. W., Eau Claire, WI 54701
Sec., Rev. James Albrecht, 66325 State Rt. 152, Dowagiac, MI 49047
Treas., Lowell Moen, 3455 Jill Ave., Eau Claire, WI 54701
Archivist-Historian, David Lau
Statistician, James Sydow

Periodicals

The Lutheran Spokesman; Journal of Theology

Church of the Nazarene

The Church of the Nazarene resulted from the merger of three independent holiness groups. The Association of Pentecostal Churches in America, located principally in New York and New England, joined at Chicago in 1907 with a largely West Coast body called the Church of the Nazarene and formed the Pentecostal Church of the Nazarene. A southern group, the Holiness Church of Christ, united with the Pentecostal Church of the Nazarene at Pilot Point, Texas, in 1908. In 1919 the word "Pentecostal" was dropped from the name. Principal leaders in the organization were Phineas Bresee, William Howard Hoople, H. F. Reynolds and C. B. Jernigan. The first congregation in Canada was organized in November 1902 by Dr. H. F. Reynolds in Oxford, Nova Scotia.

The Church of the Nazarene emphasizes the doctrine of entire sanctification or Christian Holiness. It stresses the importance of a devout and holy life and a positive witness before the world by the power of the Holy Spirit. Nazarenes express their faith through evangelism, compassionate ministries, and education.

Nazarene government is representative, a studied compromise between episcopacy and congregationalism. Quadrennially, the various districts elect delegates to a general assembly at which six general superintendents are elected.

The international denomination has 9 liberal arts colleges, two graduate seminaries, 43 Bible colleges, three schools of nursing, a teacher's training college, and a junior college. The church maintains over 600 missionaries in 112 world areas. World services include medical, educational and religious ministries. Books, periodicals and other Christian literature are published at the Nazarene Publishing House.

The church is a member of the Christian Holiness Partnership and the National Association of Evangelicals.

Headquarters

6401 The Paseo, Kansas City, MO 64131 Tel. (816)333-7000 Fax (816)822-9071
Media Contact, Gen. Sec./Headquarters Operations Officer (HOO), Dr. Jack Stone, Tel. (816)333-7000, Ext. 2517

Officers

Gen. Supts.: John A. Knight; William J. Prince; James H. Diehl; Paul G. Cunningham; Jerry D. Porter; Jim L. Bond
Gen. Sec. (HOO), Jack Stone
Gen. Treas. (HFO), Robert Foster

OTHER ORGANIZATIONS

General Bd.: Sec., Jack Stone; Treas., Robert Foster
Evangelism & Church Growth Div., Dir., Bill Sullivan
Chaplaincy Min., Dir., Curt Bowers
Pastoral Min., Dir., Wilbur Brannon
Communications Div., Dir., Michael Estep
NCN Productions, Dir., David Anderson
World Literature Ministries, Dir., Ray Hendrix
Int. Bd. of Educ., Ed. Commissioner, Jerry Lambert
Pensions & Benefits Services USA & Intl., Don Walter
Stewardship Development, Dir., Steve Weber
Sunday School Min. Div., Dir., Talmadge Johnson
Adult Min., Dir., David Felter
Children's Min., Dir., Lynda Boardman
Cirriculum Dir., Randy Cloud
NYI Min., Dir., Fred Fullerton
World Mission Div., Dir., Louie Bustle
Nazarene World Missionary Soc., Dir., Nina Gunter
Multi-Cultural Ministries, Dir., Tom Nees

Periodicals

Holiness Today; Preacher's Magazine; Cross Walk; Grow Magazine

Church of the United Brethren in Christ

The Church of the United Brethren in Christ had its beginning with Philip William Otterbein and Martin Boehm, who were leaders in the revival movement in Pennsylvania and Maryland from the late 1760s into the early 1800s.

On Sept. 25, 1800, they and others associated with them formed a society under the name of United Brethren in Christ. Subsequent conferences adopted a Confession of Faith in 1815 and a constitution in 1841. The Church of the United Brethren in Christ adheres to the original constitution as amended in 1957, 1961 and 1977.

Headquarters

302 Lake St., Huntington, IN 46750 Tel. (219) 356-2312 Fax (219)356-4730
Media Contact, Communications Dir., Steve Dennie
E-mail: sdennie@ub.org
Website: http:// www.ub.org

Officers

Bishop, Dr. Ray A. Seilhamer

Gen. Treas./Office Mgr., Marda J. Hoffman
Dept. of Education, Dir., Dr. G. Blair Dowden
Dept. of Church Services, Dir., Rev. Paul Hirschy
Dept. of Missions, Dir., Rev. Kyle McQuillen

Churches of Christ

Churches of Christ are autonomous congregations whose members appeal to the Bible alone to determine matters of faith and practice. There are no central offices or officers. Publications and institutions related to the churches are either under local congregational control or independent of any one congregation.

Churches of Christ shared a common fellowship in the 19th century with the Christian Churches/Churches of Christ and the Christian Church (Disciples of Christ). Fellowship was gradually estranged following the Civil War due to theistic evolution, higher critical theories, centralization of church-wide activities through a missionary society and addition of musical instruments.

Members of Churches of Christ believe in one God, one Lord and Savior, Jesus Christ, one Holy Spirit, one body or church of God, one baptism by immersion into Christ, one faith revealed in the Holy, inspired, inerrant scriptures and one hope of eternal life based on the grace of God in Christ and a response by each individual of faith and obedience to God's gracious instructions in scripture. The New Testament pattern is followed for salvation and church membership, church organization and standards of Christian living.

Headquarters

Media Contact, Ed., Gospel Advocate, Dr. F. Furman Kearley, P.O. Box 726, Kosciusko, MS 39090

Periodicals

Action; Christian Woman; Christian Bible Teacher; The Christian Chronicle; Firm Foundation; Gospel Advocate; Guardian of Truth; Restoration Quarterly; 21st Century Christian; Upreach; Rocky Mountain Christian; The Spiritual Sword; Word and Work

Churches of Christ in Christian Union

Organized in 1909 at Washington Court House, Ohio, as the Churches of Christ in Christian Union, this body believes in the new birth and the baptism of the Holy Spirit for believers. It is Wesleyan, with an evangelistic and missionary emphasis.

The Reformed Methodist Church merged with the Churches of Christ in Christian Union in 1952.

Headquarters

1426 Lancaster Pike, Box 30, Circleville, OH 43113 Tel. (614)474-8856 Fax (614)477-7766
Media Contact, Dir. of Comm., Rev. Ralph Hux

Officers

Gen. Supt., Dr. Daniel Tipton

93

Asst. Gen. Supt., Rev. Ron Reese
Gen. Treas., Beverly R. Salley
Gen. Bd. of Trustees: Chpsn., Dr. Daniel Tipton;
Vice-Chpsn., Rev. Ron Reese
District Superintendents: West Central District,
Rev. Ron Reese; South Central District, Rev.
Jack Norman; Northeast District, Rev. Don
Seymour

Periodical
The Evangelical Advocate

Churches of God, General Conference

The Churches of God, General Conference (CGGC) had its beginnings in Harrisburg, Pa., in 1825.

John Winebrenner, recognized founder of the Church of God movement, was an ordained minister of the German Reformed Church. His experience-centered form of Christianity, particularly the "new measures" he used to promote it, his close connection with the local Methodists, his "experience and conference meetings" in the church and his "social prayer meetings" in parishioners' homes resulted in differences of opinion and the establishment of new congregations. Extensive revivals, camp meetings and mission endeavors led to the organization of additional congregations across central Pennsylvania and westward through Ohio, Indiana, Illinois and Iowa.

In 1830 the first system of cooperation between local churches was initiated as an "eldership" in eastern Pennsylvania. The organization of other elderships followed. General Eldership was organized in 1845, and in 1974 the official name of the denomination was changed from General Eldership of the Churches of God in North America to its present name.

The Churches of God, General Conference, is composed of 16 conferences in the United States and 1 conference in Haiti. The polity of the church is presbyterial in form. The church has mission ministries in the southwest among native Americans and is extensively involved in church planting and whole life ministries in Bangladesh, Brazil, Haiti and India.

The General Conference convenes in business session triennially. An Administrative Council composed of 16 regional representatives is responsible for the administration and ministries of the church between sessions of the General Conference.

Headquarters

Legal Headquarters, United Church Center, Rm. 213, 900 S. Arlington Ave., Harrisburg, PA 17109 Tel. (717)652-0255
Administrative Offices, General Conf. Dir., Pastor Wayne W. Boyer, 700 E. Melrose Ave., P.O. Box 926, Findlay, OH 45839 Tel. (419)424-1961 Fax (419)424-3343
Media Contact, Exec. Sec., Roberta G. Bakies, P.O. Box 926, Findlay, OH 45839 Tel. (419) 424-1961 Fax (419)424-3343

E-mail: cggc@bright.net
Website: http://www.cggc.org

Officers

Pres., Glenn E. Beatty, 1114 Circle Dr., Latrobe, PA 15650 Tel. (412)539-9400
Journalizing Sec., Dr. C. Darrell Prichard, 2412 Sweetwater Dr., Findlay, OH 45840 Tel. (419)424-9777
Treas., Robert E. Stephenson, 700 E. Melrose Ave., P.O. Box 926, Findlay, OH 45839 Tel. (419)424-1961

DEPARTMENTS

Cross-Cultural Ministries, Pastor Don Dennison
Pensions, Mr. James P. Thomas
Denominational Comm., Evelyn J. Sloat
Church Renewal, Pastor Jim G. Martin
Church Planting, Pastor Harley (Jay) E. Nickless, Jr.
Youth & Family Life Ministries, Susan L. Callaway

Periodicals

The Church Advocate; The Gem; The Missionary Signal

Congregational Holiness Church

This body was organized in 1921 and embraces the doctrine of Holiness and Pentecost. It carries on mission work in Mexico, Honduras, Costa Rica, Cuba, Brazil, Guatemala, India, Nicaragua, El Salvador, Belize, Venezuela and Haiti.

Headquarters

3888 Fayetteville Hwy., Griffin, GA 30223 Tel. (404)228-4833 Fax (404)228-1177
Media Contact, Gen. Supt., Bishop Chet Smith
E-mail: chchurch@bellsouth.net
Website: http://personal.atl.bellsouth.net/atl/c/h/chchurch/church.htm

EXECUTIVE BOARD

Gen. Supt., Bishop Chet Smith
1st Asst. Gen. Supt., Rev. William L. Lewis
2nd Asst. Gen. Supt., Rev. Wayne Hicks
Gen. Sec., Rev. Leslee Bailey
Gen. Treas., Rev. Ronald Wilson

Periodical

The Gospel Messenger

Conservative Baptist Association of America

The Conservative Baptist Association of America (now known as CBAmerica) was organized May 17, 1947 at Atlantic City, N.J. The Old and New Testaments are regarded as the divinely inspired Word of God and are therefore infallible and of supreme authority. Each local church is independent, autonomous and free from ecclesiastical or political authority.

CBAmerica provides wide-ranging support to its affiliate churches and individuals through nine regional associations. CBA offers personnel to assist churches in areas such as growth and

94

health conflict resolution and financial analysis. The association supports its clergy with retirement planning, referrals for new places of ministry and spiritual counseling. The Conservative Baptist Women's Ministries assists women in the church to be effective in their personal growth and leadership.

Each June or July there is a National Conference giving members an opportunity for fellowship, inspiration and motivation.

Headquarters
25W560 Geneva Rd., P.O. Box 66, Wheaton, IL 60189 Tel. (630)260-3800 Fax (630)653-5387 Media Contact, Executive Administrator, Rev. Ed Mitchell
E-mail: cbamerica@aol.com
Website: http://www.cbamerica.org

OTHER ORGANIZATIONS
CBInternational, Exec. Dir., Dr. Hans Finzel, Box 5, Wheaton, IL 60189
Mission to the Americas, Exec. Dir., Rev. Rick Miller, Box 828, Wheaton, IL 60189
Conservative Baptist Higher Ed. Council, Dr. Brent Garrison, Southwestern College, 2625 E. Cactus Rd., Phoenix, AZ 85032

Periodicals
Spectrum; Front Line

Conservative Congregational Christian Conference

In the 1930s, evangelicals within the Congregational Christian Churches felt a definite need for fellowship and service. By 1945, this loose association crystallized into the Conservative Congregational Christian Fellow-ship, committed to maintaining a faithful, biblical witness.

In 1948 in Chicago, the Conservative Congregational Christian Conference was established to provide a continuing fellowship for evangelical churches and ministers on the national level. In recent years, many churches have joined the Conference from backgrounds other than Congregational. These Community or Bible Churches are truly congregational in polity and thoroughly evangelical in conviction. The CCCC welcomes all evangelical churches that are, in fact, congregational. The CCCC believes in the necessity of a regenerate membership, the authority of the Holy Scriptures, the Lordship of Jesus Christ, the autonomy of the local church and the universal fellowship of all Christians.

The Conservative Congregational Christian Conference is a member of the World Evangelical Congregational Fellowship (formed in 1986 in London, England) and the National Association of Evangelicals.

Headquarters
7582 Currell Blvd., Ste. #108, St. Paul, MN 55125 Tel. (612)739-1474 Fax (612)739-0750 Media Contact, Conf. Min., Rev. Clifford R. Christensen

Officers
Pres., Rev. Clarence Schultz, 7023 Pershing Blvd., Kenosha, WI 53142-1723
Vice-Pres., Rev. Edward Whitman, 59 Provence Rd., Barrington, NH 03825
Conf. Min., Rev. Clifford R. Christensen, 457 S. Mary St., Maplewood, MN 55119
Controller, Mr. Leslie Pierce, 5220 E. 105th St. S., Tulsa, OK 74137
Treas., Tay Kersey, 8450 Eastwood Rd., Moundsview, MN 55112
Rec. Sec., Peter Murdy, PO Box 953, Eastford, CT 06242
Editor, Walter Smith, 10944 St. Hwy 37, Lisbon, NY 13658
Historian, Rev. Milton Reimer, P.O. Box 4456, Lynchburg, VA 24502

Periodical
Foresee

Conservative Lutheran Association

The Conservative Lutheran Association (CLA) was originally named Lutheran's Alert National (LAN) when it was founded in 1965 by 10 conservative Lutheran pastors and laymen meeting in Cedar Rapids, Iowa. Its purpose was to help preserve from erosion the basic doctrines of Christian theology, including the inerrancy of Holy Scripture. The group grew to a worldwide constituency, similarly concerned with maintaining the doctrinal integrity of the Bible and the Lutheran Confessions.

Headquarters
Trinity Lutheran Church, 4101 E. Nohl Ranch Rd., Anaheim, CA 92807 Tel. (714)637-8370 Media Contact, Pres., Rev. P. J. Moore
E-mail: PastorPJ@ix.netcom.com

Officers
Pres., Rev. P. J. Moore, 420 Fernhill La., Anaheim, CA 92807 Tel. (714)637-8370
Vice-Pres., Rev. Dr. R. H. Redal, 409 Tacoma Ave. N., Tacoma, WA 98403 Tel. (206)383-5528
Sec., Rev. Marc Clayton, 115 McKean Ct., Apt. A, Enumclaw, WA 98022 Tel. (360)825-0175
Faith Seminary, Dean, Rev. Dr. Michael J. Adams, 3504 N. Pearl St., P.O. Box 7186, Tacoma, WA 98407 Tel. (800)228-4650 Fax (206)759-1790

Coptic Orthodox Church

This body is part of the ancient Coptic Orthodox Church of Egypt which is currently headed by His Holiness Pope Shenouda III, 116th Successor to St. Mark the Apostle. Egyptian immigrants have organized many parishes in the United States. Copts exist outside Egypt in Ethiopia, Europe, Asia, Australia, Canada and the United States. The total world Coptic community is estimated at 27 million. The church is in full communion with the other members of The Oriental Orthodox Church

Family, The Syrian Orthodox Church, Armenian Orthodox Church, Ethiopian Orthodox Church, the Syrian Orthodox Church in India and the Eritrean Orthodox Church.

Headquarters
427 West Side Ave., Jersey City, NJ 07304 Tel. (201)333-0004 Fax (201)333-0502
Media Contact, Fr. Abraam D. Sleman

CORRESPONDENT
Fr. Abraam D. Sleman

Cumberland Presbyterian Church

The Cumberland Presbyterian Church was organized in Dickson County, Tenn., on Feb. 4, 1810. It was an outgrowth of the Great Revival of 1800 on the Kentucky and Tennessee frontier. The founders were Finis Ewing, Samuel King and Samuel McAdow, ministers in the Presbyterian Church who rejected the doctrine of election and reprobation as taught in the Westminster Confession of Faith.

By 1813, the Cumberland Presbytery had grown to encompass three presbyteries, which constituted a synod. This synod met at the Beech Church in Sumner County, Tenn., and formulated a "Brief Statement" which set forth the points in which Cumberland Presbyterians dissented from the Westminster Confession. These points are:

1. That there are no eternal reprobates;
2. That Christ died not for some, but for all people;
3. That all those dying in infancy are saved through Christ and the sanctification of the Spirit;
4. That the Spirit of God operates on the world, or as coextensively as Christ has made atonement, in such a manner as to leave everyone inexcusable.

From its birth in 1810, the Cumberland Presbyterian Church grew to a membership of 200,000 at the turn of the century. In 1906 the church voted to merge with the then-Presbyterian Church. Those who dissented from the merger became the nucleus of the continuing Cumberland Presbyterian Church.

Headquarters
1978 Union Ave., Memphis, TN 38104 Tel. (901)276-4572 Fax (901)272-3913
Media Contact, Stated Clk., Rev. Robert D. Prosser, Fax (901)276-4578
E-mail: assembly@cumberland.org
Website: http://www.webmaster@cumberland.org

Officers
Mod., Rev. Masaharu Asayama, 3-15-9 Higashi, Kunitachi-shi, Tokyo, Japan, Tel. 011-81-42-572-7616 Fax. 011-81-42-575-5049; E-mail: ipcc@po.eis.or.jp
Stated Clk., Rev. Robert D. Prosser, Tel.(901)352-4572 Fax (901) 276-4578
General Assembly Council, Exec. Dir., Davis Gray, Tel.(901)352-4572 Fax (901) 272-3913

INSTITUTIONS
Cumberland Presbyterian Children's Home, Exec. Dir., Rev. Stan E. Rush, Drawer G, Denton, TX 76202 Tel. (940)382-5112 Fax (940)387-0821; E-mail: cpch@gte.net
Cumberland Presbyterian Center, Tel.(901)276-4572 Fax (901)276-4578
Memphis Theological Seminary, Pres., Dr. Larry Blakeburn, 168 E. Parkway S., Memphis, TN 38104 Tel. (901)458-8232 Fax (901)452-4051; E-mail: wa4mff@aol.com
Bethel College, Interim Pres., Robert Prosser, 325 Cherry St., McKenzie, TN 38201 Tel. (901)352-4004 Fax (901)352-4069; E-mail: walkermc@bethel-college.edu
BOARDS
Bd. of Christian Education, Exec. Dir., Claudette Pickle
Bd. of Missions, Exec. Dir., Rev. Jack Barker
Bd. of Stewardship, Exec. Sec., Rev. Richard Magrill

Periodicals
The Cumberland Presbyterian; The Missionary Messenger

Cumberland Presbyterian Church in America

This church, originally known as the Colored Cumberland Presbyterian Church, was formed in May 1874. In May 1869, at the General Assembly meeting in Murfreesboro, Tenn., Moses Weir of the black delegation sucessfully appealed for help in organizing a separate African church so that: blacks could learn self-reliance and independence; they could have more financial assistance; they could minister more effectively among blacks; and they could worship close to the altar, not in the balconies. He requested that the Cumberland Presbyterian Church organize blacks into presbyteries and synods, develop schools to train black clergy, grant loans to assist blacks to secure hymnbooks, Bibles and church buildings and establish a separate General Assembly.

In 1874 the first General Assembly of the Colored Cumberland Presbyterian Church met in Nashville. The moderator was Rev. P. Price and the stated clerk was Elder John Humphrey.

The denomination's General Assembly, the national governing body, is organized around its three program boards and agencies: Finance, Publication and Christian Education, and Missions and Evangelism. Other agencies of the General Assembly are under these three program boards.

The church has four synods (Alabama, Kentucky, Tennessee and Texas), 15 presbyteries and 153 congregations. The CPC extends as far north as Cleveland, Ohio, and Chicago, as far west as Marshalltown, Iowa, and Dallas, Tex., and as far south as Selma, Ala.

Headquarters

Media Contact, Stated Clk., Rev. Dr. Robert. Stanley Wood, 226 Church St., Huntsville, AL 35801 Tel. (205)536-7481 Fax (205)536-7482

Officers

Mod., Rev. Endia Scruggs, 1627 Carroll Rd., Harvest, AL 35749

Stated Clk., Rev. Dr. Rorbert. Stanley Wood, 226 Church St., Huntsville, AL 35801 Tel. (205) 536-7481

SYNODS

Alabama, Stated Clk., Arthur Hinton, 511 10th Ave. N.W., Aliceville, AL 35442

Kentucky, Stated Clk., Mary Martha Daniels, 8548 Rhodes Ave., Chicago, IL 60619

Tennessee, Stated Clk., Elder Clarence Norman, 145 Jones St., Huntington, TN 38334

Texas, Stated Clk., Arthur King, 2435 Kristen, Dallas, TX 75216

Periodical

The Cumberland Flag

Diocese of the Armenian Church of America

The Armenian Apostolic Church was founded at the foot of the biblical mountain of Ararat in the ancient land of Armenia, where two of Christ's Holy Apostles, Saints Thaddeus and Bartholomew, preached Christianity. In A.D. 303 the historic Mother Church of Etchmiadzin was founded by Saint Gregory the Illuminator, the first Catholicos of All Armenians. This cathedral still stands and serves as the center of the Armenian Church. A branch of this Church was established in North America in 1889. The first church building was consecrated in 1891 in Worcester, MA. The first Armenian Diocese was set up in 1898 by the then-Catholicos of All Armenians, Mgrditch Khrimian (Hairig). Armenian immigrants built the first Armenian church in the new world in Worcester, MA, under the jurisdiction of Holy Etchmiadzin.

In 1927, the churches and the parishes in California were formed into a Western Diocese and the parishes in Canada formed their own diocese in 1984. Other centers of major significance of the Armenian Apostolic Church are the Catholicate of Cilicia, now located in Lebanon, the Armenian Patriarchate of Jerusalem and the Armenian Patriarchate of Constantinople.

Headquarters

Eastern Diocese: 630 Second Ave., New York, NY 10016-4885 Tel. (212)686-0710 Fax (212) 779-3558

Western Diocese: 3325 North Glenoaks Blvd., Burbank, CA 91504 Tel. (818) 558-7474 FAX (818) 558-6333

Canadian Diocese: 615 Stuart Ave., Outremont, QC H2V 3H2 Tel. (514)276-9479 Fax (514)276-9960

Media Contact, Dir., Zohrab Information Ctr., V. Rev. Fr. Krikor Maksoudian, Eastern Diocese

Officers

Eastern Diocese

Primate, Archbishop Khajag Barsamian, Eastern Diocese Ofc.

Chancellor, Rev. Fr. Garabed Kochakian

Diocesan Council, Chpsn., Haig Dadourian, 415 Madison Ave., 7th Fl., New York, NY 10017

Western Diocese

Primate, His Em. Archbishop Vatche Hovsepian, Western Diocese Ofc.

Diocesan Council, Chpsn., Dn. Dr. Varouj Altebarmakian, 7290 North San Pedro, Fresno, CA 93011

Diocesan Council, Sec., Mr. John Yaldezian, 23221 Aetna St., Woodland Hills, CA 91367 Tel. (B) (818) 346-6163

Canadian Diocese

Primate, His Em. Archbishop Hovnan Derderian

Diocesan Council Chpsn, Mr. Takvor Hopyan, 20 Pineway,Blvd., Willowdale, ON M2H 1A1, Canada Tel (B) (416) 222-2639

Diocesan Council secretary., Mr. Vahe Ketli, 750 Montpellier, # 909, St. Laurens, QC H4L 5A7, Canada Tel (R) (514) 7i47-1347

Periodicals

The Armenian Church; The Mother Church

Elim Fellowship

The Elim Fellowship, a Pentecostal Body established in 1947, is an outgrowth of the Elim Missionary Assemblies formed in 1933.

It is an association of churches, ministers and missionaries seeking to serve the whole Body of Christ. It is of Pentecostal conviction and charismatic orientation, providing ministerial credentials and counsel and encouraging fellowship among local churches. Elim Fellowship sponsors leadership seminars at home and abroad and serves as a transdenominational agency sending long-term, short-term and tent-making missionaries to work with national movements.

Headquarters

1703 Dalton Rd., Lima, NY 14485 Tel. (716)582-2790 Fax (716)624-1229

Media Contact, Gen. Sec., Paul Anderson

Officers

Gen. Chairman, Bernard J. Evans

Asst. Gen. Chairman, George Veach

Gen. Treas., Michael McDonald

Periodical

Elim Herald

Episcopal Church

The Episcopal Church entered the colonies with the earliest settlers at Jamestown, Va., in 1607 as the Church of England. After the American Revolution, it became autonomous in 1789 as The Protestant Episcopal Church in the United States of America. (The Episcopal Church became the official alternate name in 1967.) Samuel Seabury of Connecticut was

97

elected the first bishop and consecrated in Aberdeen by bishops of the Scottish Episcopal Church in 1784.

In organizing as an independent body, the Episcopal Church created a bicameral legislature, the General Convention, modeled after the new U.S. Congress. It comprises a House of Bishops and a House of Deputies and meets every three years. A 38-member Executive Council, which meets three times a year, is the interim governing body. An elected presiding bishop serves as Primate and Chief Pastor.

After severe setbacks in the years immediately following the Revolution because of its association with the British Crown and the fact that a number of its clergy and members were Loyalists, the church soon established its own identity and sense of mission. It sent missionaries into the newly settled territories of the United States, establishing dioceses from coast to coast, and also undertook substantial missionary work in Africa, Latin America and the Far East. Today, the overseas dioceses are developing into independent provinces of the Anglican Communion, the worldwide fellowship of 36 churches in communion with the Church of England and the Archbishop of Canterbury.

The beliefs and practices of The Episcopal Church, like those of other Anglican churches, are both Catholic and Reformed, with bishops in the apostolic succession and the historic creeds of Christendom regarded as essential elements of faith and order, along with the primary authority of Holy Scripture and the two chief sacraments of Baptism and Eucharist.

EPISCOPAL CHURCH CENTER

815 Second Ave., New York, NY 10017 Tel. (212)867-8400 Fax (212)949-8059
Media Contact, Dir. of News & Info., James Solheim
Website: http://www.ecusa.anglican.org

Officers

Presiding Bishop & Primate, Most Rev. Frank Tracy Griswold III
Treas., Stephen Duggan
Sec., Rev. Canon Donald A. Nickerson, Jr.
House of Deputies: Pres., Pamela P. Chinnis; Vice-Pres., Ven. George Werner

OFFICE OF THE PRESIDING BISHOP

Presiding Bishop, Most Rev. Frank Tracy Griswold III
Admn. Asst., Rev. Canon Carl Gerdau
Exec. Dir., Office of Pastoral Dev., Rt. Rev. Harold Hopkins
Suffragan Bishop for the Armed Forces, Rt. Rev. Charles L. Keyser
Suffragan Bishop for American Churches in Europe, Rt. Rev. Jeffery Rowthorn
Office of Prof. Ministry Dev., Rev. John Docker

ADMINISTRATION AND FINANCE

Treas., Stephen Duggan
Asst. Treas., Catherine Lynch

Controller, Tony Perfetti
Archivist, Mark Duffy
Human Resources, John Colon

SERVICE, EDUCATION AND WITNESS

Congregational Ministries, Rev. Winston Ching
Hispanic Ministries, Rev. Herbert Arrunategui
Jubilee Centers, Ntsiki Kabane-Langford
Native American Ministries, Owanah Anderson
Peace & Justice, Rev. Brian Grieves
Rural Workers Fellowship, Rev. Allen Brown
Washington Ofc., Rev. Robert Brooks
Media Services, Sonia Francis
Electronic Media, Rev. Clement Lee
Dir. of News & Info., James Solheim
Episcopal Life, Jerrold Hames
Ministries with Young persons, Rev. Sheryl Kujawa
Evangelism Office, Rev. Hugh Magers
Liturgy & Music, Rev. Clayton Morris
Theological Education, —
Dir. of Anglican/Global Relations, Rev. Patrick Mauney
Ecumenical Office, Rev. David Perry
Mission Personnel, Dorothy Gist
Dep. Dir. of Anglican/Global Relations, Rev. Ricardo Potter
Women in Mission & Ministry, Ann Smith
Dir. of Bishops Fund for World Relief, Nancy Marvel
Planning Officer, Vernon Hazelwood
Stewardship, Terry Parsons

BISHOPS IN THE U.S.A.

C, Coadjutor; S, Suffragan; A Assistant
Address: Right Reverend
Presiding Bishop & Primate, Most Rev. Frank Tracy Griswold III; Pastoral Dev., Rt. Rev. Harold Hopkins; S. Bishop for Chaplaincies to Military\Prisons\Hosp., Rt. Rev. Charles L. Keyser
Alabama: Robert O. Miller, 521 N. 20th St., Birmingham, AL 35203
Alaska: Mark MacDonald, David Elsensohn, 1205 Denali Way, Fairbanks, AK 99701-4137
Albany: David S. Ball, 68 S. Swan St., Albany, NY 12210
Arizona: Robert Shahan, 114 W.Roosevelt, Phoenix, AZ 85003-1406
Arkansas: Larry E. Maze, P.O. Box 162668, Little Rock, AR 72216
Atlanta: Frank Kellog Allan, 2744 Peachtree Rd. N.W., Atlanta, GA 30363
Bethlehem: Paul Marshall, 333 Wyandotte St., Bethlehem, PA 18015
California: William E. Swing, 1055 Taylor St., San Francisco, CA 94115
Central Florida: John H. Howe, 1017 E. Robinson St., Orlando, FL 32801
Central Gulf Coast: Charles F. Duvall, P.O. Box 13330, Pensacola, FL 32591-3330
Central New York: David B. Joslin, 310 Montgomery St., Ste. 200, Syracuse, NY 13202
Central Pennsylvania: Michael Creighton, P.O. Box 11937, Harrisburg, PA 17108

Chicago: 65 E. Huron St., Chicago, IL 60611

Colorado: William J. Winterrowd, 1300 Washington St., Denver, CO 80203

Connecticut: Clarence N. Coleridge, 1335 Asylum Ave., Hartford, CT 06105

Dallas: James M. Stanton, 1630 Garrett St., Dallas, TX 75206

Delaware: Calvin Cabell Tennis, 2020 Tatnall St., Wilmington, DE 19802

East Carolina: B. Sidney Sanders, P.O. Box 1336, Kinston, NC 28501

East Tennessee: Robert Tharp, 401 Cumberland Ave., Knoxville, TN 37902-2302

Eastern Michigan: Edward Leidel, 4611 Swede Ave., Midland, MI 48642

Eastern Oregon: Rustin R. Kimsey, P.O. Box 620, The Dalles, OR 97058

Easton: Martin G. Townsend, P.O. Box 1027, Easton, MD 21601

Eau Claire: William C. Wantland, 510 S. Farwell St., Eau Claire, WI 54701

El Camino Real: Richard Shimpfky, P.O. Box 1903, Monterey, CA 93940

Florida: Stephen H. Jecko, 325 Market St., Jacksonville, FL 32202

Fond du Lac: Russell E. Jacobus, P.O. Box 149, Fond du Lac, WI 54936

Fort Worth: Jack Iker, 6300 Ridgelea Pl., Ste. 1100, Fort Worth, TX 76116

Georgia: Henry Louttit, Jr., 611 East Bay St., Savannah, GA 31401

Hawaii: Richard Chang, 229 Queen Emma Square, Honolulu, HI 96813

Idaho: John S. Thornton, P.O. Box 936, Boise, ID 83701

Indianapolis: 1100 W. 42nd St., Indianapolis, IN 46208

Iowa: C. Christopher Epting, 225 37th St., Des Moines, IA 50312

Kansas: William E. Smalley, 833-35 Polk St., Topeka, KS 66612

Kentucky: Edwin F. Gulick, 600 E. Maine, Louisville, KY 40202

Lexington: Don A. Wimberly, P.O. Box 610, Lexington, KY 40586

Long Island: Orris G. Walker, 36 Cathedral Ave., Garden City, NY 11530

Los Angeles: Frederick H. Borsch; Chester Talton, (S), P.O. Box 2164, Los Angeles, CA 90051

Louisiana: James Barrow Brown, 1623 7th St., New Orleans, LA 70115-4411

Maine: James Moodey, 143 State St., Portland, ME 04101

Maryland: Bob Ihloff, 4 East University Pkwy., Baltimore, MD 21218-2437

Massachusetts: M. Thomas Shaw, SSJE; Barbara Harris, (S), 138 Tremont St., Boston, MA 02111

Michigan: R. Stewart Wood, Jr., 4800 Woodward Ave., Detroit, MI 48201

Milwaukee: Roger J. White, 804 E. Juneau Ave., Milwaukee, WI 53202

Minnesota: James L. Jelinek; 430 Oak Grove St., #306, Minneapolis, MN 55403

Mississippi: Alfred C. Marble, P.O. Box 23107, Jackson, MS 39225-3107

Missouri: Hays Rockwell, 1210 Locust St., St. Louis, MO 63103

Montana: Charles I. Jones, 515 North Park Ave., Helena, MT 59601

Nebraska: James E. Krotz, 200 N. 62nd St., Omaha, NE 68132

Nevada: Stewart C. Zabriskie, P.O. Box 6357, Reno, NV 89513

New Hampshire: Douglas E. Theuner, 63 Green St., Concord, NH 03301

New Jersey: Joe M. Doss, 808 W. State St., Trenton, NJ 08618

New York: Richard F. Grein; Walter D. Dennis, (S), Catherine Roskam,(S), 1047 Amsterdam Ave., New York, NY 10025; Don Taylor

Newark: John Shelby Spong; Jack McKelvey, (S), 24 Rector St., Newark, NJ 07102

North Carolina: Robert C. Johnson, Jr., 201 St. Albans Dr., Raleigh, NC 27619

North Dakota: Andrew H. Fairfield, P.O. Box 10337, Fargo, ND 58106-0337

Northern California: Jerry A. Lamb, P.O. Box 161268, Sacramento, CA 95816

Northern Indiana: Francis C. Gray, 117 N. Lafayette Blvd., South Bend, IN 46601

Northern Michigan: Thomas K. Ray, 131 E. Ridge St., Marquette, MI 49855

Northwest Texas: P.O. Box 1067, Lubbock, TX 79408

Northwestern Pennsylvania: Robert D. Rowley, 145 W. 6th St., Erie, PA 16501

Ohio: J. Clark Grew; Arthur B. Williams, (S), 2230 Euclid Ave., Cleveland, OH 44115

Oklahoma: Robert M. Moody; William J. Cox, (A), 924 N. Robinson, Oklahoma City, OK 73102

Olympia: Vincent W. Warner, P.O. Box 12126, Seattle, WA 98102

Oregon: Robert Louis Ladehoff, P.O. Box 467, Portland, OR 97034

Pennsylvania: Allen L. Bartlett, Charles Bennison (Coady), 240 S. 4th St., Philadelphia, PA 19106

Pittsburgh: Alden M. Hathaway; Franklin D. Turner, (S), 325 Oliver Ave., Pittsburgh, PA 15222

Quincy: Keith Ackerman, 3601 N. North St., Peoria, IL 61604

Rhode Island: Geralyn Wolf, 275 N. Main St., Providence, RI 02903

Rio Grande: Terence Kelshaw, 4304 Carlisle St. NE, Albuquerque, NM 87107

Rochester: William G. Burrill, 935 East Ave., Rochester, NY 14607

San Diego: Gethin B. Hughes, St. Paul's Church, 2728 6th Ave., San Diego, CA 92103

San Joaquin: John-David Schofield, 4159 East Dakota Ave., Fresno, CA 93726

South Carolina: Edward L. Salmon; G. Edward Haynesworth, (A), P.O. Box 20127, Charleston, SC 29413-0127

South Dakota: Creighton Robertson, 500 S. Main St., Sioux Falls, SD 57102-0914

Southeast Florida: Calvin O. Schofield, Jr., 525 NE 15th St., Miami, FL 33132

Southern Ohio: Herbert Thompson, Jr.; Kenneth Price, (S), 412 Sycamore St., Cincinnati, OH 45202

Southern Virginia: Frank H. Vest, 600 Talbot Hall Rd., Norfolk, VA 23505

Southwest Florida: Rogers S. Harris, P.O. Box 491, St. Petersburg, FL 33731

Southwestern Virginia: Frank Powell, P.O. Box 2279, Roanoke, VA 24009

Spokane: Frank J. Terry, 245 E. 13th Ave., Spokane, WA 99202

Springfield: Peter H. Beckwith, 821 S. 2nd St., Springfield, IL 62704

Tennessee: Bertram M. Herlong, One LaFleur Bldg., Ste. 100, 50 Vantage Way, Nashville, TN 37228

Texas: Claude E. Payne, 3203 W. Alabama St., Houston, TX 77098

Upper South Carolina: Dorsey F. Henderson, Jr., P.O. Box 1789, Columbia, SC 29202

Utah: Carolyn Irish, 231 E. First St. S., Salt Lake City, UT 84111

Vermont: Mary Adelia McLeod, Rock Point, Burlington, VT 05401

Virginia: Peter J. Lee; Clayton Matthews, (S), 110 W. Franklin St., Richmond, VA 23220

Washington: Ronald Haines; Jane H. Dixon, (S), Episc. Church House, Mt. St. Alban, Washington, DC 20016

West Missouri: John Buchanan, P.O. Box 413216, Kansas City, MO 64141

West Tennessee: James M. Coleman, 692 Poplar Ave., Memphis, TN 38105

West Texas: James E. Folts; Earl N. MacArthur, (S), P.O. Box 6885, San Antonio, TX 78209

West Virginia: John H. Smith, P.O. Box 5400, Charleston, WV 25361-0400

Western Kansas: Vernon Strickland, P.O. Box 2507, Salina, KS 67402

Western Louisiana: Robert J. Hargrove, Jr., P.O. Box 2031, Alexandria, LA 71309-2031

Western Massachusetts: Gordon P. Scruton, 37 Chestnut St., Springfield, MA 01103

Western Michigan: Edward L. Lee, 2600 Vincent Ave., Kalamazoo, MI 49008

Western New York: David C. Bowman, 1114 Delaware Ave., Buffalo, NY 14209

Western North Carolina: Robert H. Johnson, P.O. Box 369, Black Mountain, NC 28711

Wyoming: William Wolfrum, 104 S. 4th St., Laramie, WY 82070

Am. Churches in Europe-Jurisdiction: Jeffery Rowthorn, The American Cathedral, 23 Avenue Georges V, 75008, Paris, France

Navajoland Area Mission: Steven Plummer, P.O. Box 720, Farmington, NM 87499

Periodical

Episcopal Life

The Estonian Evangelical Lutheran Church

For information on the Estonian Evangelical Lutheran Church (EELC), please see the listing in Chapter 4, "Religious Bodies in Canada."

Headquarters

383 Jarvis St., Toronto, ON M5B 2C7

THE EVANGELICAL CHURCH

The Evangelical Church was born June 4, 1968 in Portland, Ore., when 46 congregations and about 80 ministers, under the leadership of V. A. Ballantyne and George Millen, met in an organizing session. Within two weeks a group of about 20 churches and 30 ministers from the Evangelical United Brethren and Methodist churches in Montana and North Dakota became a part of the new church. Richard Kienitz and Robert Strutz were the superintendents.

Under the leadership of Superintendent Robert Trosen, the former Holiness Methodist Church became a part of the Evangelical Church in 1969, bringing its membership and a flourishing mission field in Bolivia. The Wesleyan Covenant Church joined in 1977, with its missionary work in Mexico, in Brownsville, Tex. and among the Navajos in New Mexico.

The Evangelical Church in Canada, where T. J. Jesske was superintendent, became an autonomous organization on June 5, 1970. In 1982, after years of discussions with the Evangelical Church of North America, a founding General Convention was held at Billings, Mont., where the two churches united. In 1993 the Canadian conference merged with the Canadian portion of the Missionary Church to form the Evangelical Missionary Church. The new group maintains close ties with their American counterparts. Currently there are nearly 150 U.S. congregations of the Evangelical Church. The headquarters is located in Minneapolis, MN.

The following guide the life, program and devotion of this church: faithful, biblical and sensible preaching and teaching of those truths proclaimed by scholars of the Wesleyan-Arminian viewpoint; an itinerant system which reckons with the rights of individuals and the desires of the congregation; local ownership of all church properties and assets.

The church is officially affiliated with the Christian Holiness Partnership, the National Association of Evangelicals, Wycliffe Bible Translators, World Gospel Mission and OMS International. The denomination has nearly 150 missionaries.

Headquarters

7733 West River Rd., Minneapolis, MN 55444 Tel. (612)561-0886 Fax (612)561-0774 Media Contact, Gen. Supt., John F. Sills

Officers

Gen. Supt., Dr. John F. Sills
Dir. of Missions, Rev. Duane Erickson

Periodicals

Heat Beat; The Evangelical Challenge

The Evangelical Church Alliance

What is known today as the Evangelical Church Alliance began in 1887 under the name "World's Faith Missionary Association." Years later, on March 28, 1928, a nonprofit organization was incorporated in the state of Missouri under the same name. In October, 1931, the name "Fundamental Ministerial Association" was chosen to reflect the organization's basis of unity.

On July 21, 1958, during the annual convention at Trinity Seminary and Bible College in Chicago, Illinois, a more comprehensive constitution was created and the name was changed to "The Evangelical Church Alliance."

The ECA licenses and ordains ministers who are qualified providing them with credentials from a recognized ecclesiastical body; provides training courses through the Bible Extension Institute for those who have not had the opportunity to attend Seminary or Bible School; provides Associate Membership for churches and Christian organizations giving opportunity for fellowship and networking with other evangelical ministers and organizations who share the same goals and mission, while remaining autonomous; provides Regional Conventions and an Annual International Convention where members can find fellowship, encouragement and training; cooperates with churches in finding new pastors when they have openings.

ECA is an international, nonsectarian, Evangelical organization. There are currently 2,238 ordained and licensed members not including churches and Christian Organizations.

Headquarters

205 W. Broadway St., P.O. Box 9, Bradley, IL 60915 Tel. (815)937-0720 Fax (815)937-0001
Media Contact, Pres./CEO, Dr. George L. Miller

Officers

Pres./CEO, Dr. George L. Miller
Chairman of the Board, Dr. Sterling L. Cauble, Sunman Bible Church, P.O. Box 216, Sunman, IN 47041
1st Vice-Chairman, Dr. Allen Hammond, 1921 Ohio St., Bluefield, WV 24701
2nd Vice-Chairman, Rev. Richard G. Sydnes, P.O. Box 355 Des Moines, IA 50302

Periodical

The Evangel

The Evangelical Congregational Church

This denomination had its beginning in the movement known as the Evangelical Association, organized by Jacob Albright in the early nineteenth century. A division which occurred in 1891 in the Evangelical Association resulted in the organization of the United Evangelical Church in 1894. An attempt to heal this division was made in 1922, but a portion of the United Evangelical Church was not satisfied with the plan of merger and remained apart, taking the above name in 1928. This denomination is Arminian in doctrine, evangelistic in spirit and Methodist in church government, with congregational ownership of local church property.

Congregations are located from New Jersey to Illinois. A denominational center, a retirement village and a seminary are located in Myerstown, Pa. Three summer youth camps and four camp meetings continue evangelistic outreach. A worldwide missions movement includes conferences in North East India, Liberia, Mexico and Japan. The denomination is a member of National Association of Evangelicals.

Headquarters

Evangelical Congregational Church Center, 100 W. Park Ave., Myerstown, PA 17067 Tel. (717)866-7581 Fax (717)866-7383
Media Contact, Bishop, Rev. Richard W. Kohl, Tel. (717)866-7581
E-mail: eccenter@eccenter.com
Website: http://www.eccenter.com/church/

Officers

Presiding Bishop, Rev. Richard W. Kohl
1st Vice-Chpsn., Rev. Jack Ward, 452 Jarvis Rd., Akron, OH 44319
Sec., Rev. Robert J. Stahl, RD 2, Box 1468, Schuylkill Haven, PA 17972
Asst. Sec.: Rev. Gregory Dimick, Hatfield, PA; Rev. Richard Reigle, Dixon, IL
Treas., Martha Metz
E.C.C. Retirement Village, Supt., Rev. Bruce Hill, Fax (717)866-6448
Evangelical School of Theology, Pres., Dr. Kirby N. Keller, Fax (717)866-4667

OTHER ORGANIZATIONS

Administrative Council: Chpsn., Bishop Richard W. Kohl; Vice-Chpsn., Rev. Keith R. Miller; Treas., Martha Metz
Div. of Evangelism & Spiritual Care, Chpsn., Bishop Richard W. Kohl
Div. of Church Ministries & Services, Chpsn., Rev. Keith R. Miller
Div. of Missions, Chpsn., Rev. John Ragsdale
Bd. of Pensions: Pres., William Kautz, New Cumberland, PA; Business Mgr., Dr. James D. Yoder, Myerstown, PA 17067

Periodical

Doors and Windows

The Evangelical Covenant Church

The Evangelical Covenant Church has its roots in historic Christianity as it emerged during the Protestant Reformation, in the biblical instruction of the Lutheran State Church of Sweden and in the great spiritual awakenings of the 19th century.

The Covenant Church adheres to the affirmations of the Protestant Reformation regarding the Holy Scriptures, believing that the Old and the

101

New Testament are the Word of God and the only perfect rule for faith, doctrine and conduct. It has traditionally valued the historic confessions of the Christian church, particularly the Apostles' Creed, while at the same time emphasizing the sovereignty of the Word over all creedal interpretations. It has especially cherished the pietistic restatement of the doctrine of justification by faith as basic to its dual task of evangelism and Christian nurture. It recognizes the New Testament emphasis upon personal faith in Jesus Christ as Savior and Lord, the reality of a fellowship of believers which acknowledges but transcends theological differences and the belief in baptism and the Lord's Supper as divinely ordained sacraments of the church.

While the denomination has traditionally practiced the baptism of infants, in conformity with its principle of freedom it has also recognized the practice of believer baptism. The principle of personal freedom, so highly esteemed by the Covenant, is to be distinguished from the individualism that disregards the centrality of the Word of God and the mutual responsibilities and disciplines of the spiritual community.

Headquarters
5101 N. Francisco Ave., Chicago, IL 60625 Tel. (773)784-3000 Fax (773)784-4366
Media Contact, Pres., Dr. Glenn R. Palmberg

Officers
Pres., Dr. Glenn R. Palmberg
Vice-Pres., Rev. Timothy C. Ek
Sec., John R. Hunt
Treas., Dean A. Lundgren

ADMINISTRATIVE BOARDS
Bd. of Christian Educ. & Discipleship: Exec. Dir., Rev. Doreen L. Olson
Bd. of Church Growth & Evangelism: Exec. Dir., Dr. James E. Persson
Bd. of Covenant Women Ministries: Exec. Dir., Rev. Deirdre M. Banks
Bd. of Human Resources: Advisory Member, John R. Hunt
Bd. of the Ministry: Exec. Dir., Rev. Donn N. Engebretson
Bd. of Pensions: Dir. of Pensions, John R. Hunt
Bd. of Communication: Exec. Dir., Donald L. Meyer
Bd. of World Mission: Exec. Dir., Rev. James W. Gustafson
Bd. of Benevolence: Pres. of Covenant Ministries of Benevolence, Paul V. Peterson, 5145 N. California Ave., Chicago, IL 60625
North Park University & Theological Sem.: Pres., Dr. David G. Horner, 3225 W. Foster Ave., Chicago, IL 60625

SERVICE ORGANIZATIONS
National Covenant Properties: Pres., David W. Johnson, 5101 N. Francisco, Chicago, IL 60625 Tel. (773)784-3000
Covenant Trust Company: Pres., Gilman G. Robinson, 5101 N. Francisco, Chicago, IL 60625 Tel. (773)784-9911

REGIONAL CONFERENCES OF THE E.C.C.
Central Conference: Supt., Herbert M. Freedholm, 3319 W. Foster Ave., Chicago, IL 60625 Tel. (773)267-3060
East Coast Conference: Supt., Robert C. Dvorak, Missionary Rd., Cromwell, CT 06416 Tel. (860)635-2691
Great Lakes Conference: Supt., David S. Dahlberg, 70 W. Streetsboro St., P.O. Box 728, Hudson, OH 44236 Tel. (330)655-9345
Midwest Conference: Supt., Kenneth P. Carlson, 13504 W. Center Rd. #229, Omaha, NE 68144 Tel. (402)334-3060
North Pacific Conference: Acting Supt., Don Robinson, 925 116th Ave. NE, # 221, Bellevue, WA 98004 Tel. (425)451-7434
Northwest Conference: Supt., Paul Erickson, 4721 E. 31st St., Minneapolis, MN 55406 Tel. (612)721-4893
Pacific Southwest Conference: Supt., John D. Notehelfer, 2120 Foothill Blvd., #215, La-Verne, CA 91750 Tel. (909)596-6790
Southeast Conference: Supt., Kurt A. Miericke, 1759 W. Broadway St., #7, Oviedo, FL 32765 Tel. (407)977-8009
E.C.C. of Canada: Supt., Jeffrey Anderson, 630 Westchester Rd., Strathmore, AB T1P 1H8 Tel. (403)934-6200
Midsouth Region: Dir. MidSouth Ministries, Rick Larson, 14400 Sylvanfield Dr., Houston, TX 77014 Tel. (281)583-4673
E.C.C. of Alaska: Field Dir., Paul W. Wilson, P.O. Box 190729, Anchorage, AK 99519 Tel. (907)562-8623

Periodicals
Covenant Companion; Covenant Quarterly; Covenant Home Altar

The Evangelical Free Church of America
In October 1884, 27 representatives from Swedish churches met in Boone, Iowa, to establish the Swedish Evangelical Free Church. In the fall of that same year, two Norwegian-Danish groups began worship and fellowship (in Boston and in Tacoma) and by 1912 had established the Norwegian-Danish Evangelical Free Church Association. These two denominations, representing 275 congregations, came together at a merger conference in 1950.

The Evangelical Free Church of America is an association of local, autonomous churches across the United States and Canada, blended together by common principles, policies and practices. A 12-point statement addresses the major doctrines but also provides for differences of understanding on minor issues of faith and practice.

Overseas outreach includes 500 missionaries serving in 31 countries.

Headquarters

901 East 78th St., Minneapolis, MN 55420-1300 Tel. (612)854-1300 Fax (612)853-8488 Media Contact, Exec. Dir. of Ministry Advancement, Timothy Addington

Officers

Acting Pres./Exec. Vice-Pres., Rev. William Hamel

Moderator, Ronald Aucutt, 3417 Silver Maple Pl., Falls Church, VA 22042

Vice-Moderator, Rev. Mark J. Wold, 41827 Higgins Way, Fremont, CA 94539

Sec., Dr. Roland Peterson, 235 Craigbrook Way, NE, Fridley, MN 55432

Vice-Sec., Rev. William S. Wick, 92 South Main, Northfield, VT 05663

Chief Fin. Ofc., Robert Peterson

Exec. Dir., Evangelical Free Church Mission, Dr. Ben Swatsky

Assoc. Dir. of Mission USA, Rev. Steve Hudson

Periodicals

Evangelical Beacon; Pursuit

Evangelical Friends International - North American Region

The organization restructured from Evangelical Friends Alliance in 1990 to become internationalized for the benefit of its world-wide contacts. The North America Region continues to function within the United States as EFA formerly did. The organization represents one corporate step of denominational unity, brought about as a result of several movements of spiritual renewal within the Society of Friends. These movements are: (1) the general evangelical renewal within Christianity, (2) the new scholarly recognition of the evangelical nature of 17th-century Quakerism, and (3) EFA, which was formed in 1965.

The EFA is conservative in theology and makes use of local pastors. Sunday morning worship includes singing, Scripture reading, a period of open worship and a sermon by the pastor.

Headquarters

5350 Broadmoor Cir. NW, Canton, OH 44709 Tel. (330)493-1660 Fax (330)493-0852 Media Contact, Gen. Supt., Dr. John P. Williams, Jr.

YEARLY MEETINGS

Evangelical Friends Church, Eastern Region, Wayne Ickes, 5350 Broadmoor Cir., N.W., Canton, OH 44709 Tel. (330)493-1660 Fax (330)493-0852

Rocky Mountain YM, John Brawner, 3350 Reed St., Wheat Ridge, CO 80033 Tel. (303)238-5200 Fax (303)238-5200

Mid-America YM, Duane Hansen, 2018 Maple, Wichita, KS 67213 Tel. (316)267-0391 Fax (316)267-0681

Northwest YM, Mark Ankeny, 200 N. Meridian St., Newberg, OR 97132 Tel. (503)538-9419 Fax (503)538-9410

Alaska YM, Sam Williams, P.O. Box 687, Kotzebue, AK 99752 Tel. (907)442-3906

Periodical

The Friends Voice

Evangelical Lutheran Church in America

The Evangelical Lutheran Church in America (ELCA) was organized April 30-May 3, 1987, in Columbus, Ohio, bringing together the 2.25 million-member American Lutheran Church, the 2.85 million-member Lutheran Church in America, and the 100,000-member Association of Evangelical Lutheran Churches.

The ELCA is, through its predecessors, the oldest of the major U.S. Lutheran churches. In the mid-17th century, a Dutch Lutheran congregation was formed in New Amsterdam (now New York). Other early congregations were begun by German and Scandinavian immigrants to Delaware, Pennsylvania, New York and the Carolinas.

The first Lutheran association of congregations, the Pennsylvania Ministerium, was organized in 1748 under Henry Melchior Muhlenberg. Numerous Lutheran organizations were formed as immigration continued and the United States grew.

In 1960, the American Lutheran Church (ALC) was created through a merger of an earlier American Lutheran Church, formed in 1930, the Evangelical Lutheran Church, begun in 1917, and the United Evangelical Lutheran Church in America started in 1896. In 1963 the Lutheran Free Church, formed in 1897, merged with the ALC.

In 1962, the Lutheran Church in America (LCA) was formed by a merger of the United Lutheran Church, formed in 1918, with the Augustana Lutheran Church, begun in 1860, the American Evangelical Lutheran Church, founded in 1872, and the Finnish Lutheran Church or Suomi Synod, founded in 1891.

The Association of Evangelical Lutheran Churches arose in 1976 from a doctrinal split with the Lutheran Church-Missouri Synod.

The ELCA, through its predecessor church bodies, was a founding member of the Lutheran World Federation, the World Council of Churches, and the National Council of the Churches of Christ in the USA.

The church is divided into 65 geographical areas or synods. These 65 synods are grouped into nine regions for mission, joint programs and service.

Headquarters

8765 W. Higgins Rd., Chicago, IL 60631 Tel. (773)380-2700 Fax (773)380-1465 Media Contact, Dir. for News, Frank Imhoff, Tel. (773)380-2955 Fax (773)380-2406 E-mail: info@elca.org Website: http://www.elca.org

103

Officers

Presiding Bishop, Rev. Dr. H. George Anderson
Sec., Rev. Dr. Lowell G. Almen
Treas., Richard L. McAuliffe
Vice-Pres., Dr. Addie J. Butler
Exec. for Admn., Rev. Dr. Robert N. Bacher
Office of the Bishop: Exec. Asst. for Federal Chaplaincies, Rev. Lloyd W. Lyngdal; Exec. Asst., Rev. Michael L. Cooper-White

DIVISIONS

Div. for Congregational Min.: Co-Exec. Dir., Rev. Mark R. Moller-Gunderson; Co-Exec. Dir., Rev. M. Wyvetta Bullock; Bd. Chpsn., Rev. Nancy I. Amacher; Lutheran Youth Organization, Pres., Rebecca Lawrence
Div. for Higher Educ. & Schools: Exec. Dir., Rev. Dr. W. Robert Sorensen; Bd. Chpsn., Rev. John G. Andreasen
Div. for Global Mission: Exec. Dir., Rev. Bonnie L. Jensen; Bd. Chpsn., Dr. Winston D. Persaud
Div. for Ministry: Exec. Dir., Rev. Dr. Joseph M. Wagner; Bd. Chpsn., Dr. Nelvin Vos
Div. for Outreach: Exec. Dir., Rev. Dr. Richard A. Magnus, Jr.; Bd. Chpsn., Rev. Julius Carroll, IV
Div. for Church in Society: Exec. Dir., Rev. Charles S. Miller, Jr.; Chpsn., Ingrid Christiansen

COMMISSIONS

Comm. for Multicultural Ministries: Exec. Dir., Rev. Frederick E.N. Rajan; Chpsn., Rev. W. Arthur Lewis
Comm. for Women: Exec. Dir., Joanne Chadwick; Chpsn., Rev. Ann M. Tiemeyer

CHURCHWIDE UNITS

Conference of Bishops: Asst. to the Bishop, Rev. Michael L. Cooper-White; Chpsn., Rev. Charles H. Maahs
ELCA Foundation: Exec. Dir., The Rev. Donald M. Hallberg, Chpsn., Ms. Barbara L. Bauer
ELCA Publishing House: Exec. Dir., Rev. Marvin L. Roloff; Bd. Chpsn., Todd P. Enedahl
ELCA Bd. of Pensions: Exec. Dir., John G. Kapanke; Bd. Chpsn, Emma Graeber Porter
Women of the ELCA: Exec. Dir., Catherine I. H. Braasch; Bd. Chpsn., Sharrol L. Bernahl

DEPARTMENTS

Dept. for Communication, Dir., Rev. Eric C. Shafer
Dept. for Ecumenical Affairs, Dir., Rev. Daniel F. Martensen; Committee Chpsn., Rev. Duane Hilarson
Dept. for Human Resources, Dir., Else Thompson
Dept. for Research & Evaluation, Dir., Kenneth W. Inskeep
Dept. for Synodical Relations, Dir., Rev. Michael L. Cooper-White

SYNODICAL BISHOPS

Region 1

Alaska, Rev. Larry J. Jorgenson (Interim), 1847 W. Northern Lights Blvd., #2, Anchorage, AK 99517-3343 Tel. (907)272-8899 Fax(907)274-3141

Northwest Washington, Rev. Donald H. Maier, 5519 Pinney Ave. N, Seattle, WA 98103-5899 Tel. (206)783-9292 Fax(206)783-9833
Southwestern Washington, Rev. David C. Wold, 420 121st St., S., Tacoma, WA 98444-5218 Tel. (253)535-8300 Fax(253)535-8315
Eastern Washington-Idaho, Rev. Robert M. Keller, 314 South Spruce St., Ste. A, Spokane, WA 99204-1098 Tel. (509)838-9871 Fax(509)838-0941
Oregon, Rev. Paul R. Swanson, 2800 N. Vancouver Ave., Ste. 101, Portland, OR 97227-1643 Tel. (503) 413-4191 Fax(503)413-2407
Montana, Rev. Dr. Mark R. Ramseth, 2415 13th Ave. S., Great Falls, MT 59405-5199 Tel. (406)453-1461 Fax(406)761-4632
Int. Regional Coord., Greig Anderson, Region 1, 766-B John St., Seattle, WA 98109-5186 Tel. (206)624-0093 Fax(206)626-0987

Region 2

Sierra Pacific, Rev. Robert W. Mattheis, 401 Roland Way, #215, Oakland, CA 94621-2011 Tel. (510)430-0500 Fax(510)430-8730
Southern California (West), Bishop, Rev. Paul W. Egertson, 1340 S. Bonnie Brae St., Los Angeles, CA 90006-5416 Tel. (213)387-8183 Fax(213)387-1963
Pacifica, Rev. Murray D. Finck, 23655 Via Del Rio, Ste. B, Yorba Linda, CA 92887-2738 Tel. (714)692-2791 Fax(714)692-9317
Grand Canyon, Rev. Dr. Howard E. Wennes, 4423 N. 24th St., Ste. 400, Phoenix, AZ 85016-5544 Tel. (602)957-3223 Fax(602)956-8104
Rocky Mountain, Rev. Allan C. Bjornberg, 455 Sherman St., Ste. 160, Denver, CO 80223 Tel. (303)777-6700 Fax(303)733-0750
Region 2, Admn. ELCA(part-time), Beverly Anderson, 18829 Grandview Dr., Sun City West, AZ 85375 Tel. (602)214-9779 Fax(602)214-7660

Region 3

Western North Dakota, Rev. Duane C. Danielson, 1614 Capitol Way, P.O. Box 370, Bismarck, ND 58502-0370 Tel. (701)223-5312 Fax(701)223-1435
Eastern North Dakota, Rev. Richard J. Foss, 1703 32nd Ave., S., Fargo, ND 58103-5936 Tel. (701)232-3381 Fax(701)232-3180
South Dakota, Rev. Andrea F. De Groot-Nesdahl, Augustana College, 29th & S. Summit, Sioux Falls, SD 57197-0001 Tel. (605)336-4011 Fax(605)336-4028
Northwestern Minnesota, Rev. Arlen D. Hermodson, Concordia College, 901 8th St. S., Moorhead, MN 56562-0001 Tel. (218)299-3019 Fax(218)299-3363
Northeastern Minnesota, Rev. E. Peter Strommen, 3900 London Rd., Duluth, MN 55804-2241 Tel. (218)525-1947 Fax(218)525-7672
Southwestern Minnesota, Rev. Stanley N. Olson,

175 E. Bridge St., P.O. Box 499, Redwood Falls, MN 56283-0499 Tel. (507)637-3904 Fax(507)637-2809

Minneapolis Area, Rev. David W. Olson, 122 W. Franklin Ave., Ste. 600, Minneapolis, MN 55404-2474 Tel. (612)870-3610 Fax(612)870-0170

Saint Paul Area, Rev. Mark S. Hanson, 105 W. University Ave., St. Paul, MN 55103-2094 Tel. (651)224-4313 Fax(651)224-5646

Southeastern Minnesota, Rev. Glenn W. Nycklemoe, Assisi Heights, 1001-14 St. NW, Rochester, MN 55901-2511 Tel. (507)280-9457 Fax(507)280-8824

Regional Coord., Rev. Craig A. Boehlke, Region 3, Luther Seminary, Bockman Hall, 2481 Como Ave., St. Paul, MN 55108-1445 Tel. (651)649-0454 Fax(651)649-0468

Region 4

Nebraska, Rev. Dr. Richard N. Jessen, 4980 S. 118th St., Ste. D, Omaha, NE 68137-2220 Tel. (402)896-5311 Fax(402)896-5354

Central States, Rev. Dr. Charles H. Maahs, 6400 Glenwood St., Ste. 210, Shawnee Mission, KS 66202-4021 Tel. (913)362-0733 Fax(913)362-0317

Arkansas-Oklahoma, Rev. Floyd M. Schoenhals, 6911 S. 66th E. Ave., Ste. 200, Tulsa, OK 74133-1748 Tel. (918)492-4288 Fax(918)491-6275

Northern Texas-Northern Louisiana, Rev. Mark B. Herbener, 1230 Riverbend Dr., Ste. 105, P.O. Box 560587, Dallas, TX 75356-0587 Tel. (214)637-6865 Fax(214)637-4805

Southwestern Texas, Rev. James E. Bennett, 8918 Tesoro Dr., Ste. 109, P.O. Box 171270, San Antonio, TX 78217-8270 Tel. (210)824-0068 Fax (210)824-7009

Texas-Louisiana Gulf Coast, Rev. Paul J. Blom, 12707 N. Freeway, #580, Houston, TX 77060-1239 Tel. (281)873-5665 Fax(281)875-4716

Regional Coord., Rev. Charles H. Maahs, Central States Synod, 6400 Glenwood St., Ste. 210, Shawnee Mission, KS 66202-4021 Tel.(913)362-0733 Fax(913)362-0317

Region 5

Metropolitan Chicago, Rev. Kenneth R. Olsen, 18 S. Michigan Ave., Rm. 605, Chicago, IL 60603-3283 Tel. (312)346-3150 Fax(312)346-3486

Northern Illinois, Rev. Gary M. Wollersheim, 103 W. State St., Rockford, IL 61101-1105 Tel. (815) 964-9934 Fax(815)964-2295

Central/Southern Illinois, Rev. Alton Zenker, 524 S. Fifth St., Springfield, IL 62701-1822 Tel. (217)753-7915 Fax(217)753-7976

Southeastern Iowa, Rev. Phillip L. Hougen, 2635 Northgate Dr., P.O. Box 3167, Iowa City, IA 52244-3167 Tel. (319)338-1273 Fax (319)351-8677

Western Iowa, Rev. Curtis H. Miller, 318 E. Fifth St., P.O. Box 577, Storm Lake, IA 50588-0577 Tel. (712)732-4968 Fax(712)732-6540

Northeastern Iowa, Rev. Steven L. Ullestad, 201-20th St. SW, P.O. Box 804, Waverly, IA 50677-0804 Tel. (319)352-1414 Fax(319)352-1416

Northern Great Lakes, Rev. Dale R. Skogman, 1029 N. Third St., Marquette, MI 49855-3588 Tel. (906)228-2300 Fax(906)228-2527

Northwest Synod of Wisconsin, Rev. Robert D. Berg, 12 W. Marshall St., P.O. Box 730, Rice Lake, WI 54868-0730 Tel. (715)234-3373 Fax(715)234-4183

East-Central Synod of Wisconsin, Rev. John C. Beem, 16 Tri-Park Way, Appleton, WI 54914-1658 Tel. (920)734-5381 Fax(920)734-5074

Greater Milwaukee, Rev. Peter Rogness, 1212 S. Layton Blvd., Milwaukee, WI 53215-1653 Tel. (414)671-1212 Fax (414)671-1756

South-Central Synod of Wisconsin, Rev. Dr. Jon S. Enslin, 2909 Landmark Pl., Ste. 202, Madison, WI 53713-4237 Tel. (608)270-0201 Fax (608)270-0202

La Crosse Area, Rev. April Ulring Larson, 3462 Losey Blvd. S., La Crosse, WI 54601-7217 Tel. (608)788-5000 Fax (608)788-4916

Regional Coord., Rev. Carl R. Evenson, Region 5, 104 E. Wisconsin Ave., Neenah, WI 54956 Tel. (920)720-9880 Fax (920)725-9210

Region 6

Southeast Michigan, Rev. Robert A. Rimbo, 218 Fisher Bldg., 3011 W. Grand Blvd., Detroit, MI 48202-3011 Tel. (313)875-1881 Fax (313)875-1889

North/West Lower Michigan, Rev. Gary L. Hansen, 801 S. Waverly Rd., Ste. 201, Lansing, MI 48917-4254 Tel. (517)321-5066 Fax (517)321-2612

Indiana-Kentucky, Rev. James R. Stuck, 911 E. 86th St., Ste. 200, Indianapolis, IN 46240-1840 Tel. (317)253-3522 Fax (317)254-5666

Northwestern Ohio, Rev. Marcus C. Lohrmann, 621 Bright Rd., Findlay, OH 45840-6987 Tel. (419) 423-3664 Fax (419)423-8801

Northeastern Ohio, Rev. Marcus J. Miller, 282 W. Bowery, 3rd Fl., Akron, OH 44307-2598 Tel. (330)253-1500 Fax (330)253-2199

Southern Ohio, Rev. Dr. Callon W. Holloway, Jr., 57 E. Main St., Columbus, OH 43215-7102 Tel. (614)464-3532 Fax (614)464-3422

Regional Coord., Marilyn Smith, Region 6, PO Box 91, Bluffton, OH 45817 Tel. (419)358-9816 Fax (419)358-9816

Region 7

New Jersey, Rev. E. Roy Riley, Jr., 1930 State Hwy. 33, Trenton, NJ 08690-1799 Tel. (609) 586-6800 Fax (609)586-1597

New England, Rev. Robert L. Isaksen, 20 Upland St., Worcester, MA 01604-1624 Tel. (508)791-1530 Fax (508)797-9295

Metropolitan New York, Rev. Stephen P. Bouman, 390 Park Ave., S., 7th Floor, New York, NY 10016-8803 Tel. (212)532-5369 Fax (212)532-5078

Upstate New York, Rev. Dr. Lee M. Miller, 3049

105

E. Genesee St., Syracuse, NY 13224-1699 Tel. (315)446-2502 Fax (315)446-4642

Northeastern Pennsylvania, Rev. Dr. David R. Strobel, 4865 Hamilton Blvd., Wescosville, PA 18106-9705 Tel. (610)395-6891 Fax (610)398-7083

Southeastern Pennsylvania, Rev. Roy G. Almquist, 506 Haws Ave., Norristown, PA 19401-4543 Tel. (610)278-7342 Fax (610)278-9994

Slovak Zion, Rev. Juan Cobrda, 8340 N. Oleander Ave., Niles, IL 60648-2552 Tel. (847)965-2475 Fax (847)583-8015

Regional Coord., Rev. Richard H. Summy, Lutheran Theol. Seminary at Philadelphia, Hagan Hall, 7301 Germantown Ave., Philadelphia, PA 19119-1794 Tel. (215)248-4616 Fax (215)248-4577

Region 8

Northwestern Pennsylvania, Rev. Paul E. Spring, Rte. 257, Salina Rd., P.O. Box 338, Seneca, PA 16346-0338 Tel. (814)677-5706 Fax (814)676-8591

Southwestern Pennsylvania, Rev. Donald J. McCoid, 9625 Perry Hwy., Pittsburgh, PA 15237-5590 Tel. (412)367-8222 Fax (412)369-8840

Allegheny, Rev. Gregory R. Pile, 701 Quail Ave., Altoona, PA 16602-3010 Tel. (814)942-1042 Fax (814)941-9259

Lower Susquehanna, Rev. Dr. Guy S. Edmiston, Jr., 900 S. Arlington Ave., Rm. 208, Harrisburg, PA 17109-5031 Tel. (717)652-1852 Fax (717)652-2504

Upper Susquehanna, Rev. Dr. A. Donald Main, Rt. 192 & Reitz Blvd., P.O. Box 36, Lewisburg, PA 17837-0036 Tel. (717)524-9778 Fax (717)524-9757

Delaware-Maryland, Rev. Dr. George P. Mocko, 7604 York Rd., Baltimore, MD 21204-7570 Tel. (410)825-9520 Fax (410)825-6745

Metropolitan Washington, D.C., Rev. Theodore F. Schneider, 224 E. Capitol St., Washington, DC 20003-1036 Tel. (202)543-8610 Fax (202)543-0786

West Virginia-Western Maryland, Rev. Ralph Dunkin, The Atrium, 503 Morganton Avenue, Ste. 100, Fairmont, WV 26554-4374 Tel. (304)363-4030 Fax (304)366-9846

Regional Coord., Dir., Rev. James E. Miley, Lutheran Theological Sem. at Gettysburg, 61 N. West Confederate Ave., Gettysburg, PA 17325-1795 Tel. (717)334-6286 Ext. 2133 Fax (717)334-0323

Region 9

Virginia, Rev. Richard F. Bansemer, Roanoke College, Bittle Hall, P.O. Drawer 70, Salem, VA 24153-0070 Tel. (540)389-1000 Fax (540)389-5962

North Carolina, Rev. Leonard H. Bolick, 1988 Lutheran Synod Dr., Salisbury, NC 28144-4480 Tel. (704)633-4861 Fax (704)638-0508

South Carolina, Rev. David A. Donges, 1003 Richland St., P.O. Box 43, Columbia, SC 29202-0043 Tel. (803)765-0590 Fax (803)252-5558

Southeastern, Rev. Ronald B. Warren, 756 W. Peachtree St. NW, Atlanta, GA 30308-1188 Tel. (404)873-1977 Fax (404)876-1734

Florida-Bahamas, Rev. William B. Trexler, 3838 W. Cypress St., Tampa, FL 33607-4897 Tel. (813)876-7660 Fax (813)870-0826

Caribbean, Rev. Francisco L. Sosa, Calle Constitucion 363, Puerto Nuevo, PR 00920 Tel. (787) 273-8300 Fax (787)273-7877

Regional Coord., Dr. Dorothy L. Jeffcoat, Region 9, Lutheran Theological So. Seminary, 4201 N. Main St., Columbia, SC 29203 Tel. (803)754-2879 Fax (803)786-6499

Periodicals

The Lutheran; Lutheran Partners; Lutheran Woman Today; Currents in Theology and Mission

Evangelical Lutheran Synod

The Evangelical Lutheran Synod had its beginning among the Norwegian settlers who brought with them their Lutheran heritage. The Synod was organized in 1853. It was reorganized in 1918 by those who desired to adhere to the synod's principles not only in word but also in deed.

The Synod owns and operates Bethany Lutheran College and Bethany Lutheran Theological Seminary. It has congregations in 20 states and maintains foreign missions in Peru, Chile, the Czech Republic and Ukraine. It operates a seminary in Lima, Peru and in Ternopil, Ukraine.

Headquarters

6 Browns Court, Mankato, MN 56001 Tel. (507) 344-5356 Fax (507)344-5426

Media Contact, Pres., Rev. George Orvick

E-mail: gorvick@blc.edu

Website: http://www.EvLuthSyn.org

Officers

Pres., Rev. George Orvick

Sec., Rev. Craig Ferkenstad, Rt. 3, Box 40, St. Peter, MN 56082

Treas., LeRoy W. Meyer, 1038 S. Lewis Ave., Lombard, IL 60148

OTHER ORGANIZATIONS

Lutheran Synod Book Co., Bethany Lutheran College, Mankato, MN 56001

Bethany Lutheran Theological Seminary, 6 Browns Court, Mankato, MN 56001

Periodicals

Lutheran Sentinel; Lutheran Synod Quarterly

Evangelical Mennonite Church

The Evangelical Mennonite Church is an American denomination in the European free church tradition, tracing its heritage to the Reformation period of the 16th century. The Swiss Brethren of that time believed that salvation could come only by repentance for sins and faith in Jesus Christ; that baptism was only for believers; and that the church should be separate from controls of the state. Their enemies called them Anabaptists, since they insisted on rebaptizing believers who had been baptized as infants. As the Anabaptist movement spread to other countries, Menno Simons became its principal leader. In time his followers were called Mennonites.

In 1693 a Mennonite minister, Jacob Amman, insisted that the church should adopt a more conservative position on dress and style of living and should more rigidly enforce the "ban"—the church's method of disciplining disobedient members. Amman's insistence finally resulted in a division within the South German Mennonite groups; his followers became known as the Amish.

Migrations to America, involving both Mennonites and Amish, took place in the 1700s and 1800s, for both religious and economic reasons. The Evangelical Mennonite Church was formed in 1866 out of a spiritual awakening among the Amish in Indiana. It was first known as the Egly Amish, after its founder Bishop Henry Egly. Bishop Egly emphasized regeneration, separation and nonconformity to the world. His willingness to rebaptize anyone who had been baptized without repentance created a split in his church, prompting him to gather a new congregation in 1866. The conference, which has met annually since 1895, united a number of other congregations of like mind. This group became The Defenseless Mennonite Church in 1898 and has been known as the Evangelical Mennonite Church since 1948.

Headquarters
1420 Kerrway Ct., Fort Wayne, IN 46805 Tel. (219)423-3649 Fax (219)420-1905
Media Contact, Admn. Asst., Karen Bohn

Officers
Pres., Rev. Donald W. Roth
Chpsn.., Rev. Gary Gates, 25281 80th Ave., Lawton, MI 49065
Vice-Chpsn., Rev. Bryce Winteregg, 11331 Coldwater Rd., Ft. Wayne, IN 46845
Sec., Gene Rupp, c/o Taylor University, 236 W. Reade Ave., Upland, IN 46989
Treas., Elmer Lengacher, 11507 Bull Rapids Rd., Grabill, IN 46741

Periodical
EMC Today

Evangelical Methodist Church
The Evangelical Methodist Church was organized in 1946 at Memphis, Tenn., largely as a movement of people who opposed modern liberalism and wished for a return to the historic Wesleyan position. In 1960, it merged with the Evangel Church (formerly Evangelistic Tabernacles) and with the People's Methodist Church in 1962.

Headquarters
P.O. Box 17070, Indianapolis, IN 46217 Tel. (317)780-8017 Fax (317)780-8078
Media Contact, Gen. Conf. Sec.-Treas., Rev. James A. Coulston

Officers
Gen. Supt., Dr. Edward W. Williamson
Gen. Conf. Sec.-Treas., Rev. James A. Coulston

Evangelical Presbyterian Church
The Evangelical Presbyterian Church (EPC), established in March 1981, is a conservative denomination of 9 geographic presbyteries - 8 in the United States and one in Argentina. From its inception with 12 churches, the EPC has grown to 186 churches with a membership of over 60,000.

Planted firmly within the historic Reformed tradition, evangelical in spirit, the EPC places high priority on church planting and development along with world missions. Fifty-six missionaries serve the church's mission.

Based on the truth of Scripture and adhering to the Westminster Confession of Faith plus its Book of Order, the denomination is committed to the "essentials of the faith." The historic motto "In essentials, unity; in nonessentials, liberty; in all things charity" catches the irenic spirit of the EPC, along with the Ephesians theme, "truth in love."

The Evangelical Presbyterian Church is a member of the World Alliance of Reformed Churches, National Association of Evangelicals, World Evangelical Fellowship and the Evangelical Council for Financial Accountability. Observers annually attend the North American Presbyterian and Reformed Council (NAPARC).

Headquarters
Office of the General Assembly, 29140 Buckingham Ave., Ste. 5, Livonia, MI 48154 Tel. (734)261-2001 Fax (734)261-3282
Media Contact, Stated Clk., Dr. L. Edward Davis, 29140 Buckingham Ave., Ste. 5, Livonia, MI 48154 Tel. (734)261-2001 Fax (734)261-3282
E-mail: EPCHURCH@aol.com
Website: http://www. epc.org

Officers
Mod., Mr. Alan Smith, 5408 Galley Ct. Fairfax, VA 22032
Administration Committee, Chmn., Dr. Richard Little, 2539 Merrimont Dr., Winston-Salem, NC 27106
Stated Clk., Dr. L. Edward Davis

PERMANENT COMMITTEES

Committee on Admn., Chmn., Dr. Richard Little, 2539 Merrimont Dr., Winston-Salem, NC 27106

Committee on National Outreach, Chmn., —

Committee on World Outreach, Chmn., Dr. Bern Draper, 8103 Saguro Ridge Rd., Parker, CO 80134

Committee on Ministerial Vocation, Chmn., Dr. William Moore, Trinity Presbyterian Church, 10101 W. Ann Arbor Rd., Plymouth, MI 48170

Comm. on Christian Educ. & Publ., Chmn., Rev. Bruce Spear, Bear Creek EPC, 3101 S. Kipling, Lakewood, CO 80227

Committee on Women's Ministries, Chmn., Anne Blackley, 323 Pine Valley Dr., Wilmington, NC 28412

Committee on Theology, Chmn., Dr. James Russell, 3228 Franklin Ave., Laurel, MI 39441

Committee on Student and Young Adult Ministries (Formerly "Committee on Youth Ministries"), Chmn., Rev. Rick Stauffer, North Park EPC, 600 Ingomer Rd., Wexford, PA 15090

PRESBYTERIES

Central South, Stated Clk., Rev. Dennis Flach, New Covenant Evangelical Presbyterian Church, 201 Magnolia Pl., Natchez, MS 39120

East, Stated Clk., Frank Johnson, 136 Chaucer Pl., Cherry Hills, NJ 08003

Florida, Stated Clk., Rev. Robert Garment, Trinity EPC, 5150 Oleander, Ft. Pierce, FL 34982

Mid-America, Stated Clk., Kenneth Breckner, Central Presbyterian Church, 7700 Davis Dr., St. Louis, MO 63105

Mid-Atlantic, Stated Clk., Llew Fischer, 3164 Golf Colony Dr., Salem, VA 24153

Midwest, Stated Clk., Alton Bennett, 29140 Buckingham Ave., Ste. 5, Livonia, MI 48154

Southeast, Stated Clk., Rev. Sam Harris, Valleybrook Pres. Church, 6100 Hixson Pike, Hixson, TN 37343

West, Stated Clk., Rev. Marc Huebl, Covenant Comm. Pres. Church, 15161 E. Hampden Ave., Aurora, CO 80014-3905

St. Andrews, Stated Clk., Rev. Juan Jose Mejias, San Antonio de Padua Mission Church, Godoy Cruz 99, 1718 San Antonio de Padua, Pica, Buenos Aires, Argentina

Fellowship of Evangelical Bible Churches

Formerly known as Evangelical Mennonite Brethren, this body emanates from the Russian immigration of Mennonites into the United States, 1873-74. Established with the emphasis on true repentance, conversion and a committed life to Jesus as Savior and Lord, the conference was founded in 1889 under the leadership of Isaac Peters and Aaron Wall. The founding churches were located in Mountain Lake, Minn., and in Henderson and Janzen, Neb. The conference has since grown to a fellowship of 39 churches with approximately 4,400 members in Argentina, Canada, Paraguay and the United States.

Foreign missions have been a vital ingredient of the total ministry. Today missions constitute about 35 percent of the total annual budget, with one missionary for every 30 members in the home churches. The conference does not develop and administer foreign mission fields of its own, but actively participates with existing evangelical "faith" mission societies. The conference has representation on several mission boards and has missionaries serving under approximately 41 different agencies around the world.

The church is holding fast to the inerrancy of Scripture, the Deity of Christ and the need for spiritual regeneration of man from his sinful natural state by faith in the death, burial and resurrection of Jesus Christ as payment for sin. Members look forward to the imminent return of Jesus Christ and retain a sense of urgency to share the gospel with those who have never heard of God's redeeming love.

Headquarters

5800 S. 14th St., Omaha, NE 68107 Tel. (402) 731-4780 Fax (402)731-1173

Admn., Robert L. Frey, 5800 S. 14th St., Omaha, NE 68107 Tel. (402)731-4780 Fax (402)731-1173

E-mail: febcoma@aol.com

Officers

Pres., Rev. C. Dwain Holsapple, 3006 Eastview St., Abbotsford, BC V2S 6W3 (U.S. Address) P.O. Box 1891, Sumas, WA 98295-1891 Tel. [O](604)859-9937, [H](604)852-1367 Fax (604)859-9108

E-mail: holsappl@uniserve.com

Vice-President, Rev. Frank Wiens, P.O. Box 50773, Billings, MT 59105-0773 Tel. (406) 254-6961

E-mail: Fewen@aol.com

Rec. Sec., Stan Seifert, 35351 Munroe Ave., Abbotsford, BC V2S 1L4 Tel. (604)852-3253 Fax (604)852-7887

Admn., Robert L. Frey, 5800 South 14th St., Omaha, NE 68107-3584 Tel. (402)731-4780 Fax (402)731-1173

E-mail: febcoma@aol.com

Commission on Churches, Chpsn., Rev. Frank Eidse, 467 2nd Ave. SE, Swift Current, SK 59H 1H3 Tel. [O](306)773-8785, [H] (306)773-0592 Fax (306)778-7403

Commission on Education, Chpsn., Rev. Ray Reimer, 5005 Adams, Lincoln, NE 68504-2126 Tel. [O](402)489-2600 [H](402)466-6409

E-mail: rayreimer@juno.com

Commission on Missions, Chpsn., Gerald Epp,

Box 86, Waldheim, SK S0K 4R0 Tel. (306)945-2023
E-mail: ggepp@sk.sympatico.ca
Commission of Trustees, Chpsn., Elvin Fast, Box 1106, Steinbach, MB R0A 2A0 Tel. (204)326-2339 Fax (204)326-6741
Commission on Church Planting, Chpsn., Rev. Randy Smart, Box 111, Stuartburn, MB R0A 2B0 Tel. [O](204)425-3383 [H](204)425-3990 E-mail: smart@aecc.escape.ca
Comm. on Women's Ministries, Chpsn., Pat Gerbrandt, Box 444, Grunthal, MB R0A 0R0 Tel. (204)434-6600
E-mail: gerbrand@mbnet.mb.ca

Periodical
Gospel Tidings

Fellowship of Fundamental Bible Churches

The churches in this body represent the 1939 separation from the Methodist Protestant Church, when some 50 delegates and pastors (approximately one- third of the Eastern Conference) withdrew to protest the union of the Methodist Protestant Church with the Methodist Episcopal Church and the Methodist Episcopal Church South, and what they considered the liberal tendencies of those churches. These churches subsequently changed their name to the Bible Protestant Church. In 1985, this group again changed its name to the Fellowship of Fundamental Bible Churches to more accurately define their position.

As fundamentalists, this group strongly adheres to the historic fundamentals of the faith, including the doctrine of separation. This group accepts a literal view of the Bible and, consequently, accepts premillennial theology and a pre-tribulational rapture.

The churches are currently located in New Jersey, New York, Pennsylvania, Virginia, and Michigan. It is a fellowship of independent Bible and Baptist churches. Baptism, by immersion, and the Lord's Supper, as a memorial, are recognized as ordinances. There are currently 21 churches representing 1500 members. This constituent body is a member of the American Council of Christian Churches.

The Fellowship of Fundamental Bible Churches owns and operates Tri-State Bible Camp and Conference Center in Montague, New Jersey, oversees a mission board called Fundamental Bible Missions, and conducts a Bible Institute called Fundamental Bible Institute.

Headquarters
P.O. Box 206, Penns Grove, NJ 08069
Media Contact, Sec., Rev. Edmund G. Cotton, 80 Hudson St., Port Jervis, NY 12771 Tel. (914)856-7695
E-mail: edgc@pikeonline.net

Officers
Pres., Rev. Mark Franklin, 284 Whig Lane, Monroeville, NJ 08343 Tel. (609)881-0057
Vice-Pres., Rev. Gary Myers, P.O. Box 191, Meshoppen, PA 18630 Tel. (717)833-4898
Sec., Rev. Edmund G. Cotton, 80 Hudson St., Port Jervis, NY 12771 Tel. (914)856-7695
Treas., William Rainey, 246 Whig Lane, Monroeville, NJ 08343 Tel. (609)881-4790

Fellowship of Grace Brethren Churches

A division occurred in the Church of the Brethren in 1882 on the question of the legislative authority of the annual meeting. It resulted in the establishment of the Brethren Church under a legal charter requiring congregational government. This body divided in 1939 with the Grace Brethren establishing headquarters at Winona Lake, Ind., and the Brethren Church at Ashland, Ohio.

Headquarters
Media Contact, Fellowship Coord., Rev. Thomas Avey, P.O. Box 386, Winona Lake, IN 46590 Tel. (219)269-1269 Fax (219)269-4066
E-mail: fgbc@fgbc.org
Website:http:// www.fgbc.org

Officers
Mod., Dr. Galen Wiley, 22713 Ellsworth Ave., Minerva, OH 44657
1st Mod.-Elect, Dr. James Custer, 2515 Carriage Rd., Powell, OH 43065
2nd Mod.-Elect, Dr. Ron Manahan, 2316 E. Kemo Ave., Warsaw, IN 46580
Fellowship Coord., Rev. Thomas Avey, P.O. Box 386, Winona Lake, IN 46590 Tel. (219)269-1269 Fax (219)269-4066
Sec., Fellowship Coord., Rev. Thomas Avey, P.O. Box 386, Winona Lake, IN 46590
Treas., Thomas Staller, 2311 S. Cost-a-Plenty Drive, Warsaw, IN 46580

OTHER BOARDS
Grace Brethren International Missions, Exec. Dir., Rev. Tom Julien, P.O. Box 588, Winona Lake, IN 46590
Grace Brethren Home Missions, Exec. Dir., Larry Chamberlain, P.O. Box 587, Winona Lake, IN 46590
Grace College & Seminary, Pres., Ronald E. Manahan, 200 Seminary Dr., Winona Lake, IN 46590 Tel. (210)372-5100
Brethren Missionary Herald Co., Pub. & Gen. Mgr., James Bustram, P.O. Box 544, Winona Lake, IN 46590
CE National, Exec. Dir., Rev. Ed Lewis, P.O. Box 365, Winona Lake, IN 46590
Grace Brethren Navajo Ministries, Dir., Steve Galegor, Counselor, NM 87018
Grace Village Retirement Community, Admn., Jeff Carroll, P.O. Box 337, Winona Lake, IN 46590
Natl. Fellowship of Grace Brethren Ministries,

Pres., Dr. Steve Taylor, 132 Summerall Ct., Aiken, SC 29801 Women's Missionary Council, Pres., Janet Minnix, 3314 Kenwick Tr., S.W., Roanoke, VA, 24015
Grace Brethren Men International, Pres., Morgan Burgess, 163 N. Franklin St., Delaware, OH 43015

Free Christian Zion Church of Christ

This church was organized in 1905 at Redemption, Ark., by a company of African-American ministers associated with various denominations. Its polity is in general accord with that of Methodist bodies.

Headquarters
1315 S. Hutchinson St., Nashville, AR 71852 Tel. (501)845-4933
Media Contact, Gen. Sec., Shirlie Cheatham

Officer
Chief Pastor, Willie Benson, Jr.

Free Methodist Church of North America

The Free Methodist Church was organized in 1860 in Western New York by ministers and laymen who had called the Methodist Episcopal Church to return to what they considered the original doctrines and lifestyle of Methodism. The issues included human freedom (anti-slavery), freedom and simplicity in worship, free seats so that the poor would not be discriminated against and freedom from secret oaths (societies) so the truth might be spoken freely at all times. The founders emphasized the teaching of the entire sanctification of life by means of grace through faith.

The denomination continues to be true to its founding principles. It communicates the gospel and its power to all people without discrimination through strong missionary, evangelistic and educational programs. Six colleges, a Bible college and numerous overseas schools train the youth of the church to serve in lay and ministerial roles.

Its members covenant to maintain simplicity in life, worship, daily devotion to Christ, responsible stewardship of time, talent and finance.

Headquarters
World Ministries Center: 770 N. High School Rd., Indianapolis, IN 46214 Tel. (317)244-3660 Fax (317)244-1247
Mailing Address, P.O. Box 535002, Indianapolis, IN 46253 Tel. (800)342-5531
Media Contact, Yearbook Ed., P.O. Box 535002, Indianapolis, IN 46253

Officers
Bishops: Gerald E. Bates; Robert Nxumalo; Noah Nzeyimana; Richard D. Snyder; Luis Uanela Nhaphale; Jim Tuan; Kevin Mannoia, Teodoro Reynoso
Gen. Conf. Sec., Melvin J. Spencer

Admn. & Finance, Gen. Dir., Gary M. Kilgore
Growth Ministries, Gen. Dir., David Harvey
Light & Life Communications, Publisher, John E. Van Valin
Light & Life Magazine, Ed.,Doug Newton
Higher Education, Gen. Sec., Timothy M. Beuthin
Men's Ministries, Exec. Dir., Lucien E. Behar
Free Methodist Foundation, Stanley B. Thompson
Women's Ministries Intl., Pres., Carollyn Ellis
World Missions, Gen. Dir., Larry Houck

Periodicals
Light and Life Magazine; Free Methodist World Mission People

Friends General Conference

Friends General Conference is an association of yearly meetings within the Religious Society of Friends, open to all Friends meetings which wish to be actively associated with its programs and services. It was organized in 1900, bringing together four associations, including the First-day School Conference (1868) and the Friends Union for Philanthropic Labor (1882).

Friends General Conference is primarily a service organization and has no authority over its constituent meetings. Its purpose is to nurture the Religious Society of Friends by developing and providing resources and opportunities for spiritual growth. A Central Committee, to which constituent yearly meetings name appointees approximately in proportion to membership, its Executive Committee, are responsible for the direction of FGC's year-round services.

There are eight standing program committees: Advancement & Outreach, Christian & Interfaith Relations, Long Range Conference Planning, Ministry & Nurture, Publications & Distribution, Religious Education, Traveling Ministries, and Friends Meeting House Fund.

Headquarters
1216 Arch St., 2B, Philadelphia, PA 19107 Tel. (215)561-1700 Fax (215)561-0759
Media Contact, Gen. Sec., Bruce Birchard
E-mail: friends@fgc.quaker.org

Officers
Gen. Sec., Bruce Birchard
Presiding Clerk, Janice Domanik
Treas., Mark Kinnucan

YEARLY MEETINGS
*Baltimore, Clerk, Lamar Matthew, 17100 Quaker Ln., Sandy Spring, MD 20860 Tel. (301)774-7663; E-mail: dianajbym@igc.org
*Canadian: Co-clerk, Gale Wills, 91A Fourth Ave., Ottawa, ON K1S 2L1 Tel. (613)235-8553; E-mail: cym@web.net Website: http://www. web.net/~cym
Central Alaska Friends Conference, Clerk, Charlie Basham, P.O. Box 25078, Ester, AK 99725 Tel. (907)429-2006; E-mail: ffcsb@ aurora.alaska.edu

Illinois, Clerk, Elizabeth Mertic, 60255 Myrtle Rd., South Bend, IN 46614 Tel. (815)882-2214; E-mail: jnurenberg@xcel.com

Lake Erie, Clerk, Janet Smith, 121 Cherry St., Perrysburg, OH 43551 Tel. (419) 874-6738

*New England, Clerk, Betsy Muench, 901 Pleasant St., Worcester, MA 01602-1908 Tel. (508)754-6760; E-mail: neym@ultranet.com

*New York, Clerk, Victoria B. Cooley, 15 Rutherford Pl., New York, NY 10003 Tel. (212)673-5750

Northern: Co-Clerks, Lorene Ludy and Jean Eden, 510 S. Dickinson, Madison, WI 53703, Tel. (608) 251-3375

Ohio Valley, Clerk, Christine Snyder, 7897 Rain Tree Rd., Centerville, OH 45459 Tel. (513)232-5348

Philadelphia, Clerk, Martha B. Bryans, 1515 Cherry St., Philadelphia, PA 19102 Tel. (215)241-7210

Piedmont Friends Fellowship, Clerk, David Bailey, 1712 Lakemont Dr., Greensboro, NC 27410 Tel. (910)854-1225

South Central, Clerk, Glenna Balch, 1202 Kinney Ave., Austin, TX 78704 Tel. (512)442-0554; E-mail: quakertx@ktc.com OR johansen@unt.edu

*Southeastern, Clerk, Cecilia Yocum, 1115 NW 40 Dr., Gainsville, FL 32605-4750 Tel. (352)336-7689; E-mail: SEYM@juno.com

Southern Appalachian, Clerk, Penny Wright, P.O. Box 1164, Bristol, TN, 37621-1164 Tel. (423)764-1625; E-mail: errol@kite.ml.org

*also affiliated with Friends United Meeting

Periodical
Friends Journal

Friends United Meeting

Friends United Meeting was organized in 1902 (the name was changed in 1963 from the Five Years Meeting of Friends) as a loose confederation of North American yearly meetings to facilitate a united Quaker witness in missions, peace work and Christian education.

Today Friends United Meeting is comprised of 27 member yearly meetings representing about half the Friends in the world. FUM's current work includes programs of mission and service and congregational renewal. FUM publishes Christian education curriculum, books of Quaker history and religious thought and a magazine, *Quaker Life*.

Headquarters
101 Quaker Hill Dr., Richmond, IN 47374-1980 Tel. (765)962-7573 Fax (765)966-1293
Media Contact, Gen. Sec., Johan Maurer
E-mail: fuminfo@xc.org
Website: www.fum.org

Officers
Presiding Clk., Wayne Carter
Treas., Ann Kendall
Gen. Sec., Johan Maurer

DEPARTMENTS
World Ministries, Assoc. Sec., Retha McCutchen
Meeting Ministries, Assoc. Sec., Mary Glenn Hadley
Quaker Hill Bookstore, Mgr., Sue Calhoun
Friends United Press, Ed., Barbara Mays

YEARLY MEETINGS
Baltimore Yearly Meeting, 17100 Quaker Ln., Sandy Spring, MD 20860 Tel. (301)774-7663 (800)962-4766 Fax (301)774-7084 Lamar Matthew, clerk; Frank Massey, Gen. Sec.

Bware Yearly Meeting, P.O. Box 179, Suna, Kenya; Fanuel L. Simidi, Gen. Sec.

Canadian Yearly Meeting: 91-A Fourth Ave., Ottawa ON K1S 2L1, Canada; Tel. and Fax (613)235-8553; Gale Wills, clerk

Central Yearly Meeting, P.O. Box 1510, Kakamega, Kenya, East Africa, Joseph Andugu, Gen. Sec.

Cuba Yearly Meeting, Ave. Libertad #110, Puerto Padre, Las Tunas, Cuba; Ramon Gonzalez-Longoria E., clerk.

East Africa Yearly Meeting of Friends, P.O. Box 35, Tiriki, Kenya, East Africa; Matthew Tsimbaji, Clerk

East Africa Yearly Meeting of Friends (North), P.O. Box 544, Kitale, Kenya, East Africa; Henry Mayabe, Gen. Sec.

East Africa Yearly Meeting of Friends (South), P.O. Box 160, Vihiga, Kenya, East Africa; Josiah Embego, Clerk; Lam Kisanya Osodo, Gen. Sec.

Elgon East Yearly Meeting, P.O. Box 2322, Kitale, Kenya, East Africa; Maurice Simiyu, Gen. Sec.

Indiana Yearly Meeting, 4715 N. Wheeling Ave., Muncie, IN 47304-1222; Tel. (765)284-6900 Fax (765)284-8925; Susan Kirkpatrick, Clerk; David Brock, Gen. Superintendent

Iowa Yearly Meeting, Box 657, Oskaloosa, IA 52577; Tel. (515)673-9717 Fax (515)673-9718; Stan Bauer, Clerk, Del Coppinger, Gen. Superintendent

Jamaica Yearly Meeting, 4 Worthington Ave., Kingston 5, Jamaica WI; Tel. (809)926-7371; Kenneth Josephs

Kakamega Yearly Meeting, P.O. Box 465, Kakamega, Kenya, East Africa; Jonathan Shisanya, Gen. Sec.

Lugari Yearly Meeting, Lugari Farmers Training Centre, P.O. Box 438, Turbo, Kenya, East Africa; Samson Atsya, Gen. Sec.

Malava Yearly Meeting, P.O. Box 26, Malava, Kenya, East Africa; Enoch Shinachi, Gen. Sec.

Nairobi Yearly Meeting, P.O. Box 8321, Nairobi, Kenya, East Africa; Stanley Ndezwa, Clerk

Nandi Yearly Meeting, P.O. Box 102, Kapsabet, Kenya, East Africa; Fredrick Inyangu, Presiding clk.

Nebraska Yearly Meeting, 423 S. Tinker St., Hominy, OK 74035; Tel. (918)885-2714; David Nagle, Clerk

New England Yearly Meeting, 901 Pleasant St., Worcester, MA 01602 Tel. (508)754-6760; Elizabeth Muench, Clerk; Jonathan Vogel-Borne, Field Secretary

New York Yearly Meeting, 15 Rutherford Pl., New York, NY 10003 Tel. (212)673-5750; Victoria B. Cooley, Clerk; Helen Garay Toppins, Admin. Sec.

North Carolina Yearly Meeting, 5506 W. Friendly Ave., Greensboro, NC 27410; Tel. (336)292-6957; Brent McKinney, Clerk; John Porter, Gen. Superintendent

Southeastern Yearly Meeting, 1115 NW 40 Dr., Gainsville, FL 32605; Tel. (904)422-1446; Cecilia Yocum, Clerk, Annie McPhearson, Sec.

Tanzania Yearly Meeting, P.O. Box 151, Mugumu, Serengeti, Tanzania; Joshua Lavuna Oguma, Gen. Sec.

Uganda Yearly Meeting, P.O. Box 605, Kampala, Uganda, East Africa; Samuel Wefwafwa, Gen. Sec.

Vokoli Yearly Meetings, P.O. Box 266, Wodanga, Vokoli, Kenya, 0331 45033; Javan Mirembe, Gen. Sec.

Western Yearly Meeting, P.O. Box 70, Plainfield, IN 46168; Tel (317)839-2789 and 839-2849 Fax (317)839-2616; Charles Heavilin, Clerk; Curt Shaw, Gen. Superintendent

Wilmington Yearly Meeting, Pyle Center Box 1194, Wilmington, OH 45177; Tel (937)382-2491 Fax (937)382-7077; Gary Farlow, Clerk; Rudy Haag, Ex. Sec.

Periodical

Quaker Life

Full Gospel Assemblies International

The Full Gospel Assemblies International was founded in 1962 under the leadership of Dr. Charles Elwood Strauser. The roots of Full Gospel Assemblies may be traced to 1947 with the beginning of the Full Gospel Church of Coatesville, Pennsylvania. As an Assemblies of God Pentecostal church, the Full Gospel Church of Coatesville was active in evangelization and educational ministries to the community. In service to the ministers and students of the Full Gospel Church ministries, the Full Gospel Trinity Ministerial Fellowship was formed in 1962, later changing its name to Full Gospel Assemblies International.

Retaining its original doctrine and faith, Full Gospel Assemblies is Trinitarian and believes in the Bible as God's infallible Word to all people, in baptism in the Holy Spirit according to Acts 2, in divine healing made possible by the sufferings of our Lord Jesus Christ and in the imminent return of Christ for those who love him.

The body of Full Gospel Assemblies is an evangelical missionary fellowship sponsoring ministry at home and abroad, composed of self governing ministries and churches. Congregations, affiliate ministries and clerical bodies are located throughout the United States and over 30 countries of the world.

Headquarters

Lincoln Hwy, RD 2, Box 520, Parkesburg, PA

Mailing Address, P.O. Box 1230, Coatesville, PA 19320 Tel. (610)857-2357

E-mail: fgfcmi@aol.com

Media Contact, Simeon Strauser

Officers

Gen. Supt., Dr. AnnaMae Strauser

Exec. Dir of Admn., Simeon Strauser

Exec. Dir. of Ministry, J. Victor Fisk

Exec. Dir. of Comm., Shirley Carozzolo

Exec. Sec., Betty Stewart

National Ministers Council & Trustees: Chpsn., Simeon Strauser, Sadsburyville, PA; Marilyn Allen, Colorado Springs, CO; Donald Campbell, Mt. Morris, PA; David Treat, Bloomington, IN; Carol Strauser, Parkesburg, PA; Paul Bryson, Gordonville, PA

Periodical

Full Gospel Ministries Outreach Report

Full Gospel Fellowship of Churches and Ministers International

In the early 1960s a conviction grew in the hearts of many ministers that there should be closer fellowship between the people of God who believed in the apostolic ministry. At the same time, many independent churches were experiencing serious difficulties in receiving authority from the IRS to give governmentally accepted tax-exempt receipts for donations.

In September 1962 a group of ministers met in Dallas, Tex., to form a Fellowship to give expression to the essential unity of the Body of Christ under the leadership of the Holy Spirit-a unity that goes beyond individuals, churches or organizations. This was not a movement to build another denomination, but rather an effort to join ministers, churches and ministry organizations of like mind across denominational lines.

To provide opportunities for fellowship and to support the objectives and goals of local and national ministries: regional conventions and an annual international convention are held.

Headquarters

4325 W. Ledbetter Dr., Dallas, TX 75233 Tel. (214)339-1200 Fax (214)339-8790

Media Contact, Exec. Sec., Dr. Chester P. Jenkins

Officers

Pres., Dr. Don Arnold, P.O. Box 324, Gadsden, AL 35901

1st Vice-Pres., Dr. Ray Chamberlain

Exec. Sec., Dr. Chester P. Jenkins

Treas., Rev. S. K. Biffle, 3833 Westerville Rd., Columbus, OH 43224

Ofc. Sec., Ms. Beverly McCune

Vice-Pres. at Large: Rev. Maurice Hart, P.O. Box 4316, Omaha, NE 68104; Rev. Don Westbrook, 3518 Rose of Sharon Rd., Durham, NC 27705
Chmn. of Evangelism, David Ellis
Past Pres., Dr. James Helton

REGIONAL VICE-PRESIDENTS
Southeast, Rev. Gene Evans, P.O. Box 813, Douglasville, GA 30133
South Central, Rev. Robert J. Miller, P.O. Box 10621, Killeen, TX 76547
Southwest, Rev. Don Shepherd, 631 Southgate Rd., Sacramento, CA 95815
Northeast, Rev. David Ellis, 3636 Winchester Rd., Allertown, PA 18104
North Central, Rev. Raymond Rothwell, P.O. Box 367, Eaton, OH 45320
Northwest, Rev. Ralph Trask, 3212 Hyacinth NE, Salem, OR 97303

Periodical
Fellowship Tidings

Fundamental Methodist Church, Inc.
This group traces its origin through the Methodist Protestant Church. It withdrew from The Methodist Church and organized on Aug. 27, 1942.

Headquarters
1034 N. Broadway, Springfield, MO 65802
Media Contact, Dist. Supt., Rev. Ronnie Howerton, 1952 Highway H, Monett, MO 65708 Tel. (417)235-3849

Officers
Treas., Wayne Blades, Rt. 1, Crane, MO 65633 Tel. (417)723-8123
Sec., Betty Nicholson, Rt. 2, Box 397, Ash Grove, MO 65604 Tel. (417)672-2268
Dist. Supt., Rev. Ronnie Howerton, 1952 Highway H, Monett, MO 65708 Tel. (417)235-3849

General Assembly of the Korean Presbyterian Church in America
This body came into official existence in the United States in 1976 and is currently an ethnic church, using the Korean language.

Headquarters
P.O. Box 457, Morganville, NJ 07951 Tel. (908)591-2771 Fax (908)591-2260
Media Contact, Gen. Sec., Rev. John Woo

Officers
Stated Clk., Rev. Sang Koo Kim, 5777 Los Arcos Way, Buena Park, CA 90620 Tel. (714)826-5714 Fax (714)680-6418

General Association of General Baptists
Similar in doctrine to those General Baptists organized in England in the 17th century, the first General Baptist churches were organized on the Midwest frontier following the Second Great Awakening. The first church was established by the Rev. Benoni Stinson, in 1823 at Evansville, Ind.

Stinson's major theological emphasis was general atonement - "Christ tasted death for every man." The group also allows for the possibility of apostasy. It practices open communion and believer's baptism by immersion.

Called "liberal" Baptists because of their emphasis on the freedom of man, General Baptists organized a General Association in 1870 and invited other "liberal" Baptists (e.g., "Free Will" and Separate Baptists) to participate.

The policy-setting body is composed of delegates from local General Baptist churches and associations. Each local church is autonomous but belongs to an association. The group currently consists of more than 60 associations in 16 states, as well as several associations in the Philippines, Guam, Saipan, Jamaica and India. Ministers and deacons are ordained by a presbytery.

A number of boards continue a variety of missions, schools and other support ministries. General Baptists belong to the Baptist World Alliance, the North American Baptist Fellowship and the National Association of Evangelicals.

Headquarters
100 Stinson Dr., Poplar Bluff, MO 63901 Tel. (573)785-7746 Fax (573)785-0564
Media Contact, Exec. Dir., Rev. Ron Black

Officers
Mod., Rev. Scott Keller
Clk., Rev. Tommy Roberts
Exec. Dir., Rev. Ron Black

OTHER ORGANIZATIONS
International Missions, Dir., Rev. Jack Eberhardt
National Missions, Dir., Rev. Gene Koker
Brotherhood Bd., Pres., —
Women's Ministries, Dir., Sandra Trivitt
Nursing Home Admn., Wanda Britt, Rt. #2, Box 230, Campbell, MO 63933
College Bd., Pres., Dr. James Murray, Oakland City College, P.O. Box 235, Oakland City, IN 47660
Congregational Ministries, Dir., Rev. Mike Warren, 100 Stinson Dr., Poplar Bluff, MO 63901
Pastoral Ministries, Dir., Rev. Fred Brittain, 100 Stinson Dr., Poplar Bluff, MO 63901
Admin./Financial Services, Financial Officer, Linda McDonough, 100 Stinson Dr., Poplar Bluff, MO 63901
Stinson Press, Inc., Pres., Rev. Sam Ramdial, 100 Stinson Dr., Poplar Bluff, MO 63901
Oakview Heights Continuing Care, Administrator, Rev. Jack Cole, 1320 West 9th St., Mt. Carmel, IL 62863
Compassionate Care Adoption Agency, Dir., Dr. John Clanton, Rt. 3, Box 12B, Oakland City, IN 47660

Periodicals
General Baptist Messenger; Capsule; Voice; The Wave

General Association of Regular Baptist Churches

This association was founded in May, 1932, in Chicago by a group of churches which had withdrawn from the Northern Baptist Convention (now the American Baptist Churches in the U.S.A.) because of doctrinal differences. Its Confession of Faith, which it requires all churches to subscribe to, is essentially the old, historic New Hampshire Confession of Faith with a premillennial ending applied to the last article.

Headquarters
1300 N. Meacham Rd., Schaumburg, IL 60173 Tel. (847)843-1600 Fax (847)843-3757
Media Contact, Asst. to Natl. Rep., Dr. Mark Jackson
E-mail: garbc@garbc.org
Website: http://www.garbc.org

Officers
Chpsn., Rev. Will M. Davis
Vice-Chpsn., Rev. David Graham
Treas.,Dr. David Gower
Sec., Rev. Bryce Augsburger
Natl. Rep., John Greening

Periodical
Baptist Bulletin

General Church of the New Jerusalem

The General Church of the New Jerusalem is the result of a reorganization in 1897 of the General Church of The Advent of the Lord. It stresses the full acceptance of the doctrines contained in the theological writings of Emanuel Swedenborg.

Headquarters
P.O. Box 711, Bryn Athyn, PA 19009 Tel. (215) 938-2620
Media Contact, Ed., Church Journal, Donald L. Rose, Box 277, Bryn Athyn, PA 19009 Tel. (215)947-6225 Fax (215)947-3078
E-mail: svsimpso@newchurch.edu
Website:http:// www.newchurch.org

Officers
Presiding Bishop, Rt. Rev. P. M. Buss
Sec., Susan V. Simpson
Treas., Neil M. Buss

Periodical
New Church Life

General Conference of Mennonite Brethren Churches

A small group, requesting that closer attention be given to prayer, Bible study and a consistent lifestyle, withdrew from the larger Mennonite Church in the Ukraine in 1860. Anabaptist in origin, the group was influenced by Lutheran pietists and Baptist teachings and adopted a quasi-congregational form of church government. In 1874 and years following, small groups of these German-speaking Mennonites left Russia, settled in Kansas and then spread to the Midwest west of the Mississippi and into Canada. Some years later the movement spread to California and the West Coast. In 1960, the Krimmer Mennonite Brethren Conference merged with this body.

Today the General Conference of Mennonite Brethren Churches conducts services in many European languages as well as in Vietnamese, Mandarin and Hindi. It works with other denominations in missionary and development projects in 25 countries outside North America.

Headquarters
4812 E. Butler Ave., Fresno, CA 93727 Tel. (209)452-1713 Fax (209)452-1752
Media Contact, Exec. Sec., Marvin Hein

Officers
Mod., Ed Boschman, 12630 N. 103rd Ave., Suite 215, Sun City, AZ 85351
Asst. Mod., Herb Kopp, 200 McIvor Ave., Winnipeg, NB R20 028
Sec., Valerie Rempel
Exec. Sec., Marvin Hein

Periodical
Christian Leader; Mennotite Bretheren Herald

Grace Gospel Fellowship

The Grace Gospel Fellowship was organized in 1944 by a group of pastors who held to a dispensational interpretation of Scripture. Most had ministries in the Midwest. Two prominent leaders were J. C. O'Hair of Chicago and Charles Baker of Milwaukee. Subsequent to 1945, a Bible Institute was founded (now Grace Bible College of Grand Rapids, Mich.), and a previously organized foreign mission (now Grace Ministries International of Grand Rapids) was affiliated with the group. Churches have now been established in most sections of the country.

The body has remained a fellowship, each church being autonomous in polity. All support for its college, mission and headquarters is on a contributory basis.

The binding force of the Fellowship has been the members' doctrinal position. They believe in the Deity and Saviorship of Jesus Christ and subscribe to the inerrant authority of Scripture. Their method of biblical interpretation is dispensational, with emphasis on the distinctive revelation to and the ministry of the apostle Paul.

Headquarters
Media Contact, Pres., Roger G. Anderson, 2125 Martindale SW, P.O. Box 9432, Grand Rapids, MI 49509 Tel. (616)245-0100 Fax (616)241-2542
E-mail: ggfinc@aol.com

Officers
Pres., Roger G. Anderson

OTHER ORGANIZATIONS

Grace Bible College, Pres., Rev. Bruce Kemper, 1011 Aldon St. SW, Grand Rapids, MI 49509

Grace Ministries Intl., Exec. Dir., Dr. Samuel Vinton, 2125 Martindale Ave. SW, Grand Rapids, MI 49509

Prison Mission Association, Gen. Dir., Nathan Whitham, P.O. Box 1587, Port Orchard, WA 98366-0140

Grace Publications Inc., Exec. Dir., Roger G. Anderson, 2125 Martindale Ave. SW, Grand Rapids, MI 49509

Bible Doctrines to Live By, Exec. Dir., Lee Homoki, P.O. Box 2351, Grand Rapids, MI 49501

Periodical

Truth

Greek Orthodox Archdiocese of America

The Greek Orthodox Archdiocese of America is under the jurisdiction of the Ecumenical Patriarchate of Constantinople in Istanbul. It was chartered in 1922 by the State of New York and has 523 parishes in the United States. The first Greek Orthodox Church was founded in New Orleans in 1864.

Headquarters

8-10 E. 79th St., New York, NY 10021 Tel. (212)570-3500 Fax (212)570-3569

Media Contact: Fr. Mark Arey, Executive Director, Dept. of Communications, Tel. (212)570-3571 Fax (212)570-3598

ARCHDIOCESAN COUNCIL

Archbishop of America and Exarch of the Ecumenical Patriarchate, His Eminence Archbishop Spyridon

SYNOD OF BISHOPS

Most Rev. Metropolitan Iakovos of Krinis, Diocese of Chicago, 40 E. Burton Place, Chicago, IL 60610

Most Rev. Metropolitan Anthony of Dardanelles, Diocese of San Francisco, 372 Santa Clara Avenue, San Francisco, CA 94127

Most Rev. Metropolitan Maximos of Aenos, Diocese of Pittsburgh, 5201 Ellsworth Avenue, Pittsburgh, PA 15232

Most Rev. Metropolitan Methodios of Aneon, Diocese of Boston, 162 Goddard Avenue, Brookline, MA 02146

Most Reverend Metropolitan Isaiah of Proikonisou, Diocese of Denver, 4310 E. Alameda Avenue, Denver, CO 80222

AUXILIARY BISHOPS

His Grace Bishop Alexios of Troas, Archdiocesan Vicar, Diocese of Atlanta; His Grace Bishop Dimitrios of Xanthou, Archdiocese, New York, NY; His Grace Bishop of George of Komanon, Bethesda, MD

EXECUTIVE COMMITTEE

John A. Catsimatidis, Vice Chairman, New York, NY; Peter J. Pappas, Sec., Syosset, NJ; Andrew A. Athens, Chicago, IL; George Behrakis, Tewksbury, MA; Michael G. Cantonis, Tarpon Springs, FL; Harry J. Pappas, Visalia, CA; James J. Paulos, Dallas, TX; George E. Safiol, Weston, MA

ARCHDIOCESE OF NEW YORK; Office of the Archbishop; Office of the Chief Secretariat; Office of the Chancellor: Chancellor, V. Rev. Protopresbyter George G. Passias

ARCHDIOCESAN DEPARTMENTS

Archives; Archdiocese Benefits Committee; Archons, Order of St. Andrew; Dept. of Communications: GOTelecom, Internet Ministries, News & Information, Office of Publications, ORTHODOX OBSERVER (bi-monthly publication); Education & Culture; Finance; Inter-Orthodox & Ecumenical Affairs; Internet Ministries; Ionian Village; Leadership 100 Endowment Fund; Management Information Systems; Registry; Religious Education/DOXA; Stewardship Ministries/LOGOS; Youth & Young Adult Ministries

ORGANIZATIONS/ INSTITUTIONS

All Saints Center; Archdiocesan Presbyters Council; Diocesan and Parish Summer Camps; Greek Orthodox Young Adult League (GOYAL); Hellenic Cultural Center; Hellenic College/Holy Cross Greek Orthodox School of Theology; Holy Cross Bookstore; Inter-Church/Inter-Faith Marriage Committee; National Ladies Philoptochos Society; National Sisterhood of Presbyters; National Forum of Greek Orthodox Church Musicians; Orthodox Christian Mission Center; Patriarch Athenagoras National Institute; Patriarch Athenagoras Orthodox Institute at the Graduate Theological Union; Standing Conference of Canonical Orthodox Bishops in the Americas (SCOBA): Chairman, His Eminence Archbishop Spyridon; St. Basil Academy; St. Michael's Home- Quality Care for the Elderly; St. Nicholas Ranch and Retreat Center; St. Photios National Shrine

OTHER JURISDICTIONS OF THE ECUMENICAL PATRIARCHATE IN THE USA

Albanian Orthodox Diocese in America; Belarusian Council of Orthodox Churches in North America; American Carpatho-Russian Orthodox Greek Catholic Diocese of the USA; Ukrainian Orthodox Church of the USA

House of God, Which is the Church of the Living God, the Pillar and Ground of the Truth, Inc.

This body, founded by Mary L. Tate in 1919, is episcopally organized.

Headquarters

1301 N. 58th St., Philadelphia, PA 19131
Media Contact, Sec., Rose Canon, 515 S. 57th St., Philadelphia, PA 19143 Tel. (215)474-8913

Officer

Bishop, Raymond W. White, 6107 Cobbs Creek Pkwy., Philadelphia, PA 19143 Tel. (215)748-6338

Hungarian Reformed Church in America

A Hungarian Reformed Church was organized in New York in 1904 in connection with the Reformed Church of Hungary. In 1922, the Church in Hungary transferred most of its congregations in the United States to the Reformed Church in the U.S. Some, however, preferred to continue as an autonomous, self-supporting American denomination, and these formed the Free Magyar Reformed Church in America. This group changed its name in 1958 to Hungarian Reformed Church in America.

This church is a member of the World Alliance of Reformed Churches, Presbyterian and Congregational, the World Council of Churches and the National Council of Churches of Christ.

Headquarters

Bishop's Office, 13 Grove St., Poughkeepsie, NY 12601 Tel. (914)454-5735

Officers

Bishop, Rt. Rev. Alexander Forro
Chief Lay-Curator, Prof. Stephen Szabo, 464 Forest Ave., Paramus, NJ 07652
Gen. Sec. (Clergy), Rt. Rev. Stefan M. Torok, 331 Kirkland Pl., Perth Amboy, NJ 08861 Tel. (908)442-7799
Gen Sec. (Lay), Zoltan Ambrus, 3358 Maple Dr., Melvindale, MI 48122
Eastern Classes: Dean (Senior of the Deans, Chair in Bishop's absence), Very Rev. Imre Bertalan, 10401 Grosvenor Pl., #1521, Rockville, MD 20852 Tel. (301)493-5036 Fax (301)571-5111; Lay-Curator, Balint Balogh, 519 N. Muhlenberg St., Allentown, PA 18104
New York Classes: Supervisor, Rt. Rev. Alexander Forro; Lay-Curator, Laszlo B. Vanyi, 229 E 82nd St., New York, NY 10028
Western Classes: Dean, V. Rev. Andor Demeter, 3921 W. Christy Dr., Phoenix, AZ 85029; Lay-Curator, Zolton Kun, 2604 Saybrook Dr., Pittsburgh, PA 15235

Periodical

Magyar Egyhaz

Hutterian Brethren

Small groups of Hutterites derive their names from Jacob Hutter, a 16th-century Anabaptist who taught true discipleship after accepting Jesus as Saviour and advocated communal ownership of property and was burned as a heretic in Austria in 1536.

Many believers are of German descent and still use their native tongue at home and in church. Much of the denominational literature is produced in German and English. "Colonies" share property, practice non-resistance, dress plainly, do not participate in politics and operate their own schools. There are 428 colonies with 42,000 members in North America. Each congregation conducts its own youth work through Sunday school. Until age 15, children attend German and English school which is operated by each colony. All youth ages 15 to 20 attend Sunday school. They are baptized as adults upon confession of faith, around age 20.

Headquarters

Media Contact, Paul S. Gross, Rt. 1, Box 6E, Reardon, WA 99029 Tel. (509)299-5400 Fax (509)299-3099
E-mail: philsig@juno.com

Officers

Smiedleut Chmn., No. 1, Jacob Waldner-Blumengard Colony, Box 13 Plum Coulee, MB R0G 1R0 Tel. (204)829-3527
Smiedleut Chmn., No. 2, Jacob Wipf, Spring Creek Colony, 36562 102 Street, Forbes, ND 58439 Tel. (701)358-8621
Dariusleut, Chmn., No. 1, Mike Stahl, Byemoor Colony, Box 70, Byemoor, AB T0J 0L0 Tel. (403)579-2130
Dariusleut, Chmn., No. 2, Martin Walter, Springpoint Colony, Box 249, Pincher Creek, AB T0K 1W0 Phone (403)553-4368
Lehrerleut, Chmn., Rev. John Wipf, Rosetown Colony, Box 1509, Rosetown, SK S0L 2V0 Tel. (306)882-3344

IFCA International, Inc.

This group of churches was organized in 1930 at Cicero, Illinois, by representatives of the American Council of Undenominational Churches and representatives of various independent churches. The founding churches and members had separated themselves from various denominational affiliations.

The IFCA provides a way for independent churches and ministers to unite in close fellowship and cooperation, in defense of the fundamental teachings of Scripture and in the proclamation of the gospel of God's grace.

Headquarters

3520 Fairlanes, Grandville, MI 49418 Tel. (616) 531-1840 Fax (616)531-1814
Mailing Address, P.O. Box 810, Grandville, MI 49468-0810
Media Contact, Exec. Dir., Dr. Richard I. Gregory
E-mail: office@ifca.org
Website: http://www.ifca.org

Officers

Exec. Dir., Dr. Richard I. Gregory, 2684 Meadow

Ridge Dr., Byron Center, MI 49315 Tel. (616)878-1285

Pres., Dr. Donald Fredericks, 3224 N. Patterson Blvd., Flagstaff, AZ 86004-2009 Tel. (520)526-1493

1st Vice-Pres., Rev.Alex Montoya, Hacienda Heoghts, CA

2nd Vice-Pres., Rev. Chip Binch, Miami, FL

Periodical

The Voice

International Church of the Foursquare Gospel

Founded by Aimee Semple McPherson in 1927, the International Church of the Foursquare Gospel proclaims the message of Jesus Christ the Savior, Healer, Baptizer with the Holy Spirit and Soon-coming King. Headquartered in Los Angeles, this evangelistic missionary body of believers consists of nearly 1,893 churches in the United States and Canada.

The International Church of the Foursquare Gospel is incorporated in the state of California and governed by a Board of Directors who direct its corporate affairs. A Foursquare Cabinet, consisting of the Corporate Officers, Board of Directors and District Supervisors of the various districts of the Foursquare Church in the United States and other elected or appointed members, serves in an advisory capacity to the President and the Board of Directors.

Each local Foursquare Church is a subordinate unit of the International Church of the Foursquare Gospel. The pastor of the church is appointed by the Board of Directors and is responsible for the spiritual and physical welfare of the church. To assist and advise the pastor, a church council is elected by the local church members.

Foursquare Churches seek to build strong believers through Christian education, Christian day schools, youth camping and ministry, Foursquare Women International who support and encourage Foursquare missionaries abroad, radio and television ministries, the Foursquare World Advance Magazine and 276 Bible Colleges worldwide.

Worldwide missions remains the focus of the Foursquare Gospel Church with 22,255 churches and meeting places, 30, 648 national Foursquare pastors/leaders and 2,222,219 members and adherents in 91 countries around the globe. The Church is affiliated with the Pentecostal Fellowship of North America, National Association of Evangelicals and the World Pentecostal Fellowship.

Headquarters

1910 W. Sunset Blvd., Ste. 200, P.O. Box 26902, Los Angeles, CA 90026-0176 Tel. (213)989-4234 Fax (213)989-4590

Media Contact, Editor, Dr. Ron Williams

Website: www.foursquare.org

Corporate Officers

Pres., Dr. Paul C. Risser

Pres. Emeritus, Dr. Donald D. Long

Vice-Pres., Dr. Harold E. Helms

Gen. Supvr., Dr. Donald D. Long

Dir. of Missions Intl., Rev. James A. Tolle

Sec., Dr. John W. Bowers

Treas., Rev. Virginia Cravens

Bd. of Directors: Dr. Paul C. Risser; Rev. James A. Tolle; Rev. Ralph Torres; Rev. Naomi Beard; Dr. John W. Bowers; Dr. Harold E. Helms; Rev. Donald D. Long; Dr. Ron Williams; Rev. Arthur Gray; Mark Simon; Rev. Alan Eastland; Rev. Lolita Frederick

District Supervisors: Eastern, Dr. Dewey Morrow; Great Lakes, Dr. Fred Parker; Midwest, Rev. Larry Spousta; Northwest, Dr. Tom Ferguson; South Central, Dr. Sidney Westbrook; Southeast, Rev. Glenn Burris, Jr.; Southern California, Rev. James C. Scott, Jr.; Southwest, Rev. Fred Donaldson; Western, Rev. Robert Booth

Foursquare Cabinet: Composed of Corp. Officers; Board of Directors; District Supervisors, Rev. Michael J. O'Brien; Dr. Ricky R. Temple; Rev. James Machen; Dr. Sterling Brackett; Rev. Beverly Bradfford; Dr. Jack W. Hayford; Rev. Loren Houltberg; Rev. Ronald Long; Dr. Ronald Mehl; Rev. Stephen Overman; Dr. Richard Scott; Dr. Roger Whitlow

SUPPORT MINISTRIES

Natl. Dept. of Youth, Natl. Youth Minister, Rev. Jerry Dirmann

Natl. Dept. of Chr. Educ., Dir., Rev. Rick Wulfestieg

Foursquare Women International, Dir., Rev. Beverly Brafford

Periodical

Foursquare World Advance

International Council of Community Churches

This body is a fellowship of locally autonomous, ecumenically minded, congregationally governed, non-creedal Churches. The Council came into being in 1950 as the union of two former councils of community churches, one formed of black churches known as the Biennial Council of Community Churches and the other of white churches known as the National Council of Community Churches.

Headquarters

21116 Washington Pky., Frankfort, IL 60423-1253 Tel. (815)464-5690 Fax (815)464-5692

Media Contact, Interim Exec. Dir., Dr. J. Ralph Shotwell

Officers

Pres., Rev. Dr. Gregory Smith

Vice-Pres., Rev. Judson Souers

Vice-Pres., Abraham Wright

117

Sec., Rev. Herbert Freitag
Treas., Martha Nolan
Interim Exec. Dir., Dr. J. Ralph Shotwell

OTHER ORGANIZATIONS

Commission on Church Relations, Dr. James MacVicar
Commission on Ecumenical Relations, Rev. Herman Harmelink
Commission on Clergy Relations, —
Commission on Laity Relations, —
Commission on Faith & Order, Rev. Dr. Kate Epperly
Comm. on Theological & Human Concerns, —
Commission on Missions, Rev. David Blanchett
Commission on Informational Services, Margaret House
Commission on Informational Services, Vermille Barnes
Women's Christian Fellowship, Pres., Shirley Fairley
Samaritans (Men's Fellowship), Pres., Al Albergottie
Young Adult Fellowship, Pres., Shantelle Harrell
Youth Fellowship, Pres., Jerry Jones

Periodical

The Christian Community

The International Pentecostal Church of Christ

At a General Conference held at London, Ohio, Aug. 10, 1976, the International Pentecostal Assemblies and the Pentecostal Church of Christ consolidated into one body, taking the name International Pentecostal Church of Christ.

The International Pentecostal Assemblies was the successor of the Association of Pentecostal Assemblies and the International Pentecostal Missionary Union. The Pentecostal Church of Christ was founded by John Stroup of Flatwoods, Ky., on May 10, 1917 and was incorporated at Portsmouth, Ohio, in 1927. The International Pentecostal Church of Christ is an active member of the Pentecostal/Charismatic Churches of North America, as well as a member of the National Association of Evangelicals.

The priorities of the International Pentecostal Church of Christ are to be an agency of God for evangelizing the world, to be a corporate body in which people may worship God and to be a channel of God's purpose to build a body of saints being perfected in the image of His Son.

The Annual Conference is held each year during the first full week of August in London, Ohio.

Headquarters

2245 St. Rt. 42 SW, P.O. Box 439, London, OH 43140 Tel. (740)852-4722 Fax (740)852-0348
Media Contact, Gen. Overseer, Clyde M. Hughes
E-mail: hqipcc@aol.com

EXECUTIVE COMMITTEE

Gen. Overseer, Clyde M. Hughes, P.O. Box 439, London, OH 43140 Tel. (740)852-4722 Fax (740)852-0348
Asst. Gen. Overseer, Thomas L. Dooley, 3200 Dueber Ave. SW, Canton, OH 44706 Tel. (330)484-6053 Fax (330)484-6053
Gen. Sec., Rev. B. G. Turner, Rt. 1, Box 260L, Charles Town, WV 25414 Tel. (304)725-4346 Fax (304)535-2221
Gen. Treas., Rev. Clifford A. Edwards, P.O. Box 18145, Atlanta, GA 30316 Tel. (404)627-2681 Fax (404)627-0702
Dir. of Global Missions, Dr. James B. Keiller, P.O. Box 18145, Atlanta, GA 30316 Tel. (404) 627-2681 Fax (404)627-0702

DISTRICT OVERSEERS

Blue Ridge District, Clyde M. Hughes, P.O. Box 439, London, OH 43140 Tel. (740)852-4722 Fax (740)852-0348
Central District, Ervin Hargrave, 2279 Seminole Ave., Springfield, OH 45506 Tel. and Fax (937)323-6433
Mid-Eastern District, H. Gene Boyce, 705 W. Grubb St., Hertford, NC 27944 Tel. (252)426-5403
Mountain District, Terry Lykins, Box 131, Staffordsville, KY 41256 Tel. (606)297-3282
New River District, Calvin Weikel, Rt. 2, Box 300, Ronceverte, WV 24970 Tel. (304)647-4301
North Central District, Edgar Kent, 67473 Red Arrow Hwy., Hartford, MI 49057 Tel. (616)621-3326
North Eastern District, Franklin Myers, Rt. 5, Box 175, Harpers Ferry, WV 25425 Tel. (304) 535-6355
South Eastern District, Chris Bowen, 7123 Lady Heidi Ct., Jonesboro, GA 30236 Tel. and Fax (404)361-0812
Tri-State District, Cline McCallister, 5210 Wilson St., Portsmouth, OH 45662 Tel. and Fax (740)776-6357

OTHER ORGANIZATIONS

Beulah Heights Bible College, Pres., Samuel R. Chand, PO Box 18145, Atlanta, GA 31306 Tel. (404)627-2681
Women's Ministries, Gen. Pres., Janice Boyce, 121 W. Hunters Tr., Elizabeth City, NC 27909 Tel. and Fax (252)338-3003
Pentecostal Ambassadors, Richard Chesney, National Youth Dir., Box 439, London, OH 43140 Tel. (740)852-0448 Fax (740)852-0348
Sunday School Dept., P.O. Box 439, London, OH 43140 Tel. (740)852-0448 Fax (740)852-0348

Periodicals

The Bridegroom's Messenger; The Pentecostal Leader

International Pentecostal Holiness Church

This body grew out of the National Holiness Association movement of the last century, with roots in Methodism. Beginning in the South and Midwest, the church represents the merger of the Fire-Baptized Holiness Church founded by B. H. Irwin in Iowa in 1895; the Pentecostal Holiness Church founded by A. B. Crumpler in Goldsboro, N.C., in 1898; and the Tabernacle Pentecostal Church founded by N. J. Holmes in 1898.

All three bodies joined the ranks of the pentecostal movement as a result of the Azusa Street revival in Los Angeles in 1906 and a 1907 pentecostal revival in Dunn, N.C., conducted by G. B. Cashwell, who had visited Azusa Street. In 1911 the Fire-Baptized and Pentecostal Holiness bodies merged in Falcon, N.C., to form the present church; the Tabernacle Pentecostal Church was added in 1915 in Canon, Ga.

The church stresses the new birth, the Wesleyan experience of sanctification, the pentecostal baptism in the Holy Spirit, evidenced by speaking in tongues, divine healing and the premillennial second coming of Christ.

Headquarters
P.O. Box 12609, Oklahoma City, OK 73157 Tel. (405)787-7110 Fax (405)789-3957
Media Contact, Admn. Asst.

Officers
E-mail: jdl@iphc.org (for Bishop Leggett)
Website: http://www.iphc.org
Gen. Supt., Bishop James D. Leggett
Vice Chpsn./Asst. Gen. Supt., Rev. M. Donald Duncan
Asst. Gen. Supt., Dr. Ronald Carpenter
Asst. Gen. Supt., Rev. Paul Howell
Gen. Sec.-Treas., Rev. Jack Goodson

OTHER ORGANIZATIONS
The Publishing House (Life Springs), Gen. Admn., Greg Hearn, Franklin Springs, GA 30639
Gen. Women's Ministries, Pres., Mary Belle Johnson
Gen. Men's Ministries, Natl. Dir., Col. Jack Kelley, P.O. Box 53307, Fayetteville, NC 28305

Periodicals
Issachar File; Helping Hand; Evangelism USA; Worldorama; CE Connection

Jehovah's Witnesses
Modern-day Jehovah's Witnesses began in the early 1870s when Charles Taze Russell was the leader of a Bible study group in Allegheny City, Pa. In July 1879, the first issue of Zion's Watch Tower and Herald of Christ's Presence (now called The Watchtower) appeared. In 1884 Zion's Watch Tower Tract Society was incorporated, later changed to Watch Tower Bible and Tract Society. Congregations spread into other states and followers witnessed from house to house.

By 1913, printed sermons were in four languages in 3,000 newspapers in the United States,

Canada and Europe. Hundreds of millions of books, booklets and tracts were distributed. Publication of the magazine now known as *Awake!* Began in 1919. Today, it is published in more than 80 languages and has a circulation of upwards of 19,000,000. In 1931 the name Jehovah's Witnesses, based on Isaiah 43:10-12, was adopted.

During the 1930s and 1940s Jehovah's Witnesses fought many court cases in the interest of preserving freedom of speech, press, assembly and worship. They have won a total of 43 cases before the United States Supreme Court. A missionary taining school was established in 1943, and it has been a major factor in the international expansion of the Witnessess. There are now 5.6 million Witnesses in 232 lands (1997).

Jehovah's Witnesses believe in one almighty God, Jehovah, who is the Creator of all things.They believe in Jesus Christ as God's Son, the first of His creations. While Jesus is now an immortal spirit in heaven, ruling as King of God's Kingdom, he is still subject to his heavenly Father, Jehovah God. Christ's human life was sacrificed as a ransom to open up for obedient mankind the opportunity of eternal life. With Christ in heaven, 144,000 individuals chosen from among mankind will rule in righteousness over an unnumbered great crowd who will survive the destruction of wickedness and receive salvation into an earth cleansed of evil. (Rev. 7:9,10; 14:1-5). These, along with the resurrected dead, will transform the earth into a global earthly paradise and will have the prospect of living forever on it.

Headquarters
25 Columbia Heights, Brooklyn, NY 11201-2483 Tel. (718)560-5600
Media Contact, Public Affairs Office, James Pellechia

Officer
Pres. Watch Tower Bible and Tract Society of Pennsylvania, Milton G. Henschel

The Latvian Evangelical Lutheran Church in America
This body was organized into a denomination on Aug. 22, 1975 after having existed as the Federation of Latvian Evangelical Lutheran Churches in America since 1955. This church is a regional constituent part of the Lutheran Church of Latvia in Exile, a member of the Lutheran World Federation and the World Council of Churches.

The Latvian Evangelical Lutheran Church in America works to foster religious life, traditions and customs in its congregations in harmony with the Holy Scriptures, the Apostles', Nicean and Athanasian Creeds, the unaltered Augsburg Confession, Martin Luther's Small and Large Catechisms and other documents of the Book of Concord.

The LELCA is ordered by its Synod (General

119

Assembly), executive board, auditing committee and district conferences.

Headquarters

2140 Okla Dr., Golden Valley, MN 55427 Tel. (612)722-0174

Media Contact, Juris Pulins, 9531 Knoll Top Rd., Union, IL 60180 Tel. (815)923-5919

Officers

Pres., Rev. Uldis Cepure, Tel. (612)546-3712

Vice-Pres., Rev. Anita Varsbergs, 9908 Shelburne Terr., 312, Gathersburg, MD 20878 Tel. (301) 251-4151

2nd Vice-Pres., Aivrs Ronis, 449 S. 40th St., Lincoln, NE 68510 Tel. (402)489-2776

Sec., Ansis Abele, 25182 Northrup Dr., Laguna Beach, CA 92653 Tel. (714)830-9712

Treas., Alfreds Trautmanis, 103 Rose St., Freeport, NY 11520 Tel. (516)623-2646

Periodical

Cela Biedrs; Leiba Zinas

The Liberal Catholic Church - Province of the United States of America

The Liberal Catholic Church was founded Feb. 13, 1916 as a reorganization of the Old Catholic Church in Great Britain with the Rt. Rev. James I. Wedgwood as the first Presiding Bishop. The first ordination of a priest in the United States was Fr. Charles Hampton, later a Bishop. The first Regionary Bishop for the American Province was the Rt. Rev. Irving S. Cooper (1919-1935).

Headquarters

Pres., Rt. Rev. Lawrence J. Smith, 9740 S. Avers Ave., Evergreen Park, IL 60805 Tel. (708)424-6548 Fax (708)423-8053

Media Contact, Regionary Bishop, Rt. Rev. Lawrence J. Smith

E-mail: regionary@aol.com

Website: http://members.aol.com/l.catholic/index.htm

Officers

Pres. & Regionary Bishop, Rt. Rev. Lawrence J. Smith

Vice-Pres., Rev. L. Marshall Heminway, P.O. Box 19957 Hampden Sta., Baltimore, MD 21211-0957

Sec. (Provincial), Rev. Lloyd Worley, 1232 24th Avenue Ct., Greeley, CO 80631 Tel. (303)356-3002

Provost, Rev. Lloyd Worley

Treas., Rev. Lloyd Worley

BISHOPS

Regionary Bishop for the American Province, Rt. Rev. Lawrence J. Smith

Aux. Bishops of the American Province: Rt. Rev. Dr. Robert S. McGinnis, Jr., 3612 N. Labarre Rd., Metaire, LA 70002; Rt. Rev. Joseph L. Tisch, P.O. Box 1117, Melbourne, FL 32901; Rt. Rev. Dr. Hein VanBeusekom, 12 Krotona

Hill, Ojai, CA 93023; Rt. Rev. Ruben Cabigting, P.O. Box 270, Wheaton, IL 60189; Rt. Rev. William S.H. Downey, 1206 Ayers Ave., Ojai, CA 93023

Periodical

Ubique

The Lutheran Church - Missouri Synod

The Lutheran Church-Missouri Synod, which was founded in 1847, has more than 6,000 congregations in the United States and works in 60 other countries. It has 2.6 million members and is the second-largest Lutheran denomination in North America.

Christian education is offered for all ages. The North American congregations operate the largest elementary and secondary school systems of any Protestant denomination in the nation, and 13,851 students are enrolled in 12 LCMS institutions of higher learning.

Traditional beliefs concerning the authority and interpretation of Scripture are important. The synod is known for mass-media outreach through "The Lutheran Hour" on radio, "This Is The Life" dramas on television, and the products of Concordia Publishing House, the third-largest Protestant publisher, whose Arch Books children's series has sold more than 55 million copies.

An extensive network of more than 1,000 volunteers in 50 work centers produces Braille, large-type, and audiocassette materials for the blind and visually impaired. 59 of the 85 deaf congregations affiliated with U.S. denominations are LCMS; and many denominations use the Bible lessons prepared for developmentally disabled persons.

The involvement of women is high, although they do not occupy clergy positions. Serving as teachers, deaconesses and social workers, women comprise approximately 48 percent of total professional workers.

The members' responsibility for congregational leadership is a distinctive characteristic of the synod. Power is vested in voters' assemblies, generally comprised of adults of voting age. Synod decision making is given to the delegates at national and regional conventions, where the franchise is equally divided between lay and pastoral representatives.

Headquarters

The Lutheran Church-Missouri Synod, International Center, 1333 S. Kirkwood Rd., St. Louis, MO 63122-7295

Media Contact, Dir., News & Information, Rev. David Mahsman, Tel. (314)965-9917 Ext. 1227; Manager, News Bureau, Mr. Joe Isenhower, Ext. 1231, Fax (314) 965-3396

E-mail: infocenter@lcms.org

Website: http://www.lcms.org

120

Officers

Pres., Dr. A.L. Barry
1st Vice-Pres., Dr. Robert T. Kuhn
2nd Vice-Pres., Dr. Robert King
3rd Vice-Pres., Dr. William C. Weinrich
4th Vice-Pres., Dr. Roger D. Pittelko
5th Vice-Pres., Dr. Wallace Schulz
Sec., Dr. Raymond L. Hartwig
Treas., Dr. Norman Sell
Admn. Officer of Bd. of Dir., Bradford L. Hewitt
Exec. Dir., Human Resources, Barb Ryan
Bd. of Directors: Dr. Karl L. Barth, Milwaukee, WI; Rev. Roosevelt Gray, Detroit, MI; Dr. Betty Duda, Oviedo, FL; Richard Peters, Amery, WI; Clifford A. Dietrich, Fort Wayne, IN; Ernest E. Garbe, Dieterich, IL; Dr. Jean Garton, Benton, AR; Oscar H. Hanson, Lafayette, CA; Ted Kober, Billings, MT; Dr. Donald K. Muchow, Austin, TX; Rev. Ulmer Marshall, Jr., Mobile, AL; Christian Preus, Plymouth, MN; Dr.
Edwin Trapp, Jr., Dallas, TX

BOARDS AND COMMISSIONS

Communication Services, Exec. Dir., Rev. Paul Devantier
Mission Services, Exec. Dir., Dr. Glenn O'Shoney
Higher Education Services, Exec. Dir., Dr. William F. Meyer
Human Care Ministries, Exec. Dir., Rev. Richard L. Krenzke
Worker Benefit Plans, Exec. Dir., Dan A. Leeman
Lutheran Church Ext. Fund-Missouri Synod, Pres., Merle Freitag
Congregational Services, Exec. Dir., Rev. Lyle Muller
Black Ministries Services, Exec. Dir., Dr. Bryant Clancy

ORGANIZATIONS

Concordia Publishing House, Pres./CEO, Dr. Stephen Carter, 3558 S. Jefferson Ave., St. Louis, MO 63118-3968
Concordia Historical Institute, Dir., Rev. Daniel Preus, Concordia Seminary, 801 De Mun Ave., St. Louis, MO 63105
Intl. Lutheran Laymen's League, Exec. Dir., Rodger W. Hebermehl, 2185 Hampton Ave., St. Louis, MO 63139-2983
KFUO Radio, Exec. Dir., Rev. Paul Devantier
Intl. Lutheran Women's Missionary League, Pres., Gloria Edwards, 3558 S. Jefferson Ave., St. Louis, MO 63118-3910

Periodicals

The Lutheran Witness; Reporter

The Malankara Mar Thoma Syrian Church

According to tradition, the Mar Thoma Church was established as a result of the apostolic mission of St. Thomas, the apostle in 52 AD. Church history attests to the continuity of the community of faithful, throughout the long centuries in India. The liturgy and faith practices of the Church were based on the relationship between the Church in Kerala, India, which St. Thomas founded, with the East-Syrian and Persian Churches. This started in the 3rd century and continued up to the 16th century. In the 17th century, the Malabar Church of St. Thomas (as the Church in Kerala was known) renewed her relationship with the Orthodox Patriarchate of Antioch as part of the resistance to forced Latinization by the Portuguese. This process also led to the development of the Kerala Episcopacy, whereby the first Indian Bishop Mar Thoma I was consecrated in Kerala.

The Mar Thoma Church retains her Eastern Orthodoxy. She follows an Orthodox (true) worship form and liturgy, believes in the catholicty of grace, is missionary and evangelistic in approach. She derives Episcopal succession from the Syrian Orthodox Church of Antioch and follows Eastern Reformed Theology. She is independent, autonomous, and indigenous, constitutionally combining democratic values and Episcopal authority. She has been in full communion with the Anglican Church since 1954.

The Diocese of North America was organized in 1988 in order to serve the needs of the immigrant community. It has a membership of around five thousand families in sixty five parishes.

Headquarters

Sinai Mar Thoma Center, 2320 S. Merrick Avenue, Merrick, New York 11566 Tel. (516)377-3311 Fax (516)377-3322

Officers

Diocesan Bishop: The Rt. Rev. Dr. Zacharias Mar Theophilus Episcopa
Diocesan/Bishop's Sec.: The Rev. Oommen Philip
Diocesan Treasurer: Kuruvilla Cherian, CPA

Mennonite Church

The Mennonite Church in North America traces its beginnings to the Protestant Reformation. Conrad Grebel, Georg Blaurock and a small band of radical believers baptized one another in Zurich, Switzerland, on Jan. 21, 1525. First nicknamed Anabaptists (Rebaptizers) by their opponents, they preferred the term Brothers and Sisters in Christ. They later took their name from the Dutch priest Menno Simons, who joined the movement in 1536.

The Mennonites' refusal to conform to majesterial decrees, including bearing of arms and the swearing of oaths, attracted fierce animosity. Thousands were martyred for their beliefs in nearly a century of persecution. They moved to many places, including the United States and Canada, where some arrived as early as 1683.

North American Mennonites began their first home mission program in Chicago, Ill., in 1893 and their first overseas mission program in India in 1899. Since the 1920s the church has established extensive emergency relief and development services in conjunction with its mission program.

Mennonites hold that the Word of God is central and that new life in Christ is available to all who believe. Adult "Believers" baptism is practiced, symbolizing a conscious decision to follow Christ. Mennonites take seriously Christ's command to witness in word and deed. They stress that Christians need the support of a faith community for encouragement and growth. They view the teachings of Jesus as directly applicable to their lives. Mennonites generally refuse to serve in the military or to use violent resistance. The largest body of Mennonites in North America, the Mennonite Church is a member of the Mennonite and Brethren in Christ World Conference, a worldwide fellowship, and the Mennonite Central Committee, an international relief and service agency. Individuals and program agencies participate in a variety of ecumenical activities at various levels of church life.

Headquarters
421 S. Second St., Ste. 600, Elkhart, IN 46516 Tel. (219)294-7131 Fax (219)293-3977
Media Contact, Churchwide Communications Dir.
E-mail: mcgb@juno.com

Officers
Mod., Dwight McFadden, Jr., 521 E. Main St., New Holland, PA 17557 Tel. (717) 859-1151

OTHER ORGANIZATIONS
Gen. Bd., Gen. Sec., George B. Stoltzfus
Historical Cmte., Dir., John E. Sharp, 1700 S. Main, Goshen, IN 46526 Tel. (219)535-7477 Fax (219)535-7477
Peace & Justice Committee, Susan Mark Landis, Minister of Peace and Justice, P.O.Box 173, Orville, OH 44667 Tel. (330) 683-6844 FAX (330) 683-6844
Bd. of Congregational Min., Pres., Everett J. Thomas, Box 1245, Elkhart, IN 46515 Tel. (219)294-7523 Fax (219)293-1892
Bd. of Educ., Pres., Orville L. Yoder, Box 1142, Elkhart, IN 46515 Tel. (219)294-7523 Fax (219)293-7446
Bd. of Missions, Pres., Stanley W. Green, Box 370, Elkhart, IN 46515 Tel. (219)294-7523
Mutual Aid Bd., Pres., Howard L. Brenneman, 1110 North Main, P.O. Box 483, Goshen, IN 46526 Tel. (219)533-9511 Fax (219)533-5264
Mennonite Publication Bd., Publisher, J. Robert Ramer, 616 Walnut Ave., Scottdale, PA 15683 Tel. (412)887-8500 Fax (412)887-3111

Periodicals
The Mennonite; Christian Living; Rejoice!; Mennonite Historical Bulletin; Mennonite Quarterly Review; Purpose; Story Friends

Mennonite Church, The General Conference

The General Conference Mennonite Church was formed in 1860, uniting Mennonites throughout the United States who were interested in doing missionary work together. Today 65,500 Christians in 410 member congregations in Canada, the United States and three countries in South America try to follow the way of Jesus in their daily lives.

The conference consists of people of many ethnic backgrounds - Swiss and German, Russian and Dutch, African-American, Hispanic, Chinese, Vietnamese and Laotian. Some native Americans in both Canada and the United States also relate to the conference.

The basic belief and practice of the conference come from the life and teachings of Jesus Christ, the early church of the New Testament and the Anabaptists of the 16th-century Reformation. Thus the conference seeks to be evangelical, guided by the Bible, led by the Holy Spirit and supported by a praying, discerning community of believers in congregations and fellowships. Peace, or shalom, is at the very heart of members, who seek to be peacemakers in everyday life.

The goals of the conference are to evangelize, teach and practice biblical principles, train and develop leaders and work for Christian unity.

The General Conference is currently working toward merger with the Mennonite Church.

Headquarters
722 Main, P.O. Box 347, Newton, KS 67114 Tel. (316)283-5100 Fax (316)283-0454
Media Contact, Dir. of Comm., David Linscheid
E-mail: gcmc@gcmc.org
Website: http://www2.southwind.net/~gcmc

Officers & Staff of General Board
Mod., Darrell Fast, 328 E. 2nd St., Newton, KS 67114
Asst. Mod., Bernie Wiebe, 46 Belair Rd., Winnipeg, MB R3T 0S2
Secretary, Norma Wiens, 17 Circle Dr., Newton, KS 67114
Gen. Sec., James Schrag
Ministerial Leadership Committee, Dir. of Ministerial Leadership, John A. Esau

OTHER ORGANIZATIONS
Commission on Home Ministries, Exec., Lois Barrett
Commission on Overseas Mission, Exec. Sec., Ron Flaming
Mennonite Women, Exec. Coords., Susan Jantzen and Lara Hall
Commission on Education,Co-Exec. Sec., Dennis Good & Ken Hawkley
Div. of General Services: Bus. Mgr., Ted Stuckey; Communications Dir., David Linscheid

Mennonite Men, Coord, Jim Gingerich
Faith & Life Press, Mgr., Dennis Good

Periodicals
The Mennonite (published jointly with the Mennonite Church)

The Metropolitan Church Association, Inc.

Organized after a revival movement in Chicago in 1894 as the Metropolitan Holiness Church, this organization was chartered as the Metropolitan Church Association in 1899. It has Wesleyan theology.

Headquarters
323 Broad St., Lake Geneva, WI 53147 Tel. (414)248-6786
Media Contact, Pres., Rev. Warren W. Bitzer

Officers
Pres., Rev. Warren W. Bitzer
Vice-Pres. & Sec., Elbert L. Ison
Treas., Gertrude J. Puckhaber

Periodical
The Burning Bush

The Missionary Church

The Missionary Church was formed in 1969 through a merger of the United Missionary Church (organized in 1883) and the Missionary Church Association (founded in 1898). It is evangelical and conservative with a strong emphasis on missionary work and church planting.

There are three levels of church government with local, district and general conferences. There are 10 church districts in the United States. The general conference meets every two years. The denomination operates one college in the United States.

Headquarters
3811 Vanguard Dr., P.O. Box 9127, Ft. Wayne, IN 46899-9127 Tel. (219)747-2027 Fax (219) 747-5331
Media Contact, Pres., Dr. John Moran
E-mail: missionary.church@internetmci.com
Officers
Pres., Dr. John Moran
Vice-Pres., Rev. William Hossler
Sec., Rev. Dave Engbrecht
Treas., Milt Gerber
Director of Church Planting, Rev. Robert Ransom
Director of World PartnersUSA: Rev. David Mann
Director of Discipling Ministries, Rev. Tom Swank
Dir. of Ad. Services, David Von Gunten
Director of Financial Services, Neil Rinehart
Bethel Church Services, Dir., Rev. Larry Avery
Youth Dir., Eric Liechty
Children's Dir., Ms. Frances Blankenbaker
Resource & Curriculum, Dr. Duane Beals
Family Life Dir., Christine Crocker

Marketing & Communication Dir., Murray Young
Sunday School/Body Building Dir., Bob Keller
Senior Adult Ministry Dir., Dr. Charles Cureton
Missionary Men Liaison, Rev. Ron Phipps
Missionary Women Intl., Pres., Barbara Reffey
Missionary Church Investment Foundation, Mr. Eric Smith

Periodicals
Emphasis on Faith and Living; Priority

Moravian Church in America (Unitas Fratrum)

In 1735 German Moravian missionaries of the pre-Reformation faith of Jan Hus came to Georgia, in 1740 to Pennsylvania, and in 1753 to North Carolina. They established the American Moravian Church, which is broadly evangelical, ecumenical, liturgical, "conferential" in form of government and has an episcopacy as a spiritual office.

Headquarters
See Provincial addresses
Media Contact, Editor, The Moravian, Roxann Miller, Tel. (610)867-7566 Fax (610)866-9223

Northern Province

Headquarters
1021 Center St., P.O. Box 1245, Bethlehem, PA 18016-1245 Tel. (610)867-7566 Fax (610)866-9223

PROVINCIAL ELDERS' CONFERENCE
Pres., Rev. R. Burke Johnson
Vice-Pres./Sec. (Eastern Dist.), Rev. David L. Wickmann
Vice-Pres. (Western Dist.), Rev. Lawrence Christianson
Comptroller, Theresa E. Kunda, 1021 Center St., P.O. Box 1245, Bethlehem, PA 18016-1245
Staff Assoc., Rev. Gary L. Harke, P.O. Box 386, Sun Prairie, WI 53590

NORTHERN PROVINCE
1021 Center St., P.O. Box 1245, Bethlehem, PA 18016-1245 Tel. (610)867-7566 Fax (610)866-9223
Eastern District Pres., Rev. David L. Wickmann, P.O. Box 1245, Bethlehem, PA 18016-1245
Western District Pres., Rev. Rev. Lawrence Christianson
Pacific Southwest District Pres., Rev. Larry Wetzel, 7142 W. Cherry Hills Dr., Peoria, AZ 85345 Tel. (602)979-0488
Canadian District Pres., Rev. Ruth Humphreys, 25 23332 Twp. Rd. 20, Sherwood Park, AB T8B 1L5
E-mail: burke@mcnp.org
Website: http://www.moravian.org

SOUTHERN PROVINCE
459 S. Church St., Winston-Salem, NC 27101 Tel. (910)725-5811 Fax (910)725-1029
E-mail: bob_sawyer@ecunet.org
Website: www.moravian.org

123

PROVINCIAL ELDERS' CONFERENCE
Pres., Rev. Dr. Robert E. Sawyer
Vice-Pres./Asst. to Pres., Rev. William H. McElveen
Sec., Lane A. Sapp
Treas., Richard Cartner, Drawer M, Salem Station, Winston-Salem, NC 27108

ALASKA PROVINCE
P.O. Box 545, Bethel, AK 99559

Officers
Pres., Rev. Frank Chingliak
Vice-Pres., Rev. Peter Green
Sec., Sarah Owens
Treas., Juanita Asicksik
Dir. of Theological Education, Rev. Will Updegrove

Periodical
The Moravian

National Association of Congregational Christian Churches

This association was organized in 1955 in Detroit, Michigan, by delegates from Congregational Christian Churches committed to continuing the Congregational way of faith and order in church life. Participation by member churches is voluntary.

Headquarters
P.O. Box 1620, Oak Creek, WI 53154 Tel. (414)764-1620 Fax (414)764-0319
Media Contact, Assoc. Exec. Sec., Rev. Dr. Donald P. Olsen, 8473 So. Howell Ave., Oak Creek, WI 53154 Tel. (414)764-1620 Fax (414)764-0319
E-mail: naccc@naccc.org
Website: http://www.naccc.org/

Officers
Exec. Sec., Rev. Dr. Douglas L. Lobb, 8473 South Howell Ave., Oak Creek, WI 53154
Assoc. Exec. Secs., Rev. Phil Jackson and Rev. Dr. Donald P. Olsen

Periodical
The Congregationalist

National Association of Free Will Baptists

This evangelical group of Arminian Baptists was organized by Paul Palmer in 1727 at Chowan, N.C. Another movement (teaching the same doctrines of free grace, free salvation and free will) was organized June 30, 1780, in New Durham, N.H., but there was no connection with the southern organization except for a fraternal relationship.

The northern line expanded more rapidly and extended into the West and Southwest. This body merged with the Northern Baptist Convention Oct. 5, 1911, but a remnant of churches reorganized into the Cooperative General Association of Free Will Baptists Dec. 28, 1916, at Pattonsburg, Mo.

Churches in the southern line were organized into various conferences from the beginning and finally united in one General Conference in 1921. Representatives of the Cooperative General Association and the General Conference joined Nov. 5, 1935 to form the National Association of Free Will Baptists.

Headquarters
5233 Mt. View Rd., Antioch, TN 37013-2306 Tel. (615)731-6812 Fax (615)731-0771
Mailing Address, P.O. Box 5002, Antioch, TN 37011-5002
Media Contact, Exec. Sec., Melvin Worthington

Officers
Exec. Sec., Dr. Melvin Worthington
Mod., Rev. Carl Cheshier, PO Box 7208, Moore, TX 73153

DENOMINATIONAL AGENCIES
Free Will Baptist Foundation, Exec. Dir., William Evans
Free Will Baptist Bible College, Pres., Dr. Tom Malone
Foreign Missions Dept., Dir., Rev. James Forlines
Home Missions Dept., Dir., Trymon Messer
Bd. of Retirement, Dir., Rev. William Evans
Historical Commission, Sec., Jack Williams
Comm. for Theological Integrity, Chpsn., Rev. Leroy Forlines, P.O. Box 50117, Nashville, TN 37205
Music Commission, Chpsn., Rev. Randy Sawyer, 2316 Union Rd., Gastonia, NC 28054
Media Comm., Chpsn., Rev. Steve Faison, PO Box 295, Cedar Springs, GA 31732
Sunday School & Church Training Dept., Dir., Dr. Alton Loveless
Women Nationally Active for Christ, Exec. Sec., Majorie Workman
Master's Men Dept., Dir., Rev. Tom Dooley

Periodicals
Attack, A Magazine for Christian Men; Contact; Free Will Bible College Bulletin; Co-Laborer; Free Will Baptist Gem; Heartbeat; Mission Grams

National Baptist Convention of America, Inc.

The National Baptist Convention of America, Inc., was organized in 1880. Its mission is articulated through its history, constitution, articles of incorporation and by-laws. The Convention (corporate churches) has a mission statement with fourteen (14) objectives including: fostering unity throughout its membership and the world Christian community by proclaiming the gospel of Jesus Christ; validating and propagating the Baptist doctrine of faith and practice, and its distinctive principles throughout the world; and harnassing and encouraging the scholarly and Christian creative skills of its membership for Christian writing and publications.

Headquarters

Media Contact, Liaison Officer, Dr. Richard A. Rollins, 777 S. R.L. Thornton Fwy., Ste. 205, Dallas, TX 75203 Tel. (214)946-8913 Fax (214)946-9619

Officers

Pres., Dr. E. Edward Jones, 1327 Pierre Ave., Shreveport, LA 71103 Tel. (318)221-3701 Fax (318)222-7512
Gen. Rec. Sec., Dr. Clarence C. Pennywell, 2016 Russell Rd., Shreveport, LA 71107
Corres. Sec., Rev. E. E. Stafford, 6614 South Western Ave., Los Angeles, CA 90047
Liaison Officer, Dr. Richard A. Rollins, 777 So. R.L. Thornton Frwy., Ste. 205, Dallas, TX 75203 Tel. (214)946-8913 Fax (214)946-9619
Pres. Aide, Rev. Dr. Joe R. Gant, 5823 Ledbetter St., Shreveport, LA 77108

Periodicals

The Lantern

National Baptist Convention, U.S.A., Inc.

The older and parent convention of black Baptists, this body is to be distinguished from the National Baptist Convention of America.

Headquarters

1700 Baptist World Center Dr., Nashville, TN 37207 Tel. (615)228-6292 Fax (615)226-5935

Officers

Pres., Dr. Henry J. Lyons, 3455 26th Ave. S., St. Petersburg, FL 33711-3550 Tel. (615)228-6292
Gen. Sec., Dr. Roscoe Cooper, Jr., 300 Grace St., Richmond, VA 23220-4908 Tel. (804)643-0192

Periodical

Mission Herald

National Missionary Baptist Convention of America

The National Missionary Baptist Convention of America was organized in 1988 as a separate entity from the National Baptist Convention of America, Inc., after a dispute over control of the convention's publishing efforts. The new organization intended to remain committed to the National Baptist Sunday Church School and Baptist Training Union Congress and the National Baptist Publishing Board.

The purpose of the National Missionary Baptist Convention of America is to serve as an agency of Christian education, church extension and missionary efforts. It seeks to maintain and safeguard full religious liberty and engage in social and economic development.

Headquarters

1404 E. Firestone, Los Angeles, CA 90001 Tel. (213)582-0090
Media Contact, Dr. W. T. Snead, Sr.

Officers

Pres., Dr. W. T. Snead, Sr.

Vice-Pres., At-large, Dr. Harvey E. Leggett, 866 Monroe St., Ypsilanti, MI 48197
Vice-Pres., Ecumenical Affairs, Dr. F. Benjamin Davis, 1535 Dr. A.J. Brown Blvd. N., Indianapolis, IN 46202
Vice-Pres., Auxiliaries, T. J. Prince, 2219 Sea Island Dr., Dallas, TX 75232
Vice-Pres., Boards, Dr. O. E. Piper, 4220 W. 18th St., Chicago, IL 60623
Vice-Pres., Financial Affairs, J. A. Boles, 2001 South J St., Tacoma, WA 98405
Pres., National Baptist Publishing Bd., Dr. T. B. Boyd, III, 6717 Centennial Blvd., Nashville, TN 37209
Gen. Sec., Dr. Melvin V. Wade, 4269 S. Figueroa, Los Angeles, CA 90037
Corres. Sec., Dr. H. J. Johnson, 2429 South Blvd., Dallas, TX 75215
Treas., Dr. W. N. Daniel, 415 W. Englewood Ave., Chicago, IL 60612
Rec. Sec., Dr. Lonnie Franks, Crocker, TX

National Organization of the New Apostolic Church of North America

This body is a variant of the Catholic Apostolic Church which began in England in 1830. The New Apostolic Church distinguished itself from the parent body in 1863 by recognizing a succession of Apostles.

Headquarters

3753 N. Troy St., Chicago, IL 60618
Media Contact, Sec. & Treas., Ellen E. Eckhardt, Tel. (773)539-3652 Fax (773)478-6691
Website: http://www.nak.org

Officers

Pres., Rev. Erwin Wagner, 330 Arlene Pl., Waterloo, ON N2J 2G6
First Vice-Pres., Rev. Richard C. Freund, 1 Mikel Ln., Glen Head, NY 11545-1591
Second Vice-Pres., Rev. Leonard E Kolb, 4522 Wood St., Erie, PA 16509-1639
Treas. & Sec., Ellen E. Eckhardt, 6380 N. Indian Rd., Chicago, IL 60646
Asst. Sec., Rev. John E. Doderer, 3753 N. Troy St., Chicago, IL 60618

National Primitive Baptist Convention, Inc.

Throughout the years of slavery and the Civil War, the Negro population of the South worshipped with the white population in their various churches. At the time of emancipation, their white brethren helped them establish their own churches, granting them letters of fellowship, ordaining their deacons and ministers and helping them in other ways.

The doctrine and polity of this body are quite similar to that of white Primitive Baptists, yet there are local associations and a national convention, organized in 1907.

Each church is independent and receives and controls its own membership. This body was formerly known as Colored Primitive Baptists.

US RELIGIOUS BODIES

125

Headquarters
6433 Hidden Forest Dr., Charlotte, NC 28213
Tel. (704)596-1508
Media Contact, Elder T. W. Samuels

Officers
Natl. Convention, Pres., Elder T. W. Samuels, Tel. (704)596-3153
Natl. Convention, Vice-Pres., Elder Ernest Ferrell, Tallahassee, FL
Natl. Convention, Chmn. Bd. of Dirs., Elder Ernest Ferrell, Tallahassee, FL
Natl. Church School Training Union, Pres., Jonathan Yates, Mobile, AL
Natl. Ushers Congress, Pres., Bro. Carl Batts, 21213 Garden View Dr., Maple Heights, OH 44137
Publishing Bd., Chpsn., Elder E. W. Wallace, Creamridge, NJ
Women's Congress, Pres., Betty Brown, Cocoa Beach, FL
Natl. Laymen's Council, Pres., Densimore Robinson, Huntsville, AL
Natl. Youth Congress, Pres., Robert White, Trenton, NJ

National Spiritualist Association of Churches

This organization is made up of believers that Spiritualism is a science, philosophy and religion based upon the demonstrated facts of communication between this world and the next.

Headquarters
NSAC General Offices, Rev. Sharon L. Snowman, Secretary, P.O. Box 217, Lily Dale, NY 14752-0217
Media Contact, Ms. Marrice Converson, 5341 S., Cornell, Chicago, IL 60615-6205
E-mail: nsac@nsac.org
Website: http://www.nsac.org

Officers
Pres., Rev. Barbara Thurman, 200 Marina Vista Rd., Larkspur, CA 94939-2144
Vice-Pres., Rev. Pamla Ashlay, 11811 Watertown Plank Rd., Milwaukee, WI 53226
Sec., Rev. Sharon L. Snowman, P.O. Box 217, Lily Dale, NY 14752 Tel. (716)595-2000 Fax (716)595-2020
Treas., Rev. Lelia Cutler, 7310 Medfield St. #1, Norfolk, VA 23505

OTHER ORGANIZATIONS
Bureau of Educ., Supt., Rev. Janet Travis, 17 Ann Court, Kings Park, NY 11754
Bureau of Public Relations, Ms. Marrice Coverson, 5341 S. Cornell, Chicago, IL 60615-6205
The Stow Memorial Foundation, Sec., Rev. Sharon L. Snowman, P.O. Box 217, Lily Dale, NY 14752 Tel. (716)595-2000 Fax (716)595-2020
Spiritualist Benevolent Society, Inc., P.O. Box 217, Lily Dale, NY 14752

Periodicals
The National Spiritualist Summit; Spotlight

Netherlands Reformed Congregations

The Netherlands Reformed Congregations organized denominationally in 1907. In the Netherlands, the so-called Churches Under the Cross (established in 1839, after breaking away from the 1834 Secession congregations) and the so-called Ledeboerian churches (established in 1841 under the leadership of the Rev. Ledeboer, who seceded from the Reformed State Church), united in 1907 under the leadership of the then 25-year-old Rev. G. H. Kersten, to form the Netherlands Reformed Congregations. Many of the North American congregations left the Christian Reformed Church to join the Netherlands Reformed Congregations after the Kuyperian presupposed regeneration doctrine began making inroads.

All Netherlands Reformed Congregations, office-bearers and members subscribe to three Reformed Forms of Unity: The Belgic Confession of Faith (by DeBres), the Heidelberg Catechism (by Ursinus and Olevianus) and the Canons of Dort. Both the Belgic Confession and the Canons of Dort are read regularly at worship services, and the Heidelberg Catechism is preached weekly, except on church feast days.

Headquarters
Media Contact, Synodical Clk., Rev. C. Vogelaar, 2281 Mapleleaf Terrace, Grand Rapids, MI 49505 Tel. (616)742-5929 Fax (616)742-5930

OTHER ORGANIZATION
Netherlands Reformed Book and Publishing, 1233 Leffingwell NE, Grand Rapids, MI 49505
The Banner of Truth, Editor, Rev. J. Den Hoed, 824 18th Ave. S., Rock Valley, IA 51247 Tel. (712)476-2442

Periodical
The Banner of Truth

North American Baptist Conference

The North American Baptist Conference was begun by immigrants from Germany. The first church was organized by the Rev. Konrad Fleischmann in Philadelphia in 1843. In 1865 delegates of the churches met in Wilmot, Ont., and organized the North American Baptist Conference. Today only a few churches still use the German language, mostly in a bilingual setting.

The Conference meets in general session once every three years for fellowship, inspiration and to conduct the business of the Conference through elected delegates from the local churches. The General Council, composed of representatives of the various Associations and Conference organizations and departments, meets annually to determine the annual budget and programs for the Conference and its departments and agencies. The General Council also makes recommendations to the Triennial Conference on policies, long-range plans and election of certain personnel, boards and committees.

Approximately 65 missionaries serve in Brazil, Cameroon, Japan, Mexico, Nigeria, Philippines, and Russia.

Ten homes for the aged are affiliated with the Conference and 12 camps are operated on the association level.

Headquarters
1 S. 210 Summit Ave., Oakbrook Terrace, IL 60181 Tel. (630)495-2000 Fax (630)495-3301
Media Contact, Marilyn Schaer

Officers
Mod., Mr. Wayne Wegner
Vice-Mod., Rev. Harvey Wilke
Exec. Dir., Dr. Philip Yntema
Treas., Jackie Loewer

OTHER ORGANIZATIONS
Intl. Missions Dept., Dir., Ron Salzman
Home Missions Dept., Dir., Rev. Jim Fann
Church Extension Investors Fund, Dir., Robert Mayforth

North American Old Roman Catholic Church (Archdiocese of New York)

This body is identical with the Roman Catholic Church in faith but differs from it in discipline and worship. The Mass is offered with the appropriate rite either in Latin or in the vernacular. All other sacraments are taken from the Roman Pontifical. This jurisdiction allows for married clergy.

Primatial Headquarters
Box 021647 GPO, Brooklyn, NY 11202-0036 Tel. (718)855-0600
Media Contact, Chancellor, Most Rev. Albert J. Berube

Officers
Primate, The Most Rev. Herve L. Quessy
Chancellor, Most Rev. Albert J. Berube
Diocese of New York: Ordinary, Most Rev. Albert J. Berube
Diocese of Montreal & French Canada: Ordinary, Most Rev. Herve L. Quessy

Old German Baptist Brethren

This group separated from the Church of the Brethren (formerly German Baptist Brethren) in 1881 in order to preserve and maintain historic Brethren Doctrine.

Headquarters
Vindicator Ofc. Ed., Steven L. Bayer, 6952 N. Montgomery County Line Rd., Englewood, OH 45322-9748 Tel. (937)884-7531

Periodical
The Vindicator

Old Order Amish Church

The congregations of this Old Order Amish group have no annual conference. They worship in private homes. They adhere to the older forms of worship and attire. This body has bishops, ministers and deacons.

INFORMATION
Der Neue Amerikanische Calendar, c/o Raber's Book Store, 2467 C R 600, Baltic, OH 43804
Telephone Contact, LeRoy Beachy, Beachy Amish Mennonite Church, 4324 SR 39, Millersburg, OH 44654 Tel. (216)893-2883

Old Order (Wisler) Mennonite Church

This body arose from a separation of Mennonites dated 1872, under Jacob Wisler, in opposition to what were thought to be innovations.

The group is in the Eastern United States and Canada. Each state, or district, has its own organization and holds semi-annual conferences.

Headquarters
Media Contact, Amos B. Hoover, 376 N. Muddy Creek Rd., Denver, PA 17517 Tel. (717)484-4849 Fax (717)484-104

Open Bible Standard Churches

Open Bible Standard Churches originated from two revival movements: Bible Standard Conference, founded in Eugene, Ore., under the leadership of Fred L. Hornshuh in 1919, and Open Bible Evangelistic Association, founded in Des Moines, Iowa, under the leadership of John R. Richey in 1932.

Similar in doctrine and government, the two groups amalgamated on July 26, 1935 as "Open Bible Standard Churches, Inc." with headquarters in Des Moines, Iowa.

The original group of 210 ministers has enlarged to incorporate over 1,902 ministers and 1,069 churches in 36 countries. The first missionary left for India in 1926. The church now ministers in Asia, Africa, South America, Europe, Canada, Mexico, Central America, and the Caribbean Islands.

Historical roots of the parent groups reach back to the outpouring of the Holy Spirit in 1906 at Azusa Street Mission in Los Angeles and to the full gospel movement in the Midwest. Both groups were organized under the impetus of pentecostal revival. Simple faith, freedom from fanaticism, emphasis on evangelism and missions and free fellowship with other groups were characteristics of the growing organizations.

The highest governing body of Open Bible Standard Churches meets biennially and is composed of all ministers and one voting delegate per 100 members from each church. A National Board of Directors, elected by the national and regional conferences, conducts the business of the organization. Official Bible College is Eugene Bible College in Oregon.

Open Bible Standard Churches is a charter member of the National Association of Evangelicals and of the Pentecostal/Charismatic Churches of North America. It is a member of the Pentecostal World Conference.

NATIONAL OFFICE

2020 Bell Ave., Des Moines, IA 50315 Tel. (515)288-6761 Fax (515)288-2510
Media Contact, Exec. Dir., Communications & Resources, Jeff Farmer, Tel. (515)288-6761 Fax (515)288-2510
E-mail: info@openbible.org
Website: http://www. openbible.org

Officers

Pres., Jeffrey E. Farmer
Sec.-Treas., Teresa A. Beyer
Dir. of Intl. Min., Paul V. Canfield

Periodicals

Message of the Open Bible

The (Original) Church of God, Inc.

This body was organized in 1886 as the first church in the United States to take the name "The Church of God." In 1917 a difference of opinion led this particular group to include the word (Original) in its name. It is a holiness body and believes in the whole Bible, rightly divided, using the New Testament as its rule and government.

Headquarters

P.O. Box 592, Wytheville, VA 24382
Media Contact, Gen. Overseer, Rev. William Dale, Tel. (800)827-9234

Officers

Gen. Overseer, Rev. William Dale
Asst. Gen. Overseer, Rev. Alton Evans

Periodical

The Messenger

The Orthodox Church in America

The Orthodox Church of America entered Alaska in 1794 before its purchase by the United States in 1867. Its canonical status of independence (autocephaly) was granted by its Mother Church, the Russian Orthodox Church, on April 10, 1970, and is now known as The Orthodox Church in America.

Headquarters

P.O. Box 675, Syosset, NY 11791-0675 Tel. (516)922-0550 Fax (516)922-0954
Media Contact, Dir. of Communications, V. Rev. John Matusiak
E-mail: jjm@oca.org
Website: http://www.oca.org

Officers

Primate, Archbishop of Washington, Metropolitan of All America & Canada, Most Blessed Theodosius

Chancellor, V. Rev. Robert S. Kondratick, P.O. Box 675, Syosset, NY 11791 Tel. (516)922-0550 Fax (516)922-0954

SYNOD

Chpsn., His Beatitude Theodosius, P.O. Box 675, Syosset, NY 11791
Archbishop of New York, Most Rev. Peter, 33 Hewitt Ave., Bronxville, NY 10708
Archbishop of Pittsburgh & Western PA, Most Rev. Kyrill, P.O. Box R, Wexford, PA 15090
Archbishop of Dallas, Archbishop Dmitri, 4112 Throckmorton, Dallas, TX 75219
Bishop of Philadelphia, Archbishop Herman, St. Tikhon's Monastery, South Canaan, PA 18459
Aux. Bishop of Anchorage, Rt. Rev. Innocent, P.O. Box 240805, Anchorage, AK 99524-0805
Bishop of Detroit, Rt. Rev. Nathaniel, P.O. Box 309, Grass Lake, MI 49240-0309
Bishop of Midwest, Rt. Rev. Job, 605 Iowa St., Oak Park, IL 60302
Bishop of San Francisco, Rt. Rev. Tikhon, 649 North Robinson St., Los Angeles, CA 90026
Bishop of Ottawa and Canada, Rt. Rev. Seraphim, P.O. Box 179, Spencerville, ON K0E 1X0 Tel. (613)925-5226
Auxiliary Bishop, Titular Bishop of Bethesda, Rt. Rev. Mark, 9511 Sun Pointe Dr., Boynton Beach, FL 33437
Auxiliary Bishop for the Diocese of Alaska, Rt. Rev. Innocent, 513 E. 24th St., Ste. #3, Ancorage, AK 99503 Tel. (907) 279-0025

Periodical

The Orthodox Church

The Orthodox Presbyterian Church

On June 11, 1936, certain ministers, elders and lay members of the Presbyterian Church in the U.S.A. withdrew from that body to form a new denomination. Under the leadership of the late Rev. J. Gresham Machen, noted conservative New Testament scholar, the new church determined to continue to uphold the Westminster Confession of Faith as traditionally understood by Presbyterians and to engage in proclamation of the gospel at home and abroad.

The church has grown modestly over the years and suffered early defections, most notably one in 1937 that resulted in the formation of the Bible Presbyterian Church under the leadership of Dr. Carl McIntire. It now has congregations throughout the states of the continental United States.

The denomination is a member of the North American Presbyterian and Reformed Council and the International Council of Reformed Churches.

Headquarters

607 N. Easton Rd., Bldg. E, Box P, Willlow Grove, PA 19090-0920 Tel. (215)830-0900 Fax (215)830-0350
Media Contact, Stated Clerk, Rev. Donald J. Duff
E-mail: duff.1@opc.org
Website: http://www.opc.org

Officers

Moderator of General Assembly, Rev. Ross W. Graham, PO Box P, Williow Grove, PA 19090-0920

Stated Clk., Rev. Donald J. Duff

Periodical

New Horizons in the Orthodox Presbyterian Church

Patriarchal Parishes of the Russian Orthodox Church in the U.S.A.

This group of parishes is under the direct jurisdiction of the Patriarch of Moscow and All Russia, His Holiness Aleksy II, in the person of a Vicar Bishop, His Grace Paul, Bishop of Zaraisk.

Headquarters

St. Nicholas Cathedral, 15 E. 97th St., New York, NY 10029 Tel. (212)831-6294 Fax (212)427-5003

Media Contact, Sec. to the Bishop, Deacon Vladimîr Tyschuk, Tel. (212)289-1915

Periodical

One Church

Pentecostal Assemblies of the World, Inc.

This organization is an interracial Pentecostal holiness of the Apostolic Faith, believing in repentance, baptism in Jesus's name and being filled with the Holy Ghost, with the evidence of speaking in tongues. It originated in the early part of the century in the Middle West and has spread throughout the country.

Headquarters

3939 Meadows Dr., Indianapolis, IN 46205 Tel. (317)547-9541

Media Contact, Admin., John E. Hampton, Fax (317)543-0512

Officers

Presiding Bishop, Paul A. Bowers

Asst. Presiding Bishop, David Ellis

Bishops: Arthus Brazier; George Brooks; Ramsey Butler; Morris Golder; Francis L. Smith, Francis L.; Brooker T. Jones; C. R. Lee; Robert McMurray; Philip L. Scott; William L. Smith; Samuel A. Layne; Freeman M. Thomas; James E. Tyson; Charles Davis; Willie Burrell; Harry Herman; Jeremiah Reed; Jeron Johnson; Clifton Jones; Robert Wauls; Ronald L. Young; Henry L. Johnson; Leodis Warren; Thomas J. Weeks; Eugene Redd; Thomas W. Weeks, Sr.; Willard Saunders; Davis L. Ellis; Earl Parchia; Vanuel C. Little; Norman Wagner; George Austin; Benjamin A. Pitt; Markose Thopil; John K. Cole; Peter Warkie; Norman Walters; Alphonso Scott; David Dawkins

Gen. Sec, Suffragan Bishop Richard Young

Gen. Treas., Elder James Loving

Asst. Treas., Suffragan Bishop Willie Ellis

Periodical

Christian Outlook

Pentecostal Church of God

Growing out of the pentecostal revival at the turn of the century, the Pentecostal Church of God was organized in Chicago on Dec. 30, 1919, as the Pentecostal Assemblies of the U.S.A. The name was changed to Pentecostal Church of God in 1922; in 1934 it was changed again to The Pentecostal Church of God of America, Inc.; and finally the name became the Pentecostal Church of God (Inc.) in 1979.

The International Headquarters was moved from Chicago to Ottumwa, Iowa, in 1927, then to Kansas City, Mo., in 1933 and finally to Joplin, Mo., in 1951.

The denomination is evangelical and pentecostal in doctrine and practice. Active membership in the National Association of Evangelicals and the Pentecostal/Charismatic Churches North America is maintained.

The church is Trinitarian in doctrine and teaches the absolute inerrancy of the Scripture from Genesis to Revelation. Among its cardinal beliefs are the doctrines of salvation, which includes regeneration; divine healing, as provided for in the atonement; the baptism in the Holy Ghost, with the initial physical evidence of speaking in tongues; and the premillennial second coming of Christ.

Headquarters

4901 Pennsylvania, P.O. Box 850, Joplin, MO 64802 Tel. (417)624-7050 Fax (417)624-7102

Media Contact, Gen. Sec., Dr. Ronald R. Minor

E-mail: peg@clandjop.com

Officers

Gen. Supt., Dr. James D. Gee

Gen. Sec., Dr. Ronald R. Minor

OTHER GENERAL EXECUTIVES

Dir. of World Missions, Dr. Charles R. Mosier

Dir. of Indian Missions, Dr. C. Don Burke

Gen. PYPA Pres., Reggie O. Powers

Dir. of Home Missions/Evangelism, Dr. H. O. (Pat) Wilson

ASSISTANT GENERAL SUPERINTENDENTS

Northwestern Division, Rev. James R. Layne

Southwestern Division, Rev. Donald D. Hamilton

North Central Division, Rev. Freddy A. Burcham

South Central Division, Rev. E. L. Redding

Northeastern Division, Rev. Thomas E. Branham

Southeastern Division, Rev. Virgil R. Kincard

OTHER DEPARTMENTAL Officers

Bus. Mgr., Rev. Alan Greagrey

Director of Women's Ministry, Diana L. Gee

Christian Educ., Dir., Mrs. Billie Palumbo

Periodical

The Pentecostal Messenger

Pentecostal Fire-Baptized Holiness Church

Organized in 1918, this group consolidated

with the Pentecostal Free Will Baptists in 1919. It maintains rigid discipline over members.

Headquarters
P.O. Box 261, La Grange, GA 30241-0261 Tel. (706)884-7742
Media Contact, Gen. Mod., Wallace B. Pittman, Jr.

Officers
Gen. Treas., K. N. (Bill) Johnson, P.O. Box 1528, Laurinburg, NC 28352 Tel. (919)276-1295
Gen. Sec., W. H. Preskitt, Sr., Rt. 1, Box 169, Wetumpka, AL 36092 Tel. (205)567-6565
Gen. Mod., Wallace B. Pittman, Jr.
Gen. Supt. Mission Bd., Jerry Powell, Rt. 1, Box 384, Chadourn, NC 28431

Periodical
Faith and Truth

The Pentecostal Free Will Baptist Church, Inc.

The Cape Fear Conference of Free Will Baptists, organized in 1855, merged in 1959 with The Wilmington Conference and The New River Conference of Free Will Baptists and was renamed the Pentecostal Free Will Baptist Church, Inc. The doctrines include regeneration, sanctification, the Pentecostal baptism of the Holy Ghost, the Second Coming of Christ and divine healing.

Headquarters
P.O. Box 1568, Dunn, NC 28335 Tel. (910)892-4161 Fax (910)892-6876
Media Contact, Gen. Supt., Preston Heath
E-mail: pheath@intrstar.net

Officers
Gen. Supt., Rev. Preston Heath
Asst. Gen. Supt., Rev. Reynolds Smith
Gen. Sec., Rev. Horace Johnson
Gen. Treas., Dr. W. L. Ellis
Christian Ed. Dir., Rev. Murray King
Gen. Services Dir., Danny Blackman
Ministerial Council Dir., —
Ladies' Auxiliary Dir., Dollie Davis
Heritage Bible College, Pres., Dr. W. L. Ellis
Crusader Youth Camp, Dir., Rev. Murray King

OTHER ORGANIZATIONS
Heritage Bible College
Crusader Youth Camp
Blessings Bookstore, 1006 W. Cumberland St., Dunn, NC 28334 Tel. (910)892-2401
Cape Fear Christian Academy, Rt 1 Box 139, Erwin, NC 28339 Tel. (910)897-5423

Periodical
The Messenger

Pillar of Fire

The Pillar of Fire was founded by Alma Bridwell White in Denver on Dec. 29, 1901 as the Pentecostal Union. In 1917, the name was changed to Pillar of Fire. Alma White was born in Kentucky in 1862 and taught school in Montana where she met her husband, Kent White, a Methodist minister, who was a University student in Denver.

Because of Alma White's evangelistic endeavors, she was frowned upon by her superiors, which eventually necessitated her withdrawing from Methodist Church supervision. She was ordained as Bishop and her work spread to many states, to England, and since her death to Liberia, West Africa, Malawi, East Africa, Yugoslavia, Spain, India and the Philippines.

The Pillar of Fire organization has a college and two seminaries stressing Biblical studies. It operates eight separate schools for young people. The church continues to keep in mind the founder's goals and purposes.

Headquarters
P.O. Box 9159, Zarephath, NJ 08890 Tel. (908) 356-0102
Western Headquarters, 1302 Sherman St., Denver, CO 80203 Tel. (303)427-5462
Media Contact, 1st Vice Pres., Robert B. Dallenbach, 3455 W. 83 Ave., Westminster, CO 80030 Tel. (303)427-5462 Fax (303)429-0910

Officers
Pres. & Gen. Supt., Bishop Donald J. Wolfram
1st Vice-Pres. & Asst. Supt., Bishop Robert B. Dallenbach
2nd Vice-Pres./Sec.-Treas., Lois R. Stewart
Trustees: Kenneth Cope; Elsworth N. Bradford; S. Rea Crawford; Lois Stewart; Dr. Donald J. Wolfram; Robert B. Dallenbach; June Blue

Periodical
The Pillar Monthly

Polish National Catholic Church of America

After a number of attempts to resolve differences regarding the role of the laity in parish administration in the Roman Catholic Church in Scranton, Pa., this Church was organized in 1897. With the consecration to the episcopacy of the Most Rev. F. Hodur, this Church became a member of the Old Catholic Union of Utrecht in 1907.

Headquarters
Office of the Prime Bishop, 1004 Pittston Ave., Scranton, PA 18505 Tel. (717)346-9131
Media Contact, Prime Bishop, Most Rev. John F. Swantek, 1002 Pittston Ave., Scranton, PA 18505 Tel. (717)346-9131 Fax (717)346-2188

Officers
Prime Bishop, Most Rev. John F. Swantek, 115 Lake Scranton Rd., Scranton, PA 18505
Central Diocese: Bishop, Rt. Rev. Anthony M. Rysz, 529 E. Locust St., Scranton, PA 18505
Eastern Diocese: Bishop, Rt. Rev. Thomas J. Gnat, 166 Pearl St., Manchester, NH 03104

Buffalo-Pittsburgh Diocese: Bishop, Rt. Rev. Thaddeus S. Peplowski, 5776 Broadway, Lancaster, NY 14086

Western Diocese: Rt. Rev. Robert M. Nemkovich, 920 N. Northwest Hwy., Park Ridge, IL 60068

Canadian Diocese: Bishop, Sede Vacante, 186 Cowan Ave., Toronto, ON M6K 2N6

Ecumenical Officer, V. Rev. Stanley Skrzypek, 206 Main Street, New York Mills, NY 13416 Tel. (315)736-9757

Periodicals

God's Field; Polka

Presbyterian Church in America

The Presbyterian Church in America has a strong commitment to evangelism, to missionary work at home and abroad and to Christian education.

Organized in December 1973, this church was first known as the National Presbyterian Church but changed its name in 1974 to Presbyterian Church in America (PCA).

The PCA made a firm commitment on the doctrinal standards which had been significant in presbyterianism since 1645, namely the Westminster Confession of Faith and Catechisms. These doctrinal standards express the distinctives of the Calvinistic or Reformed tradition.

The PCA maintains the historic polity of Presbyterian governance, namely rule by presbyters (or elders) and the graded courts which are the session governing the local church. The presbytery is responsible for regional matters and the general assembly for national matters. The PCA has taken seriously the position of the parity of elders, making a distinction between the two classes of elders, teaching and ruling.

In 1982, the Reformed Presbyterian Church, Evangelical Synod (RPCES) joined the PCA. It brought with it a tradition that had antecedents in Colonial America. It also included Covenant College in Lookout Mountain, Ga., and Covenant Theological Seminary in St. Louis, both of which are national denominational institutions of the PCA.

Headquarters

1852 Century Pl., Atlanta, GA 30345-4305 Tel. (404)320-3366 Fax (404)329-1275

Media Contact: Rev. J. Robert Fiol

E-mail: info@ac.pca-atl.org

Website: http://www.pcanet.org

Officers

Mod., Rev. Kennedy Smartt

Stated Clk., Dr. L. Roy Taylor, 1852 Century Pl., Ste. 190, Atlanta, GA 30345-4305 Tel. (404)320-3366

PERMANENT COMMITTEES

Admn., Dr. L. Roy Taylor, 1852 Century Pl., Ste. 190, Atlanta, GA 30345-4305 Tel. (404) 320-3366 Fax (404)329-1275

Christian Educ. & Publ., Dr. Charles Dunahoo, 1852 Century Pl., Ste. 190, Atlanta, GA 30345-4305 Tel. (404)320-3388

Mission to North America, Dr. Cortez Cooper, 1852 Century Pl., Ste. 205, Atlanta, GA 30345-4305 Tel. (404)320-3330

Mission to the World, Dr. Paul D. Kooistra, 1852 Century Pl., Ste. 201, Atlanta, GA 30345-4305 Tel. (404)320-3373

Presbyterian Church (U.S.A.)

The Presbyterian Church (U.S.A.) was organized June 10, 1983, when the Presbyterian Church in the United States and the United Presbyterian Church in the United States of America united in Atlanta. The union healed a major division which began with the Civil War when Presbyterians in the South withdrew from the Presbyterian Church in the United States of America to form the Presbyterian Church in the Confederate States.

The United Presbyterian Church in the United States of America had been created by the 1958 union of the Presbyterian Church in the United States of America and the United Presbyterian Church of North America. Of those two uniting bodies, the Presbyterian Church in the U.S.A. dated from the first Presbytery organized in Philadelphia, about 1706. The United Presbyterian Church of North America was formed in 1858, when the Associate Reformed Presbyterian Church and the Associate Presbyterian Church united.

Strongly ecumenical in outlook, the Presbyterian Church (U.S.A.) is the result of at least 10 different denominational mergers over the last 250 years. A restructure, adopted by the General Assembly meeting in June 1993, has been implemented. The Presbyterian Church (U.S.A.) dedicated its new national offices in Louisville, Ky. in 1988.

Headquarters

100 Witherspoon St., Louisville, KY 40202 Tel. (502)569-5000 Fax (502)569-5018

Media Contact, Assoc. Dir. for Communications, Gary W. Luhr, Tel. (502)569-5515 Fax (502) 569-8073

E-mail: presytel@pcusa.org

Website: http://www.pcusa.org

Officers

Mod., Douglas W. Oldenburg

Vice-Mod., James E. Mead

Stated Clk., Clifton Kirkpatrick

Assoc. Stated Clks., C. Fred Jenkins, Eugene G. Turner, Jan De Vries

THE OFFICE OF THE GENERAL ASSEMBLY

Tel. (502)569-5360 Fax (502)569-8005

Stated Clk., Clifton Kirkpatrick

Dept. of the Stated Clerk: Dir., —

Dept. of Administration & Assembly Services: Dir., Jan De Vries

Dept. of Constitutional Servicess: Dir., C. Fred Jenkins

Dept. of Governing Bodies, Ecumenical & Agency Rel.: Dir., Eugene G. Turner

Dept. of Hist., Philadelphia: 425 Lombard St., Philadelphia, PA 19147 Tel. (215)627-1852 Fax (215)627-0509; Dir., Frederick J. Heuser, Jr.

Deputy Dir., Kristin Gleeson

Deputy Dir., Michelle Francis, PO Box 849, Montreat, NC 28757

GENERAL ASSEMBLY COUNCIL

Exec. Dir., John J. Detterick, Fax (502)569-8080

Worldwide Ministries Division, Dir., Marian McClure

Congregational Ministries Division, Dir., Richard M. Ferguson

National Ministries Division, Dir., Curtis A. Kearns, Jr.

Corp. & Admn. Services, Interim Dir., Robert McKee

BOARD OF PENSIONS

Pres., —, 2000 Market St., Philadelphia, PA 19103-3298 Tel. (215)587-7200

Chpsn. of the Bd., Eugene Sibery

PRESBYTERIAN CHURCH (U.S.A.) FOUNDATION

Ofc., 200 E. Twelfth St., Jeffersonville, IN 47130 Tel. (812)288-8841 Fax (502)569-5980

Chpsn. of the Bd., Georgette Huie

Pres. & CEO, Larry Carr

PRESBYTERIAN CHURCH (U.S.A.) INVESTMENT/LOAN PROGRAM, INC.

Chpsn. of the Board, Alvin Puryear

Pres. & CEO, Kenneth G.Y. Grant, Tel. (800)903-7457 Fax (502)569-8868

PRESBYTERIAN PUBLISHING CORPORATE

Pres. & CEO, Davis Perkins, Fax (502)569-5113

Chpsn. of the Bd., Robert Bohl

SYNOD EXECUTIVES

Alaska-Northwest, Rev.Gary Skinner, 233 6th Ave. N., Ste. 100, Seattle, WA 98109-5000 Tel. (206)448-6403

Covenant, Rev. Lowell Simms, 6172 Busch Blvd., Ste. 3000, Columbus, OH 43229-2564 Tel. (614)436-3310

Lakes & Prairies, Rev. Margaret J. Thomas, 8012 Cedar Ave. S., Bloomington, MN 55425-1210 Tel. (612)854-0144

Lincoln Trails, Rev. Verne E. Sindlinger, 1100 W. 42nd St., Indianapolis, IN 46208-3381 Tel. (317)923-3681

Living Waters, Rev. William Giles, P.O. Box 1207, Brentwood, TN 37024 Tel. (615)370-4008

Mid-America, Rev. John L. Williams, 6400 Glenwood, Ste. 111, Overland Park, KS 66202-4072 Tel. (913)384-3020

Mid-Atlantic, Rev. Carroll D. Jenkins, P.O. Box 27026, Richmond, VA 23261-7026 Tel. (804)342-0016

Northeast, Rev. Robert Howell White, Jr., 5811 Heritage Landing Dr., East Syracuse, NY 13057-9360 Tel. (315)446-5990

Pacific, Rev. Philip H. Young, 8 Fourth St., Petaluma, CA 94952-3004 Tel. (707)765-1772

Puerto Rico (Boriquen in Puerto Rico), Rev. Harry Fred Del Valle, Ave. Hostos Edificio 740, Cond. Medical Center Plaza, Ste. 216, Mayaguez, PR 00680 Tel. (787)832-8375

Rocky Mountains, Rev. Richard O. Wyatt, 3025 West 37th Ave., Ste.206, Denver, CO 80211-2799 Tel. (303)477-9070

South Atlantic, Rev. John Niles Bartholomew, 118 E. Monroe St., Jacksonville, FL 32202 Tel. (904)356-6070

Southern California, Hawaii, Rev. John N. Langfitt, 1501 Wilshire Blvd., Los Angeles, CA 90017-2293 Tel. (213)483-3840

Southwest, Jane F. Odell, 4423 N. 24th St., Ste. 800, Phoenix, AZ 85016-5592 Tel. (602)468-3800

Sun, Rev. Judy R. Fletcher (Interim), 920 S. I 35 E, Denton, TX 76205-7898 Tel. (940)382-9656

Trinity, Rev. Thomas M. Johnston, Jr., 3040 Market St., Camp Hill, PA 17011-4599 Tel. (717)737-0421

Periodicals

American Presbyterians: Journal of Presbyterian History; Presbyterian News Service "News Briefs"; Church & Society Magazine; Horizons; Monday Morning; Presbyterians Today; Interpretation; Presbyterian Outlook; "Presbyterians: Being Faithful to Jesus Christ"

Primitive Advent Christian Church

This body split from the Advent Christian Church. All its churches are in West Virginia. The Primitive Advent Christian Church believes that the Bible is the only rule of faith and practice and that Christian character is the only test of fellowship and communion. The church agrees with Christian fidelity and meekness; exercises mutual watch and care; counsels, admonishes, or reproves as duty may require and receives the same from each other as becomes the household of faith. Primitive Advent Christians do not believe in taking up arms.

The church believes that three ordinances are set forth by the Bible to be observed by the Christian church: (1) baptism by immersion; (2) the Lord's Supper, by partaking of unleavened bread and wine; (3) feet washing, to be observed by the saints' washing of one another's feet.

Headquarters

Media Contact, Sec.-Treas., Roger Wines, 1971 Grapevine Rd., Sissonville, WV 25320 Tel. (304)988-2668

Officers

Pres., Herbert Newhouse, 7632 Hughart Dr., Sissonville, WV 25320 Tel. (304)984-9277

Vice-Pres., Roger Hammons, 273 Frame Rd., Elkview, WV 25071 Tel. (304)965-6247

Sec. & Treas., Roger Wines, 1971 Grapevine Rd., Sissonville, WV 25320 Tel. (304)988-2668

Primitive Baptists

This large group of Baptists, located throughout the United States, opposes all centralization and modern missionary societies. They preach salvation by grace alone.

Headquarters

P.O. Box 38, Thornton, AR 71766 Tel. (501)352-3694

Media Contact, Elder W. Hartsel Cayce

Officers

Elder W. Hartsel Cayce

Elder Lasserre Bradley, Jr., Box 17037, Cincinnati, OH 45217 Tel. (513)821-7289

Elder S. T. Tolley, P.O. Box 68, Atwood, TN 38220 Tel. (901)662-7417

Periodicals

Baptist Witness; The Christian Baptist; The Primitive Baptist; For the Poor

Primitive Methodist Church in the U.S.A.

Hugh Bourne and William Clowes, local preachers in the Wesleyan Church in England, organized a daylong meeting at Mow Cop in Staffordshire on May 31, 1807, after Lorenzo Dow, a Methodist preacher from America, told them of American camp meetings. Thousands attended and many were converted but the Methodist church, founded by the open-air preacher John Wesley, refused to accept the converts and reprimanded the preachers.

After waiting for two years for a favorable action by the Wesleyan Society, Bourne and Clowes established The Society of the Primitive Methodists. This was not a schism, Bourne said, for "we did not take one from them...it now appeared to be the will of God that we...should form classes and take upon us the care of churches in the fear of God." Primitive Methodist missionaries were sent to New York in 1829. An American conference was established in 1840. Missionary efforts reach into Guatemala, Spain and other countries. The denomination joins in federation with the Evangelical Congregational Church, the United Brethren in Christ Church and the Southern Methodist Church and is a member of the National Association of Evangelicals.

The church believes the Bible is the only true rule of faith and practice, the inspired Word of God. It believes in one Triune God, the Deity of Jesus Christ, the Deity and personality of the Holy Spirit, the innocence of Adam and Eve, the Fall of the human race, the necessity of repentance, justification by faith of all who believe, regeneration witnessed by the Holy Spirit, sanctification by the Holy Spirit, the second coming of the Lord Jesus Christ, the resurrection of the dead and conscious future existence of all people and future judgments with eternal rewards and punishments.

Headquarters

Media Contact, Pres./Exec. Dir., Rev. Wayne Yarnall, 1045 Laurel Run Rd., Wilkes-Barre, PA 18702 Tel. (717)472-3436 Fax (717)472-9283 E-mail: exdir1@juno.com

Officers

Pres./Exec. Dir., Rev. Wayne Yarnall, 1045 Laurel Run Rd., Wilkes-Barre, PA 18702 Tel. (717)472-3436 Fax (717)472-9283

Vice-Pres., Rev. James G. Johnson, 516 Jackson St., Sdickson City, PA 18519-1435

General. Secretary.: Rev. David Allen, Jr., 1199 Lawrence St., Lowell, MA 01522-5526 Tel. (978) 453-2052

E-mail: pahson@banet.net

Treas., Mr. Raymond C. Baldwin, 11012 Langton Arms Ct., Oakton, VA 22124

E-mail: Rbaldwin32@aol.com

Progressive National Baptist Convention, Inc.

This body held its organizational meeting in Cincinnati in November, 1961. Subsequent regional sessions were followed by the first annual session in Philadelphia in 1962.

Headquarters

601 50th Street, N.E., Washington, DC 20019 Tel. (202)396-0558 Fax (202)398-4998

Media Contact, Gen. Sec., Dr. Tyrone S. Pitts

Officers

Pres., Dr. Bennett W. Smith, Sr., St. John Baptist Church, 184 Goodell St., Buffalo, NY 14204

Gen. Sec., Dr. Tyrone S. Pitts

OTHER ORGANIZATIONS

Dept. of Christian Education, Exec. Dir., Dr. C. B. Lucas, Emmanuel Baptist Church, 3815 W. Broadway, Louisville, KY 40211

Women's Dept., Mildred Wormley, 218 Spring St., Trenton, NJ 08618

Home Mission Bd., Exec. Dir., Rev. Archie LeMone, Jr.

Congress of Christian Education, Pres., Rev. Harold S. Diggs, Mayfield Memorial Baptist Church, 700 Sugar Creek Rd. W., Charlotte, NC 28213

Baptist Global Mission Bureau, Dr. Ronald K. Hill, 161-163 60th St., Philadelphia, PA 19139

Nannie Helen Burroughs School, Tel. (202)398-5266

Periodical

Baptist Progress

Protestant Reformed Churches in America

The Protestant Reformed Churches (PRC) have their roots in the sixteenth century

Reformation of Martin Luther and John Calvin, as it developed in the Dutch Reformed churches. The denomination originated as a result of a controversy in the Christian Reformed Church in 1924 involving the adoption of the "Three Points of Common Grace." Three ministers in the Christian Reformed Church, the Reverends Herman Hoeksema, George Ophoff, and Henry Danhof, and their consistories (Eastern Avenue, Hope, and Kalamazoo, respectively) rejected the doctrine. Eventually these men were deposed, and their consistories were either deposed or set outside the Christian Reformed Church. The denomination was formed in 1926 with three congregations. Today the denomination is comprised of some twenty-seven churches (more than 6,000 members) in the USA and Canada.

The presbyterian form of church government as determined by the Church Order of Dordt is followed by the PRC. The doctrinal standards of the PRC are the Reformed confessions - the Heidelberg Catechism, Belgic Confession of Faith, and Canons of Dordrecht. The doctrine of the covenant is a cornerstone of their teaching. They maintain an unconditional, particular covenant of grace that God establishes with His elect.

Headquarters
16511 South Park Ave., South Holland, IL 60473 Tel. (708)333-1314
Media Contact, Stat. Clk., Don Doezema, 4949 Ivanrest Ave., Grandville, MI 49418 Tel. (616) 531-1490
E-mail: doezema@prca.org

Officer
Stat. Clk., Don Doezema

Periodical
The Standard Bearer

Reformed Church in America
The Reformed Church in America was established in 1628 by the earliest settlers of New York. It is the oldest Protestant denomination with a continuous ministry in North America. Until 1867 it was known as the Reformed Protestant Dutch Church.

The first ordained minister, Domine Jonas Michaelius, arrived in New Amsterdam from The Netherlands in 1628. Throughout the colonial period, the Reformed Church lived under the authority of the Classis of Amsterdam. Its churches were clustered in New York and New Jersey. Under the leadership of Rev. John Livingston, it became a denomination independent of the authority of the Classis of Amsterdam in 1776. Its geographical base was broadened in the 19th century by the immigration of Reformed Dutch and German settlers in the midwestern United States. The Reformed Church now spans the United States and Canada.

The Reformed Church in America accepts as its standards of faith the Heidelberg Catechism, Belgic Confession and Canons of Dort. It has a rich heritage of world mission activity. It claims to be loyal to reformed tradition which emphasizes obedience to God in all aspects of life.

Although the Reformed Church in America has worked in close cooperation with other churches, it has never entered into merger with any other denomination. It is a member of the World Alliance of Reformed Churches, the World Council of Churches and the National Council of the Churches of Christ in the United States of America.

Headquarters
475 Riverside Dr., New York, NY 10115 Tel. (212)870-2841 Fax (212)870-2499
Media Contact, Dir., Stewardship & Communication Services, E. Wayne Antworth, 475 Riverside Dr., Rm. 1815, New York, NY 10115 Tel. (212)870-2954 Fax (212)870-2499
E-mail: rcags475@aol.com
Website: http://www.rca.org

Officers and Staff of General Synod
Pres., Frederick Kruithof, 475 Riverside Dr., Rm. 1814, New York, NY 10115
Gen. Sec., Wesley Granberg- Michaelson

OTHER ORGANIZATIONS
Bd. of Directors, Pres., Frederick Kruithof, 475 Riverside Dr., Rm. 1814, New York, NY 10115
Bd. of Pensions: Pres., Gregg Mast; Sec., Wesley Granberg- Michaelson
General Synod Council: Mod., Charles Van Engen, 475 Riverside Dr., Rm. 1812, New York, NY 10115
Office of Policy, Planning & Admn. Serv., Kenneth R. Bradsell
Ofc. of Ministry & personnel Services, Dir., Alvin J. Poppen
Office of Evangelism & Church Dev. Ser., Richard Welscott
Ofc. of Finance Services, Treas., Susan Converse
Ofc. of Stewardship & Comm. Services, Dir., E. Wayne Antworth
Ofc. of Congregational Ser., Dir., Jeffrey Japinga
Reformed Church Women's Ministries, Exec. Dir., Arlene Waldorf
African-American Council, Exec. Dir., Glen Missick
Council for Hispanic Ministries, Natl. Sec., Luis Perez
American Indian Council, Natl. Sec., —
Council for Pacific/Asian-American Min., Natl. Sec., Ella Campbell

Periodicals
Perspectives; The Church Herald

Reformed Church in the United States
Lacking pastors, early German Reformed immigrants to the American colonies were led in

worship by "readers." One reader, schoolmaster John Philip Boehm, organized the first congregations near Philadelphia in 1725. A Swiss pastor, Michael Schlatter, was sent by the Dutch Reformed Church in 1746. Strong ties with the Netherlands existed until the formation of the Synod of the German Reformed Church in 1793.

The Eureka Classis, organized in North and South Dakota in 1910 and strongly influenced by the writings of H. Kohlbruegge, P. Geyser and J. Stark, refused to become part of the 1934 merger of the Reformed Church with the Evangelical Synod of North America, holding that it sacrificed the Reformed heritage. (The merged Evangelical and Reformed Church became part of the United Church of Christ in 1957.) Under the leadership of pastors W. Grossmann and W. J. Krieger, the Eureka Classis in 1942 incorporated as the continuing Reformed Church in the United States.

The growing Eureka Classis dissolved in 1986 to form a Synod with four regional classes. An heir to the Reformation theology of Zwingli and Calvin, the Heidelberg Catechism, the Belgic Confession and the Canons of Dort are used as the confessional standards of the church. The Bible is strictly held to be the inerrant, infallible Word of God.

The RCUS supports Dordt College and Mid-America Reformed Seminary in Iowa. The RCUS is the official sponsor to the Reformed Confessing Church of Zaire.

Headquarters
Media Contact, Rev. Frank Walker Th.M., 5601 Spring Blossom St., Bakersfield, CA 93313-6041 Tel. (805)827-9885
E-mail: fhw@iname.com
Website: http://www.rcus.org

Officers
Pres., Rev. Vernon Pollema, 235 James Street, Shafter, CA 93263 Tel. (805)746-6907
Vice-Pres., Rev. Paul Treick, 1515 Carlton Ave., Modesto, CA 95350 Tel. (209)526-0637
Stated Clk., Rev. Frank Walker Th.M., 5601 Spring Blossom St., Bakersfield, CA 93313-6025 Tel. (805)827-9885
Treas., Clayton Greiman, 2115 Hwy. 69, Garner, IA 50438 Tel. (515)923-2950

PERIODICAL
Reformed Herald

Reformed Episcopal Church
The Reformed Episcopal Church was founded Dec. 2, 1873 in New York City by Bishop George D. Cummins, an assistant bishop in the Protestant Episcopal Church from 1866 until 1873. Cummins and other evangelical Episcopalians viewed with alarm the influence of the Oxford Movement in the Protestant Episcopal Church, for the interest it stimulated in Roman Catholic ritual and doctrine and for intol-

erance it bred toward evangelical Protestant doctrine.

Throughout the late 1860s, evangelicals and ritualists clashed over ceremonies and vestments, exchanges of pulpits with clergy of other denominations, the meaning of critical passages in the Book of Common Prayer, interpretation of the sacraments and validity of the Apostolic Succession.

In October, 1873, other bishops publicly attacked Cummins in the church newspapers for participating in an ecumenical Communion service sponsored by the Evangelical Alliance. Cummins resigned and drafted a call to Episcopalians to organize a new Episcopal Church for the "purpose of restoring the old paths of their fathers." On Dec. 2, 1873, a Declaration of Principles was adopted and Dr. Charles E. Cheney was elected bishop to serve with Cummins. The Second General Council, meeting in May 1874 in New York City, approved a Constitution and Canons and a slightly amended version of the Book of Common Prayer. In 1875, the Third General Council adopted a set of Thirty-Five Articles.

Cummins died in 1876. The church had grown to nine jurisdictions in the United States and Canada at that time. The Reformed Episcopal Church is a member of the National Association of Evangelicals.

Headquarters
7372 Henry Ave., Philadelphia, PA 19128-1401 Tel. (215)483-1196 Fax (215)483-5235
Media Contact, Rt. Rev. Leonard Riches
Media Contact, Rt. Rev. Royal U. Grote, Jr., Church Growth Office, 211 Byrne Ave., Houston, TX 77009 Tel. (713)862-4929
E-mail: nicaea@aol.com
Website: http://www/geopages.com/capitol-hill/1125/

Officers
Pres. & Presiding Bishop, Rt. Rev. Leonard W. Riches
Vice-Pres., Bishop Sanco K. Rembert, 705 S. Main St., Summerville, SC 29483 Tel. (803) 873-3451 Fax (803)875-6200
Sec., Bonnie C. Abboud
Treas., Rev. Jon W. Abboud, Tel. (610)449-6267

OTHER ORGANIZATIONS
Bd. of Foreign Missions: Pres., Dr. Barbara J. West, 316 Hunters Rd., Swedesboro, NJ 08085 Tel. (609) 467-1641
Bd. of Natl. Church Extension: Pres., Rt. Rev. Royal U. Grote, Jr., 211 Byrne Ave., Houston, TX 77009 Tel. (713)862-4929
Publication Society: Pres., Rt. Rev. Gregory K. Hotchkiss, 318 Main St., Somerville, NJ 08876 Tel. (908)725-2678 Fax (908)725-4641; Orders, Rev. David S. Ayres, 25 S. 43rd St., Philadelphia, PA 19104 Tel. (215)387-2707

The Reapers: Pres., Susan Higham, 3144 Jasper St., Philadelphia, PA 19134 Tel. (215)634-6690

Committee on Women's Work: Pres., Joan Workowski, 1162 Beverly Rd., Rydal, PA 19046

BISHOPS

William H.S. Jerdan, Jr., 414 W. 2nd South St., Summerville, SC 29483

Sanco K. Rembert, P.O. Box 20068, Charleston, SC 29413

Franklin H. Sellers, Sr., 81 Buttercup Ct., Marco Island, FL 33937-3480

Leonard W. Riches, Sr., 85 Smithtown Rd., Pipersville, PA 18947 Tel. (610)483-1196 Fax (610)294-8009

Royal U. Grote, Jr., 211 Byrne Ave., Houston, TX 77009

James C. West, Sr., 91 Anson St., Charleston, SC 29401

Robert H. Booth, 1222 Haworth St., Philadelphia, PA 19124

Gregory K. Hotchkiss, 318 E. Main St., Somerville, NJ 08876

George B. Fincke, 155 Woodstock Circle, Vacaville, CA 95687-3381

Daniel R. Morse, P.O.Box 38615, Germantown, TN 38183-0615

Michael Fedechko, Box 2532, New Liskeard, ON P0J 1P0

Charles W. Dorrington, 626 Blanshard St., Victoria, BC V8W 3G6

Ted Follows, 626 Blanshard St., Victoria, BC V8W 3G6

Periodical

The Evangelical Episcopalian

Reformed Mennonite Church

This is a small group of believers in Pennsylvania, Ohio, Michigan, Illinois, and Ontario, Canada who believe in non-resistance of evil, and non-conformity to the world and who practice separation from unfaithful worship. They believe that Christian unity is the effect of brotherly love and are of one mind and spirit. Their church was established in 1812 by John Herr who agreed with the teachings of Menno Simon as well as those of Jesus Christ.

Headquarters

Lancaster County only, Reformed Mennonite Church, 602 Strasburg Pike, Lancaster, PA 17602

Media Contact, Bishop, Glenn M. Gross, Tel. (717)697-4623

Officer

Bishop Glenn M. Gross, 906 Grantham Rd., Mechanicsburg, PA 17055

Reformed Methodist Union Episcopal Church

The Reformed Methodist Union Episcopal church was formed after a group of ministers

withdrew from the African Methodist Episcopal Church following a dispute over the election of ministerial delegates to the General Conference.

These ministers organized the Reformed Methodist Union church during a four-day meeting beginning on Jan. 22, 1885 at Hills Chapel (now known as Mt. Hermon RMUE church), in Charleston, S.C. The Rev. William E. Johnson was elected president of the new church. Following the death of Rev. Johnson in 1896, it was decided that the church would conform to regular American Methodism (the Episcopacy). The first Bishop, Edward Russell Middleton, was elected, and "Episcopal" was added to the name of the church. Bishop Middleton was consecrated on Dec. 5, 1896, by Bishop P. F. Stephens of the Reformed Episcopal Church.

Headquarters

1136 Brody Ave., Charleston, SC 29407

Media Contact, Gen. Secretary, Brother Willie B. Oliver, P.O. Box 1995, Orangeburg, SC 29116 Tel. (803)536-3293

Officers

Bishop, Rt. Rev. Leroy Gethers, Tel. (803)766-3534

Asst. Bishop, Rt.Rev. Jerry M. DeVoe, Jr.

Gen. Sec., Brother Willie B. Oliver

Treas., Rev. Daniel Green

Sec. of Education, Rev. William Polite

Sec. of Books Concerns, Sister Ann Blanding

Sec. of Pension Fund, Rev. Joseph Powell

Sec. of Church Extension, Brother William Parker

Sec. of Sunday School Union, Sister Wine

Sec. of Mission, Rev. Warren Hatcher

Reformed Presbyterian Church of North America

Also known as the Church of the Covenanters, this church's origin dates back to the Reformation days of Scotland when the Covenanters signed their "Covenants" in resistance to the king and the Roman Church in the enforcement of state church practices. The Church in America has signed two "Covenants" in particular, those of 1871 and 1954.

Headquarters

Media Contact, Stated Clk., Louis D. Hutmire, 7408 Penn Ave., Pittsburgh, PA 15208 Tel. (412)731-1177 Fax (412)731-8861

Officers

Mod., Rev. William J. Edgar, 25 Lawrence Rd., Broomall, PA 19008 Tel. (610) 353-1371

Clk., J. Bruce Martin, 310 Main St., Ridgefield Park, NJ 07660 Tel. (201) 440-5993

Asst. Clk., Raymond E. Morton, 411 N. Vine St., Sparta, IL 62286 Tel. (618)443-3419

Stated Clk., Louis D. Hutmire, 7408 Penn Ave., Pittsburgh, PA 15208 Tel. (412)731-1177

Periodical

The Covenanter Witness

Reformed Zion Union Apostolic Church

This group was organized in 1869 at Boydton, Va., by Elder James R. Howell of New York, a minister of the A.M.E. Zion Church, with doctrines of the Methodist Episcopal Church.

Headquarters
Rt. 1, Box 64D, Dundas, VA 23938 Tel. (804)676-8509
Media Contact, Bishop G. W. Studivant

Officer
Exec. Brd., Chair, Rev. Hilman Wright, Tel. (804)447-3988
Sec., Joseph Russell, Tel. (804)634-4520

Religious Society of Friends (Conservative)

These Friends mark their present identity from separations occurring by regions at different times from 1845 to 1904. They hold to a minimum of organizational structure. Their meetings for worship, which are unprogrammed and based on silent, expectant waiting upon the Lord, demonstrate the belief that all individuals may commune directly with God and may share equally in vocal ministry.

They continue to stress the importance of the Living Christ and the experience of the Holy Spirit working with power in the lives of individuals who obey it.

YEARLY MEETINGS
North Carolina YM, Deborah L. Shaw, 1009 W. McGee St., Greensboro, NC 27403 Tel. (910) 273-2199
Iowa YM: Bill Deutsch, 1478 Friends End Rd., Decorah, IA 52101 Tel. (319)382-3699
Ohio YM, John Brady, 61830 Sandy Ridge Rd., Barnesville, OH 43713 Tel. (614)425-3655

Religious Society of Friends (Unaffiliated Meetings)

Though all groups of Friends acknowledge the same historical roots, 19th-century divisions in theology and experience led to some of the current organizational groupings. Many newer yearly meetings, often marked by spontaneity, variety and experimentation and hoping for renewed Quaker unity, have chosen not to identify with past divisions by affiliating in traditional ways with the larger organizations within the Society. Some of these unaffiliated groups have begun within the past 25 years.

YEARLY MEETINGS
Central Yearly Meeting (I), Supt., Cecil Hinshaw, Rt. 2, Box 232, Winchester, IN 46394 Tel. (317)584-1089
Intermountain Yearly Meeting(I), Clerk, Chuck Rostkowski, 962 26th St., Ogden, UT 84401 Tel. (801)399-9491
North Pacific Yearly Meeting (I), Contact:, Helen Dart, 3311 NW Polk, Corvallis, OR 97330 Tel. (206)633-4860

Pacific Yearly Meeting (I), Clerk, Eric Moon, 2314 Eighth St., Apt. B, Berkeley, CA 94710 Tel. (510) 841-5471

Periodical
Friends Bulletin

Reorganized Church of Jesus Christof Latter Day Saints

This church was founded April 6, 1830, by Joseph Smith, Jr., and reorganized under the leadership of the founder's son, Joseph Smith III, in 1860. The church, with headquarters in Independence, Mo., is established in 36 countries in addition to the United States and Canada. A biennial world conference is held in Independence, Mo. The current president is W. Grant McMurray. The church has a world-wide membership of approximately 245,000.

Headquarters
World Headquarters, P.O. Box 1059, Independence, MO 64051 Tel. (816)833-1000 Fax (816)521-3096
Media Contact, Publ. Rel. Commissioner, Shirlene Flory

Officers
First Presidency: Pres., W. Grant McMurray; Counselor, Howard S. Sheehy, Jr.; Counselor, Kenneth R. Robinson
Council of 12 Apostles, Pres., A. Alex Kahtava
Presiding Bishopric: Presiding Bishop, Larry R. Norris; Counselor, Orval G. Fisher; Counselor, Dennis D. Piepergerdes
Presiding Evangelist, Everett S. Graffeo
World Church Sec., A. Bruce Lindgren
Public Relations, Shirlene Flory

Periodicals
Saints Herald; Restoration Witness

The Roman Catholic Church

The largest single body of Christians in the United States, the Roman Catholic Church, is under the spiritual leadership of His Holiness the Pope. Its establishment in America dates back to the priests who accompanied Columbus on his second voyage to the New World. A settlement, later discontinued, was made at St. Augustine, Florida. The continuous history of this Church in the Colonies began at St. Mary's in Maryland, in 1634.

(The following information has been furnished by the editor of The Official Catholic Directory, published by P. J. Kenedy & Sons, 3004 Glenview Rd., Wilmette, IL 60091. Reference to this complete volume will provide additional information.)

INTERNATIONAL ORGANIZATION
His Holiness the Pope, Bishop of Rome, Vicar of Jesus Christ, Supreme Pontiff of the Catholic Church.
Pope John Paul II, Karol Wojtyla (born May 18, 1920; installed Oct. 22, 1978)

137

APOSTOLIC PRO NUNCIO TO THE UNITED STATES

Archbishop Agostino Cacciavillan, 3339 Massachusetts Ave., N.W., Washington, DC 20008 Tel. (202)333-7121 Fax (202)337-4036

U.S. ORGANIZATION

National Conference of Catholic Bishops, 3211 Fourth St., Washington, DC 20017-1194. (202)541-3000

The National Conference of Catholic Bishops (NCCB) is a canonical entity operating in accordance with the Vatican II Decree, Christus Dominus. Its purpose is to foster the Church's mission to mankind by providing the Bishops of this country with an opportunity to exchange views and insights of prudence and experience and to exercise in a joint manner their pastoral office.

Officers

Pres., Bishop Anthony M. Pilla
Vice-Pres., Bishop Joseph A. Fiorenza
Treas., Bishop Robert J. Banks
Sec., Archbishop Harry J. Flynn

NCCB GENERAL SECRETARIAT

Gen. Sec., Rev. Msgr.Dennis M. Schnurr
Assoc. Gen. Sec., Rev. William P. Fay, Sr. Sharon A. Euart, R.S.M., Mr. Bruce Egnew
Sec. for Communication, Rev. Msgr. Francis J. Maniscalco

NCCB COMMITTEES

Administrative Committee: Chmn., Bishop Anthony M. Pilla
Executive Committee: Chmn., Bishop Anthony M. Pilla,
Committee on Budget and Finance: Chmn., Bishop Robert J. Banks
Committee on Personnel: Bishop Joseph A. Fiorenza
Committee on Priorities and Plans: Chmn., Bishop Anthony M. Pilla
American College Louvain: Chmn., Bishop Frank J. Rodimer
Bishop's Welfare Emergency Relief: Chmn., Bishop Anthony M. Pilla
Aid to the Church in Central and Eastern Europe: Chmn., Adam Cardinal Meida
Diaconate: Chmn., Bishop Edward U. Kmiee
African American Catholics: Chmn., Bishop George Murray
Bishop's Life and Ministry: Chmn. Bishop Robert Morneau
Catholic Charismatic Renewal: Chmn., Bishop Sam G. Jacobs
Canonical Affairs: Chmn., Bishop David E. Fellhauer
Church in Latin America: Chmn., Bishop Roberto O. Cronzalez, OFM
Consecrated Life: Chmn., Bishop Joseph J. Gerry, OSB
Doctrine: Chmn., Archbishop Daniel E. Pilarczyk

Economic Concerns of the Holy See: Chmn. Archbishop James P. Keleher
Ecumenical and Interreligious Affairs: Chmn., Archbishop Alexander Brunett
Evangelization: Chmn., Archbishop Michael J. Sheehan
Hispanic Affairs: Chmn., Bishop Gerald R. Barnes
Home Missions: Chmn., Bishop Edward J. Slattery
Laity: Chmn. Bishop G. Patrick Ziemann
Lay Ministry Subcommittee: Chmn., Bishop Phillip R. Straling
Liturgy: Chmn., Archbishop Jerome G. Hanus, O.S.B.
Marriage and Family Life: Chmn., Bishop Thomas J. O'Brien
Migration: Chmn., Bishop John S. Cummins
Native American Catholics: Chmn. Bishop Donald Pelotte, SSS
Nomination of Conference Offices: Chmn. Bishop Dale J. Melczek
North American College Rome: Chmn., William Cardinal Keeler
Pastoral Practices: Chmn., Bishop Joseph L. Imesch
Priestly Formation: Chmn., Archbishop John C. Favalora
Priestly Life and Ministry: Chmn.,Bishop Richard C. Hanifen
Pro-Life Activities: Chmn., Bernard Cardinal Law
Relationship Between Eastern and Latin Catholic Churches: Chmn., Bishop Andrew Pataki
Review of Scripture Translations: Chmn., Bishop Richard J. Sklba
Ex Corde Ecclesiae: Chmn., Bishop John J. Leibrecht
Forum on the Principles of Translation: Chmn., Archbishop Jerome G. Hanus
Healthcare Issues and the Church: Chmn., Bishop Donald W. Wuerl
Oversee and Use of the Catechism: Chmn., Archbishop Daniel M. Buechlein
Science and Human Values: Chmn., Bishop Edward M. Egan
Selection of Bishops: Chmn., Bishop Anthony M. Pilla
Sexual Abuse: Chmn. Bishop John F. Kinney
Shrines: Chmn. Archbishop James P. Keleher
Stewardship: Chmn. Bishop Sylvester D. Ryan
Subcommittee on Youth: Bishop Roger L. Schweitz, OMI
Vocations: Chmn. Bishop Paul S. Loverde
Women in Society and in the Church: Chmn., Bishop John C. Dunne
World Missions: Chmn., Bishop Sean P. O'Malley, OFMCap

United States Catholic Conference, 3211 Fourth St., Washington, DC 20017, Tel. (202)541-3000
The United States Catholic Conference

(USCC) is a civil entity of the American Catholic Bishops assisting them in their service to the Church in this country by uniting the people of God where voluntary, collective action on a broad diocesan level is needed. The USCC provides an organizational structure and the resources needed to insure coordination, cooperation and assistance in the public, educational and social concerns of the church at the national, regional, state and, as appropriate, diocesan levels.

Officers
Pres., Bishop Anthony M. Pilla
Vice-Pres., Bishop Joseph A. Fiorenza
Treas., Bishop Robert J. Banks
Sec., Archbishop Harry J. Flynn

GENERAL SECRETARIAT
Gen. Sec., Dennis M. Schnurr
Assoc. Gen. Sec., Rev. William P. Fay, Sr. Sharon A. Euart, R.S.M., Mr. Bruce Egnew
Sec. for Communications, Rev. Msgr. Francis J. Maniscalco

USCC COMMITTEES AND DEPARTMENTS
Administrative Board: Chmn., Bishop Anthony M. Pilla
Executive Committee: Chmn., Bishop Anthony M. Pilla
Committee on Budget and Finance: Chmn. Bishop Robert J. Banks
Committee on Personnel: Chmn., Bishop Joseph A. Fiorenza
Committee on Priorities and Plans: Chmn., Bishop Anthony M. Pilla
Catholic Campaign for Human Development: Chmn., Bishop Ricardo Ramirez, CSB
Committee on Communications: Chmn., Bishop Robert N. Lynch
Committee on Education: Chmn., Archbishop Francis B. Schulte
Bishops and Catholic College and University Presidents: Chmn., Archbishop Francis B. Schulte
Advisory Committee on Public Policy and Catholic Schools: Chmn., Archbishop Francis B. Schulte
Sapientia Christiana: Chmn., Bishop John P. Boles
Committee of Domestic Policy: Chmn., Bishop William S. Skylstad
Committee on International Policy: Chmn., Archbishop Theodore E. McCarrick

RELATED ORGANIZATIONS

U.S.CATHOLIC BISHOPS' NATIONAL ADVISORY COUNCIL
Chmn., Ms. Helen Boettcher

NATIONAL ORGANIZATIONS
Catholic Legal Immigration Network, Inc., 3211 4th St. NE, Washington, D.C. 20017-1194 Tel. (202)541-3317 Fax (202)541-3055

Catholic Relief Services, Exec. Dir., Mr. Kenneth Hackett, 209 W. Fayette St., Baltimore, MD 21201 Tel. (401)625-2220 Fax (401)685-1635
American Catholic Correctional Chaplains Association, Pres., Bro. Peter Donohue, C.F.X., 1717 N.E. 9th St., Ste. 123, Gainesville, FL 32609
American Catholic Historical Association, Pres., Jay P. Dolan, The Catholic University of America, Washington, D.C. 20064
The American College of the Roman Catholic Church of the United States - North American College, Chmn., Most Rev. Edward M. Egan, 238 Jewett Ave., Bridgeport, CT 06606
Association of Catholic Diocesan Archivists, Pres., Rev. Msgr. Francis J. Weber, 5150 Northwest Hwy., Chicago, IL 60630 Tel. (312)736-5150 Fax (312)736-0488
Catholic Association of Teachers of Homiletics, Pres., Rev. Thomas A. Kane, Weston School of Theology, 3 Phillips Pl., Cambridge, MA 02138 Tel. (617)492-1960 Fax (617)492-5833
Catholic Campus Ministry Association, Exec. Dir., Donald R. McCrabb, 300 College Park Ave., Dayton, OH 45469-2515 Tel. (937)229-4648 Fax (937)229- 4024
Catholic Charities,-USA Episcopal Liaison, Rev. Joseph M. Sullivan, 1731 King St., Ste. 200, Alexandria, VA 22314 Tel. (703)549-1390 Fax (703)549-1656
Catholic Communications Foundation, Chmn., Most Rev. Anthony G. Bosco, P.O. Box 374, Pawling, NY 12564 Tel. (203)746-6685
Catholic Health Association of the United States, Pres., John E. Curley, 4455 Woodson Rd., St. Louis MO 63134 Tel. (314)427-2500 Fax (314)427-0029
Catholic Kolping Society of America, Sec., —
Catholic Network of Volunteer Service, Exec. Dir., Sr. Ellen Cavanaugh, 4121 Harewood Rd. N.E., Washington, D.C. 20017 Tel. (202)529-1100 Fax (202)526-1094
Catholic Theological Society of America, Pres., Elizabeth Johnson,Creighton University, 2500 California Plaza, Omaha, NE 68178-0116 Tel. (402)280-2505 Fax (402) 280-2502.
Center For Human Development, Pres., —
Conference of Diocesan Coordinators of Health Affairs, Chmn., Rev. Frank Godic, 1031 Superior Ave. Cleveland, OH 44114 Tel. (216)696-6525
Conference of Major Religious Superiors of Men's Institutes of the United States, Inc., Exec. Dir., Rev. Gregory Reisert, 8808 Cameron St., Silver Spring, MD 20910. Tel. (301)588-4030. Fax (301)587-4575
Confraternity of Christian Doctrine, Inc., Msgr. Charles A. Bugge, 3211 4th St. N.E., Washington, D.C. 20017 Tel. (202)541-3090
Council of Major Superiors of Women Religious in the United States of America, Pres., Mother Vincent Marie Finnegan, 4200 Harewood Rd.

N.E., Washington, D.C. 20017-0467 Tel. (202)832-2575 Fax (202)832-6325

Federation of Diocesan Liturgical Commissions, Exec. Sec., Rev. Michael Spillane, 401 Michigan Ave. N.E., Washington, D.C. 20017 Tel. (202)635- 6990

Diocesan Fiscal Management Conference, Exec. Dir., Rev. Robert J. Yeager, 3225 Pickle Rd., Oregon, OH 43616-4099 Tel. (419)693-0465

Instituto de Liturgia Hispana, Pres., Rev. Raul Gomez, P.O. Box 29387,Washington, D.C. 20017-0387 Tel. (202)526-1995 Fax (202)529-8729

International Catholic Migration Commission, Pres., Michael Whiteley, 1319 F St. N.W., Washington, D.C. 20004.

Jesuit Conference Inc., Pres., Rev. Gregory F. Lucey, 1616 P St. N.W., Washington, D.C. 20036-1405 Tel. (202)462-0400 Fax (202)328-9212

Ladies of Charity of the United States of America, Pres., John E. Hoag, 910 Carnoustie Dr. Kansas City, MS 64145

Leadership Conference of Women Religious, Exec. Dir., Sr. Margaret Cafferty, 8808 Cameron St., Silver Spring, MD 20910 Tel. (301)588-4955 Fax (301)587-4575

Lithuanian Roman Catholic Federation of America, Pres., Saulius V. Kuprys, 4545 W. 63rd St. Chicago, IL 60629 Tel. (312)585-9500

Mariological Society of America, Exec. Sec., Rev. Thomas A. Thompson, Marian Library, University of Dayton, Dayton, OH 45469-1390 Fax (937)229-4590

Mexican American Cultural Center, Chmn., Most Rev. Patrick F. Flores, 3019 W. French Pl., San Antonio, TX 78228 Tel. (512)732-2156

National Apostolate with People with Mental Retardation, Exec. Dir., Michela M. Perrone, 4516 30th St. N.W., Washington D.C. 20008 Tel. (800)736-1280 Fax (202)686-6716

National Assembly of Religious Brothers, Pres., Br. Thomas J. Sullivan, 1337 W. Ohio St. Chicago, IL 60622-6490 Tel. (312)829-8525 Fax (312)829-8915

National Assembly of Religious Women, Natl. Coord., Sr. Judith Vaughan, 529 S. Wabash, Rm. 404, Chicago, IL 60605 Tel. (312)663-1980 Fax (312)663-9161

National Assoc. of African American Catholic Deacons, Inc. Pres., Deacon John P. Stewart, 4323 Chaplin St. N.E., Washington D.C. 20019 Tel. (202)575-1296 Fax (202)678-3325

National Association of Catholic Chaplains, Exec. Dir., Joseph J. Driscoll, 3501 South Lake Dr., Milwaukee, WI 53207 Tel. (414)483-4898

National Association of Catholic Family Life Ministers, Pres., Joan McGuiness Wagner, 300 College Park, Dayton, OH 45469-1445

National Association of Church personnel

Administrators, Exec. Dir., Sr. Ann White, 100 E. 8th St. Cincinnati, OH 45202 Tel. (513)421-3134 Fax (513)421-6225

National Association of Deacon Organizations, Pres., Deacon Ron Lesjak, 4410 89th St. Kenosha, WI 53142 Tel. (414)694-9143

National Association of Diocesan Directors of Campus Ministry, Pres., Rev. Frederick J. Pennett, Jr., 6 Madbury Rd., P.O. Box 620, Durham, NH 03824-0620 Tel. (603)862-1310

National Association of Diocesan Ecumenical Officers, Pres., Rev. Vincent A. Heier, 462 N. Taylor St., St. Louis, MO 63108 Tel. (314)531-9700 Fax (314)531-2269

National Association of the Holy Name Society, Mod., Most Rev. Michael A. Saltarelli, P.O. Box 26038, Baltimore, MD 21224-0738

National Association of Pastoral Musicians, Exec. Dir.,al Rev. Virgil C. Funk, 225 Sheridan St. N.W., Washington, D.C. 20011 Tel. (202)723-5800 Fax (202)723-2262

National Association of Diaconate Directors, Exec. Dir., Deacon John Pistone, 1337 W. Ohio St., Chicago, IL 60622 Tel. (312)226-4033 Fax (312)829-8915

National Black Catholic Clergy Caucus, Exec. Dir., Rev. Albert J. McKnight, 343 N. Walnut St., P.O. Box 1088, Opelousas, LA 70571-1088 Tel. (318)942- 2481 Fax (318)942-9201

National Catholic Cemetery Conference, Exec. Dir., Leo A. Droste, 710 N. River Rd., Des Plaines, IL 60016 Tel. (708)824-8131

National Catholic Conference of Airport Chaplains, Pres., Rev. John A. Jamnicky, Chicago O'Hare Intl. Airport, P.O. Box 66353, Chicago, IL 60666-0353 Tel. (312)686-2636 Fax (312)686-0130

National Catholic Conference for Seafarers, Pres., Rev. Sinclair Oubre, 545 Savannah Ave., Port Arthur, TX 77640 Tel. (409)985-9661 Fax (409)985-9691

National Catholic Committee on Scouting Executive Committee, Advisor, Most Rev. Robert Carlson, P.O. Box 152079, Irving, TX 75015-2079 Fax (214)580-2502

National Catholic Conference for Total Stewardship, Inc., Pres., Rev. Francis A. Novak,1633 N. Cleveland Ave., Chicago IL 60614 Tel. (312)363-8046 Fax (312)363-2123

National Catholic Council on Alcoholism and Related Drug Problems, Treas., Rev. Msgr. Kieran Martin, 1550 Hendrickson St., Brooklyn, NY 11234-3514 Tel. (718)951-7177 Fax (718)951-7233

National Catholic Development Conference, Pres., Peter A. Eltink, 86 Front St., Hempstead, NY 11550 Tel. (516)481-6000

National Catholic Educational Association, Pres., Sr. Catherine McNamee, 1077 30th St., N.W., Ste. 100, Washington, DC 20007 Tel. (202)337-6232 Fax (202)333-6706

National Catholic Office for the Deaf, Exec. Dir., Nora Letourneau, 7202 Buchanan St.

Landover Hills, MD 20784-2236 Tel. (301)577-1684(voice) (301)577-4184 (TTY only)

National Catholic Office for persons with Disabilities, Exec. Dir., Mary Jane Owen, P.O. Box 29113, Washington, D.C. 20017 Tel. (202)529-2933 (TT-voice) Fax (202)529-4678

National Catholic Rural Life Conference, Exec. Dir., Bro. David G. Andrews, 4625 Beaver Ave., Des Moines, IA 50310 Tel. (515)270-2634 Fax (515)270-9447

National Catholic Stewardship Council, Inc., Nat'l. Dir., Matthew R. Paratore, 1275 K St. N.W., Ste. 980, Washington, D.C. 20005 Tel. (202)289-1093 Fax (202)682- 9018

National Catholic Student Coalition, Dir., Jamie Williams, 300 College Park Ave., Dayton, OH 45469-2515 Tel.(513)229-3590 Fax (513)229-4024

National Center for Urban Ethnic Affairs, Pres., John A. Kromkowski, P.O. Box 20, Cardinal Station, Washington, D.C. 20064 Tel. (202)232-3600

National Conference of Catechetical Leadership, Exec. Dir., Neil Parent, 3021 4th St. N.E., Washington, D.C. 20017-1102 Tel. (202)636-3826 Fax (202)832-2712

National Council for Catholic Evangelization, Exec. Dir., John Simon, 905 E. 166th St., South Holland, IL. 60473-2420

National Council of Catholic Men, Pres., William Sandweg, 4712 Randolph Dr., Annandale, VA 22003

National Council of Catholic Women, Exec. Adm., Annette Kane, 1275 K. St. NW, Ste. 975, Washington, DC 20005 Tel. (202)682-0334 Fax (202)682-0338

National Federation of Catholic Physicians' Guilds, Exec. Dir., Robert H. Herzog, 850 Elm Grove Rd., Elm Grove, WI 53122 Tel. (414)784-3435 Fax (414)782-8788

National Federation for Catholic Youth Ministry, Inc. Exec. Dir., Rev. Leonard C. Wenke, 3700-A Oakview Ter. N.E., Washington, D.C.20017-2591 Tel. (202)636-3825

National Federation of Spiritual Directors, Pres., Rev. George P. Evans, 127 Lake St., Brighton, MA 02135. Fax (617)787-2336

National Foundation for Catholic Youth, Exec. Dir., Rev. Leonard C. Wenke, 3700-A Oakview Ter., Washington, D.C. 20017 Tel. (202)636-3825

National Office for Black Catholics, Exec. Dir., Walter T. Hubbard, The Paulist Center, 3025 4th St., N.E., Washington, D.C. 20017 Tel. (202)635-1778

National Organization for Continuing Education of Roman Catholic Clergy, Inc., Exec. Dir., Br. Paul J. Murray, 1337 W. Ohio St., Chicago, IL 60622 Tel. (312)226-1890

National Pastoral Center for the Chinese Apostolate, Inc., Dir. Rev. Joseph Chiang, 5

Monroe St. Rm. 52, New York, NY 10002-7303 Tel. (212)233-3303

National Pastoral Life Center, Dir. Rev. Philip Murnion, 299 Elizabeth St., New York, NY 10012. Tel. (212)431-7825 Fax (212)274-9786

Papal Foundation, Exec. Dir., Rev. Msgr. Thomas J. Benestad, 222 N. 17th St., Philadelphia, PA 19103 Tel. (215)587-2491

Parish Evaluation Project, Dir. Rev. Thomas P. Sweetser, O'Hare Lake Office Plaza, 2200 E. Devon, Ste. 283, Des Plaines, IL 60018 Tel. (847)297-2080 Fax (847)297-2107

Pax Christi U.S.A., National Catholic Peace Movement, Intl. Sec. Mr. Etienne De'Jonghe, 348 E. 10th St., Erie, PA 16503-1110 Tel. (814)453- 4955 Fax (814)452-4784

Religious Formation Conference, Exec. Dir. Sr. Jane Finnery, 8820 Cameron St., Silver Spring, MD 20910 Tel. (301)588-4938 Fax (301)585-7649

Retreats International Inc., Dir., Most Rev. Thomas W. Gedeon, National Office, Box 1067, Notre Dame, IN 46556 Tel. (219)631-5320

Slovak Catholic Federation, Pres., Rev. Msgr. Thomas V. Banick, 134 S. Washington St., P. O. Box 348, Wilkes-Barre, PA 18701 Tel. (717)823-4168

UNDA-USA National Catholic Association for Communicators, Pres., William G. Halpin, National Office, 901 Irving Ave., Dayton, OH 45409-2316 Tel. (513)229-2303 Fax (513)229-2300

USCC Commission on Certification and Accreditation, Exec. Dir., Sr. Kay L. Sheskaitis, 3501 S. Lake Dr., P.O. Box 07058, Milwaukee WI 53207-0058 Tel.(414)486-0139 Fax (414)483-6712

United States Catholic Mission Association, Exec. Dir., Lou F. McNeil, 3029 4th St. N.E., Washington, D.C. 20017 Tel. (202)832-3112 Fax (202)832-3688

CATHOLIC ORGANIZATIONS WITH INDIVIDUAL I.R.S. RULINGS

Apostleship of the Sea in the United States, Dir. Deacon Robert Mario Balderas, 3211 4th St. N.W., Washington, D.C. 20017. Tel.(202)541-3226. Fax (202)541-3399

The Beginning Experience, Episcopal Moderator, Rev. A. Edward Pevec, 305 Michigan Ave., Detroit, MI 48226 Tel. (313)965-5110 Fax (313)965-5557

Canon Law Society of America, Exec. Coord., Rev. Patrick J. Cogan, Catholic University, Washington, DC 20064 Tel. (202)269-3491 Fax (202)319-5719

Catholic Coalition on Preaching, Inc., Pres., Rev. Eugene F. Lauer, University of Notre Dame, 1201 Hesburgh Library, Notre Dame, IN 46556 Tel. (219)631-5328

Catholic Engaged Encounter, Inc., Exec. Dir.,

Dave Florijan, 5 Tara Dr., Pittsburgh, PA 15209 Tel. (412)487-5116

Catholic Library Association, Pres. Br. Paul J. Osterdorf, 461 W. Lancaster Ave., Haverford, PA 19041 Tel. (215)649-5250

Catholic Mutual Relief Society of America, Pres., Donald E. Ruth, 4223 Center St., Omaha, NE 68105 Tel. (402)551-8765

Catholic Relief Insurance Company of America, Pres., Donald E. Ruth, 4223 Center St., Omaha, NE 68105 Tel. (402)551-8765

Conference for Pastoral Planning and Council Development, Exec. Dir., Arthur X. Deegan II, 625 Cleveland St., Clearwater, FL 34615 Tel. (813)461-5000 Fax (813)462-6037

National Association for Lay Ministry, Chmn., Linda Perrone Rooney, 5420 S. Cornell Ave. Chicago Il 60615 Tel. (312)241-6050

National Catholic Conference for Interracial Justice, Exec. Dir., Jerome B. Ernst, 3033 4th St. N.E., Washington, D.C. 20017-1102 Tel. (202)529-6480 Fax (202)526-1262

National Catholic Risk Retention Group, Inc., Dir., Henry P. Devlin, 1500 N. Woodward Ave., Ste. 209, P.O. Box 0864, Bloomfield Hills, MI 48303-0864 Tel.(810)642-6676. Fax (810)642-6412

National Catholic Young Adult Ministry Association, Inc. Pres., James Breen, 3700 - A Oakview Ter. N.E. Washington, D.C. 20017-2591 Tel. (202)636- 3825 Fax (202)526-7544

National Conference of Diocesan Vocation Directors, Pres., Rev. Patrick Zurek, 1603 S. Michigan Ave. #400, Chicago, IL 60616 Tel. (312)663-5456

National Federation of Priests' Councils, Exec. Dir., Bro. Bernard F. Stratman, 1337 W. Ohio, Chicago, IL 60622 Tel.(312)226-3334 Fax (312)829-8915

National Institute for the Word of God, Exec. Dir., Rev. John Burke, O. P., 487 Michigan Ave., NE, Washington, DC 20017 Tel. (202)529-0001

National Service Committee of the Catholic Charismatic Renewal of the United States Inc., Dir., Walter Matthews, P.O. Box 628, Locust Grove, VA 22508-0628

North American Forum on the Catechumenate, Exec. Dir., Thomas H. Morris,7115 Leesburg Pike, Ste. 308, Falls Church, VA 22043-2301 Tel (703)534-8082

Catholic Committee for Refugees & Children, Pres., John Swenson, 3211 4th St. NE, Washington, D.C. 20017-1194 Fax (202)541-3245

Worldwide Marriage Encounter, Mod., Most Rev. G. Patrick Ziemann, 1908 E. Highland Ave., Ste. A, San Bernardino, CA 92404 Tel. (909)881-3456 Fax (909)881-3531

ARCHDIOCESES AND DIOCESES

Each Archdiocese or Diocese contains the following information in sequence: Name of incumbent Bishop; name of Auxiliary Bishop or Bishops, and the Chancellor or Vicar General of the Archdiocese or Diocese, or just the address and telephone number of the chancery office.

Cardinals are addressed as His Eminence and Archbishops and Bishops as Most Reverend.

Albany, Bishop Howard J. Hubbard. Chancellor, Rev. Randall P. Patterson. Chancery Office, Pastoral Center, 40 N. Main Ave., Albany, NY 12203 Tel. (518)453-6600 Fax (518)453-6795

Diocese of Alexandria, Bishop Sam G. Jacobs. Chancellor, Rev. Msgr. Joseph M. Susi. Chancery Office, 4400 Coliseum Blvd., P.O. Box 7417, Alexandria, LA 71306 Tel. (318)445-2401 Fax (318)448-6121

Allentown, Bishop Edward P. Cullen. Chancellor, Rev. Msgr. Joseph M. Whalen. Chancery Office, 202 N. 17th St., P.O. Box F, Allentown, PA 18105 Tel. (610)437-0755 Fax (610)433-7822

Altoona-Johnstown, Bishop Joseph V. Adamec. Chancellor, Rev. Dennis P. Boggs. Chancery Office, 126 Logan Blvd., Hollidaysburg, PA 16648 Tel. (814)695-5579 Fax (814)695-8894

Amarillo, Bishop John W. Yanta. Chancellor, Sr. Christine Jensen. Chancery Office, 1800 N. Spring St., P.O. Box 5644, Amarillo, TX 79117-5644 Tel.(806)383-2243 Fax (806)383-8452

Archdiocese of Anchorage, Archbishop Francis T. Hurley. Chancellor-Vacant, Chancery Office, 225 Cordova St., Anchorage, AK 99501 Tel. (907)258-7898 Fax (905)279-3885

Arlington, ——. Chancellor, Rev. Robert J. Rippy. Chancery, Ste. 704, 200 N. Glebe Rd., Arlington, VA 22203 Tel. (703)841-2500 (703)524-5028

Archdiocese of Atlanta, Most Rev. John Frances Donoghue. Chancellor, Rev. Donald A. Kenny. Chancery Office, 680 W. Peachtree St., N.W., Atlanta, GA 30308 Tel. (404)888-7804 Fax (404)885-7494

Austin, Bishop John E. McCarthy. Vicar General, Rev. Msgr. Edward C. Matocha. Chancery Office, N. Congress and 16th, P.O. Box 13327 Capital Sta. Austin, TX 78711 Tel. (512)476-4888 Fax(512)469-9537

Baker, Bishop Thomas J. Connolly. Chancellor, Mary Ann Davis. Chancery Office, 911 S.E. Armour, Bend, OR 97702, P.O. Box 5999, Bend, OR 97708 Tel. (541)388-4004 Fax (541)388-2566

Archdiocese of Baltimore, William Cardinal Keeler; Auxiliary Bishops: John H. Ricard; P. Francis Murphy, William C. Newman. Chancellor, Rev. Msgr. W. Francis Malooly. Chancery Office, 320 Cathedral St., Baltimore, MD 21201 Tel. (410)547-5446

Baton Rouge, Most Rev. Alfred C. Hughes. Chancellor, Rev. Msgr. Robert Berggreen. Chancery Office, 1800 S. Acadian Thruway, P.O. Box 2028, Baton Rouge, LA 70821-2028 Tel. (504)387-0561 Fax (504)336-8789

Beaumont, Most Rev. Joseph A. Galante. Chancellor, Sr. Esther Dunegan. Chancery Office, 703 Archie St., P.O. Box 3948, Beaumont, TX 77704-3948 Tel. (409)838-0451 Fax (409)838-4511.

Belleville, Bishop Wilton D. Gregory. Chancellor, Rev. Kenneth J. York. Chancery Office, 222 S. Third St., Belleville IL 62220-1985 Tel. (618)277-8181 Fax (618)277-0387

Biloxi, Bishop Joseph L. Howze. Chancellor, Rev. Msgr. Andrew Murray. Chancery Office, 120 Reynoir St., P.O. Box 1189, Biloxi, MS 39533 Tel. (601)374-0222 Fax (601)435-7949

Birmingham, Most Rev. David E. Foley. Chancellor, Sr. Mary Frances Loftin. Chancery Office, 8131 Fourth Ave. S., P.O. Box 12047, Birmingham, AL 35202-2047 Tel. (205)838-8322 Fax (205)836-1910

Bismarck, Bishop Paul A. Zipfel, Chancellor, Sr. Joanne Graham. Chancery Office, 420 Raymond St., Box 1575, Bismarck, ND 58502-1575 Tel. (701)223-1347 Fax (701)223-3693

Boise, —. Chancellor, Deacon James Bowen; Chancery Office, 303 Federal Way, Boise, ID 83705-5925 Tel. (208)342-1311 Fax (208)342-0224

Archdiocese of Boston, Archbishop Bernard Cardinal Law; Auxiliary Bishops: Lawrence J. Riley; Daniel A. Hart; John B. McCormack, John P. Boles; John R. McNamara. Chancellor, William F. Murphy. Chancery Office, 2121 Commonwealth Ave., Brighton, MA 02135 Tel. (617)254-0100 Fax (617)783-4564

Bridgeport, Bishop Edward M. Egan. Chancellor, Rev. Msgr. Thomas J. Driscoll. Chancery Office, 238 Jewett Ave., Bridgeport CT 06606-2892 Tel. (203)372-4301 Fax (203)371-8698

Brooklyn, Bishop Thomas V. Daily; Auxiliary Bishops: Joseph M. Sullivan; Rene A. Valero; Ignatius A. Catanello; Gerald M. Barbarito. Chancellor, Rev. Msgr. Otto L. Garcia. Chancery Office, 75 Greene Ave., Box C, Brooklyn, NY 11202 Tel. (718)399-5990 Fax (718)399-5934

Brooklyn, St. Maron of, Bishop Francis M. Zayek; Auxiliary Bishop Joseph M. Sullivan. Chancellor, James B. Namie. Chancery Office, 294 Howard Ave., Staten Island, NY 10301 Tel. (718)815-0436 Fax (718)815-0536

Brownsville, Bishop Raymundo J. PeÒa. Chancellor, Sylvia W. Garcia. Chancery, P.O. Box 2279, Brownsville, TX 78522-2279 Tel. (210)542-2501 Fax (210)542-6751

Buffalo, Bishop Henry J. Mansell; Auxiliary Bishops Edward D. Head; Bernard J. McLaughlin. Chancellor, Rev. Msgr. Robert J. Cunningham. Chancery Office, 795 Main St., Buffalo, NY 14203 Tel. (716)847-5500 Fax (716)847-5557

Burlington, Bishop Kenneth A. Angell. Chancellor, Rev. Jay C. Haskin. Chancery Office, 351 North Ave., Burlington, VT 05401 Tel. (802)658-6110 Fax (802)658-0436

Camden, Bishop James T. McHugh. Chancellor, Rev. Msgr. Joseph W. Pokusa. Chancery Office, 1845 Haddon Ave., P.O. Box 709, Camden, NJ 08101-0709 Tel. (609)756-7900 Fax (609)963-2655

Canton, Romanian Diocese of, Bishop John Michael Botean; 1121 44th St., NE, Canton, OH 44714 Tel. (216)492-4086

Charleston, Bishop David B. Thompson. Vicar General, Rev. Msgr. Sam R. Miglarese; Chancellor for Administration, Miss Cleo C. Cantey. Chancery Office, 119 Broad St., P.O. Box 818, Charleston, SC 29402 Tel. (803)723-3488 Fax (803)724- 6387

Charlotte, Bishop William G. Curlin. Chancellor, Very Rev. Mauricio W. West. Chancery Office P.O. Box 36776, Charlotte, NC 28236 Tel. (704)377-6871 Fax (704)358-1208

Cheyenne, Bishop Joseph H. Hart. Chancellor, Rev. Carl Beavers. Chancery Office, 2121 Capitol Ave., Box 426, Cheyenne, WY 82003-0426 Tel. (307)638-1530 Fax (307)637-7936

Archdiocese of Chicago, — Francis Cardinal George; Bishop John R. Manz; Bishop Edwin M. Conway; Bishop Thad J. Jakubowski; Bishop John R. Gorman; Bishop Raymond E. Goedert; Bishop Gerald Kicanas; Bishop Edwin M. Conway; Bishop Joseph N. Perry. Chancellor, Rev. Thomas J. Paprocki. Chancery Office, P.O. Box 1979, Chicago, IL 60690 Tel. (312)751- 7999

Chicago, St. Nicholas for Ukrainians, Bishop Michael Wiwchar. Chancellor, Sonia Ann Peczeniuk. Chancery Office, 2245 W. Rice St., Chicago, IL 60622 Tel. (312)276-5080 Fax (312)276-6799

Archdiocese of Cincinnati, Archbishop Daniel E. Pilarczyk; Chancellor, Most Rev. Carl K. Moeddel. Chancery Office, 100 E. 8th St., Cincinnati, OH 45202 Tel. (513)421-3131 Fax (513)421-6225.

Cleveland, Bishop Anthony M. Pilla. Auxiliary Bishops: Bishop A. Edward Pevec, Bishop A. James Quinn; Chancellor, Rev. Ralph E. Wiatrowski. Chancery Office, 350 Chancery Bldg., Cathedral Square, 1027 Superior Ave., Cleveland, OH 44114 Tel. (216)696-6525 Fax (216)621-7332

Colorado Springs, Bishop Richard C. Hanifen. Chancellor, Rev. George V. Fagan. Chancery Office, 29 West Kiowa St., Colorado Springs, CO 80903-1498 Tel. (719)636-2345 Fax (719)636-1216

Columbus, Bishop James A. Griffin. Chancellor, Rev. Joseph M. Hendricks. Chancery Office, 198 E. Broad St., Columbus, OH 43215 Tel. (614)224-2251 Fax (614)224-6306

Corpus Christi, Bishop Roberto O. Gonzalez. Chancellor, Deacon Roy M. Grassedonio. Chancery Office, 620 Lipan St., P.O. Box 2620, Corpus Christi, TX 78403-2620 Tel. (512)882-6191 Fax (512)882-1018

143

Covington, Bishop Robert W. Muench. Chancellor, Rev. Roger L. Kriege. Chancery Office, The Catholic Center, P. O. Box 18548, Erlanger, KY 41018-0548 Tel. (606)283-6210 Fax (606)283-6334

Crookston, Bishop Victor H. Balke. Chancellor, Rev. Michael H. Foltz. Chancery Office, 1200 Memorial Dr., P.O. Box 610, Crookston, MN 56716 Tel. (218) 281-4533 Fax (218)281-3328

Dallas, Bishop Charles V. Grahmann. Chancellor, Rev. Msgr. John P. Bell. Chancery Office, 3725 Blackburn, P.O. Box 190507, Dallas, TX 75219 Tel. (214) 528-2240 Fax (214)526-1743

Davenport, Bishop William E. Franklin. Chancellor, Rev. Msgr. Leo J. Feeney. Chancery Office, 2706 N. Gaines St., Davenport, IA 52804-1998 Tel. (319)324-1911 Fax (319)324-5842

Archdiocese of Denver, Archbishop Charles J. Charut. Chancellor, Sr. Rosemary Wilcox. Chancery Office, 200 Josephine St., Denver, CO 80206 Tel. (303) 388-4411 Fax (303)388-0517

Des Moines, Bishop Joseph J. Charron. Chancellor, Lawrence Breheny. Chancery Office, 601 Grand Ave., P.O. Box 1816, Des Moines, IA 50306 Tel. (515)243-7653 Fax (515)237-5070

Archdiocese of Detroit, Archbishop Adam Cardinal Maida; Auxiliary Bishops: Moses B. Anderson; Thomas J. Gumbleton; Bishop John C. Mienstedt; Allen H. Vigneron; Kevin Britt; Bernard Harrington. Chancery Office, 1234 Washington Blvd., Detroit, MI 48226 Tel. (313) 237-5800 Fax (313)237-4642

Dodge City, Bishop Ronald M. Gilmore. Chancellor, Rev. Warren L. Stecklein. Chancery Office, 910 Central Ave., P.O. Box 137, Dodge City, KS 67801-0137 Tel. (316) 227-1500 Fax (316)227-1570

Archdiocese of Dubuque, Archbishop Jerome G. Hanus. Chancellor, Rev. Joseph L. Hauer, P.O. Box 479, Dubuque IA 52004-0479 Tel. (319) 556-2580 Fax (319)556-5464

Duluth, Bishop Roger L. Schwietz. Chancellor, Rev. Dale Nau, Chancery Office, 2830 E. 4th St., Duluth, MN 55812 Tel. (218)724-9111 Fax (218)724-1056

El Paso, Armande X. Ochoa, Chancellor, Rev. Richard A. Matty. Chancery Office, 499 St. Matthews, El Paso, TX 79907 Tel. (915)595-5000 Fax (915)595-5095

Erie, Bishop Donald W. Trautman. Chancellor, Rev. Msgr. Lawrence E. Brandt. Chancery Office, P.O. Box 10397, Erie, PA 16514 Tel. (814)824-1111 Fax (814)824-1128

Evansville, Bishop Gerald A. Gettelfinger. Chancellor, Sr. Judith A. Neff. Chancery Office, 4200 N. Kentucky Ave., P.O. Box 4169, Evansville, IN 47724-0169 Tel. (812)424-5536 Fax (812)421-1334

Fairbanks, Bishop Michael Kaniecki. Chancellor, Sr. Marilyn Marx. Chancery Office, 1316 Peger Rd., Fairbanks, AK 99709 Tel. (907) 474-0753 Fax (907)474-8009

Fall River, Bishop Sean P. O'Malley. Chancellor, Rev. Msgr. John J. Oliveira. Chancery Office, 410 Highland Ave., Box 2577, Fall River, MA 02722 Tel. (508) 675-1311 Fax (508)679-9220

Fargo, Bishop James S. Sullivan. Chancellor, Rev. Richard M. Goellen. Chancery Office, 1310 Broadway, P.O. Box 1750, Fargo, ND 58107. Tel (701)235-6429. (701)235-0296

Fort Wayne-South Bend, Bishop John M. D'Arcy and Daniel R. Jenky; Auxiliary Bishop — Chancellor, Rev. Msgr. J. William Lester. Chancery Office, 1103 S. Calhoun St., P.O. Box 390, Fort Wayne, IN 46801 Tel. (219)422-4611 Fax (219)423-3382

Fort Worth, Bishop Joseph P. Delaney. Chancellor, Rev. Robert W. Wilson. Chancery Office, 800 W. Loop 820 S., Fort Worth, TX 76108 Tel. (817)560-3300 Fax (817)244-8839

Fresno, Bishop John T. Steinbock. Chancellor, Rev. Perry Kavookjian. Chancery Office, 1550 N. Fresno St., Fresno, CA 93703-3788 Tel. (209)488-7400 Fax (209)488-7464

Gallup, Bishop Donald E. Pelotte. Chancellor, Br. Duane Torisky. Chancery Office, 711 S. Puerco Dr., P.O. Box 1338, Gallup, NM 87305 Tel. (505)863-4406 Fax (505)722-9131

Galveston-Houston, Bishop Joseph A. Fiorenza; Auxiliary Bishops: Bishop Curtis J. Guillory, James A. Tamayo; Chancellor, Rev. Frank H. Rossi. Chancery Office, 1700 San Jacinto St., Houston, TX 77002-8291, P.O. Box 907, Houston, TX 77001-0907 Tel. (713)659-5461 Fax (713)759-9151

Gary, Bishop Dale J. Melezek; Chancellor, Rev. Gerald H. Schweitzer. Chancery Office, 9292 Broadway, Merrillville, IN 46410 Tel. (219)769-9292 Fax (219)738-9034

Gaylord, Bishop Patrick R. Cooney. Vicar Gen., James L. Brucksch. Chancery Office, 1665 West M-32, Gaylord, MI 49735 Tel. (517)732-5147 Fax (517)732-1706

Grand Island, Bishop Lawrence J. McNamara. Chancellor, Rev. Richard L Pionkowski, Chancery Office, 311 W. 17th St., P.O. Box 996, Grand Island, NE 68802 Tel. (308)382-6565 Fax (308)382-6569

Grand Rapids, Bishop Robert J. Rose; Auxiliary Bishop Joseph McKinney; Chancellor, Sr. Patrice Konwinski. Chancery Office, 660 Burton St. S.E., Grand Rapids, MI 49507 Tel. (616)243-0491 Fax (616)243- 4910

Great Falls-Billings, Bishop Anthony M. Milone. Chancellor, Rev. Robert D. Grosch. Chancery Office, 121 23rd St. S., P.O. Box 1399, Great Falls, MT 59403 Tel. (406)727-6683 Fax (406)454-3480

Green Bay, Bishop Robert J. Banks; Auxiliary Bishop Robert F. Morneau; Chancellor, Sr. Lisa Lucht. Chancery Office, Box 23066, Green Bay, WI 54305-3066 Tel. (414)435-4406 Fax (414)435-1330

144

Greensburg, Bishop Anthony G. Bosco. Chancellor, Rev. Lawrence T. Persico. Chancery Office, 723 E. Pittsburgh St., Greensburg, PA 15601 Tel. (412)837-0901 Fax (412)837-0857

Harrisburg, Bishop Nicholas C. Dattilo. Chancellor, Carol Houghton. Chancery Office, P.O. Box 2557, Harrisburg, PA 17105-2557 Tel. (717)657-4804 Fax (717)657-7673

Archdiocese of Hartford, Archbishop Daniel A. Cronin; Auxiliary Bishop Peter A. Rosazza and Christie A. Maealoso. Chancellor, Rev. Msgr. Daniel J. Plocharaczyk. Chancery Office, 134 Farmington Ave., Hartford, CT 06105-3784 Tel. (860) 541-6491 Fax (860)541-6309

Helena, ——. Chancellor, Rev. John W. Robertson. Chancery Office, 515 N. Ewing, P.O. Box 1729, Helena, MT 59624 Tel. (406)442-5820 Fax (406)442-5191

Honolulu, Bishop Francis X. Di Lorenzo. Chancellor, Sr. Grace Dorothy Lim. Chancery Office, 1184 Bishop St., Honolulu, HI 96813 Tel. (808)533-1791 Fax (808)521-8428

Houma-Thibodaux, Bishop Michael Jarrell. Chancellor, Rev. Msgr. Albert G. Bergeron. Chancery Office, P.O. Box 9077, Houma, LA 70361 Tel. (504)868-7720 Fax (504)868-7727

Archdiocese of Indianapolis, Archbishop Daniel M. Buechlein. Chancellor, Suzanne L. Magnant. Chancery Office, 1400 N. Meridian St., P.O. Box 1410, Indianapolis, IN 46206 Tel. (317)236-1400 Fax (317)236-1401

Jackson, Bishop William R. Houck. Chancellor, Rev. Michael Flannery. Chancery Office, 237 E. Amite St., P.O. Box 2248, Jackson, MS 39225-2248 Tel. (601)969-1880 Fax (601)960-8455

Jefferson City, Bishop John R. Gaudos. Chancellor, Sr. Virginia Bartolac Chancery Office, 605 Clark Ave., P.O. Box 417, Jefferson City, MO 65101 Tel. (314)635-9127 Fax (314)635-2286

Joliet, Bishop Joseph L. Imesch; Auxiliary Bishop Roger L. Kaffer. Chancellor, Sr. Judith Davies. Chancery Office, 425 Summit St., Joliet, IL 60435 Tel. (815) 722-6606 Fax (815)722-6602

Juneau, Michael Wartel; Judicial Vicar, Rev. Patrick J. Travers. Chancery Office, 419 6th St., #200, Juneau, AK 99801 Tel. (907)586-2227 Fax (907)463-3237

Kalamazoo, Bishop James A. Murray. Chancellor, Rev. Msgr. Dell F. Stewart. Chancery Office, 215 N. Westnedge Ave. Kalamazoo, MI 49007-3760 Tel. (616)349-8714 Fax (616) 349-6440

Archdiocese of Kansas City in Kansas, Archbishop James P. Keleher. Chancellor, Rev. Msgr. William T. Curtin. Chancery Office, 12615 Parallel, Kansas City, KS 66109 Tel. (913)721-1570 Fax (913)721-1577

Kansas City-St. Joseph, Bishop Raymond J.

Boland. Chancellor, Rev. George M. Noonan. Chancery Office, P.O. Box 419037, Kansas City, MO 64141-6037 Tel. (816)756-1850 Fax(816)756-0878

Knoxville, Bishop Anthony J. O'Connell. Chancellor, Rev. F. Xavier Mankel. Chancery Office, 805 Northshore Dr., P.O. Box 11127, Knoxville, TN 37939-1127 Tel. (615)584-3307.

La Crosse, Bishop Raymond L. Burke. Chancellor, Rev.Michael J. Gorman. Chancery Office. 3710 East Ave. S., P.O.Box 4004, La Crosse, WI 54602-4004 Tel. (608)788-7700 Fax (608)788-8413

Lafayette in Indiana, Bishop William L. Higi. Chancellor, Rev. Robert L. Sell. Chancery Office, P. O. Box 260, Lafayette, IN 47902 Tel. (317) 742-0275 Fax (317)742-7513

Lafayette, Bishop Edward Joseph O'Donnell. Chancellor, Sr. Joanna Valoni. Chancery Office, Diocesan Office Bldg., 1408 Carmel Ave., Lafayette, LA 70501 Tel. (318)261-5500 Fax (318) 261-5635

Lake Charles, Bishop Jude Speyrer. Chancellor Deacon George Stearns. Chancery Office, 414 Iris St., P.O. Box 3223, Lake Charles, LA 70602 Tel. (318)439-7400 Fax(318)439-7413

Lansing, Bishop Carl F. Mengeling. Chancellor, Rev. James A. Murray. Chancery Office, 300 W. Ottawa, Lansing, MI 48933 Tel. (517)342-2440 Fax (517)342-2515

Las Cruces, Bishop Ricardo Ramirez. Chancellor, Sr. Mary Ellen Quinn. Chancery Office, 1280 Med Park Dr., Las Cruces, NM 88005 Tel. (505)523-7577 Fax (505)524-3874

Las Vegas, Bishop Daniel F. Walsh. Chancellor, Jean Delli Bovi. Chancery Office 336 Cathedral Way, Las Vegas, NV 89109 Tel. (702)735-3500 Fax (702)735-8941

Lexington, Bishop James K. Williams. Chancellor, Sr. Mary Kevan Seibert. Chancery Office, 1310 Leestown Rd., P.O. Box 12350, Lexington, KY 40582-2350 Tel. (606)253-1993 Fax (606)254-6284

Lincoln, Fabian W. Bruskewitz. Chancellor, Rev. Timothy J. Thorburn. Chancery Office, 3400 Sheridan Blvd., Lincoln, NE 68506, P.O. Box 80328, Lincoln, NE 68501 Tel. (402)488-0921 Fax (402)488-3569

Little Rock, Bishop Andrew J. McDonald. Chancellor, Francis I. Malone. Chancery Office, 2415 N. Tyler St., P.O. Box 7239, Little Rock, AR 72217 Tel. (501) 664-0340

Archdiocese of Los Angeles, Roger Cardinal Mahony; Auxiliary Bishops: Gerald E. Wilkerson; Gabino Zavala; Stephen E. Blaire; Thomas J. Curry; Joseph M. Sartoris. Chancellor, Rev. Msgr. Terrance Fleming. Chancery Office, 1531 W. Ninth St., Los Angeles, CA 90015-1194 Tel. (213) 251-3200 Fax (213)251-2607

Archdiocese of Louisville, Archbishop Thomas C. Kelly; Auxiliary Bishop Charles G.

145

Maloney; Chancellor, Rev. Robert Dale Cieslik. Chancery Office, 212 E. College St., P.O. Box 1073, Louisville, KY 40201 Tel. (502)585-3291

Lubbock, Bishop Pacido Rodriguez. Chancellor, Sr. Antonio Gonzalez. Chancery Office. 4620 4th St., Lubbock, TX 79416, P.O. Box 98700, Lubbock, TX 79499- 8700 Tel. (806)792-3943 Fax (806)792-8109

Madison, Bishop William H. Bullock; Auxiliary Bishop George O. Wirz; Chancellor, Rev. Joseph P. Higgins. Chancery Office, 15 E. Wilson St., Box 111, Madison, WI 53701 Tel. (608)256-2677 Fax (608)256-1006

Manchester, Bishop John B. McCormick; Auxiliary Bishop Francis J. Christian. Chancellor Rev. Msgr. Francis J. Christian. Chancery Office, 153 Ash St., P.O. Box 310, Manchester, NH 03105 Tel. (603)669-3100 Fax (603)669-0377

Marquette, Bishop James H. Garland. Chancellor, Rev. Peter Oberto. Chancery Office, 444 S. Fourth St., P.O. Box 550, Marquette, MI 49855 Tel. (906)225-1141 Fax (906)225-0437

Memphis, Bishop J. Terry Steib. Chancellor, Rev. Robert D. Ponticello. Chancery Office, 1325 Jefferson Ave., P.O. Box 41679, Memphis, TN 38174-1679 Tel. (901)722-4700 Fax (901)722-4769

Metuchen, Bishop Vincent D. Breen. Chancellor, Sr. M. Michaelita Wiechetek. Chancery Office, P.O. Box 191, Metuchen, NJ 08840 Tel. (908)283-3800 Fax (908)283-2012

Archdiocese of Miami, Archbishop John C. Favalora; Auxiliary Bishops Agustin A. Rom·n; Thomas Wensk; Gilberto Fernandez. Chancellor, Very Rev. Tomas M. Marin. Chancery Office, 9401 Biscayne Blvd., Miami Shores, FL 33138 Tel. (305)757-6241 Fax (305)754-1897.

Archdiocese for the Military Services, Bishop Edwin F. O'Brien; Auxiliary Bishops: Francis X. Roque; Joseph J. Madera; John J. Glynn. Chancellor, Rev. Msgr. Aloysius R.Callaghan. Chancery Office, P.O. Box 4469, Washington, D.C. 20017-0469 Tel. (301)853-0400 Fax (301)853-2246

Archdiocese of Milwaukee, Archbishop Rembert G. Weakland, Auxiliary Bishop Richard J. Sklba. Chancellor, Ms. Barbara Anne Cusack, J.C.D. Chancery Office, 3501 S. Lake Dr., P.O. Box 07912, Milwaukee, WI 53207-0912 Tel. (414)769-3340 Fax (414)769-3408

Archdiocese of Mobile, Archbishop Oscar H. Lipscomb. Chancellor, Very Rev. G. Warren Wall. Chancery Office, 400 Government St., P.O. Box 1966, Mobile, AL 36633 Tel. (334)434-1585 Fax (334) 434-1588

Monterey, Bishop Sylvester D. Ryan. Chancellor, Rev. Charles G. Fatooh. Chancery Office, 580 Fremont St., P.O. Box 2048, Monterey, CA 93942-2048 (408)373-4345 Fax (408)373-1175

Nashville, Bishop Edward U. Kmiec. Chancellor, Ann K. Krenson. Chancery Office, 2400 21st Ave., S., Nashville, TN 37212 Tel. (615)383-6393 Fax (615)292-8411

Archdiocese of Newark, Archbishop Theodore E. McCarrick, Auxiliary Bishops: Dominic A. Marconi; David Arias; Charles J. Mc Donnell. Chancellor, Sr. Thomas Mary Salerno, P.O. Box 9500, Newark, NJ 07104-9500. Tel (201)497-4000 Fax (201)497-4033

Archdiocese of New Orleans, Archbishop Francis B. Schulte; Auxiliary Bishop: Dominic Carmon. Chancellor, Rev. Msgr. Thomas J. Rodi. Chancery Office, 7887 Walmsley Ave., New Orleans, LA 70125 Tel. (504)861-9521 Fax (504)866-2906

Newton, Melkite Diocese of, Bishop John A. Elya; Auxiliary Bishop: Nicholas J. Samra. Chancellor, Deacon Paul F. Lawler. Chancery Office, 19 Dartmouth St., West Newton, MA 02165 Tel. (617)969-8957 Fax (617)969-4115

New Ulm, Bishop Raymond A. Lucker. Chancellor, Rev. Dennis C. Labat. Chancery Office, 1400 Sixth St. N., New Ulm, MN 56073-2099 Tel. (507)359-2966 Fax (507)354-3667

Archdiocese of New York, John Cardinal O'Connor; Auxiliary Bishops: Patrick V. Ahern; Francis Garmendia; Austin B. Vaughan; Anthony F. Mestice; William J. McCormack; Patrick J. Sheridan. Robert A. Brucato. Chancery Office, 1011 First Ave., New York, NY 10022 Tel. (212)371-1000 Fax (212)826-6020

Norwich, Bishop Daniel A. Hart. Chancellor, Rev. Msgr. Robert L. Brown. Chancery Office, 201 Broadway, P.O. Box 587, Norwich, CT 06360 Tel. (203)887-9294 Fax (203)886-1670

Oakland, Bishop John S. Cummins. Chancellor, Sr. Barbara Flannery, C.S.J. Chancery Office, 2900 Lakeshore Ave., Oakland, CA 94610 Tel. (510)893-4711 Fax (510)893-0945

Ogdensburg, Bishop Paul S. Loverde. Chancellor, Rev. Robert H. Aucoin. Chancery Office, P.O. Box 369, 622 Washington St., Ogdensburg, NY 13669 Tel. (315)393-2920 Fax (315)394-7401

Archdiocese of Oklahoma City, Archbishop Eusebius J. Beltran, Chancellor, Rev. John A. Steichen. Chancery Office, 7501 Northwest Expressway, P.O. Box 32180, Oklahoma City, OK 73123 Tel. (405)721-5651 Fax (405)721-5210

Archdiocese of Omaha, Archbishop Elden Francis Curtiss; Chancellor, Msgr. Michael F. Gutgsell. Chancery Office, 100 N. 62nd St., Omaha, NE 68132-2795 Tel. (402)558-3100 Fax (402)551-4212

Orange, Bishop Tod Brown; Auxiliary Bishop Michael P. Driscoll. Chancellor, Rev. John Urell. Chancery Office, 2811 E. Villa Real Dr., P.O. Box 14195, Orange, CA 92613-1595 Tel. (714)282-3000 Fax (714)282-3029

146

Orlando, Bishop Norbert M. Dorsey. Chancellor, Sr. Lucy Vazquez. Chancery Office, 421 E. Robinson, P.O. Box 1800, Orlando, FL 32802-1800 Tel. (407)425-3556 Fax (407)649-7846

Owensboro, Bishop John J. McRaith. Chancellor, Sr. Joseph Angela Boone. Chancery Office, 600 Locust St., Owensboro, KY 42301 Tel. (502)683-1545 Fax (502)683-6883

Palm Beach, —. Chancellor, Rev. Charles Hawkins. Chancery Office, P.O. Box 109650, Palm Beach Gardens, FL 33410-9650 Tel. (407)775-9500 Fax (407)775-9556

Parma, Byzantine Eparchy of, Bishop Andrew Pataki. Chancellor, Vacant See. Chancery Office, 1900 Carlton Rd., Parma, OH 44134-7180 Tel. (216)741-8773 Fax (216)741-9356

Parma, Ukrainian Diocese of St. Joseph, Bishop Robert M. Moskal. Chancellor, Rev. Msgr. Thomas A. Sayuk.

Chancery Office 5720 State Rd., P.O. Box 347180, Parma, OH 44134-7180 Tel. (216)888-1522 Fax (216)888-3477

Passaic, Byzantine Diocese of, Bishop Michael J. Dudick; Chancellor, Rev. Msgr. Raymond Misulich. Chancery Office, 445 Lackawanna Ave., West Paterson, NJ 07424 Tel. (201)890-7777 Fax (201)890- 7175

Paterson, Bishop Frank J. Rodimer. Chancellor, Rev. Msgr. Herbert K. Tillyer. Chancery Office, 777 Valley Rd., Clifton, NJ 07013 Tel. (201)777-8818 Fax (201)777-8976

Pensacola-Tallahassee, Bishop John H. Ricard; Chancellor, Rev. Msgr. James Amos. Chancery Office, P.O. Drawer 17329, Pensacola, FL 32522 Tel. (904)432-1515 Fax (904)436-6424

Peoria, Bishop John J. Myers. Chancellor, Rev. James F. Campbell. Chancery Office, P.O. Box 1406, 607 NE Madison Ave., Peoria, IL 61655 Tel. (309)671-1550 Fax (309)671-5079

Archdiocese of Philadelphia, Archbishop Anthony Cardinal Bevilacqua; Auxiliary Bishops: Robert P. Maginnis, Joseph F. Martino. Chancellor, Rev. Steven J. Harris. Chancery Office, 222 N. 17th St. Philadelphia, PA 19103 Tel. (215)587-4538 Fax (215)587-3907

Phoenix, Bishop Thomas J. O'Brien. Chancellor, Sr. Mary Ann Winters. Chancery Office, 400 E. Monroe St., Phoenix, AZ 85004 Tel. (602)257-0030 Fax (602)258-3425

Pittsburgh, Bishop Donald W. Wuerl; Auxiliary Bishops: William J. Winter, David A Zubik. Chancellor, Rev. David A. Zubik. Chancery Office, 111 Blvd. of Allies, Pittsburgh, PA 15222 Tel. (412)456-3000

Archdiocese of Pittsburgh, Byzantine, Bishop Judson M. Procyk. Chancellor. Rev. Msgr. Raymond Balta. Chancery Office, 925 Liberty Ave., Pittsburgh, PA 15222 Tel. (412)281-1000 Fax (412)281-0388

Portland, Bishop Joseph J. Gerry; Aux. Bishop,

Most Rev. Michael R. Cote. Co-Chancellors, Rev. Michael J. Henchal, Sr. Rita-Mae Bissonnette. Chancery Office, 510 Ocean Ave., P.O. Box 11559, Portland, ME 04104-7559 Tel. (207)773-6471 Fax (207)773-0182

Archdiocese of Portland in Oregon, Bishop John G. Vlazny; Auxiliary Bishop Kenneth Steiner. Chancellor, Mary Jo Tully. Chancery Office, 2838 E. Burnside St., Portland, OR 97214-1895 Tel. (503)234-5334 Fax(503)234-2545

Providence, Bishop Robert G. Mulvee; Chancellor, Rev. Msgr. William I. Varsanyi. Chancery Office, 1 Cathedral Sq., Providence, RI 02903-3695 Tel. (401)278-4500 Fax (401)278-4548

Pueblo, Bishop Arthur N. Tafoya. Vicar General, Rev. Edward H. Nunez. Chancery Office, 1001 N. Grand Ave., Pueblo, CO 81003 Tel. (719)544-9861 Fax (719)544-5202

Raleigh, Bishop F. Joseph Gossman. Chancellor, John P. Riedy. Chancery Office, 300 Cardinal Gibbons Dr., Raleigh, NC 27606 Tel. (919)821-9703 Fax (919)821-9705

Rapid City, Bishop BlasÈ Cupich. Chancellor, Sr. M. Celine Erk. Chancery Office, 606 Cathedral Dr., P.O. Box 678, Rapid City, SD 57709 Tel. (605)343-3541 Fax (605)348-7985

Reno, Bishop Phillip F. Straling. Chancellor, Bro. Matthew Cunningham. Chancery Office, 515 Court St., Reno, NV 89501, P.O. Box 1211, Reno, NV 89504 Tel. (702)329-9274 Fax (702)348-8619

Richmond, Bishop Walter F. Sullivan. Chancellor, Rev. Thomas F. Shreve. Chancery Office, 811 Cathedral Pl., Richmond, VA 23220-4898 Tel. (804)359-5661 Fax (804)358-9159

Rochester, Bishop Matthew H. Clark. Chancellor, Rev. Kevin E. McKenna. Chancery Office, 1150 Buffalo Rd., Rochester, NY 14624-1890 Tel. (716)328-3210 Fax (716)328-3149

Rockford, Bishop Thomas G. Doran. Chancellor, V. Rev. Charles W. McNamee. Chancery Office, 1245 N. Court St., Rockford, IL 61103 Tel. (815)962-3709 Fax (815)968-2824

Rockville Centre, Bishop John R. McGann; Auxiliary Bishops: James J. Daly; Emil A. Wcela; John C. Dunne. Chancellor, Rev. Francis J. Schneider. Chancery Office, 50 N. Park Ave. Rockville Centre, NY 11570 Tel. (516)678-5800 Fax (516)678-1786

Sacramento, Bishop William K. Weigand; Auxilliary Bishop: Richard J. Garcia; Chancellor; Sr. Eileen Enright. Chancery Office, 2110 Broadway. Sacramento, CA 95818 Tel. (916)733-0200 Fax (916)733-0215

Saginaw, Bishop Kenneth E. Untener. Chancellor, Rev. Msgr. Thomas P. Schroeder. Chancery Office, 5800 Weiss St., Saginaw, MI 48603-2799 Tel. (517)799-7910 Fax (517)797-6670

St. Augustine, Bishop John J. Snyder. Chancellor,

147

Rev. Keith R. Brennan. Chancery Office, 11625 Old St. Augustine Rd., Jacksonville, FL 32258, P.O. Box 24000, Jacksonville, FL 32241-3200 Tel. (904)262-3200 Fax (904)262-0698

St. Cloud, Bishop John F. Kinney. Chancellor, Rev. Severin Schwieters. Chancery Office, P.O. Box 1248, 214 Third Ave. S., St. Cloud, MN 56302 Tel. (612)251-2340 Fax (612)251-0470

Archdiocese of St. Louis, Most Rev. Justin Rigali; Auxiliary Bishops: Joseph Naumann; Michael J. Sheridan; Edward K. Braxton. Chancellor, Rev. Richard F. Stika. Chancery Office, 4445 Lindell Blvd., St. Louis, MO 63108-2497 Tel. (314)533-1887 Fax (314)533-1889

Archdiocese of St. Paul and Minneapolis, Archbishop Harry J. Flynn; Auxiliary Bishop: Lawrence H. Welsh. Chancellor, William S. Fallon. Chancery Office, 226 Summit Ave., St. Paul, MN 55102 Tel. (612)291-4400 Fax (612)290-1629

St. Petersburg, Bishop Robert N. Lynch. Chancellor, V. Rev. Robert C. Gibbons. Chancery Office, 6363 9th Ave. N., St. Petersburg, FL 33710, P.O. Box 40200, St. Petersburg, FL 33743-0200 Tel. (813)344-1611 Fax (813)345-2143

Salina, Bishop George K. Fitzsimons. Chancellor, Rev. Msgr. James E. Hake. Chancery Office, 103 N. 9th, P.O. Box 980, Salina, KS 67402-0980 Tel. (913)827- 8746 Fax (913)827-6133

Salt Lake City, Bishop George H. Niederauer. Chancellor, Deacon Silvio Mayo. Chancery Office, 27 C. St., Salt Lake City, UT 84103 Tel. (801)328-8641 Fax (801)328-9680

San Angelo, Bishop Michael Pfeifer. Chancellor, Rev. Msgr. Larry J. Droll. Chancery Office, 804 Ford, Box 1829, San Angelo, TX 76902 Tel. (915)651-7500 Fax (915)651-6688

Archdiocese of San Antonio, Archbishop Patrick F. Flores; Auxiliary Bishops: Thomas J. Flanagan; Patrick J. Zurek. Chancellor, Rev. Msgr. Patrick J. Murray. Chancery Office, 2718 W. Woodlawn Ave., P.O. Box 28410, San Antonio, TX 78228-0410 Tel. (210)734-2620 Fax (210)734-0231

San Bernardino, Bishop Gerald R. Barnes; Chancellor, Rev. Donald Webber. Chancery Office, 1201 E. Highland Ave., San Bernardino, CA 92404 Tel. (909)475-5300 Fax (909)475-5833

San Diego, Bishop Robert Brom; Auxiliary Bishop Gilbert E. Chavez. Chancellor, Rev. Msgr. Daniel J. Dillabough. Chancery Office, P.O. Box 85728, San Diego, CA 92186-5728 Tel. (619)490-8200 Fax (619)490-8272

Archdiocese of San Francisco, Archbishop William J. Levada; Auxiliary Bishops: John C. Wester; Patrick J. McGrath. Chancellor, Sr. Mary B. Flaherty. Chancery Office, 445

Church St., San Francisco, CA 94114 Tel. (415)565-3600 Fax (415)565-3633

San Jose, Bishop Pierre DuMaine. Chancellor, Sr. Patricia Marie Mulpeters. Chancery Office, 900 Lafayette St., Ste. 301, Santa Clara, CA 95050-4966 Tel. (408)983-0100 Fax (408)983-0295

Archdiocese of Santa Fe, Archbishop Michael J. Sheehan. Chancellor, Rev. Richard Olona. Chancery Office, 4000 St. Joseph Pl., NW, Albuquerque, NM 87120 Tel. (505)831-8100

Santa Rosa, Bishop Patrick G. Ziemann. Chancellor, Rev. Msgr. James E. Pulskamp. Chancery Office, 547 B St., P.O. Box 1297, Santa Rosa, CA 95402 Tel. (707)545-7610 Fax (707)542-9702

Savannah, Bishop J. Kevin Boland. Chancellor, Rev. Jeremiah J. McCarthy. Chancery Office, 601 E. Liberty St., Savannah, GA 31401-5196 Tel. (912)238-2320 Fax (912)238-2335

Scranton, Bishop James C. Timlin; Auxiliary Bishop, Most Rev. John Dougherty. Chancellor, Rev. Msgr. Neil J. Van Loon. Chancery Office, 300 Wyoming Ave., Scranton, PA 18503 Tel. (717)346-8910

Archdiocese of Seattle, Archbishop Alexander J. Brunett. Chancellor, V. Rev. George L. Thomas. Chancery Office, 910 Marion St., Seattle, WA 98104 Tel. (206)382-4560 Fax (206)382-4840

Shreveport, Bishop William B. Friend. Chancellor, Sr. Margaret Daues. Chancery Office, 2500 Line Ave., Shreveport, LA 71104-3043 Tel. (318)222-2006 Fax (318)222-2080

Sioux City, Bishop Lawrence D. Soens. Chancellor, Rev. Kevin C. McCoy. Chancery Office, 1821 Jackson St., P.O. Box 3379, Sioux City, IA 51102-3379 Tel. (712)255-7933 Fax (712)233-7598

Sioux Falls, Bishop Robert J. Carlson. Chancellor, Rev. Jerome Klein. Chancery Office, 3100 W. 41st St., Box 5033, Sioux Falls, SD 57105 Tel. (605)334-9861 Fax (605)334-2092

Spokane, Bishop William S. Skylstad. Chancellor, Rev. Mark Pautler. Chancery Office, 1023 W. Riverside Ave., P.O. Box 1453, Spokane, WA 99210-1453 Tel. (509)456-7100

Springfield-Cape Girardeau, Bishop John J. Leibrecht. Chancellor, Rev. Msgr. Thomas E. Reidy. Chancery Office, 601 S. Jefferson, Springfield, MO 65806-3143 Tel. (417)866-0841 Fax (417)866-1140

Springfield in Illinois, Bishop Daniel L. Ryan. Vicar Gen., V. Rev. John Renken. Chancery Office, 1615 W. Washington, P.O. Box 3187, Springfield, IL 62708-3187 Tel. (217)698-8500 Fax (217)698-8620

Springfield in Massachusetts, Bishop Thomas L. Dupre. Chancellor, Rev. Daniel P. Liston. Chancery Office, 76 Elliot St., Springfield,

MA 01105, P.O. Box 1730, Springfield, MA 01101 Tel. (413)732-3175 Fax (413)737-2337

Stamford, Ukrainian, Bishop Basil H. Losten. Chancellor, Rt. Rev. Mitred Matthew Berko. Chancery Office, 14 Peveril Rd., Stamford, CT 06902-3019 Tel. (203)324-7698 Fax (203)967- 9948

Steubenville, Bishop Gilbert I. Sheldon. Chancellor, Linda A. Nichols. Chancery Office, 422 Washington St., P.O. Box 969, Steubenville, OH 43952 Tel. (614)282-3631 Fax (614)282-3327

Stockton, Bishop Donald W. Montrose. Chancellor, Rev. Richard J. Ryan. Chancery Office, 1105 N. Lincoln St., Stockton, CA 95203, P.O. Box 4237, Stockton, CA 95204-0237 Tel. (209)466-0636 Fax (209)941-9722

Superior, Bishop Raphael M. Fliss. Chancellor, Sr. Eileen Lang. Chancery Office, 1201 Hughitt Ave., Box 969, Superior, WI 54880 Tel. (715)392-2937 Fax (715)392-2015

Syracuse, Bishop James M. Moynihan; Auxiliary Bishop Thomas J. Costello. Chancellor, Rev. Richard M. Kopp. Chancery Office, 240 E. Onondaga St., Syracuse, NY 13202, P.O. Box 511, Syracuse, NY 13201 Tel. (315)422-7203 Fax (315)478-4619

Toledo, Bishop James R. Hoffman; Auxiliary Bishop Robert W. Donnelly. Chancery Office, P.O. Box 985, Toledo, OH 43697-0985 Tel. (419)244-6711 Fax (419)244- 4791

Trenton, Bishop John M. Smith. Chancellor, Rev. Msgr. William F. Fitzgerald. Chancery Office, 701 Lawrenceville Rd., P.O. Box 5309, Trenton, NJ 08638 Tel. (609)882-7125 Fax (609)771-6793

Tucson, Bishop Manuel D. Moreno. Chancellor, Rev. John P. Lyons, Chancery Office, 192 S. Stone Ave., Box 31, Tucson, AZ 85702 Tel. (602)792-3410

Tulsa, Bishop Edward J. Slattery. Chancellor, Dr. Edward L. Maillet. Chancery Office, 820 S. Boulder St., Tulsa, OK 74119, P.O. Box 2009, Tulsa, OK 74101 Tel. (918)587-3115 Fax (918)587-6692

Tyler, Bishop Edmond Carmody. Chancellor, Rev. Gavin Vaverek. Chancery Office, 1015 E.S.E. Loop 323, Tyler, TX 75701-9663 Tel. (903)534-1077 Fax (903)534-1370

Van Nuys Eparchy, Byzantine Rite, Bishop George M. Kuzma. Chancellor, Rev. Wesley Izer. Chancery Office, 8131 N. 16th St., Phoenix, AZ 85020 Tel. (602)861-9778 Fax (602)861-9796

Venice, Bishop John J. Nevins. Chancellor, V. Rev. Jerome A. Carosella. Chancery Office, 1000 Pinebrook Rd., Venice, FL 34292, P.O. Box 2006, Venice, FL 34284 Tel. (941) 484-9543 Fax (941)484-1121

Victoria, Bishop David E. Fellhauer. Chancellor, Rev. Msgr. Thomas C. McLaughlin. Chancery Office, 1505 E. Mesquite Lane, P.O. Box 4070, Victoria, TX 77903 Tel. (512)573-0828 Fax (512)573-5725

Archdiocese of Washington, Archbishop James Cardinal Hickey; Auxiliary Bishops: Alvaro Corrada; Leonard J. Olivier; Rev. William E. Lori. Chancellor Rev. Msgr. Bernard C. Gerhardt. Chancery Office, 5001 Eastern Ave., P.O. Box 29260, Washington, DC 20017 Tel. (301)853-4500 Fax (301)853-3246

Wheeling-Charleston, Bishop Bernard W. Schmitt. Chancellor, Rev. Robert C. Nash. Chancery Office, 1300 Byron St., P.O. Box 230, Wheeling, WV 26003 Tel. (304) 233-0880 Fax (304)233-0890

Wichita, Bishop Eugene J. Gerber. Chancellor, Rev. Robert E. Hemberger. Chancery Office, 424 N. Broadway, Wichita, KS 67202 Tel. (316)269-3900 Fax (316)269- 3936

Wilmington, Bishop Michael A. Saltarelli. Chancellor, Rev. Msgr. Joseph F. Rebman. Chancery Office, P.O. Box 2030, 1925 Delaware Ave., Ste. 1A, Wilmington, DE 19899 Tel. (302)573-3100 Fax (302)573-3128

Winona, Bishop —. Chancellor, Mr. John M.Vitek. Chancery Office, 55 W. Sanborn, P.O. Box 588, Winona, MN 55987 Tel. (507)454-4643 Fax (507)454-8106

Worcester, Bishop Daniel P. Reilly; Auxiliary Bishop George E. Rueger. Chancery Office, 49 Elm St., Worcester, MA 01609 Tel. (508)791-7171 Fax (508)753-7180

Yakima, Bishop Carlos A. Sevilla. Chancellor, V. Rev. Perron J. Auve. Chancery Office, 5301-A Tieton Dr., Yakima, WA 98908 Tel. (509)965-7117 Fax (509)966-8334

Youngstown, Bishop Thomas J. Tobin; Auxiliary Bishop Benedict C. Franzetta. Chancellor, Rev. Robert J. Siffrin. Chancery Office, 144 W. Wood St., Youngstown, OH 44503 Tel. (216)744-8451 Fax (216)744-2848

Periodicals

Nuestra Parroquia; The Pilot; Clarion Herald; Our Sunday Visitor; The New World; The Criterion; Commonweal; Maryknoll; Columbia; Clarion Herald; The Evangelist; Catholic Universe Bulletin; National Catholic Reporter; Catholic Worker; The Catholic Transcript; Catholic Standard and Times; Liguorian; The Catholic Review; Catholic Light; Homiletic and Pastoral Review; Catholic Herald; Extension; Catholic Digest; Catholic Chronicle; New Oxford Review; The Long Island Catholic; Pastoral Life; Columban Mission; Salt of the Earth; The Pilot; Praying; Providence Visitor; The Tidings; Worship; Saint Anthony Messenger; Review for Religious; The Tablet; Theology Digest; U.S. Catholic

The Romanian Orthodox Church in America

The Romanian Orthodox Church in America is an autonomous Archdiocese chartered under the name of "Romanian Orthodox Archdiocese in America."

The diocese was founded in 1929 and approved by the Holy Synod of the Romanian Orthodox Church in Romania in 1934. The Holy Synod of the Romanian Orthodox Church of July 12, 1950, granted it ecclesiastical autonomy in America, continuing to hold only dogmatical and canonical ties with the Holy Synod and the Romanian Orthodox Patriarchate of Romania. In 1951, approximately 40 parishes with their clergy from the United States and Canada separated from this church. In 1960, they joined the Russian Orthodox Greek Catholic Metropolia, now called the Orthodox Church in America, which reordained for these parishes a bishop with the title "Bishop of Detroit and Michigan."

The Holy Synod of the Romanian Orthodox Church, on June 11, 1973, elevated the Bishop of Romanian Orthodox Missionary Episcopate in America to the rank of Archbishop.

Headquarters

19959 Riopelle St., Detroit, MI 48203 Tel. (313) 893-8390
Media Contact, Archdiocesan Dean & Secretary, V. Rev. Fr. Nicholas Apostola, 44 Midland St., Worcester, MA 01602-4217 Tel. (508)799-0040 Fax (508)756-9866

Officers

Archbishop, His Eminence Victorin Ursache
Vicar, V. Rev. Archim. Dr. Vasile Vasilachi, 45-03 48th Ave., Woodside, Queens, NY 11377 Tel. (718)784-4453
Inter-Church Relations, Dir., Rev. Fr. Nicholas Apostola, 14 Hammond St., Worcester, MA 01610 Tel. (617)799-0040
Sec., V. Rev. Fr. Nicholas Apostola, 44 Midland St., Worchester, MA 01602 Tel. (508)756-9866 Fax (508)799-0040

Periodical

Credinta-The Faith

The Romanian Orthodox Episcopate of America

This body of Eastern Orthodox Christians of Romanian descent was organized in 1929 as an autonomous Diocese under the jurisdiction of the Romanian Patriarchate. In 1951 it severed all relations with the Orthodox Church of Romania. Now under the canonical jurisdiction of the autocephalous Orthodox Church in America, it enjoys full administrative autonomy and is headed by its own Bishop.

Headquarters

P.O. Box 309, Grass Lake, MI 49240 Tel. (517) 522-4800 Fax (517)522-5907
Media Contact, Ed./Sec., Dept. of Publications, Rev. Deacon David Oancea, P.O. Box 185, Grass Lake, MI 49240-0185 Tel. (517)522-3656 Fax (517)522-5907
E-mail: roeasolia@aol.com
Website: http://www.roea.org

Officers

Ruling Bishop, His Grace Bishop Nathaniel Popp
Dean of all Canada, V. Rev. Nicolae Marioncu, Box 995, Ste. 1, 709 First St., W., Assiniboia, SK S0H 0B0

OTHER ORGANIZATIONS

The American Romanian Orthodox Youth, Pres., Joe Bologa, 4730 Tahiti Dr., Akron, OH 44319
Assoc. of Romanian Orthodox Ladies' Aux., Pres., Mary Ellen Rosco, 625 Centralia, Dearborn Hts., MI 48127
Orthodox Brotherhood U.S.A., Pres., Tom Carto, 865 Bonnie Brae Ave. NE, Warren, OH 44483
Orthodox Brotherhood of Canada, Pres., William Murray, 2 Cowrie Rd., Regina, SK S4S 6Y1

Periodical

Solia-The Herald

The Russian Orthodox Church Outside of Russia

This group was organized in 1920 to unite in one body of dioceses the missions and parishes of the Russian Orthodox Church outside of Russia. The governing body, set up in Constantinople, was sponsored by the Ecumenical Patriarchate. In November 1950, it came to the United States. The Russian Orthodox Church Outside of Russia emphasizes being true to the old traditions of the Russian Church. It is not in communion with the Moscow Patriarchate.

Headquarters

75 E. 93rd St., New York, NY 10128 Tel. (212)534-1601 Fax (212)426-1086
Media Contact, Dep. Sec., Bishop Gabriel

SYNOD OF BISHOPS

Pres., His Eminence Metropolitan Vitaly
Sec., Archbishop of Syracuse and Trinity, Laurus
Dep. Sec., Bishop of Manhattan, Gabriel, Tel. (212)722-6577

Periodicals

Living Orthodoxy; Orthodox Family; Orthodox Russia (Russian); Orthodox Voices; Pravoslavnaya Rus; Pravoslavnaya Zhisn; Orthodox America

The Salvation Army

The Salvation Army, founded in 1865 by William Booth (1829-1912) in London, England, and introduced into America in 1880, is an international religious and charitable movement organized and operated on a paramilitary pattern and is a branch of the Christian church. To carry out its purposes, The Salvation Army has established a widely diversified program of religious and social welfare services which are designed to meet the needs of children, youth and adults in all age groups.

Headquarters

615 Slaters Ln., Alexandria, VA 22313 Tel. (703)684-5500 Fax (703)684-5538

Media Contact, Community Relations & Devel., Lt. Colonel Tom Jones, Tel. (703)684-5521 Fax (703)684-5538

Officers

Natl. Commander, Commissioner Robert A. Watson
Natl. Chief Sec., Col. John M. Bate
Natl. Community Relations, Dir., Lt. Colonel Tom Jones

TERRITORIAL ORGANIZATIONS

Central Territory: 10 W. Algonquin Rd., Des Plaines, IL 60016 Tel. (708)294-2000 Fax (708)294-2299; Territorial Commander, Commissioner Harold D. Hinson
Eastern Territory: 440 W. Nyack Rd., P.O. Box C-635, West Nyack, NY 10994 Tel. (914)623-4700 Fax (914)620-7466; Territorial Commander, Commissioner Joseph Noland
Southern Territory: 1424 Northeast Expressway, Atlanta, GA 30329 Tel. (404)728-1300 Fax (404)728-1331; Territorial Commander, Commissioner John Busby
Western Territory: 30840 Hawthorne Blvd., Ranchos Palos Verdes, CA 90274 Tel. (310)541-4721 Fax (310)544-1674; Territorial Commander, Commissioner David Edwards

Periodical

The War Cry

The Schwenkfelder Church

The Schwenkfelders are the spiritual descendants of the Silesian nobleman Caspar Schwenkfeld von Ossig (1489-1561), a scholar, reformer, preacher and prolific writer who endeavored to aid in the cause of the Protestant Reformation. A contemporary of Martin Luther, John Calvin, Ulrich Zwingli and Phillip Melanchthon, Schwenkfeld sought no following, formulated no creed and did not attempt to organize a church based on his beliefs. He labored for liberty of religious belief, for a fellowship of all believers and for one united Christian church.

He and his cobelievers supported a movement known as the Reformation by the Middle Way. Persecuted by state churches, ultimately 180 Schwenkfelders exiled from Silesia emigrated to Pennsylvania. They landed at Philadelphia Sept. 22, 1734. In 1782, the Society of Schwenkfelders, the forerunner of the present Schwenkfelder Church, was formed. The church was incorporated in 1909.

The General Conference of the Schwenkfelder Church is a voluntary association for the Schwenkfelder Churches at Palm, Worcester, Lansdale, Norristown and Philadelphia, Pennsylvania.

They practice adult baptism and dedication of children, and observe the Lord's Supper regularly with open Communion. In theology, they are Christo-centric; in polity, congregational; in missions, world-minded; in ecclesiastical organization, ecumenical.

The ministry is recruited from graduates of colleges, universities and accredited theological seminaries. The churches take leadership in ecumenical concerns through ministerial associations, community service and action groups, councils of Christian education and other agencies.

Headquarters

105 Seminary St., Pennsburg, PA 18073 Tel. (215)679-3103
Media Contact, Dennis Moyer

Officers

Mod., John Graham, Collegeville, PA 19426
Sec., Frances Witte, Central Schwenkfelder Church, Worcester, PA 19490
Treas., Syl Rittenhouse, 1614 Kriebel Rd., Lansdale, PA 19446

Periodical

The Schwenkfeldian

Separate Baptists in Christ

The Separate Baptists in Christ are a group of Baptists found in Indiana, Ohio, Kentucky, Tennessee, Virginia, West Virginia, Florida and North Carolina dating back to an association formed in 1758 in North Carolina and Virginia. Today this group consists of approximately 100 churches. They believe in the infallibility of the Bible, the divine ordinances of the Lord's Supper, feetwashing, baptism and that those who endureth to the end shall be saved.

The Separate Baptists are Arminian in doctrine, rejecting both the doctrines of predestination and eternal security of the believer.

At the 1991 General Association, an additional article of doctrine was adopted. "We believe that at Christ's return in the clouds of heaven all Christians will meet the Lord in the air, and time shall be no more," thus leaving no time for a literal one thousand year reign. Seven associations comprise the General Association of Separate Baptists.

Headquarters

Media Contact, Clk., Rev. Mark Polston, 787 Kitchen Rd., Mooresville, IN 46158 Tel. (317)834-0286

Officers

Mod., Rev. Jim Goff, 1020 Gagel Ave., Louisville, KY 40216
Asst. Mod., Rev. Jimmy Polston, 785 Kitchen Rd., Mooresville, IN 46158 Tel. (317)831-6745
Clk., Greg Erdman, 10102 N. Hickory Ln., Columbus, IN 47203 Tel. (812)526-2540
Asst. Clk., Rev. Mark Polston, 787 Kitchen Rd., Mooresville, IN 46158 Tel. (317)834-0286

Serbian Orthodox Church in the U.S.A. and Canada

The Serbian Orthodox Church is an organic part of the Eastern Orthodox Church. As a local church it received its autocephaly from Constantinople in 1219 A.D.

In 1921, a Serbian Orthodox Diocese in the United States of America and Canada was organized. In 1963, it was reorganized into three dioceses, and in 1983 a fourth diocese was created for the Canadian part of the church. The Serbian Orthodox Church in the USA and Canada received its administrative autonomy in 1928. The Serbian Orthodox Church is in absolute doctrinal unity with all other local Orthodox Churches.

Headquarters
St. Sava Monastery, P.O. Box 519, Libertyville, IL 60048 Tel. (847)367-0698

BISHOPS
Metropolitan of Midwestern America, Most Rev. Metropolitan Christopher

Bishop of Canada, Georgije, 5A Stockbridge Ave., Toronto, ON M8Z 4M6 Tel. (416)231-4009

Bishop of Eastern America, Rt. Rev. Bishop Mitrophan, P.O. Box 368, Sewickley, PA 15143 Tel. (412)741-5686

Diocese of Western America, Bishop Jovan, 2541 Crestline Terr., Alhambra, CA 91803 Tel. (818)264-6825

OTHER ORGANIZATIONS
Brotherhood of Serbian Orth. Clergy in U.S.A. & Canada, Pres., V. Rev. Lazar Kostur, Merrilville, IN

Federation of Circles of Serbian Sisters

Serbian Singing Federation

Periodical
The Path of Orthodoxy

Seventh-day Adventist Church

The Seventh-day Adventist Church grew out of a worldwide religious revival in the mid-19th century. People of many religious persuasions believed Bible prophecies indicated that the second coming or advent of Christ was imminent.

When Christ did not come in the 1840s, a group of these disappointed Adventists in the United States continued their Bible studies and concluded they had misinterpreted prophetic events and that the second coming of Christ was still in the future. This same group of Adventists later accepted the teaching of the seventh-day Sabbath and became known as Seventh-day Adventists. The denomination organized formally in 1863.

The church was largely confined to North America until 1874, when its first missionary was sent to Europe. Today, over 42,000 congregations meet in 204 countries. Membership exceeds 9 million and increases between five and six percent each year.

In addition to a mission program, the church has the largest worldwide Protestant parochial school system with approximately 5,500 schools with more than 914,000 students on elementary through college and university levels.

The Adventist Development and Relief Agency (ADRA) helps victims of war and natural disasters, and many local congregations have community service facilities to help those in need close to home.

The church also has a worldwide publishing ministry with 55 printing facilities producing magazines and other publications in over 230 languages and dialects. In the United States and Canada, the church sponsors a variety of radio and television programs, including "Christian Lifestyle Magazine," "It Is Written," "Breath of Life," "Ayer, Hoy, y MaÒana," "Voice of Prophecy," and "La Voz de la Esperanza."

The North American Division of Seventh-day Adventist includes 58 Conferences which are grouped together into 9 organized Union Conferences. The various Conferences work under the general direction of these Union Conferences.

Headquarters
12501 Old Columbia Pike, Silver Spring, MD 20904-6600 Tel. (301)680-6000

Media Contact, Act. Dir., Archives & Statistics, Bert Haloviak

World-Wide Officers
Pres., Robert S. Folkenberg

Sec., G. Ralph Thompson

Treas., Robert L. Rawson

WORLD-WIDE DEPARTMENTS
Adventist Chaplaincy Ministries, Dir., Richard O. Stenbakken

Children's Ministries, Dir., Virginia L. Smith

Education, Dir., Humberto M. Rasi

Communication, Dir., Rajmund Dabrowski

Family Ministries, Dir., Ronald M. Flowers

Health and Temperance, Dir., Allan R. Handysides

Ministerial Assoc., Dir., James A. Cress

Public Affairs & Religious Liberty, Dir., John Graz

Publishing, Dir., Ronald E. Appenzeller

Sabbath School & Personal Ministries, James W. Zackrison

Stewardship, Dir., Benjamin C. Maxson

Trust Services, G. Tom Carter

Women's Ministries, Ardis D. Stenbakken

Youth, Baraka G. Muganda

North American Officers
Pres., Alfred C. McClure

Vice-Pres.: Cyril Miller; Richard C. Osborn; Rose M. Otis; Manuel Vasquez

Sec., Harold W. Baptiste

Assoc. Sec., Rosa T. Banks

Treas., Juan R. Prestol

Assoc. Treas.: Marshall Chase; Kenneth W. Osborn; Donald R. Pierson

NORTH AMERICAN ORGANIZATIONS
Atlantic Union Conf.: P.O. Box 1189, South Lancaster, MA 01561-1189; Pres., Theodore T. Jones

Canada: Seventh-day Adventist Church in Canada (see Ch. 4)
Columbia Union Conf.: 5427 Twin Knolls Rd., Columbia, MD 21045; Pres., Harold L. Lee
Lake Union Conf.: P.O. Box C, Berrien Springs, MI 49103; Pres., Don C. Schneider
Mid-America Union Conf.: P.O. Box 6128, Lincoln, NE 68506; Pres., Charles Sandefur
North Pacific Union Conf.: Pres., Jere D. Patzer, P.O. Box 16677, Portland, OR 97216;
Pacific Union Conf.: P.O. Box 5005, Westlake Village, CA 91359; Pres., Thomas J. Mostert, Jr
Southern Union Conf.: P.O. Box 849, Decatur, GA 30031; Pres., Malcolm D. Gordon
Southwestern Union Conf.: P.O. Box 4000, Burleson, TX 76097; Pres., Max A. Trevino

Periodicals

Collegiate Quarterly; Adra Today; Sabbath School Leadership; Adventist Review; Christian Record; Cornerstone Connections; Guide; Insight; Journal of Adventist Education; Liberty; Listen; Message; Ministry; Adult, Youth, and Children's Editions Mission; Our Little Friend; Primary Treasure; Signs of the Times; Vibrant Life; Youth Ministry Accent; Children's Friend; The Student; Women of Spirit; Young & Alive; Lifeglow; Vida Radiante

Seventh Day Baptist General Conference, USA and Canada

Seventh Day Baptists emerged during the English Reformation, organizing their first churches in the mid-1600s. The first Seventh Day Baptists of record in America were Stephen and Ann Mumford, who emigrated from England in 1664. Beginning in 1665 several members of the First Baptist Church at Newport, R.I. began observing the seventh day Sabbath, or Saturday. In 1671, five members, together with the Mumfords, formed the first Seventh Day Baptist Church in America at Newport.

Beginning about 1700, other Seventh Day Baptist churches were established in New Jersey and Pennsylvania. From these three centers, the denomination grew and expanded westward. They founded the Seventh Day Baptist General Conference in 1802.

The organization of the denomination reflects an interest in home and foreign missions, publications and education. Women have been encouraged to participate. From the earliest years religious freedom has been championed for all and the separation of church and state, advocated.

Seventh Day Baptists are members of the Baptist World Alliance and Baptist Joint Committee. The Seventh Day Baptist World Federation which has 17 member conferences on six continents.

Headquarters

Seventh Day Baptist Center, 3120 Kennedy Rd., P.O. Box 1678, Janesville, WI 53547-1678
Tel. (608)752-5055 Fax (608)752-7711

Media Contact, Ex. Sec., Calvin Babcock
E-mail: sdbgen@inwave.com
Website: http://www.seventhdaybaptist.org

OTHER ORGANIZATIONS

Seventh Day Baptist Missionary Society, Exec. Dir., Kirk Looper, 119 Main St., Westerly, RI 02891
Seventh Day Bapt. Bd. of Christian Ed., Exec. Dir., Dr. Ernest K. Bee, Jr., Box 115, Alfred Station, NY 14803
Women's Soc. of the Gen. Conference, Pres., Mrs. Ruth Probasco, 858 Barrett Run Rd., Bridgeton, NJ 08302
American Sabbath Tract & Comm. Council, Dir. of Communications, Rev. Kevin J. Butler, 3120 Kennedy Rd., P.O. Box 1678, Janesville, WI 53547
Seventh Day Baptist Historical Society, Historian, Don A. Sanford, 3120 Kennedy Rd., P.O. Box 1678, Janesville, WI 53547
Seventh Day Baptist Center on Ministry, Dir. of Pastoral Services, Rev. Rodney Henry, 3120 Kennedy Rd., P.O. Box 1678, Janesville, WI 53547

Periodical

Sabbath Recorder

Southern Baptist Convention

The Southern Baptist Convention was organized on May 10, 1845, in Augusta, GA.

Cooperating Baptist churches are located in all 50 states, the District of Columbia, Puerto Rico, American Samoa and the Virgin Islands. The members of the churches work together through 1,216 district associations and 39 state conventions and/or fellowships. The Southern Baptist Convention has an Executive Committee and 12 national agencies - four boards, six seminaries, one commission, and one associated organization.

The purpose of the Southern Baptist Convention is "to provide a general organization for Baptists in the United States and its territories for the promotion of Christian missions at home and abroad and any other objects such as Christian education, benevolent enterprises, and social services which it may deem proper and advisable for the furtherance of the Kingdom of God". (Constitution, Article II)

The Convention exists in order to help the churches lead people to God through Jesus Christ.

From the beginning, there has been a mission desire to share the Gospel with the peoples of the world. The Cooperative Program is the basic channel of mission support. In addition, the Lottie Moon Christmas Offering for Foreign Missions and the Annie Armstrong Easter Offering for Home Missions support Southern Baptists' world mission programs.

In 1997, there were over 4,100 foreign missionaries serving in 126 foreign countries and over 4,800 home missionaries serving within the United States.

In 1987, the Southern Baptist Convention adopted themes and goals for the major denominational emphasis of Bold Mission Thrust for 1990-2000. Bold Mission Thrust is an effort to enable every [person]in the world to have opportunity to hear and to respond to the Gospel of Christ by the year 2000.

Headquarters
901 Commerce St., Ste. 750, Nashville, TN 37203 Tel. (615)244-2355
Media Contact, Vice-Pres. for Convention Relations, A. William Merrell, Tel. (615)244-2355 Fax (615)742-8919
E-mail: 70423.2763@compuserve.com
Website: http://www.sbcnet.org

Officers
Pres., Paige Patterson, PO Box 1889, Wake Forest, NC 27588-1889 Tel. (919)556-3101
Recording Sec., John Yeats, P.O. Box 12130, Oklahoma City, OK 73112
Executive Committee: Pres., Morris H. Chapman; Vice-Pres., Business & Finance, Jack Wilkerson; Vice-Pres., Convention News, Herb V. Hollinger; Vice-Pres., Convention Relations, A. William Merrell; Vice-Pres., Convention Policy, Augie Boto; Vice-Pres., Cooperative Program, David E. Hankins

GENERAL BOARDS AND COMMISSION
International Mission Board: Pres., Jerry A. Rankin, Box 6767, Richmond, VA 23230 Tel. (804)353-0151
North American Mission Board: Pres., Robert E. Reccord, 4200 No. Point Pkwy., Alpharetta, GA 30202 Tel. (770) 410-6519
Annuity Board: Pres., O. S. Hawkins, P.O. Box 2190, Dallas, TX 75221 Tel. (214)720-0511
Lifeway Christian Resources: Pres., James T. Draper, 127 Ninth Ave., N., Nashville, TN 37234 Tel. (615)251-2000
Ethics and Religious Liberty Commission: Pres., Richard D. Land, 901 Commerce St., Nashville, TN 37203 Tel. (615)244-2495

STATE CONVENTIONS
Alabama, Troy L. Morrison, 2001 E. South Blvd., Montgomery, AL 36116 Tel. (334)288-2460
Alaska, Cloyd Sullins, 1750 O'Malley Rd., Anchorage, AK 99516 Tel. (907)344-9627
Arizona, Steve Bass, 3031 W. Northern Ave., Ste. 131, Phoenix, AZ 85051 Tel. (602)864-0337
Arkansas, Emil Turner, P.O. Box 552, Little Rock, AR 72203 Tel. (501)376-4791
California, Fermin A. Whittaker, 678 E. Shaw Ave., Fresno, CA 93710 Tel. (209)229-9533
Colorado, David T. Bunch, 7393 So. Alton Way, Englewood, CO 80112 Tel. (303)771-2480
District of Columbia, W. Jere Allen, 1628 16th St. NW, Washington, DC 20009 Tel. (202)265-1526

Florida, John Sullivan, 1230 Hendricks Ave., Jacksonville, FL 32207 Tel. (904)396-2351
Georgia, Dr. J. Robert White, 2930 Flowers Rd., S, Atlanta, GA 30341 Tel. (770)455-0404
Hawaii, O. W. Efurd, 2042 Vancouver Dr., Honolulu, HI 96822 Tel. (808)946-9581
Illinois, Bob Wiley, P.O. Box 19247, Springfield, IL 62794 Tel. (217)786-2600
Indiana, Charles Sullivan, P.O. Box 24189, Indianapolis, IN 46224 Tel. (317)241-9317
Iowa Southern Baptist Convention, O. Wyndell Jones, Westview #27, 2400 86th St., Des Moines, IA 50322 Tel. (515)278-1566
Kansas-Nebraska, R. Rex Lindsay, 5410 W. Seventh St., Topeka, KS 66606 Tel. (913)273-4880
Kentucky, James A. Hawkins, P.O. Box 43433, Middletown, KY 40243 Tel. (502)245-4101
Louisiana, Dean Doster, Box 311, Alexandria, LA 71301 Tel. (318)448-3402
Maryland-Delaware, Charles R. Barnes, 10255 S. Columbia Rd., Columbia, MD 21064 Tel. (301)290-5290
Michigan, Michael Collins, 15635 W. 12 Mile Rd., Southfield, MI 48076 Tel. (810)557-4200
Minnesota-Wisconsin, William C. Tinsley, 519 16th St. SE, Rochester, MN 55904 Tel. (507)282-3636
Mississippi, William W. Causey, P.O. Box 530, Jackson, MS 39205 Tel. (601)968-3800
Missouri, James Hill, 400 E. High, Jefferson City, MO 65101 Tel. (573)635-7931
Nevada, David Meacham, 406 California Ave., Reno, NV 89509 Tel. (702)786-0406
New England, Kenneth R. Lyle, 5 Oak Ave., Northboro, MA 01532 Tel. (508)393-6013
New Mexico, Claude Cone, P.O. Box 485, Albuquerque, NM 87103 Tel. (505)924-2300
New York, J. B. Graham, 6538 Collamer Dr., East Syracuse, NY 13057 Tel. (315)433-1001
North Carolina, James Royston, 205 Convention Dr., Cary, NC 27511 Tel. (919)467-5100
Northwest, Jeff Iorg, 3200 NE 109th Ave., Vancouver, WA 98682 Tel. (360)882-2100
Ohio, Exec. Dir., Jack P. Kwok, 1680 E. Broad St., Columbus, OH 43203 Tel. (614)258-8491
Oklahoma, Anthony Jordan, 3800 N. May Ave., Oklahoma City, OK 73112 Tel. (405)942-3800
Pennsylvania-South Jersey, David C. Waltz, 4620 Fritchey St., Harrisburg, PA 17109 Tel. (717)652-5856
South Carolina, B. Carlisle Driggers, 190 Stoneridge Dr., Columbia, SC 29210 Tel. (803)765-0030
Tennessee, James M. Porch, P.O. Box 728, Brentwood, TN 37024 Tel. (615)371-2090
Texas, William M. Pinson, 333 N. Washington, Dallas, TX 75246 Tel. (214)828-5100
Utah-Idaho, Jim Harding, 12401 S. 450 E. Bldg. G1, Draper, UT 84020 Tel. (801)572-5350
Virginia, Reginald M. McDonough, P.O. Box 8568, Richmond, VA 23226 Tel. (804)672-2100

West Virginia, Jere L. Phillips, Number One Mission Way, Scott Depot, WV 25560 Tel. (304)757-0944

Wyoming, John W. Thomason, Box 4779, Casper, WY 82604 Tel. (307)472-4087

FELLOWSHIPS

Dakota Southern Baptist Fellowship, James Goodson, Interim,, P.O. Box 7187, Bismark, ND 58507 Tel. (701)255-3765

Montana Southern Baptist Fellowship, C. Clyde Billingsley, P.O. Box 99, Billings, MT 59103 Tel. (406)252-7537

Canadian Convention of Southern Baptists, Gerry Taillon, Postal Bag 300, Cochrane, Alberta T0L 0W0 Tel. (403)932-5688

Periodicals

The Commission; SBC Life; MissionsUSA

Southern Methodist Church

Organized in 1939, this body is composed of congregations desirous of continuing in true Biblical Methodism and preserving the fundamental doctrines and beliefs of the Methodist Episcopal Church, South. These congregations declined to be a party to the merger of the Methodist Episcopal Church, The Methodist Episcopal Church, South and the Methodist Protestant Church into The Methodist Church.

Headquarters

P.O. Box 39, Orangeburg, SC 29116-0039 Tel. (803)536-1378 Fax (803)535-3881

Media Contact, Pres., Rev. Bedford F. Landers

E-mail: smchq@juno.com

Officers

Pres., Rev. Bedford F. Landers

Admn. Asst. to Pres., Philip A. Rorabaugh

Director of Foreign Missions, Rev. Franklin D. McLellan, P.O. Box 39, Orangeburg, SC 29116-0039

Southern Methodist College Pres., Rev. Daniel H. Shapley, PO Box 1027, Orangeburg, SC 29116-1027

The Eastern Conf., Vice-Pres., Rev. John T. Hucks, Jr., 221 Pinewood Dr., Rowesville, SC 29133

Alabama-Florida-Georgia Conf., Vice-Pres., Rev. Glenn A Blank, 2275 Scenic Highway, Apt. 109, Pensacola, FL 32502

Mid-South Conf., Vice-Pres., Rev. Dr. Ronald R. Carrier, 5030 Hillsboro Rd., Nashville, TN 37215

South-Western Conf., Vice-Pres., Rev. Ira Schilling, 106 Albert Dr., Haughton, LA 71037

Gen. Conf., Treas., Rev. Philip A. Rorabaugh, P.O. Drawer A, Orangeburg, SC 29116-0039

PERIODICAL

The Southern Methodist

Sovereign Grace Believers

The Sovereign Grace Believers are a contemporary movement which began its stirrings in the mid-1950s when some pastors in traditional Baptist churches returned to a Calvinist-theological perspective.

The first "Sovereign Grace" conference was held in Ashland, Kentucky, in 1954 and since then, conferences of this sort have been sponsored by various local churches on the West Coast, Southern and Northern states and Canada. This movement is a spontaneous phenomenon concerning reformation at the local church level. Consequently, there is no interest in establishing a Reformed Baptist "Convention" or "Denomination." Each local church is to administer the keys to the kingdom.

Most Sovereign Grace Believers formally or informally relate to the "First London" (1646), "Second London" (1689) or "Philadelphia" (1742) Confessions.

There is a wide variety of local church government in this movement. Many Calvinist Baptists have a plurality of elders in each assembly. Other Sovereign Grace Believers, however, prefer to function with one pastor and several deacons.

Membership procedures vary from church to church but all require a credible profession of faith in Christ, and proper baptism as a basis for membership.

Calvinistic Baptists financially support gospel efforts (missionaries, pastors of small churches at home and abroad, literature publication and distribution, radio programs, etc.) in various parts of the world.

Headquarters

Media Contact, Corres., Jon Zens, P.O. Box 548, St. Croix Falls, WI 54024 Tel. (612)465-6516 Fax (612)465-5101

E-mail: jon@searchingtogether.org

Website: http://www.cet.com.~dlavoie/solo.christo

Periodicals

Reformation Today; Kindred Minds; Searching Together

The Swedenborgian Church

Founded in North America in 1792 as the Church of the New Jerusalem, the Swedenborgian Church was organized as a national body in 1817 and incorporated in Illinois in 1861. Its biblically-based theology is derived from the spiritual, or mystical, experiences and exhaustive biblical studies of the Swedish scientist and philosopher Emanuel Swedenborg (1688-1772).

The church centers its worship and teachings on the historical life and the risen and glorified present reality of the Lord Jesus Christ. It looks with an ecumenical vision toward the establishment of the kingdom of God in the form of a universal Church, active in the lives of all people of good will who desire and strive for freedom, peace and justice for all. It is a member of the NCCC and active in many local councils of churches.

155

With churches and groups throughout the United States and Canada, the denomination's central administrative offices and its seminary- Swedenborg School of Religion- are located in Newton, Massachusetts. Affiliated churches are found in Africa, Asia, Australia, Canada, Europe, the United Kingdom, Japan, South Korea and South America. Many philosophers and writers have acknowledged their appreciation of Swedenborg's teachings.

Headquarters
48 Sargent St., Newton, MA 02158 Tel. (617)969-4240 Fax (617)964-3258
Media Contact, Central Ofc. Mgr., Martha Bauer
E-mail: manager@centraloffice.swedenborg.org
Website: http://www.swedenborg.org

Officers
Pres., Rev. Ronald P. Brugler, 489 Franklin St., N., Kitchener, ON, Canada N2A 1Z2
Vice-Pres., Christine Laitner, 10 Hanna Court, Midland, MI 48642
Rec. Sec., Gloria Toot, 10280 Gentlewind Dr., Montgomery, OH 45242
Treas., Polly Baxter, 4720 Bel Pre Rd., Rockville, MD 20853
Ofc. Mgr., Martha Bauer

Periodicals
The Messenger; Our Daily Bread

Syrian Orthodox Church of Antioch
The Syrian Orthodox Church of Antioch traces its origin to the Patriarchate established in Antioch by St. Peter the Apostle. It is under the supreme ecclesiastical jurisdiction of His Holiness the Syrian Orthodox Patriarch of Antioch and All the East, now residing in Damascus, Syria. The Syrian Orthodox Church- composed of several archdioceses, numerous parishes, schools and seminaries- professes the faith of the first three Ecumenical Councils of Nicaea, Constantinople and Ephesus, and numbers faithful in the Middle East, India, the Americas, Europe and Australia.

The first Syrian Orthodox faithful came to North America during the late 1800s, and by 1907 the first Syrian Orthodox priest was ordained to tend to the community's spiritual needs. In 1949, His Eminence Archbishop Mor Athanasius Y. Samuel came to America and was soon appointed Patriarchal Vicar. The Archdiocese was officially established in 1957. In 1995, the Archdiocese of North America was divided into three separate Patriarchal Vicariates (Eastern United States, Western United States and Canada), each under a hierarch of the Church.

There are 18 official archdiocesan parishes and three mission congregations in the United States, located in California, District of Columbia, Florida, Illinois, Massachusetts, Michigan, New Jersey, New York, Oregon,

Rhode Island and Texas. In Canada, there are five official parishes: three in the Province of Ontario and two in the Province of Quebec and a mission congregation in the Province of Alberta.

Headquarters
Archdiocese for the Eastern U.S., 260 Elm Avenue, Teaneck, NJ 07666 Tel. (201)801- 0660 Fax (201)801-0603
E-mail: syrianoc@syrianorthodoxchurch.org
Website: http://www.syrianorthodoxchurch.org
Archdiocese of Los Angeles and Environs, 417 E. Fairmont Rd., Burbank, CA 91501 Tel. (818)845-5089 Fax (818)845-5436
Media Contact, Archdiocesan Gen. Sec., V. Rev. Chorepiscopus John Meno, 260 Elm Ave., Teaneck, NJ 07666 Tel. (201)907-0122 Fax (201)907-0551

Officers
Archdiocese for Eastern U.S.: Archbishop, Mor Cyril Aphrem Karim
Archdiocese of Los Angeles and Environs: Archbishop, Mor Clemis Eugene Kaplan

Triumph the Church and Kingdom of God in Christ Inc. (International)
This church was given through the wisdom and knowledge of God to the Late Apostle Elias Dempsey Smith on Oct. 20, 1897, in Issaquena County, Mississippi, while he was pastor of a Methodist church.

The Triumph Church, as this body is more commonly known, was founded in 1902. Its doors opened in 1904 and it was confirmed in Birmingham, Alabama, with 225 members in 1915. It was incorporated in Washington, D.C., in 1918 and currently operates in 31 states and overseas. The General Church is divided into 13 districts, including the Africa District.

Triumphant doctrine and philosophy are based on the principles of life, truth and knowledge; the understanding that God is in man and expressed through man; the belief in manifested wisdom and the hope for constant new revelations. Its concepts and methods of teaching the second coming of Christ are based on these and all other attributes of goodness.

Triumphians emphasize that God is the God of the living, not the God of the dead.

Headquarters
213 Farrington Ave. S.E., Atlanta, GA 30315
Media Contact, Bishop C. W. Drummond, 7114 Idlewild, Pittsburg, PA 15208 Tel. (412)731- 2286

Officers
Chief Bishop, Bishop C. W. Drummond, 7114 Idlewild, Pittsburgh, PA 15208 Tel. (412)731- 2286
Gen. Bd of Trustees, Chmn., Bishop Leon Simon, 1028 59th St., Oakland, CA 94608 Tel. (415)652-9576
Gen. Treas., Bishop Hosea Lewis, 1713

Needlewood Ln., Orlando, FL 32818 Tel. (407)295-5488

Gen. Rec. Sec., Bishop Zephaniah Swindle, Box 1927, Shelbyville, TX 75973 Tel. (409)598-3082

True Orthodox Church of Greece (Synod of Metropolitan Cyprian), American Exarchate

The American Exarchate of the True (Old Calendar) Orthodox Church of Greece adheres to the tenets of the Eastern Orthodox Church, which considers itself the legitimate heir of the historical Apostolic Church.

When the Orthodox Church of Greece adopted the New, or Gregorian, Calendar in 1924, many felt that this breach with tradition compromised the Church's festal calendar, based on the Old, or Julian, Calendar, and its unity with world Orthodoxy. In 1935, three State Church Bishops returned to the Old Calendar and established a Synod in Resistance, the True Orthodox Church of Greece. When the last of these Bishops died, the Russian Orthodox Church Abroad consecrated a new Hierarchy for the Greek Old Calendarists and, in 1969, declared them a Sister Church.

In the face of persecution by the State Church, some Old Calendarists denied the validity of the Mother Church of Greece and formed two synods, now under the direction of Archbishop Chrysostomos of Athens and Archbishop Andreas of Athens. A moderate faction under Metropolitan Cyprian of Oropos and Fili does not maintain communion with the Mother Church of Greece, but recognizes its validity and seeks a restoration of unity by a return to the Julian Calendar and traditional ecclesiastical polity by the State Church. About 1.5 million Orthodox Greeks belong to the Old Calendar Church.

The first Old Calendarist communities in the United States were formed in the 1930s. The Exarchate under Metropolitan Cyprian was established in 1986. Placing emphasis on clergy education, youth programs, and recognition of the Old Calendarist minority in American Orthodoxy, the Exarchate has encouraged the establishment of monastic communities and missions. Cordial contacts with the New Calendarist and other Orthodox communities are encouraged. A center for theological training and Patristic studies has been established at the Exarchate headquarters in Etna, California.

In July 1994, the True Orthodox Church of Greece (Synod of Metropolitan Cyprian), the True Orthodox Church of Romania, the True Orthodox Church of Bulgaria, and the Russian Orthodox Church Abroad entered into liturgical union, forming a coalition of traditionalist Orthodox bodies several million strong.

Headquarters

St. Gregory Palamas Monastery, P.O. Box 398, Etna, CA 96027-0398 Tel. (530)467-3228 Fax (530) 467-3996

Media Contact, Exarch in America, His Eminence, Archbishop Chrysostomos

Officers

Synodal Exarch in America, His Eminence, Archbishop Chrysostomos

Asst. to the Exarch, His Grace Bishop Auxentios of Photiki

Chancellor of the Exarchate, The Very Rev. Raphael Abraham, 3635 Cottage Grove Ave., S.E., Cedar Rapids, IA 52403-1612

Ukrainian Orthodox Church of America (Ecumenical Patriarchate)

This body was organized in the United States in 1928, when the first convention was held. In 1932, Dr. Joseph Zuk was consecrated as first Bishop. His successor was the Most Rev. Bishop Bohdan, Primate, who was consecrated by the order of the Ecumenical Patriarchate of Constantinople in 1937, in New York City. He was succeeded by the Most Rev. Metropolitan Andrei Kuschak, consecrated by the blessing of Ecumenical Patriarch by Archbishop Iakovos, Metropolitan Germanos and Bishop Silas of the Greek-Orthodox Church, in 1967. His successor is Bishop Vsevolod, ordained in 1987 by Archbishop Iakovos, Metropolitan Silas and Bishops Philip and Athenagoras.

Headquarters

Ukrainian Orthodox Church of America, 3 Davenport Ave., Ste. 2A, New Rochelle, NY 10805 Tel. (914)636-7813 Fax (914)636-7813

Media Contact, Very Rev. Arihimandrite Lev, 10 Oakwood St., Bridgeport, CT 06006

Officer

Primate, Rt. Rev. Bishop Vsevolod

Periodical

Ukrainian Orthodox Herald

Ukrainian Orthodox Church of the U.S.A.

The church was formally organized in the United States in 1919. Archbishop John Theodorovich arrived from Ukraine in 1924.

Headquarters

P.O. Box 495, South Bound Brook, NJ 08880 Tel. (908)356-0090 Fax (908)356-5556

135 Davidson Ave., Somerset, NJ 08873

Media Contact, Archbishop, His Eminence Antony

Officers

Metropolitan, His Beatitude Constantine [Buggan], Archbishop of Chicago & Philadelphia

Archbishop, His Eminence Antony

United Christian Church

The United Christian Church originated about 1864. There were some ministers and laymen in the United Brethren in Christ Church who disagreed with the position and practice of the church on infant baptism, voluntary bearing of arms and belonging to oath-bound secret combinations. This group developed into United Christian Church, organized at a conference held in Campbelltown, Pa., on May 9, 1877. The principal founders of the denomination were George Hoffman, John Stamn and Thomas Lesher. Before they were organized, they were called Hoffmanites.

The United Christian Church has district conferences, a yearly general conference, a general board of trustees, a mission board, a board of directors of the United Christian Church Home, a camp meeting board, a young peoples' board and local organized congregations.

It believes in the Holy Trinity and the inspired Holy Scriptures with the doctrines they teach. The church practices the ordinances of Baptism, Holy Communion and Foot Washing.

It welcomes all into its fold who are born again, believe in Jesus Christ as Savior and Lord and have received the Holy Spirit.

Headquarters
c/o John P. Ludwig, Jr., 523 W. Walnut St., Cleona, PA 17042 Tel. (717)273-9629
Media Contact, Presiding Elder, John P. Ludwig, Jr.

Officers
Presiding Elder, Elder John P. Ludwig, Jr.
Conf. Sec., Mr. Lee Wenger, 1625 Thompson Ave., Annville, PA 17003
Conf. Moderator, Elder Gerald Brinser, RR 1, Box 225, Annville, PA 17003

OTHER ORGANIZATIONS
Mission Board: Pres., Elder John P. Ludwig, Jr.; Sec., Elder David Heagy, R.R. 4, Box 100, Lebanon, PA 17042; Treas., Mark Copenhaver, RR 4, Box 195, Lebanon, PA 17042

United Church of Christ

The United Church of Christ was constituted on June 25, 1957 by representatives of the Congregational Christian Churches and of the Evangelical and Reformed Church, in Cleveland, Ohio.

The Preamble to the Constitution states: "The United Church of Christ acknowledges as its sole head, Jesus Christ... It acknowledges as kindred in Christ all who share in this confession. It looks to the Word of God in the Scriptures, and to the presence and power of the Holy Spirit ... It claims ... the faith of the historic Church expressed in the ancient creeds and reclaimed in the basic insights of the Protestant Reformers. It affirms the responsibility of the Church in each generation to make this faith its own in... worship, in honesty of thought and expression, and in purity of heart before God.... it recognizes two sacraments: Baptism and the Lord's Supper."

The creation of the United Church of Christ brought together four unique traditions:

(1) Groundwork for the Congregational Way was laid by Calvinist Puritans and Separatists during the late 16th-early 17th centuries, then achieved prominence among English Protestants during the civil war of the 1640s. Opposition to state control prompted followers to emigrate to the United States, where they helped colonize New England in the 17th century. Congregationalists have been self-consciously a denomination from the mid-19th century.

(2) The Christian Churches, an 18th-century American restorationist movement emphasized Christ as the only head of the church, the New Testament as their only rule of faith, and "Christian" as their sole name. This loosely organized denomination found in the Congregational Churches a like disposition. In 1931, the two bodies formally united as the Congregational Christian Churches.

(3) The German Reformed Church comprised an irenic aspect of the Protestant Reformation, as a second generation of Reformers drew on the insights of Zwingli, Luther and Calvin to formulate the Heidelberg Catechism of 1563. People of the German Reformed Church began immigrating to the New World early in the 18th century, the heaviest concentration in Pennsylvania. Formal organization of the American denomination was completed in 1793. The church spread across the country. In the Mercersburg Movement, a strong emphasis on evangelical catholicity and Christian unity was eveloped.

(4) In 19th-century Germany, Enlightenment criticism and Pietist inwardness decreased longstanding conflicts between religious groups. In Prussia, a royal proclamation merged Lutheran and Reformed people into one United Evangelical Church (1817). Members of this new church way migrated to America. The Evangelicals settled in large numbers in Missouri and Illinois, emphasizing pietistic devotion and unionism; in 1840 they formed the German Evangelical Church Society in the West. After union with other Evangelical church associations, in 1877 it took the name of the German Evangelical Synod of North America.

On June 25, 1934, this Synod and the Reformed Church in the U.S. (formerly the German Reformed Church) united to form the Evangelical and Reformed Church. They blended the Reformed tradition's passion for the unity of the church and the Evangelical tradition's commitment to the liberty of conscience inherent in the gospel.

Headquarters
700 Prospect Avenue, Cleveland, OH 44115 Tel. (216)736-2100 Fax (216)736-2120
Media Contact, UCC-Sec., Edith A. Guffey, 700 Prospect Ave., Cleveland, OH 44115 Tel. (216)736-2110 Fax (216)736-2120
E-mail: langa @ucc.org
Website: http://www.apk.net/ucc/

Officers

Pres., Rev. Paul H. Sherry
Sec., Edith A. Guffey
Dir. of Fin. & Treas., Rev. Doris R. Powell
Exec. Assoc. to Pres., Rev. Vilma M. Machin
Asst. to Pres. for Ecumenical Concerns, Rev. John H. Thomas
Asst. to Pres., Lorin W. Cope
Chpsn. Exec. Council, Rev. Linda S. Gruber
Vice-Chpsn., Ms. Iris M. Branch
Mod., Ms. Denise Page Hood
Asst. Mod.: Rev. Jana L. Norman-Richardson; Mr. Robert Frieberg

ORGANIZATIONS

United Church Board for World Min.: 700 Prospect Ave., Cleveland, OH 44115 Tel. (216)736-3200; 475 Riverside Dr., New York, NY 10115 Tel. (212)870-2637; Exec. Vice-Pres., Rev. David Y. Hirano; Mission Program Unit, Gen. Sec., Dale L. Bishop; Support Services Unit, Treas., Bruce Foresman

United Church Board for Homeland Min.: 700 Prospect Ave., Cleveland, OH 44115 Tel. (216)736-3800 Fax (216)736-3803; Office of Exec. Vice-Pres., Exec. Vice-Pres., Rev. Thomas E. Dipko; Gen. Sec., Rev. Robert P. Noble, Jr.; Office of the Treasurer, Treas., Matthew O'Brien; Div. of Evangelism & Local Church Dev., Gen. Sec., Rev. Jose A. Malayang; Div. of Education & Publication, Gen. Sec., Audrey Miller; Div. of American Missionary Association, Gen. Sec., Rev. F. Allison Phillips

Commission for Racial Justice: 700 Prospect Ave., Cleveland, OH 44115; Ofc. for Urban & Natl. Racial Justice, 5113 Georgia Ave. NW, Washington, DC 20011 Tel. (202)291-1593; Ofc. for Constituency Dev./Rural Racial Justice, Franklinton Center, P.O. Box 187, Enfield, NC 27823 Tel. (919)437-1723; Ofc. for Ecumenical Racial Justice, 475 Riverside Dr., Room 1948, New York, NY 10115 Tel. (212) 870-2077; Exec. Dir., Bernice Powell Jackson

Council for American Indian Ministry: 471 3rd Street, Box 412, Excelsior, MN 55331 Tel. (612)474-3532; Exec. Dir., Rev. Armin L. Schmidt

Council for Health & Human Service Min.: 700 Prospect Ave., Cleveland, OH 44115 Tel. (216)736-2250; Exec. Dir., Rev. Bryan Sickbert

Coord. Center for Women in Church & Soc.: 700 Prospect Ave., Cleveland, OH 44115 Tel. (216)736-2150; Exec. Dir., Rev. Lois M. Powell

Office for Church in Society: Exec. Dir., Rev. Wallace Ryan Kuroiwa, 700 Prospect Ave., Cleveland, OH 44115; 110 Maryland Ave. NE, Washington, DC 20002; Dir., Washington Ofc., Rev. Jay E. Lintner

Office for Church Life & Leadership: 700 Prospect Ave., Cleveland, OH 44115; Exec. Dir., Rev. William A. Hulteen, Jr.

Office of Communication: 700 Prospect Ave., Cleveland, OH 44115 Tel. (216)736-2222 Fax (216)736-2223; 475 Riverside Dr., 16th Fl., New York, NY 10115 Tel. (212)870-2137; Dir., Rev. Arthur L. Cribbs, Jr.

Stewardship Council: 700 Prospect Ave., Cleveland, OH 44115; 412 Orange St., New Haven, CT 06511; Exec. Dir., Rev. Earl D. Miller

Commission on Development: Dir. Planned Giving, Rev. Donald G. Stoner

Historical Council: Office of Archivist, 700 Prospect Ave., Cleveland, OH 44115

Pension Boards: 475 Riverside Dr., New York, NY 10115; Exec. Vice-Pres., Joan F. Brannick

United Church Foundation, Inc.: 475 Riverside Dr., New York, NY 10115; Financial Vice-Pres. & Treas., Donald G. Hart

CONFERENCES

Western Region

California, Nevada, Northern, Rev. Mary Susan Gast, 9260 Alcosta Blvd.,#C18, San Ramon, CA 94583-4143

California, Southern, Rev. Daniel F. Romero, 2401 N. Lake St., Altadena, CA 91001

Hawaii, Rev. David P. Hansen, 15 Craigside Pl., Honolulu, HI 96817

Montana-Northern Wyoming, Rev. John M. Schaeffer, 2016 Alderson Ave., Billings, MT 59102

Central Pacific, Rev. Hector Lopez, 0245 SW Bancroft St., Ste. E, Portland, OR 97201

Rocky Mountain, Rev. William A. Dalke, 7000 Broadway, Ste. 420, ABS Bldg., Denver, CO 80221

Southwest, Rev. Ann C. Rogers-Witte, 4423 N. 24th St., Ste. 600, Phoenix, AZ 85016

Washington-North Idaho, Rev. Lynne S. Fitch, 720 14th Ave. E., Seattle, WA 98102; Rev. Randall Hyvonen, S. 412 Bernard St., Spokane, WA 99204

West Central Region

Iowa, Rev. Susan J. Ingham, 600 42nd St., Des Moines, IA 50312

Kansas-Oklahoma, Rev. John H. Krueger, 1248 Fabrique, Wichita, KS 67218

Minnesota, Rev. William Kaseman, 122 W. Franklin Ave., Rm. 323, Minneapolis, MN 55404

Missouri, Rev. A. Gayle Engel, 461 E. Lockwood Ave., St. Louis, MO 63119

Nebraska, Rev. George S. Worcester, 825 M St., Lincoln, NE 68508

North Dakota, Rev. Jack J. Seville, Jr., 227 W. Broadway, Bismarck, ND 58501

South Dakota, Rev. Gene E. Miller, 3500 S. Phillips Ave., #121, Sioux Falls, SD 57105-6864

Great Lakes Region

Illinois, Rev. Charlene Burch, 1840 Westchester Blvd., Westchester, IL 60154

Illinois South, Rev. Ronald L. Eslinger, Box 325, 1312 Broadway, Highland, IL 62249

Indiana-Kentucky, Rev. Stephen C. Gray, 1100 W. 42nd St., Indianapolis, IN 46208

Michigan, Rev. Kent J. Ulery, P.O. Box 1006, East Lansing, MI 48826

Ohio, Rev. Ralph C. Quellhorst, 6161 Busch Blvd.,#95, Columbus, OH 43229

Wisconsin, Rev. Frederick R. Trost, 4459 Gray Rd., Box 495, De Forest, WI 53532-0495

Southern Region

Florida, Rev. M. Douglas Borko, 222 E. Welbourne Ave., Winter Park, FL 32789

South Central, Rev. Mark H. Miller, 6633 E. Hwy. 290, #200, Austin, TX 78723-1157

Southeast, Rev. Timothy C. Downs, 756 W. Peachtree St., NW, Atlanta, GA 30308

Southern, Rev. Rollin O. Russell, 217 N. Main St., Box 658, Graham, NC 27253

Middle Atlantic Region

Central Atlantic, Rev. John R. Deckenback, 916 S. Rolling Rd., Baltimore, MD 21228

New York, Rev. William Briggs, The Church Center, Rm. 202, 3049 E. Genesee St., Syracuse, NY 13224

Penn Central, Rev. Lyle J. Weible, The United Church Center, Rm. 126, 900 S. Arlington Ave., Harrisburg, PA 17109

Penn Northeast, Rev. Donald E. Overlock, 431 Delaware Ave., P.O. Box 177, Palmerton, PA 18071

Penn Southeast, Rev. Franklin R. Mittman, Jr., 505 Second Ave., P.O. Box 400, Collegeville, PA 19426

Penn West, Rev. Paul L. Westcoat, Jr., 320 South Maple Ave., Greensburg, PA 15601

Puerto Rico, Rev. Osvaldo Malave-Rivera, Box 5427, Hato Rey, PR 00919

New England Region

Connecticut, Rev. Davida Foy Crabtree, 125 Sherman St., Hartford, CT 06105

Maine, Rev. Jean M. Alexander, Rev. David R. Gaewski, 68 Main St., P.O. Box 966, Yarmouth, ME 04096

Massachusetts, Rev. Bennie E. Whiten, Jr., P.O. Box 2246, 1 Badger Rd., Framingham, MA 01701

New Hampshire: Rev. Carole C. Carlson; Rev. Benjamin C. L. Crosby; Rev. John W. Lynes, 314 S. Main, P.O. Box 465, Concord, NH 03302

Rhode Island, Rev. H. Dahler Hayes, 56 Walcott St., Pawtucket, RI 02860

Vermont, Rev. Richard B. Crocker, 285 Maple St., Burlington, VT 05401

Nongeographic

Calvin Synod, Rev. Louis Medgyesi, 607 Plum St., Fairport Harbor, OH 44077

Periodicals

United Church News; Common Lot; Courage in the Struggle for Justice and Peace

United Holy Church of America, Inc.

The United Holy Church of America, Inc. is an outgrowth of the great revival that began with the outpouring of the Holy Ghost on the Day of Pentecost. The church is built upon the foundation of the Apostles and Prophets, Jesus Christ being the cornerstone.

During a revival of repentence, regeneration and holiness of heart and life that swept through the South and West, the United Holy Church was born. The founding fathers had no desire to establish a denomination but were pushed out of organized churches because of this experience of holiness and testimony of the Spirit-filled life.

On the first Sunday in May 1886, in Method, N.C., what is today known as the United Holy Church of America, Inc. was born. The church was incorporated on Sept. 25, 1918.

Baptism by immersion, the Lord's Supper and feet washing are observed. The premillennial teaching of the Second Coming of Christ, Divine healing, justification by faith, sanctification as a second work of grace and Spirit baptism are accepted.

Headquarters

5104 Dunstan Rd., Greensboro, NC 27405 Tel. (919)621-0669

Mailing Address, Bishop Thomas E. Talley, P.O. Box 1035, Portsmouth, VA 23705

Media Contact, Gen. Rec. Sec., Beatrice S. Faison, 224 Wenz Rd., Toledo, OH 43615 Tel. (419)531-1859

Officers

Gen. Pres., Bishop Thomas E. Talley, P.O. Box 1035, Portsmouth, VA 23705 Tel. (804)399-3644

1st Vice-Pres., Bishop Odell McCollum, 3206 Blueridge Rd., Columbus, OH 43219 Tel. (614) 475-4713

2nd Vice-Pres., Bishop Elijah Williams, 901 Briarwood St., Reidsville, NC 27320 Tel. (919) 349-7275

Gen. Rec. Sec., Beatrice S. Faison, 224 Wenz Rd., Toledo, OH 43615 Tel. (419)531-1859

Asst. Rec. Sec., Elsie M. Harris, 2304 8th St., Portsmouth, VA 23704 Tel. (804)399-0926

Gen. Fin. Sec., Vera Perkins-Hughes, 3425 Rosedale Rd., Cleveland Hts., OH 44112 Tel. (216) 851-7448

Gen. Asst. Fin. Sec., Bertha Williams, 4749 Shaw Dr., Wilmington, NC 28405 Tel. (919)395-4462

Gen. Corres. Sec., Gloria Rainey, 198 Easton South/102, Laurel, MD 20707 Tel. (301)725-6982

Gen. Treas., Louis Bagley, 8779 Wales Dr., Cincinnati, OH 45249 Tel. (513)247-0588

Gen Pres. Missionary Dept., Rev. Ardelia M. Corbett, 519 Madera Dr., Youngstown, OH 44504 Tel. (216)744-3284

Gen. Supt. Bible Church School, Robert L. Rollins, 1628 Avondale Ave., Toledo, OH 43607 Tel. (419)246-4046

Gen. Pres. Y.P.H.A., Elder James W. Brooks, Rt.
3 Box 105, Pittsboro, NC 27312 Tel.
(919)542-5357
Gen. Educ. Dept., Elder Franklin R. Freeman,
2805 Collingwood Blvd., Toledo, OH 43610
Tel. (419)244-4498
Gen. Usher's Dept., Sherly Hughes, 1491 E.
191st St., Apt. H-604, Euclid, OH 44117 Tel.
(216) 383-0038
Gen. Statistician, Sheila Y. Holt-Williams, P.O.
Box 76421, Milwaukee, WI 53216 Tel. (414)
445-4467
Music Dept., Gen. Chair, Rosie Johnson, 2009
Forest Dale Dr., Silver Spring, MD 20932

PRESIDENTS OF CONVOCATIONAL DISTRICTS

Barbados, New England & Northern Dist.,
Bishop Joseph T. Bowens, 825 Fairoak Ave.,
Chillum, MD 20783
Bermuda Dist., Bishop Norris N. Dickenson,
P.O. Box Cr32, 27 Old Road, Crawl CR BX,
Bermuda, CR01
Central Western Dist., Bishop Bose Bradford,
6279 Natural Bridge, Pine Lawn, MO 63121
Tel. (314)355-1598
Haiti Dist., Bishop Cannier Guillaume, 108 Bas
Fort National, Port-au-Prince, Haiti, West
Indies
Florida/Georgia Dist., Bishop Elijah Williams,
901 Briarwood St., Reidsville, NC 27320 Tel.
(919)349-7275
Northwestern Dist., Bishop Odell McCollum,
3206 BlueRidge Rd., Columbus, OH 43219
Southern Dist./W. North Carolina Dist., Bishop
Jesse Jones, 608 Cecil St., Durham, NC 27707
Tel. (919)682-8249
Virginia Dist., Bishop Thomas E. Talley, 2710
Magnolia St., Portsmouth, VA 23705
West Virginia Dist., Bishop Irvin Evans, 207
Carnegie St., Linden, NJ 07036 Tel. (908)925-
6138
Western Dist., Bishop Irvin Evans, 207 Carnegie
St., Linden, NJ 07036 Tel. (908)925-6138

Periodical
The Holiness Union

United House of Prayer

The United House of Prayer was founded and
organized as a hierarchical church in the 1920s
by the late Bishop C. M. Grace, who had built the
first House of Prayer in 1919 in West Wareham,
MA, with his own hands. The purpose of the
organization is to establish, maintain and perpetuate the doctrine of Christianity and the
Apostolic Faith throughout the world among all
people; to erect and maintain houses of prayer
and worship where all people may gather for
prayer and to worship the almighty God in spirit
and in truth, irrespective of denomination or
creed, and to maintain the Apostolic faith of the
Lord and Savior, Jesus Christ.

Headquarters
1117 7th St. NW, Washington, DC 20001 Tel.
(202)289-0238 Fax (202)289-8058
Media Contact, Apostle S. Green

Officers
CEO, Bishop S. C. Madison, 1665 N. Portal Dr.
NW, Washington, DC 20012 Tel. (202)882-
3956 Fax (202)829-4717

NATIONAL PROGRAM STAFF
The General Assembly, Presiding Officer,
Bishop S. C. Madison, 1665 N. Portal Dr. NW,
Washington, DC 20012 Tel. (202)882-3956
Fax (202)829-4717
General Council Ecclesiastical Court, Clerk,
Apostle R. Price, 1665 N. Portal Dr. NW,
Washington, DC 20012 Tel. (202)882-3956
Fax (202)829-4717
Annual Truth & Facts Publication, Exec. Editor,
Bishop S. C. Madison, 1665 N. Portal Dr. NW,
Washington, DC 20012 Tel. (202)882-3956
Fax (202)829-4717
Nationwide Building Program, General Builder,
Bishop S. C. Madison, 1665 N. Portal Dr. NW,
Washington, DC 20012 Tel. (202)882-3956
Fax (202)829-4717
Special Projects, Dir., Apostle S. Green

The United Methodist Church

The United Methodist Church was formed April
23, 1968, in Dallas by the union of The Methodist
Church and The Evangelical United Brethren
Church. The two churches shared a common historical and spiritual heritage. The Methodist Church
resulted in 1939 from the unification of three
branches of Methodism - the Methodist Episcopal
Church, the Methodist Episcopal Church, South,
and the Methodist Protestant Church.

The Methodist movement began in 18th-centu-
ry England under the preaching of John Wesley,
but the Christmas Conference of 1784 in Baltimore
is regarded as the date on which the organized
Methodist Church was founded as an ecclesiastical
organization. It was there that Francis Asbury was
elected the first bishop in this country.

The Evangelical United Brethren Church was
formed in 1946 with the merger of the
Evangelical Church and the Church of the United
Brethren in Christ, both of which had their beginnings in Pennsylvania in the evangelistic movement of the 18th and early 19th centuries. Philip
William Otterbein and Jacob Albright were early
leaders of this movement among the German-
speaking settlers of the Middle Colonies.

Headquarters
Information InfoServ, Dir., Mary Lynn Holly,
Tel. 1-800-251-8140
E-mail: infoserv@umcom.umc.org
Website: http://www.umc.org
Media Contact, Dir., United Methodist News
Service, Thomas S. McAnally,
Tel. (615)742-5470 Fax (615)742-5469

Officers

Gen. Conference, Sec., Carolyn M. Marshall, 204 N. Newlin St., Veedersburg, IN 47987

Council of Bishops: Pres., Bishop George W. Bashore, 1204 Freedom Rd., Cranberry Township, PA 16066; Sec., Bishop Sharon Zimmerman Rader, 750 Windsor St., Ste. 303, Sun Prairie, WI 53590

BISHOPS AND CONFERENCE COUNCIL DIRECTORS

North Central Jurisdiction

Sec., Judith McCartney, 240 N. Sandusky St., Delaware, OH 43015 Tel. (614)363-0864

Dakotas: Bishop Michael J. Coyner, 815 25th St. S., Fargo, ND 58103-2303 Tel. (701)232-2241 Fax (701)232-2615; Richard W. Fisher, 1331 W. University Ave., P.O. Box 460, Mitchell, SD 57301-0460 Tel. (605)996-6552 Fax (605) 996-1766

Detroit: Bishop Donald A. Ott, Tel. (248)559-7000 Fax (248)569-4830; Jeffery Regan, 21700 Northwestern Hwy., Ste. 1200, Southfield, MI 48075-4917 Tel. (248)559-7000 Fax (248)569-4830

East Ohio: Bishop Jonathan D. Keaton, Tel. (330)499-3972 Fax (330)499-3279; Judith A. Olin, 8800 Cleveland Ave. NW, P.O. Box 2800, North Canton, OH 44720 Tel. (330)499-3972 Fax (330)499-3279

Illinois Great Rivers: Bishop Sharon Brown Christopher, 400 Chatham Rd., Ste. 100, Springfield, IL 62704 Tel. (217)726-8071 Fax (217)726-8074; Rev. Raymond P. Owens, P.O. Box 515, Bloomington, IL 61702-0515 Tel. (309)828-5092 Fax (309)829-8369

Iowa: Bishop Charles W. Jordan, Tel. (515)283-1991 Fax (515)283-8672; Don Mendenhall, 500 E. Court Ave., Ste. C, Des Moines, IA 50309-2019 Tel. (515)283-1991 Fax (515)288-1906

Minnesota: Bishop John L. Hopkins, Tel. (612) 870-4007 Fax (612)870-3587; James H. Perry, 122 W. Franklin Ave., #400, Minneapolis, MN 55404-2472 Tel. (612)870-0058 Fax (612)870-1260

North Indiana: Bishop Woodie W. White, 1100 W. 42nd St., Indianapolis, IN 46208 Tel. (317)924-1321 Fax (317)924-4859; Steven Burris, P.O. Box 869, Marion, IN 46952 Tel. (765)664-5138 Fax (765)664-2307

Northern Illinois: Bishop C. Joseph Sprague, 77 W. Washington St., Ste. 1820, Chicago, IL 60602 Tel. (312)346-9766 Fax (312)214-9031; Phillip Blackwell, 8765 W. Higgins Rd., Ste. 650, Chicago, IL 60631 Tel. (773)380-5060 Fax (773)380-5067

South Indiana: Bishop Woodie W. White, 1100 W. 42nd St., Indianapolis, IN 46208 Tel. (317)924-1321 Fax (317)924-4859; Susan W.N. Ruach, Box 5008, Bloomington, IN 47407-5008 Tel. (812)336-0186 Fax (812)336-0216

West Michigan: Bishop Donald A. Ott, 21700 Northwestern Hwy., Ste. 1200, Southfield, MI 48075-4917 Tel. (248)559-7000 Fax (810)569-4830; John R. Thompson, P.O. Box 6247, Grand Rapids, MI 49516-6247 Tel. (616)459-4503 Fax (616)459-0191

West Ohio: Bishop Judith Craig, Tel. (614)844-6200 Fax (614)781-2625; Stanley T. Ling, 32 Wesley Blvd., Worthington, OH 43085 Tel. (614)844-6200 Fax (614)781-2642

Wisconsin: Bishop Sharon Z. Rader, 750 Windsor St., Ste. 303, Sun Prairie, WI 53590 Tel. (608)837-8526 Fax (608)837-0281; Jane Follmer Zekoff, P.O. Box 620, Sun Prairie, WI 53590-0620 Tel. (608)837-7328 Fax (608)837-8547

Northeastern Jurisdiction

Baltimore-Washington: Bishop Felton Edwin May, 110 Maryland Ave., NE, Ste. 311, Washington, DC 20002 Tel. (202)546-3110 Fax (202)546-3186; Marcus Matthews, 9720 Patuxent Woods Dr., Ste. 100, Columbus, MD 21046 Tel. (410)309-3400 Fax (410)309-9430

Central Pennsylvania: Bishop Neil L. Irons, Tel. (717)652-6705 Fax (717)652-5109; G. Edwin Zeiders, 900 S. Arlington Ave., Harrisburg, PA 17109-5086 Tel. (717)652-0460 Fax (717)652-3499

Eastern Pennsylvania: Bishop Peter D. Weaver, Tel. (610)666-9090 Fax (610)666-9181; Michelle Barlow, P.O. Box 820, Valley Forge, PA 19482-0820 Tel. (610)666-9090 Fax (610) 666-9093

New England: Bishop Susan W. Hassinger, PO Box 249, Lawrence, MA 01842-0449 Tel. (978)682-7555 Fax (978)682-9555; Lornagrace Stuart, PO Box 249, Lawrence, MA 01842-0449 Tel. (978)682-7555 Fax (978)682-9555

New York: Bishop Ernest S. Lyght, Tel. (914) 684-6922 Fax (914)997-1628; Clayton Miller, 252 Bryant Ave., White Plains, NY 10605 Tel. (914)997-1570 Fax (914)684-6874

North Central New York: Bishop Hae-Jong Kim, 1010 East Ave., Rochester, NY 14607 Tel. (716)271-3400 Fax (716)271-3404; c/o CCOM Director, P.O. Box 1515, Cicero, NY 13039 Tel. (315)699-8715 Fax (315)699-8774

Northern New Jersey: Bishop Alfred Johnson, 112 W. Delaware Ave., Pennington, NJ 08534 Tel. (609)737-3940 Fax (609)737-6962; Sherrie Dobbs, 22 Madison, Madison, NJ 07940 Tel. (201)377-3800 Fax (201)765-9868

Peninsula-Delaware: Bishop Peter D. Weaver, P.O. Box 820, Valley Forge, PA 19482-0820 Tel. (610)666-9090 Fax (610)666-9181; Jonathan Baker, 139 N. State St., Dover, DE 19901 Tel. (302)674-2626 Fax (302)674-1573

Southern New Jersey: Bishop Alfred Johnson, 112 W. Delaware Ave., Pennington, NJ 08534 Tel. (609)737-3940 Fax (609)737-6962; John A. Janka, 1995 E. Marlton Pike East, Cherry Hill, NJ 08003-1893 Tel. (609)424-1700 Fax (609)424-9282

Troy: Bishop Susan M. Morrison, 215 Lancaster St., Albany, NY 12210-1131 Tel. (518)426-0386 Fax (518)426-0347; Garry Campbell, P.O. Box 560, Saratoga Springs, NY 12866 Tel. (518)584-8214 Fax (518)584-8378

West Virginia: Bishop S. Clifton Ives, 900 Washington St., East, Charleston, WV 25301 Tel. (304)344-8330 Fax (304)344-8330; Randall Flanagan, P.O. Box 2313, Charleston, WV 25328 Tel. (304)344-8331 Fax (304)344-8338

Western New York: Bishop Hae-Jong Kim, 1010 East Ave., Rochester, NY 14607 Tel. (716)271-3400 Fax (716)271-3404; James M. Pollard, 8499 Main St., Buffalo, NY 14221 Tel. (716)633-8558 Fax (716)633-8581

Western Pennsylvania: Bishop George W. Bashore, Tel. (724)776-2300 Fax (724)776-1355; Larry Homitsky, PO Box 5002, Cranberry Township, PA 16066 Tel. (724)776-2300 Fax (724)776-1355

Wyoming: Bishop Susan M. Morrison, 215 Lancaster St., Albany, NY 12210-1131 Tel. (518) 426-0386 Fax (518)426-0347; Charles Johns, 1700 Monroe St., Endicott, NY 13761-0058 Tel. (607)757-0608 Fax (607)757-0752

South Central Jurisdiction

Exec. Sec.: Thalia Matherson, 5646 Milton St., #240, Dallas, TX 75206 Tel. (214)692-9081

Central Texas: Bishop Joe A. Wilson, Tel. (817) 877-5222 Fax (817)332-4609; Henry Radde, 464 Bailey, Ft. Worth, TX 76107-2153 Tel. (817)877-5222 Fax (817)338-4541

Kansas East: Bishop Albert F. Mutti, Tel. (913) 272-0587 Fax (913)272-9135; Dale L. Fooshee, P.O. Box 4187, Topeka, KS 66604-0187 Tel. (913)272-9111 Fax (913)272-9135

Kansas West: Bishop Albert F. Mutti, P.O. Box 4187, Topeka, KS 66604 Tel. (913)272-0587 Fax (913)272-9135; Barbara Sheldon, 9440 E. Boston, #150, Wichita, KS 67207-3600 Tel. (316)684-0266 Fax (316)684-0044

Little Rock: Bishop Janice K. Riggle Huie, 723 Center St., Little Rock, AR 72201-4399 Tel. (501)324-8019 Fax (501)324-8018; Lewis T. See, Jr., 715 Center St., Ste. 202, Little Rock, AR 72201 Tel. (501)324-8027 Fax (501)324-8018

Louisiana: Bishop Dan E. Solomon, Tel. (504) 346-1646 Fax (504)387-3662; Leslie Nichols Akin, 527 North Blvd., Baton Rouge, LA 70802-5720 Tel. (504)346-1646 Fax (504)383-2652

Missouri East: Bishop Ann B. Sherer, PO Box 6039, Chesterfield, MO 63006 Tel. (314) 891-8001 Fax (314)891-8003; Elmer E. Revelle, 870 Woods Mill Rd., #400, Ballwin, MO 63011 Tel. (314)891-1207 Fax (314)891-1211

Missouri West: Bishop Ann B. Sherer, PO Box 6039, Chesterfield, MO 63006 Tel. (314)891-8001 Fax (314)891-8003; Keith T. Berry, 1512 Van Brunt Blvd., Kansas City, MO 64127 Tel. (816)241-7650 Fax (816)241-4086

Nebraska: Bishop Joel L. Martinez, Tel. (402) 466-4955 Fax (402)466-7931; Mel Luetchens, P.O. Box 4553, Lincoln, NE 68504 Tel. (402)464-5994 Fax (402)466-7931

New Mexico: Bishop Alfred L. Norris, Tel. (505)255-8786 Fax (505)255-8738; James E. Large, 7920 Mountain Rd. NE, Albuquerque, NM 87110-7805 Tel. (505)255-8786 Fax (505) 255-8738

North Arkansas: Bishop Janice K. Riggle Huie, 723 Center St., Little Rock, AR 72201-4399 Tel. (501)324-8019 Fax (501)324-8018; Lewis T. See, 715 Center St., Ste. 202, Little Rock, AR 72201 Tel. (501)324-8034 Fax (501) 324-8018

North Texas: Bishop William B. Oden, 3300 Mockingbird Ln., P.O. Box 600127, Dallas, TX 75360-0127 Tel. (214)522-6741 Fax (214)528-4435; Mary Brooke Casad, P.O. Box 516069, Dallas, TX 75251-6069 Tel. (972)490-3438 Fax (972) 490-7216

Northwest Texas: Bishop Alfred L. Norris, 7920 Mountain Rd. NE, Albuquerque, NM 87110-7805 Tel. (505)255-8786 Fax (505)255-8738; Louise Schock, 1415 Ave. M, Lubbock, TX 79401-3939 Tel. (806)762-0201 Fax (806)762-0205

Oklahoma: Bishop Bruce P. Blake, Tel. (405)525-2252 Fax (405)525-2216; David Severe, 2420 N. Blackwelder, Oklahoma City, OK 73106-1499 Tel. (405)525-2252 Fax (405)525-4164

Oklahoma Indian Missionary: Bishop Bruce P. Blake, 2420 N. Blackwelder Ave., Oklahoma City, OK 73106-1499 Tel. (405)525-2252 Fax (405)525-2216; David L. Severe, 2420 N. Blackwelder Ave., Oklahoma City, OK 73106-1499 Tel. (405)525-2252 Fax (405)525-2216

Rio Grande: Bishop Raymond H. Owen, P.O. Box 781688, San Antonio, TX 78278 Tel. (210)408-4500 Fax (210)408-4515; Francisco Estrada, P.O. Box 781974, San Antonio, TX 78278 Tel. (210)408-5313 Fax (210)408-4515

Southwest Texas: Bishop Raymond H. Owen, P.O. Box 781688, San Antonio, TX 78278 Tel. (210)408-4500 Fax (210)408-4501; Jerry Jay Smith, P.O. Box 78149, San Antonio, TX 78278 Tel. (210)408-4500 Fax (210)408-4501

Texas: Bishop J. Woodrow Hearn, Tel. (713)529-7736 Fax (713)521-3724; James Foster, 5215 Main St., Houston, TX 77002-9792 Tel. (713) 521-9383 Fax (713)521-3724

Southeastern Jurisdiction

Exec. Dir.: Gordon C. Goodgame, P.O. Box 67, Lake Junaluska, NC 28745 Tel. (704)452-2881

Alabama-West Florida: Bishop William W. Morris, 424 Interstate Park Dr., Montgomery, AL 36109 Tel. (334)277-1787 Fax (334)277-0109; James William Carpenter, P.O. Drawer 700, Andalusia, AL 36420-0700 Tel. (334)222-3127 Fax (334)222-0469

Florida: Bishop Cornelius L. Henderson, P.O.

163

Box 1747, Lakeland, FL 33802-1747 Tel. (941) 688-4427 Fax (941)687-0568; James Jennings, P.O. Box 3767, Lakeland, FL 33802 Tel. (941) 688-5563 Fax (941)680-1912

Holston: Bishop Ray W. Chamberlain, Jr., P.O. Box 51787, Knoxville, TN 37950-1787 Tel. (423)525-1809 Fax (423)673-4474; Calvin W. Maas, P.O. Box 1178, Johnson City, TN 37605-1178 Tel. (423)928-2156 Fax (423)928-8807

Kentucky: Bishop Robert C. Morgan, 2000 Warrington Way, #280, Louisville, KY 40222 Tel. (502)425-4240 Fax (502)426-5181; Rhoda Peters, 2000 Warrington Way, #280, Louisville, KY 40222 Tel. (502)425-3884 Fax (502)426-5181

Memphis: Bishop Kenneth L. Carder, 520 Commerce St., Ste. 201, Nashville, TN 37203 Tel. (615)742-8834 Fax (615)742-3726; Benny Hopper, PO Box 1257, Jackson, TN 38302 Tel. (901)427-8589 Fax (901)423-2419

Mississippi: Bishop Marshall L. Meadows, Jr., P.O. Box 931, Jackson, MS 39205-0931 Tel. (601)948-4561 Fax (601)948-5981; c/o CCOM Dir., P.O. Box 1147, Jackson, MS 39215 Tel. (601) 354-0515 Fax (601)948-5982

North Alabama: Bishop Robert E. Fannin, Tel. (205)322-8665 Fax (205)322-8938; Michael Stewart, 898 Arkadelphia Rd., Birmingham, AL 35204 Tel. (205)226-7954 Fax (205)226-7975

North Carolina: Bishop Marion M. Edwards, P.O. Box 10955, Raleigh, NC 27605-0955 Tel. (919)832-9560 Fax (919)834-7989; Hope Morgan Ward, P.O. Box 10955, Raleigh, NC 27605-0955 Tel. (919)832-9560 Fax (919)834-7989

North Georgia: Bishop G. Lindsey Davis, Tel. (404)659-0002 Fax (404)577-0068; Douglas Brantley, 159 Ralph McGill Blvd. NE, Atlanta, GA 30308 Tel. (404)659-0002 Fax (404) 577-0131

Red Bird Missionary: Bishop Robert C. Morgan, 2000 Warrington Way, #280, Louisville, KY 40222 Tel. (502)425-4240 Fax (502)426-5181; Ruth Wiertzema, 6 Queendale Ctr., Beverly, KY 40913 Tel. (606)598-5915 Fax (606)598-6405

South Carolina: Bishop J. Lawrence McCleskey, Tel. (803)786-9486 Fax (803)754-9327; Charles L. Johnson, Sr., 4908 Colonial Dr., Columbia, SC 29203 Tel. (803)786-9486 Fax (803)691-0220

South Georgia: Bishop Richard C. Looney, P.O. Box 13616, Macon, GA 31208-3616 Tel. (912) 738-0048 Fax (912)738-9033; James T. Pennell, P.O. Box 20408, St. Simons Island, GA 31522-0008 Tel. (912)638-8626 Fax (912)638-5258

Tennessee: Bishop Kenneth L. Carder, 520 Commerce St., Ste. 201, Nashville, TN 37203 Tel. (615)742-8834 Fax (615)742-3726; Randall C. Ganues, P.O. Box 120607,

Nashville, TN 37212 Tel. (615)329-1177 Fax (615)329-0884

Virginia: Bishop Joe E. Pennel, Jr., Tel. (804) 359-9451 Fax (804)358-7736; F. Douglas Dillard, P.O. 11367, Richmond, VA 23230-1367 Tel. (804)359-9451 Fax (804)359-5427

Western North Carolina: Bishop Charlene P. Kammerer, P.O. Box 18750, Charlotte, NC 28218 Tel. (704)535-2260 Fax (704)567-6117; Thomas R. Sigmon, P.O. Box 18005, Charlotte, NC 28218-0005 Tel. (704)535-2260 Fax (704) 567-6117

Western Jurisdiction

Alaska Missionary: Bishop Edward W. Paup, 1505 SW 18th Ave., Portland, OR 97201-2599 Tel. (503)226-1530 Fax (503)228-3189; Dale Kelley, 3402 Wesleyan Dr., Anchorage, AK 99508-4866 Tel. (907)333-5050 Fax (907) 333-2304

California-Nevada: Bishop Melvin G. Talbert, Tel. (916)374-1510 Fax (916)372-5544; James H. Corson, P.O. Box 980250, West Sacramento, CA 95798-0250 Tel. (916)374-1516 Fax (916)372-5544

California-Pacific: Bishop Roy I. Sano, Tel. (626)568-7300 Fax (626)796-7297; Marilynn Huntington, P.O. Box 6006, Pasadena, CA 91102 Tel. (626)568-7300 Fax (626)796-7297

Desert Southwest: Bishop William W. Dew, Jr., Tel. (602)266-6956 Fax (602)266-5343; Thomas G. Butcher, 1550 E. Meadowbrook Ave., Ste. 200, Phoenix, AZ 85014-4040 Tel. (602)266-6956 Fax (602)266-5343

Oregon-Idaho: Bishop Edward W. Paup, 1505 SW 18th Ave., Portland, OR 97201-2599 Tel. (503) 226-7931 Fax (503)228-3189; James Wenger-Monroe, 1505 SW 18th Ave., Portland, OR 97201-2599 Tel. (503) 226-7931 Fax (503)226-4158

Pacific Northwest: Bishop Elias G. Galvan, 2112 Third Ave. Ste. 301, Seattle, WA 98121-2333 Tel. (206)728-7674 Fax (206)728-8442; Daniel P. Smith, 2112 Third Ave., Ste. 300, Seattle, WA 98121-2333 Tel. (206)728-7462 Fax (206) 728-8442

Rocky Mountain: Bishop Mary Ann Swenson, Tel. (303)733-5035 Fax (303)733-5047; Gary M. Keene, 2200 S. University Blvd., Denver, CO 80210-4797 Tel. (303)733-3736 Fax (303)733-1730

Yellowstone: Bishop Mary Ann Swenson, 2200 S. University Blvd., Denver, CO 80210-4797 Tel. (303)733-5035 Fax (303)733-5047; Thomas Boller, P.O. Box 2540, Billings, MT 59103 Tel. (406)256-1385 Fax (406)256-4948

AGENCIES

Judicial Council: Pres., Tom Matheny; Sec., Sally Curtis AsKew, P.O. Box 58, Bogart, GA 30622 Tel. (770)725-1543 Fax (770)725-1685

Council on Finance & Administration: Pres., Bishop Richard C. Looney; Gen. Sec., Sandra Kelley Lackore, 1200 Davis St., Evanston, IL

60201-4193 Tel. (847)869-3345 Fax (847) 869-6972

Council on Ministries: Pres., Bishop J. Woodrow Hearn; Gen. Sec., C. David Lundquist, 601 W. Riverview Ave., Dayton, OH 45406 Tel. (937) 227-9400 Fax (937)227-9407

Board of Church & Society: Pres., Bishop Charles W. Jordan; Gen. Sec., Thomas White Wolf Fassett, 100 Maryland Ave. NE, Washington, DC 20002 Tel. (202)488-5623 Fax (202)488-5619

Board of Discipleship: Pres., Bishop Mary Ann Swenson; Gen. Sec., Ezra Earl Jones, P.O. Box 840, Nashville, TN 37202 Tel. (615)340-7200 Fax (615)304-7006

Board of Global Ministries: Pres., Bishop Dan E. Solomon; Gen. Sec., Randolph Nugent, 475 Riverside Dr., New York, NY 10115 Tel. (212)870-3600 Fax (212)870-3748

Board of Higher Education & Ministry: Pres., Bishop William B. Oden; Gen. Sec., Roger Ireson, P.O. Box 871, Nashville, TN 37202 Tel. (615)340-7400 Fax (615)340-7048

Board of Pension & Health Benefits: Pres., Bishop Bruce P. Blake; Gen. Sec., Barbara Boigegrain, 1201 Davis St., Evanston, IL 60201 Tel. (847) 869-4550 Fax (847)475-5061

Board of Publications: Chpsn., W. Randolph Smith; United Methodist Publishing House, Pres. & Publisher, Neil M. Alexander, P.O. Box 801, Nashville, TN 37202 Tel. (615)749-6000 Fax (615)749-6079

Commission on Archives & History: Pres., Bishop Emilio de Carvalho; Gen. Sec., Charles Yrigoyen, P.O. Box 127, Madison, NJ 07940 Tel. (973)408-3189 Fax (973)408-3909

Comm. Christian Unity/Interrel. Concerns: Pres., Bishop Roy I. Sano; Gen. Sec., Bruce Robbins, 475 Riverside Dr., Rm. 1300, New York, NY 10115 Tel. (212)749-3553 Fax (212)749-3556

Comm. on Communication/UM Communications: Pres., Bishop Sharon Z. Rader; Gen. Sec., Judith Weidman, 810 12th Ave. S., Nashville, TN 37203 Tel. (615)742-5400 Fax (615)742-5469

Commission on Religion & Race: Pres., Bishop S. Clifton Ives; Gen. Sec., Barbara R. Thompson, 100 Maryland Ave. NE, Washington, DC 20002 Tel. (202)547-2271 Fax (202)547-0358

Commission on the Status & Role of Women: Pres., Joyce Waldon Bright; Gen. Sec., Stephanie Anna Hixon; Cecelia M. Long, 1200 Davis St., Evanston, IL 60201 Tel. (847)869-7330 Fax (847)869-1466

Commission of United Methodist Men: Pres., Bishop Raymond H. Owen; Gen. Sec., Joseph L. Harris, PO Box 860, Nashville, TN 37202-0860 Tel. (615)340-7145 Fax (615)340-1770

Periodicals

Mature Years; El Intérprete; New World Outlook; Newscope; Interpreter; Methodist History; *Christian Social Action; Pockets; Response; Social Questions Bulletin; United Methodist Reporter; United Methodist Review; Quarterly Review; Alive Now; Circuit Rider; El Aposento Alto; Weavings:A Journal of the Christian Spiritual Life; The Upper Room*

United Pentecostal Church International

The United Pentecostal Church International came into being through the merger of two oneness Pentecostal organizations - the Pentecostal Church, Inc., and the Pentecostal Assemblies of Jesus Christ. The first of these was known as the Pentecostal Ministerial Alliance from its inception in 1925 until 1932. The second was formed in 1931 by a merger of the Apostolic Church of Jesus Christ with the Pentecostal Assemblies of the World.

The church contends that the Bible teaches that there is one God who manifested himself as the Father in creation, in the Son in redemption and as the Holy Spirit in regeneration; that Jesus is the name of this absolute deity and that water baptism should be administered in his name, not in the titles Father, Son and Holy Ghost (Acts 2:38, 8:16, and 19:6).

The Fundamental Doctrine of the United Pentecostal Church International, as stated in its Articles of Faith, is "the Bible standard of full salvation, which is repentance, baptism in water by immersion in the name of the Lord Jesus Christ for the remission of sins, and the baptism of the Holy Ghost with the initial sign of speaking with other tongues as the Spirit gives utterance."

Further doctrinal teachings concern a life of holiness and separation, the operation of the gifts of the Spirit within the church, the second coming of the Lord and the church's obligation to take the gospel to the whole world.

Headquarters
8855 Dunn Rd., Hazelwood, MO 63042 Tel. (314)837-7300 Fax (314)837-4503

Media Contact, Gen. Sec.-Treas., Rev. C. M. Becton

Officers
Gen. Supt., Rev. Nathaniel A. Urshan

Asst. Gen. Supts.: Rev. Kenneth Haney, 7149 E. 8 Mile Rd., Stockton, CA 95212; Jesse Williams, P.O. Box 64277, Fayetteville, NC 28306

Gen. Sec.-Treas., Rev. C. M. Becton

Dir. of Foreign Missions, Rev. Harry Scism

Gen. Dir. of Home Missions, Rev. Jack Cunningham

Editor-in-Chief, Rev. J. L. Hall

Gen. Sunday School Dir., Rev. E. J. McClintock

OTHER ORGANIZATIONS
Pentecostal Publishing House, Mgr., Rev. Marvin Curry

Youth Division (Pentecostal Conquerors), Pres., Brian Kinsey, Hazelwood, MO 63042

Ladies Auxiliary, Pres., Gwyn Oakes, P.O. Box 247, Bald Knob, AR 72010

Harvestime Radio Broadcast, Dir., Rev. J. Hugh Rose, 698 Kerr Ave., Cadiz, OH 43907

Stewardship Dept., Contact Church Division, Hazelwood, MO 63042

Education Division, Supt., Rev. Arless Glass, 4502 Aztec, Pasadena, TX 77504

Public Relations Division, Contact Church Division, Hazelwood, MO 63042

Historical Society & Archives

Periodicals

World Harvest Today; The North American Challenge; Homelife; Conqueror; Reflections; Forward

The United Pentecostal Churches of Christ

In a time when the Church of Jesus Christ is challenged to send the "Evening Light Message" to the uppermost part of the Earth, a group of men and women came together on May 29, 1992 at the Pentecostal Church of Christ in Cleveland, Ohio to form what is now called The United Pentecostal Churches of Christ.

Organized and established by Bishop Jesse Delano Ellis, II, the United Pentecostal Churches of Christ is about the business of preparing people to see the Lord of Glory. The traditional barriers of yesteryear must not keep saints or like faith apart, ever again and this fellowship of Pentecostal, Apostolic Independent Churches have discovered the truth of Our Lord's Prayer in the seventeenth chapter of Saint John: "that they may all be One."

The United Pentecostal Churches of Christ is a fellowship of holiness assemblies which has membership in the universal Body of Christ. As such, we preserve the message of Christ's redeeming love through His atonement and declare holiness of life to be His requirement for all men who would enter into the Kingdom of God. We preach repentence from sin, baptism in the Name of Jesus Christ, a personal indwelling of the Holy Spirit, a daily walk with the Lord and life after death. Coupled with the cardinal truths of the Church are the age old customs of ceremony and celebration.

Headquarters

10515 Chester Ave., (at University Circle), Cleveland, OH 44106 Tel. (216)721-5935 Fax (216)721-6938

Contact Person, Asst. Gen. Sec., Rev. W. Michelle James Williams

REGIONAL OFFICE

493-5 Monroe St., Brooklyn, New York 11221 Tel. (718)574-4100 Fax (718)574-8504

Contact Person, Asst. Gen. Sec., Rev. Rodney McNeil Johnson

Officers

Presiding Bishop and Gen. Overseer, Bishop J. Delano Ellis, II, Cleveland, OH

Asst. Presiding Bishop, Bishop Carl Halloway Montgomery, II, Baltimore, MD

Secretary Gen., Bishop James R. Chambers, Brookyn, NY

Supervisor of Women's Department, Rev. Sabrina J. Ellis, Cleveland, OH

Pres. Of Pentacostal Youth Congress, Overseer Gregory Dillard, Chicago, IL

Periodical

THE PENTACOSTAL FLAME

United Zion Church

A branch of the Brethren in Christ which settled in Lancaster County, Pa., the United Zion Church was organized under the leadership of Matthias Brinser in 1855.

Headquarters

United Zion Retirement Community, 722 Furnace Hills Pk., Lititz, PA 17543

Media Contact, Bishop, Carl Eberly, 270 Clay School Rd., Ephrata, PA 17522 Tel. (717)733-3932

Officers

Gen. Conf. Mod., Bishop Carl Eberly, 270 Clay School Rd., Ephrata, PA 17522 Tel. (717)733-3932

Asst. Mod., Rev. John Leisey

Gen. Conf. Sec., Rev. Clyde Martin

Gen. Conf. Treas., Kenneth Kleinfelter, 919 Sycamore Lane, Lebanon, PA 17042

Periodical

Zion's Herald

Unity of the Brethren

Czech and Moravian immigrants in Texas (beginning about 1855) established congregations which grew into an Evangelical Union in 1903, and with the accession of other Brethren in Texas, into the Evangelical Unity of the Czech-Moravian Brethren in North America. In 1959, it shortened the name to the original name used in 1457, the Unity of the Brethren (Unitas Fratrum, or Jednota Bratrska).

Headquarters

4009 Hunter Creek, College Station, TX 77845

Media Contact, Sec. of Exec. Committee, Georgia Anderson, 2501 Davis St., #42, Taylor, TX 76574 Tel. (512)352-3239

Officers

Pres., Kent Laza, 4009 Hunter Creek, College Station, TX 77845

1st Vice Pres., Rev. Michael Groseclose, 902 Church St., Belleville, TX 77418 Tel. (512)365-6890

Sec., Georgia Anderson, 2501 Davis St., #42, Taylor, TX 76574 Tel. (512)352-3239

Fin. Sec., Rev. Joseph Polasek, 4241 Blue Heron, Bryan, TX 77807

Treas., Frank McKay, III, 148 North Burnett, Baytown, TX 77520

OTHER ORGANIZATIONS

Bd. of Christian Educ., Dr., Donald Ketcham, 900 N. Harrison, West, TX 76691

Brethren Youth Fellowship, Pres., Marcia Hailey, 113 Oak Lane, Elm Mott, TX 76640

Young Adult Fellowship, Pres., Kimberly Stewart, 3719 Thursa Ln., Friendswood, TX 77546

Christian Sisters Union, Pres., Catherine Holubec, 1810 Hood, Taylor, TX 76574

Sunday School Union, Pres., Marvin Chlapek, 11026 Elm Bridge Ct., Houston, TX 77065

Periodical

Brethren Journal, Editor, Rev.Milton Maly, 6703 FM 2502, Brenham, TX 77833; Bus Mngr., Jean Maly, 6703 FM 2502, Brenham, TX 77833

Universal Fellowship of Metropolitan Community Churches

The Universal Fellowship of Metropolitan Community Churches was founded Oct. 6, 1968 by the Rev. Troy D. Perry in Los Angeles, with a particular but not exclusive outreach to the gay community. Since that time, the Fellowship has grown to include congregations throughout the world.

The group is trinitarian and accepts the Bible as the divinely inspired Word of God. The Fellowship has two sacraments, baptism and holy communion, as well as a number of traditionally recognized rites such as ordination.

This Fellowship acknowledges "the Holy Scriptures interpreted by the Holy Spirit in conscience and faith, as its guide in faith, discipline, and government." The government of this Fellowship is vested in its General Council (consisting of Elders and District Coordinators), clergy and church delegates, who exert the right of control in all of its affairs, subject to the provisions of its Articles of Incorporation and By-Laws.

Headquarters

8704 Santa Monica Blvd. 2nd Floor, West Hollywood, CA 90069-4548 Tel. (310)360-8640 Fax (310)360-8680 E-mail: ufmcchq@aol.com Website: http://www.ufmcc.com

Officers

Mod., Rev. Elder Troy D. Perry

Vice-Mod., Rev. Elder Nancy L. Wilson

Treas., Rev. Elder Donald Eastman

Clk., Rev. Elder Darlene Garner, 7245 Lee Hwy., Falls Church, VA 22046

Elder Clarke Friesen, P.O. Box 90685, Tucson, AZ 85752

Rev. Elder Jorge Sosa Morato, Apartado Postal 7-1421/06090, Mexico City, Mexico

Rev. Elder Hong Kia Tan, 72 Fleet Rd., Hampstead, London, NW3 2QT England

Chief Operating Officer, Ravi Verma, 8704 Santa Monica Blvd., 2nd Floor, West Hollywood, CA 90069-4548

Press Officer, James Birkitt, 8704 Santa Monica Blvd., 2nd Floor, West Hollywood, CA 90069-4548

US National Ecumenical Officer, Dr. Gwynne Guibord, 4311 Wilshir Blvd., Ste. 308, Los Angeles, CA 90010 Tel. (213)932-1516

DISTRICT COORDINATORS

Australian District, Rev. Greg Smith, MCC Sydney, P.O. Box 1237, Darlinghurst NSW 2010, Australia

Eastern Canadian District, Rev. Diane Fisher, 179 Palmer Rd. No. 411, Belleville, ON K8P 4S8 Canada

European District, Ms. Cecilia Eggleston, E-Mail: c.m.e@btinternet.com

Great Lakes District, Judy Dale, 1300 Ambridge Dr., Louisville, KY 40207-2410 Tel. (502)897-3821

Gulf Lower Atlantic District, Rev. Jay Neely, c/o First MCC of Atlanta, 1379 Tullie Rd., Atlanta, GA 30329

Mid-Atlantic District, Rev. Arlene Ackerman, P.O. Box 276, Landsville, PA 17538

Mountains & Plains District, Rev. L. Robert Arthur, P.O. Box 8291, Omaha, NE 68108

Northeast District, Rev. Ron Helms, Moderator, E-Mail: nedufmcc@aol.com

Northwest District, Rev. Janet Suess-Pierce

South Central District, Rev. Eleanor Nealy, P.O. Box 7441, Houston, TX 77248-7441

Southeast District, Rev. Judy Davenport, P.O. Box 12768, St. Petersburg, FL 33733-2768

Southwest District, Don Pederson, 3600 S. Harbor Blvd., No. 183, Oxnard, CA 93035-4136

OTHER COMMISSIONS & COMMITTEES

Min. of Global Outreach, Field Dir., Rev. Judy Dahl

Commission on the Laity, Chpsn., JoNee Shelton, 1969 Alston Ave., Ft. Worth, TX 76110

Clergy Credentials & Concerns, Admn., Rev. Justin Tanis

Bd. of Pensions, Admn., J. Hulsey-Mazur, 8704 Santa Monica Blvd. 2nd Floor, West Hollywood, CA 90069-4548

Ecumenical Witness & Ministry: Dir., Rev. Elder Nancy L. Wilson

UFMCC AIDS Ministry: AIDS Liaison., Frank Zerilli

Women's Secretariat, Chair, Rev. Diane Fisher, 179 Palmer Rd. #411, Bellville, ON K8P 4S8

Periodicals

Keeping in Touch; UFMCC E-Mail News Service (FREE)

Volunteers of America

Volunteers of America, founded in 1896 by Ballington and Maud Booth, provides spiritual and material aid for those in need in more than

300 communities across the United States. As one of the nation's largest and most diversified human-service organizations, Volunteers of America offers more than 400 programs for the elderly, families, youth, alcoholics, drug abusers, offenders and the disabled.

Headquarters
110 South Union St., Alexandria, VA 22314-3324 Tel. (800)899-0089

Officers
Chpsn., Jean Galloway
Pres., Charles W. Gould

Periodical
Spirit

The Wesleyan Church

The Wesleyan Church was formed on June 26, 1968, through the union of the Wesleyan Methodist Church of America (1843) and the Pilgrim Holiness Church (1897). The headquarters was established at Marion, Ind., and relocated to Indianapolis in 1987.

The Wesleyan movement centers around the beliefs, based on Scripture, that the atonement in Christ provides for the regeneration of sinners and the entire sanctification of believers. John Wesley led a revival of these beliefs in the 18th century.

When a group of New England Methodist ministers led by Orange Scott began to crusade for the abolition of slavery, the bishops and others sought to silence them. This led to a series of withdrawals from the Methodist Episcopal Church. In 1843, the Wesleyan Methodist Connection of America was organized and led by Scott, Jotham Horton, LaRoy Sunderland, Luther Lee and Lucius C. Matlack.

During the holiness revival in the last half of the 19th century, holiness replaced social reform as the major tenet of the Connection. In 1947 the name was changed from Connection to Church and a central supervisory authority was set up.

The Pilgrim Holiness Church was one of many independent holiness churches which came into existence as a result of the holiness revival. Led by Martin Wells Knapp and Seth C. Rees, the International Holiness Union and Prayer League was inaugurated in 1897 in Cincinnati. Its purpose was to promote worldwide holiness evangelism and the Union had a strong missionary emphasis from the beginning. It developed into a church by 1913.

The Wesleyan Church is now spread across most of the United States and Canada and 41 other countries. The Wesleyan World Fellowship was organized in 1972 to unite Wesleyan mission bodies developing into mature churches. The Wesleyan Church is a member of the Christian Holiness Partnership, the National Association of Evangelicals and the World Methodist Council.

Headquarters
P.O. Box 50434, Indianapolis, IN 46250 Tel. (317)842-0444
E-mail: gensecoff@aol.com
Website: http://www.wesleyan.org
Media Contact, Gen. Sec., Dr. Ronald R. Brannon, Tel. (317)570-5154 Fax (317)570-5280

Officers
Gen. Supts.: Dr. Earle L. Wilson; Dr. Lee M. Haines; Dr. Thomas E. Armiger
Gen. Sec., Dr. Ronald R. Brannon
Gen. Treas., Donald M. Frase
Gen. Director of Communications, Dr. Norman G. Wilson
Gen. Publisher, Rev. Nathan Birky
Evangelism & Church Growth, Gen. Dir., Dr. B. Marlin Mull
World Missions, Gen. Dir., Dr. Donald L. Bray
Local Church Educ., Gen. Dir., Dr. Ray E. Barnwell, Sr.
Student Ministries, Gen. Dir., Rev. Ross DeMerchant
Education & the Ministry, Gen. Dir., Rev. Kerry D. Kind
Estate Planning, Gen. Dir., Howard B. Castle
Wesleyan Pension Fund, Gen. Dir., Mr. Bobby L. Temple
Wesleyan Investment Foundation, Gen. Dir., Dr. John A. Dunn

Periodicals
Wesleyan Woman; The Wesleyan Advocate; Wesleyan World

Wesleyan Holiness Association of Churches

This body was founded Aug. 4, 1959 near Muncie, Ind. by a group of ministers and laymen who were drawn together for the purpose of spreading and conserving sweet, radical, scriptural holiness. These men came from various church bodies. This group is Wesleyan in doctrine and standards.

Headquarters
RR 2, Box 9, Winchester, IN 47394 Tel. (765)584-3199 Fax (717)966-4147
Media Contact, Gen. Sec.-Treas., Rev. Robert W. Wilson, R.D. 1, Box 98A, Mifflinburg, PA 17844

Officers
Gen. Supt., Rev. John Brewer
Asst. Gen. Supt., Rev. Jack W. Dulin, Rt. 2, Box 309, Milton, KY 40045 Tel. (502)268-5826
Gen. Sec.-Treas., Rev. Robert W. Wilson, R D 1, Box 98A, Mifflinburg, PA 17844 Tel. (717)966-4147
Gen. Youth Pres., Rev. Nathan Shockley, 504 W. Tyrell St., St. Louis, MI 48880 Tel. (517)681-2591

Periodical
Eleventh Hour Messenger

Wisconsin Evangelical Lutheran Synod

Organized in 1850 at Milwaukee, Wis., by three pastors sent to America by a German mission society, the Wisconsin Evangelical Lutheran Synod still reflects its origins, although it now has congregations in 50 states and three Canadian provinces. It supports missions in 26 countries.

The Wisconsin Synod federated with the Michigan and Minnesota Synods in 1892 in order to more effectively carry on education and mission enterprises. A merger of these three Synods followed in 1917 to give the Wisconsin Evangelical Lutheran Synod its present form.

Although at its organization in 1850 WELS turned away from conservative Lutheran theology, today it is ranked as one of the most conservative Lutheran bodies in the United States. WELS confesses that the Bible is the verbally inspired, infallible Word of God and subscribes without reservation to the confessional writings of the Lutheran Church. Its interchurch relations are determined by a firm commitment to the principle that unity of doctrine and practice are the prerequisites of pulpit and altar fellowship and ecclesiastical cooperation. It does not hold membership in ecumenical organizations.

Headquarters

2929 N. Mayfair Rd., Milwaukee, WI 53222 Tel. (414)256-3888 Fax (414)256-3899
E-mail: webbin@sab.wels.net
Website: http://www.wels.net
Dir. of Communications, Rev. Gary Baumler

Officers

Pres., Rev. Karl R. Gurgel
1st Vice-Pres., Rev. Richard E. Lauersdorf
2nd Vice-Pres., Rev. Jon Mahnke, 6001 Blossom Ave., San Jose CA 95123
Sec., Rev. Douglas L. Bode, 1005 E. Broadway, Prairie du Chien, WI 53821

OTHER ORGANIZATIONS

Executive Dir. Of Support Services, (to be named)
Bd. for Ministerial Education, Admn., Rev. John Lawrenz
Bd. for Parish Services, Admn., Rev. Wayne Mueller
Bd. for Home Missions, Admn., Rev. Harold J. Hagedorn
Bd. for World Missions, Admn., Rev. Daniel Koelpin

Periodicals

Wisconsin Lutheran Quarterly; Lutheran Parent; Lutheran Parent's Wellspring; Northwestern Lutheran; The Lutheran Educator; Mission Connection

Religious Bodies in the United States Arranged by Families

The following list of religious bodies appearing in the Directory Section of the Yearbook shows the "families," or related clusters into which American religious bodies can be grouped. For example, there are many communions that can be grouped under the heading "Baptist" for historical and theological reasons. It is not to be assumed, however, that all denominations under one family heading are similar in belief or practice. Often, any similarity is purely coincidental. The family clusters tend to represent historical factors more often than theological or practical ones. The family categories provided one of the major pitfalls of church statistics because of the tendency to combine the statistics by "families" for analytical and comparative purposes. Such combined totals are almost meaningless, although often used as variables for sociological analysis.

Religious bodies not grouped under family headings appear alphabetically and are not indented in the following list.

Adventist Bodies

Advent Christian Church
Church of God General Conference
(Oregon, IL and Morrow, GA)
Primitive Advent Christian Church
Seventh-day Adventist Church

American Evangelical Christian Churches
American Rescue Workers
American Catholic Church

Anglican

The Anglical Orthodox Church
Episcopal Church
Reformed Episcopal Church

Apostolic Christian Church (Nazarene)
Apostolic Christian Churches of America

Baptist Bodies

American Baptist Association
American Baptist Churches in the U.S.A.
Baptist Bible Fellowship International
Baptist General Conference
Baptist Missionary Association of America
Conservative Baptist Association of America
General Association of General Baptists
General Association of Regular Baptist Churches
National Association of Free Will Baptists
National Baptist Convention of America, Inc.
National Baptist Convention, U.S.A., Inc.
National Missionary Baptist Convention of America
National Primitive Baptist Convention, Inc.
North American Baptist Conference
Primitive Baptists
Progressive National Baptist Convention, Inc.
Separate Baptists in Christ
Seventh Day Baptist General Conference, USA and Canada
Southern Baptist Convention
Sovereign Grace Baptists

Berean Fundamental Church

Brethren (German Baptists)

Brethren Church (Ashland, Ohio)
Church of the Brethren
Fellowship of Grace Brethren Churches
Old German Baptist Brethren

Brethren, River

Brethren in Christ Church
United Zion Church

Christadelphians
The Christian and Missionary Alliance
Christian Brethren (also known as Plymouth Brethren)
Christ Community Church (Evangelical-Protestant)
The Christian Congregation, Inc.
Christian Union
Church of Christ, Scientist
The Church of Illumination
Church of the Living God (Motto: Christian Workers for Fellowship)
Church of the Nazarene
Churches of Christ in Christian Union

Churches of Christ—Christian Churches

Christian Church (Disciples of Christ)
Christian Churches and Churches of Christ
Churches of Christ

Churches of God

Church of God (Anderson, Ind.)
Church of God by Faith, Inc.
The Church of God (Seventh Day), Denver, Colo.
Churches of God, General Conference

Churches of the New Jerusalem

General Church of the New Jerusalem
The Swedborgian Church

Conservative Congregational Christian Conference

Eastern Churches

Albanian Orthodox Archdiocese in America
Albanian Orthodox Diocese of America
The American Carpatho-Russian Orthodox
Greek Catholic Church
The Antiochian Orthodox Christian Arch-
diocese of North America
Apostolic Catholic Assyrian Church of the
East, North American Dioceses
Apostolic Orthodox Catholic Church
Armenian Apostolic Church of America
Apostolic Orthodox Catholic Church
Armenian Apostolic Church of America
Coptic Orthodox Church
Diocese of the Armenian Church of America
Greek Orthodox Archdiocese of North and
South America
The Orthodox Church in America
Patriarchal Parishes of the Russian Orthodox
Church in the U.S.A.
The Romanian Orthodox Church in America
The Romanian Orthodox Episcopate of
America
The Russian Orthodox Church Outside
Russia
Serbian Orthodox Church in the U.S.A. and
Canada
Syrian Orthodox Church of Antioch
True Orthodox Church of Greece (Synod of
Metropolitan Cyprian), American
Exarchate
Ukrainian Orthodox Church of America
(Ecumenical Patriarchate)
Ukrainian Orthodox Church of the U.S.A.

The Evangelical Church
The Evangelical Church Alliance
The Evangelical Congregational Church
The Evangelical Covenant Church
The Evangelical Free Church of America
Fellowship of Fundamental Bible Churches
Free Christian Zion Church of Christ

Friends

Evangelical Friends International-North
America Region
Friends General Conference
Friends United Meeting
Religious Society of Friends (Conservative
Religious Society of Friends (Unaffiliated
Meetings)

Grace Gospel
House of God, Which is the Church of the
Living God, the Pillar and Ground of
the Truth, Inc.
Independent Fundamental Churches of
America
International Council of Community
Churches
Jehovah's Witnesses

Latter Day Saints

Church of Christ
The Church of Jesus Christ (Bickertonites)
The Church of Jesus Christ of Latter-day
Saints
Reorganized Church of Jesus Christ of Latter
Day Saints

The Liberal Catholic Church—Province of
the United States of America

Lutherans

The American Association of Lutheran
Churches
Apostolic Lutheran Church of America
The Association of Free Lutheran
Congregations
Church of the Lutheran Brethren of America
Church of the Lutheran Confession
Conservative Lutheran Association
The Estonian Evangelical Lutheran Church
Evangelical Lutheran Church in America
Evangelical Lutheran Synod
The Latvian Evangelical Lutheran Church in
America
The Lutheran Church—Missouri Synod
Wisconsin Evangelical Lutheran Synod

Malankara Mar Thoma Syrian Church

Mennonite Bodies

Beachy Amish Mennonite Churches
Bible Fellowship Church
Church of God in Christ (Mennonite)
Evangelical Mennonite Church
Fellowship of Evangelical Bible Churches
General Conference of Mennonite Brethren
Churches
Hutterian Brethren
Mennonite Church
Mennonite Church, General Conference
Old Order Amish Church
Old Order (Wisler) Mennonite Church
Reformed Mennonite Church

Methodist Bodies

African Methodist Episcopal Church
African Methodist Episcopal Zion Church
Allegheny Wesleyan Methodist Connection
(Original Allegheny Conference)
Bible Holiness Church
Christian Methodist Episcopal Church
Evangelical Methodist Church
Free Methodist Church of North America
Fundamental Methodist Church, Inc.
Primitive Methodist Church in the U.S.A.
Reformed Methodist Union Episcopal Church
Reformed Zion Union Apostolic Church
Southern Methodist Church
The United Methodist Church
The Wesleyan Church

The Metropolitan Church Association, Inc.
The Missionary Church

Moravian Bodies

Moravian Church in America (Unitas Fratrum)
Unity of the Brethren

National Association of Congregational Christian Churches
National Organization of the New Apostolic Church of North America
National Spiritualist Association of Churches

Old Catholic Churches

Christ Catholic Church

Pentecostal Bodies

Apostolic Episcopal Church
Apostolic Faith Mission Church of God
Apostolic Faith Mission of Portland, Oregon
Apostolic Overcoming Holy Church of God, Inc.
Assemblies of God
Assemblies of God International Fellowship (Independent/Not Affiliated)
The Bible Church of Christ, Inc.
Bible Way Church of Our Lord Jesus Christ, World Wide, Inc.
Christian Church of North America, General Council
Church of God (Cleveland, Tenn.)
The Church of God in Christ
Church of God in Christ, International
Church of God, Mountain Assembly, Inc.
The Church of God of Prophecy
Church of Our Lord Jesus Christ of the Apostolic Faith, Inc.
Congregational Holiness Church
Elim Fellowship
Full Gospel Assemblies International
Full Gospel Fellowship of Churches and Ministers International
International Church of the Foursquare Gospel
The International Pentecostal Church of Christ
International Pentecostal Holiness Church
Open Bible Standard Churches, Inc.
The (Original) Church of God, Inc.
Pentecostal Assemblies of the World, Inc.
Pentecostal Church of God
Pentecostal Fire-Baptized Holiness Church
The Pentecostal Free Will Baptist Church, Inc.
United Holy Church of America, Inc.
United Pentecostal Church International
United Pentecostal Churches of Christ

Pillar of Fire
Polish National Catholic Church of America

Presbyterian Bodies

Associate Reformed Presbyterian Church (General Synod)
Cumberland Presbyterian Church
Cumberland Presbyterian Church in America
Evangelical Presbyterian Church
General Assembly of the Korean Presbyterian Church in America
The Orthodox Presbyterian Church
Presbyterian Church in America
Presbyterian Church (U.S.A.)
Reformed Presbyterian Church of North America

Reformed Bodies

Christian Reformed Church in North America
Hungarian Reformed Church in America
Netherlands Reformed Congregations
Protestant Reformed Churches in America
Reformed Church in America
Reformed Church in the United States
United Church of Christ

The Roman Catholic Church
The Salvation Army
The Schwenkfelder Church
Triumph the Church and Kingdom of God in Christ Inc. (International)
United House of Prayer
Universal Fellowship of Metropolitan Community Churches

United Brethren Bodies

Church of the United Brethren in Christ
United Christian Church

Volunteers of America
Wesleyan Holiness Association of Churches

4. Religious Bodies in Canada

A large number of Canadian religious bodies were organized by immigrants from Europe and elsewhere, and a smaller number sprang up originally on Canadian soil. In the case of Canada, moreover, many denominations that overlap the U.S.-Canada border have headquarters in the United States.

If you have difficulty finding a particular denomination, check the index of organizations. In some cases alternative names for denominations are listed there. A final section lists denominations according to denominational families. This can be a helpful tool in finding a particular denomination.

Complete statistics for Canadian denominations are found in the table "Canadian Current and Non-current Statistics" in the statistical section of the Yearbook.

Addresses for periodicals are found in the listing of Canadian Religious Periodicals. Information about finances for some of the denominations is in the Church Finance statistical section.

The Anglican Church of Canada

Anglicanism came to Canada with the early explorers such as Martin Frobisher and Henry Hudson. Continuous services began in Newfoundland about 1700 and in Nova Scotia in 1710. The first Bishop, Charles Inglis, was appointed to Nova Scotia in 1787. The numerical strength of Anglicanism was increased by the coming of American Loyalists and by massive immigration both after the Napoleonic wars and in the later 19th and early 20th centuries.

The Anglican Church of Canada has enjoyed self-government for over a century and is an autonomous member of the worldwide Anglican Communion. The General Synod, which normally meets triennially, consists of the Archbishops, Bishops and elected clerical and lay representatives of the 30 dioceses. Each of the Ecclesiastical Provinces-Canada, Ontario, Rupert's Land and British Columbia-is organized under a Metropolitan and has its own Provincial Synod and Executive Council. Each diocese has its own Diocesan Synod.

Headquarters

Church House, 600 Jarvis St., Toronto, ON M4Y 2J6 Tel. (416)924-9192 Fax (416)968-7983
Media Contact, Dir. of Information Resources, Douglas Tindal
E-mail: dtindal@national.anglican.ca

GENERAL SYNOD Officers

Primate of the Anglican Church of Canada, Most Rev. Michael G. Peers
Prolocutor, Ven. Rodney O. Andrews, Box 1168, Sault Ste. Marie, ON P6A 5N7
Gen. Sec., Ven. James B. Boyles
Treas., Gen. Synod, Mr. James Cullen

DEPARTMENTS AND DIVISIONS

Faith, Worship & Ministry, Dir., Rev. Canon Alyson Barnett-Cowan
Financial Management and Dev., Dir., Mr. James Cullen
Inform. Resources Dir., Mr. Douglas Tindal
Partnerships, Dir., Dr. Eleanor Johnson
Pensions, Dir., Mrs. Jenny Mason
Primate's World Relief and Dev. Fund, Dir., Mr. Robin Gibson

METROPOLITANS (ARCHBISHOPS)

Ecclesiastical Province of: Canada, The Most Rev. Arthur G. Peters, 5732 College St., Halifax, NS B3H 1X3; Rupert's Land, The Most Rev. J. Barry Curtis, 3015 Glencoe Rd. SW, Calgary, AB T2S 2L9 Tel. (403)243-3673 Fax (403)243-2182; British Columbia, The Most Rev. David P. Crawley, 1876 Richter St., Kelowna, BC V1Y 2M9 Tel. (250)762-3306 Fax (250)762-4150; Ontario, The Most Rev. Percy R. O'Driscoll, One London Place, 903-255 Queens Ave., London, ON N6A 5R8 Tel. (519)434-6893 Fax (519)673-4151

DIOCESAN BISHOPS

Algoma: The Rt. Rev. Ronald Ferris, Box 1168, Sault Ste. Marie, ON P6A 5N7 Tel. (705)256-5061 Fax (705)946-1860
Arctic: The Rt. Rev. Christopher Williams, 4910 51st St., Box 1454, Yellowknife, NT X1A 2P1 Tel. (867)873-5432 Fax (867)873-8478
Athabasca: The Right Rev. John R. Clarke, Box 6868, Peace River, AB T8S 1S6 Tel. (403)624-2767 Fax (403)624-2365
Brandon: The Rt. Rev. Malcolm Harding, 341-13th St., Brandon, MB R7A 4P8 Tel. (204)727-7550 Fax (204)727-4135
British Columbia: The Rt. Rev. Barry Jenks, 900 Vancouver St., Victoria, BC V8V 3V7 Tel. (250)386-7781 Fax (250)386-4013
Caledonia: The Rt. Rev. John E. Hannen, Box 278, Prince Rupert, BC V8J 3P6 Tel. (250)624-6013 Fax (250)624-4299
Calgary: Archbishop, The Most Rev. J. Barry Curtis, 3015 Glencoe Rd. SW, Calgary, AB T2S 2L9 Tel. (403)243-3673 Fax (403)243-2182
Cariboo: The Right Rev. James D. Cruickshank, 5-618 Tranquille Rd., Kamloops, BC V2B 3H6 Tel. (250)376-0112 Fax (250)376-1984
Central Newfoundland: The Rt. Rev. Edward Marsh, 34 Fraser Rd., Gander, NF A1V 2E8 Tel. (709)256-2372 Fax (709)256-2396
Eastern Newfoundland and Labrador: The Rt. Rev. Donald F. Harvey, 19 King's Bridge Rd., St. John's, NF A1C 3K4 Tel. (709)576-6697 Fax (709)576-7122
Edmonton: The Rt. Rev. Victoria Matthews, 10033 - 84 Ave., Edmonton, AB T6E 2G6 Tel. (403)439-7344 Fax (403)439-6549

Fredericton: The Rt. Rev. George C. Lemmon, 115 Church St., Fredericton, NB E3B 4C8 Tel. (506)459-1801 Fax (506)459-8475

Huron: Archbishop, The Most Rev. Percy R. O'Driscoll, One London Place, 903-255 Queens Ave., London, ON N6A 5R8 Tel. (519)434-6893 Fax (519)673-4151

Keewatin: The Rt. Rev. Gordon Beardy, 915 Ottawa St., Keewatin, ON P0X 1C0 Tel. (807)547-3353 Fax (807)547-3356

Kootenay: Archbishop, The Most Rev. David P. Crawley, 1876 Richter St., Kelowna, BC V1Y 2M9 Tel. (250)762-3306 Fax (250)762-4150

Montreal: The Rt. Rev. Andrew S. Hutchison, 1444 Union Ave., Montreal, QC H3A 2B8 Tel. (514)843-6577 Fax (514)843-3221

Moosonee: The Rt. Rev. Caleb J. Lawrence, Box 841, Schumacher, ON P0N 1G0 Tel. (705)360-1129 Fax (705)360-1120

New Westminster: The Rt. Rev. Michael C. Ingham, 580-401 W. Georgia St., Vancouver, BC V6B 5A1 Tel. (250)684-6306 Fax (250)684-7017

Niagara: The Rt. Rev. Ralph Spence, 252 James St. N., Hamilton, ON L8R 2L3 Tel. (905)527-1278 Fax (905)527-1281

Nova Scotia: The Most Rev. Arthur G. Peters, 5732 College St., Halifax, NS B3H 1X3 Tel. (902)420-0717 Fax (902)425-0717

Ontario: The Rt. Rev. Peter Mason, 90 Johnson St., Kingston, ON K7L 1X7 Tel. (613)544-4774 Fax (613)547-3745

Ottawa: The Rt. Rev. John A. Baycroft, 71 Bronson Ave., Ottawa, ON K1R 6G6 Tel. (613)232-7124 Fax (613)232-7088

Qu'Appelle: The Rt. Rev. Duncan D. Wallace, 1501 College Ave., Regina, SK S4P 1B8 Tel. (306)522-1608 Fax (306)352-6808

Quebec: The Rt. Rev. Bruce Stavert, 31 rue des Jardins, Quebec, QC G1R 4L6 Tel. (418)692-3858 Fax (418)692-3876

Rupert's Land: The Rt. Rev. Patrick V. Lee, 935 Nesbitt Bay, Winnipeg, MB R3T 1W6 Tel. (204)453-6130 Fax (204)452-3915

Saskatchewan: The Rt. Rev. Anthony Burton, Box 1088, Prince Albert, SK S6V 5S6 Tel. (306)763-2455 Fax (306)764-5172

Saskatoon: The Rt. Rev. Thomas O. Morgan, Box 1965, Saskatoon, SK S7K 3S5 Tel. (306)244-5651 Fax (306)933-4606

Toronto: The Rt. Rev. Terence E. Finlay, 135 Adelaide St. East, Toronto, ON M5C 1L8 Tel. (416)363-6021 Fax (416)363-3683

Western Newfoundland: The Rt. Rev. Leonard Whitten, 25 Main St., Corner Brook, NF A2H 1C2 Tel. (709)639-8712 Fax (709)639-1636

Yukon: The Rt. Rev. Terry Buckle, Box 4247, Whitehorse, YT Y1A 3T3 Tel. (867)667-7746 Fax (867)667-6125

Periodicals

Anglican Journal (National Newspaper); *Ministry Matters*

The Antiochian Orthodox Christian Archdiocese of North America

The approximately 100,000 members of the Antiochian Orthodox community in Canada are under the jurisdiction of the Antiochian Orthodox Christian Archdiocese of North America with headquarters in Englewood, N.J. There are churches in Edmonton, Winnipeg, Halifax, London, Ottawa, Toronto, Windsor, Montreal Saskatoon, and Hamilton.

Headquarters

Metropolitan Philip Saliba, 358 Mountain Rd., Englewood, NJ 07631 Tel. (201)871-1355 Fax (201)871-7954

Website: http://www.antiochian.com

Media Contact, Rev. Fr. Thomas Zain, 52 78th St., Brooklyn, NY 11209 Tel. (718)748-7940 Fax (718)855-3608

Periodicals

The Word; Again; Handmaiden

Apostolic Christian Church (Nazarene)

This church was formed in Canada as a result of immigration from various European countries. The body began as a movement originated by the Rev. S. H. Froehlich, a Swiss pastor, whose followers are still found in Switzerland and Central Europe.

Headquarters

Apostolic Christian Church Foundation, 1135 Sholey Rd., Richmond, VA 23231 Tel. (804)222-1943

Media Contact, James Hodges

Officer

Exec. Dir., James Hodges

The Apostolic Church in Canada

The Apostolic Church in Canada is affiliated with the worldwide organization of the Apostolic Church with headquarters in Great Britain. A product of the Welsh Revival (1904 to 1908), its Canadian beginnings originated in Nova Scotia in 1927. Today its main centers are in Nova Scotia, Ontario and Quebec. This church is evangelical, fundamental and Pentecostal, with special emphasis on the ministry gifts listed in Ephesians 4:11-12.

Headquarters

27 Castlefield Ave., Toronto, ON M4R 1G3

Media Contact, Pres., Rev. John Kristensen, 685 Park St. S., Peterborough, ON K9J 3S9 Tel. (705)742-1618

Officers

Pres., Rev. John Kristensen, 685 Park St. S., Peterborough, ON K9J 3S9 Tel. (705)742-1618

Natl. Sec., Rev. J. Karl Thomas, 22 Malamute Cres., Scarborough, ON M1T 2C7 Tel. (416)298-0977

174

Apostolic Church of Pentecost of Canada Inc.

This body was founded in 1921 at Winnipeg, Manitoba, by Pastor Frank Small. Doctrines include belief in eternal salvation by the grace of God, baptism of the Holy Spirit with the evidence of speaking in tongues, water baptism by immersion in the name of the Lord Jesus Christ.

Headquarters
200-809 Manning Rd. NE, Calgary, AB T2E 7M9
E-mail: acop@compuserve.com
Website: http://www.illuminart.com/acop
Media Contact, Admn., Rev. Wes Mills, Tel. (403)273-5777 Fax (403)273-8102

Officers
Mod., Rev. G. Killam
Admin., Rev. Wes Mills

Armenian Holy Apostolic Church—Canadian Diocese

The Canadian branch of the ancient Church of Armenia founded in A.D. 301 by St. Gregory the Illuminator was established in Canada at St. Catharines, Ontario, in 1930. The diocesan organization is under the jurisdiction of the Holy See of Etchmiadzin, Armenia. The Diocese has churches in St. Catharines, Hamilton, Toronto, Ottawa, Vancouver, Mississauga, Montreal, Brossard, Laval and Windsor.

Headquarters
Diocesan Offices: Primate, Canadian Diocese, Archbishop Hovnan Derderian, 615 Stuart Ave., Outremont, QC H2V 3H2 Tel. (514)276-9479 Fax (514)276-9960
Media Contact, Exec. Dir., ArminÈ Keuchgerian

Periodical
Pourastan

Armenian Evangelical Church

Founded in 1960 by immigrant Armenian evangelical families from the Middle East, this body is conservative doctrinally, with an evangelical, biblical emphasis. The polity of churches within the group differ with congregationalism being dominant, but there are presbyterian Armenian Evangelical churches as well. Most of the local churches have joined main-line denominations. All of the remaining Armenian Evangelical (congregational or presbyterian) local churches in the United States and Canada have joined with the Armenian Evangelical Union of North America.

Headquarters
Armenian Evangelical Church of Toronto, 2851 John St., P.O. Box 42015, Markham, ON L3R 5R0 Tel. (905)305-8144
Media Contact, Chief Editor, Rev. Yessayi Sarmazian

A.E.U.N.A. Officers
Min. to the Union, Rev. Karl Avakian, 1789 E. Frederick Ave., Fresno, CA 93720
Mod., Rev. Bernard Geulsgeugian

Officer
Min., Rev. Yessayi Sarmazian

Periodical
Armenian Evangelical Church

Associated Gospel Churches

The Associated Gospel Churches (AGC) traces its historical roots to the 1890s. To counteract the growth of liberal theology evident in many established denominations at this time, individuals and whole congregations seeking to uphold the final authority of the Scriptures in all matters of faith and conduct withdrew from those denominations and established churches with an evangelical ministry. These churches defended the belief that "all Scripture is given by inspiration of God" and also declared that the Holy Spirit gave the identical word of sacred writings of holy men of old, chosen by Him to be the channel of His revelation to man.

At first this growing group of independent churches was known as the Christian Workers' Churches of Canada, and by 1922 there was desire for forming an association for fellowship, counsel and cooperation. Several churches in southern Ontario banded together under the leadership of Dr. P. W. Philpott of Hamilton and Rev. H. E. Irwin, K. C. of Toronto.

When a new Dominion Charter was obtained on March 18, 1925, the name was changed to Associated Gospel Churches. Since that time the AGC has steadily grown, spreading across Canada by invitation to other independent churches of like faith and by actively beginning new churches.

Headquarters
3228 South Service Rd., Burlington, ON L7N 3H8 Tel. (905)634-8184 Fax (905)634-6283
E-mail: agc@ftn.net
Website: http://www.agcofcanada.com/home
Media Contact, Rev. Tim Davis, c/o 3228 South Service Rd., Burlington, ON L7N 3H8 Tel. (905)634-8184 Fax (905)634-6283

Officers
Pres., —
Mod., Rev. Vern Trafford, 55 Leonard St., Kitchener, ON N2H 6C7 Tel. (519)744-8061
Sec.-Treas., Rev. Don Ralph, Box 3203, Stn. C, Hamilton, ON L8H 7K6 Tel. (905)549-4516

Association of Regular Baptist Churches (Canada)

The Association of Regular Baptist Churches was organized in 1957 by a group of churches for the purpose of mutual cooperation in missionary activities. The Association believes the Bible to be God's word, stands for historic Baptist principles and opposes modern ecumenism.

Headquarters
130 Gerrard St. E., Toronto, ON M5A 3T4 Tel. (416)925-3261
Media Contact, Sec., Rev. W. P. Bauman, Tel. (416)925-3263 Fax (416)925-8305

Officers
Chmn., Rev. S. Kring, 67 Sovereen St., Delhi, ON N4B 1L7
Sec., Rev. W. P. Bauman

Baptist General Conference of Canada

The Baptist General Conference was founded in Canada by missionaries from the United States. Originally a Swedish body, BGC Canada now includes people of many nationalities and is conservative and evangelical in doctrine and practice.

Headquarters
4306-97 St. NW, Edmonton, AB T6E 5R9 Tel. (403)438-9127 Fax (403)435-2478
Media Contact, Exec. Dir., Rev. Abe Funk

Officers
Exec. Dir., Rev. Abe Funk, 27-308 Jackson Rd. NW, Edmonton, AB T6L 6W1 Tel. (403)466-6244

DISTRICTS
Central Canada Baptist Conference: Exec. Min., Rev. Alf Bell, 19-130 Ulster St., Winnipeg, MB R3T 3A2 Tel. (204)261-9113 Fax (204)261-9176
Baptist General Conference in Alberta: Exec. Min., Dr. Cal Netterfield, 5011 122nd A St., Edmonton, AB T6H 3S8 Tel. (403)438-9126 Fax (403)438-5258
British Columbia Baptist Conference: Exec. Min., Rev. Walter W. Wieser, 7600 Glover Rd., Langley, BC V2Y 1Y1 Tel. (604)888-2246 Fax (604)888-0046
Baptist General Conf. in Saskatchewan: Exec. Min., Rev. Charles Lees, Box 419, Loon Lake, SK S0M 1L0 Tel. (306)837-4711

Periodicals
BGC Canada News

The Bible Holiness Movement

The Bible Holiness Movement, organized in 1949 as an outgrowth of the city mission work of the late Pastor William James Elijah Wakefield, an early-day Salvation Army officer, has been headed since its inception by his son, Evangelist Wesley H. Wakefield, its bishop-general.

It derives its emphasis on the original Methodist faith of salvation and scriptural holiness from the late Bishop R. C. Horner. It adheres to the common evangelical faith in the Bible, the Deity and the atonement of Christ. It stresses a personal experience of salvation for the repentant sinner, of being wholly sanctified for the believer and of the fullness of the Holy Spirit for effective witness.

Membership involves a life of Christian love and evangelistic and social activism. Members are required to totally abstain from liquor and tobacco. They may not attend popular amusements or join secret societies. Divorce and remarriage are forbidden. Similar to Wesley's Methodism, members are, under some circumstances, allowed to retain membership in other evangelical church fellowships. Interchurch affiliations are maintained with a number of Wesleyan-Arminian Holiness denominations.

Year-round evangelistic outreach is maintained through open-air meetings, visitation, literature and other media. Noninstitutional welfare work, including addiction counseling, is conducted among minorities. There is direct overseas famine relief, civil rights action, environment protection and antinuclearism. The movement sponsors a permanent committee on religious freedom and an active promotion of Christian racial equality.

The movement has a world outreach with branches in the United States, India, Nigeria, Philippines, Ghana, Liberia, Cameroon, Kenya, Zambia, South Korea, Mulawi, and Tanzania. It ministers to 89 countries in 42 languages through literature, radio and audiocassettes.

Headquarters
Box 223, Postal Stn. A, Vancouver, BC V6C 2M3 Tel. (250)498-3895
Media Contact, Bishop-General, Evangelist Wesley H. Wakefield, P.O. Box 223, Postal Station A, Vancouver, BC V6C 2M3 Tel. (250)498-3895

DIRECTORS
Bishop-General, Evangelist Wesley H. Wakefield, (Intl. Leader)
Evangelist M. J. Wakefield, Oliver, BC
Pastor Vincente & Mirasal Hernando, Phillipines
Pastor & Mrs. Daniel Stinnett, 1425 Mountain View W., Phoenix, AZ 85021
Evangelist I. S. Udoh, Abak, Akwalbom, Nigeria, West Africa
Pastor Richard & Laura Wesley, Protem, Monrovia, Liberia
Pastor Choe Chong Dee, Cha Pa Puk, S. Korea
Pastor S. A. Samuel, Andra, India
Pastors Heinz and Catherine Speitelsbach, Sardis, BC V2R 3W2
Pastor and Mrs. Daniel Vandee, Ghana, W. Africa

Periodical
Hallelujah

Brethren in Christ Church, Canadian Conference

The Brethren in Christ, formerly known as Tunkers in Canada, arose out of a religious awakening in Lancaster County, Pa. late in the

18th century. Representatives of the new denomination reached Ontario in 1788 and established the church in the southern part of the present province. Presently the conference has congregations in Ontario, Alberta, Quebec and Saskatchewan. In theology they have accents of the Pietist, Anabaptist, Wesleyan and Evangelical movements.

Headquarters

Brethren in Christ Church, Gen. Ofc., P.O. Box 290, Grantham, PA 17027-0290 Tel. (717)697-2634 Fax (717)697-7714

Canadian Headquarters, Bishop's Ofc., 2619 Niagara Pkwy., Ft. Erie, ON L2A 5M4 Tel. (905)871-9991

Media Contact, Mod., Dr. Warren L. Hoffman, Brethren in Christ Church Gen. Ofc.

Officers

Mod., Bishop Darrell S. Winger, 2619 Niagara Pkwy., Ft. Erie, ON L2A 5M4 Tel. (905)871-9991

Sec., Betty Albrecht, RR 2, Petersburg, ON N0B 2H0

British Methodist Episcopal Church of Canada

The British Methodist Episcopal Church was organized in 1856 in Chatham, Ontario and incorporated in 1913. It has congregations across the Province of Ontario.

Headquarters

460 Shaw St., Toronto, ON M6G 3L3 Tel. (416)534-3831

Gen. Sec., Rev. Maurice M. Hicks, 3 Boxdene Ave., Scarborough, ON M1V 3C9 Tel. (416)298-5715 Fax (416)298-2276

Officers

Gen. Supt., Rev. Dr. D. D. Rupwate, 66 Golfwood Dr., Hamilton, ON L9C 6W3 Tel. (905)383-6856

Asst. Gen. Supt., Rev. Livingston Yearwood, 16 Lynvalley Cres., Scarborough, ON M1R 2V3 Tel. (416)445-2646

Gen. Sec., Rev. Maurice M. Hicks, 3 Boxdene Ave., Scarborough, ON M1V 3C9 Tel. (416)298-5715

Gen. Treas., —

Canadian and American Reformed Churches

The Canadian and American Reformed Churches accept the Bible as the infallible Word of God, as summarized in The Belgic Confession of Faith (1561), The Heidelberg Cathechism (1563) and The Canons of Dordt (1618-1619). The denomination was founded in Canada in 1950 and in the United States in 1955.

Headquarters

Synod: 607 Dynes Rd., Burlington, ON L7N 2V4

Canadian Reformed Churches: Ebenezer Canadian Reformed Church, 607 Dynes Rd., Burlington, ON L7N 2V4

American Reformed Churches: American Reformed Church, 3167-68th St. S.E., Caledonia, MI 46316

Theological College, Dr. N. H. Gootjes, 110 W. 27th St., Hamilton, ON L9C 5A1 Tel. (905)575-3688 Fax (905)575-0799

Media Contact, Rev. G. Nederveen, 3089 Woodward Ave., Burlington, ON L7N 2M3 Tel. (905)681-7055 Fax (905)681-7055

Periodicals

Reformed Perspective: A Magazine for the Christian Family; In Holy Array; Evangel: The Good News of Jesus Christ; Clarion: The Canadian Reformed Magazine; Diakonia-A Magazine of Office-Bearers

Canadian Baptist Ministries

The Canadian Baptist Ministries has four federated member bodies: (1) Baptist Convention of Ontario and Quebec, (2) Baptist Union of Western Canada, (3) the United Baptist Convention of the Atlantic Provinces, (4) Union d'...glises Baptistes FranÁaises au Canada (French Baptist Union). Its main purpose is to act as a coordinating agency for the four groups for mission in all five continents.

HEADQUARTERS

7185 Millcreek Dr., Mississauga, ON L5N 5R4 Tel. (905)821-3533 Fax (905)826-3441

Website: http://www.cbmin.org

Media Contact, Communications, David Rogelstad

E-mail: daver@cbmin.org

Officers

Pres., Dr. Carmen Moir

Gen. Sec., Rev. David Phillips

E-mail: dphillips@cbmin.org

1) Baptist Convention of Ontario and Quebec

The Baptist Convention of Ontario and Quebec is a family of 386 churches in Ontario and Quebec, united for mutual support and encouragement and united in missions in Canada and the world.

The Convention was formally organized in 1888. It has two educational institutions-McMaster Divinty College founded in 1887, and the Baptist Leadership Education Centre at Whitby. The Convention works through the all-Canada missionary agency, Canadian Baptist Ministries. The churches also support the Sharing Way, its relief and development arm of Canadian Baptist Ministries.

Headquarters

195 The West Mall, Ste. 414, Etobicoke, ON M9C 5K1 Tel. (416)622-8600 Fax (416)622-2308

Media Contact, Exec. Min., Dr. Ken Bellous

Officers

Pres., Rev. Rosetta O'Neal
1st Vice-Pres., Mr. Keith Hillyer
2nd Vice-Pres., Rev. Don Crisp
Treas./Bus. Admn., Nancy Bell
Exec. Min., Dr. Ken Bellous
Past Pres., Rev. Ralph Neil

Periodical
The Canadian Baptist

2) Baptist Union of Western Canada

Headquarters

605-999 8th St. SW, Calgary, AB T2R 1J5
Media Contact, Exec. Min., Rev. Gerald Fisher

Officers

Pres., Rev. Jake Kroeker
Exec. Min., Rev. Gerald Fisher, 605,999 8St. SW, Calgary, AB T2R 1J5
Area Min., Alberta, Dr. Keith Churchill, 307, 10328-81 Ave., Edmonton, AB T6E 1X2
Area Min., British Columbia, Rev. Paul Pearce, 201, 20349-88th Ave., Langley, BC VlM 2K5
Area Min., Saskatchewan, Rev. Wayne Larson, 2155 Cross Pl., Regina, SK S4S 4C8
Carey Theological College, Principal, Dr. Brian Stelck, 5920 Iona Dr., Vancouver, BC V6T 1J6
Baptist Resources Centre, Dr. Bernie Potrin, Director of Learning Services, 605, 999-8 Street SW, Calgary, AB T2R 1J5

3) United Baptist Convention of the Atlantic Provinces

The United Baptist Convention of the Atlantic Provinces is the largest Baptist Convention in Canada. Through the Canadian Baptist Ministries, it is a member of the Baptist World Alliance.

In 1763 two Baptist churches were organized in Atlantic Canada, one in Sackville, New Brunswick and the other in Wolfville, Nova Scotia. Although both these churches experienced crises and lost continuity, they recovered and stand today as the beginning of organized Baptist work in Canada.

Nine Baptist churches met in Lower Granville, Nova Scotia in 1800 and formed the first Baptist Association in Canada. By 1846 the Maritime Baptist Convention was organized, consisting of 169 churches. Two streams of Baptist life merged in 1905 to form the United Baptist Convention. This is how the term "United Baptist" was derived. Today there are 554 churches within 21 associations across the Convention.

The Convention has two educational institutions: Atlantic Baptist University in Moncton, New Brunswick, a Christian Liberal Arts University, and Acadia Divinity College in Wolfville, Nova Scotia, a Graduate School of Theology. The Convention engages in world mission through Canadian Baptist Ministries, the all-Canada mission agency. In addition to an active program of home mission, evangelism, training, social action and stewardship, the Convention operates ten senior citizen complexes and a Christian bookstore.

Headquarters

1655 Manawagonish Rd., Saint John, NB E2M 3Y2 Tel. (506)635-1922 Fax (506)635-0366
E-mail: ubcap@fundy.net
Media Contact, Interim Dir. of Communications, Dr. Eugene M. Thompson

Officers

Pres., Dr. Robert Wilson
Vice-Pres., Dr. Rick Thomas
Exec. Min., Dr. Harry G. Gardner
Dir. of Admn. & Treas., Daryl MacKenzie
Dir. of Home Missions & Church Planting, Rev. David Cook
Dir. of Evangelism, Dr. Malcolm Beckett
Dir. of Training, Rev. Marilyn McCormick

4) Union d'Eglises Baptistes Françaises au Canada

Baptist churches in French Canada first came into being through the labors of two missionaries from Switzerland, Rev. Louis Roussy and Mme. Henriette Feller, who arrived in Canada in 1835. The earliest church was organized in Grande Ligne (now St.-Blaise), Quebec in 1838.

By 1900 there were 7 churches in the province of Quebec and 13 French-language Baptist churches in the New England states. The leadership was totally French Canadian.

By 1960, the process of Americanization had caused the disappearance of the French Baptist churches. During the 1960s, Quebec as a society, began rapidly changing in all its facets: education, politics, social values and structures. Mission, evangelism and church growth once again flourished. In 1969, in response to the new conditions, the Grande Ligne Mission passed control of its work to the newly formed Union of French Baptist Churches in Canada, which then included 8 churches. By 1990 the French Canadian Baptist movement had grown to include 25 congregations.

The Union d'Églises Baptistes Françaises au Canada is a member body of the Canadian Baptist Ministries and thus is affiliated with the Baptist World Alliance.

Headquarters

2285 avenue Papineau, Montreal, QC H2K 4J5 Tel. (514)526-6643 Fax (514)526-9269
Media Contact, Gen. Sec., Rev. David Affleck

Officers

Sec. Gen., Rev. David Affleck

Periodical
Le Trait d'Union

Canadian Conference of Mennonite Brethren Churches

The conference was incorporated Nov. 22, 1945.

Headquarters

3-169 Riverton Ave., Winnipeg, MB R2L 2E5 Tel. (204)669-6575 Fax (204)654-1865
Media Contact, Conf. Min., Reuben Pauls

Officers

Mod., Ike Bergen, 32025 Bahlstrom Ave., Rm. 302, Abbotsford, BC V2T 2K7 Tel. (604)853-6959 Fax (604)853-6990
Asst. Mod., Ralph Gliege, Box 67, Hepburn, SK S0K 1Z0 Tel. (306)947-2030
Sec., Diana MacFarlane, 46100 Chilliwack Central Rd., Chilliwack, BC V2P 1J6 Tel. (604)792-8037 Fax (604)792-4145

Periodicals

Mennonite Brethren Herald; Mennonitische Rundschau; IdeaBank; Le Lien; Expression; Chinese Herald

Canadian Convention of Southern Baptists

The Canadian Convention of Southern Baptists was formed at the Annual Meeting, May 7-9, 1985, in Kelowna, British Columbia. It was formerly known as the Canadian Baptist Conference, founded in Kamloops, British Columbia, in 1959 by pastors of existing churches.

Headquarters

Postal Bag 300, Cochrane, AB T0L 0W0 Tel. (403)932-5688 Fax (403)932-4937
E-mail: 70420.2230@compuserve.com
Media Contact, Exec. Dir.-Treas., Rev. Allen E. Schmidt

Officers

Exec. Dir.-Treas., Allen E. Schmidt, 128 Riverview Cir., Cochrane, AB T0L 0W4
Pres., Mr. Clarke Cremer, 2 Timmins Ave., Winnipeg, MB R2R 2M2

Periodical

The Baptist Horizon

Canadian District of the Moravian Church in America, Northern Province

The work in Canada is under the general oversight and rules of the Moravian Church, Northern Province, general offices for which are located in Bethlehem, PA. For complete information, see "Religious Bodies in the United States" section of the *Yearbook*.

Headquarters

1021 Center St., P.O. Box 1245, Bethlehem, PA 18016-1245
Media Contact, Ed., *The Moravian*, Roxann Miller

Officer

Pres., Ruth Humphreys, 25-23332 Twp. Rd. 520, Sherwood Park, AB T8B 1L5 Tel. (403)467-6745 Fax (403)467-0411

Canadian Evangelical Christian Churches

The Canadian Evangelical Christian Churches are associated through a common doctrine that is a combination of Calvinistic and Arminian beliefs.

Each congregation is managed independently, however ordination is supervised by the national body.

Headquarters

Moderator, Rev. David Lavigne, 103 Riverside Dr., Box 313, New Hamburg, N0B 2G0 1V5 Tel. (519)662-4780
E-mail: cecc@orc.ca

Canadian Yearly Meeting of the Religious Society of Friends

Canadian Yearly Meeting of the Religious Society of Friends was founded in Canada as an offshoot of the Quaker movement in Great Britain and colonial America. Genesee Yearly Meeting, founded 1834, Canada Yearly Meeting (Orthodox), founded in 1867, and Canada Yearly Meeting, founded in 1881, united in 1955 to form the Canadian Yearly Meeting. Canadian Yearly Meeting is affiliated with Friends United Meeting and Friends General Conference. It is also a member of Friends World Committee for Consultation.

Headquarters

91A Fourth Ave., Ottawa, ON K1S 2L1 Tel. (613)235-8553 OR (613)296-3222 Fax (613)235-1753
E-mail: cym@web.net
Website: http://www.web.net/-cym
Media Contact, Gen. Sec.-Treas., -

Officers

Gen. Sec.-Treas., -
Clerk: Gale Wills
Archivist, Jane Zavitz Bond
Archives, Arthur G. Dorland, Pickering College, 389 Bayview St., Newmarket, ON L3Y 4X2 Tel. (416)895-1700

Periodicals

The Canadian Friend; Quaker Concern

Christ Catholic Church International

The Christ Catholic Church International, with Cathedral, churches, missions and oratories in Canada, the United States, Norway, Australia, Bosnia and Colombia South America, is an Orthodox-Catholic Communion tracing Apostolic Succession through the Old Catholic and Orthodox Catholic Churches.

The church ministers to a growing number of people seeking an experiential relationship with their Lord and Savior Jesus Christ in a Sacramental and Scripture based church. As one of the three founding members of FOCUS: Federation of Orthodox Catholic Churches United Sacramentally, CCCI is working to bring together Old and Orthodox Catholicism into one united church under the headship of Jesus Christ.

Headquarters

5165 Palmer Ave., P.O. Box 73, Niagara Falls, ON L2E 6S8 Tel. (905)354-2329 Fax (905)354-9934

E-mail: dwmullan@sympatico.ca

Website: http://www3.sympatico.ca/dwmullan

Media Contact, The Rt. Rev. John W. Brown, 1504-75 Queen St., Hamilton, ON L8R 3J3 Tel. (905)527-9089 Fax (905)354-9934

Officers

Presiding Bishop, The Most Rev. Donald Wm. Mullan, 6190 Barker St., Niagara Falls, ON L2E 1Y4

Archbishop, The Most Rev. Jose Ruben Garcia Matiz, Calle 52 Sur #24 A-35 - Bq. #1, Ap. 301, Santa Fe de Bogota, D.C., Colombia, South America

Episcopal Vicar, The Rt. Rev. John Wm. Brown, 1504-75 Queen St. N., Hamilton, ON L8R 3J3

Auxiliary Bishop, The Rt. Rev. Acie Angel, 1085 Wiethaupt Rd., Florissant, MO 63031

Auxiliary Bishop, The Rt. Rev. Curtis Bradley, 145 S. Garfield St., Denver, CO 80209

Auxiliary Bishop, The Rt. Rev. Gerard Laplante, 715 E. 51st Ave., Vancouver, BC V5X 1E2

Auxiliary Bishop, The Rt. Rev. Luis Fernando Hoyos Maldonado, A.A. 2437 Santa Fe de Bogota, D.C., Colombia, South America

Auxiliary Bishop, The Rt. Rev. L.M. McFerran, #206-6020 East Boulevard, Vancouver, BC C6M 3V5

Auxiliary Bishop, The Rt. Rev. Ronald K. Pace, 1411 Nursery Rd., Clearwater, FL 33756

Auxiliary Bishop, The Rt. Rev. Jose Moises Moncada Quevedo, A.A. 2437 Santa Fe de Bogota, D.C., Colombia, South America

Auxiliary Bishop, The Rt. Rev. Roger Robberstad, Pb 2624 St. Hanshaugen N-0131 Oslo, Norway

Periodical

St. Luke Magazine

The Franciscan

SEMINARY

St. Mary's Seminary: The Very Rev. Del Baier, 8287 Lamont, Niagara Falls, ON L2G 7L4 (offering on-site and correspondence programs)

The New Order of St. Francis: (Priests, Brothers and Sisters), Sec. General, Rev. Bro. Sean Ross, 5768 Summer St., Niagara Falls, ON L2G 1M2

Christian and Missionary Alliance in Canada

A Canadian movement, dedicated to the teaching of Jesus Christ the Saviour, Sanctifier, Healer and Coming King, commenced in Toronto in 1887 under the leadership of the Rev. John Salmon. Two years later, the movement united with The Christian Alliance of New York, founded by Rev. A. B. Simpson, becoming the Dominion Auxiliary of the Christian Alliance, Toronto, under the presidency of the Hon. William H. Howland. Its four founding branches were Toronto, Hamilton, Montreal, and Quebec. By Dec. 31, 1997, there were 386 churches across Canada, with 1211 official workers, including a worldwide missionary force of 240.

In 1980, the Christian and Missionary Alliance in Canada became autonomous. Its General Assembly is held every two years.

NATIONAL OFFICE

Box 7900 Stn. B, Willowdale, ON M2K 2R6 Tel. (905)771-6747 Fax (905) 771-9874

E-mail: nationaloffice@cmacan.org

Media Contact, Vice-Pres. General Services, Kenneth Paton

Officers

Pres., Dr. Arnold Cook, Box 7900, Postal Sta. B, Willowdale, ON M2K 2R6

Vice-Pres./Personnel & Missions, Rev. Wallace C.E. Albrecht

Vice-Pres./Fin., Paul D. Lorimer

Vice-Pres./Canadian Ministries, Rev. C. Stuart Lightbody

Vice-Pres./Gen. Services, Kenneth Paton

DISTRICT SUPERINTENDENTS

Canadian Pacific: Rev. Brian Thom

Western Canadian: Rev. Arnold Downey

Canadian Midwest: Rev. Bob Peters

Central Canadian: Rev. David Lewis

East Canadian District: Rev. Doug Wiebe

St. Lawrence: Rev. Yvan Fournier

Christian Brethren (also known as Plymouth Brethren)

The Christian Brethren are a loose grouping autonomous local churches, often called "assemblies." They are firmly committed to the inerrancy of Scripture and to evangelical doctrine of salvation by faith alone apart from works or sacrament. Characteristics and common elements are a weekly Breaking of Bread and freedom of ministry without a requirement of ordination. For their history, see "Religious Bodies in the United States" in the Directories section of this Yearbook.

CORRESPONDENT

James A Stahr, 327 W. Prairie Ave., Wheaton, IL 60187-3408 Tel. (630)665-3757

RELATED ORGANIZATIONS

Christian Brethren Church in the Province of Quebec, Exec. Sec., Marj Robbins, P.O. Box 1054, Sherbrooke, QC J1H 5L3 Tel. (819)820-1693 Fax (819)821-9287

MSC Canada, Administrator, William Yuille, 509-3950 14th Ave., Markham, ON L3R 0A9 Tel. (905)947-0468 Fax (905)947-0352

Vision Ministries Canada, Dir., Gord Martin, P.O. Box 28032, Waterloo, ON N2L 6J8 Tel. (519)725-1212 Fax (519)725-9421

News of Quebec

Christian Church (Disciples of Christ) in Canada

Disciples have been in Canada since 1810, and were organized nationally in 1922. This national church seeks to serve the Canadian context as part of the whole Christian Church (Disciples of Christ) in the United States and Canada.

Headquarters

128 Woolwich St., #202, P.O. Box 64, Guelph, ON N1H 6J6 Tel. (519)823-5190 Fax (519)823-5766

Media Contact, Exec. Min., Robert W. Steffer

Officers

Mod., Mervin Bailey, 1205 Jubilee Ave., Regina, SK S4S 3S7

Vice-Mod., John Dick, RR#4, Thamesdill, ON N0P 2K0

Exec. Min., Rev. Dr. Robert W. Steffer, P.O. Box 30013, 2 Quebec St., Guelph, ON N1H 8J5

Periodical

Canadian Disciple

Christian Reformed Church in North America

Canadian congregations of the Christian Reformed Church in North America have been formed since 1908. For detailed information about this denomination, please refer to the listing for the Christian Reformed Church in North America in Chapter 3, "Religious Bodies in the United States."

Headquarters

United States Office: 2850 Kalamazoo Ave., S.E., Grand Rapids, MI 49560 Tel. (616)224-0744 Fax (616)224-5895

Canadian Office: 3475 Mainway, P.O. Box 5070 STN LCR 1, Burlington, ON L7R 3Y8 Tel. (905)336-2920 Fax (905)336-8344

Website: http://www.crcna.org

Media Contact, Gen. Sec., Dr. David H. Engelhard, U.S. Office

OFFICERS

Gen. Sec., Dr. David H. Engelhard, U.S. Office

Exec. Dir./Ministries, Dr. Peter Borgdorff, U.S.Office

Canadian Ministries Director, Raymond Elgersma, Canadian Office

Dir. of Fin.& Administration, Kenneth Horjus, U.S. Office

Periodical

The Banner

Church of God (Anderson, Ind.)

This body is one of the largest of the groups which have taken the name "Church of God." Its headquarters are at Anderson, Ind. It originated about 1880 and emphasizes Christian unity.

Headquarters

Western Canada Assembly, Chpsn., Hilda Nauenburg, 4717 56th St., Camrose, AB T4V 2C4 Tel. (780)672-0772 Fax (780)672-6888

Eastern Canada Assembly, Chpsn., Jim Wiebe, 38 James St., Dundas, ON L9H 2J6

E-mail: wcdncog@cable-lynx.net

Website: http://www.cable-lynx.net/~wcdncog

Media Contact for Western Canada, Church Service/Mission Coordinator, John D. Campbell, 4717 56th St., Camrose, AB T4V 2C4 Tel. (780)672-0772 Fax (780)672-6888

Periodicals

College News & Updates; The Gospel Contact; The Messenger

Church of God (Cleveland, Tenn.)

This body began in the United States in 1886 as the outgrowth of the holiness revival under the name Christian Union. Reorganized in 1902 as the Holiness Church, in 1907 the church adopted the name Church of God. Its doctrine is fundamental and Pentecostal. It maintains a centralized form of government and an evangelistic and missionary program.

The first church in Canada was established in 1919 in Scotland Farm, Manitoba. Paul H. Walker became the first overseer of Canada in 1931.

Headquarters

Intl. Offices: 2490 Keith St., NW, Cleveland, TN 37311 Tel. (423)472-3361

Media Contact, Dir. of Publ. Relations, Michael L. Baker, P.O. Box 2430, Cleveland, TN 37320-2430 Tel. (423)478-7112 Fax (423)478-7066

Officers

Canada-Eastern, Rev. Canute Blake, P.O. Box 2036, Brampton, ON L6T 3TO Tel. (905)793-2213

Canada-Western, Rev. Raymond W. Wall, Box 54055, 2640 52 St. NE, Calgary, AB T1Y 6S6 Tel. (403)293-8817 Fax (403)293-8832

Canada-Quebec/Maritimes, Rev. Jacques Houle, 19 Orly, Granby, QC J2H 1Y4 Tel. (514)378-4442 Fax (514)378-8646

Periodical

Church of God Beacon

Church of God in Christ (Mennonite)

The Church of God in Christ, Mennonite was organized by the evangelist-reformer John Holdeman in Ohio. The church unites with the faith of the Waldenses, Anabaptists and other such groups throughout history. Emphasis is placed on obedience to the teachings of the Bible, including the doctrine of the new birth and spiritual life, noninvolvement in government or the military, a head-covering for women, beards for men and separation from the world shown by simplicity in clothing, homes, possessions and lifestyle. The church has a worldwide membership of about 17,000, largely concentrated in the United States and Canada.

Headquarters

P.O. Box 313, 420 N. Wedel Ave., Moundridge, KS 67107 Tel. (316)345-2532 Fax (316)345-2582

Media Contact, Dale Koehn, P.O.Box 230, Moundridge, KS 67107 Tel. (316)345-2532 Fax (316)345-2582

Periodical

Messenger of Truth

The Church of God of Prophecy in Canada

In the late 19th century, people seeking God's eternal plan as they followed the Reformation spirit began to delve further for scriptural light concerning Christ and his church. A small group of people emerged which dedicated and covenanted themselves to God and one another to be the Church of God. On June 13, 1903, A.J. Tomlinson joined them during a period of intense prayer and Bible study. Under Tomlinson's dynamic leadership, the church enjoyed tremendous growth.

In 1923 two churches emerged. Those that opposed Tomlinson's leadership are known today in Canada as the New Testament Church of God. Tomlinson's followers are called the Church of God of Prophecy.

In Canada, the first Church of God of Prophecy congregation was organized in Swan River, Manitoba, in 1937. Churches are now established in British Columbia, Manitoba, Alberta, Saskatchewan, Ontario, Quebec and all 50 states.

The church accepts the whole Bible rightly divided, with the New Testament as the rule of faith and practice, government and discipline. The membership upholds the Bible as the inspired Word of God and believes that its truths are known by the illumination of the Holy Spirit. The Trinity is recognized as one supreme God in three persons-Father, Son and Holy Ghost. It is believed that Jesus Christ, the virgin-born Son of God, lived a sinless life, fulfilled his ministry on earth, was crucified, resurrected and later ascended to the right hand of God. Believers now await Christ's return to earth and the establishment of the millenial kingdom.

Headquarters

World Headquarters: Bible Place, P.O. Box 2910, Cleveland, TN 37320-2910

National Office: Bishop Adrian L. Varlack, P.O. Box 457, Brampton, ON L6V 2L4 Tel. (905)843-2379 Fax (905)843-3990

Media Contact, Bishop Mirriam Bailey, P.O. Box 457, Brampton, ON L6V 2L4 Tel. (905)843-2379 Fax (905)843-3990

Officers

Pres., Bishop Adrian L. Varlack

V. Pres & Sec., Aston R. Morrison
Asst. Sec. & Treas., Mirriam Bailey

Periodical

Canada Update

The Church of Jesus Christ of Latter-day Saints in Canada

The Church has had a presence in Canada since the early 1830's. Joseph Smith and Brigham Young both came to Eastern Canada as missionaries. There are now 145,000 members in Canada in more than 400 congregations.

Leading the Church in Canada are the presidents of nearly 40 stakes (equivalent to a diocese). World headquarters is in Salt Lake City, UT (See U.S. Religious Bodies chapter of the Directories section of this Yearbook).

Headquarters

50 East North Temple St., Salt Lake City, UT 84150

Media Contact, Public Affairs Dir., Bruce Smith, 1185 Eglinton Ave., Box 116, North York, ON M3C 3C6 Tel. (416)424-2485 Fax (416)424-3326

Church of the Lutheran Brethren

The Church of the Lutheran Brethren of America was organized in December 1900. Five independent Lutheran congregations met together in Milwaukee, WI, and adopted a constitution patterned very closely to that of the Lutheran Free Church of Norway.

The spiritual awakening in the Midwest during the 1890s crystallized into convictions that led to the formation of a new church body. Chief among the concerns were church membership practices, observance of Holy Communion, confirmation practices and local church government.

The Church of the Lutheran Brethren practices a simple order of worship with the sermon as the primary part of the worship service. It believes that personal profession of faith is the primary criterion for membership in the congregation. The Communion service is reserved for those who profess faith in Christ as savior. Each congregation is autonomous and the synod serves the congregations in advisory and cooperative capacities.

The synod supports a world mission program in Cameroon, Chad, Japan and Taiwan. Approximately 40 percent of the synodical budget is earmarked for world missions. A growing home mission ministry is planting new congregations in the United States and Canada. Affiliate organizations operate several retirement/nursing homes, conference and retreat centers.

Headquarters

1020 Alcott Ave., W., P.O. Box 655, Fergus Falls, MN 56538 Tel. (218)739-3336 Fax (218)739-5514

E-mail: rmo@clba.org

182

Website: http://www.clba.org
Media Contact, Asst. to Pres., Rev. Luther
Larson

Officers

Pres., Rev. Arthur Berge, 72 Midridge Close SE,
Calgary, AB T2X 1G1
Vice-Pres., Rev. Luther Stenberg, PO Box 75,
Hagen, SK S0J 1B0
Sec., Mr. Alvin Herman, 3105 Taylor Street E.,
Saskatoon, SK S7H 1H5
Treas., Edwin Rundbraaten, Box 739, Birch
Hills, SK S0J 0G0
Youth Coord., Rev. Harold Rust, 2617 Preston
Ave. S., Saskatoon, SK S7J 2G3

Periodical

Faith and Fellowship

Church of the Nazarene in Canada

The first Church of the Nazarene in Canada
was organized in November, 1902, by Dr. H. F.
Reynolds. It was in Oxford, Nova Scotia. The
Church of the Nazarene is Wesleyan Arminian in
theology, representative in church government
and warmly evangelistic.

Headquarters

20 Regan Rd., Unit 9, Brampton, ON L7A 1C3
Tel. (905)846-4220 Fax (905)846-1775
E-mail: nazarene@interlog.com
Website:http://web.1-888.com.nazarene/nation-
al/
Media Contact, Gen. Sec., Dr. Jack Stone, 6401
The Paseo, Kansas City, MO 64131 Tel.
(816)333-7000 Fax (816)822-9071

Officers

Natl. Dir., Dr. William E. Stewart, 20 Regan Rd.
Unit 9, Brampton, ON L7A 1C3 Tel.
(905)846-4220 Fax (905)846-1775
Exec. Asst., John T. Martin, 20 Regan Rd. Unit 9,
Brampton, ON L7A 1C3 Tel. (905)846-4220
Fax (905)846-1775
Chmn., Rev. Wesley G. Campbell, #205, 1255
56th St., Delta, BC V4L 2B9
Vice-Chmn., Rev. Ronald G. Fry, 1280 Finch
Ave. W. Ste. 416, North York, ON M3J 3K6
Sec., Rev. Larry Dahl, 14320 94th St.,
Edmonton, AL T5E 3W2

Churches of Christ in Canada

Churches of Christ are autonomous congregations, whose members appeal to the Bible alone
to determine matters of faith and practice. There
are no central offices or officers. Publications
and institutions related to the churches are either
under local congregational control or independent of any one congregation.

Churches of Christ shared a common fellowship in the 19th century with the Christian
Churches/Churches of Christ and the Christian
Church (Disciples of Christ). Fellowship was
broken after the introduction of instrumental
music in worship and centralization of church-

wide activities through a missionary society.
Churches of Christ began in Canada soon after
1800, largely in the middle provinces. The few
pioneer congregations were greatly strengthened
in the mid-1800s, growing in size and number.

Members of Churches of Christ believe in the
inspiration of the Scriptures, the divinity of Jesus
Christ, and immersion into Christ for the remission of sins. The New Testament pattern is followed in worship and church organization.

Headquarters

Media Contact, Man. Ed., Gospel Herald,
Eugene C. Perry, 4904 King St., Beansville,
ON L0R 1B6 Tel. (416)563-7503 Fax
(416)563-7503
E-mail: eperry9953@aol.com

Periodicals

Gospel Herald; Sister Triangle

Conference of Mennonites in Canada

The Conference of Mennonites in Canada
began in 1902 as an organized fellowship of
Mennonite immigrants from Russia clustered in
southern Manitoba and around Rosthern,
Saskatchewan. The first annual sessions were
held in July, 1903. Its members hold to traditional Christian beliefs, believer's baptism and congregational polity. They emphasize practical
Christianity: opposition to war, service to others
and personal ethics. Further immigration from
Russia in the 1920s and 1940s increased the
group which is now located in all provinces from
New Brunswick to British Columbia. In recent
years a variety of other ethnic groups, including
native Canadians, have joined the conference.
This conference is affiliated with the General
Conference Mennonite Church whose offices are
at Newton, Kan.

Headquarters

600 Shaftesbury Blvd., Winnipeg, MB R3P 0M4
Tel. (204)888-6781 Fax (204)831-5675
Media Contact, Roma Quapp

Officers

Chpsn., Ron Sawatsky, 134 Woodbend Cresc.,
Waterloo, ON N2T 1G9
Vice-Chpsn., Gerd Bartel, 6250 49 Ave., Delta,
BC V4K 4S5
Sec., Mary Anne Loeppky, Box 973, Altona, MB
R0G 0B0
Gen. Sec., Helmut Harder

Periodicals

Mennonite Reporter; NEXUS

Congregational Christian Churches in Canada

This body originated in the early 18th century
when devout Christians within several denominations in the northern and eastern United States,
dissatisfied with sectarian controversy, broke
away from their own denominations and took the

183

simple title "Christians." First organized in 1821 at Keswick, Ontario, the Congregational Christian Churches in Canada was incorporated on Dec. 4, 1989, as a national organization. In doctrine the body is evangelical, being governed by the Bible as the final authority in faith and practice. It believes that Christian character must be expressed in daily living; it aims at the unity of all true believers in Christ that others may believe in Him and be saved. In church polity, the body is democratic and autonomous. It is also a member of The World Evangelical Congregational Fellowship.

Headquarters
241 Dunsdon St. Ste. 405, Brantford, ON N3R 7C3 Tel. (519)751-0606 Fax (519)751-0852
Media Contact, Pres., Jim Potter, 8 Church St., Waldemar, ON L0N 1G0 Tel. (519)928-561

Officers
Pres., Jim Potter
Exec. Dir., Rev. Bruce Robertson
Sec., Rev. Alan McInnes

Periodical
Spirit Catalyst Bi Monthly
Editor, Rev. Russ Bailey

The Coptic Orthodox Church in Canada

The Coptic Orthodox Church in North America was begun in Canada in 1964 and was registered in the province of Ontario in 1965. The Coptic Orthodox Church has spread rapidly since then. The total number of local churches in both Canada and the USA have reached seventy-four. Besides two dioceses were established a monastery with a bishop, monks and novices, as well as two theological seminaries.

The Coptic Orthodox Church is a hierarchical church and the administrative governing body of each local church is an elected Board of Deacons approved by the Bishop.

Headquarters
St. Mark's Coptic Orthodox Church, 41 Glendinning Ave., Scarborough, ON M1W 3E2 Tel. (416)494-4449 Fax (416)494-2631
Media Contact, Fr. Ammonius Guirguis, Tel. (416)494-4449 Fax (416)494-2631

OFFICER
Archpriest, Fr. Marcos A. Marcos
Officer, Fr. Ammonius Guirguis, 41 Glendinning Ave., Agincourt, ON M1W 3E2 Tel. (416)494-4449
Officer, Fr. Misael Ataalla

Elim Fellowship of Evangelical Churches and Ministers

The Elim Fellowship of Evangelical Churches and Ministers, a Pentecostal body, was established in 1984 as a sister organization of Elim Fellowship in the United States.

This is an association of churches, ministers and missionaries seeking to serve the whole body of Christ. It is Pentecostal and has a charismatic orientation.

Headquarters
30 Amelia St., Paris, ON N3L 3V5 Tel. (519)442-3288 Fax (519)442-1487
E-mail:—
Website: http://Bfree.ON.ca/comdir/churches/elim
Ofc. Mgr., Larry Jones
Sec., Debbie Jones

Officers
Pres., Errol Alchin
Vice-Pres., Winston Nunes, 4 Palamino Cres., Willowdale, ON M2K 1W1
Sec., John Woods, 3G Crestlea Cres. Nepean, ON N2G 4N1
Treas., Aubrey Phillips, P.O. Box 208, Blairsville, GA 30512
President Emeritus, Carlton Spencer

COUNCIL OF ELDERS
Errol Alchin, Tel. (519)442-3288
Howard Ellis, Tel. (519)579-9844
Winston Nunes, Tel. (416)225-4824
Aubrey Phillips, Tel. (706)745-2473
John Woods, Tel. (613)228-1796
Bernard Evans, Tel. (716)528-2790

The Estonian Evangelical Lutheran Church

The Estonian Evangelical Lutheran Church (EELC) was founded in 1917 in Estonia and reorganized in Sweden in 1944. The teachings of the EELC are based on the Old and New Testaments, explained through the Apostolic, Nicean and Athanasian confessions, the unaltered Confession of Augsburg and other teachings found in the Book of Concord.

Headquarters
383 Jarvis St., Toronto, ON M5B 2C7 Tel. (416)925-5465 Fax (416)925-5688
Media Contact, Archbishop, Rev. Udo Petersoo

Officers
Archbishop, The Rev. Udo Petersoo
Gen. Sec., Dean Edgar Heinsoo

Periodical
Eesti Kirik

The Evangelical Covenant Church of Canada

A Canadian denomination organized in Canada at Winnipeg in 1904 which is affiliated with the Evangelical Covenant Church of America and with the International Federation of Free Evangelical Churches, which includes 31 federations in 26 countries.

This body believes in the one triune God as confessed in the Apostles' Creed, that salvation is received through faith in Christ as Saviour, that the Bible is the authoritative guide in all matters of faith and practice. Christian Baptism and the Lord's Supper are accepted as divinely ordained sacraments of the church. As descendants of the 19th century northern European pietistic awakening, the group believes in the need of a personal experience of commitment to Christ, the development of a virtuous life and the urgency of spreading the gospel to the "ends of the world."

Headquarters
630 Westchester Rd., Strathmore, AB T1P 1H8 Tel. (403)934-5845 Fax (403)934-5847
Media Contact, Supt., Rev. Jerome Johnson

Officers
Supt., Rev. Jerome W. Johnson
Chpsn., Les Doell, RR 2, Wetaskiwin, AB T9A 1W9
Sec., Lori Koop, 6568 Claytonwood Pl., Surrey, BC V3S 7T5
Treas., Rod Johnson, Box 196, Norquay, SK S0A 2V0

Periodical
The Covenant Messenger

Evangelical Free Church of Canada
The Evangelical Free Church of Canada traces its beginning back to 1917 when the church in Enchant, Alberta opened its doors. Today the denomination has nearly 140 churches from the West Coast to Quebec. Approximately 45 missionaries are sponsored by the EFCC in 10 countries. The Evangelical Free Church is the founding denomination of Trinity Western University in Langley, British Columbia. Church membership is 7,123, average attendance is 16,375.

Headquarters
Mailing Address, Box 56109, Valley Centre P.O., Langley, BC V3A 8B3 Tel. (604)888-8668 Fax (604)888-3108
Location, 7600 Glover Rd., Langley, BC
E-mail: efcc@twa.ca
Website: http://www.twu.ca/efcc/efcc.htm
Media Contact, Exec. Sec., Wilma Kits, Box 56109, Valley Centre P.O., Langley, BC V3A 8B3 Tel. (604)888-8668 Fax (604)888-3108

Officers
Pres., Dr. Richard J. Penner
Mod., David Enns, 920 Cottonwood Rd., Winnipeg, MB R2J 1G2

Periodical
The Pulse

Evangelical Lutheran Church in Canada
The Evangelical Lutheran Church in Canada was organized in 1985 through a merger of The Evangelical Lutheran Church of Canada (ELCC) and the Lutheran Church in America-Canada Section.

The merger is a result of an invitation issued in 1972 by the ELCC to the Lutheran Church in America-Canada Section and the Lutheran Church-Canada. Three-way merger discussions took place until 1978 when it was decided that only a two-way merger was possible. The ELCC was the Canada District of the ALC until autonomy in 1967.

The Lutheran Church in Canada traces its history back more than 200 years. Congregations were organized by German Lutherans in Halifax and Lunenburg County in Nova Scotia in 1749. German Lutherans, including many United Empire Loyalists, also settled in large numbers along the St. Lawrence and in Upper Canada. In the late 19th century, immigrants arrived from Scandinavia, Germany and central European countries, many via the United States. The Lutheran synods in the United States have provided the pastoral support and help for the Canadian church.

Headquarters
302-393 Portage Avenue, Winnipeg, MB R3B 3H6 Tel. (204)984-9150 Fax (204)984-9185
Media Contact, Bishop, Rev. Telmor G. Sartison

Officers
Bishop, Rev. Telmor G. Sartison
Vice-Pres., Janet Morley
Sec., Mr. Robert H. Granke
Treas., William C. Risto

ASSISTANTS TO THE BISHOPS
Rev. Cynthia Halmarson
Rev. Richard Stetson

DIVISIONS AND OFFICES
Evangelical Lutheran Women, Pres., Carolyn Hertzberger
Exec. Dir., Diane Doth

SYNODS
Alberta and the Territories: Bishop, Rev. Stephen P. Kristenson, 10014-81 Ave., Edmonton, AB T6E 1W8 Tel. (403)439-2636 Fax (403)433-6623
Eastern: Bishop, Rev. Michael J. Pryse, 50 Queen St. N., Kitchener, ON N2H 6P4 Tel. (519)743-1461 Fax (519)743-4291
British Columbia: Bishop, Rev. Raymond L. Schultz, 80-10th Ave., E., New Westminster, BC V3L 4R5 Tel. (604)524-1318 Fax (604)524-9255
Manitoba/Northwestern Ontario: Bishop, Rev. Richard M. Smith, 201-3657 Roblin Blvd., Winnipeg, MB R3G 0E2 Tel. (204)889-3760 Fax (204)869-0272
Saskatchewan: Bishop, Rev. Allan A. Grundahl, Bessborough Towers, Rm. 707, 601 Spadina Cres. E., Saskatoon, SK S7K 3G8 Tel. (306)244-2474 Fax (306)664-8677

Periodicals
Canada Lutheran; Esprit

The Evangelical Mennonite Conference
The Evangelical Mennonite Conference began as a renewal movement among a small group of

Dutch-German (DG) Mennonites in Southern Russia. Klaas Reimer, a Mennonite minister, was concerned about what he saw as a decline of spiritual life and discipline in the church, and inappropriate involvement in the Napoleonic War. Around 1812, Reimer and several others began separate worship services, emphasizing a stricter discipline and separation from values and beliefs seen as dangerous. By 1814, they were organized as a separate group, called the Kleine Gemeinde (KG, small church).

Increasing pressure from the government, particularly about military conscription, led to the group's migration to North America in 1874 to 1875. Fifty families settled in Manitoba and 36 families settled in Nebraska. Ties between the two groups weakened, and eventually the U.S. group gave up its KG identity.

The KG passed through pioneer hardships and then suspicions, because of its pacifism, during times of war. It survived several schisms and migrations. Beginning in the 1940s, the church began to move away from a pattern of isolation. It developed a vision for foreign missions, began to support higher education (initially, in the area of Bible School Training), developed congregations in non-DG communities, and began to work in cooperation with other evangelical denominations and missions. It is a supporting member of Mennonite Central Committee, the relief, development, and education agency.

There has been a growing rural to urban shift. The cultural make-up of congregations is changing, though the DG background is still dominant nationally. Ten churches have pastors or ministers of non-DG background. Some churches have a multiple leadership pattern; others have new patterns. Most churches now support the leading minister full-time.

A German language magazine was published from 1935 to 1984. An English language magazine began in 1963 and continues today. The common language used in worship is English. Among churches developed among people of DG Mennonite background returning from Mexico, services can be in a mixture of Low German, High German, and English.

The church's name was changed to Evangelical Mennonite Church in 1952 and Evangelical Mennonite Conference in 1960. The conference has roughly 134 mission workers in 20 countries of the world. It has 53 congregations across British Columbia to Ontario, with 33 being in Manitoba. In 1997 its membership passed 6,600. Membership is for people baptized on confession of faith (not infants). Children are considered safe in Christ until they reach the age of accountability and opt out.

Headquarters

Box 1268, 440 Main St., Steinbach, MB R0A 2A0 Tel. (204)326-6401 Fax (204)326-1613
E-mail: emconf@mts.net
Media Contact, Conf. Pastor, John Koop

Officers

Acting Conf. Mod., Ralph Unger, Box 18, Grp. 3 R.R. 1, Steinbach, MB R0A 2A0
Bd. of Missions, Exec. Sec., Henry Klassen
Bd. of Missions, Foreign Sec., Lester Olfert
Bd. of Church Ministries, Exec. Sec./Editor, Terry M. Smith
Canadian Sec., Conf. Pastor, John Koop

Periodical

The Messenger

Evangelical Mennonite Mission Conference

This group was founded in 1936 as the Rudnerweider Mennonite Church in Southern Manitoba and organized as the Evangelical Mennonite Mission Conference in 1959. It was incorporated in 1962. The Annual Conference meeting is held in July.

Headquarters

Box 52059, Niakwa P.O., Winnipeg, MB R2M 5P9 Tel. (204)253-7929 Fax (204)256-7384
E-mail: emmc@mb.sympatico.ca
Media Contact, John Bergman, Box 206, Niverville, MB R0A 1E0 Tel. (204)388-4775 Fax (204)388-4775
E-mail: jbergman@mb.sympatico.ca

Officers

Mod., David Penner, 906-300 Sherk St., Leamington, ON N8H 4N7
Vice-Mod., Carl Zacharias, R.R. 1, Box 205, Winkler, MB R6W 4A1
Sec., Darrell Dyck, R.R. 1, Box 186, Winkler, MB R6W 4A1
Dir. of Conference Ministries, Jack Heppner
Dir. of Missions, Rev. Leonard Sawatzky
Business Admin., Henry Thiessen

OTHER ORGANIZATIONS

The Gospel Message: Box 1622, Saskatoon, SK S7K 3R8 Tel. (306)242-5001 Fax (306)242-6115; 210-401-33rd St. W., Saskatoon, SK S7L 0V5 Tel. (306)242-5001;
Radio Pastor, Rev. Ed Martens

Periodical

EMMC Recorder

The Evangelical Missionary Church of Canada

This denomination was formed in 1993 with the merger of The Evangelical Church of Canada and The Missionary Church of Canada. The Evangelical Missionary Church of Canada maintains fraternal relations with the worldwide body of the Missionary Church and with the Evangelical Church in the U.S. The Evangelical Church of Canada was among those North American Evangelical United Brethren Conferences which did not join the EUB in merging with the Methodist Church in 1968. The Missionary Church of Canada is Anabaptist in heritage. Its practices and theology were shaped by the Holiness Revivals of the late 1800s. The Evangelical Missionary Church consists of 135 churches in two conferences in Canada.

Headquarters
#550 1212-31st Ave. NE, Calgary, AB T2E 7S8 Tel. (403)250-2759 Fax (403)291-4720
Media Contact, Missions Liaison, Glenn Gibson

Officers
Pres., Rev. Mark Bolender, #550, 1212-31st Ave. NE, Calgary, AB T2E 7S8 Tel. (403)250-2759 Fax (403)291-4720
Canada East District, Dist. Supt., Rev. Phil Delsaut, 130 Fergus Ave., Kitchener, ON N2A 2H2 Tel. (519)894-9800
Canada West District, Dist. Supt., Rev. David Crouse, #550, 1212-31st Ave. NE, Calgary, AB T2E 7S8 Tel. (403)291-5525

The Fellowship of Evangelical Baptist Churches in Canada

This organization was founded in 1953 by the merging of the Union of Regular Baptist Churches of Ontario and Quebec with the Fellowship of Independent Baptist Churches of Canada.

Headquarters
679 Southgate Dr., Guelph, ON N1G 4S2 Tel. (519)821-4830 Fax (519)821-9829
Media Contact, Pres., Rev. Terry D. Cuthbert
E-Mail: president@fellowship.ca

Officers
Pres., Rev. Terry D. Cuthbert
Chmn., Rev. G. Leslie Somers

Periodicals
B.C. Fellowship Baptist; The Evangelical Baptist; Intercom

Foursquare Gospel Church of Canada

The Western Canada District was formed in 1964 with the Rev. Roy Hicks as supervisor. Prior to 1964 it had been a part of the Northwest District of the International Church of the Foursquare Gospel with headquarters in Portland, Oregon.

A Provincial Society, the Church of the Foursquare Gospel of Western Canada, was formed in 1976; a Federal corporation, the Foursquare Gospel Church of Canada, was incorporated in 1981 and a national church formed.

Headquarters
#100 8459 160th St., Surrey, BC V3S 3T9
E-mail: fgcc@portal.ca
Media Contact, Pres. & Gen. Supervisor, Timothy J. Peterson, #100-8459 160th St., Surrey, BC V4N 1B4 Tel. (604)543-8414 Fax (604)543-8417

Officers
Pres. & Gen. Supervisor, Timothy J. Peterson

Periodical
VIP Communique

Free Methodist Church in Canada

The Free Methodist Church was founded in New York in 1860 and expanded in 1880. It is Methodist in doctrine, evangelical in ministry and emphasizes the teaching of holiness of life through faith in Jesus Christ.

The Free Methodist Church in Canada was incorporated in 1927 after the establishment of a Canadian Executive Board. In 1959 the Holiness Movement Church merged with the Free Methodist Church. Full autonomy for the Canadian church was realized in 1990 with the formation of a Canadian General Conference. Mississauga, Ontario, continues to be the location of the Canadian Headquarters.

The Free Methodist Church ministers in 28 countries through its World Ministries Center in Indianapolis, Indiana.

Headquarters
4315 Village Centre Ct., Mississauga, ON L4Z 1S2 Tel. (905)848-2600 Fax (905)848-2603
E-mail: fmccan@inforamp.net
Website: http://www.fmc-canada.org
Media Contact, Norman Bull

Officers
Pres., Bishop Keith Elford
Dir. of Admn. Ser., Norman Bull
Dir. of Development, Mary-Elsie Fletcher
Dir. of Pastoral Ser., Rev. Dennis Camplin

Periodical
The Free Methodist Herald

Free Will Baptists

As revival fires burned throughout New England in the mid- and late 1700s, Benjamin Randall proclaimed his doctrine of Free Will to large crowds of seekers. In due time, a number of Randall's converts moved to Nova Scotia. One such believer was Asa McGray, who was to become instrumental in the establishment of several Free Baptist churches. Local congregations were organized in New Brunswick. After several years of numerical and geographic gains, disagreements surfaced over the question of music, Sunday school, church offerings, salaried clergy and other issues. Adherents of the more progressive element decided to form their own fellowship. Led by George Orser, they became known as Free Christian Baptists.

The new group faithfully adhered to the truths and doctrines which embodied the theological basis of Free Will Baptists. Largely through Archibald Hatfield, contact was made with Free Will Baptists in the United States in the 1960s. The association was officially welcomed into the Free Will Baptist family in July 1981, by the National Association.

187

Headquarters
5233 Mt. View Rd., Antioch, TN 37013-2306
Tel. (615)731-6812 Fax (615)731-0771
Media Contact, Mod., Dwayne Broad, RR 3,
Bath, NB E0J 1E0 Tel. (506)278-3771

Officers
Mod., Dwayne Broad
Promotional Officer, Dwayne Broad

General Church of the New Jerusalem

The Church of the New Jerusalem is a Christian Church founded on the Bible and the Writings of Emanuel Swedenborg (1688-1772). These Writings were first brought to Ontario in 1835 by Christian Enslin.

Headquarters
c/o Olivet Church, 279 Burnhamthorpe Rd., Etobicoke, ON M9B 1Z6 Tel. (416)239-3054 Fax (416)239-4935
E-mail: Mgladish@interlog.com
Website: http://www.newchurch.org
Media Contact, Exec. Vice-Pres., Rev. Michael D. Gladish

Officers
Pres., Rt. Rev. P. M. Buss, Bryn Athyn, PA 19009
Exec. Vice-Pres., Rev. Michael D. Gladish
Sec., Suzanna Hill, 55 Chapel Hill Dr., Kitchener, ON N2G 3W5
Treas., James Bellinger, 2 Shaver Court, Etobicoke, ON M9B 4P5

Periodical
New Church Canadian

Greek Orthodox Metropolis of Toronto (Canada)

Greek Orthodox Christians in Canada are under the jurisdiction of the Ecumenical Patriarchate of Constantinople (Istanbul).

Headquarters
86 Overlea Blvd., Toronto, ON M4H 1C6 Tel. (416)429-5757 Fax (416)429-4588
E-mail: gocanada@total.net
Media Contact, Orthodox Way Committee

Officers
Metropolitan Archbishop of the Metropolis of Toronto (Canada), His Eminence Metropolitan Archbishop Sotirios

Periodical
Orthodox Way

Independent Assemblies of God International (Canada)

This fellowship of churches has been operating in Canada for over 52 years. It is a branch of the Pentecostal Church in Sweden. Each church within the fellowship is completely independent.

Headquarters
1211 Lancaster St., London, ON N5V 2L4 Tel. (519)451-1751 Fax (519)453-3258

Media Contact, Gen. Sec., Rev. Harry Wuerch
E-mail: rwuerch@odyssey.on.ca

Officers
Gen. Sec., Rev. Harry Wuerch
Treas., Rev. David Ellyatt, 1795 Parkhurst Ave., London, ON N5V 2C4
E-mail: david.ellyatt@odyssey.on.ca

Periodical
The Mantle

Independent Holiness Church

The former Holiness Movement of Canada merged with the Free Methodist Church in 1958. Some churches remained independent of this merger and they formed the Independent Holiness Church in 1960, in Kingston, Ontario. The doctrines are Methodist and Wesleyan. The General Conference is every three years, next meeting in 1998.

Headquarters
Rev. R. E. Votary, 1564 John Quinn Rd., R.R.1, Greely, ON K4P 1J9 Tel. (613)821-2237
Media Contact, Gen. Sec., Dwayne Reaney, 5025 River Rd. RR #1, Manotick, ON K4M 1B2 Tel. (613)692-3237

Officers
Gen. Supt., Rev. R. E. Votary, 1564 John Quinn Rd., Greeley, ON K4P 1J9
Gen. Sec., Dwayne Reaney
Additional Officers: E. Brown, 104-610 Pesehudoff Cresc., Saskatoon, SK S7N 4H5; D. Wallace, 1456 John Quinn Rd., R#1, Greely, ON K4P 1J9

Periodical
Gospel Tidings

Jehovah's Witnesses

For details on Jehovah's Witnesses see "Religious Bodies in United States" in this edition of the *Yearbook*.

Headquarters
25 Columbia Heights, Brooklyn, NY 11201-2483 Tel. (718)560-5600 Fax (718)560-5619
Canadian Branch Office: Box 4100, Halton Hills, ON L7G 4Y4
Media Contact, Director, Public Affairs Office, James N. Pellechia

Lutheran Church-Canada

Lutheran Church-Canada was established in 1959 at Edmonton, Alberta, as a federation of Canadian districts of the Lutheran Church - Missouri Synod; it was constituted in 1988 at Winnipeg, Manitoba, as an autonomous church.

The church confesses the Bible as both inspired and infallible, the only source and norm of doctrine and life and subscribes without reservation to the Lutheran Confessions as contained in the Book of Concord of 1580.

Headquarters

3074 Portage Ave., Winnipeg, MB R3K 0Y2 Tel. (204)895-3433 Fax (204)897-4319
Media Contact, Dir. of Comm., Ian Adnams

Officers

Pres., Rev. Ralph Mayan, 8631 Wagner Dr., Richmond, BC V7A 4N2
Vice-Pres., Rev. Dennis Putzman, 24 Valencia Dr., St. Catharines, ON L2T 3X8
2nd Vice-Pres., Rev. James Fritsche, 30 Dayton Dr., Winnipeg, MB R2J 3N1
3rd Vice-Pres., Rev. Daniel Rinderknecht, Box 1 Site 11 R.R. 4, Stony Plain, AB T7Z 1X4
Sec., Robert Hallman, 478 Greenbrook Dr., Kitchener, ON N2M 4K6
Treas., Ken Werschler

DISTRICT OFFICES

Alberta-British Columbia: Pres., Dr. H. Ruf, 7100 Ada Blvd., Edmonton, AB T5B 4E4 Tel. (403)474-0063 Fax (403)477-9829
Central: Pres., Dr. R. Holm, 1927 Grant Dr., Regina, SK S4S 4V6 Tel. (306)586-4434 Fax (306)586-0656
East: Pres., Dr. R. Winger, 275 Lawrence Ave., Kitchener, ON N2M 1Y3 Tel. (519)578-6500 Fax (519)578-3369

Periodical

Canadian Lutheran

Mennonite Church (Canada)

This body has its origins in Europe in 1525 as an outgrowth of the Anabaptist movement. It was organized in North America in 1898.(See: Mennonite Church description in the section "Religious Bodies in the United States")

Headquarters

421 S. Second St., Ste. 600, Elkhart, IN 46516 Tel. (219)294-7131 Fax (219)293-3977
E-mail: mcgb@juno.com
Media Contact, Churchwide Communications Director

Officers

Mod., Dwight McFadden Jr., 521 E. Main St., New Holland, PA 17557 Tel. (717)859-1151, Ext. 338

Periodical

Canadian Mennonite

North American Baptist Conference

Churches belonging to this conference emanated from German Baptist immigrants of more than a century ago. Although scattered across Canada and the U.S., they are bound together by a common heritage, a strong spiritual unity, a Bible-centered faith and a deep interest in missions.

Note: The details of general organization, officers, and periodicals of this body will be found in the North American Baptist Conference directory in the "Religious Bodies in the United States" section of this Yearbook.

Headquarters

1 S. 210 Summit Ave., Oakbrook Terrace, IL 60181 Tel. (630)495-2000 Fax (630)495-3301
Media Contact, Marilyn Schaer

Officer

Exec. Dir., Dr. Philip Yntema

Periodicals

N.A.B. Today

The Old Catholic Church of Canada

The church was founded in 1948 in Hamilton, Ontario. The first bishop was the Rt. Rev. George Davis. The Old Catholic Church of Canada accepts all the doctrines of the Eastern Orthodox Churches and, therefore, not Papal Infallibility or the Immaculate Conception. The ritual is Western (Latin Rite) and is in the vernacular language. Celibacy is optional.

Headquarters

RR #1, Midland, ON L4R 4K3 Tel. (705)835-6940
Media Contact, Bishop, The Most Rev. David Thomson

Officer

Vicar General and Auxiliary Bishop, The Rt. Rev. A.C. Keating, PhD., 5066 Forest Grove Crest, Burlington, ON L7L GG6 Tel. (905)331-1113

Old Order Amish Church

This is the most conservative branch of the Mennonite Church and direct descendants of Swiss Brethren (Anabaptists) who emerged from the Reformation in Switzerland in 1525. The Amish, followers of Bishop Jacob Ammann, became a distinct group in 1693. They began migrating to North America about 1720; all of them still reside in the United States or Canada. They first migrated to Ontario in 1824 directly from Bavaria, Germany and also from Pennsylvania and Alsace-Lorraine. Since 1953 some Amish have migrated to Ontario from Ohio, Indiana and Iowa.

In 1998 there were 22 congregations in Ontario, each being autonomous. No membership figures are kept by this group, and there is no central headquarters. Each congregation is served by a bishop, two ministers and a deacon, all of whom are chosen from among the male members by lot for life.

CORRESPONDENT

Pathway Publishers, David Luthy, Rt. 4, Aylmer, ON N5H 2R3

Periodicals

Blackboard Bulletin; Herold der Wahreit; The Budget; The Diary; Die Botschaft; Family Life; Young Companion

Open Bible Faith Fellowship of Canada

This is the Canadian branch of the Open Bible Standard Churches, Inc., USA of Des Moines,

Iowa. It is an evangelical, full gospel denomination emphasizing evangelism, missions and the message of the Open Bible. The Canadian Branch was chartered Jan. 7, 1982.

Headquarters
Word of Life Church, 310 Scott St., St. Catharines, ON L2R 6Z4 Tel. (905)646-0970
Media Contact, Gen. Overseer, George Woodward

Officers
Pres., . Peter Youngren
Sec., George Woodward
Treas., Ron Cosby, 1100 Gorham St., Ste. 11B, Newmarket, ON L3Y 7V1 Tel. (905)836-9337

Orthodox Church in America (Canada Section)

The Archdiocese of Canada of the Orthodox Church in America was established in 1916. First organized by St. Tikhon, martyr Patriarch of Moscow, previously Archbishop of North America, it is part of the Russian Metropolia and its successor, the autocephalous Orthodox Church in America.

The Archdiocesan Council meets twice yearly, the General Assembly of the Archdiocese takes place every three years. The Archdiocese is also known as "Orthodox Church in Canada."

Headquarters
P.O. Box 179, Spencerville, ON K0E 1X0 Tel. (613)925-5226 Fax (613)925-1521
E-mail: zoe@mulberry.com

Officers
Bishop of Ottawa & Canada, The Rt. Rev. Seraphim Chancellor, V. Rev. John Tkachuk, P.O. Box 1390, Place Bonaventure, Montreal, QC H5A 1H3 Tel. (514)481-5093 Fax (514) 481-2256
Treas., Nikita Lopoukhine, 55 Clarey Ave., Ottawa, ON K1S 2R6
Eastern Sec., Olga Jurgens, P.O. Box 179, Spencerville, ON K0E 1X0
Western Sec., Deacon Andrew Piasta, #3, 27004 Township Rd. 514, Spruce Grove, AB Tel. (403)987-4833

ARCHDIOCESAN COUNCIL
Clergy Members: Rev. Lawrence Farley; V. Rev. Andrew Morbey; Rev. Dennis Pihach; Rev. Larry Reinheimer; Deacon Philip Eriksson
Lay Members: Audrey Ewanchuk; Nicholas Ignatieff; David Grier; John Hadjinicolaou; Denis-Michel Lessard; Sister Theodora (Zion)
Ex Officio: Chancellor; Treas.; Eastern Sec.; Western Sec.

REPRESENTATIVES TO METROPOLITAN COUNCIL
V. Rev. Andrew Morbey
Mary Ann Lopoukhine

Periodical
Canadian Orthodox Messenger

Patriarchal Parishes of the Russian Orthodox Church in Canada

This is the diocese of Canada of the former Exarchate of North and South America of the Russian Orthodox Church. It was originally founded in 1897 by the Russian Orthodox Archdiocese in North America.

Headquarters
St. Barbara's Russian Orthodox Cathedral, 10105 96th St., Edmonton, AB T5H 2G3
Media Contact, Sec.-Treas., Victor Lopushinsky, #303 9566-101 Ave., Edmonton, AB T5H 0B4 Tel. (403)455-9071

Officer
Admn., Bishop of Kashira, Most Rev. Mark, 10812-108 St., Edmonton, AB T5H 3A6 Tel. (403)420-9945

The Pentecostal Assemblies of Canada

This body is incorporated under the Dominion Charter of 1919 and is also recognized in the Province of Quebec as an ecclesiastical corporation. Its beginnings are to be found in the revivals at the turn of the century, and most of the first Canadian Pentecostal leaders came from a religious background rooted in the Holiness movements.

The original incorporation of 1919 was implemented among churches of eastern Canada only. In the same year, a conference was called in Moose Jaw, Saskatchewan, to which the late Rev. J. M. Welch, general superintendent of the then-organized Assemblies of God in the U.S., was invited. The churches of Manitoba and Saskatchewan were organized as the Western District Council of the Assemblies of God. They were joined later by Alberta and British Columbia. In 1921, a conference was held in Montreal, to which the general chairman of the Assemblies of God was invited. Eastern Canada also became a district of the Assemblies of God, joining Eastern and Western Canada as two districts in a single organizational union.

In 1920, at Kitchener, Ontario, eastern and western churches agreed to dissolve the Canadian District of the Assemblies of God and unite under the name The Pentecostal Assemblies of Canada.

Today the Pentecostal Assemblies of Canada operates throughout the nation and in about 30 countries around the world. Religious services are conducted in more than 25 different languages in the 1,100 local churches in Canada. Members and adherents number about 230,000. The number of local churches includes approximately 100 Native congregations.

Headquarters
6745 Century Ave., Mississauga, ON L5N 6P7 Tel. (905)542-7400 Fax (905)542-7313
Media Contact, Public Relations, Rev. W. A. Griffin
E-mail: wgriffin@paoc.org

Officers

Gen. Supt., Rev. William D. Morrow
Asst. Gen. Supt., Rev. E. Stewart Hunter
Gen. Sec.-Treas., Rev. David Ball

DISTRICT SUPERINTENDENTS

British Columbia: Rev. William R. Gibson, 5641 176 A St., Surrey, BC V3S 4G8 Tel. (604)576-9421 Fax (604)576-1499
Alberta: Rev. Lorne D. McAlister, 10585-111 St., #101, Edmonton, AB T5H 3E8 Tel. (403)426-0084 Fax (403)420-1318
Saskatchewan: Rev. Samuel O. Biro, 3488 Fairlight Dr., Saskatoon, SK S7M 3Z4 Tel. (306)652-6088 Fax (306)652-0199
Manitoba: Rev. Gordon V. Peters, 187 Henlow Bay, Winnipeg, MB R3Y 1G4 Tel. (204)488-6800 Fax (204)489-0499
Western Ontario: Rev. David Shepherd, 3214 S. Service Rd., Burlington, ON L7M 3J2 Tel. (905)637-5566 Fax (905)637-7558
Eastern Ontario and Quebec: Rev. Richard Hilsden, Box 13250, Kanata, ON K2K 1X4 Tel. (613)599-3422 Fax (613)599-7284
Maritime Provinces: Rev. David C. Slauenwhite, Box 1184, Truro, NS B2N 5H1 Tel. (902)895-4212 Fax (902)897-0705

BRANCH CONFERENCES

German Conference: Rev. Philip F. Kniesel, #310, 684 Belmont Ave., W, Kitchener, ON N2M 1N6
Slavic Conferences: Eastern District, Rev. A. Muravski, 44 Glenabbey Dr. Courtice, ON L1E 1B7; Western District, Rev. Michael Brandebura, 4108-134 Ave., Edmonton, AB T5A 3M2
Finnish Conference: Rev. E. Ahonen, 1920 Argyle Dr., Vancouver, BC V5P 2A8

Periodicals

Pentecostal Testimony; Resource: The National Leadership Magazine

Pentecostal Assemblies of Newfoundland

This body began in 1911and held its first assembly at the Bethesda Mission at St. John's. It was incorporated in 1925 as The Bethesda Pentecostal Assemblies of Newfoundland and changed its name in 1930 to the Pentecostal Assemblies of Newfoundland.

Headquarters

57 Thorburn Rd., Box 8895, Stn. "A", St. John's, NF A1B 3T2 Tel. (709)753-6314 Fax (709)753-4945
Media Contact, Gen. Sup't., A. E. Batstone, 57 Thorburn Rd., Box 8895, Stn. "A", St. John's, NF A1B 3T2

Executive Officers

Gen. Sup't. A. Earl Batstone, 57 Thorburn Rd., Box 8895, Stn. "A", St. John's, NF A1B 3T2
Gen. Sec.-Treas., Clarence Buckle, P.O. Box 8895, Stn. A, St. John's, NF A1B 3T2

Ex. Dir. of Home Missions, Barry Q. Grimes, 57 Thorburn Rd., Box 8895, Stn. "A", St. John's, NF A1B 3T2
Ex. Dir. of Ch. Ministries, Robert H. Dewling, 57 Thorburn Rd., Box 8895, Stn. "A", St. John's, NF A1B 3T2

PROVINCIAL DIRECTORS

Sunday school Ministry, Eric A. Dawe, Box 299, Deer Lake, NF A0K 2E0
Children's Ministry, Lorinda R. Moulton, 669 Tamarack Dr., Apt. 304, Labrador City, Labrador A2V 2V2
Women's Ministries, Nancy Hunter, 10 Hardy Ave., Grand Falls-Windsor, NF A2A 2P9
Men's Ministries, Norman C. Joy, 54 Premier Dr., Corner Brook, NF A2H 1S4
Youth Ministry, B. Dean Brenton, 14 Wickham Place, St. John's, NF A1B 3L5
Mature Adult Ministry, Clayton Rice, 29 Diana Rd., St. John's, NF A1B 1H7
Family Ministry, Eva M. Winsor, 26 Ireland Dr., Grand Falls-Windsor, NF A2A 2S6

AUXILIARY SERVICES

Chaplain for Institutions, Roy A. Burden, 293 Frecker Dr., St. John's NF A1E 5T8
Pentecostal Senior Citizens Home Administrator, Beverly Bellefleur, Box 130, Clarke's Beach, NF A0A 1W0
Evergreen Manor, Summerford, NF A0G 4E0
Pastoral Enrichment Ministry, Gary D. & Eva M. Winsor, 26 Ireland Dr., Grand Falls-Windsor, NF A2A 2S6
Chaplain, Memorial University of Newfoundland, Calvin T. Andrews, Thompson Student Centre, Room T 3036, Memorial University of Newfoundland, Box 102, St. John's, NF A1C 5S7
Emmanuel Convention Centre Administrator, Ronald M. Dicks, Box 248, Lewisporte, NF A0G 3A0
World Missions Promotions, A. Scott Hunter, 10 Hardy Ave., Grand Falls-Windsor, NF A2A 2P9

Periodical

Good Tidings

Presbyterian Church in America (Canadian Section)

Canadian congregations of the Reformed Presbyterian Church, Evangelical Synod, became a part of the Presbyterian Church in America when the RPCES joined PCA in June 1982. Some of the churches were in predecessor bodies of the RPCES, which was the product of a 1965 merger of the Reformed Presbyterian Church in North America, General Synod and the Evangelical Presbyterian Church. Others came into existence later as a part of the home missions work of RPCES. Congregations are located in seven provinces, and the PCA is continuing church extension work in Canada. The denomination is committed to world evangelization and to a continuation of historic Presbyterianism. Its officers are required to subscribe to the Reformed faith as set forth in the Westminster Confession of Faith and Catechisms.

Headquarters

Media Contact, Correspondent, Doug Codling, Faith Reformed Presbyterian Church, 2581 E. 45th St., Vancouver, BC V5R 3B9 Tel. (604)438-8755

Periodicals

Equip for Ministry; Multiply; Network

Presbyterian Church in Canada

This is the nonconcurring portion of the Presbyterian Church in Canada that did not become a part of The United Church of Canada in 1925.

Headquarters

50 Wynford Dr., North York, ON M3C 1J7 Tel. (416)441-1111 Fax (416)441-2825
Website: http://www.presbycan.cal
Media Contact, Principal Clk., Rev. Stephen Kendall

Periodicals

Channels; The Presbyterian Message; Presbyterian Record; Glad Tidings; La Vie Chrétienne

Reformed Church in Canada

The Canadian branch of the Reformed Church in America consists of 41 churches organized under the Council of the Reformed Church in Canada and within the classis of Ontario (24 churches), British Columbia (10 churches), Canadian Prairies (7 churches). The Reformed Church in America was established in 1628 by the earliest Dutch settlers in America as the Reformed Protestant Dutch Church. It is evangelical in theology and presbyterian in government.

Headquarters

Gen. Sec., Rev. Wesley Granberg- Michaelson, 475 Riverside Dr., Rm. 1812, New York, NY 10115 Tel. (212)870-2841 Fax (212)870-2499
Council of the Reformed Church in Canada, Exec. Sec., Rev. James Moerman, Reformed Church Center, RR #4, Cambridge, ON N1R 5S5 Tel. (519)622-1777
Media Contact, Dir., Stewardship & Communication Services, Rev. E. Wayne Antworth, 475 Riverside Dr., Rm. 1815, New York, NY 10115 Tel. (212)870-2954 Fax (212)870-2499

The Reformed Episcopal Church of Canada

The Reformed Episcopal Church is a separate entity. It was established in Canada by an act of incorporation given royal assent on June 2, 1886. It maintains the founding principles of episcopacy (in historic succession from the apostles), Anglican liturgy and Reformed doctrine and evangelical zeal. In practice it continues to recognize the validity of certain nonepiscopal orders of evangelical ministry. The Church has reunited with the Reformed Episcopal Church and is now composed of two Dioceses in this body—the Diocese of Central and Eastern Canada and the Diocese of Western Canada and Alaska. The current Presiding Bishop is Bishop Leonard Riches in Philadelphia.

Headquarters

Box 2532, New Liskeard, ON P0J 1P0 Tel. (705)647-4565 Fax (705)647-4565
E-mail: fed@nt.net
Website: http://www.recus.org
Media Contact, Pres., Rt. Rev. Michael Fedechko, M.Div., D.D.

Officers

Pres., Rt. Rev. Michael Fedechko, 320 Armstrong St., New Liskeard, ON P0J 1P0
Sec., Janet Dividson, 224 Haliburton,New Liskeard, ON P0J 1P0

BISHOPS

Diocese of Central & Eastern Canada: Rt. Rev. Michael Fedechko, Highway 11B, New Liskeard, ON P0J 1P0
Diocese of Western Canada & Alaska: Rt. Rev. Charles W. Dorrington, 54 Blanchard St., Victoria, BC V8X 4R1 Tel. (604)744-5014 Fax (604)388-5891

Periodical

The Messenger

Reinland Mennonite Church

This group was founded in 1958 when 10 ministers and approximately 600 members separated from the Sommerfelder Mennonite Church. In 1968, four ministers and about 200 members migrated to Bolivia. The church has work in five communities in Manitoba and one in Ontario.

Headquarters

Bishop William H. Friesen, P.O. Box 96, Rosenfeld, MB R0G 1X0 Tel. (204)324-6339
Media Contact, Deacon, Henry Wiebe, Box 2587, Winkler, MB R6W 4C3 Tel. (204)325-8487

Reorganized Church of Jesus Christ of Latter Day Saints

Founded April 6, 1830, by Joseph Smith, Jr., the church was reorganized under the leadership of the founder's son, Joseph Smith III, in 1860. The Church is established in 38 countries including the United States and Canada, with nearly a quarter of a million members. A biennial world conference is held in Independence, Missouri. The current president is W. Grant McMurray.

Headquarters

World Headquarters Complex: P.O. Box 1059,

Independence, MO 64051 Tel. (816)833-1000
Fax (816)521-3095
Ontario Regional Ofc.: 390 Speedvale Ave. E.,
Guelph, ON N1E 1N5
Media Contact, Public Relations Coordinator,
Susan Naylor

CANADIAN REGIONS AND DISTRICTS
North Plains & Prairie Provinces Region:
Regional Admn., Kenneth Barrows, 84
Hidden Park NW, Calgary, AB T3A 5K5;
Alberta District, R.A.(Ryan) Levitt, #325,
51369 Range Rd., Sherwood Park, AB T8C
1H3; Saskatchewan District, Robert G.
Klombies, 202 Saskatchewan Crescent W.,
Saskatoon, SK S7M 0A4
Pacific Northwest Region: Regional Admn.,
Raymond Peter, P.O. Box 18469, 4820
Morgan, Seattle, WA 98118; British Columbia
District, E. Carl Bolger, 410-1005 McKenzie
Ave., Victoria, BC V8X 4A9
Ontario Region: Regional Admn., Larry D.
Windland, 390 Speedvale Ave. E., Guelph, ON
N1E 1N5; Chatham District, David R. Wood,
127 Mount Pleasant Crescent, Wallaceburg,
ON N8A 5A3; Grand River District, C. Allen
Taylor, R R 2, Orangeville, ON L9W 2Y9;
London District, William T. Leney, Jr., 18
Glendon Road, Stratford, ON N5A 5B3;
Niagara District, Willis L. Hopkin, 765 Rymal
Rd. E., Hamilton, ON L8W 1B6; Northern
Ontario District, Douglas G. Bolger, 482
Timmins St., North Bay, ON P1B 4K7; Ottawa
District, Marion Smith, 70 Mayburry St., Hull,
QC J9A 2E9; Owen Sound District, Robin M.
Duff, P.O. Box 52, Owen Sound, ON N1K
5P1; Toronto Metropole, Kerry J. Richards, 74
Parkside Dr., Brampton, ON L6Y 2G9

Periodical
Saints Herald

The Roman Catholic Church in Canada
The largest single body of Christians in
Canada, the Roman Catholic Church is under the
spiritual leadership of His Holiness the Pope.
Catholicism in Canada dates back to 1534, when
the first Mass was celebrated on the GaspÈ
Peninsula on July 7, by a priest accompanying
Jacques Cartier. Catholicism had been implanted
earlier by fishermen and sailors from Europe.
Priests came to Acadia as early as 1604. Traces
of a regular colony go back to 1608 when
Champlain settled in Quebec City. The Recollets
(1615), followed by the Jesuits (1625) and the
Sulpicians (1657), began the missions among the
native population. The first official Roman document relative to the Canadian missions dates
from March 20, 1618. Bishop FranÁois de
Montmorency-Laval, the first bishop, arrived in
Quebec in 1659. The church developed in the
East, but not until 1818 did systematic missionary work begin in western Canada.

In the latter 1700s, English-speaking Roman
Catholics, mainly from Ireland and Scotland,
began to arrive in Canada's Atlantic provinces.
After 1815 Irish Catholics settled in large numbers in what is now Ontario. The Irish potato
famine of 1847 greatly increased that population
in all parts of eastern Canada.

By the 1850s the Catholic Church in both
English- and French-speaking Canada had begun
to erect new dioceses and found many religious
communities. These communities did educational, medical and charitable work among their own
people as well as among Canada's native peoples. By the 1890s large numbers of non-English
and non-French-speaking Catholics had settled
in Canada, especially in the Western provinces.
In the 20th century the pastoral horizons have
continued to expand to meet the needs of what
has now become a very multiracial church.

Headquarters
Media Contact, Dir. Communications Service,
Rev. Mr. William Kokesch
Dir. Service des Communications, Sylvain
Salvas

Officers
General Secretariat of the Episcopacy
Secrétaire général (French Sector), Father Émilius
Goulet
General Secretary (English Sector), Msgr. Peter
Schonenbach
Assistant General Secretary (English Sector),
Bede Martin Hubbard
Secrétaire général adjoint (French Sector), M.
Gerald Baril

CANADIAN ORGANIZATION
Canadian Conference of Catholic Bishops:
(Conférence des évêques cath. du Canada), 90
Parent Ave., Ottawa, ON K1N 7B1 Tel.
(613)241-9461 Fax (613)241-8117

EXECUTIVE COMMITTEE
National Level
Pres., Most Rev. M. le Cardinal Jean-Claude
Turcotte (Montreal)
Vice-Pres., Most Rev. Gerald Wiesner, o.m.i.
(Prince George)
Co-Treas.: Most Rev. Anthony F. Tonnos
(Hamilton)

EPISCOPAL COMMISSIONS
National Level
Social Affairs, Mgr. Francois Thibodeau
Canon Law, Most Rev. Francis J. Spence
Relations with Assoc. of Priests, Religious, &
Laity, Most Rev. Terrence Prendergast
Evangelization of Peoples, Mgr. Andre Gaumond
Ecumenism, Most Rev. Brendan O'Brien
Theology, —
Sector Level
Comm. sociales, Mgr. Robert Lebel
Social Comm., Most Rev. Fred Colli
Éducation chrétienne, Mgr. Paul Marchand

Christian Education, Most Rev. Anthony Tonnos
Liturgie, Mgr. Antoine Hacault
Liturgy, Most Rev. Marcel A.J. Gervais

OFFICES
Secteur français
Evangélisation des peuples, Dir., Mme. AdËle Bolduc
Office des communications sociales, Dir. général, M. Bertrand Ouellet
Office national de liturgie, coordonnateur, M. l'abbé Paul Boily, 3530, rue Adam, Montréal, QC H1W 1Y8 Tel. (514)522-4930 Fax (514)522-1557
Oecuménisme, Sr. Donna Geernaert
Services des relations publiques, Dir., M. Sylvain Salvas
Service des Editions, Dir., Mme Johanne Gnassi
Théologie Dir., P. Gilles Langevin
Tribunal d'appel du Canada, P. Maurice Dionne, C.Ss.R.
Éducation chrétienne Dir., F. Jean-Claude Éthier
Affaires sociales, Dir., M. Bernard Dufresne
English Sector
Natl. Liturgical Ofc., Dir., Sr. Donna Kelly, c.n.d.
Natl. Ofc. of Religious Educ., Dir., Bernadette Tourangeau
Evangelization of peoples, Dir., Ms. AdËle Bolduc
Ecumenism, Sr. Donna Geernaert
Theology Dir., P. Gilles Langevin, S.J.
Canadian Appeal Tribunal, Maurice Dionne, C.Ss.R.
Public Information Ofc., Dir., Rev. William Kokesch
Social Affairs, Dir., Joe Gunn

REGIONAL EPISCOPAL ASSEMBLIES
Atlantic Episcopal Assembly: Pres., Mgr. André Richard; Vice-Pres., Most Rev. Raymond Lahey et Magr. Francois Thibodeau; Sec.-Treas., Daniel Deveau, c.s.c., Tel. (506)758-2589 Fax (506)758-2580
Assemblée des ÈvÍques du Que: PrÈs., Mgr. Pierre Morissette; Vice-Pres., Mgr. Robert Ébacher; Sécretaire général, M. Guy St. Onge, prêtre; Secrétariat, 1225 Boulevard Saint Joseph est, Montréal, QC H2J 1L7 Tel. (514)274-4323 Fax (514)274-4383
E-mail: aeq@eveques.qc.ca
Ontario Conference of Catholic Bishops: Pres., Bishop Anthony Tonnos; Vice-Pres., Most Rev. Brendan O'Brien; Sec., Thomas J. Reilly; Secretariat, Ste. 800, 10 St. Mary St., Toronto, ON M4Y 1P9 Tel. (416)923-1423 Fax (416)923-1509
E-mail: occb@pathcom.com
Western Catholic Conference: Pres., Bishop Blaise Morand; Vice-Pres., Mgr. Raymond Roussin; Sec., Abbot Peter Novecosky, O.S.B., P.O. Box 10, Muenster, SK S0K 2Y0 Tel. (306)682-1788 Fax (306)682-1766

MILITARY ORDINARIATE
Ordinaire aux forces canadiennes: Mgr. Donald Thériault, National Defence Headquarters, Ottawa, ON K1A 0K2 Tel. (613)990-7824 Fax (613)990-7824
Canadian Religious Conference: Sec. Gen., Sr. Hélène Robitaille, F.D.L.S., 219 Argyle St., Ottawa, ON K2P 2H4 Tel. (613)236-0824 Fax (613)236-0825
E-mail: crcn@web.net

LATIN RITE
Alexandria-Cornwall: Msgr. Eugene P. LaRocque, Centre diocésain, 220 Chemin Montréal, C. P. 1388, Cornwall, ON K6H 5V4 Tel. (613)933-1138
Amos: Evêché, Msgr. Gérard Drainville, 450, Principale Nord, Amos, QC J9T 2M1 Tel. (819)732-6515
Antigonish: Bishop Colin Campbell, Chancery Office, 161 Hawthorne St., P.O. Box 1330, Antigonish, NS B2G 1B1 Tel. (902)863-4818
E-mail: Colin.campbell@ns.sympatico.ca
Baie-Comeau: EvÍchÈ, Msgr. Pierre Morissette, 639 Rue de Bretagne, Baie-Comeau, QC G5C 1X2 Tel. (418)589-5744
Bathurst: Evêché, Msgr. André Richard, 645, avenue Murray, C.P. 460, Bathurst, NB E2A 3Z4 Tel. (506)546-3493
Calgary: Bishop Most Rev. Drederick Henry, Rm. 290-120, 17th Ave SW, Calgary, AB T2S 2T2 Tel. (403)218-5524
Charlottetown: Bishop Joseph Vernon Fougere, D.D., P.O. Box 907, Charlottetown, PE C1A 7L9 Tel. (902)368-8005
E-mail: bishopfh@rcdiocese-calgary.ab.ca
Website: http://www.rcdiocese-calgary.ab.ca
Chicoutimi: EvÍchÈ, Msgr. Jean-Guy Couture, 602 est, rue Racine, C.P. 278, Chicoutimi, QC G7H 6J6 Tel. (418)543-0783
E-mail: diocese@saglac.ca
Churchill-Baie D'Hudson: Evêché, Msgr. Reynald Rouleau, O.M.I., C.P. 10, Churchill, MB R0B 0E0 Tel. (204)675-2541
Archdiocese of Edmonton: Archbishop, Joseph N. MacNeil, Archdiocesan Office, 8421-101st Ave., Edmonton, AB T6A 0L1 Tel. (403)469-1010
E-mail: mmccaff@ibm.net
Edmundton: Evêché, Mgr. François Thibodeau, C.J.M., Centre diocésain, Edmundston, NB E3V 3K1 Tel. (506)735-5578
E-mail: diocese@nbnet.nb.ca
Website: http://www.francophone.net/diocese
Gaspé: Evêché, Mgr. Raymond Dumais, C.P. 440, Gaspé, QC G0C 1R0 Tel. (418)368-2274
Gatineau-Hull: Archévêché, Mgr. Roger Ébacher, 180, boulevard Mont-Bleu, Hull, QC J8Z 3J5 Tel. (819)771-8391
E-mail: diocesegh@inexpress.net
Grand Falls: Bishop, Joseph Faber MacDonald, Chancery Office, P.O. Box 397, Grand Falls-Windsor, NF A2A 2J8 Tel. (709)489-4019

E-mail: rcdiocese.gf@thezone.net
Website: http://www.stemnet.nf.ca/CAP/central/
GrandWin/rcd-gf/rcd-gf.htm
ArchidiocËse de Grouard-McLennan: Admin.
diocesain, M. Arthé Guimond, ptre, C.P. 388,
McLennan, AB T0H 2L0 Tel. (403)324-3002
Archdiocese of Halifax: Archbishop, Most Rev.
Terrence Prendergast, Archbishop's Residence,
6541 Coburg Rd., P.O. Box 1527, Halifax, NS
B3J 2Y3 Tel. (902)429-9388
Hamilton: Bishop, Bishop Anthony Tonnos, 700
King St. W., Hamilton, ON L8P 1C7 Tel.
(416)528-7988
E-mail: mglover@netcom.ca
Hearst: Evêché, Mgr. André Vallée, 76, 7 rue C.P.
1330, Hearst, ON P0L 1N0 Tel. (705)362-4903
E-mail: ev1330@ntl.sympatico.ca
Website: http://www.designer.com/diocesehearst
Joliette: Evêché, Mgr. Gilles Lussier, 2 rue St.-
Charles Borromée, Nord. C.P. 470, Joliette,
QC J6E 6H6 Tel. (450)753-7596
E-mail: diocesejo1@pandore.qc.ca
Kamloops: Bishop, Lawrence Sabatini, Bishop's
Residence, 635A Tranquille Rd., Kamloops,
BC V2B 3H5 Tel. (604)376-3351
Archidiocèse de Keewatin-LePas: Archbishop,
Peter-Alfred Sutton, Résidence, 108 1st St. W.,
C.P. 270, Le
Pas, MB R9A 1K4 Tel. (204)623-3529
Archdiocese of Kingston: Archbishop, Francis J.
Spence, 390 Palace Rd., Kingston, ON K7L
4T3 Tel. (613)548-4461
rcdiokgn@limestone.kosone.com
Labrador City-Schefferville: Mgr. Douglas
Crosby, 318 Ave. Elizabeth, Labrador City,
Labrador, NF A2V 2K7 Tel. (709)944-2046
London: Bishop, John M. Sherlock, Chancery
Office, 1070 Waterloo St., London, ON N6A
3Y2 Tel. (519)433-0658
E-mail: bketelaa@rcec.london.on.ca
Website: http://www.rcec.london.on.ca
Mackenzie-Fort Smith (T.No.O.): Evêché, Mgr.
Denis Croteau, 5117, 52 rue, Yellowknife,
T.N.O., X1A 1T7 Tel. (867)920-2129
Archidiocèse de Moncton: Administrateur
Diocéshin, P. Ernest LÈger, C.P. 248,
Moncton, NB E1C 8K9 Tel. (506)857-9531
E-mail: erns@mon.auracom.com
Mont-Laurier: Evêché, Mgr. Jean Gratton, 435
rue de la Madone, C.P. 1290, Mont Laurier,
QC J9L 1S1 Tel. (819)623-5530
Archidiocèse de Montréal: Archévêché,
Monsieur le cardinal Jean-Claude Turcotte,
2000 ouest rue Sherbrooke, Montréal, QC
H3H 1G4 Tel. (514)931-7311
E-mail: chanc@cam.org
Website: http://www.archeveche-mtl.qc.ca
Monsonee: Mgr. Vincent Cadieux, Résidence,
C.P. 40, Moosonee, ON P0L 1Y0 Tel.
(705)336-2908
Nelson: Diocesan Admn., Bishop Eugene J.
Cooney, Chancery Office, 813 Ward St.,
Nelson, BC V1L 1T4 Tel. (250)354-4740

Nicolet: Evêché, Msr. Raymond Saint Gelais, 49
rue Brunault, Nicolet, QC J3T 1X7 Tel.
(819)293-4234
Archidiocèse D'Ottawa: Chancellerie, Msr.
Marcel A.J. Gervais, 1247, avenue Kilborn,
Ottawa, ON K1H 6K9 Tel. (613)738-5025
E-mail: guyleval@sympatico.ca
Website: http://www.trytel.com/~ado150
Pembroke: Bishop, Brendon M. O'Brien,
Bishop's Residence, 188 Renfrew St., P.O.
Box 7, Pembroke, ON K8A 6X1 Tel.
(613)735-6313
Peterborough: Bishop, James L. Doyle, Bishop's
Residence, 350 Hunter St. W., P.O. Box 175
Peterborough, ON K9J 6Y8 Tel. (705)745-
5123
Prince-Albert: Evêché, Mgr. Blaise Morand,
1415-ouest, 4e Ave. West, Prince-Albert, SK
S6V 5H1 Tel. (306)922-4747
E-mail: bmorand@sympatico.ca
Prince-George: Bishop Gerald Wisner, Chancery
Office, 2935 Highway 16 West, P.O. Box
7000, Prince George, BC V2N 3Z2 Tel.
(604)964-4424
E-mail: pgbishop@netbistro.com
Archidiocèse de Québec: Archévêché, Mgr.
Maurice Couture, 2 rue Port Dauphin, C.P.
459, Québec, QC G1R 4R6 Tel. (418)692-
3935
E-mail: Diocesedequebec@videotron.ca
Website: http://www.diocesequebec.qc.ca
Archdiocese of Regina: Archbishop, Peter
Mallon, D.D., Chancery Office, 455 Broad St.
North, Regina, SK S4R 2X8 Tel. (306)352-
1651
E-mail: archregina@sk.sympatico.ca
Archidiocèse de Rimouski: Archévêché, Mgr.
Bertrand Blanchet, 34 ouest, rue de L'évêché,
ouest C.P. 730, Rimouski, QC G5L 7C7 Tel.
(418)723-3320
Rouyn-Noranda: Evêché, Mgr. Jean-Guy
Hamelin, 515 avenue Cuddihy, C.P. 1060,
Rouyn-Noranda, QC J9X 5W9 Tel. (819)764-
4660
E-mail: diocese.rouyn-noranda@sympatico.ca
Ste-Anne de la Pocatière: Evêché, Mgr. Clément
Fecteau, C.P. 430 La Pocatière, Pocatière, QC
G0R 1Z0 Tel. (418)856-1811
E-mail: diocesap@globetrotter.qc.ca
Archidiocèse de Saint-Boniface: Archevêché,
Mgr. Antoine Hacault, 151 ave de la
Cathédrale, St-Boniface, MB R2H 0H6 Tel.
(204)237-9851
E-mail: arch@tbf.net
St. Catharine's: Bishop, John A. O'mara,
Bishop's Residence, 122 Riverdale Ave., St.
Catharines, ON L2R 4C2 Tel. (416)684-0154
Website: http://www.romancatholic.niagara.on.ca
St. George's: Bishop, Raymond J. Lahey,
Bishop's Residence, 16 Hammond Dr., Corner
Brook, NF A2H 2W2 Tel. (709)639-8662
E-mail: diocese@nf.sympatico.ca
Website: http://members.aol.com/diosg/

195

Saint Hyacinthe: Evêché, Mgr. Francois Lapierre, 1900 ouest Girouard, C. P. 190, Saint-Hyacinthe, QC J2S 7B4 Tel. (514)773-8581
E-mail: lapierre@ntic.qc.ca
Saint-Jean- Longueuil: Evêché, Jacques Berthelet, 740 boul. Ste-Foy, C.P. 40, Longueuil, QC J4K 4X8 Tel. (450)679-1100
E-mail: dsj1@sympatico.ca
Website: http://planete.qc.ca/diocese
Saint-Jérome: Evêché, Mgr. Gilles Cazabon, 355 rue St-Georges, C.P. 580, Saint-Jérome, QC J7Z 5V3 Tel. (450)432-9742
Saint John: Bishop, —, Chancery Office, 1 Bayard Dr., Saint John, NB E2L 3L5 Tel. (506)653-6800
E-mail: jwk@brunnet.net (temporary)
Website: http://www.brunnet.net/dsj/
Archdiocese of St. John's: Archbishop, James H. MacDonald, Archbishop's Residence, P.O. Box 37, Basilica Residence, St. John's, NF A1C 5H5 Tel. (709)726-3660
Website: http://www.delweb.com/rcec
Saint-Paul: Evêché, Mgr. Thomas Collins, 4410 51e Ave., St-Paul, AB T0A 3A2 Tel. (403)645-3277
E-mail: diospaul@incentre.net
Saskatoon: Diocesan Admn., Bishop V. James Weisgerber, Chancery Office, 106 - 5th Ave. N., Saskatoon, SK S7K 2N7 Tel. (306)242-1500
E-mail: Chancery@sk.sympatico.ca
Sault Ste. Marie: Mgr. Jean-Louis Plouffe, Bishop's Residence, P.O. Box 510, North Bay, ON P1B 8J1 Tel. (705)476-1300
E-mail: Pastoral@isys.ca
Website: http://www.isys.ca/cathcom.htm
Archidiocèse de Sherbrooke: Archévêché, Mgr. André Gaumond, 130 rue de la Cathedrale, C.P. 430, Sherbrooke, QC J1H 5K1 Tel. (819)563-9934
E-mail: dioscher@login.net
Thunder Bay: Admin. diocesain, Mgr. Roger Bazin, P.O. Box 10400, Thunder Bay, ON P7B 6T8 Tel. (807)622-8144
E-mail: dotb.baynet.net
Website: http://www.dotb.baynet.net
Timmins: Admin. Diocesain, L'abbe Maurice Magnan, 65, avenue Jubilee est, Timmins, ON P4N 5W4 Tel. (705)267-6224
E-mail: dioctims@ntl.sympatico.ca
Website: http://www.nt.net/~dioctims
Archdiocese of Toronto: Archbishop, Aloysius M. Ambrozic, Chancery Office, 1155 Yonge St., Toronto, ON M4T 1W2 Tel. (416)934-0606
E-mail: spiritua@idirect.com
Trois-Rivières: Evêché, Mgr. Laurent Noel, 362 rue Bonaventure, C.P. 879, Trois-Rivièrès, QC G9A 5J9 Tel. (819)374-9847
Valleyfield: Evêché, Mgr. Robert Lebel, 11 rue de l'Eglise, Valleyfield, QC J6T 1J5 Tel. (450)373-8122

E-mail: diovall@rocler.qc.ca
Archdiocese of Vancouver: Archbishop, Adam Exner, Chancery Office, 150 Robson St., Vancouver, BC V6B 2A7 Tel. (604)683-0281
Victoria: Bishop, Remi J. De Roo, Bishop's Office, 1 - 4044 Nelthorpe St., Victoria, BC V8X 2A1 Tel. (604)479-1331
Coadjutor Bishop, Raymond Roussin
Whitehorse (Yukon): Bishop, Thomas Lobsinger, O.M.I. Bishop's Residence, 5119 5th Ave., Whitehorse, YT Y1A 1L5 Tel. (403)667-2052
Archdiocese of Winnipeg: Archbishop, Leonard J. Wall, 1495 Pembina Hwy, Winnipeg, MB R3T 2C6 Tel. (204)452-2227
E-mail: rcacwpg@mb.sympatico.ca
Yarmouth: Bishop James Wingle, 53 rue Park, Yarmouth, NS B5A 4B2 Tel. (902)742-7163
Website: http://www.dioceseyarmouth.org

EASTERN RITES

Eparchy of Edmonton Eparch: —, V Eparch's Residence, 9645-108 Ave., Edmonton, AB T5H 1A3 Tel. (403)424-5496
Eparchy of New Westminster: Eparch, Severian S. Yakymyshyn, O.S.B.M., Eparch's Residence, 502 5th Ave., New Westminster, BC V3L 1S2 Tel. (604)524-4158
Eparchy of Saskatoon: Eparch, — Eparch's Residence, 866 Saskatchewan. Crescent East, Saskatoon, SK S7N 0L4 Tel. (306)665-2569
Ukrainian Eparchy of Toronto: Eparch, Most Rev. Cornelius John Pasichny, Eparch's Residence, 139 Franklin Ave., Toronto, ON M6P 3Y9 Tel. (416)538-1436
Toronto, Ontario Eparchy: For Slovaks, Eparch, Apostolic Administrator, Rev. John Fetsco, Chancery Office, 223 Carlton Rd., Unionville, ON L3R 3M2 Tel. (416)477-4867
Ukrainian Archeparchy of Winnipeg: Most Rev. Michael Bzdel, Archeparch's Residence, 235 Scotia St., Winnipeg, MB R2V 1V7 Tel. (204)338-7801
Montréal (Qué) Archéparchie: Pour Les Grecs-Melkites,Eparque, Mgr. Sleiman Hajjar, Chancelerie: 34 Maplewood, Montréal, QC H2V 2M1 Tel. (514)272-6430
Archéparchie de Montréal: Pour les Maronites, Éparque, Mgr. Joseph Khoury, 12475, rue Grenet, Montréal, QC H4J 2K4 Tel. (514)331-2807
E-mail: beitmaroun@aei.ca
Canada/États-Unis, Mgr. Hovhannes Tertzakian, 110 E. 12th St., New York, NY 10003 Tel. (212)477-2030

Periodicals

Cahiers de Spiritualité Ignatienne; The Catholic Register; The Catholic Times (Montreal); Companion Magazine; Global Village Voice; Discover the Bible; L'Église Canadienne; The Monitor; National Bulletin on Liturgy; The New Freeman; Messenger (of the Sacred Heart); Foi et Culture (Bulletin natl. de liturgie) Liturgie; Prairie Messenger; Vie Liturgique; La Vie des Communautés religieuses; Relations; Présence; The Communicator; Scarboro Missions; Missions Today

Romanian Orthodox Church in America (Canadian Parishes)

The first Romanian Orthodox immigrants in Canada called for Orthodox priests from their native country of Romania. Between 1902 and 1914, they organized the first Romanian parish communities and built Orthodox churches in different cities and farming regions of western Canada (Alberta, Saskatchewan, Manitoba) as well as in the eastern part (Ontario and Quebec).

In 1929, the Romanian Orthodox parishes from Canada joined with those of the United States in a Congress held in Detroit, Michigan, and asked the Holy Synod of the Romanian Orthodox Church of Romania to establish a Romanian Orthodox Missionary Episcopate in America. The first Bishop, Policarp (Morushca), was elected and consecrated by the Holy Synod of the Romanian Orthodox Church and came to the United States in 1935. He established his headquarters in Detroit with jurisdiction over all the Romanian Orthodox parishes in the United States and Canada.

In 1950, the Romanian Orthodox Church in America (i.e. the Romanian Orthodox Missionary Episcopate in America) was granted administrative autonomy by the Holy Synod of the Romanian Orthodox Church of Romania, and only doctrinal and canonical ties remain with this latter body.

In 1974 the Holy Synod of the Romanian Orthodox Church of Romania recognized and approved the elevation of the Episcopate to the rank of the Romanian Orthodox Archdiocese in America and Canada.

Headquarters

Canadian Office: Descent of the Holy Ghost, Romanian Orthodox Church, 2895 Seminole St., Windsor, ON N8Y 1Y1

Media Contact, Most Rev. Archbishop Victorin, 19959 Riopelle St., Detroit, MI 48203 Tel. (313)893-8390

Officers

Archbishop, Most Rev. Archbishop Victorin, 19959 Riopelle St., Detroit, MI 48203 Tel. (313)893-8390

Vicar, V. Rev. Archim., Dr. Vasile Vasilachi, 45-03 48th Ave., Woodside, Queens, NY 11377 Tel. (718)784-4453

Cultural Councilor, Very Rev. Fr. Nicolae Ciurea, 19 Murray St. W., Hamilton, ON L8L 1B1 Tel. (416)523-8268

Admn. Councilor, V. Rev. Fr. Mircea Panciuk, 11024-165th Ave., Edmonton, AB T5X 1X9

Sec., Rev. Fr. Simion John Catau, 31227 Roan Dr., Warren, MI 48093 Tel. (810)264-1924

The Romanian Orthodox Episcopate of America (Jackson, MI)

This body of Eastern Orthodox Christians of Romanian descent is part of the Autocephalous Orthodox Church in America. For complete description and listing of officers, please see chapter 3, "Religious Bodies in the United States."

Headquarters

2522 Grey Tower Rd., Jackson, MI 49201 Tel. (517)522-4800 Fax (517)522-5907

E-mail: roeasolia@aol.com

Website: http://www.roea.org

Mailing Address, P.O. Box 309, Grass Lake, MI 49240-0309

Media Contact, Ed./Sec., Rev. Dea. David Oancea, P.O. Box 185, Grass Lake, MI 49240-0185 Tel. (517)522-3656 Fax (517)522-5907

Officers

Ruling Bishop, Rt. Rev. Nathaniel Popp

Deans for the Deanery of Canada, Western Provinces, Very Rev. Daniel Nenson, 2855 Helmsing St., Regina, SK S4V 0W7 Tel. (306)761-2379; Eastern Provinces, Very Rev. Dumitru Paun, 47 Adelaide S., London, ON N5Z 3K1 Tel. (519)858-4065

Periodical

Solia - The Herald

The Salvation Army in Canada

The Salvation Army, an evangelical branch of the Christian Church, is an international movement founded in 1865 in London, England. The ministry of Salvationists, consisting of clergy (officers) and laity, comes from a commitment to Jesus Christ and is revealed in practical service, regardless of race, color, creed, sex or age.

The goals of The Salvation Army are to preach the gospel, disseminate Christian truths, instill Christian values, enrich family life and improve the quality of all life.

To attain these goals, The Salvation Army operates local congregations, provides counseling, supplies basic human needs and undertakes spiritual and moral rehabilitation of any needy people who come within its influence.

A quasi-military system of government was set up in 1878, by General William Booth, founder (1829-1912). Converts from England started Salvation Army work in London, Ontario, in 1882. Two years later, Canada was recognized as a Territorial Command, and since 1933 it has included Bermuda. An act to incorporate the Governing Council of The Salvation Army in Canada received royal assent on May 19, 1909.

Headquarters

2 Overlea Blvd., Toronto, ON M4H 1P4 Tel. (416)425-2111

Media Contact, Colonel William Ratcliffe, Tel. (416)425-6153 Fax (416)425-6157

E-mail: wgratcli@sallynet.org

Website: http://www.sallynet.org

197

Officers
Territorial Commander, Commissioner Norman Howe
Territorial Pres., Women's Organizations, Commissioner Marian Howe
Chief Sec., Col. Clyde Moore
Sec. for Personnel, Col. John Carew
Bus. Adm. Sec., Lt. Col. Peter Wood
Fin. Sec., Major Susan McMillan
Program Sec., Lt. Col. Merv Leach
Community Rel. and Dev. Sec., Col. William Ratcliffe
Property Sec., Major Donald Copple

Periodicals
The War Cry; Faith & Friends; En Avant!; The Young Soldier; The Edge; Catherine; Horizons

Serbian Orthodox Church in the U.S.A. and Canada, Diocese of Canada

The Serbian Orthodox Church is an organic part of the Eastern Orthodox Church. As a local church it received its autocephaly from Constantinople in A.D. 1219. The Patriarchal seat of the church today is in Belgrade, Yugoslavia. In 1921, a Serbian Orthodox Diocese in the United States of America and Canada was organized. In 1963, it was reorganized into three dioceses, and in 1983 a fourth diocese was created for the Canadian part of the church. The Serbian Orthodox Church is in absolute doctrinal unity with all other local Orthodox Churches.

Headquarters
7470 McNiven Rd., RR 3, Campbellville, ON L0P 1B0 Tel. (905)878-0043 Fax (905)878-1909
E-mail: vladika@istocnik.com
Website: http://www. istocnik.com
Media Contact, Rt. Rev. Georgije

Officers
Serbian Orthodox Bishop of Canada, Rt. Rev. Georgije
Dean of Western Deanery, V. Rev. Mirko Malinovic, 924 12th Ave., Regina, SK S4N 0K7 Tel. (306)352-2917
Dean of Eastern Deanery, V. Rev. Zivorad Subotic, 351 Mellville Ave., Westmount, QC H3Z 2Y7 Tel. + Fax (514)931-6664

Seventh-day Adventist Church in Canada

The Seventh-day Adventist Church in Canada is part of the worldwide Seventh-day Adventist Church with headquarters in Washington, D.C. (See "Religious Bodies in the United States" section of this *Yearbook* for a fuller description.) The Seventh-day Adventist Church in Canada was organized in 1901 and reorganized in 1932.

Headquarters
1148 King St., E., Oshawa, ON L1H 1H8 Tel. (905)433-0011 Fax (905)433-0982
Media Contact, Orville Parchment

Officers
Pres., Orville Parchment
Sec., Claude Sabot
Treas., Donald Upson

DEPARTMENTS
Under Treas., Brian Christenson
Asst. Treas., Clareleen Ivany
Computer Services, Brian Ford
Coord. of Ministries, John Howard
Education, Mike Lekic
Public Affairs/Religious Liberty Trust, Karnik Doukmetzian

Periodical
Canadian Adventist Messenger

Syrian Orthodox Church of Antioch

The Syrian Orthodox Church professes the faith of the first three ecumenical councils of Nicaea, Constantinople and Ephesus and numbers faithful in the Middle East, India, the Americas, Europe and Australia. It traces its origin to the Patriarchate established in Antioch by St. Peter the Apostle and is under the supreme ecclesiastical jurisdiction of His Holiness the Syrian Orthodox Patriarch of Antioch and All the East, now residing in Damascus, Syria.

The Archdiocese of the Syrian Orthodox Church in the U.S. and Canada was formally established in 1957. In 1995, the Archdiocese of North America was divided into three separate Patriarchal Vicariates, including one for Canada. The first Syrian Orthodox faithful came to Canada in the 1890s and formed the first Canadian parish in Sherbrooke, Quebec. Today five official parishes of the Archdiocese exist in Canada-two in Quebec and three in Ontario. There is also an official mission congregation in Calgary, Alberta.

Headquarters
Archdiocese of Canada, 4829 Rue Resther, Montreal, QB H2J 2V6 Tel. (514)521-0515

Officer
Archbishop Mor Timotheos Aphrem Aboodi

Ukrainian Orthodox Church of Canada

Toward the end of the 19th century many Ukrainian immigrants settled in Canada. In 1918, a group of these pioneers established the Ukrainian Orthodox Church of Canada (UOCC), today the largest Ukrainian Orthodox Church beyond the borders of Ukraine. In 1990, the UOCC entered into a eucharistic union with the Ecumenical Patriarchate at Constantinople (Istanbul).

Headquarters
Ukrainian Orthodox Church of Canada, Office of the Consistory, 9 St. Johns Ave., Winnipeg, MB R2W 1G8 Tel. (204)586-3093 Fax (204)582-5241
E-mail: consistory@uocc.ca

Website: http://www. uocc.ca
Media Contacts, V. Rev. Dr. Ihor Kutash, 6270-
12th Ave., Montreal, QC H1X 3A5 Tel.
(514)727-2236 Fax (514)728-9834; Ms. M.
Zurek, 9 St. Johns Ave., Winnipeg, MB R2W
1G8 Tel. (204)586-3093 Fax (204)582-5241

Officers
Primate, Most Rev. Metropolitan Wasyly Fedak,
9 St. Johns Ave., Winnipeg, MB R2W 1G8
Tel. (204)586-3093 Fax (204)582-5241
Chancellor, Rt. Rev. Dr. Oleg Krawchenko

Periodical
Visnyk/The Herald/Le Messager (newspaper)
Ridna Nyva (almanac/annual)

Union of Spiritual Communities of Christ (Orthodox Doukhobors in Canada)

The Doukhobors are groups of Canadians of
Russian origin living in the western provinces of
Canada, but their beginnings in Russia are
unknown. The name "Doukhobors," or "Spirit
Wrestlers," was given in derision by the Russian
Orthodox clergy in Russia as far back as 1785.
Victims of decades of persecution in Russia, about
7,500 Doukhobors arrived in Canada in 1899.

The teaching of the Doukhobors is penetrated
with the Gospel spirit of love. Worshiping God in
the spirit, they affirm that the outward church
and all that is performed in it and concerns it has
no importance for them; the church is where two
or three are gathered together, united in the name
of Christ. Their teaching is founded on tradition,
which they call the "Book of Life," because it
lives in their memory and hearts. In this book are
sacred songs or chants, partly composed independently, partly formed out of the contents of
the Bible, and these are committed to memory by
each succeeding generation. Doukhobors
observe complete pacifism and non-violence.

The Doukhobors were reorganized in 1938 by
their leader, Peter P. Verigin, shortly before his
death, into the Union of Spiritual Communities
of Christ, commonly called Orthodox
Doukhobors. It is headed by a democratically
elected Executive Committee which executes the
will and protects the interests of the people.

At least 99 percent of the Doukhobors are law-
abiding, pay taxes, and "do not burn or bomb or
parade in the nude" as they say a fanatical offshoot called the "Sons of Freedom" does.

Headquarters
USCC Central Office, Box 760, Grand Forks,
BC V0H 1H0 Tel. (250)442-8252 Fax
(250)442-3433
Media Contact, John J. Verigin, Sr.

Officers
Hon. Chmn. of the Exec. Comm., John J.
Verigin, Sr.
Chpsn., Andrew Evin

Periodical
ISKRA

United Brethren Church in Canada

Founded in 1767 in Lancaster County, Pa.,
missionaries came to Canada about 1850. The
first class was held in Kitchener in 1855, and the
first building was erected in Port Elgin in 1867.

The Church of the United Brethren in Christ
had its beginning with Philip William Otterbein
and Martin Boehm, who were leaders in the
revivalistic movement in Pennsylvania and
Maryland during the late 1760s.

Headquarters
302 Lake St., Huntington, IN 46750 Tel.
(219)356-2312 Fax (219)356-4730

General Officers
Pres., Rev. Brian Magnus, 120 Fife Rd., Guelph,
ON N1H 6Y2 Tel. (519)836-0180
Treas., Brian Winger, 2233 Hurontario St., Apt.
916, Mississauga, ON L5A 2E9 Tel. (905)275-
8140

The United Church of Canada

The United Church of Canada was formed on
June 10, 1925, through the union of the
Methodist Church, Canada, the Congregational
Union of Canada, the Council of Local Union
Churches and 70 percent of the Presbyterian
Church in Canada. The union culminated years
of negotiation between the churches, all of which
had integral associations with the development
and history of the nation.

In fulfillment of its mandate to be a uniting as
well as a United Church, the denomination has
been enriched by other unions during its history.
The Wesleyan Methodist Church of Bermuda
joined in 1930. On January 1, 1968, the Canada
Conference of the Evangelical United Brethren
became part of The United Church of Canada. At
various times, congregations of other Christian
communions have also become congregations of
the United Church.

The United Church of Canada is a full member
of the World Methodist Council, the World
Alliance of Reformed Churches (Presbyterian
and Congregational), and the Canadian and
World Councils of Churches.

The United Church is the largest Protestant
denomination in Canada.

NATIONAL OFFICES
The United Church House, 3250 Bloor St. W.,
Ste. 300, Etobicoke, ON M8X 2Y4 Tel.
(416)231-5931 Fax (416)231-3103
E-mail: info@uccan.org
Website: http://www.uccan.org
Media Contact, Manager Public Relations &
Info. Unit, Mary-Frances Denis

GENERAL COUNCIL
Mod., William F. Phipps
Gen. Sec., K. Virginia Coleman
Human Resources, Sec., Anne Shirley Sutherland
Theology, Faith & Ecumenism, Sec., Rev. S.
Peter Wyatt

Archivist, Jean E. Dryden, 73 Queen's Park Cr., E., Toronto, ON M5C 1K7 Tel. (416)585-4563 Fax (416)585-4584
E-mail: uccvu.archives@utoronto.ca
Website: http://www. vicu.utoronto.ca/archives. archives.htm

ADMINISTRATIVE DIVISIONS

Communication: Gen. Sec., Linda E. Slough
Finance: Gen. Sec., Steven Adams
Ministry Personnel & Education: Gen. Sec., Rev. Steven Chambers
Mission in Canada: Gen. Sec., Rev. David Iverson
World Outreach: Gen. Sec., Rhea Whitehead

CONFERENCE EXECUTIVE SECRETARIES

Alberta and Northwest: Rev. George H. Rodgers, 9911-48 Ave., Edmonton, AB T6E 5V6 Tel. (403)435-3995 Fax (403)438-3317
E-mail: anconf@web.net
All Native Circle: Speaker, Rev. Arlene J. Granbois, 367 Selkirk Ave., Winnipeg, MB R2W 2N3 Tel. (204)582-5518 Fax (204)582-6649
E-mail: ancc@mb.sympatico.ca
Bay of Quinte: Wendy Bulloch, P.O. Box 700, Frankford, ON K0K 2C0 Tel. (613)398-7051 Fax (613)398-8894
E-mail: bayq.conference@sympatico.ca
British Columbia: Rev. Brian D. Thorpe, 4383 Rumble St., Burnaby, BC V5J 2A2 Tel. (604)431-0434 Fax (604)431-0439
E-mail: bcconf@infoserve.net
Hamilton: Rev. Roslyn A. Campbell, Box 100, Carlisle, ON L0R 1H0 Tel. (905)659-3343 Fax (905)659-7766
E-mail: office@hamconf.org
London: W. Peter Scott, 359 Windermere Rd., London, ON N6G 2K3 Tel. (519)672-1930 Fax (519)439-2800
E-mail: lonconf@execulink.com
Manitoba and Northwestern Ontario: Rev. Roger A. Coll, 170 Saint Mary's Rd., Winnipeg, MB R2H 1H9 Tel. (204)233-8911 Fax (204)233-3289
E-mail: confmnwo@mb.sympatico.ca
Manitou: Rev. George H. Lavery, 1402 Regina St., North Bay, ON P1B 2L5 Tel. (705)474-3350 Fax (705)497-3597
E-mail: manitou@efni.com
Maritime: Rev. Catherine H. Graw, 32 York St., Sackville, NB E4L 4R4 Tel. (506)536-1334 Fax (506)536-2900
E-mail: marconf@nbnet.nb,ca
Montreal and Ottawa: Rev. Gordon J. Roberts, 225-50 Ave., Lachine, QC H8T 2T7 Tel. (514)634-7015 Fax (514)634-2489
E-mail: lachine@istar.ca
Newfoundland and Labrador: Rev. Clarence R. Sellers, 320 Elizabeth Ave., St. John's, NF A1B 1T9 Tel. (709)754-0386 Fax (709)754-8336
E-mail: newlab@seascape.com

Saskatchewan: Rev. Wilbert R. Wall, 418 A. McDonald St., Regina, SK S4N 6E1 Tel. (306)721-3311 Fax (306)721-3171
E-mail: ucskco@sk.sympatico.ca
Toronto: Rev. David W. Allen, 65 Mayall Ave., Downsview, ON M3L 1E7 Tel. (416)241-2677 Fax (416)241-2689
E-mail: torconf@web.net

Periodicals

Fellowship Magazine; United Church Observer; Mandate; Aujourd'hui Credo

United Pentecostal Church in Canada

This body, which is affiliated with the United Pentecostal Church, International, with headquarters in Hazelwood, Mo., accepts the Bible standard of full salvation, which is repentance, baptism by immersion in the name of the Lord Jesus Christ for the remission of sins and the baptism of the Holy Ghost, with the initial signs of speaking in tongues as the Spirit gives utterance. Other tenets of faith include the Oneness of God in Christ, holiness, divine healing and the second coming of Jesus Christ.

Headquarters

United Pentecostal Church Intl., 8855 Dunn Rd., Hazelwood, MO 63042 Tel. (314)837-7300 Fax (314)837-4503
Media Contact, Gen. Sec.-Treas., Rev. C. M. Becton

DISTRICT SUPERINTENDENTS

Atlantic: Rev. Harry Lewis, P.O. Box 1046, Perth Andover, NB E0J 1V0
British Columbia: Rev. Paul V. Reynolds, 13447-112th Ave., Surrey, BC V3R 2E7
Canadian Plains: Rev. Johnny King, 615 Northmount Dr., NW, Calgary, AB T2K 3J6
Central Canadian: Rev. Clifford Heaslip, 4215 Roblin Blvd., Winnipeg, MB R3R 0E8
Newfoundland: Jack Cunningham
Nova Scotia: Superintendent, Rev. John D. Mean, P.O. Box 2183, D.E.P.S., Dartmouth, NS B2W 3Y2
Ontario: Rev. Carl H. Stephenson, 63 Castlegrove Blvd., Don Mills, ON M3A 1L3

Universal Fellowship of Metropolitan Community Churches

The Universal Fellowship of Metropolitan Community Churches is a Christian church which directs a special ministry within, and on behalf of, the gay and lesbian community. Involvement, however, is not exclusively limited to gays and lesbians; U.F.M.C.C. tries to stress its openness to all people and does not call itself a "gay church."

Founded in 1968 in Los Angeles by the Rev. Troy Perry, the U.F.M.C.C. has over 300 member congregations worldwide. Congregations are in Vancouver, Edmonton, Windsor, London, Toronto, Ottawa (2), Guelph, Fredericton, Winnipeg, Halifax, Barrie and Belleville.

Theologically, the Metropolitan Community Churches stand within the mainstream of Christian doctrine, being "ecumenical" or "interdenominational" in stance (albeit a "denomination" in their own right).

The Metropolitan Community Churches are characterized by their belief that the love of God is a gift, freely offered to all people, regardless of sexual orientation and that no incompatibility exists between human sexuality and the Christian faith.

The Metropolitan Community Churches in Canada were founded in Toronto in 1973 by the Rev. Robert Wolfe.

Headquarters

Media Contact, Marcie Wexler, 33 Holly St., #1117, Toronto, ON M4S 2G8 Tel. (416)487-8429 Fax (416)932-1836

Officer

Eastern Canadian District: Rev. Marcie Wexler, 33 Holly St., #1117, Toronto, ON M4S 2G8 Tel. (416)487-8429

The Wesleyan Church of Canada

This group is the Canadian portion of The Wesleyan Church which consists of the Atlantic and Central Canada districts. The Central Canada District of the former Wesleyan Methodist Church of America was organized at Winchester, Ontario, in 1889 and the Atlantic District was founded in 1888 as the Alliance of the Reformed Baptist Church, which merged with the Wesleyan Methodist Church in July, 1966.

The Wesleyan Methodist Church and the Pilgrim Holiness Church merged in June, 1968, to become The Wesleyan Church. The doctrine is evangelical and Wesleyan Arminian and stresses holiness beliefs. For more details, consult the U.S. listing under The Wesleyan Church.

Headquarters

The Wesleyan Church Intl. Center, P.O. Box 50434, Indianapolis, IN 46250-0434

Media Contact, Dist. Supt., Central Canada, Rev. Donald E. Hodgins, 3 Applewood Dr., Ste. 101, Belleville, ON K8P 4E3 Tel. (613)966-7527 Fax (613)968-6190

DISTRICT SUPERINTENDENTS

Central Canada: Rev. Donald E. Hodgins, 3 Applewood Dr., Ste.101, Belleville, ON K8P 4E3

E-mail: central.canada.district@sympatico.ca

Atlantic: Rev. Dr. H. C. Wilson, P.O. Box 20, 41 Summit Ave., Sussex, NB E0E 1P0 Tel. (506)433-1007

E-mail: ncwilson@nbnet.nb.ca

Periodical

Central Canada; The Clarion

Religious Bodies in Canada
Arranged by Families

The following list of religious bodies appearing in the preceding directory, "Religious Bodies in Canada," shows the "families," or related clusters into which Canadian religious bodies can be grouped. For example, there are many bodies that can be grouped. For example, there are many bodies that can be grouped under the heading "Baptist" for historical and theological reasons. It is not to be assumed, however, that all denominations under one family heading are necessarily similar in belief or practice. Often any similarity is purely coincidental since ethnicity, theological divergence and even political and personality factors have shaped the directions denominational groups have taken.

Family categories provide one of the major pitfalls of church statistics because of the tendency to combine statistics by "families" for analytical and comparative purposes. Such combined totals are almost meaningless, although often used as variables for sociological analysis.

Religious bodies not grouped under family headings appear alphabetically and are not indented in the following list.

The Anglican Church of Canada
Apostolic Christian Church (Nazarene)
Armenian Evangelical Church
Associated Gospel Churches
Adventist Bodies

Baptist Bodies

Association of Regular Baptist Churches (Canada)
Baptist General Conference of Canada
Canadian Baptist Ministries
  Baptist Convention of Ontario and Québec
  Baptist Union of Western Canada
  Union d'Églises Baptistes Françaises au Canada
  United Baptist Convention of the Atlantic Provinces
Canadian Convention of Southern Baptists
The Fellowship of Evangelical Baptist Churches in Canada
Free Will Baptists
North American Baptist Conference

The Bible Holiness Movement
Brethren in Christ Church, Canadian Conference
Canadian District of the Moravian Church in America, Northern Province
Canadian Evangelical Christian Churches
Canadian Yearly Meeting of the Religious Society of Friends
Christ Catholic Church International
Christian and Missionary Alliance in Canada
Christian Brethren (Plymouth Brethren)
Church of God (Anderson, Ind.)
Church of the Nazarene Canada

Churches of Christ—Christian Churches

Christian Church (Disciples of Christ) in Canada
Churches of Christ in Canada

Congregational Christian Churches in Canada

Doukhobors

Union of Spiritual Communities of Christ (Orthodox Doukhobors in Canada)

Eastern Churches

The Antiochian Orthodox Christian Archdiocese of North America
Armenian Holy Apostolic Church—Canadian Diocese
The Coptic Orthodox Church in Canada
Greek Orthodox Metropolis of Toronto (Canada)
Orthodox Church in America (Canada Section)
Patriarchal Parishes of the Russian Orthodox Church in Canada
Romanian Orthodox Church in America (Canadian Parishes)
The Romanian Orthodox Episcopate of America (Jackson, MI)
Serbian Orthodox Church in the U.S.A. and Canada, Diocese of Canada
Syrian Orthodox Church of Antioch
Ukrainian Orthodox Church of Canada

The Evangelical Covenant Church of Canada
The Evangelical Missionary Church of Canada
Evangelical Free Church of Canada
Independent Holiness Church
Jehovah's Witnesses

Latter-Day Saints

The Church of Jesus Christ of Latter-Day Saints in Canada
Reorganized Church of Jesus Christ of Latter-Day Saints

Lutherans

Church of the Lutheran Brethren
The Estonian Evangelical Lutheran Church

Evangelical Lutheran Church in Canada
The Latvian Evangelical Lutheran Church in
America
Lutheran Church—Canada

Mennonite Bodies

Canadian Conference of Mennonite Brethren
Churches
Church of God in Christ (Mennonite)
Conference of Mennonites in Canada
The Evangelical Mennonite Conference
Evangelical Mennonite Mission Conference
Mennonite Church (Canada)
Old Order Amish Church
Reinland Mennonite Church

Methodist Bodies

British Methodist Episcopal Church of
Canada
Free Methodist Church in Canada
The Wesleyan Church of Canada

The Old Catholic Church of Canada

Pentecostal Bodies

The Apostolic Church in Canada
Apostolic Church of Pentecost of Canada,
Inc.
Church of God (Cleveland, Tenn.)
The Church of God of Prophecy in Canada
Elim Fellowship of Evangelical Churches and
Ministers
Foursquare Gospel Church of Canada
Independent Assemblies of God International
(Canada)
The Pentecostal Assemblies of Canada
Pentecostal Assemblies of Newfoundland
United Pentecostal Church of Canada

Presbyterian Bodies

Presbyterian Church in America (Canadian
Section)
The Presbyterian Church in Canada

Reformed Bodies

Canadian and American Reformed Churches
Christian Reformed Church in North America
Reformed Church in Canada
The United Church of Canada

The Reformed Episcopal Church of Canada
The Roman Catholic Church in Canada
The Salvation Army in Canada
Seventh-Day Adventist Church in Canada
United Brethren Church in Canada
Universal Fellowship of Metropolitan
Community Churches

203

5. The Emerging Electronic Church

Information from religious bodies and cooperative organizations in Canada and the United States is now widely available "on line" and in electronic form. With phenomenal speed and little cost one can have instantaneous contact for news, disaster updates, research data, program information, bulletin notes for the Sunday service or contact with a staff member of a local church or a regional, national, or international body.

The "home page" addresses listed here are but the tip of the iceberg. From making one contact you will find a variety of additional World Wide Web addresses and active links to local and international bodies. For example, a query to the home page of the Evangelical Lutheran Church in America will enable you to find the name and map location of the local congregation nearest your home. You may also find that congregation has its own "home page" providing information you would want to consider before deciding to visit or affiliate. A different example is provided by The United Methodist Church Board of Church and Society. From their home page you can link to the text for all of the legislation currently being considered in the House and Senate of the United States. From the National Council of the Churches of Christ U.S.A. home page you can link to the Yearbook pages, Church World Service, and the World Council of Churches and from these to many other sites as you will see below. The "home pages" may include only text or may have color graphics, color photos, sound, and/or animation.

Almost every Internet service provider (America On Line, for example) lists a variety of sources on religion including a variety of real time "chat rooms" where one can meet to discuss spirituality, theology, or any other topic that seems of interest. Further, most service providers, but particularly Yahoo and Alta Vista, list links to Roman Catholic, Buddhist, Muslim, Evangelical, and Interfaith groups. One can contact mission organizations, teen groups, women's groups and other special interest groups.

Space here is limited so only a few key addresses are being provided. Additional E-mail and Website information is provided in separate chapters (see "United States Cooperative Organizations"). With these addresses, however, your connection is virtually limitless.

Databases and search engines are listed first followed by religious bodies, regional and local ecumenical bodies, seminaries, and finally periodicals. A special feature includes contact information for disaster response agencies and world religious bodies.

Helpful Databases and Search Engines for Local Churches and Denominations

A good place to begin your search if you are looking for general information is with one of the following church search engines. Links to some of these search engines are available at the World Council of Churches site. You can go directly to http://www.wcc-coe.org and then link to these.

Christian Connection—Website: http://www.amherst.edu/~drsharp/cc/churches.html
This resource, sponsored by Amherst University and Christianity.Net, includes a directory of over 7,000 local churches, and provides maps and information on most of the listed churches.

Christianity.Net Church Locator—Website: http://www.christianity.net/churchlocator/CLhelp.html
Sponsored by Christianity.Net, this resource lets one browse all the United States churches by region, denomination, and key word searches, provides registry for persons wishing to add churches to the list, and offers help with building church websites.

Christian Web Directory—Churches—Website: http://www.goshen.net/WebDirectory/den.html
Sponsored by Goshen.Net, this resource offers a rather brief list of denominations and independent churches. It also offers free web space for churches wishing to add their pages to the Internet. The grouping of denominations into categories is at times misleading or confusing. It has a church locator to help in finding local churches by region, tradition, and denomination.

Church Online!—Links to Denominational Sites and Resources—Website: http://www.churchonline.com/linksden.html
This page was last updated in November 1997, and many of the links on it are no longer working, while the working ones often point to relay pages, which will gradually expire over time. Lists by region and denomination.

Church Surf Christian Directory—Website: http://www.churchsurf.com/churches/
Churchsurf.Com lists over 8000 congregations worldwide and is searchable by location and denomination. While churches are listed worldwide, the lion's share of the congregations listed is in the United States and Canada.

Cross Search Church andDenominational Resources—Website: http://www.crosssearch.com/Church_and_Denominational_Resources/
This site has listings for congregations, denominations, church service and related organizations. Social and community groups are also included in this partial listing.

In the Footsteps of the Lord Churches and Organizations—Website: http://www.xensei.com/ users/Angel/Churches.html
A worldwide general listing of Christian organizations, evangelism outreaches, denominations, and ministries.

Net Ministries Church Directory—Website: http://netministries.org/churches.htm#denoms
Consists primarily of lists of congregations and local churches, mainly in the United States, but some worldwide. Listings are given by region and denomination.

Yahoo! Society and Culture Directory—Website: http://www.yahoo.com/Society_ and_ Culture/ Religion/Faiths_and_Practices/Christianity/Denominations _and_Sects/
This is a large, high-level resource that is rather thorough, though the links relate mostly to United States churches and may not always be active.

Houses of Worship, Sponsored by the American Bible Society—Website: http://www.hows.net/

U.S. Religious Bodies

Advent Christian Church (Official)—Website: http://www.adventchristian.org/index.htm

Advent Christian Fellowship (Official)—E-mail: mbalasa@ix.netcom.com
Website: http://acf.net/

African Methodist Episcopal Church (Official)—E-mail: rsh@amenet.org
Website: http://www.amenet.org/ame.htm

African Methodist Episcopal Zion Church (Official)—E-mail: whoms@nonprofit.net
Website: http://www.nonprofit.net/whoms/

Albanian Orthodox Archdiocese in America (Official)—Website: http://www.oca.org/oca/al/

Allegheny Wesleyan Methodist Connection—E-mail: awmc@juno.com
Website: http://c1web.com/local_info/churches/aw.html

Amana Colonies Online Resource—Website: http://www.jeonet.com/amanas/

American Baptist Association (Official)—E-mail: bssc@abaptist.org
Website: http://www.abaptist.org/

American Baptist Churches in the U. S. A (Official)—E-mail: abcusa@icdc.com
Website: http://www.abc-usa.org

American Evangelical Christian Churches (Directory)—E-mail: alpha@strato.net

American Orthodox Church—E-mail: PatriarchV@webtv.net
Website: http://www.freeyellow.com/members2/aocinc/page1.html

American Rescue Workers (Official)—E-mail: amerscwk@csrlink.net
Website: http://www.arwus.org/

Anglican Catholic Church (Official)—E-mail: FrShort@anglicancatholic.org
Website: http://www.anglicancatholic.org/

Anglican Church in America (Official)—E-mail: cluesing@jetcity.com
Website: http://www.acahome.org/

Anglican Orthodox Church (Official)—E-mail: JCRyle1816@aol.com
Website: http://www.netministries.org/churches/ch01051/

Anglican Province of Christ the King (Official)—E-mail: webmaster@episcopalnet.org
Website: http://www.episcopalnet.org/

Antiochian Orthodox Christian Archdiocese of North America—
E-mail: archdiocese@antiochian.org
Website: http://www.aaron.org/

Apostolic Catholic Assyrian Church of the East (Official)
—Website: http://www.cired.org/ace.html

Apostolic Catholic Church in America (Official)—E-mail: apcathch@aol.com
Website: http://members.aol.com/apcathch/index.html

Apostolic Catholic Church of America (Official)—E-mail: rmgubala@aol.com
Website: http://netministries.org/see/churches/ch01792

Apostolic Christian Church of America (Official)—E-mail: Webmaster@ApostolicChristian.org
Website: http://www.apostolicchristian.org/

Apostolic Christian Church (Official)—E-mail: webmaster@bibleviews.com
Biblical Viewpoints Publications/Bible Views Website: http://www.mich.com/~lhaines/index.html

Apostolic Faith Mission Church of God (Official)—E-mail: webmaster@antioch.com.sg

Apostolic Faith (Mission of Portland, OR) Church (Official)—E-mail: webmaster@apostolicfaith.org
Website: http://www.apostolicfaith.org/

Apostolic Lutheran Church of America (Official)—
Website: http://www.digitmaster.com/church/apostolic.html

Apostolic Orthodox Catholic Church—E-mail: idyll@pe.net
Website: http://www.pe.net/~idyll/para1.htm

Apostolic Orthodox Church (Official)—E-mail: olmercyrjb@aol.com
Our Lady of Mercy Retreat Center—Website: http://www.interinc.com/Allfaiths/AOC/

Apostolic Overcoming Holy Church of God, Inc. (Unofficial)—E-mail: aoh@pdnt.com
AOH Church of God Homepage (Sheriff Temple)—Website: http://www.prairienet.org/staoh/

Armenian Apostolic Church of America (Official)—E-mail: prelacy@gis.net
Armenian Prelacy Home Page—Website: http://www.armprelacy.org/

Armenian Evangelical Church (Unofficial Links Page)—Website: http://cacc-sf.org/c-alinks.html

Assemblies of God Church General Council (Official)—E-mail: opr@ag.org

Assemblies of God Online! (General Council of the Assemblies of God—USA)—
Website: http://www.ag.org/

Associate Reformed Presbyterian Church (Official)—E-mail: leland@arpsynod.org
Website: http://www.arpsynod.org/

Association of Free Lutheran Congregations (Official)—E-mail: webmaster@aflc.org
Website: http://www.aflc.org/

Baptist Bible Fellowship International (Official)—Website: http://www.bbfi.org/

Baptist General Conference (Official)—E-mail: rsrbgc@aol.com
Website: http://www.bgc.bethel.edu/

Baptist Missionary Association (Official)—E-mail: webmaster@bmaweb.net
Website: http://www.bmaweb.net/

Baptist Missionary Association of America (Official)—E-mail: jwadams1@concentric.net
Website: http://www.concentric.net/~Jwadams1/

Berean Fellowship Church (Berean Fundamental Church)—E-mail: webmaster@bereanfellowship.org
Welcome To Berean Fellowship Church OnLine!—
Website: http://home.sprynet.com/sprynet/barryj/ber__new.htm

Bible Church of Christ, Inc. (Official)—Website: http://www.tbcc.org/

Bible Fellowship Church (Official)—E-mail: EricClontz@juno.com
Website: http://www.bfc.org/

Bible Fellowship Evangelical Free Church (Official)—Website: http://www.bfefc.org/

Bible Holiness Church (Unofficial)- Nashville, CitySearch—
Website: http://www.nashville.citysearch.com/e/v/nastn/0003/01/19/

Bible Presbyterian Church (Official)—E-mail: moderator@bpc.org
Website: http://www.bpc.org/

Bible Way Church of Our Lord Jesus Christ World Wide, Inc. (Directory)
ChurchSurf Church Search Results—
Website: http://www.churchsurf.com/cgi-bin/topical.pl?denomination=Church+of+Our+Lord+Jesus+Christ+of+the+Apostolic+Faith

Brethren Church National Office (Official)—E-mail: brethren@bright.net
Website: http://www.apollotrust.com/~brethren/

Bruderhof Community (Official)—Plough Online—Website: http://www.bruderhof.org/

Byzantine Catholic Church in America (Unofficial)—E-mail: 73004.1253@Compuserve.com.
Website: http://www.byzcath.org/

Byzantine—Melkite Orthodox Church, Eparchy of Newton (Official)—
E-mail: stamm01@dsha.k12.wi.useparchy
Website: http://www.dsha.k12.wi.us/Melkite/eparchy.htm

Romanian Byzantine Catholic Parishe—Website: http://www.epix.net/~byzantin/rom.html

Byzantine-Catholic Eparchy (Official)—E-mail: byzruth@aol.com
The Eparchy of Passaic—Website: http://members.aol.com/byzruth/index.htm

Calvary Chapel Churches (Unofficial and Directory)—Website: http://calvarychapel.com/

Canterbury Shaker Village (Official)—E-mail: csv@newww.com
Website: http://www.shakers.org/

Cathars (Assemblies of Good Christians) (Official)—E-mail: assembly@surfsup.net
Website: http://www.surfsup.net/cathar/welcome.htm

Catholic Apostolic Church of Antioch—E-mail: antioch1@swcp.com
Website: http://www.swcp.com/~antioch1/

Catholic Church of the Americas (Official)—E-mail: CCA1196@aol.com
Website: http://207.55.155.28/cca/

Celtic Christian Orthodox Catholic Church (Official)—E-mail: MotherRebecca@celticrite.org
Website: http://www.celticrite.org/

Charismatic Episcopal Church International Communion—E-mail: webdeacon@iccec.org
Website: http://www.iccec.org/

Chinese Christian Fellowship (Official)—E-mail: mitccf-core@mit.edu
Website: http://www.mit.edu/afs/athena/activity/m/mitccf/www/home.html

Christ Catholic Church International (Official)—E-mail: dwmullan@sympatico.ca
Website: http://www3.sympatico.ca/dwmullan/#menu

Christadelphians (Official)—E-mail: rhoades@christadelphian.com
Website: http://www.christadelphian.com/

Christian and Missionary Alliance (Official)—E-mail: 70570.3457@compuserve.com
Alliance Denomination Page—Website: http://cma-world.com/wel-1.htm

Christian Brethren (Plymouth Brethren) (Unofficial Information Page)—
E-mail: dwyman@cloudnet.com
Website: http://www.cloudnet.com/~dwyman/anonymous1.html)

Christian Catholic Church USA [Old Catholic] (Official)—E-mail: wings19@intellinet.com
Website: http://www.interinc.com/Allfaiths/cccusa

Christian Church (Disciples of Christ) (Official)—E-mail: cmiller@oc.disciples.org
Website: http://www.disciples.org/

Christian Church of North America (Official)—E-mail: ccna@nauticom.net
Website: http://www.ccna.org/

Christian Churches and Churches of Christ (Official—E-mail: garcia@church-of-christ.org
Website: http://church-of-christ.org/christ.html

Christian Holiness Partnership (Official)—E-mail: bbpa28a@prodigy.com
Website: http://www.holiness.org/

Christian International Ministries and Churches (Official)—E-mail: cinpm@arc.net
Christian International, FL—A Prophetic & Apostolic—Website: http://www.ci-ministries.org/

Christian Methodist Episcopal Church (Official)—E-mail: lake42@avana.net
Website: http://clever.net/thelake/cme/index2.htm

Christian Reformed Church in North America (Official)—E-mail: btgh@crcna.org
Website: http://www.crcna.org/

Christian Union (Christian Union Bible College) (Information Page)—
E-mail:greenoh@rocketmail.com
Website: http://www.greenfield-ohio.com/green/p197.htm

Church of Antioch (Official)—E-mail: jhjensen@teleport.com
Website: http://www.teleport.com/~jhjensen/gnosis/sri/antioch.htm

Church of the Brethren (Official)—E-mail: cobweb@brethren.org
Website: http://www.brethren.org/

Church of Christ in Christian Union (Official)—E-mail: steinbpa@juno.com
Website: http://www.bright.net/~cccuhq/

Church of Christ, Scientist (Official)—E-mail: clerk@csps.com
Website: http://www.tfccs.com/

Church of God [Anderson, Indiana] (Official)—E-mail: baird@netdirect.net
Welcome To The Church of God Online—Website: http://www.chog.org/

Church of God [Charleston, Tennessee] (Official)—Website: http://www.thechurchofgod.org/

Church of God by Faith, Inc. (Official)—Website: http://www.cogbf.org/

Church of God in Christ (Official)—Website: http://www.cogic.org/

Church of God in Christ, Mennonite (Unofficial)—E-mail: webmaster@bibleviews.com
Website: http://www.bibleviews.com/holdeman.html

Church of God, in Truth (Official)—E-mail: cogintruth@kiwi.net
Welcome to the Church of God, in Truth—Website: http://www.flash.net/~cogit/

Church of God International [Cleveland, TN] (Official)—E-mail: atlbc@mindspring.com
Welcome to the Church of God, General Conference Web—Website: http://www.abc-coggc.org/

Church of God of Prophecy (Official)—E-mail: cogopinfo@cogop.org
Website: http://www.cogop.org/

Church of God [Seventh Day] (Official)—E-mail: bible@bible.ca
Official beliefs of the church of God (Seventh day)—
Website: http://www.bible.ca/cr-church-God-7thday.htm

Church of Our Lord Jesus Christ (Directory)—
Website: http://www.churchsurf.com/cgi-bin/topical.pl?denomination=Church+of+Our+Lord+Jesus+
Christ+of+the+Apostolic+Faith

Church of Jesus Christ of Latter-day Saints (Official)—Website: http://www.lds.org/

Church of Our Lord Jesus Christ of the Apostolic Faith, Inc. (Directory)∏
Website: http://www.churchsurf.com/cgi-bin/topical.pl?denomination=Church+of+Our+Lord+Jesus+
Christ+of+the+Apostolic+Faith

Church of the Brethren (Official)—E-mail: cobweb@brethren.org
Website: http://www.brethren.org/

Church of the Lutheran Brethren in America (Official)—E-mail: clba@clba.org
Website: http://www.clba.org/

Church of the Lutheran Confession (Official)—E-mail: JohnHLau@juno.com
Website: http://www.primenet.com/~mpkelly/clc/clc.html

Church of the Nazarene (Official)—E-mail: webmaster@nazarene.org
Website: http://www.nazarene.org/

Churches of God General Conference (Official)—E-mail: wwb@brt.bright.net
Website: http://www.cggc.org/

Communion of Evangelical Episcopal Churches (Official)—E-mail: info@theceec.org
Website: http://www.theceec.org/

Concordia Lutheran Conference—Scriptural Publications—
Website: http://lonestar.texas.net/~dsteinke/scrippub/

Congregational Holiness Church, Inc. (Official)—E-mail: chchurch@bellsouth.net
Website: http://personal.atl.bellsouth.net/atl/c/h/chchurch/church.htm

Conservative Baptist Association of America (Official)—E-mail: cba@cb.usa.com
Website: http://www.cbamerica.org/

Conservative Congregational Christian Conference (Unofficial)—E-mail: cccc4@juno.com
About the Conservative Congregational Christian Conference—
Website: http://members.aol.com/cypreschap/cypresshtml/cypress3.htm

Conservative Lutheran Association—E-mail: fsinfo@FaithSeminary.edu
Website: http://www.faithseminary.edu/

Coptic Orthodox Churches in the Diaspora (Official)—E-mail: Webmaster@coptic.org
Website: http://www.coptic.org/

Cumberland Presbyterian Church (Official)—E-mail: pmj@cumberland.org
Website: http://www.cumberland.org/

Cumberland Presbyterian Church in America (Official)—E-mail: mleslie598@aol.com
Website: http://www.cumberland.org/cpca/

Diocese of the Armenian Church of America (Official)—E-mail: amyag@stleon.org
Website: http://www.100anniversary.com/

Elim Fellowship (Mid-Atlantic Regional Home Page)—
Website: http://www.cyberenet.net/~revival/elim.htm

Episcopal Church (Official)—E-mail: Questions@episcopalian.org
Website: http://www.episcopalian.org/

Estonian Evangelical Lutheran Church in Exile (Official)—
E-mail: eelk.Toronto@churchoffice.com
Website: http://www.churchoffice.com/eelk/eelkto.html

Evangelical Anglican Church in America (Official)—
Website: http://www.dircon.co.uk/aglo/evangeli.htm

Evangelical Catholic Church (Official)—Website: http://members.aol.com/EvCathCh/index.html

Evangelical Church Alliance (OFFICIAL)—E-mail: eca@keynet.net
Website: http://www.keynet.net/~eca/

Evangelical Congregational Church (Official)—Website: http://www.eccenter.com/church/

Evangelical Covenant Church (Official)—Website: http://www.covchurch.org/

Evangelical Free Church of America (Official)—E-mail: webmaster@efca.org
Website: http://www.efca.org/

Evangelical Friends International (Official)—E-mail: carym@earthlink.net
Website: http://www.evangelical-friends.org/

Evangelical Lutheran Church in America (Official)—E-mail: info@elca.org
Website: http://www.elca.org/

Evangelical Lutheran Synod (Official)—E-mail: elsmedia@blc.edu
Evangelical Lutheran Synod—Website: http://www.evluthsyn.org/

Evangelical Mennonite Church Page (Official)—Website: http://www.brookside.org/emc.htm

Evangelical Methodist Church (Official)
About Evangelical Methodist Church and it's conservative and Christian
Bible teachings about Jesus Christ—Website: http://www.emchurch.org/

Evangelical Presbyterian Church (Official)—Website: http://www.epc.org/

Fellowship of Evangelical Bible Churches—E-mail address: <febcoma@aol.com>
Website: http://www.lib.uwaterloo.ca/mhsc/contents/F4553ME.html

Fellowship of Grace Brethren Churches (Official)—Website: http://207.51.167.37/

Fire-Baptized Holiness Church of God of the Americas (Official)—Website: http://www.fbhchurch.org/

First Evangelical Church Association (Official)—Website: http://www.feca.org

Free Methodist Church of North America (Official)—Website: http://www.fmcna.org/

Free Presbyterian Church (Official)—Website: http://www.freepres.org/

Free Reformed Churches of North America (Official)—Website: http://www.frcna.org/

Friends General Conference (Official)—Website: http://www.quaker.org/fgc/

Friends United Meeting (Official)—Website: http://www.fum.org/

Full Gospel Fellowship of Churches and Ministers International—E-mail: fgfcmi@aol.com

General Association of General Baptist Churches (Unofficial)—
Website: http://www.angelfire.com/mo/genbap/

General Association of Regular Baptist Churches (Official)—Website: http://www.garbc.org/

General Association of Separate Baptists in Christ (Official)—Website: http://www.separatebaptist.org/

General Church of the New Jerusalem (Official)—Website: http://www.newchurch.org/

General Conference of Mennonite Brethren Churches (Official)—
Website: http://www.mobynet.com/mbms/genconf.html

Global Church of God (World Ahead—Publishing House for the Denomination)—
Website: http://www.worldahead.org

Gospel Hall Churches- Gospel Hall FAQ (Frequently Asked Questions and Links)—
Website: http://www.lookup.com/Homepages/85793/home.html

Grace Church (Official)- THE GRACELIFE(tm) INTERNET MINISTRIES MENU PAGE—
Website: http://www.mindspring.com/~mamcgee/gracelife.html

Grace Gospel Fellowship (Official)—E-mail: ggf@iserv.net
Website: http://www.iserv.net/~ggf/

Greek Orthodox Archdiocese of America (Official)—E-mail: archdiocese@goarch.org
Website: http://www.goarch.org/

Holy Church of Christ, Apostolic Faith (Official)—E-mail: sstreet@netpath.net
Website: http://www.netpath.net/~sstreet/hcc.htm

Holy Ukrainian Autocephalous Orthodox Church in Exile (Official)—
Website: http://www.atlantis-bbs.com/uaoc/

House of God the Holy Church of the Living God, the Pillar and Ground of the Truth, Inc.—
E-mail: dayton@houseofgod.org
Website: http://www.concentric.net/~whouston/

Hungarian Reformed Church in America (Information Page)—
Website: http://www.egyed.com/magyar/szerv/am/nj/nj.amre.html

Hutterian Brethren (Hutterites) (Unofficial)—E-mail: mb000476@mb.sympatico.ca
Website: http://www.hutterianbrethren.com/

Independent Catholic Churches of America (Links Page)—
Website: http://www.wp.com/wdpeck/c_links.htm

Independent Fundamental Churches of America (Official)—E-mail:gregory@ifca.org
Website: http://www.ifca.org/

Indonesian Full Gospel Fellowship (Official)—E-mail: webmaster@hartanto.com
Website: http://www.ifgf.org/

International Church of the Foursquare Gospel (Official)—Website: http://www.foursquare.org/

International Churches of Christ (Official)—Website: http://www.icoc.org/index.html

International Conference of Reformed Churches (Official)—E-mail: rcjanssen@compuserve.com
Website: http://ourworld.compuserve.com/homepages/rcjanssen/icrc.htm

International Council of Community Churches (Official)—
Website: http://www.akcache.com/community/iccc-nat.html

International Ministerial Fellowship—E-mail: info@i-m-f.org
Website: http://www.i-m-f.org/

International Pentecostal Church of Christ (Official)—E-mail: ipcc@aol.com
Website: http://members.aol.com/hqipcc/index.htm

International Pentecostal Holiness Church (Official)—E-mail: webman@iphc.org
Website: http://www.iphc.org/

Latvian Evangelical Lutheran Church in America (Unofficial Web Page)—E-mail: lirs@lirs.org
Website: http://www.lirs.org/

Liberal Catholic Church (Official)—E-mail: warnon@eideti.com
Website: http://annex1-18.infi-net.com/English/Organizations/lcc.gb/lcc.html

Light of the World Christian Churches (Official)—Website: http://www.ltw.org/home.html

Lutheran Church—Missouri Synod (Official)—E-mail: webmaster@lcms.org
Website: http://www.lcms.org/

Lutheran Churches of the Reformation (Official)—Website: http://www.willinet.net/~pella/lcr.html

Lutheran Confessional Synod (Official)—E-mail: lcsbish@aol.com
Website: http://www.luthconf.org/

Lutheran Ministerium and Synod (Official)—E-mail: revralphs@juno.com
Website: http://www.aurorawdc.com/lms-usa/lmsintro.htm

Lutheran World Federation (Official)—E-mail: info@lutheranworld.org
Website: http://www.lutheranworld.org/

Mar Thoma Church (Official)—E-mail: webmaster@marthomachurch.org
Website: http://www.marthomachurch.org/

Mennonite Church (Official)—E-mail: mcgb@juno.com
The Mennonite Churches—Website: http://www.mennonites.org/

Missionary Church (Official)—E-mail: mcdenomusa@aol.com
Website: http://www.sweetwater.com/mcusa

Moravian Church in America (Official)—E-mail: illumination@compuserve.com
Website: http://www.moravian.org/

National Association of Free Will Baptists (Official)—E-mail: webmaster@nafwb.org
Website: http://www.nafwb.org/

National Baptist Convention of America, Inc. (Official)—E-mail: nbyc1@aol.com
Website: http://members.aol.com/nbyc1/nbca.html

National Baptist Convention, U. S. A., Inc. (Official)—Website: http://www.nbcusa.org/nbcusa.html

National Spiritualist Association of Churches (Official)—E-mail: pcook@nsac.org
Website: http://www.nsac.org/chrchg_l.htm

Netherlands Reformed Congregations (List of Congregations and Links)—
Website: http://206.67.165.122/nrc/nrc.html

New Apostolic Church—International (Official)—E-mail: info@www.nak.org
http://www.nak.org/home-gb.html

New Testament Association of Independent Baptist Churches—E-mail: church@ibnet.org
Website: http://www.ibnet.org/nta.htm

North American Baptist Conference (Unofficial)—Website: http://www.fbceg.org/nab.htm

Open Bible Standard Churches (Official)—E-mail: Webmaster@OpenBible.org
Website: http://www.openbible.org/

Orthodox American Church (Information Page)—Website: http://www.qc.edu/~mmlqc/oac/

Orthodox Catholic Church in North America—E-mail: oldroman@postmark.net
Orthodox Catholic Church in North America—Monkton, MD—
Website: http://www.netministries.org/see/churches/ch04408

Orthodox Catholic Church of America (Official)—E-mail: PatriarchV@webtv.net
    The Orthodox Catholic Church—Bay City, MI—
    Website: http://netministries.org/see/churches/ch04589
Orthodox Church in America (Official)—E-mail: info@oca.org
    Website: http://www.oca.org/oca/
Orthodox Presbyterian Church (Official)—Website: http://www.opc.org/
Patriarchal Parishes of the Russian Orthodox Church in the U. S. A. (Official)
    A Worldwide Directory of Parishes in the Russian Orthodox Church Abroad ROCOR) —
    Website: http://www.orthodox.net/directry/index.htm
Pentecostal Assemblies of the World (Directory)—
    Website: http://php.indiana.edu/~kbraddy/churches.html
Pentecostal Church of God (Official)—E-mail: pcg@clandjop.com
    Website: http://www.churchsurf.com/host/mo/derek2_html/index.html
Polish National Catholic of America (Official)—Website: http://www.pncc.org/
Presbyterian Church in America (Official)—Website: http://www.pcanet.org/
Presbyterian Church (U. S. A.) (Official)—Website: http://www.pcusa.org/pcusa/pcusa.htm
Primitive Methodist Church in the U. S. A. (Unofficial)—
    Website: http://www.hostme.com/primmethod/
Progressive National Baptist Convention, Inc. (Official)—E-mail: info@pnbc.org
    Website: http://www.pnbc.org/
Protestant Reformed Churches in America (Official)—Website: http://www.iserv.net/~prc/prc.html
Reformed Church in America (Official)—E-mail: rcamail@iserv.net
    Website: http://www.rca.org/pages/page.idc?page=homepage.index.html
Reformed Church in the United States (Official)—E-mail: Frank.Walker@mci2000.com
    Website: http://www.geocities.com/Heartland/1136/rcus.html
Reformed Episcopal Church (Official)—Website: http://recus.org/
Reformed Presbyterian Church of North America (Official)—Website: http://www.reformed.com/rpcna/
Refuge Temple Church (OFFICIAL)—E-mail: refuge-temple@usa.net
    Website: http://www.churchsurf.com/host/world/refuge/
Religious Society of Friends (Yearly Meetings Listings for the Americas)—
    E-mail: wsamuel@cpcug.org
    Calendar of Friends' (Quaker) Yearly Meetings—
    Website: http://cpcug.org/user/wsamuel/cym.html#Am
Religious Society of Friends (Unaffiliated Meetings) (Official)—E-mail: simon@csc.liv.ac.uk
    Quaker FWCC page index—Website: http://www.quaker.org/fwcc/
Reorganized Church of Jesus Christ of Latter Day Saints—E-mail: snaylor@rlds.org
    Website: http://www.rlds.org/
Roman Catholic Church (Official)—E-mail: webmaster@nccbuscc.org
    National Conference of Catholic Bishops/United States Catholic Conference—
    Website: http://www.nccbuscc.org/
Romanian Orthodox Church in America - The Trinity: Episcopate—
    Website: http://www.itp.tsoa.nyu.edu/~student/simi/sfantamaria/episcopate.html
Romanian Orthodox Episcopate of America (Official)—E-mail: roeasolia@aol.com
    Website: http://www.roea.org/roea.html
Russian Orthodox Church Outside of Russia (Official)—Website: http://www.synod.com/
Salvation Army International Headquarters (Official)—E-mail: websa@SalvationArmy.org
    Website: http://www.sarmy.org/
Separate Baptists in Christ (Official)—E-mail: mail@separatebaptist.org
    General Association of Separate Baptists in Christ—Website: http://www.separatebaptist.org/
Serbian Orthodox Church in the U. S. A. and Canada (Official)—E-mail: gsladic@mcs.com
    The Diocesan Observer—Website: http://www.mcs.net/~gsladic/
Seventh-day Adventist Church (Official)—E-mail: info@adventist.org
    Website: http://www.adventist.org/
Seventh Day Baptist General Conference, USA and Canada (Official)—E-mail: sdbgen@inwave.com
    Seventh Day Baptist Church—Website: http://www.seventhdaybaptist.org/
Southern Baptist Convention (Official)—E-mail: webmaster@bssb.com
    Website: http://www.sbcnet.org/

Sovereign Grace Baptists (Links Page)—E-mail: libcfl@aol.com
LIBC—Church Directory—Website: http://users.aol.com/libcfl/direct.htm

Swedenborgian Church (Official)—E-mail: manager@centraloffice.swedenborg.org
Website: http://www.swedenborg.org/

New Church (Swedenborgian) (Official)—E-mail: ncquest@aol.com
The New Church—Website: http://www.newchurch.org/

Syrian Orthodox Church of Antioch (Official)—
Website: http://wwwstaff.murdoch.edu.au/~t-issa/syr/syr.htm

Triumph the Church and Kingdom of God in Christ, Inc., (International)—
Website: http://www.1411.com/cities\zzbiz/ZZ123083.htm

Ukrainian Orthodox Church of USA (Official)—E-mail: Consistory@uocofusa.org
Website: http://www.uocofusa.org/

Unitarian Universalist Association (Official)—E-mail: info@uua.org
Website: http://www.uua.org/

United Brethren in Christ Church (Official)—Website: http://www.ub.org/

United Church of Christ (Official)—Website: http://www.ucc.org/

United Church of God (Official)—E-mail: webmaster@ucgstp.org
Website: http://www.ucgstp.org/united.htm

United House of Prayer (Official)—E-mail: dayton@houseofgod.org
The House of God Main Page—Website: http://www.concentric.net/~whouston/

United Methodist Church (Official)—E-mail: infoserv@umcom.umc.org
United Methodist Information—Website: http://www.umc.org/

United Pentecostal Church, International (Official)—Website: http://www.upci.org/

United Zion Church (Official)—E-mail: archbishopgregory@usa.net
United Zion Retirement Community—Website: http://www.uzrc.org/

Universal Fellowship of Metropolitan Community Churches (Official)—
E-mail: charles.bidwell@ualberta.ca
Website: http://www.ualberta.ca/~cbidwell/ufmcc/uf-home.htm

Universal Spiritualist Association (Official)—Website: http://www.spiritualism.org/

Wesleyan Church (Official)—Website: http://www.wesleyan.org/

Wesleyan Holiness Association of Churches (Official)—E-mail: webadmin@wesley.nnc.edu
The Wesley Center for Applied Theology—Website: http://wesley.nnc.edu/

Western Orthodox Church in America (Official)—E-mail: info@woca.org
Website: http://www.woca.org/

Wisconsin Evangelical Lutheran Synod (Official)—E-mail: webbin@sab.wels.net
Website: http://www.wels.net/

Worldwide Church of God (Official)—E-mail: info@wcg.org
Website: http://www.wcg.org/

Canadian Religious Bodies

American Evangelical Christian Churches of Canada (Official Home Page)—
Website: http://home.istar.ca/~mbittle/aecc.htm

Anglican Catholic Church of Canada (Official Home Page)—Website: http://www.zeuter.com/~accc/

Anglican Church of Canada (Official Home Page)—Website: http://www.anglican.ca/

Antiochian Orthodox Christian Archdiocese of North America (Official Home Page)—
Website: http://www.antiochian.org/

Apostolic Christian Church (Nazarene)—Biblical Viewpoints Publications/Bible Views—
Website: http://www.mich.com/~lhaines/index.html

Apostolic Church in Canada—Website: http://www.apostolic.ca/

Apostolic Church of Pentecost of Canada, Inc. (Official Home Page) —
Website: http://www.illuminart.com/acop/index.htm

Armenian Evangelical Church
ARMENIAN EVANGELICAL CHURCH OF MONTREAL—Montreal,QC—
Website: http://netministries.org/see/churches/ch01243

Armenian Holy Apostolic Church—Canadian Diocese—http://www.100anniversary.com/slic.htm

Assemblies of God International Fellowship (Independent/Not Affiliated)—
E-mail: david.ellyatt@odyssey.on.ca
Independent Assemblies of God International (Canada)—
Website: http://www.odyssey.on.ca/~david.ellyatt/internat.html

Associated Gospel Churches (Official Home Page)—Website: http://www.octonet.com/home/

Association of Regular Baptist Churches (Official Home Page)
Welcome to the General Association of Regular Baptist Churches—
Website: http://www.garbc.org/garbc/index.html

Baptist Bible Fellowship International (Official Home Page)—Website: http://www.bbfi.org/

Baptist General Conference of Canada (Official Home Page)—
Website: http://skylite.datanet.ab.ca/users/bgcc/

Bible Presbyterian Church (Official Home Page)—Website: http://www.bpc.org/

Brethren in Christ Church, Canadian Conference (Official Home Page)
Mennonite and Brethren in Christ Resource Centre—
Website: http://www.imagitek.com/mcc/

Bruderhof Communities (Official Home Page)
Bruderhof Communities: Plough Online—Website: http://www.bruderhof.org/

Canadian and American Reformed Churches (Official Home Page)—
Website: http://www.cuug.ab.ca:8001/~hoogerdj/carc.html

Canadian Baptist Ministries (Official Home Page)—Website: http://www.cbmin.org/

Canadian Conference of Mennonite Brethren Churches (Official Home Page)—
Website: http://www.cdnmbconf.ca/mb/mbdoc.htm

Canadian Yearly Meeting of the Religious Society of Friends (Official Home Page)—
Website: http://www.web.net/~cym/

Christ Catholic Church International (Official Home Page)—
Website: http://www3.sympatico.ca/dwmullan/#menu

Christadelphia Worldwide (Official Home Page)—Website: http://www.christadelphia.org/

Christian and Missionary Alliance (Official Home Page) —
Website: http://www.gospelcom.net/cmalliance/message/simpson.shtml

Christian Brethren [Plymouth Brethren] (Unofficial Information Page)
PLYMOUTH BRETHREN: Exclusive Raven/Taylor Sect—
Website: http://www.cloudnet.com/~dwyman/anonymous1.html

Christian Church (Disciples of Christ) (Official Home Page)—Website: http://www.disciples.org/

Christian Church of North America (Official Home Page)—Website: http://www.ccna.org/

Christian Churches and Churches of Christ (Official Home Page)—
Website: http://church-of-christ.org/christ.html

Christian International Ministries and Churches (Official Home Page)
WWW pages of Christian International related Ministries and Churches—
Website: http://www.oru.edu/CI/www/www.html

Christian Reformed Church in North America (Official Home Page)—Website: http://www.crcna.org/

Church of God [Anderson, Indiana] (Official Home Page)—Website: http://www.chog.org/

Church of God [Cleveland, Tennessee]—Index Page—Website: http://www.chofgod.org/

Church of God in Christ, Mennonite (Unofficial Home Page)—
Website: http://www.bibleviews.com/holdeman.html

Church of God of Prophecy (Official Home Page)—Website: http://www.cogop.org/

Church of Jesus Christ of Latter-day Saints (Official Home Page)—Website: http://www.lds.org/

Church of the Lutheran Brethren in America (Official Home Page)—Website: http://www.clba.org/

Church of the Nazarene (Official Home Page)—Website: http://www.nazarene.org/

Churches of Christ in Canada [Non-Instrumental] (Official Home Page)—
Website: http://church-of-christ.org/

Conference of Mennonites in Canada (Official Home Page)—
Website: http://www2.southwind.net/~gcmc/index.html

Congregational Christian Churches in Canada—Website: http://www.io.org/~jimamy/Ccccbeta.html

Coptic Orthodox Churches in the Diaspora (Official Home Page)—Website: http://www.coptic.org/

Elim Fellowship (Official Home Page)—Website: http://www.frontiernet.net/~elim/efexec.htm

Estonian Evangelical Lutheran Church in Exile (Official Home Page)—
Website: http://www.churchoffice.com/eelk/eelkto.html

Evangelical Baptist Missions International (Official Home Page)—Website: http://www.ebm.org/

Evangelical Covenant Church of Canada (Listing of Local Congregations)—
Website: http://www.npcts.edu/cov/chchsa-g.htm

Evangelical Fellowship of Canada (Official)—Website: http://www.efc-canada.com/index.html

Evangelical Free Church of Canada (Official Home Page)—
Website: http://www.twu.ca/efcc/efcc.htm

Evangelical Lutheran Church in Canada [ELCIC] (Official Home Page)—
Website: http://www.wlu.ca/~wwwsem/elcic/ehome.html

Evangelical Mennonite Conference of Canada (Official Home Page)—
Website: http://www.sbcollege.mb.ca/emc/

Evangelical Mennonite Mission Conference (Official Home Page)—
Website: http://www.sbcollege.mb.ca/emmc///

Evangelical Missionary Church of Canada (Official Home Page)—
Website: http://www.cadvision.com/emcc/index.html

Fellowship of Evangelical Baptist Churches in Canada—Website: http://www.fellowship.ca/

Foursquare Gospel Church, District of Canada—E-mail: fgcc@portal.ca

Free Methodist Church in Canada (Official Home Page)—Website: http://www.fmc-canada.org/

Free Presbyterian Church (Official Home Page)—Website: http://www.freepres.org/

Free Will Baptists (Official Home Page)
  International Fellowship of Free Will Baptist Churches—Website: http://www.ifofwbc.org/

General Church of the New Jerusalem—Website: http://www.newchurch.org/

Global Church of God, Canada (Official Home Page)—Website: http://www.globalchurch.ca/

Greek Orthodox Metropolis of Toronto (Official Home Page)—Website: http://www.gocanada.org/

Independent Assemblies of God International [Canada] (Official Home Page)—
Website: http://www.odyssey.on.ca/~david.ellyatt/internat.html

Independent and Nondenominational Churches in Canada (Directory)—
Website: http://www.churchonline.com/canadad/nd/nd.html

Independent Baptist Network (Official Home Page)—Website: http://www.ibnet.org/

Indonesian Full Gospel Fellowship and Indonesian Harvest Outreach (Official Home Page)—
Website: http://ifgfhou.ifgf.org/index.html

International Council of Community Churches of Canada (Official Home Page)
  **Official Site of the Bishop Ordinary, Christian Catholic Rite of Community Churches, &
  General Superintendent for Canada, International Council of Community Churches Site offi-
  ciel de l'évêque ordinaire du rite catholique-chrétien d'églises communautaires et responsable
  du Conseil international des Églises communautaires au Canada**—
  Website: http://www.angelfire.com/biz/saterio/

Lutheran Church - Canada (Official Home Page)—Website: http://www.lutheranchurch-canada.ca/

Mar Thoma Churches of North America and Europe Diocese (Directory)—
  Members list of Trinity Mar Thoma Church, Edmonton, Alberta, Canada—
  Website: http://www.ee.ualberta.ca/~ralex/Members1.html

Mennonite Church (Canada) (Official Home Page)
  Mennonite Central Committee—Website: http://www.mennonitecc.ca/mcc/

Moravian Church (Official Home Page)
  About the Moravian Church—Website: http://home.ptd.net/~boddie/moravians.html
  **Canadian District of the Moravian Church in North America, Northern Province (Official
  Home Page)**—Website: http://www.moravian.org//index.htm

New Church [Swedeborgian] (Official Home Page)—Website: http://www.newchurch.org/

North American Baptist Conference—A Profile (Unofficial Home Page)—
Website: http://www.fbceg.org/nab.htm

Old Catholic Church of Canada—Website: http://netministries.org/see/churches/ch05841

Open Bible Faith Fellowship of Canada (OFFICIAL)—
Website: http://www.obff.com/contents/introduction.htm

Orthodox Church in America—Archdiocese of Canada (Official Home Page)—
Website: http://www.oca.org/OCA/CA/

Patriarchal Parishes of the Russian Orthodox Church in Canada (Official Home Page)—
Website: http://www.cybertap.com/handyman/bishop/
Pentecostal Assemblies of Canada (Official Home Page)—Website: http://www.paoc.org/
Pentecostal Assemblies of Newfoundland (Official Home Page)—Website: http://www.paon.nf.ca/
Presbyterian Church in America (Official Home Page)—Website: http://www.pcanet.org/
Presbyterian Church in Canada (Official Home Page)—Website: http://www.presbycan.ca/
Reformed Church in Canada (Official Home Page)—Website: http://www.reformed-church.ca/
Reformed Episcopal Church of Canada (Diocesan Official Home Pages)
  The Diocese of Central and Eastern Canada—Website: http://www.recus.org/ec.html
  Diocese of Western Canada—Website: http://www.recus.org/wc.html
Reorganized Church of Jesus Christ of Latter Day Saints—Website: http://www.rlds.org/
Roman Catholic Church in Canada (Official Home Page of the Canadian Conference of Catholic Bishops)—Website: http://www.cccb.ca/
Romanian Orthodox Church in America
  The Trinity: Episcopate—
  Website: http://www.itp.tsoa.nyu.edu/~student/simi/sfantamaria/episcopate.html
Romanian Orthodox Episcopate of America (Official Home Page)—
  Website: http://www.roea.org/roea.html
Salvation Army in Canada and Bermuda (Official Home Page)—Website: http://www.sallynet.org/
Serbian Orthodox Church in the U. S. A. and Canada (Official Home Page)
  The Diocesan Observer—Website: http://www.mcs.net/~gsladic/
Seventh-Day Adventist Church in Canada (Official Database of Churches)
  Graphical Seventh-day Adventist Church Finder: Canada—
  Website: http://www.sdanet.org/locator/country.cgi?country=ca
Spiritualist Churches in Canada (Directory)—
  Website: http://www.nucleus.com/~gateway/chur_can.html#directory
Standard Church of America in Canada (Directory)—
  Website: http://www.churchonline.com/canadad/st/st.html
Syrian Orthodox Church of Antioch (Official Home Page)—
  Website: http://www.SyrianOrthodoxChurch.org/
Ukrainian Orthodox Church of Canada (Official Home Page)—Website: http://uocc.ca/
United Brethren Church (Official Home Page)—
  Website: http://www.ub.org/ubcweb/ubcsite.site/index.html
United Church of Canada (Official Home Page)—Website: http://www.uccan.com/
United Pentecostal Church, International (Official Home Page)—Website: http://www.upci.org/
Universal Fellowship of Metropolitan Community Churches (Official Home Page)—
  Website: http://www.ualberta.ca/~cbidwell/ufmcc/uf-home.htm
Wesleyan Church (Official Home Page)—Website: http://www.wesleyan.org/

U.S. Cooperative Organizations

Alban Institute, Inc.—Website: http://www.alban.org
American Bible Society—Website: http://www.americanbible.org
American Council of Christian Churches—Website: http://www.amcouncilc.org
American Friends Service Committee—Website: http://www.afsc.org
The American Theological Library Association, Inc.—
  Website: http://atla.library.vanderbilt.edu/alta/home.html
ADRIS/Association for the Development of Religious Information Services—
  Website: http://www.firestormcom.com/adris
The Association of Theological Schools in the United States and Canada—Website: http://www.ats.edu
Bread For The World—Website: http://www.bread.org
Campus Crusade for Christ International—Website: http://www.ccci.org
CARA-Center for Applied Research in the Apostolate—
  Website: http://www.georgetown.edu/research/cara/index.html
Christian Holiness Partnership—Website: http://www.holiness.org

Christian Management Association—Website: http://www.CMAonline.org

A Christian Ministry in the National Parks—Website: http://www.coolworks.com/showme/acmnp/

Church Women United in the U.S.A.—Website: http://www.churchwomen.org

Evangelical Council for Financial Accountability—Website: www.ecfa.org

Evangelical Press Association—Website: http://www.epassoc.org

Fellowship of Reconciliation—Website: http://www.nonviolence.org/~nvweb/for

International Union of Gospel Missions—Website: http://www.iugm.org

Interreligious Foundation for Community Organization (IFCO)—Website: http://www.ifconews.org

The Lord's Day Alliance of the United States—Website: http://www.gabaptist.org

Lutheran World Relief—Website: http://www.lwr.org/

The Mennonite Central Committee—Website: http://www.mennonitecc.ca/mcc/

National Association of Congregational Christian Churches (Official)—E-mail: naccc@naccc.org
    Website: http://www.naccc.org/

National Association of Evangelicals (Official)—E-mail: nae@nae.net
    Website: http://nae.goshen.net/

National Bible Association—Website: http://www.biblenet.org

National Council of the Churches of Christ in the U.S.A.—Website: http://www.ncccusa.org

National Institute of Business and Industrial Chaplains—Website: http://www.nibic.com

National Interfaith Committee for Worker Justice—Website: http://www.igc.org/nicwi

National Interfaith Hospitality Network—Website: http://www.nihn.org

National Interreligious Service Board for Conscientious Objectors—Website: http://www.nisbco.org

National Religious Broadcasters—Website: http://www.nrb.org

National Woman's Christian Temperance Union—Website: http://www.wctu.org

North American Baptist Fellowship—Website: http://www.bwanet.org

North American Broadcast Section, World Association for Christian Communication—
    Website: http://www.united.edu/nabs/nabs1.htm

Pentecostal/Charismatic Churches of North America—Website: http://www.iphc.org/pccna/index.html

Project Equality, Inc.—Website: http://www.projectequality.org

The Religion Communicators Council, Inc.—Website: http://www.rprc.org

Religion News Service—Website: http://www.religionnews.com

Religion Newswriters Association—Website: http://www.rna.org

Religious Conference Management Association, Inc.—

Standing Conference of Canonical Orthodox Bishops in the Americas—Website: http://www.goarch.org

Vellore Christian Medical College Board (USA), Inc.—Website: http://www.vellorecmc.org

World Council of Churches, United States Office—Website: http://www.wcc-coe.org

YMCA of the USA—Website: http://www.ymca.net

Canadian Cooperative Organizations

Aboriginal Rights Coalition (Project North)—E-mail: arc@istar.ca

The Canadian Council of Churches—E-mail: ccchurch@web.net
    Website: http://www.web.net/~ccchurch

Canadian Society of Biblical Studies/Société Canadienne des Études Bibliques—
    E-mail: mdesjard@mach1.wlu.ca

The Churches' Council on Theological Education in Canada: An Ecumenical Foundation—
    E-mail: ccte@web.net
    Website: www.web.net/~ccte

Ecumenical Coalition for Economic Justice (ECEJ)—E-mail:gattfly@web.net

Evangelical Fellowship of Canada—E-mail: efc@efc-canada.com

Interchurch Communications—E-mail: doug_tindal@national.anglican.ca

Lutheran Council in Canada—E-Mail: sartison@elcic.ca

Project Ploughshares—E-mail: plough@watserv1.uwaterloo.ca
    Website: http://www.ploughshares.ca

Religious Television Associates—E-mail:rbooth@uccan.org

Scripture Union—E-mail: sucan@istar.ca
Website: http://home.istar.ca/~sucan

Student Christian Movement of Canada—E-mail: scmcan@web.net
Website: http://www.web.net/~scmcan/

Taskforce on the Churches and Corporate Responsibility—E-mail: tccr@web.net

Ten Days for Global Justice—E-mail: tendays@web.net
Website: http://www.web.net/~tendays

World Vision Canada—E-mail:info@worldvision.ca

Website: http://www.worldvision.capar

U.S. Local and Regional Ecumenical Bodies

CALIFORNIA
Ecumenical Council of San Diego County—Website: http://home.earthlink.net/~searay1/
CONNECTICUT
Council of Churches and Synagogues of Southwestern Connecticut—
Website: http://www.interfaithcouncil.org
DISTRICT OF COLUMBIA
InterFaith Conference of Metropolitan Washington—Website: http://www.interfaith-metrodc.org/
ILLINOIS
Evanston Ecumenical Action Council—Website: http://members.aol.com/eeachome/eeac.html
Oak Park-River Forest Community of Congregation—
Website: http://www.mcs.net/~grossman/comcong.htm
INDIANA
Indiana Partners for Christian Unity and Mission—
Website: http://members.aol.com/indunity/ipcymhomepage.html
MAINE
Maine Council of Churches—Website: http://www.mainetoday.koz.com/maine/mcc
MICHIGAN
Christian Communication Council of Metropolitan Detroit Churches—
Website: http://users.aol.com/councilweb/index.htm
Grand Rapids Area Center for Ecumenism (GRACE)—Website: http://www.grcmc.org/grace
MINNESOTA
Minnesota Council of Churches—Website: http://www.mnchurches.org
Greater Minneapolis Council of Churches—Website: http://www.gmcc.org
The Joint Religious Legislative Coalition—Website: http://www.jrlc.org
Metropolitan Interfaith Council on Affordable Housing (MICAH)—
Website: http://www.micah.org
St. Paul Area Council of Churches—Website: http://www.center.hamline.edu/spacc
Tri-Council Coordinating Commission—Website: http://www.amcc.org/tcc.html
MISSOURI
Council of Churches of the Ozarks—Website: http://www.anetweb.com/ccozarks
Interfaith Community Services—Website: http://www.inter-serv.org
MONTANA
Montana Association of Churches—
NEW HAMPSHIRE
New Hampshire Council of Churches—Website: http://www.nhchurches.org
NEW MEXICO
New Mexico Conference of Churches—Website: http://www.rt66.com/~nmcc
NEW YORK
New York State Community of Churches, Inc.- A Household of Christians—
Website: http://www.nyscommunityofchurches.org
Schenectady Inner City Ministry—Website: http://www.crisny.org
NORTH CAROLINA
Greensboro Urban Ministry—Website: http://www.greensboro.com/gum
OHIO
Akron Area Association of Churches—Website: http://www.triple-ac.org

OKLAHOMA
Tulsa Metropolitan Ministry—Website: http://www.tumm.org

PENNSYLVANIA
Pennsylvania Conference on Interchurch Cooperation—Website: http://www.pachurches.org
The Pennsylvania Council of Churches—Website: http://www.pachurches.org
Christian Associates of Southwest Pennsylvania—Website: http://www.casp.org
Hanover Area Council of Churches—Website: http://www.netrax.net/~bouchord/hacc.htm
Metropolitan Christian Council of Philadelphia—Website: http://www.mccp.org

VIRGINIA
Virginia Council of Churches, Inc.—Website: http://www.vcc-net.org

WASHINGTON
Associated Ministries of Tacoma-Pierce County—Website: http://www.associatedministries.org
Center for the Prevention of Sexual and Domestic Violence—Website: www.cpsdv.org
Northwest Harvest/ E. M. M.—Website: http://www.northwestharvest.org
Spokane Council of Ecumenical Ministries—Website: http://www.tincan.org/~seem

WEST VIRGINIA
West Virginia Council of Churches—Website: www.wvcc.org

US Seminaries

Abilene Christian University—E-mail: moneyr@nicanor.acu.edu
Website: http://www.acu.edu

Alaska Bible College—E-mail: info@akbible.edu
Website: http://www.akbible.edu

Andover Newton Theological School—E-mail: admissions@ants.edu
Website: http://www.ants.edu

The Anglican Theological Seminary International—E-mail: AOCCranmer@aol.com
Website: http://www.netministries.org/churches/ch01051

Appalachian Bible College—E-mail: abc@appbibco.edu

Asbury Theological Seminary—
E-mail: First Name_Last Name@ats.wilmore.ky.us (see directory listing for names)
Website: http://www.ats.wilmore.ky.us

Associated Mennonite Biblical Seminary—E-mail: nkraybill@ambs.edu
Website: http://www.ambs.edu

Austin Presbyterian Theological Seminary—Website: http://www.austinseminary.edu/

Bangor Theological Seminary—E-mail: jwiebe@bts.edu
Website: http://www.bts.edu

Baptist Bible College and Seminary—E-mail: bbc@bbc.edu
Website: http://www.bbc.edu

Baptist Missionary Association Theological Seminary—
E-mail: prbryan@E-tex.com OR bmaisem@flash.net
Website: http://www.geocities.com/Athens/Acropolis/3386

Baptist Theological Seminary at Richmond—E-mail: btsr@mindspring.com

Barclay College—E-mail: barclaycollege@havilandtalco.com

Bethany Lutheran Theological Seminary—E-mail: gschmeli@blc.edu
Website: http://sem-09.blc.edu/default.html

Bethany Theological Seminary—E-mail: roopge@earlham.edu

Bethel Theological Seminary—E-mail: webmaster@bethel.edu
Website: http://www.bethel.edu

Beulah Heights Bible College—E-mail: b.h.b.c@beulah.org

Boise Bible College—E-mail: boibible@micron.net
Website: http://netnow.micron.net/~boibible

Boston University (School of Theology)—Website: http://web.bu.edu/

Brite Divinity School, Texas Christian University—E-mail: L.Perdue@tcu.edu
Website: http://www.brite.tcu.edu/brite/

Calvin Theological Seminary—E-mail: kprg@calvin.edu
Website: http://www.calvin.edu/seminary

Candler School of Theology, Emory University—E-mail: candler@emory.edu
Website: http://www.emory.edu/candler

Catholic University of America—E-mail: cua-deansrs@cua.edu
Website: http://www.cua.edu/www/srs/

Central Baptist Theological Seminar—E-mail: central@cbts.edu
Website: http://www.cbts.edu

Chicago Theological Seminary—E-mail: ksmith@chgosem.edu
Website: http://www.chgosem.edu

Church of God Theological Seminary—E-mail: cogseminary@wingnet.com
Website: http://www.wingnet.net/~cogseminary

Cincinnati Bible College and Seminary—E-mail: info@cincybible.edu
Website: http://www.cincybible.edu

Circleville Bible College—E-mail: cbc@biblecollege.edu
Website: http://www.biblecollege.edu

Claremont School of Theology—E-mail: Kbronson@cst.edu
Website: http://www.est.edu

Clear Creek Baptist Bible College—E-mail: ccbbc@tcnet.net
Website: http://www.ccbbc.edu

Concordia Theological Seminary—E-mail: sem_relations@ctsfw.edu
Website: http://www.ctsfw.edu

Cranmer Seminary—Website: http://members.tripod.com/~AnglicanOrthodox/index.html

Crown College—E-mail: crown@gw.crown.edu
Website: http://www.crown.edu

Denver Seminary—E-mail: info@densem.edu
Website: http://www.gospelcom.net/densem/

Earlham School of Religion—E-mail: woodna@earlham.edu
Website: http://www.esr.earlham.edu/esr

Eastern Baptist Theological Seminary—Website: http://www.ebts.edu

Eastern Mennonite Seminary—E-mail: info@emu.edu
Website: http://www.emu.edu/units/sem/sem.htm

Emmanuel School of Religion—E-mail: emmanuel.johnson-city.tn.us
Website: http://www.emmanuel.johnson-city.tn.us

Episcopal Divinity School—Website: http://www.episdivschool.org

Erskine Theological Seminary—E-mail: ruble@erskine.edu

Florida Christian College—E-mail: fcc@fcc.edu

Free Will Baptist Bible College—E-mail: president@fwbbc.edu
Website: http://www.fwbcc.edu

Garrett-Evangelical Theological Seminary—E-mail: seminary@nwu.edu
Website: http://www.garrett.nwu.edu

God's Bible School and College—E-mail: gbs.po@juno.com
Website: http://www.gbs.edu

Golden Gate Baptist Theological Seminary—E-mail: seminary@ggbts.edu
Website: http://www.ggbts.edu/index.html

Gordon-Conwell Theological Seminary—E-mail: info@gcts.edu
Website: http://www.gcts.edu

Grace Bible College—E-mail: gbc@gbcol.edu
Website: http://www.gbcol.edu

Grace Theological Seminary—Website: http://www.grace.edu

Graduate Theological Union—E-mail: maloney@gtu.edu
Website: http://www.gtu.edu

Greenville College—E-mail: rsmith@Greenville.edu
Website: http://www.greenville.edu

Hartford Seminary—E-mail: hartsem@mail.hartsem.edu
Website: http://www.hartsem.edu

Harvard Divinity School—Website: http://www.divweb.harvard.edu

Hebrew Union College-Jewish Institute of Religion—E-mail: rabbiz@cn.huc.edu
Website: http://www.huc.edu

Holy Cross Greek Orthodox School of Theology—E-mail: admissions@hchc.edu

Huntington College, Graduate School of Christian Ministries—E-mail: gscm@huntington.edu
Website: http://www.huntington.edu/academics/gscm

Indiana Wesleyan University—E-mail: jbarnes@indwes.edu
Website: http://www.indwes.edu

Interdenominational Theological Center—E-mail: rfranklin@itc.edu

Jewish Theological Seminary of America—E-mail: webmaster@jtsa.edu
Website: http://www.jtsa.edu

Johnson Bible College—E-mail: jbc@jbc.edu
Website: http://www.jbc.edu

Lancaster Bible College—Website: http://www.lbc.edu

Lancaster Theological Sem. of the United Church of Christ—E-mail: dean@lts.org

Lincoln Christian College and Seminary—E-mail: psnyder@lccs.edu
Website: http://www.lccs.edu

Logos Evangelical Seminary—E-mail: logos@sprynet.com

Luther Seminary—E-mail: sbooms@luthersem.edu
Website: http://www.luthersem.edu/

Lutheran Bible Institute of Seattle—E-mail: admissn@lbi.edu
Website: http://www.lbi.edu

Lutheran Theological Seminary—Website: http://www.ltsg.edu

Lutheran Theological Seminary at Philadelphia—E-mail: mtairy@ltsp.edu
Website: http://www.ltsp.edu

Lutheran Theological Southern Seminary—E-mail: Freisz@ltss.edu
Website: http://www.ltss.edu

Manhattan Christian College—Website: http://www.mccks.edu

Memphis Theol. Sem. of the Cumberland Presbyterian Church—E-mail: wa4mff@aol.com

Mennonite Brethren Biblical Seminary—E-mail: mbseminary@aol.com
Website: http://www.fresno.edu/mbseminary

Methodist Theological School in Ohio—E-mail: pres@mtso.edu
Website: http://www.mtso.edu

Minnesota Bible College—E-mail: academic@mnbc.edu
Website: http://www.mnbc.edu

Moravian Theological Seminary—E-mail: merge01@moravian.edu
Website: http://www.moravian.ed

Mt. St. Mary's Seminary—Website: http://www.msmary.edu

Multnomah Bible College and Biblical Seminary—Website: http://www.multnomah.edu

Nashotah House (Theological Seminary)—E-mail: nashotah@nashotah.edu
Website: http://www.nashotah.edu

Nazarene Bible College—E-mail: nbc@rmii.com
Website: http://www.members.aol.com/nazbibleco

New Brunswick Theological Seminary—E-mail: rsh@nbts.edu
Website: http://www.nbts.edu

New Orleans Baptist Theological Seminary—E-mail: nobts@nobts.edu
Website: http://www.nobts.edu

New York Theological Seminary—Website: http://www.nyts.edu

North American Baptist Seminary—E-mail: train@nabs.edu
Website: http://www.nabs.edu

North Park Theological Seminary—E-mail: jphelan@northpark.edu
Website: http://www.northpark.edu/cs

Northwest College—E-mail: mail@ncag.edu
Website: http://www.nwcollege.edu

Oral Roberts University School of Theology and Missions—E-mail: jhorner@oru.edu
Website: http://www.oru.edu

Pacific Christian College—E-mail: rlawson@pacificc.edu

Pacific Lutheran Theological Seminary—E-mail: president@plts.edu
Website: http://www.plts.edu

Pacific School of Religion—E-mail: comm@psr.edu
Website: http://www.psr.edu

Payne Theological Seminary—E-mail: dbalsbau@wu.wilberforce.edu

Pepperdine University—E-mail: rmarrs@pepperdine.edu
Website: http://www.pepperdine.edu/seaver/religion/main.html

Perkins School of Theology (Southern Methodist University)—E-mail: theoadms@smu.edu
Website: http://www.smu.edu/~theology

Philadelphia College of Bible—E-mail: president@pcb.edu

Philadelphia Theological Seminary—E-mail: info@ptsorec.edu
Website: http://www.ptsofrec.edu

Piedmont Baptist College—E-mail: admissions@pbc.edu
Website: http://www.pbc.edu

Point Loma Nazarene College—Website: http://www.ptloma.edu

Practical Bible College—E-mail: pbc@lakenet.org
Website: http://www.lakenet.org/~pbc

Puget Sound Christian College—E-mail: psccpres@ricochet.ent

Reconstructionist Rabbinical College—E-mail: rrcinfo@rrc.edu

Reformed Presbyterian Theological Seminary—E-mail: rpseminary@aol.com

Reformed Theological Seminary—E-mail: rtsjackson@aol.com
Website: http://www.rts.edu

Regent University School of Divinity—E-mail: uinssyn@regent.edu
Website: http://www.regent.edu

SS. Cyril and Methodius Seminary—
E-mail: 103244.3555@compuserve.com OR deansoff@sscms.edu
Website: http://www.metronet.lib.mi.us/aml.html (Library)
Website: http://www.sscms.edu/deansoff (Seminary)

Sacred Heart School of Theology—E-mail: shst@msn.com
Website: http://www.execpc.com./~rakirsch/shst

Saint Paul School of Theology—E-mail: spst@spst.edu
Website: http://www.spst.edu

St. Tikhon's Orthodox Theological Seminary—E-mail: stots@stots.edu (Admin.)
stotsfac@stots.edu (Faculty)
stotscat@stots.edu (Library)
Websites: http://www.stots.edu AND http://www.oca.org/oca/pim/oca-stostots.html

St. Vladimir's Orthodox Theological Seminary—E-mail: thopko@svots.edu
Website: http://www.svots.edu

San Francisco Theological Seminary—E-mail: sftsinfo@sfts.edu
Website: http://www.sfts.edu

Seabury-Western Theological Seminary—Website: http://www.swts.nwu.edu

Seattle University School of Theology and Ministry—E-mail: jancoski@seattleu.edu

Seventh-day Adventist Theological Seminary—E-mail: seminary@andrews.edu
Website: http://www.andrews.edu/sem

Southeastern Baptist Theological Seminary—Website: http://www.sebts.edu

Southern Baptist Theological Seminary—E-mail: mohler@sbts.edu
Website: http://www.sbts.edu

Southern Christian University—E-mail: scuniversity@mindspring.com
Website: http://www.southernchristian.edu

Southern Wesleyan University—Website: http://www.swu.edu

Southwestern Baptist Theological Seminar—Website: http://www.swbts.edu

Swedenborg School of Religion—E-mail: maryk59988@aol.com

Talbot School of Theology—E-mail: biola.edu/biola/talbot/
Website: http://www.talbot.edu

Theological School of the Protestant Reformed Churches—E-mail: decker@prca.org

Toccoa Falls College—E-mail: president@toccoafalls.edu
Website: http://www.toccoafalls.edu

Trinity College of Florida—E-mail: trinity@gte.net

Trinity Episcopal School for Ministry—E-mail: tinalockett@tesm.edu
Website: http://www.episcopalian.org

Trinity International University—E-mail: tedsadm@tiu.edu
Website: http://www.tiu.edu

United Theological Seminary—E-mail: utsadmis@united.edu
Website: http://www.united.edu

United Theological Seminary of the Twin Cities—E-mail: general@unitedseminary-mn.org
Website: http://www.unitedseminary-mn.org

University of Chicago (Divinity School)—Website: http://www2.uchicago.edu/divinity

University of the South School of Theology—E-mail: glytle@seraphl.sewanee.edu
Website: http://www.sewanee.edu

Vanderbilt University Divinity School—E-mail: Houghjc@ctrvax.vanderbilt.edu
Website: http://www.vanderbilt.edu

Vennard College—E-mail: Vennard@kds:.net
Website: http://www.kds:.net/VennardCollege/

Walla Walla College (School of Theology)—E-mail: burser@wwc.edu
Website: http://www.wwc.edu

Wartburg Theological Seminary—E-mail: Roger_Fjeld.parti@ecunet.org

Washington Theological Consortium—E-mail: wtconsort@aol.com

Washington Theological Union—Website: http://www.wtu.edu

Wesley Theological Seminary—E-mail: admiss@clark.net
Website: http://www.wesleysem.org

Western Theological Seminary—Website: http://www.westernsem.org

Weston Jesuit School of Theology—E-mail: rmanning@wjst.edu

Winebrenner Theological Seminary—E-mail: wtseminary@aol.com
Website: http://www.winebrenner.edu

Canadian Seminaries

Acadia Divinity College—E-mail: mashley@acadiau.ca
Website: http://ace.acadiau.ca/divcol

Alberta Bible College—E-mail: abbible@cadvision.com
Website: http://www.abc-ca.org

Baptist Leadership Training School—E-mail: blts@imag.net
Website: http://www.yet.ca

Bethany Bible Institute—E-mail: bethany@sk.sympatico.ca
Website: http://www.bethany.sk.ca

Briercrest Bible College—Website: http://www.briercrest.ca

Briercrest Biblical Seminary—Website: http://www.briercrest.ca

Canadian Lutheran Bible Institute—E-mail: clbi@cable-lynx.net

Canadian Nazarene College—E-mail: cncoff@cnaz.ab.ca

Centre for Christian Studies—E-mail: centre@escape.ca

College of Emmanuel and St. Chad—E-mail: christen@duke.usask.ca

Columbia Bible College—E-mail: info@columbiabc.edu
Website: http://www.columbiabc.edu

Concordia Lutheran Seminary—E-mail: clsadmin@connect.ab.ca

Covenant Bible College—E-mail: covbibco@cadvision.com OR 103354.2431@compuserve.com
Website: http://www.covenantbiblecollege.ab.ca

Emmanuel Bible College—E-mail: dmin@ebcollege.on.ca
Website: http://www.ebcollege.on.ca

Emmanuel College—E-mail: ec.office@utoronto.ca
Website: http://vicu.utoronto.ca

Gardner College, A Centre for Christian Studies—E-mail: gardnerc@cable-lynx.net
Website: http://cable-lynx/~gardnerc

Great Lakes Bible College—E-mail: info@glcc.vaxxine.com

Heritage Baptist College/Heritage Theological Seminary—E-mail: admin@heritage-theo.edu
Website: http://www.heritage-theo.edu

Institute for Christian Studies—E-mail: wcoffeybailey@icscanada.edu
Website: http://icscanada.edu

Joint Board of Theological Colleges—E-mail: dio@colba.net
Website: http://www.mcgill.ca/religion/jbtc.htm

Knox College—E-mail: knox.college@utoronto.ca
Website: http://www.utoronto.ca/knox

Living Faith Bible College—E-mail: livfaith@telusplanet.net
Website: http://www.telusplanet.net/public/livfaith.htm

Lutheran Theological Seminary—E-mail: rohrb@duke.usask.ca

McMaster Divinity College—E-mail: divinity@mcmaster.ca
Website: http://www.mcmaster.ca/divinity

Mount Carmel Bible School—E-mail: carmel@worldgate.com

Newman Theological College—E-mail: admin@newman.edu
Website: http://www.newman.edu

Northwest Bible College—E-mail: northwest@oanet.com
Website: http://www.nwbc.ab.ca

Pacific Life Bible College—E-mail: paclife@smartt.com

Peace River Bible Institute—E-mail: prbi@telusplanet.net

Providence College and Theological Seminary—E-mail: info@providence.mb.ca
Website: http://www.providence.mb.ca

Queen's Theological College—E-mail: theology@post.queensu.ca
Website: http://info.queensu.ca/theology/qtchome.html

Reformed Episcopal Theological College—E-mail: fed@nt.net

Regent College—E-mail: regentcollege@compuserve.com
Website: http://www.regent-college.edu

Regis College—Website: http://www.utornonto.ca/regis

St. Augustine's Seminary of Toronto—Website: http://www.canxsys.com/staugust.htm

Steinbach Bible College—E-mail: pr@sbcollege.mb.ca
Website: http://www.sbcollege.mb.ca

The Salvation Army William and Catherine Booth Bible College—E-mail: wcbc@cc.umanitoba.ca

Toronto Baptist Seminary and Bible Colleg—E-mail: tbs@tbs.edu
Website: http://www.tbs.edu

Toronto School of Theology—E-mail: registrar.tst@utoronto.ca
Website: http://www.utoronto.ca/tst

Tyndale College and Seminary—E-mail: info@tyndale-canada.edu
Website: http://www.tyndale-canada.edu

Université de Montréal, Faculté de théologie—E-mail: theologie@post.umontreal.ca
Website: http://mistral.ere.umontreal.ca/davidrob/theo

University of St. Michael's College, Faculty of Theology—
Website: http://www.utoronto.ca/stmikes/index.html

The University of Winnipeg, Faculty of Theology—E-mail: ray.whitehead@uwinnipeg.ca

Waterloo Lutheran Seminary—Website: http://www.wlu.ca/~wwwsem/

Western Pentecostal Bible College—E-mail: wpbcr@uniserve.com

US Periodicals

Adult Lessons Quarterly—Website: http://www.jmsblind.org

A.M.E. Review—E-mail: E-mail: amervw@aol.com

Baptist Bulletin—E-mail: baptistbulletin@garbc.org
Website: http://www.garbc.org

Catholic Digest—E-mail: cdigest@stthomas.edu
Website: http://www.catholicdigest.org

Catholic Herald—E-mail: chn@execpc.com

Church Advocate, The—E-mail: ejs@brt.bright.net

Co-Laborer—E-mail: colaborer@nafwb.org

Covenant Companion—E-mail: covcom@compuserve.com

Covenant Home Altar—E-mail: covcom@compuserve.com

Currents in Theology and Mission—E-mail: currents@lstc.edu

Discovery—Website: http://www.jmsblind.org

Evangelist, The—E-mail: evannews@global2000.net
Website: http://www.evangelist.org

Forum Letter—E-mail: Saltzman@midmo.net

Friends Journal—E-mail: friendsjnl@aol.com

Front Line—E-mail: chapalruss@aol.com

Gem, The—E-mail: ejs@brt.bright.net

Guide—E-mail: guide@rhpa.org

Insight—E-mail: insight@rhpa.org

John Milton Magazine—Website: http://www.jmsblind.org

Liguorian—E-mail: 104626.1547@compuserve.com

Lutheran, The—E-mail: lutheran@elca.org
Website/ Online Edition: http://www.thelutheran.org

Lutheran Spokesman, The—E-mail: pgflei@prairie.lakes.com

Mennonite, The—E-mail: themennonite@gcmc.org OR themennonite@mph.org
Website: http://www.mph.lm.com/themenno.html

Mature Years—E-mail: mcropsey@umpublishing.org

Mennonite Historical Bulletin—E-mail: johnes@goshen.edu
Website: http://www.goshen.edu/mcarchives

New World Outlook—E-mail: nwo@gbgm-umc.org
Website: http://gbgm-umc.org/nwo

Newscope—E-mail: rpeck@umpublishing.org

Northwestern Lutheran—Email: nl@sab.wels.net

Other Side, The—E-mail: editors@theotherside.org
Website: http://www.theotherside.org

Presbyterian News Service "News Briefs"—E-mail: jerryv@ctr.pcusa.org

Presbyterian Outlook—E-mail: outlook.parti@pcusa.org
Website: http://www.pres-outlook.com

Quaker Life—E-mail: quakerlife@xc.org

Sabbath School Leadership—E-mail: fcrumbly@rhpa.org
Website: http://www.rhpa.org

Sojourners—Website http://www.sojourners.com

Standard Bearer, The—E-mail: engelsma@prca.org

Timbrel: The Publication of Mennonite Women—E-mail: dhwert@oregon.uoregon.edu

Wesleyan World—E-mail: wwm@iquest.net

Canadian Periodicals

Anglican Journal—E-mail: editor@national.anglican.ca

Aujourd hui Credo—E-mail: copermit@sympatico.ca
Website: http://www.egliseunie.org

The Baptist Horizon—E-mail: office@ccsb.ca

CLBI-Cross Roads—E-mail: clbipbad@cable-lynx.net

Canada Lutheran—E-Mail: canaluth@elcic.ca

Connexions—Website: http://www.connexions.org

Edge, The—E-mail: edge@sallynet.org

Evangelical Baptist, The—E-mail: president@fellowship.ca

Faith and Friends—E-mail: faithandfriends@salleynet.org

Faith Today—E-mail: ft@efc-canada.com

Glad Tidings—E-mail: jsterens@presbyterian.ca

Good Tidings—E-mail: paon@paon.nf.ca

Gospel Contact, The—E-mail: wcdncog@cable-lynx.net
Website: http://www.cable-lynx.net/~wcdncog

Gospel Herald—E-mail: eperry9953@aol.com OR wpgwayne@aol.com

The Grape Vine—E-mail: bbrennan@islandnet.com

InfoMission—E-mail: dlpancorvo@cbmin.org
Website: http://www.cbmin.org

Intercom—E-mail: president@fellowship.com

Mandate—E-mail: rchevali@uccan.org

Messenger, The—E-mail: emconf@mts.net

Missions Today—E-mail: missions@eda.net
Website: http://www.eda.net/~missions

Orthodox Way—E-mail: gocanada@total.net.ca
Website: http://www.gocanada.org

Passport—Website: http://www.briercrest.ca

Presbyterian Message, The—E-mail: mjcarter@nb.sympatico.ca

Pulse, The—E-mail: efcc@twu.ca
Website: http://www.twu.ca/efcc/efcc.htm

RESCUE—E-mail: iugm@iugm.org
Website: http://www.iugm.org

War Cry, The—E-mail: warcry@salleynet.org

Relief and Disaster Response Agencies

Including Aid, Advocacy, Relief, Development, UN and other Organizations. The World Council of Churches website (http://www.wcc-coe.org/wcc/otherorg.html) can also access many Development organizations. In Europe websites can be accessed through http://www.oneworld.org/aprodev/indes.html which has excellent links to many world wide bodies including some of those listed below.

Adventist Development and Relief Agency—Website: http://www.adra.org/
American Friends Service Committee—Website: http://www.afsc.org./
    Links to Britain and Canada.
Bread for the World—Website: http://www.Ucaqld.com.au/trendz/issue2/socialjustice.html
Catholic Campaign for Human Development—Website: http://www.nccbuscc.org/chd/
Catholic Charities USA—Website: http://www.catholiccharitiesusa.org/
Catholic Fund for Overseas Development—Website: http://www.oneworld.org/cafod/
Catholic Relief Services—Website: http://www.catholicrelief-crs.org/
Christian Aid (WCC)—Website: http://www.oneworld.org/christian-aid/
Christian Relief Services—Website: http://www.christianrelief.org
    Assists 20 Native American groups.
Church World Service—Website: http://www.ncccusa.org/cws/
    Excellent links to 34 cooperating partners. Including Crop Walks across the country. For NCC information go here first.
Interfaith Hunger Appeal—Website: http://www.ihaglobal.org/
Lutheran World Relief—Website: http://www.lwr.org/
Mennonite Central Committee—Website: http://www.mbnet.mb.ca/mcc/
Oxfam International—Website: http://www.oneworld.org/oxfam
One Great Hour of Sharing—Website: http://www.oghs.org/
Red Cross International Committee—Website: http://www.icrc.org/
Salvation Army—Website: http://www.sarmy.org
World Vision Canada—Website: http:www. worldvision.ca/default.htm
World Vision International—Website: http://www.wvi.org/
World Vision USA—Website: http://www.worldvision.org/

World Religious Bodies with Websites

The following is a list of website information for some Religious bodies with worldwide websites. To recieve an up-to-date directory of International congregations, e-mail your request to 102412.3531@compuserve.com

Anglican Communion World Wide—Website: http://www.aco.org/
  Provides connections with the Lambeth Conference, the Primates Meeting, the Church of England, the Archbishop of Canterbury and Anglican communions around the world.
Armenian Church Worldwide—Website: http://www.stleon.org/ACWW.html
Baptist World Alliance—Website: http://www.baptistnet.org
  When contacted message is that server was not available.
Billy Graham Evangelistic Association—Website: http://www.graham-assn.org/
Church of the Province of South Africa (Anglican)—Website: http://www.aztec.co.za/cpsa
Consejo Latinoamerican de Iglesias—Website: http://www. ecuanex.apc.org/clai
Coptic Orthodox Church of Egypt—Website: http://www. bu.edu/faculty/best/pub/cn
  Through this site one can connect to the Coptic network and several other oriental Orthodox religious bodies.
Ecumenical Patriarchate of Constantinople—Website: http://www. goarch.org/patriarchate
Eglise Nationale Protestante Geneve—Website: http://www. wcc-coe.org/enpaq
Ethiopian Orthodox Church—Website: http://www.students.vivc.edu/~mages/orth.html
Evangelische Kirche in Deutschland (EKD)—Website: http://www. ekd.de/
  Information is available in English
Hong Kong Christian Council—Website: http://www.hk.super.net/~hkcc
Lutheran World Federation—Website: http://www.lwf.org/
National Council of Churches in Korea—Website: http://www. peacenet.or.kr/ncck/
Presbyterian Church of Brazil—Website: http://www.ipb.org.br/
Russian Orthodox Church—Website: http://www.russian-orthodox-church.org.ru/
Salvation Army—Website: http://www.sarmy.org
Seventh Day Adventists—Website: http://www.adventist.org
South African Council of Churches—Website: http://www.sacc.org.za/
Syrian Orthodox Church Antioch—Website: http://www.syrianorthodoxchurch.org/soc.htm
United Reformed Church (United Kindgom)—
  Website: http://www. compulink.co.uk/~urc/urc-home.html
Uniting Church of Australia—Website: http://www.jbce.com.au/~jbce
World Alliance of Reformed Churches—Website: http://www.Wcc-coe.org/warc

6. United States Regional and Local Ecumenical Bodies

One of the many ways Christians and Christian churches relate to one another locally and regionally is through ecumenical bodies. The membership in these ecumenical organizations is diverse. Historically, councils of churches were formed primarily by Protestants, but many local and regional organizations now include Orthodox and Roman Catholics. Many are made up of congregations or judicatory units of churches. Some have a membership base of individuals. Others foster cooperation between ministerial groups, community ministries, coalitions, or church agencies. While Council of Churches is a term still commonly used to describe this form of cooperation, other terms such as "conference of churches," "ecumenical councils," "churches united," "metropolitan ministries," are coming into use. Ecumenical organizations that are national in scope are listed in chapter 1 of the Directories section, "Cooperative Organizations."

An increasing number of ecumenical bodies have been exploring ways to strengthen the interreligious aspect of life in the context of religious pluralism in the U.S. today. Some organizations in this listing are interfaith agencies primarily through the inclusion of Jewish congregations in their membership. Other organizations nurture partnerships wit a broader base of religious groups in their communities, especially in the areas of public policy and interreligious dialogue.

This list does not include all local and regional ecumenical and interfaith organizations in existence today. For information about other groups contact the Ecumenical Networks Commission of the National Council of the Churches of Christ in the U.S.A., 475 Riverside Dr., New York, NY 10115-0050. Tel. (212)870-2155 Fax (212)870-2690

The terms regional and local are relative, making identification somewhat ambiguous. Regional councils may cover sections of large states or cross-state boarders. Local councils may be made up of several counties, towns, or clusters of congregations. State councils or state-level ecumenical contacts exist in 43 of the 50 states. These state-level or multi-state organizations are marked with a " * " and are the first listing for each state. Other listings are in alphabetical order under the state.

ALABAMA

Greater Birmingham Ministries
2304 12th Ave. N, Birmingham, AL 35234-3111
Tel. (205)326-6821 Fax (205)252-8458
E-mail: —
Website: —
Media Contact, Scott Douglas
Exec. Dir., Scott Douglas
Economic Justice, Co-Chpsn.: Helen Holdefer; Karnie Smith
Direct Services, Chpsn., Benjamin Greene
Finance & Fund-Raising, Chpsn., Dick Sales
Pres., Richard Ambrose
Sec., Lois Martin
Treas., Chris Hamlin
Major activities: Direct Service Ministries (Food, Utilities, Rent and Nutrition Education, Shelter); Alabama Arise (Statewide legislative network focusing on low income issues); Economic Justice Issues (Low Income Housing and Advocacy, Health Care, Community Development, Jobs Creation, Public Transportation); Faith in Community Ministries (Interchurch Forum, Interpreting and Organizing, Bible Study)

Interfaith Mission Service
411-B Holmes Ave. NE, Huntsville, AL 35801
Tel. (256)536-2401 Fax (256)536-2284

Exec. Dir., Susan J. Smith
Pres., Rev. William McWeeny
E-mail: —
Website: —
Major activities: Foodline & Food Pantry; Emergency Funds; Local FEMA Committee; Ministry Development; Clergy Luncheon; Workshops; Response to Community Needs; Information and Referral; Interfaith Understanding; Christian Unity; Gang, Violence & Drug Taskforce; Homeless Needs

ALASKA

Alaska Christian Conference
3012 Riverview Drive, Fairbanks, AK 99709-4735 Tel. (907)474-0700 Fax (907)474-0700
E-mail: akimpact@mosquitonet.com
Website: —
Media Contact, Pres., Richard K. Heacock, Jr.
Pres., Richard K. Heacock, Jr.
Vice-Pres., Rev. Uelyss Reed, Jr., Box 56019, North Pole, AK 99705 Tel. (907)488-1588 Fax (907)488-5529
Sec., Rev. Leo A. Walsh, S.T.L., 825 South Klevin Street, Anchorage, AK 99508-2698 Tel. (907) 333-5544 Fax(907) 338-3864
Treas., Carolyn M. Winters, 2133 Bridgewater Drive, Fairbanks, AK 99709-4101 Tel. (907) 456-8555

227

Major activities: Legislative & Social Concerns; Resources and Continuing Education; New Ecumenical Ministries; Communication; Alcoholism (Education & Prevention); Family Violence (Education & Prevention); Native Issues; Ecumenical/Theological Dialogue; HIV/AIDS Education and Ministry; Criminal Justice

ARIZONA

*Arizona Ecumenical Council

4423 N. 24th St., Ste. 750, Phoenix, AZ 85016 Tel. (602)468-3818 Fax (602)468-3839
E-mail: —
Website: —
Media Contact, Exec. Dir., Dr. Paul Eppinger, Tel. (602)967-6040 Fax (602)468-3839
Exec. Dir., Dr. Paul Eppinger
Pres., Rev. Gail Davis, 4423 N. 24th St. Ste. 700, Phoenix, AZ 85016
Major activities: Donohoe Ecumenical Forum Series; Political Action Team; Legislative Workshop; Arizona Ecumenical Indian Concerns Committee; Mexican/American Border Issues; ISN-TV; Disaster Relief; Break Violence-Build Community; Truckin' for Kids; "Souper Bowl"; Gun Info. and Safety Program

ARKANSAS

*Arkansas Interfaith Conference

P.O. Box 151, Scott, AR 72142 Tel. (501)961-2626 Fax (501)961-1040
E-mail: —
Website: —
Media Contact, Conf. Exec., Mimi Dortch, Tel. (501)961-2626
Conf. Exec., Mimi Dortch
Pres., Rev. Jesse Yarborough, Christ Episcopal Church, 501 S. Scott St., Little Rock, AR 72201
Sec., Rabbi Eugene Levy, Temple B'nai Israel, 3700 Rodney Pauhan Rd., Little Rock, AR 72212
Treas., Jim Davis, Box 7239, Little Rock, AR 72217
Major activities: Task Force on Hunger; Task Force on Violence; Institutional Ministry; Interfaith Executives' Advisory Council; Drug Abuse, Interfaith Relations; Church Women United; IMPACT; AIDS Task Force; Our House-Shelter; Legislative Liaison; Task Force on Civil Political Dialogue; Ecumenical Choir Camp; Tornado Disaster Relief; Camp for Jonesboro School Children Massacre

CALIFORNIA

*California Council of Churches/ California Church Impact

2700 "L" Street, Sacramento, CA 95816 Tel. (916)442-5447 Fax (916)442-3036

E-mail: hn0029@handsnet.org
Website: —
Media Contact, Exec. Dir., Scott D. Anderson
Exec. Dir., Scott D. Anderson
Major activities: Monitoring State Legislation; Calif. IMPACT Network; Legislative Principles; Food Policy Advocacy; Family Welfare Issues; Health; Church/State Issues; Violence Prevention

*Northern California Interreligious Conference

965 Mission St., #711, San Francisco, CA 94103 Tel. (415)512-7110 Fax (415)512-1172
E-mail: NCIC@igc.org
Website: —
Media Contact, Robert Forsberg
Coordinator, Elizabeth Friedman
Pres., Rev. Phil Lawson
Vice-Pres.: E.J. Hilliard
Sec., Robert Forsberg
Treas., John Lanehart
Major activities: Peace with Justice; Faith and Witness; Unlearning Racism Training; Public Policy Advocacy

*Southern California Ecumenical Council

54 N. Oakland Ave., Pasadena, CA 91101-2086 Tel. (626)578-6371 Fax (626)578-6358
E-mail: —
Website: —
Media Contact, Exec. Dir., Rev. Albert G. Cohen
Exec. Dir., Rev. Albert G. Cohen
Pres., Rev. Sally Welch
Ecology Task Force, Dir., Rev. Peter Moore-Kochlacs
Ecology Task Force, Dir., Rev. Albert G. Cohen
Faith & Order Commission, Dir., Rev. Rod Parrott
Faith & Values Cable TV Regional Comm., Dir., Nila LaDuke
Hope Publishing, Dir., Faith Sand
Interreligious Disaster Response Coord., Dir. (Southern CA), —
Major activities: Consultation with the regional religious sector concerning the well being and spiritual vitality of this most diverse and challenging area

The Council of Churches of Santa Clara County

1229 Naglee Ave., San Jose, CA 95126 Tel. (408)297-2660 Fax (408)297-2661
E-mail: ccscc@aol.com
Website: —
Media Contact, Ex. Dir., Rev. Vaughn F. Beckman
Exec. Dir., Rev. Vaughn F. Beckman
Pres., Rev. John L. Freesemann
Assoc. Dir., —
Major activities: Social Education/Action; Ecumenical and Interfaith Witness; Affordable

Housing; Environmental Ministry; Family/ Children; Refugee Immigration Ministry; Interfaith Study Project; Convalescent Hospital Ministries; Gay Ministry

Ecumenical Council of San Diego County
1880 Third Ave., San Diego, CA 92101
E-mail: —
Website: http://home.earthlink.net/~searay1/
Media Contact, Exec. Dir., Rev. Glenn S. Allison, P.O. Box 3628, San Diego, CA 92163 Tel. (619)238-0649 Fax (619)238-1526 OR Rosemary Johnston, Editor, *ECUMENEWS*, (619)702-5399
Exec. Dir., Rev. Glenn S. Allison
Admn., Patricia R. Munley
Pres., George Mitrovich
Treas., Joseph Ramsey
Major activities: Interfaith Shelter Network/El Nido Transitional Living Program; Emerging Issues; Faith Order & Witness; Worship & Celebration; Ecumenical Tribute Dinner; Advent Prayer Breakfast; AIDS Chaplaincy Program; Third World Opportunities; Seminars and Workshops; Called to Dance Assn.; S.D. Names Project *Quilt*; Children's Sabbath Workshops and events; Edgemoor Chaplaincy; Stand for Children events; Continuing Education for clergy and laypersons

The Ecumenical Council of Pasadena Area Churches
P.O. Box 41125, 444 E. Washington Blvd., Pasadena, CA 91114-8125 Tel. (626)797-2402 Fax (626)797-7353
E-mail: zyhv76@prodigy.com
Website: —
Exec. Dir., Rev. Frank B. Clark
Major activities: Christian Education; Community Worship; Community Concerns; Christian Unity; Ethnic Ministries; Hunger; Peace; Food, Clothing Assistance for the Poor; Emergency Shelter

Fresno Metro Ministry
1055 N. Van Ness, Ste. H, Fresno, CA 93728 Tel. (209)485-1416 Fax (209)485-9109
E-mail: metromin@qnis.net
Website: —
Media Contact, Exec. Dir., Rev. Walter P. Parry
Exec. Dir., Rev. Walter P. Parry
Admn. Asst., Linda Jimenez
Pres., Rev. Delman Howard
Major activities: Hunger Relief Advocacy; Human Relations and Anti-Racism; Health Care Advocacy; Public Education Concerns; Children's Needs; Biblical and Theological Education For Laity;; Ecumenical & Interfaith Celebrations & Cooperation; Youth Needs; Community Network Building; Human Services Facilitation; Anti-Poverty Efforts; Hate Crime Prevention and Response

Interfaith Council of Contra Costa County
1543 Sunnyvale Ave., Walnut Creek, CA 94596 Tel. (925)933-6030
E-mail: —
Website: —
Media Contact, Dir., Rev. Machrina L. Blasdell
Dir., Rev. Machrina L. Blasdell
Chaplains: Rev. Charles Tinsley; Rev. Duane Woida; Rev. Harold Wright; Laurie Maxwell
Pres., Rev. Steve Harms
Treas., Robert Bender
Major activities: Institutional Chaplaincies; Community Education, Interfaith Cooperation; Social Justice

Interfaith Service Bureau
3720 Folsom Blvd., Sacramento, CA 95816 Tel. (916)456-3815 Fax (916)456-3816
E-mail: —
Website: —
Media Contact, Interim Dir., Dexter McNamara
Interim Dir., Dexter McNamara
Pres.: Rabbi Brad Bloom
Vice-Pres.: Patricia Hill
Major activities: Welfare Reform Concerns; Refugee Resettlement & Support; Religious Cable Television; Violence Prevention; Graffiti Abatement; Religious and Racial Cooperation and Understanding

Marin Interfaith Council
650 Las Gallinas, San Rafael, CA 94903 Tel. (415)492-1052 Fax (415)492-8907
E-mail: —
Website: —
Media Contact, Exec. Dir., Rev. Kevin F. Tripp, 650 Las Gallinas, San Rafael, CA 94903 Tel. (415)492-1052 Fax (415)492-8907
Exec. Dir., Rev. Kevin F. Tripp
Major activities: Interfaith Dialogue; Education; Advocacy; Convening; Interfaith Worship Services & Commemorations

Pacific and Asian American Center for Theology and Strategies (PACTS)
Graduate Theological Union, 2400 Ridge Rd., Berkeley, CA 94709 Tel. (510)849-0653 Fax —
E-mail: pacts@igc.org
Website: —
Media Contact, Deborah Lee
Dir., Deborah Lee
Pres., Ron Nakasone
Major activities: Collect and Disseminate Resource Materials; Training Conferences; Public Seminars; Women in Ministry; Racial and Ethnic Minority Concerns; Journal and Newsletter; Hawaii & Greater Pacific Programme; Sale of Sadao Watanabe Calendars; Informational Forums on Peace & Social Justice in Asian Pacific American Community and Asia/Pacific Internationally;

229

Forums & Conferences for Seminarians Asian Pacific Heritage

Pomona Inland Valley Council of Churches

1753 N. Park Ave., Pomona, CA 91768 Tel. (909)622-3806 Fax (909)622-0484
E-mail: —
Website: —
Media Contact, Dir. of Development, Mary Kashmar
Pres., The Rev. Henry Rush
Acting Exec. Dir., The Rev. La Quetta Bush-Simmons
Sec., Ken Coates
Treas., Anne Ashford
Major activities: Advocacy and Education for Social Justice; Ecumenical Celebrations; Hunger Advocacy; Emergency Food and Shelter Assistance; Farmer's Market; Affordable Housing; Transitional Housing

San Fernando Valley Interfaith Council

10824 Topanga Canyon Blvd., No. 7, Chatsworth, CA 91311 Tel. (818)718-6460 Fax (818)718-0734
E-mail: —
Website: —
Media Contact, Dir., Public Relations, Arlene C. Quinn, Ext. 3302, Fax (818)718-0734
Exec. Dir., Barry Smedberg; Ext. 3011
Pres., Rev. Dr. Jeffrey Utter
Major activities: Seniors Multi-Purpose Centers; Nutrition & Services; Meals to Homebound; Meals on Wheels; Interfaith Reporter; Interfaith Relations; Social Adult Day Care; Hunger/Homelessness; Volunteer Care-Givers; Clergy Gatherings; Food Pantries and Outreach; Social Concerns; Aging; Hunger; Human Relations; Child Abuse Program; Medical Service; Homeless Program; Disaster Response Preparedness; Immigration Services; Self-Sufficiency Program for Section 8 Families

South Coast Ecumenical Council

3300 Magnolia Ave., Long Beach, CA 90806 Tel. (562)595-0268 Fax (562)490-9920
Website: —
Media Contact, Exec. Dir., Rev. Ginny Wagener
E-mail:REVGW@aol.com
Exec. Dir., Rev. Ginny Wagener
Agape Theater Ministries, Dr. Ralph Mosby
Farmers' Markets, Rev. Dale Whitney
Pres., Rev. Ken McMillan
Centro Shalom, Amelia Nieto
Women & Children First, Dr. Anneka Davidson
New Communion, David Satchwell
Major activities: Homeless Support Services; Farmers' Markets; Hunger Projects; Church Athletic Leagues; Community Action; Hunger Walks; Christian Unity Worships; Inter-religious Dialogue; Justice Advocacy; Martin Luther King, Jr. Celebration; Violence Prevention; Long Beach Church Women United; Long Beach Interfaith Clergy; Agape Theater Ministries

Westside Interfaith Council

P.O. Box 1402, Santa Monica, CA 90406 Tel. (310)394-1518 Fax (310)576-1895
E-mail: —
Website: —
Media Contact, Rev. Janet A. Bregar
Exec. Dir., Rev. Janet A. Bregar
Major activities: Meals on Wheels; Community Religious Services; Convalescent Hospital Chaplaincy; Homeless Partnership; Hunger & Shelter Coalition

COLORADO

*Colorado Council of Churches

1234 Bannock St., Denver, CO 80204-3631 Tel. (303)825-4910 Fax (303)534-1266
E-mail: council@diac.com
Website: —
Media Contact, Exec. Dir., Rev. Lucia Guzman
Pres., Rev. Louise Barger
Staff Assoc, Robert Hunter
Major activities: Institutional Ministries; Human Needs and Economic Issues (Includes Homelessness, Migrant Ministry, Justice in the Workplace); World Peace and Global Affairs; Religion in the Media; Interreligious Dialogue;Covenant with Children

Interfaith Council of Boulder

3700 Baseline Rd., Boulder, CO 80303 Tel. (303)494-8094 Fax —
E-mail: —
Website: —
Media Contact, Pres., Stan Grotegut, 810 Kalma Ave., Boulder, CO 80304 Tel. (303)443-2291
Pres., Stan Grotegut
Major activities: Interfaith Dialogue and Programs; Thanksgiving Worship Services; Food for the Hungry; Share-A-Gift; Monthly Newsletter

CONNECTICUT

*Christian Conference of Connecticut (CHRISCON)

60 Lorraine St., Hartford, CT 06105 Tel. (860)236-4281 Fax (860)236-9977
E-mail: chconf@aol.com
Website: —
Media Contact, Exec. Dir., Rev. Stephen J. Sidorak, Jr., Tel. (203)236-4281
Exec. Dir., Rev. Stephen J. Sidorak, Jr.
Pres., The Rt. Rev. Clarence N. Coleridge
Vice-Pres., Most Rev. Daniel A. Cronin
Sec., The Rev. Dr. Lowell H. Fewster
Treas., Thomas F. Sarubbi
Major activities: Communications; Institutional Ministries; Conn. Bible Society; Conn.

Council on Alcohol Problems; Ecumenical Forum; Faith & Order; Social Concerns; Public Policy; Peace and Justice Convocation

Association of Religious Communities

325 Main St., Danbury, CT 06810 Tel. (203)792-9450 Fax (203)792-9452
E-mail: —
Website: —
Media Contact, Exec. Dir., Samuel E. Deibler, Jr.
Exec. Dir., Samuel E. Deibler, Jr.
Pres., The Rev. James Stinson
Major activities: Refugee Resettlement, Family Counseling; Family Violence Prevention; Affordable Housing

The Capitol Region Conference of Churches

30 Arbor St., Hartford, CT 06106 Tel. (860)236-1295 Fax (860)236-8071
E-mail: —
Website: —
Media Contact, Exec. Dir., Rev. Roger W. Floyd
Exec. Dir., Rev. Roger W. Floyd
Pastoral Care & Training, Dir., Rev. Kathleen Davis
Aging Project, Dir., Barbara Malcolm
Community Organizer, Joseph Wasserman
Broadcast Ministry Consultant, Ivor T. Hugh
Pres., Valentine Doyle
Major activities: Organizing for Peace and Justice; Aging; Legislative Action; Cooperative Broad cast Ministry; Ecumenical Cooperation; Inter-faith Reconciliation; Chaplaincies; Low-Income Senior Empower-ment; Anti-Racism Education

Center City Churches

100 Constitution Plaza, Suite 721, Hartford, CT 06103-1721 Tel. (860)728-3201 Fax (860)549-8550
E-mail: —
Website: —
Media Contact, Exec. Dir., Paul C. Christie
Exec. Dir., Paul C. Christie
Pres., The Rev. Dr. Jay Terbush
Sec., John Hunt
Treas., Ann Thomas
Major activities: Senior Services; Family Support Center; Energy Bank; Crisis Intervention; After School Tutoring; Summer Day Camp; Housing for persons with AIDS; Mental Health Residence; Community Soup Kitchen; Job Training for Homeless

Christian Community Action

98 S. Main St., South Norwalk, CT 06854 Tel. (203)854-1811 Fax (203)854-1870
E-mail: —
Website: —
Dir., Jacquelyn P. Miller
Major activities: Emergency Food Program; Used Furniture; Loans for Emergencies; Loans for Rent, Security

Christian Community Action

168 Davenport Ave., New Haven, CT 06519 Tel. (203)777-7848 Fax (203)777-7923
E-mail: cca168@aol.com
Website: —
Media Contact, Exec. Dir., The Rev. Bonita Grubbs
Exec. Dir., The Rev. Bonita Grubbs
Major activities: Emergency Food Program; Used Furniture & Clothing; Security and Fuel; Emergency Housing for Families; Advocacy; Transitional Housing for Families

Council of Churches and Synagogues of Southwestern Connecticut

628 Main St., Stamford, CT 06901 Tel. (203)348-2800 Fax (203)358-0627
E-mail: council@flvax.ferg.lib.ct.us
Website: http://www.interfaithcouncil.org
Media Contact, Communications Ofc., Lois Alcosser
Exec. Dir., The Rev. Dr. Jeffrey C. Wood
Major activities: Partnership Against Hunger; The Food Bank of Lower Fairfield County; Table to Table; Friendly Visitors and Friendly Shoppers; Senior Neighborhood Support Services; Christmas in April; Adopt-A-House; Interfaith Programming; Prison Visitation; Friendship House; Help a Neighbor; Operation Fuel

Council of Churches of Greater Bridgeport, Inc.

180 Fairfield Ave., Bridgeport, CT 06604 Tel. (203)334-1121 Fax (203)367-8113
E-mail: ccgb@snet.net
Website: —
Media Contact, Exec. Dir., Rev. John S. Kidd
Exec. Dir., Rev. John S. Kidd
Pres., Rev. Michael Stevens
Sec., Dorothy Allsop
Treas., Roger Perry
Major activities: Youth in Crisis; Youth Shelter; Criminal Justice; Hospital, Nursing Home and Jail Ministries; Local Hunger; Ecumenical Relations, Prayer and Celebration; Covenantal Ministries; Homework Help; Summer Programs; Race Relations/Bridge Building; Good Jobs / First Jobs

Interfaith Cooperative Ministries of Greater New Haven

57 Olive St., New Haven, CT 06511 Tel. (203)776-9526 Fax —
E-mail: —
Website: —
Pres., Patricia Anderson, Interfaith Volunteer Caregivers, 30 Gillies Rd., Hamden, CT 06517
Major activities: Mission to Poor and Dispos-sessed; Criminal Justice; Elderly; Sheltering Homeless; Soup Kitchen; Low Income Housing; AIDS Residence; Summer Children's Program; Pastoral Counseling Center

231

Manchester Area Conference of Churches

P.O. Box 773, Manchester, CT 06045-0773 Tel. (860)649-2093 Fax —
E-mail: —
Website: —
Media Contact, Exec. Dir., Denise Cabana
Exec. Dir., Denise Cabana
Dir. of Community Ministries, Joseph Piescik
Dept.of Ministry Development, Dir., Karen Bergin
Pres., Rev. Charles Ericson
Vice-Pres., Theresa Ghabrial
Sec., Jean Richert
Treas., Clive Perrin
Major activities: Provision of Basic Needs (Food, Fuel, Clothing, Furniture); Emergency Aid Assistance; Emergency Shelter; Soup Kitchen; Reentry Assistance to Ex-Offenders; Pastoral Care in Local Institutions; Interfaith Day Camp; Advocacy for the Poor; Ecumenical Education and Worship

New Britain Area Conference of Churches (NEWBRACC)

830 Corbin Ave., New Britain, CT 06052 Tel. (860)229-3751 Fax (860)223-3445
E-mail: —
Website: —
Media Contact, Exec. Dir., Michael Gorzoch
Exec. Dir., Michael Gorzoch
Pastoral Care/Chaplaincy: Rev. Ron Smith; Rev. Will Baumgartner; Rev. Rod Rinnel
Pres., Alton Brooks
Treas., Lynne Alexander
Major activities: Worship; Social Concerns; Emergency Food Bank Support; Communications-Mass Media; Hospital and Nursing Home Chaplaincy; Elderly Programming; Homelessness and Hunger Programs; Telephone Ministry; Thanksgiving Vouchers

Greater Waterbury Interfaith Ministries, Inc.

84 Crown St., Waterbury, CT 06704 Tel. (203)757-6413 Fax —
E-mail: —
Website: —
Media Contact, Exec. Dir., Carroll E. Brown
Exec. Dir., Carroll E. Brown
Pres., Virginia Slavin
Major activities: Emergency Food Program; Emergency Fuel Program; Soup Kitchen; Ecumenical Worship; Christmas Toy Sale

DELAWARE

*The Christian Council of Delaware and Maryland's Eastern Shore

Media Contact, Pres., Bishop George Mocko, Evangelical Lutheran Church in America, 7604 York Rd., Baltimore, MD 21204 Tel. (410)825-9520 Fax (410)825-6745

E-mail: —
Website: —
Pres., Bishop George Mocko
Major activities: Exploring Common Theological, Ecclesiastical and Community Concerns; Racism

DISTRICT OF COLUMBIA

The Council of Churches of Greater Washington

5 Thomas Circle N.W., Washington, DC 20005 Tel. (202)722-9240 Fax (202)722-9241
E-mail: —
Website: —
Media Contact, Exec. Dir., The Rev. Rodger Hall Reed, Sr.
Pres., The Rev. Lewis Anthony
Exec. Dir., The Rev. Rodger Hall Reed, Sr.
Program Officer, Daniel M. Thompson
Major activities: Promotion of Christian Unity/Ecumenical Prayer & Worship; Coordination of Community Ministries; Summer Youth Employment; Summer Camping/Inner City Youth; Supports wide variety of social justice concerns

InterFaith Conference of Metropolitan Washington

1419 V St. NW, Washington, DC 20009 Tel. (202)234-6300 Fax (202)234-6303
E-mail: ifc@interfaith-metrodc.org
Website: http://www.interfaith-metrodc.org/
Media Contact, Exec. Dir., Rev. Dr. Clark Lobenstine
Exec. Dir., Rev. Dr. Clark Lobenstine
Admn. Sec., Najla Robinson
Pres., Dr. Sulayman S. Nyang
1st Vice-Pres., Laura Nell Morris
Chpsn., Fr. Paul Lee
Sec., Dr. Reba Carrath
Treas., Jack Serber
Major activities: Interfaith Dialogue; Interfaith Concert; Racial and Ethnic Polarization; Youth Leadership Training; Hunger; Homelessness; Church-State Zoning Issues

FLORIDA

*Florida Council of Churches

924 N. Magnolia Ave., Ste. 236, Orlando, FL 32803 Tel. (407)839-3454 Fax (407)246-0019
E-mail: fced@aol.com
Website: —
Media Contact, Exec. Dir., Rev. Fred Morris, Tel. (407)839-3454 Fax (407)246-0019
Exec. Dir., Rev. Fred Morris
Refugee Employment Service, Staff Assoc, H. Basil Nichols
Major activities: Justice and Peace; Refugee Resettlement; Disaster Response; Legislation & Public Policy; Local Ecumenism; Farmworker Ministry

Christian Service Center for Central Florida, Inc.
808 W. Central Blvd., Orlando, FL 32805-1809
Tel. (407)425-2523
E-mail: —
Website: —
Media Contact, Exec. Dir., Robert F. Stuart, Tel. (407)425-2523 Fax (407)425-9513
Exec. Dir., Robert F. Stuart
Family Emergency Services, Dir., LaVerne Sainten
Alzheimers Respite, Dir., Mary Ellen Ort-Marvin
Fresh Start, Dir., Rev. Haggeo Gautier
Dir. of Mktg., Margaret Ruffier-Farris
Pres., Dr. Charles Horton
Treas., Rick Crandall
Sec., Annie Harris
Major activities: Provision of Basic Needs (food, clothing, shelter); Emergency Assistance; Noon-time Meals; Sunday Church Services at Walt Disney World; Collection and Distribution of Used Clothing; Shelter & Training for Homeless; Respite for Caregivers of Alzheimers

GEORGIA

*Georgia Christian Council
P.O. Box 7193, Macon, GA 31209-7193 Tel. (912)743-2085 Fax (912)743-2085
E-mail: lccollins@juno.com
Website: —
Media Contact, Exec. Dir., Rev. Leland C. Collins
Exec. Dir., Rev. Leland C. Collins
Pres., Bishop Henry Louttit, 611 Bay Street, Savannah, GA 31401
Sec., Rev. Scudder Edwards, 6865 Turner Ct., Cumming, GA 30131
Major activities: Local Ecumenical Support and Resourcing; Legislation; Rural Development; Racial Justice; Networking for Migrant Coalition; Aging Coalition; GA To GA With Love; Medical Care; Prison Chaplaincy; Training for Church Development; Souper Bowl; Disaster Relief; Clustering; Development of Local Ecumenism

Christian Council of Metropolitan Atlanta
465 Boulevard, S.E., Atlanta, GA 30312 Tel. (404)622-2235 Fax (404)627-6626
E-mail: dojccma@aol.com
Website: —
Media Contact, Dir. of Development & Communication, Jane Hopson Enniss
Exec. Dir., Rev. Dr. David O. Jenkins
Assoc. Dir., Rev. Bernard McLendon
Pres., Dr. Shan R.F. Yohan
Major activities: Refugee Services; Commission on Children and Youth, Supervised Ministry; Homeless; Ecumenical and Interreligious Events; persons with Handicapping Conditions; Women's Concerns; Task Force on Prison Ministry; Quarterly Forums on Ecumenical Issues; Faith and Order Concerns; Interracial & Intercultural Emphasis

IDAHO

The Regional Council for Christian Ministry, Inc.
237 N. Water, Idaho Falls, ID 83403 Tel. (208)524-9935 Fax —
E-mail: —
Website: —
Exec. Sec., Wendy Schoonmaker
Major activities: Island Park Ministry; Community Food Bank; Community Observances; Community Information and Referral Service; F.I.S.H.

ILLINOIS

*Illinois Conference of Churches
615 S. 5th St., Springfield, IL 62703 Tel. (217)544-3423 Fax (217)544-9307
E-mail: ICCExDir.DAA@juno.com
Website: —
Media Contact, Exec. Dir., Rev. David A. Anderson
Exec. Dir., Rev. David A. Anderson
Assoc. Dir., Nancy Tegtmeier
Pres., Rev. Dr. Edgar L. Hiestand, Jr. Tel. (815)943-5422
Major activities: Unity and Relationships Commission; Church and Society Commission; Public Policy Ecumenical Network; Harvesting Hope; Disaster Relief; Annual Parish Clergy Ecumenical Forum; Triennial State-wide Ecumenical Assembly

Churches United of the Quad City Area
630-9th St., Rock Island, IL 61201 Tel. (309)786-6494 Fax (309)786-5916
E-mail: clandon@revealed.net OR dmccarthy@revealed.net
Website: —
Media Contact, Exec. Dir., Rev. Charles R. Landon, Jr, 630 9th St., Rock Island, IL 61201 Tel. (309)786-6494
Exec. Dir., Rev. Charles R. Landon, Jr.
Program Manager, Diane R. McCarthy
Pres., Connie M. Avey
Treas., Rev. Robert Pearson
Major activities: Jail Ministry; Hunger Projects; Minority Enablement; Criminal Justice; Radio-TV; Peace; Local Church Development

Contact Ministries of Springfield
1100 E. Adams, Springfield, IL 62703 Tel. (217)753-3939 Fax (217)753-8643
E-mail: —
Website: —
Media Contact, Exec. Dir., Ethel Butchek
Exec. Dir., Ethel Butchek

Major activities: Information; Referral and Advocacy; Ecumenical Coordination; Low Income Housing Referral; Food Pantry Coordination; Prescription & Travel Emergency; Low Income Budget Counseling; 24 hours on call; Emergency On-site Family Shelter

Evanston Ecumenical Action Council

P.O. Box 1414, Evanston, IL 60204 Tel. (847)475-1150 Fax (847)475-1150
E-mail: —
Website: http://members.aol.com/eeachome/eeac. html
Media Contact, Comm. Chpsn., Donna Spicuzza
Dir. Hospitality Cntr. for the Homeless, Mary E. Senn
Co-Pres.: Rev. Mark Adams; Ms. Kathryn Hirn
Treas., James Lindholm
Admn. Dir., Barbara O'Neill, M.DIV.
Major activities: Interchurch Communication and Education; Peace and Justice Ministries; Coordinated Social Action; Soup Kitchens; Multi-Purpose Hospitality Center for the Homeless; Worship and Renewal

Greater Chicago Broadcast Ministries

112 E. Chestnut St., Chicago, IL 60611-2014 Tel. (312)988-9001 Fax —
E-mail: —
Website: —
Media Contact, Exec. Dir., Lydia Talbot
Pres., Bd. of Dir., Eugene H. Winkler
Exec. Dir., Lydia Talbot
Admn. Asst., Margaret Early
Major activities: Television, Cable, Interfaith/Ecumenical Development; Social/Justice Concerns

The Hyde Park & Kenwood Interfaith Council

1448 E. 53rd St., Chicago, IL 60615 Tel. (773)752-1911 Fax (773)752-2676
E-mail: —
Website: —
Media Contact, Exec. Dir., Lesley M. Radius
Exec. Dir., Lesley M. Radius
Pres., Rev. David Grainger
Sec., Barbara Krell
Major activities: Interfaith Work; Hunger Projects; Community Development

Oak Park-River Forest Community of Congregations

P.O. Box 3365, Oak Park, IL 60303-3365 Tel. (708)386-8802
E-mail: —
Website: http://www.mcs.net/~grossman/com-cong.htm
Media Contact, Patricia C. Koko
Admn. Sec., Patricia C. Koko
Pres., Rev. Joseph Ruiz
Treas., Rev. Robert Long

Major activities: Community Affairs; Ecumenical/ Interfaith Affairs; Youth Education; FOOD PANTRY; Senior Citizens Worship Services; Interfaith Thanksgiving Services; Good Friday Services; UNICEF Children's Fund Drive; ASSIST (Network); Blood Drive; Literacy Training; CROP/CWS Hunger Walkathon; Austin Community Table (feeding hungry); Work with Homeless Through PADS (Public Action to Deliver Shelter); Senior Resource Coordinator Program

Peoria Friendship House of Christian Service

800 N.E. Madison Ave., Peoria, IL 61603 Tel. (309)671-5200 Fax (309)671-5206
E-mail: —
Website: —
Media Contact, Exec. Dir., Beverly Isom
Pres. of Bd., David Dadds
Major activities: Children's After-School; Teen Programs; Recreational Leagues; Senior Citizens Activities; Emergency Food/Clothing Distribution; Emergency Payments for Prescriptions, Rent, Utilities; Community Outreach; Economic Development; Neighborhood Empowerment; GED Classes; Family Literacy; Mother's Group

INDIANA

The Associated Churches of Fort Wayne & Allen County, Inc.

602 E. Wayne St., Fort Wayne, IN 46802 Tel. (219)422-3528 Fax (219)422-6721
E-mail: —
Website: —
Media Contact, Exec. Dir., Rev. Vernon R. Graham
Exec. Dir., Rev. Vernon R. Graham
Sec., Deborah Morse
Foodbank: Ellen Graham; Marv Phillips; Ed Pease
Prog. Development, Ellen Graham
WRE Coord., Maxine Bandemer
Pres., Rev. Dick Jones, 11060 North State Rd. #1, Ossian, IN 46777
Treas., Mel McFall, 2702 Chichester Lane, Fort Wayne, IN 46804
Major activities: Weekday Religious Ed.; Radio & TV; Church Clusters; Church and Society Commission; Overcoming Racism; A Baby's Closet; Widowed-to-Widowed; CROP; Campus Ministry; Feeding the Babies; Food Bank System; Peace & Justice Commission; Welfare Reform; Endowment Devel.; Habitat for Humanity; Child Care Advocacy; Advocates Inc.; Ecumenical Dialogue; Feeding Children; Vincent House (Homeless); A Learning Journey (Literacy); Reaching Out in Love; The Jail Ministry

Christian Ministries
of Delaware County

401 E. Main St., Muncie, IN 47305 Tel.
(317)288-0601 Fax (317)282-4522
E-mail: —
Website: —
Media Contact, Exec. Dir., Susan Hughes
Exec. Dir., Susan Hughes
Pres., Sue Klein
Treas., Dr. J. B. Black
Major activities: Baby Care Program; Youth
Ministry at Detention Center; Community
Church Festivals; Community Pantry;
Community Assistance Fund; CROP Walk;
Social Justice; Family Life Education;
Combined Clergy; Homeless Shelter (sleeping
room only); Clothing and household items
available free; workshops for low income
clients; homeless people apartments available-
short stays only at no cost; provide programs
and workshops for pastors and churches in
community; work with schools sponsoring
programs such as Teen Mom Program; plays
about child abuse/conflict resolution

Church Community Services

1703 Benham Ave., Elkhart, IN 46516 Tel.
(219)295-3673 Fax —
E-mail: —
Website: —
Media Contact, Dir., Trisha Leasor
Exec. Dir., Rosalie J. Day
Major activities: Advocacy for Low Income per-
sons; Financial Assistance for Emergencies;
Food Pantry; Used Furniture; Information and
Referral; Clothing Referral; Laundry Voucher;
Medication; Transportation Vouchers; Rent
Funds; Classes on Cooking; Budget and
Money; Credit; Managing a Checking
Account

The Church Federation of
Greater Indianapolis, Inc.

1100 W. 42nd St., Ste. 345, Indianapolis, IN
46208 Tel. (317)926-5371 Fax (317)926-5373
E-mail: —
Website: —
Media Contact, Comm. Consultant, Julie Foster
Exec. Dir., Rev. Dr. Angelique Walker-Smith
Pres., Rev. Dr. James B. Lemler
Treas., R. Wayne Reynolds
Major activities: "Sacred Spaces" (A Christian
Partnership of Neighborhood Action) Reclaim-
ing Our Neighborhoods through Community
Formation, Community Resourcing, Com-
munity Education, and Communications; The
Sanctuary Church Movement; "Loving Our
Children": An Educational Partnership
Between Church and Public Schools for "at
risk" Children; Indianapolis Prayer Network
to Stop the Violence

Evansville Area Community
of Churches, Inc.

414 N.W. Sixth St., Evansville, IN 47708-1332
Tel. (812)425-3524 Fax (812)425-3525
E-mail: —
Website: —
Media Contact, Dir. of Programs & Church
Relations, Barbara G. Gaisser
Dir. of Programs/Ofc. Mgr., Barbara G. Gaisser
Exec. Dir., Rev. William F. Bower
Weekday Dir., Linda M. Schenk
Pres., Rev. Steve Lintzench
V. Pres., John Musgrove
Sec., Rev. Shane O'Neill
Treas., Ms. Julia Wood
Major activities: Christian Education;
Community Responsibility & Service; Public
Relations; Interpretation; Church Women
United; Institutional Ministries; Interfaith
Dialogue; Earth Care Ethics; Public Education
Support; Disaster Preparedness; Job Loss
Networking Support Group; Interfaith TV
Program; Women in Ministry Support Group;
Intl. Women's Day Celebration Events

Indiana Partners for
Christian Unity and Mission

P.O. Box 88790, Indianapolis, IN 46208-0790
Tel. (800)746-2310 Fax (317)687-8337
E-mail: indunity@aol.com
Website: http://members.aol.com/indunity/ipcum
homepage.html
Media Contact, James Dougans
Pres., Rev. Andy Kinsey
Treas., Rev. Robert Kirk
Major activities: Spring Celebration of Christian
Unity; Fall Educational Conference; Network
the 117 ministerial Associations in Indiana;
Initiate dialogue and the building of relation-
ships between ecumenical officers and judicato-
ry leaders; Task Force on Racial Reconciliation

Interfaith Community Council,
Inc.

702 E. Market St., New Albany, IN 47150 Tel.
(812)948-9248 Fax (812)948-9249
E-mail: —
Website: —
Media Contact, Exec. Dir., David Bos
Exec. Dir., Rev. Dr. David Bos
Child Dev. Center, Dir., Dee Wright
Programs/Emergency Assistance, Jane Alcorn
Hedden House, Dir., Stephanie Al-Uqdah
RSVP, Dir., Matie Watts
Major activities: Child Development Center;
Emergency Assistance; Hedden House
(Transitional Shelter for Recovering
Substance Abuse Women);Retired Senior
Volunteer Program; New Clothing and Toy
Drives; Convalescent Sitter & Mother's Aides;
Senior Day College; Emergency Food
Distribution; Homeless Prevention

235

Lafayette Urban Ministry
525 N. 4th St., Lafayette, IN 47901 Tel. (317)423-2691 Fax (317)423-2693
E-mail: —
Website: —
Media Contact, Exec. Dir., Joseph Micon
Exec. Dir., Joseph Micon
Advocate Coord., Rebecca Smith
Public Policy Coord., Harry Brown
Pres., John Wilson
Major activities: Social Justice Ministries with and among the Poor

United Religious Community of St. Joseph County
2015 Western Ave., South Bend, IN 46629 Tel. (219)282-2397 Fax (219)282-8014
E-mail: —
Website: —
Media Contact, Exec. Dir., Dr. James J. Fisko
Exec. Dir., Dr. James J. Fisko
Pres., Mary Lou Deardorff
Victim Offender Reconciliation Prog., Victim Impact Panel Coord., Martha Sallows
Volunteer Advocacy Project: Coord., Sara Goetz; Coord., Linda Jung-Zimmerman
Major activities: Religious Understanding; Interfaith/Ecumenical Education; CROP Walk; Hunger Education; Housing and Homelessness Issues; Clergy Education and Support; Refugee Resettlement; Victim Assistance; Advocacy for the Needy

West Central Neighborhood Ministry, Inc.
1316 Broadway, Fort Wayne, IN 46802-3304 Tel. (219)422-6618 Fax (219)422-9319
E-mail: —
Website: —
Media Contact, Exec. Dir., Andrea S. Thomas
Exec. Dir., Andrea S. Thomas
Ofc. Mgr., J. R. Stopperich
Neighborhood Services Dir., Carol Salge
Senior Citizens Dir., Gayle Mann
Youth Director, Bevaun Graves
Major activities: After-school Programs; Teen Drop-In Center; Summer Day Camp; Summer Overnight Camp; Information and Referral Services; Food Pantry; Nutrition Program for Senior Citizens; Senior Citizens Activities; Tutoring; Developmental Services for Families & Senior Citizens; Parent Club

IOWA

*Ecumenical Ministries of Iowa (EMI)
3816-36th St., Ste. 202, Des Moines, IA 50310-4722 Tel. (515)255-5905 Fax (515)255-1421
E-mail: emi.parti@ecunet.org
Website: —
Media Contact, Exec. Dir., Dr. James R. Ryan
Exec. Dir., Dr. James R. Ryan
Admn. Asst., Martha E. Jungck

Major activities: Facilitating the denominations'-cooperative agenda of resourcing local expression of the church; Assess needs & develop responses through Justice and Unity Commissions

*Iowa Religious Media Services
3816 36th St., Des Moines, IA 50310 Tel. (515)277-2920 Fax —
E-mail: —
Website: —
Media Contact, Dir., Sue Sonner
Educ. Consultant, Joanne Talarico, CHM
Production Mgr., Dr. Richard Harbart
Major activities: Media Library for Churches in 6 Denominations in Iowa; Provide Video Production Services for Churches, Non-profit & Educational organizations

Churches United, Inc.
866 4th Ave. SE, Cedar Rapids, IA 52403 Tel. (319)366-7163 Fax —
E-mail: —
Website: —
Media Contact, Admn. Sec., Marcey Luxa
Admn. Sec., Marcey Luxa
Pres., Rev. Carroll Brown
Treas., Joseph Luxa, 450 19th St. NW, Cedar Rapids, IA 52405
Major activities: Communication/resource center for member churches; Community Information and Referral; Community Food Bank; L.E.A.F. (Local Emergency Assistance Fund; Care Center Ministry; Radio/TV Ministry; Ecumenical City-wide Celebrations; CROP/World Hunger; Jail Chaplaincy Ministry

Des Moines Area Religious Council
3816 - 36th St., Des Moines, IA 50310 Tel. (515)277-6969 Fax (515)255-1421
E-mail: dmreligions@juno.com
Website: —
Media Contact, Exec. Dir., Forrest Harms
Exec. Dir., Forrest Harms
Pres., Sharon Baker
Treas., Bill Corwin
Major activities: Outreach and Nurture; Education; Social Concerns; Mission; Emergency Food Pantry; Ministry to Widowed; Child Care Assistance

KANSAS

*Kansas Ecumenical Ministries
5833 SW 29th St., Topeka, KS 66614-2499 Tel. (785)272-9531 Fax (785)272-9533
E-mail: —
Website: —
Media Contact, Exec. Dir., Dr. Joe M. Hendrixson
E-mail: joe_hendrixson@ecunet.org
Exec. Dir., Dr. Joe M. Hendrixson

Pres., Rev. Art Jaggard
Vice-Pres., Rev. Sally Fahrenthold
Sec., Rev. Jane Ireland
Major activities: State Council of Churches; Legislative Activities; Program Facilitation and Coordination; Higher Education Concerns; Education; Mother-to-Mother Program; Peacemaking; Rural Concerns; Housing; Health Care

Cross-Lines Cooperative Council
736 Shawnee Ave., Kansas City, KS 66105 Tel. (913)281-3388 Fax (913)281-2344
E-mail: xlines@TFS.net
Website: —
Media Contact, Dir. of Dev., Bill Scholl
Exec. Dir., Marilynn Rudell
Dir. of Programs, Rev. Robert L. Moore
Major activities: Emergency Assistance; Family Support Advocacy; Crisis Heating/Plumbing Repair; Thrift Store; Workcamp Experiences; Adult Education (GED and Basic English Literacy Skills); School Supplies; Christmas Store; Institute for Poverty and Empowerment Studies (Education on poverty for the non-poor)

Inter-Faith Ministries-Wichita
829 N. Market, Wichita, KS 67214-3519 Tel. (316)264-9303 Fax (316)264-2233
E-mail: —
Website: —
Media Contact, Exec. Dir., Sam Muyskens
Exec. Dir., Rev. Sam Muyskens
Ofc. Mgr., Patricia Chebultz
Care Coordination Team: Dir., Cody Patton
Inter-Faith Inn (Homeless Shelter), Dir., Sandy Swank
Operation Holiday, Dir., Sally Dewey
Dev./Communications, Dir., James D. Marler
Campaign to End Childhood Hunger, Karen Fitzgerald
Community Ministry, —
Racial Justice, Coord., Rev. Lucius Woodard
Major activities: Communications; Urban Education; Inter-religious Understanding; Community Needs and Issues; Theology and Worship; Hunger; HIV/AIDS Ministry; Family Life; Multi-Cultural Concerns

KENTUCKY

*Kentucky Council of Churches
412 Rose St., Lexington, KY 40508 Tel. (606)253-3027 Fax (606)231-5028
E-mail: kycnclch@internetMCI.com
Website: —
Media Contact, Exec. Dir., Nancy Jo Kemper
Exec. Dir., Rev. Nancy Jo Kemper
Disaster Recovery Prog., Coord., Rev. John Kays
Pres., Fr. Jude Weisenbeck
Major activities: Christian Unity; Public Policy; Justice; Disaster Response; Peace Issues; Racism; Health Care Issues; Local Ecumenism; Rural Land/Farm Issues; Gambling; Capital Punishment

Eastern Area Community Ministries
P.O. Box 43049, Louisville, KY 40253-0049 Tel. (502)244-6141 Fax (502)254-5141
E-mail: —
Website: —
Media Contact, Exec. Dir., Rev. Judy Sutherlin
Exec. Dir., Rev. Judy Sutherlin
Board Pres., Rev. John Allen
Board Sec., Tina Drozdz
Board Treas., Homer Lacy, Jr.
Youth and Family Services, Prog. Dir., Bill Jewell
Older Adult Services, Associate Program Dir., Sharon Eckler
Neighborhood Visitor Program, Prog. Dir., Kathy Raymond
Major activities: Food Pantry; Clothes Closet; Meals on Wheels; Teen Court; Community Worship Services; Good Start for Kids; Juvenile Court Diversion; Community Development; Transient Fund; Ministerial Association

Fern Creek/Highview United Ministries
7502 Tangelo Dr., Louisvlle, KY 40228 Tel. (502)239-7407 Fax (502)239-7454
E-mail: FernCreek.Ministries@crnky.org
Website: —
Exec. Dir., Kay Sanders, 7502 Tangelo Dr., Louisville, KY 40228 Tel. (502)239-7407
Exec. Dir., Kay Sanders
Pres., Linda Masterson
Major activities: Ecumenically supported social service agency providing services to the community, including Emergency Financial Assistance, Food/Clothing, Health Aid Equipment Loans, Information/Referral, Advocacy, Monthly Blood-Pressure Checks; Holiday Programs, Life Skills Training; Mentoring Care Management; Adult Day-Care Program

Hazard-Perry County Community Ministries, Inc.
P.O. Box 1506, Hazard, KY 41702-1506 Tel. (606)436-0051 Fax (606)436-0071
E-mail: —
Website: —
Media Contact, Gerry Feamster-Roll
Exec. Dir., Gerry Feamster-Roll
Chpsn., Sarah Hughes
V. Chpsn., Susan Duff
Sec., Virginia Campbell
Treas., Margaret Adams
Major activities: Food Pantry/Crisis Aid Program; Day Care; Summer Day Camp; After-school Program; Christmas Tree; Family Support Center; Adult Day Care; Transitional Housing

237

Highlands Community Ministries

1140 Cherokee Rd., Louisville, KY 40204 Tel. (502)451-3695 Fax —
E-mail: IFADIR@iglou.com
Website: —
Media Contact, Exec. Dir., Stan Esterle
Exec. Dir., Stan Esterle
Major activities: Welfare Assistance; Day Care; Counseling with Youth, Parents and Adults; Adult Day Care; Social Services for Elderly; Housing for Elderly and Handicapped; Ecumenical Programs; Community Classes; Activities for Children; Neighborhood and Business organization

Kentuckiana Interfaith Community

1113 South 4th St., Louisville, KY 40203 Tel. (502)587-6265 Fax (502)540-5017
E-mail: —
Website: —
Media Contact, Exec. Dir.,—
Pres., Annette Turner
Vice-Pres., Cantor Elihu Flax
Sec., Rev. Dr. Wallace Garner
Treas., J. Patrick Serey
Admn. Sec./Program Asst., Ms. Karin Talbott-Hill
Major activities: Christian/Jewish Ministries in KY, Southern IN; Consensus Advocacy; Interfaith Dialogue; InterChurch Family Ministries; Community Hunger Walk; Racial Justice Forums; Network for Neighborhood-based Ministries; Community Winterhelp; LUAH/Hunger & Racial Justice Commission; *Faith Channel*-Cable TV Station, *Horizon* and *Ark* Newspapers; Police/Comm. Relations Task Force; Ecumenical Strategic Planning; Networking with Seminaries & Religious-Affiliated Institutions

Ministries United South Central Louisville (M.U.S.C.L., Inc.)

1207 Hart Avenue, Louisville, KY 42013 Tel. (502)363-9087 Fax (502)363-9087 (call first)
Media Contact, Ex. Dir., Rev. Antonio (Tony) Aja, M.Div. Tel. (502)363-2383
E-mail: Tony_Aja@pcusa.org
Website: —
Ex. Dir., Rev. Antonio (Tony) Aja, M.Div.
Airport Relocation Ombudsman, Rev. Phillip Garrett, M.Div. Tel. (502)361-2706; E-mail: philombud@aol.com
Senior Adults Programs, Dir., Mrs. Jeannine Blakeman, BSSW
Emergency Assistance, Dir., Mr. Michael Hundley
Low-Income Coord., Ms. Wanda Irvio
Youth Services, Dir., Rev. Bill Sanders, M.Div.
Volunteers Coord., Mrs. Carol Stemmle
Case Manager, —

Northern Kentucky Interfaith Commission, Inc.

901 York St., Newport, KY 41072 Tel. (606)581-2237 Fax (606)261-6041
E-mail: —
Website: —
Media Contact, Exec. Dir., Rev. William C. Neuroth
Pres., Rev. Donald Smith
Sec., Ms. Jo Shade
Treas., Sister Marilyn Hoffman
Admin. Asst., Karen Yates
Major activities: Understanding Faiths; Meeting Spiritual and Human Needs; Enabling Churches to Greater Ministry

Paducah Cooperative Ministry

1359 S. 6th St., Paducah, KY 42003 Tel. (502)442-6795 Fax (502)442-6812
E-mail: —
Website: —
Media Contact, Dir., Heidi Suhrheinrich
Dir., Heidi Suhrheinrich
Chpsn., Dr. Rick C. Dye
Vice-Chpsn., Father Brian Johnson
Major activities: Programs for: Hungry, Elderly, Poor, Homeless, Handicapped, Undereducated

South East Associated Ministries (SEAM)

6500 Six Mile Ln., Ste.A, Louisville, KY 40218 Tel. (502)499-9350 Fax —
E-mail: —
Website: —
Media Contact, Mary Beth Helton
Exec. Dir., Mary Beth Helton
Life Skills Center, Dir., Robert Davis
Youth Services, Dir., Tracey Frazier
Pres., Bud McCord
Treas., Joe Hays
Major activities: Emergency Food, Clothing and Financial Assistance; Life Skills Center (Programs of Prevention and Case Management and Self-Sufficiency Through Education, Empowerment, Support Groups, etc.); Bloodmobile; Ecumenical Education and Worship; Juvenile Court Diversion; TEEN Court; Teen Crime & the Community

South Louisville Community Ministries

Peterson Social Services Center, 204 Seneca Trail, Louisville, KY 40214 Tel. (502)367-6445 Fax (502)361-4668
E-mail: slcm@crnky.org
Website: —
Media Contact, Exec. Dir., J. Michael Jupin
Bd. Chair., Jane Davis
Bd. Vice-Chair., Cyndi Marlow
Bd. Treas., Eugene Wells
Exec. Dir., Rev. J. Michael Jupin
Major activities: Food, Clothing & Financial Assistance; Home Delivered Meals, Transportation, Refugee Resettlement; Ecumenical Worship; Juvenile Diversion Program; Affordable Housing; Adult Day Care; Truancy Prevention; Case Management

St. Matthews Area Ministries
201 Biltmore Rd., Louisville, KY 40207 Tel. (502)893-0205 Fax (502)893-0206
E-mail: —
Website: —
Media Contact, Dan G. Lane
Exec. Dir., Dan G. Lane
Child Care, Dir., Janet Hennessey
Dir. Assoc., Eileen Bartlett
Major activities: Child Care; Emergency Assistance; Youth Services; Interchurch Worship and Education; Housing Development; Counseling; Information & Referral; Mentor Program; Developmentally Disabled

LOUISIANA

*Louisiana Interchurch Conference
660 N. Foster Dr., Ste. A-225, Baton Rouge, LA 70806 Tel. (504)924-0213 Fax (504)927-7860
Website: —
Media Contact, Exec. Dir., Rev. C. Dana Krutz
E-mail: dan_krutz@ecunet.org
Exec. Dir., Rev. C. Dana Krutz
Pres., Bishop Thomas L. Hoyt, Jr.
Major activities: Ministries to Aging; Prison Reform; Liaison with State Agencies; Ecumenical Dialogue; Institutional Chaplains; Racism

Greater Baton Rouge Federation of Churches and Synagogues
P.O. Box 626, Baton Rouge, LA 70821 Tel. (504)925-3414 Fax (504)925-3065
E-mail: —
Website: —
Media Contact, Exec. Dir., Rev. Jeff Day
Exec. Dir., Rev. Jeff Day
Admn. Asst., Marion Zachary
Pres., Bette Lavine
Pres.-Elect, Tom Sylvest
Treas., Randy Trahan
Major activities: Combating Hunger; Housing (Helpers for Housing); Interfaith Relations; Interfaith Concert; Race Relations

Greater New Orleans Federation of Churches
4545 Magnolia St., #206, New Orleans, LA 70115 Tel. (504)897-4488 Fax (504)897-4208
E-mail: —
Website: —
Exec. Dir., Rev. J. Richard Randels
Major activities: REACH (Religious Ecumenical Access Channel); Information and Referral; Food Distribution(FEMA); Forward Together TV Program; Sponsors seminars for pastors (e.g. church growth, clergy taxes,etc.); Police Chaplaincy; Fire Chaplaincy

MAINE

*Maine Council of Churches
15 Pleasant Ave., Portland, ME 04103 Tel. (207)772-1918 Fax (207)772-2947
E-mail: mecchurchs@aol.com
Website: http://www. mainetoday.koz.com/maine/mcc
Media Contact, Communications Director, Karen Caouette
Exec. Dir., Thomas C. Ewell
Assoc. Dir., Douglas Cruger
Admin. Asst., —
Pres., Elizabeth Ring
Sec., —
Treas., Rev. Thomas Merrill
Major activities: Criminal Justice Reform and Restorative Justice; Legislative Work and Coalition Work in Health, Homelessness, and Children; Advocacy

MARYLAND

*Central Maryland Ecumenical Council
Cathedral House, 4 E. University Pkwy., Baltimore, MD 21218 Tel. (410)467-6194 Fax (410)554-6387
E-mail: —
Website: —
Media Contact, Admn., Martha Young
Pres., Rev. H.J. Siegfried Otto
Major activities: Interchurch Communications and Collaboration; Information Systems; Ecumenical Relations; Urban Mission and Advocacy; Staff for Judicatory Leadership Council; Commission on Dialogue; Commission on Church & Society; Commission on Admin. & Dev.; Ecumenical Choral Concerts; Ecumenical Worship Services

Community Ministries of Rockville
114 West Montgomery Ave., Rockville, MD 20850 Tel. (301)762-8682 Fax (301)762-2939
E-mail: —
Website: —
Media Contact, Christine Tetrault
Exec. Dir. & Comm. Min., Mansfield M. Kaseman
Managing Dir., Christine L. Tetrault
Major activities: Shelter Care; Emergency Assistance; Elderly Home Care; Affordable Housing; Political Advocacy; Community Education

Community Ministry of Montgomery County
114 West Montgomery Ave., Rockville, MD 20850 Tel. (301)762-8682 Fax (301)762-2939
E-mail: —
Website: —
Media Contact, Exec. Dir., Lincoln S. Dring, Jr.
Exec. Dir., Lincoln S. Dring, Jr.
Major activities: Interfaith Clothing Center; Emergency Assistance Coalition; The Advocacy Function; Information and Referral Services; Friends in Action; The Thanksgiving

239

Hunger Drive; Thanksgiving in February; Congregation Based Shelters

MASSACHUSETTS

*Massachusetts Council of Churches

14 Beacon St., Rm. 416, Boston, MA 02108 Tel. (617)523-2771 Fax (617)523-1483
E-mail: ecumass@juno.com
Website: —
Media Contact, Exec. Dir., Rev. Diane C. Kessler
Exec. Dir., Rev. Diane C. Kessler
Assoc. Dir., Dr. Ruy Costa
Ecum. Working Group to Counter Racism, Adjunct Assoc., Rev. W. C. Watson, Jr.
Consultant, Rev. Betsy Sowers
Pres., Mrs. Mary Alice Stahleker
Vice-Pres., Rev. Canon Edward Rodman
Sec., Rev. William Perkins
Treas., Rev. James Pannell
Major activities: Christian Unity; Education and Evangelism; Defend Social Justice & Individual Rights; Ecumenical Worship; Services and Resources for Individuals and Churches

Attleboro Area Council of Churches, Inc.

505 N. Main St., Attleboro, MA 02703 Tel. (508)222-2933 Fax (508)222-2933
E-mail: —
Website: —
Media Contact, Executive Director, Carolyn L. Bronkar
Exec. Dir., Carolyn L. Bronkar
Admn. Sec., Joan H. Lindstrom
Staff Asst., Emergency Food Program, Lynne F. Sias
Hosp. Chplns., Rev. Dr. William B. Udall and Rev. Janet Long
Pres., Rev. David Hill, 52 Glendale Rd., Attleboro, MA 02703
Treas., Ray Larson, 33 Watson Ave., Attleboro, MA 02703
Major activities: Hospital Chaplaincy; personal Growth/Skill Workshops; Ecumenical Worship; Media Resource Center; Referral Center; Communications/Publications; Community Social Action; Food'n Friends Kitchens; Nursing Home Volunteer Visitation Program; Lay School of Christian Theology

The Cape Cod Council of Churches, Inc.

320 Main St., P.O. Box 758, Hyannis, MA 02601 Tel. (508)775-5073 Fax —
E-mail: —
Website: —
Media Contact, Exec. Dir., Rev. Susan Royce Scribner
Exec. Dir., Rev. Susan Royce Scribner
Pres., Mr. Barry Jones-Henry, Sr.
Chaplain, Cape Cod Hospital, Rev. William Wilcox
Chaplain, Falmouth Hospital, Rev. Allen Page

Chaplain, House of Correction & Jail, Rev. Thomas Shepherd
Chaplain, Rehabilitation Hospital of the Cape and Islands, Mrs. Elizabeth Stommel
Service Center & Thrift Shop: P.O. Box 125, Dennisport, MA 02639 Tel. (508)394-6361
Major activities: Pastoral Care; Social Concerns; Religious Education; Emergency Distribution of Food, Clothing, Furniture; Referral and Information; Church World Service; Interfaith Relations; Media Presence; Hospital & Jail Chaplaincy; Arts & Religion

Cooperative Metropolitan Ministries

474 Centre St., Newton, MA 02158 Tel. (617)244-3650 Fax (617)244-0569
E-mail: —
Website: —
Media Contact, Exec. Dir., Claire Kashuck
Exec. Dir., Claire Kashuck
Bd. Pres., Sr. Joyceyn McMullen
Treas., Karen Gunn
Clk., Barbara Baker
Major activities: Low Income, Legislative Advocacy; Networking; Volunteerism; Publications on Elder Housing Options; Suburban/Urban Bridges; Racial Justice

Council of Churches of Greater Springfield

39 Oakland St., Springfield, MA 01108 Tel. (413)733-2149 Fax (413)733-9817
E-mail: —
Website: —
Media Contact, Asst. to Dir., Sr. John Bridgid
Exec. Dir., Rev. Ann Geer
Community Min., Dir., Rev. L. Edgar Depaz
Pres., The Rev. Dr. Ledyard Baxter
Treas., John Pearson, Esq
Major activities: Christian Education Resource Center; Advocacy; Emergency Fuel Fund; Peace and Justice Division; Community Ministry; Task Force on Racism; Hospital and Jail Chaplaincies; Pastoral Service; Crisis Counseling; Christian Social Relations; Relief Collections; Ecumenical and Interfaith Relations; Ecumenical Dialogue with Roman Catholic Diocese; Mass Media; Church/ Community Projects and Dialogue

Greater Lawrence Council of Churches

117A S. Broadway, Lawrence, MA 01843 Tel. (508)686-4012 Fax —
E-mail: glcclawrence@juno.com
Website: —
Media Contact, Exec. Dir., David Edwards
Exec. Dir., David Edwards
Pres., Carol Rabs
Vice-Pres., Rev. Michael Graham
Admn. Asst., Linda Sullivan
Major activities: Ecumenical Worship; Radio Ministry; Hospital and Nursing Home Chaplaincy; Church Women United;

Afterschool Children's Program; Vacation Bible School

Inter-Church Council of Greater New Bedford

412 County St., New Bedford, MA 02740-5096 Tel. (508)993-6242 Fax (508)991-3158
E-mail: —
Website: —
Media Contact, Exec. Min., Rev. Edward R. Dufresne, Ph.D.
Exec. Min., Rev. Edward R. Dufresne, Ph.D.
Pres., Pamela Pollock
Treas., Christopher Bunnell
Major activities: Pastoral Counseling; Chaplaincy; Housing for Elderly; Urban Affairs; Community Development; Parish Nurse Ministry; Accounting for the Developmentally Challenged

Massachusetts Commission on Christian Unity

82 Luce St., Lowell, MA 01852-3034 Tel. (978)453-5423 Fax (978)453-5423
E-mail: —
Website: —
Media Contact, Exec. Dir., Rev. K. Gordon White
Exec. Sec., Rev. K. Gordon White
Major activities: Faith and Order Dialogue with Church Judicatories; Guidelines & Pastoral Directives for Inter-Church Marriages

Worcester County Ecumenical Council

4 Caroline St., Worcester, MA 01604 Tel. (508)757-8385 Fax (508)795-7704
E-mail: —
Website: —
Media Contact, Sec., Eleanor G. Bird
Dir., Rev. Steven Alspach
Pres., Rev. Dr. Jonathan Wright-Gray
Major activities: Clusters of Churches; Electronic Media; Ecumenical Worship and Dialogue; Interfaith Activities; Resource Connection for Churches; Hunger Ministries; Group Purchasing Consortium

MICHIGAN

*Michigan Ecumenical Forum
809 Center St., Ste. 5, Lansing, MI 48906 Tel. (517)485-4395 Fax (517)482-8751
E-mail: ecumenical@earthlink.net
Website: —
Media Contact, Coord./Exec. Dir., Rev. Steven L. Johns-Boehme, 809 Centre St., Ste. 5, Lansing, MI 48906 Tel. (517)485-4395
Coord./Exec. Dir., Rev. Steven L. Johns-Boehme
Major activities: Communication and Coordination; Support and Development of Regional Ecumenical Fora; Ecumenical Studies; Fellowship and Celebration; Church and Society Issues; Continuing Education

ACCORD-Area Churches Together-Serving

312 Capital Ave., NE, Battle Creek, MI 49017 Tel. (616)966-2500 Fax —
E-mail: —
Website: —
Media Contact, Exec. Dir., —
Exec. Dir., —
Pres., Rev. Erick Johnson
Vice-Pres./Church, Rev. Joy Rogers
Vice-Pres./Admn., —
Vice-Pres./Community, Rev. Susan Valiquette
Major activities: CROP Walk; Food Closet; Christian Sports; Week of Prayer for Christian Unity; Nursing Home Vesper Services; Ecumenical Worship

Bay Area Ecumenical Forum

103 E. Midland St., Bay City, MI 48706 Tel. (517)686-1360 Fax —
E-mail: —
Website: —
Media Contact, Rev. Karen Banaszak
Major activities: Ecumenical Worship; Community Issues; Christian Unity; Education; CROP Walk

Berrien County Association of Churches

275 Pipestone, Benton Harbor, MI 49022 Tel. (616)926-0030 Fax —
E-mail: —
Website: —
Media Contact, Sec., Mary Ann Hinz
Pres., Evelyn Maki
Dir., Street Ministry, Rev. James Atterberry
Major activities: Street Ministry; CROP Walk; Community Issues; Fellowship; Christian Unity; Camp Warren; Hospital Chaplaincy Program; Publish *Annual County Church Directory* and Monthly Newsletter; Resource Guide for Helping Needy; Distribution of *Worship Opportunity—Brochure for Tourists*

Christian Communication Council of Metropolitan Detroit Churches

1300 Mutual Building, 28 W. Adams, Detroit, MI 48226 Tel. (313)962-0340
E:mail: councilweb@aol.com
Website: http://users.aol.com/councilweb/index.htm
Media Contact, Rev. Richard Singleton, 28 W. Adams, Detroit, MI 48226 Tel. (313)962-0340 Fax (313)962-9044
Exec. Dir., Rev. Richard Singleton
Meals for Shut-ins, Prog. Dir., John Simpson
Major activities: Theological and Social Concerns; Ecumenical Worship; Educational Services; Electronic Media; Print Media; Meals for Shut-Ins; Summer Feeding Program

Grand Rapids Area Center for Ecumenism (GRACE)

38 Fulton West, Grand Rapids, MI 49503-2628
Tel. (616)774-2042 Fax (616)774-2883
E-mail:dbaak@ecunet.org
Website: http://www.grcmc.org/grace
Media Contact, Exec. Dir., Rev. David P. Baak
Exec. Dir., Rev. David P. Baak
Prog. Dir., Lisa H. Mitchell
Major activities: AIDS Pastoral Care Network (Client Services Education/ Volunteer Coordination); Hunger Walk ; Education /Relationships; (Ecumenical Lecture, Christian Unity Worship/Events, Interfaith Dialogue Conference, Prayer Against Violence); (Affiliates: ACCESS-All County Churches Emergency Support System, FISH for My People-transportation); Publications (Religious Community Directory, Grace Notes); Racial Justice Institute; Project Zero Mentoring (Welfare Reform Response)

Greater Flint Association of Christian Churches

308 W. Third Ave., Flint, MI 48502 Tel. (810)238-3691 Fax (810)238-4463
E-mail: —
Website: —
Media Contact, Rev. Charlotte VanDyke or Mrs. Constance D. Neely
Pres., Rev. James F. Offrink
Major activities: Christian Education; Christian Unity; Christian Missions; Hospital and Nursing Home Visitors; Church in Society; American Bible Society Materials; Interfaith Dialogue; Church Teacher Exchange Sunday; Directory of Area Faiths and Clergy; Thanksgiving & Easter Sunrise Services; CROP Walks

The Jackson County Interfaith Council

425 Oakwood, P.O. Box 156, Clarklake, MI 49234-0156 Tel. (517)529-9721 Fax —
E-mail: —
Website: —
Media Contact, Exec. Dir., Rev. Loyal H. Wiemer, Box 156, Clarklake, MI 49234 Tel. (517)529-9721
Exec. Dir., Rev. Loyal H. Wiemer
Major activities: Chaplaincy at Institutions and Senior Citizens Residences; Martin L. King, Jr. Day Celebrations; Ecumenical Council Representation; Radio and TV Programs; Food Pantry; Interreligious Events; Clergy Directory

Muskegon County Cooperating Churches

1218 Jefferson St., Muskegon, MI 49441 Tel. (616)727-6000 Fax (616)727-6011
E-mail: —
Website: —
Media Contact, Program Coordinator, Delphine Hogston

Pres., Rev. Dr. James Harwood
Major activities: Prison Ministry; CROP Walk; Ecumenical Worship; Education; Jewish-Christian Dialogue; AIDS Ministry; Community Issues; Senior Issues; Racial Reconciliation; Faith News TV Ministry; Tutoring

MINNESOTA

*Minnesota Council of Churches

122 W. Franklin Ave., Rm. 100, Minneapolis, MN 55404 Tel. (612)870-3600 Fax (612)870-3622,
E-mail: mcc@mnchurches.org
Website: http://www.mnchurches.org
Media Contact, Exec. Dir., Rev. Peg Chemberlin
E-mail: peg.chemberlin@ecunet.org
Exec. Dir., Rev. Peg Chemberlin
Life & Work, Dir., Robert Hulteen
Unity & Relationships, Dir., Rev. Lydia Veliko, E-mail: veliko@ecunet.org
Refugee Services, Dir., Tatiana Pigoreva
Indian Ministry, Dir., —
Communications, Dir., Dr. Robert M. Frame, II
Facilities, Dir., Cynthia Darrington-Ottinger
Tri-Council Coordinating Commission: Co-Dirs., James and Nadine Addington
Research Dir. & Admn. Asst., James Casebolt
Joint Religious Legislative Coalition, Dir., Brian A. Rusche
Pres., Rev. William Kaseman
Major activities: Minnesota Church Center; Local Ecumenism; Life & Work: Anti-Racism; Hispanic Ministries, Indian Ministry; Legislative Advocacy; Refugee Services; Service to Newly Legalized/Undocumented persons; Sexual Exploitation within the Religious Community; Unity & Relationships: Chaplaincy; Clergy Support; Consultation on Church Union; Ecumenical Study & Dialogue; Jewish-Christian Relations; Muslim-Christian Relations; State Fair Ministry; Tri-Council Coordinating Commission (Minnesota Churches Anti-Racism Initiative, Religious Initiative for Gender Justice); Active Non-Violence; No-Interest Small Loan Program; Child Labor Discussions

Arrowhead Interfaith Council

230 E. Skyline Pkwy., Duluth, MN 55811 Tel. (218)727-5020 Fax (218)727-5022
E-mail: —
Website: —
Media Contact, Pres., Alan Cutter
Pres., Alan Cutter
Vice-Pres., Amy Berstein
Sec., John H. Kemp
Major activities: InterFaith Dialogue; Joint Religious Legislative Coalition; Corrections Chaplaincy; Human Justice and Community Concerns; Community Seminars; Children's Concerns

Community Emergency Assistance Program (CEAP)

7231 Brooklyn Blvd., Brooklyn Center, MN 55429 Tel. (612)566-9600 Fax (612)566-9604
E-mail: —
Website: —
Media Contact, Exec. Dir., Tia Henry-Johnson
Exec. Dir., Tia Henry-Johnson
Major activities: Provision of Basic Needs (Food, Clothing); Emergency Financial Assistance for Shelter; Home Delivered Meals; Chore Services and Homemaking Assistance; Family Loan Program; Volunteer Services

Greater Minneapolis Council of Churches

1001 E. Lake St., P.O. Box 7509, Minneapolis, MN 55407-0509 Tel. (612)721-8687 Fax (612)722-8669
Website: http://www.gmcc.org
Media Contact, Dir. of Communications, Darcy Hanzlik
Exec. Dir., Rev. Dr. Gary B. Reierson
E-mail: reierson@gmcc.org
Pres., David Nasby
Treas., Dorothy Bridges
Indian Work: Sr.Assoc. Exec. Dir., Mary Ellen Dumas; Assoc. Dir., Noya Woodrich
Programs, Assoc. Exec. Dir., Edward Duren, Jr.
Minnesota FoodShare, Dir., Rev. Christopher Morton
Handyworks, Dir., Mary Jo Tarasar
Correctional Chaplains: Rev. Susan Allers Hatlie; Rev. Thomas Van Leer; Imam Charles El-Amin; Rev. Lonnie Branch; Susan Jourdain
Congregations In Community, Dir., Rev. Bruce Bjork
Shared Ministries Tutorial Program, Dir., Katherine Beecham
Div. of Indian Work: Family Violence Prog., Dir., Herb Grant; Teen Parents Prog., Dir., Leroy LaPlante, Jr.; Youth Leadership Dev. Prog., Dir., Vivinnie Crowe; Horizons Unlimited, Dir., Monica Guilhot-Chartrand; Ampau (New Beginnings) House, Dir., Leroy LaPlante, Jr.
Finance & Admin., Assoc. Exec. Dir., Dennis Anderson
Institutional Advancement: Assoc. Exec. Dir., Don R. Riggs
Metro Paint-A-Thon, Coord., Beth Storey
Minnesota Churches Anti-Racism Initiative, Dir., James and Nadine Addington
Religious Initiative for Gender Justice, Assoc. Dir., Rev. Linda Gesling
Congregations Concerned for Children Child Advocacy Network, Coord., Norma Bourland
Project Restoration, Dir., Rev. Bruce Bjork
Center for Urban Service, Dir., Rev. Bruce Bjork
Child Care Center Challenge Grant Fund, Exec. Dir., Rev. Dr. Gary B. Reirson
Major activities: Indian Work (Emergency Assistance, Youth Leadership, self-sufficiency, Jobs Program, Teen Indian Parents

Program, and Family Violence Program); Minnesota FoodShare; Metro Paint-A-Thon; Shared Ministries Tutorial Program; Congregations In Community; Correctional Chaplaincy Program; HandyWorks; Education and Celebration; Anti-racism Initiative; Anti-sexism Program; Child Advocacy; Social Justice Advocacy; Child Care Center Start-up; Home Renovation; Affordable Housing; Urban Immersion Service Retreats; Welfare Reform; Economic Self-Sufficiency

The Joint Religious Legislative Coalition

122 W. Franklin Ave., Rm. 315, Minneapolis, MN 55404 Tel. (612)870-3670, (888)870-1402
Media Contact, Exec. Dir., Brian A. Rusche
E-mail: jrlc@ecunet.org
Website: http://www.jrlc.org
Exec. Dir., Brian A. Rusche
Research Dir., James Casebolt
Congregational Organizer, Rev. Becky Myrick
Major activities: Lobbying at State Legislature; Researching Social Justice Issues and Preparing Position Statements; Organizing Grassroots Citizen's Lobby

Metropolitan Interfaith Council on Affordable Housing (MICAH)

122 W. Franklin Ave., #310, Minneapolis, MN 55404 Tel.(612)871-8980 Fax (612)871-8984
E-mail: info@micah.org
Website: http://www.micah.org
Media Contact, Ex. Dir., Joy Sorensen Navarre
Ex. Dir., Joy Sorensen Navarre
Assoc. Dir., JosÇ Trejo
Congregational Organizer, Jodi Nelson
Congregational Organizer, Elaine Lyford-Nojima, Jean Pearson
Pres., Sue Watlov Phillips
Sec., Denise Miller
Treas., Dick Little
Major activities: MICAH is a regional advocacy organization made up of over 100 Catholic, Islamic, Jewish, and Protestant congregations dedicated to ensuring decent, safe, and affordable housing for everyone in our community. In 1998, MICAH began an 18 month education project using live theater to inform faith audiences about fair housing. The play entitled, "Like Waters Rolling Down will be shown in seven congregation across the Twin Cities metropolitan region.

St. Paul Area Council of Churches

1671 Summit Ave., St. Paul, MN 55105 Tel. (651)646-8805 Fax (651)646-6866
E-mail: rwalz@pioneerplanet.infi.net
Website: http://www.center.hamline.edu/spacc
Media Contact, Sandy Lucas
Exec. Dir., Rev. Thomas A. Duke
Dir. of Development, Kristi Anderson

Congregations in Community, Bob Walz
Congregations Concerned for Children, Peg Wangensteen
Project Spirit, Rev. Paulette Ajavon
Project Home, Margaret Lovejoy
Dept. of Indian Work, Sheila White Eagle
Criminal Justice Care Services, Rev. Kathleen Gatson
Pres. of the Board, Rev. Dick Goebel
Treas., Bert Nienaber
Sec., Charles Hawkins
Major activities: Chaplaincy at Detention and Corrections Authority Institutions; Police Chaplaincy; Education and Advocacy Regarding Children and Poverty; Assistance to Churches Developing Children's Parenting Care Services; Ecumenical Encounters and Activities; Indian Ministries; Leadership in Forming Cooperative Ministries for Children and Youth; After School Tutoring; Assistance to Congregations Developing Shared Ministry Activities; Training Programs in Anti-racism; Shelters for homeless

Tri-Council Coordinating Commission

122 W. Franklin, Rm. 100, Minneapolis, MN 55404 Tel. (612)871-0229 Fax (612)870-3622
E-mail: —
Media Contact, Co-Dir., Nadine Addington
Website: http://www.amcc.org/tcc.html
Co-Dir., R. James Addington
Pres., Rev. Thomas Duke, 1671 Summit Ave., St. Paul, MN 55105
Major activities: Anti-Racism Training; Organizing & Resource; Anti- Sexism Education and Resource Center

MISSISSIPPI

*Mississippi Religious Leadership Conference

P.O. Box 68123, Jackson, MS 39286-8123 Tel. (601)948-5954 Fax (601)354-3401
E-mail: —
Website: —
Media Contact, Exec. Dir., Rev. Canon Thomas E. Tiller, Jr.
Exec. Dir., Rev. Canon Thomas E. Tiller, Jr.
Chair, Bishop Marshall Meadors
Treas., Rev. Tom Clark
Major activities: Cooperation among Religious Leaders; Lay/Clergy Retreats; Social Concerns Seminars; Disaster Task Force; Advocacy for Disadvantaged

MISSOURI

Council of Churches of the Ozarks

P.O. Box 3947, Springfield, MO 65808-3947 Tel. (417)862-3586 Fax (417)862-2129
Media Contact, Comm. Dir., Susan Jackson
E-mail:CCOZARKS@DIALUS.com
Website: http://www.ANETWEB.com/CCOZARKS

Exec. Dir., Rev. Jesse Thorton
Dev. Officer, Vicki Riley
Operations Dir., Noel Chase
Major activities: Ministerial Alliance; Retired Sr. Volunteer Prog.; Treatment Center for Alcohol and Drug Abuse; Helping Elderly Live More Productively; Daybreak Adult Day Care Services; Ombudsman for Nursing Homes; Homesharing; Family Day Care Homes; USDA Food Program; Youth Ministry; Disaster Aid and Counseling; Homebound Shoppers; Food and Clothing Pantry; Ozarks Food Harvest

Ecumenical Ministries

#2 St. Louis Ave., Fulton, MO 65251 Tel. (573)642-6065 Fax —
E-mail: em_fulton@ecunet.org
Website: —
Media Contact, Ofc. Mgr., Karen Luebbert
Exec. Dir., Andrea Langton
Pres., William Jessop
Major activities: Kingdom Hospice; CROP Hunger Walk; Little Brother and Sister; Unity Service; Senior Center Bible Study; County Jail Ministry; Fulton High School Baccalaureate Service, HAVEN House; Galloway County Youth Treatment Center Ministry

Interfaith Community Services

200 Cherokee St., P.O. Box 4038, St. Joseph, MO 64504-0038 Tel. (816)238-4511 Fax (816)238-3274
E-mail: DaveB@PonyExpress.net
Website: http://www.inter-serv.org
Media Contact, Exec. Dir., David G. Berger, P.O. Box 4038, St. Joseph, MO 64504-0038 Tel. (816)238-4511
Exec. Dir., David G. Berger
Major activities: Child Development; Neighborhood Family Services; Group Home for Girls; Retired Senior Volunteer Program; Nutrition Program; Mobile Meals; Southside Youth Program; Church and Community; Housing Development; Homemaker Services to Elderly;; Emergency Food, Rent, Utilities; AIDS Assistance; Family Respite; Family and Individual Casework

MONTANA

*Montana Association of Churches

Andrew Square, Ste. G, 100 24th St. W., Billings, MT 59102 Tel. (406)656-9779 Fax (406)656-2156
Media Contact, Exec. Dir., Margaret MacDonald
E-mail: zmac@wtp.net
Website: www.wtp.net/~zmac
Exec. Dir., Margaret E. MacDonald
Admn. Asst., Larry D. Drane
Pres., Rev. Ken Moore, First Christian Church, 311 Power, Helena, MT 59601
Treas., Rev. Paul Everett, 401 Riverview, Glendive, MT 59330

244

Christian Witness for Humanity, Mark Nagasawa
Christian Advocates Network, Betty Waddell
Major activities: Montana Christian Advocates
Network; Christian Unity; Junior Citizen
Camp; Public Information; Ministries
Development; Social Ministry; Faith
Responses to Extremism and Racism through
Christian Witness For Humanity

NEBRASKA

*Interchurch Ministries of Nebraska
215 Centennial Mall S., Rm. 411, Lincoln, NE
68508-1888 Tel. (402)476-3391 Fax
(402)476-9310
Website: —
Media Contact, Exec. Sec.,Rev. Fred E. Loder
E-mail: im50427@navix.net
Exec. Sec.,Fred E. Loder
Admin. Asst., Sharon K. Kalcik
Pres.,Bishop James E. Krotz
Treas., Mrs. Shirley Mac Marsh
Major activities: Interchurch Planning and
Development; Comity; Indian Ministry; Rural
Church Strategy; Hunger; United Ministries
in Higher Education; Disaster Response;
Farm Families Response Network; Pantry
Network; Farm Mediation Services; Rural
Health

Lincoln Interfaith Council
140 S. 27th St., Ste. B, Lincoln, NE 68510-1301
Tel. (402)474-3017 Fax (402)475-3262
Website: —
Media Contact, David Hancock
E-mail: AsianCtr@navix.net
Exec. Dir., Rev. Dr. Norman E. Leach
Pres., Mr. Gene Crump
Vice-Pres., Rev. Dr. Roger Harp
Sec., Amrita Mahapatra
Treas., The Rev. Clip Higgins
Media Specialist, David Hancock
Urban Ministries, Rev. Dr. Norman E. Leach
Admn. Asst., Jean Scali
Fiscal Mgr., Jean Scali
Asian Community & Cultural Center, Maria Vu
Family Outreach Workers:Bich Tang; Tan Pham
Police Community Liaison,Toan Tran
Migrant Child Education Outreach, Mai-Huong
Sullivan
Major activities: Asian Community & Cultural
Center; Emergency Food Pantries System;
MLK, Jr. Observance; Interfaith Passover
Seder; Week of Prayer Christian Unity; Center
for Spiritual Growth; Festival of Faith &
Culture; Holocaust Memorial Observance;
Citizens Against Racism & Prejudice;
HIV/AIDS Healing Worship Services;
Community organization; Anti-Drug & Anti-
Alcohol Abuse Projects; Youth Gang &
Violence Prevention; Domestic Abuse
Prevention; Migrant Child Education;
American Citizenship Classes; Survival

English for Pre-literate AmerAsians and
Ederly Refugees; Ecumenical Dear Ministry

NEW HAMPSHIRE

*New Hampshire Council of Churches
316 S. Main St., P.O. Box 1087, Concord, NH
03302 Tel. (603)224-1352 Fax (603)224-9161
Website: http://www.nhchurches.org
Media Contact, Exec. Sec., David Lamarre-Vincent
E-mail:davidlv@ecunet.com
Exec. Sec., David Lamarre-Vincent
Pres., Rev. Bensamin C. L. Crosby, 314 S. Main
St., Concord, NH 03301-3468
Treas., Richard Couser
Major activities: Ecumenical Work

NEW JERSEY

*New Jersey Council of Churches
176 W. State St., Trenton, NJ 08608 Tel.
(609)396-9546 Fax (609)396-7646
E-mail: —
Website: —
Media Contact, Public Policy Dir., Joan
Diefenbach, Esq.
Pres., Rev. Jack Johnson
Vice-Pres., —
Sec., Beverly McNally
Treas., Marge Christie
Major activities: Racial Justice; Children's
Issues; Theological Unity; Ethics Public
Forums; Advocacy; Economic Justice

Bergen County Council of Churches
165 Burton Ave., Hasbrouck Hts., NJ 07604 Tel.
(201)288-3784
E-mail: —
Website: —
Media Contact, Pres., Rev. Stephen Giordano,
Clinton Avenue Reformed Church, Clinton
Ave. & James St., Bergenfield, NJ 07621 Tel.
(201)384-2454 Fax (201)384-2585
Exec. Sec., Anne Annunziato
Major activities: Ecumenical and Religious
Institute; Brotherhood/Sisterhood Breakfast;
Center for Food Action; Homeless Aid;
Operation Santa Claus; Aging Services; Boy
& Girl Scouts; Easter Dawn Services; Music;
Youth; Ecumenical Representation; Support of
Chaplains in Jails & Hospitals

Council of Churches of Greater Camden
P.O. Box 1208, Merchantville, NJ 08109 Tel.
(609)985-5162 Fax —
E-mail: —
Website: —
Media Contact, Exec. Sec., Rev. Dr. Samuel A.
Jeanes, Braddock Bldg., 205 Tuckerton Road,
Medford, NJ 08055 Tel. (609)985-7724
Exec. Sec., Rev. Dr. Samuel A. Jeanes
Pres., Rev. Lawrence L. Dunn

245

Treas., William G. Mason
Major activities: Radio & T.V.; Hospital
Chaplaincy; United Services; Good Friday
Breakfast; Mayors' Prayer Breakfast; Public
Affairs; Easter Sunrise Service

Metropolitan Ecumenical Ministry
525 Orange St., Newark, NJ 07107 Tel.
(201)481-6650 Fax (201)481-7883
E-mail: —
Website: —
Media Contact, Pam Smith
Exec. Dir., C. Stephen Jones
Major activities: Community Advocacy (educa-
tion, housing, environment); Church Mission
Assistance; Community and Clergy
Leadership Development; Economic
Development; Affordable Housing

**Metropolitan Ecumenical Ministry
Community Development Corp.**
525 Orange St., Newark, NJ 07107 Tel.
(201)481-6650 Fax (201)481-7883
Website: —
Exec. Dir., Jacqueline Jones
E-mail: memcdc@juno.com
Major activities: Housing Development;
Neighborhood Revitalization; Commercial/
Small Business Development; Economic
Development; Community Development;
Credit Union; Home Ownership Counseling;
Credit Repair; Mortgage Approval; Technical
Assitance To Congregations

**Trenton Ecumenical Area Ministry
(TEAM)**
1001 Pennnington Rd., Trenton, NJ 08618-2629
Tel. (609)882-5942 Fax —
E-mail: —
Website: —
Media Contact, Exec. Dir., Rev. Dr. John R.
Norwood, Jr.
Exec. Dir., Rev. Dr. John R. Norwood, Jr.
Pres., Rev. Dr. J. Evans Dodds
Campus Chaplains: Rev. Nancy Schulter; Rev.
Joanne B. Bullock
Sec., Tina Swan
Major activities: Racial Justice; Children & Youth
Ministries; Advocacy; CROP Walk; Ecumenical
Worship; Hospital Chaplaincy; Church Women
United; Campus Chaplaincy; Congregational
Empowerment; Prison Chaplaincy; Substance
Abuse Ministry Training

NEW MEXICO

***New Mexico Conference of
Churches**
124 Hermosa SE, Albuquerque, NM 87108-2610
Tel. (505)255-1509 Fax (505)256-0071
Media Contact, Exec. Sec., Dr. Wallace Ford
E-mail: wford@ecunet.org
Website: http://www.rt66.com/~nmcc

Pres., The Rev. Ann Calvin Rogers-Witte,124
Hermosa, SE, Albuquerque, NM 87108-2610
Treas., Ruth Tribeou
Exec. Sec.,Rev. Dr. Wallace Ford
Major activities: State Task Forces: Poverty,
Legislative Concerns, Faith and Order, AIDS,
Eco-Justice, Ecumenical Continuing
Education; Regional Task Forces: Aging,
Ecumenical Worship and Spiritual Life,
Refugees, Emergency Care

**Inter-Faith Council of
Santa Fe, New Mexico**
PO Box 4637, Santa Fe, NM 87502 Tel.
(505)983-2892
E-mail: —
Website: —
Media Contact, Barbara A. Robinson, Fax
(505)473-5637
Treas., Marcia Mize
Major activities: Faith Community Assistance
Center; Interfaith Dialogues/Celebrations/
Visitations; Peace Projects; Understanding
Hispanic Heritage; Newsletter

NEW YORK

***New York State Community of
Churches, Inc.-A Household of
Christians**
Program Ofc.: 362 State St., Albany, NY 12210
Tel. (518)436-9319 Fax (518)427-6705
Center Printing: 3049 E. Genesee St., Syracuse,
NY 13224 Tel. (315)446-6126 Fax (315)446-
5789
E-mail: nyscc_albany@ecunet.org
Website: http://www. nyscommunityofchurch-
es.org
Media Contact, Rev. Daniel Hahn
Interim Exec. Steward, Ms. Mary Lu Bower
Pres., The Rev. Dr. Robert White
Corp. Sec., Rev. Dr. Jon Norton
Treas., Bishop Susan Morrison
New York State Interfaith IMPACT, The Rev.
Daniel Hahn
Dir. of Chaplaincy Services, Rev. James Miller
Dir. of Public Policy, Mary Lu Bowen
Admn. Asst., Sylvenia Cochran
Major activities: Public Policy and Ecumenical
Ministries; Chaplaincy in State Institutions;
Rural Poor and Migrants; Homeless; AIDS;
Universal Health Care; Life and Law; U.S.-
Canadian Border Concerns; Single Parent
Families; Faith and Order; Environmental
Issues; The Family, Education, Violence;
Covenanting Congregations; Casino Gambling

Brooklyn Council of Churches
125 Ft. Greene Pl, Brooklyn, NY 11217 Tel.
(718)625-5851 Fax —
E-mail: —
Website: —
Media Contact, Dir., Charles Henze

Program Dir., Charles Henze
Pres., Adele S. Hester
Treas., Rev. Charles H. Straut , Jr.
Major activities: Education Workshops; Food
Pantries; Welfare Advocacy; Hospital and
Nursing Home Chaplaincy; Church Women
United; Legislative Concerns

Broome County Council of Churches, Inc.

81 Main St., Binghamton, NY 13905 Tel.
(607)724-9130 Fax (607)724-9148
E-mail: —
Website: —
Media Contact, Exec. Dir., William H. Stanton
Exec. Dir., William H. Stanton
Dir. of Development, Billie L. Briggs
Hospital Chaplains: Rev. Charles Heier; Betty
Pomeroy
Jail Chaplain, Rev. Philip Singer
Aging Ministry Coord., Dorothy Myers
CHOW Prog. Coord., Dee Jester
Pres., Rev. Mark Ridley
Treas., Rachel Light
Office Mgr., Joyce M. Besemer
Caregiver Program Coord., Jan Aerie
Major activities: Hospital and Jail Chaplains;
Youth and Aging Ministries; CHOW
(Emergency Hunger Program); Christian
Education; Ecumenical Worship and
Fellowship; Media; Community Affairs; Peace;
Day by Day Marriage; Prep Program; Interfaith
Coalition Against Hate; Neighborhood
Volunteer Interfaith Caregiver Program

Buffalo Area Council of Churches

1272 Delaware Ave., Buffalo, NY 14209-2496
Tel. (716)882-4793 Fax (716)882-7671
Website: —
Media Contact, Exec. Dir., Rev. Dr. G. Stanford
Bratton
E-mail: WNYFaiths@aol.com
Exec. Dir., Rev. Dr. G. Stanford Bratton
Pres.,Rev. Donald Garrett
1st Vice-Pres., Rev.Jeff Carter
2nd Vice-Pres., Rev. Dr. Kenneth Neal
Sec., Deborah Dill
Treas., Eula Hooker
Chpsn. of Trustees, Emerson Barr
Church Women United: Coord., Sally Giordano;
Pres., Bobbie Grimm
Community Witness & Ministry, Chpsn.,Rev. Dr.
Kenneth Neal
Adminisration, Rev. Jeff Carter
Roll Call Against Racism,Chpsn.,Rev. Jeff
Carter
Radio & TV: Coord., Linda Velazquez; Chpsn.,
Rev. Robert Hutchinson
Development of Network of Religious
Communities, Rev. Dr. G. Stanford Bratton
Major activities: Radio-TV; Social Services;
Chaplains; Church Women United; Ecumeni-
cal Relations; Refugees; Public Policy;
Community Development; Lay/Clergy Educa-
tion; Interracial Dialogue; Police/ Community
Relations; Buffalo Coalition for Common
Ground

Buffalo Area Metropolitan Ministries, Inc.

775 Main St., Ste. 204, Buffalo, NY 14203-1310
Tel. (716)854-0822 Fax (716)854-0823
E-mail: —
Website: —
Media Contact, Interim Exec. Dir., Rev. Francis
X. Mazur
Interim Exec. Dir., Rev. Francis X. Mazur
Pres., Rev. Daniel Budd
Vice-Pres. for Plng. & Prog., Rev. James Croglio
Vice-Pres. for Admn. & Fin., Patricia Greenspan
Sec., Rev. Pierre Albrecht-Carrie
Treas., Rev. Amos Acree
Chair, Food for All Prog., Mrs. Judy Metzger,
Interim
Major activities: An association of religious
communities in Western New York with
Bahai, Jewish, Muslim, Christian, Unitarian-
Univeralist, Hindu, and Jain membership pro-
viding a united religious witness through these
major activities: Hunger; Economic Issues;
Interreligious Dialogue; Interfaith AIDS
Network; Multifaith Forums; Fair Housing;
Interfaith Holocaust Commemoration; Child-
ren's Sabbath; Resource for Hospital Chaplains

Capital Area Council of Churches, Inc.

646 State St., Albany, NY 12203 Tel. (518)462-
5450 Fax —
E-mail: —
Website: —
Media Contact, Admn. Asst.,Kitt Jackson
Exec. Dir., Rev. Dr. Robert C. Lamar
Admn. Asst.,Kitt Jackson
Pres.,Marlene Shilling
Treas.,Edward Cameron
Major activities: Hospital Chaplaincy; Food
Pantries; CROP Walk; Jail and Nursing Home
Ministries; Martin Luther King Memorial
Service and Scholarship Fund; Emergency
Shelter for the Homeless; Campus Ministry;
Ecumenical Dialogue; Forums on Social
Concerns; Peace and Justice Education; Inter-
Faith Programs; Legislative Concerns; Comm.
Thanksgiving Day and Good Friday Services;
Annual Ecumenical Musical Celebration

CAPITAL Region Ecumenical Organization (CREO)

Box 2199, Scotia, NY 12302 Tel. (518)382-7505
Fax (518)382-7505
E-mail: TishMurph@aol.com
Website: —
Media Contact, Coord., Jim Murphy
Coord., Jim Murphy

247

Major activities: Promote Cooperation/ Coordination Among Member Judicatories and Ecumenical Organizations in the Capital Region in Urban Ministries, Social Action

Chautaugua County Rural Ministry
127 Central Ave., P.O. Box 362, Dunkirk, NY 14048 Tel. (716)366-1787 Fax —
E-mail: —
Website: —
Media Contact, Exec. Dir., Kathleen Peterson
Exec. Dir., Kathleen Peterson
Major activities: Chautaugua County Food Bank; Collection/Distribution of Furniture, Clothing, & Appliances; Homeless Services; Advocacy for the Poor; Soup Kitchen; Emergency Food Pantry; Thrift Store

Concerned Ecumenical Ministry to the Upper West Side
286 LaFayette Ave., Buffalo, NY 14213 Tel. (716)882-2442 Fax (716)882-2477
E-mail: —
Website: —
Media Contact, Interim Exec. Dir., The Rev. Catherine Rieley-Goddard
Interim Exec. Dir., The Rev. Catherine Rieley-Goddard
Pres., Mr. Robert Grimm
Major activities: Community Center Serving Youth, Young Families, Seniors and the Hungry

Cortland County Council of Churches, Inc.
7 Calvert St., Cortland, NY 13045 Tel. (607)753-1002 Fax —
E-mail: —
Website: —
Media Contact, Office Mgr., Joy Niswender
Exec. Dir., Rev. Donald M. Wilcox
Major activities: College Campus Ministry; Hospital Chaplaincy; Nursing Home Ministry; Newspaper Column; Interfaith Relationships; Hunger Relief; CWS; Crop Walk; Leadership Education; Community Issues; Mental Health Chaplaincy; Grief Support; Jail Ministry

Council of Churches of Chemung County, Inc.
330 W. Church St., Elmira, NY 14901 Tel. (607)734-2294 Fax —
E-mail: —
Website: —
Media Contact, Exec. Dir., Joan Geldmacher, Tel. (607)734-7622
Exec. Dir., Joan Geldmacher
Pres., Rev. Doris Washington, Tel. (607)733-6155
Major activities: CWS Collection; CROP Walk; UNICEF; Institutional Chaplaincies; Radio; Easter Dawn Service; Communications Network; Produce & Distribute Complete Church Directories; Representation on Community Boards and Agencies; Ecumenical Services; Interfaith Coalition; Taskforce on Children & Families; Multicultural Committee

Council of Churches of the City of New York
475 Riverside Dr., Rm. 1950, New York, NY 10115 Tel. (212)870-2120 Fax (212)870-3433
E-mail: JEHiemstra@aol.com
Website: —
Media Contact, Exec. Dir., Dr. John E. Hiemstra
Exec. Dir., Dr. John E. Hiemstra
Pres., Rev. Calvin O. Butts
1st Vice-Pres., Friend Carol Holmes
2nd Vice-Pres., Rev. Carolyn Holloway
3rd Vice-Pres., Ven. Michael Kendall
Sec., Rev.N.J. L'Heureux
Treas., Dr. John Blackwell
Major activities: Radio & TV; Pastoral Care; Protestant Chapel, Kennedy International Airport; Coordination and Strategic Planning; Religious Conferences; Referral & Advocacy; Youth Development; Building Great Minds Tutoring Program; Directory of Churches and Database Available

Dutchess Interfaith Council, Inc.
9 Vassar St., Poughkeepsie, NY 12601 Tel. (914)471-7333 Fax —
E-mail: —
Website: —
Media Contact, Exec. Dir., Rev. Gail A. Burger
Exec. Dir., Rev. Gail A. Burger
Pres.,Marguerite T. Palmore
Treas., Elizabeth M. DiStefano
Major activities: CROP Hunger Walk; Interfaith Music Festival; Public Worship Events; Interfaith Dialogue; Christian Unity; Interfaith Youth Evening; Oil Purchase Group; HIV/AIDS Work; Weekly Radio Program; Racial Unity Work

Genesee County Churches United, Inc.
P.O. Box 547, Batavia, NY 14021 Tel. (716)343-6763 Fax —
E-mail: —
Website: —
Media Contact, Pres.,Captain Leonard Boynton, Salvation Army, 529 East Main St., Batavia, NY 14020 Tel. (716)343-6284
Pres.,Leonard Boynton
Exec. Sec., Helen H. Mullen
Chaplain (Temporary), Rev. Bert Tidlund
Major activities: Jail Ministry.; Food Pantries; Serve Needy Families; Radio Ministry; Pulpit Exchange; Community Thanksgiving; Ecumenical Services at County Fair

Genesee-Orleans Ministry of Concern
118 S. Main St., Box 245, Albion, NY 14411-0245 Tel. (716)589-9210 Fax —
E-mail: —

Website: —
Media Contact, Exec. Dir., Marian M. Adrian, GNSH
Exec. Dir., Marian M. Adrian, GNSH
Advocates: JoAnn McCowan; Margaret Grauerholz, Esq.
Pres., John W. Cebula, Esq.
Chaplains: Orleans County Jail, Rev. Wilford Moss; Orleans Albion Correctional Facility, Sr. Dolores O'Dowd
Major activities: Advocacy Services for the Disadvantaged, Homeless, Ill, Incarcerated and Victims of Family Violence; Emergency Food, Shelter, Utilities, Medicines

Graymoor Ecumenical & Interreligious Institute
475 Riverside Dr., Rm. 1960, New York, NY 10115-1999 Tel. (212)870-2330 Fax (212)870-2001
E-mail: 104075,2312@compuserve.com
Website: —
Media Contact, Walter Gange, SA, Graymoor, Route 9, PO Box 300, Garrison, NY 10524-0300 Tel. (914)424-3671 ext. 3540 Fax (914)424-3433
(See Listing in US Cooperative Directory)

Greater Rochester Community of Churches
2 Riverside St., Rochester, NY 14613-1222 Tel. (716)254-2570 Fax (716)254-6551
Website: —
Media Contact, Coord., Marie E. Gibson
E-mail: grcc@juno.com
Major activities: Ecumenical Worship; Refugee Resettlement; Chaplaincy Services; Christian Unity; Beyond Racism Project; Interfaith Cooperation; Community Economic Development; Crossroads Program; Rochester's Religious Community Directory; Religious Information/Resources

InterReligious Council of Central New York
3049 E. Genesee St., Syracuse, NY 13224 Tel. (315)449-3552 Fax (315)449-3103
E-mail: IRCCNY@aol.com
Website: —
Media Contact, Chrissie Rizzo
Interim CEO, Dr. Stephen Schneeweiss
Pres., Rabbi Daniel A. Jezer
Bus. Mgr., Arthur A. West
Associate Director, John Landesman
Pastoral Care Prog., Acting Dir., The Rev. John Hoffenstein
Refugee Resettlement Prog., Dir., Nona Stewart
Senior Companion Prog., Dir., Virginia Frey
Long Term Ombudsman Prog., Dir., Linda Kashdin
Covenant Housing Prog., Dir., Kimberlee Dupcak
Southeast Asia Center, Dir., Joey Tse
Community Wide Dialogue on Racism, Race

Relations and Racial Healing, Dir., Arthea Brown
Major activities: Pastoral Ministries; Community Ministries; Interreligious and Ecumenical Relations; Diversity Education; Worship; Community Advocacy and Planning

The Long Island Council of Churches
1644 Denton Green, Hempstead, NY 11550 Tel. (516)565-0290 Fax call for instructions
Eastern Office, 235 Sweezy Ave., Riverhead, NY 11901 Tel. (516)727-2210
E-mail: —
Website: —
Media Contact, Admn. Asst., Barbara McLaughlin
Interim Exec. Dir., Rev. William H. Perkins
Admn. Asst., Barbara McLaughlin
Pastoral Care, Interim Dir., Rev. Richard Lehman
Clinical Pastoral Educ., Dir.,-
Social Services, Dir., Lillian Sharik, Tel. (516)565-0390
Project REAL, Dir., Mr. Frank Ruggiero
Nassau County Ofc., Social Services Sec.,Mary Ann Venohr
Suffolk County Ofc., Food Program & Family Support, Carolyn Gumbs
Nassau County Blood Prog. Coord., Nancy Schaffer
Suffolk County Blood Prog. Coord.: Joan McHugh
Dev. Dir.,,Kenneth Lewis
Major activities: Pastoral Care in Hospitals and Jails; Clinical Pastoral Education; Emergency Food; Family Support & Advocacy; Advocacy for Domestic and International Peace & Justice; Blood Donor Coordination; Church World Service; Multifaith Cooperation; Clergy/Laity Training; Newsletter; Church Directory; Community Residences for Adults with Psychiatric Disabilities (Project REAL); HIV Education Projects;AIDS Interfaith of L.I.; Special Projects

The Niagara Council of Churches Inc.
St. Paul UMC, 723 Seventh St., Niagara Falls, NY 14301 Tel. (716)285-7505
E-mail: —
Website: —
Media Contact, Pres., Nessie S. Bloomquist, 7120 Laur Rd., Niagara Falls, NY 14304 Tel. (716)297-0698 Fax (716)298-1193
Exec. Dir., Ruby Babb
Pres., Nessie S. Bloomquist
Treas., Shirley Bathurst
Trustees Chpsn., Rev. Vincent Mattoni, 834 19th St., Niagara Falls, NY 14304
Major activities: Ecumenical Worship; Bible Study; Christian Ed. & Social Concerns; Church Women United; Evangelism & Mission; Institutional Min. Youth Activities; Hymn Festival; Week of Prayer for Christian

249

Unity; CWS Projects; Audio-Visual Library; UNICEF; Food Pantries and Kitchens; Community Missions, Inc.; Political Refugees; Eco-Justice Task Force; Migrant/ Rural Ministries; Interfaith Coalition on Energy

Niagara County Migrant Rural Ministry

6507 Wheeler Rd., Lockport, NY 14094 Tel. (716)434-4405 Fax —
E-mail: —
Website: —
Media Contact, Exec. Dir., Grayce M. Dietz
Chpsn., Lois Farley
Vice-Chpsn., Beverly Farnham
Sec., Anne Eifert
Treas., Rev. Patricia Ludwig
Major activities: Migrant Farm Worker Program; Assist with Immigration Problems and Application Process for Social Services; Monitor Housing Conditions; Assist Rural Poor; Referrals to Appropriate Service Agencies; Children's Daily Enrichment Program

Queens Federation of Churches

86-17 105th St., Richmond Hill, NY 11418-1597 Tel. (718)847-6764 Fax (718)847-7392
E-mail: qfc@ecunet.org
Website: —
Media Contact, Rev. N. J. L'Heureux, Jr.
Exec. Dir., Rev. N. J. L'Heureux, Jr.
York College Chaplain, Rev. Dr. Hortense Merritt
Pres., Annie Lee Phillips
Treas., Lloyd W. Patterson, Jr.
Major activities: Emergency Food Service; York College Campus Ministry; Blood Bank; Scouting; Christian Education Workshops; Planning and Strategy; Church Women United; Community Consultations; Seminars for Church Leaders; Directory of Churches and Synagogues; Christian Relations (Prot/RC); Chaplaincies; Public Policy Issues; N.Y.S. Interfaith Commission on Landmarking of Religious Property; Queens Interfaith Hunger Network

Rural Migrant Ministry

P.O. Box 4757, Poughkeepsie, NY 12601 Tel. (914)485-8627 Fax (914)485-1963
E-mail: —
Website: —
Media Contact, Exec. Dir., Rev. Richard Witt
Exec. Dir., Rev. Richard Witt
Pres., Karen Maxwell
Major activities: Serving the Rural Poor and Migrants Through a Ministry of Advocacy & Empowerment; Youth Program; Latino Committee; Organization and Advocacy with and for Rural Poor and Migrant Farm Workers

Schenectady Inner City Ministry

930 Albany St., Schenectady, NY 12307-1514

Tel. (518)374-2683 Fax (518)382-1871
E-mail: sicm@crisny.org
Website: http://www. crisny.org
Media Contact, Marianne Comfort
Urban Agent, Rev. Phillip N. Grigsby
Off. Mgr., Collen Pickett
Fiscal, Joan LeMonica
Emergency Food Liaison, Patricia Obrecht
Church/Community Worker, Jim Murphy
Co-Pres.: James and Judy Depasquale
Bethesda House, Margaret Anderton
Save and Share, Cathy Bryson
Damien Center, Laurie Bacheldor
Jobs, Etc., David Coplon, Cynthia Blair
Summer Food, Joan LeMonica
Major activities: Emergency Food; Advocacy; Housing; Neighborhood and Economic Issues; Ecumenical Worship and Fellowship; Community Research; Education in Churches on Faith Responses to Social Concerns; Legislative Advocacy; Food Buying Coop; Homeless Day Shelter; CROP Walk; HIV/AIDS Ministry; Teen Theatre; Job Training and Placement Center; Summer Lunch for Youth

Southeast Ecumenical Ministry

25 Westminster Rd., Rochester, NY 14607 Tel. (716)271-5350 Fax (716)271-8526
E-mail: boys7@frontiernet.net
Website: —
Media Contact, Laurie Kennedy
Dir., Laurie Kennedy
Pres., Rev. James Widboom
Major activities: Transportation of Elderly; Emergency Food Cupboard; Supplemental Nutrition Program

Staten Island Council of Churches

2187 Victory Blvd., Staten Island, NY 10314 Tel. (718)761-6782 Fax —
E-mail: —
Website: —
Media Contact, Exec. Sec., Mildred J. Saderholm, 94 Russell St., Staten Island, NY 10308 Tel. (718)761-6782
Pres., Rev. Dr. Claude A. Knight
Exec. Sec., Mildred J. Saderholm
Major activities: Support; Christian Education; Pastoral Care; Congregational Concerns; Urban Affairs

Troy Area United Ministries

17 First St., #2, Troy, NY 12180 Tel. (518)274-5920 Fax (518)271-1909
E-mail: TAUMMS@juno.com OR TAUM@crisny.org
Website: —
Media Contact, Exec. Dir., Margaret T. Stoner
Exec. Dir., Margaret T. Stoner
Pres., Dorcas Rose
Chaplain, R.P.I., Rev. Paul Fraser
Chaplain, Russell Sage College, Rev. Paul Fraser

Major activities: Community Dispute Settlement (mediation) Program; College Ministry; Nursing Home Ministry; CROP Walk; Homeless and Housing Concerns; Weekend Meals Program at Homeless Shelter; Community Worship Celebrations; Racial Relations; Furniture Program; Damien Center of Troy Hospitality for persons with HIV/AIDS

Wainwright House
260 Stuyvesant Ave., Rye, NY 10580 Tel. (914)967-6080 Fax (914)967-6114
E-mail: —
Website: —
Media Contact, Exec. Dir., Judith W. Milinowski
Exec. Dir., Judith W. Milinowski
Pres., Dr. Robert A. Rothman
Exec. Vice-Pres., Beth Adams Smith
Major activities: Educational Program and Conference Center; Intellectual, Psychological, Physical and Spiritual Growth; Healing and Health

NORTH CAROLINA
*North Carolina Council of Churches
Methodist Bldg., 1307 Glenwood Ave., Ste. 162, Raleigh, NC 27605-3258 Tel. (919)828-6501 Fax —
E-mail: nccck@aol.com
Website: —
Media Contact, Exec. Dir., Rev. S. Collins Kilburn
Exec. Dir., Rev. S. Collins Kilburn
Program Associates,Sr. Evelyn Mattern, Rev. George Reed
Pres., Dr. Rollin Russell, P.O. Box 658, Graham, NC 27253
Treas., Dr. James W. Ferree, 5108 Huntcliff Tr., Winston-Salem, NC 27104
Major activities: Children and Families; Health Care Justice; Christian Unity; Equal Rights; Legislative Program; Criminal Justice; Farmworker Ministry; Rural Crisis; Racial Justice; Disaster Response; AIDS Ministry; Death Penalty; Poverty and Response to Welfare Changes.

Asheville-Buncombe Community Christian Ministry (ABCCM)
30 Cumberland Ave., Asheville, NC 28801 Tel. (704)259-5300 Fax (704)259-5923
E-mail: —
Website: —
Media Contact, Exec. Dir., Rev. Scott Rogers, Fax (704)259-5323
Exec. Dir., Rev. Scott Rogers
Pres., Dr. John Grant
Major activities: Crisis Ministry; Jail/Prison Ministry; Shelter Ministry; Medical Ministry

Greensboro Urban Ministry
305 West Lee St., Greensboro, NC 27406 Tel.

(910)271-5959 Fax (910)271-5920
E-mail: Guministry@aol.com
Website: http://www.greensboro.com/gum
Media Contact, Exec. Dir., Rev. Mike Aiken
Exec. Dir., Rev. Mike Aiken
Major activities: Emergency Financial Assistance; Emergency Housing; Hunger Relief; Inter-Faith and Inter-Racial Understanding; Justice Ministry; Chaplaincy with the Poor

NORTH DAKOTA
*North Dakota Conference of Churches
227 W. Broadway, Bismarck, ND 58501 Tel. (701)255-0604 Fax (701)223-6075
E-mail: —
Website: —
Media Contact, Office Mgr., Eunice Brinckerhoff
Pres., Rev. Marvin Klemmer
Treas., Harriet McClelland
Ofc. Mgr., Eunice Brinckerhoff
Major activities: Prison Chaplaincy; Rural Life Ministry; Faith and Order; North Dakota 101; Current Ecumenical Proposals

OHIO
*Ohio Council of Churches
6877 N. High St., Ste. 206, Columbus, OH 43085-2516 Tel. (614)885-9590 Fax (614)885-6097
E-mail: Ohio_Council_of_Churches@compuserve.com
Website: —
Exec. Dir., Rev. Rebecca J. Tollefson
Public Policy, Dir., Tom Smith
Social Advocacy, Dir., Hugh Gibbs
Pres., Joyce Slaughter
Vice Pres., Rev. George Lambert
Treas., Jack Davis
Major activities: Agricultural Issues; Economic & Social Justice; Ecumenical Relations; Health Care Reform; Public Policy Issues; Criminal Justice Issues; Welfare Reform; African American Males; Theological Dialogue; Racial Relations; Education Childcare/Children Issues; Environment; Poverty

Akron Area Association of Churches
350 S. Portage Path, Akron, OH 44320 Tel. (330)535-3112 Fax (330)374-5041
E-mail: aaac1@juno.com
Website: http://www.triple-ac.org
Media Contact, Admin. Asst., Chloe Ann Kriska
Exec. Dir., Rev. Dennis D. Sparks
Bd. of Trustees, Pres., Rev. Raymond Kovach
Vice-Pres., Rev. David Frees
Sec., Dale Kline
Treas., Dr. Stephen Laning
Program Dir., Rev. Dennis D. Sparks
Christian Ed., Dir., Chloe Ann Kriska

251

Major activities: Messiah Sing; Interfaith Council; Newsletters; Resource Center; Community Worship; Training of Local Church Leadership; Radio Programs; Clergy and Lay Fellowship Luncheons; Cable TV; Interfaith Caregivers; Neighborhood Development; Community Outreach; Church Interracial Partnerships

Alliance of Churches

470 E. Broadway, Alliance, OH 44601 Tel. (330)821-6648 Fax —
E-mail: —
Website: —
Media Contact, Dir., Lisa A. Oyster
Dir., Lisa A. Oyster
Pres., Rev. Bud Hoffman
Treas., Betty Rush
Major activities: Christian Education; Community Relations & Service; Ecumenical Worship; Community Ministry; Peacemaking; Medical Transportation for Anyone Needing It; Emergency Financial Assistance

Churchpeople for Change and Reconciliation

326 W. McKibben, Box 488, Lima, OH 45802 Tel. (419)229-6949 Fax —
E-mail: —
Website: —
Media Contact, Exec. Dir., Richard Keller
Exec. Dir., Richard Keller
Major activities: Developing Agencies for Minorities, Poor, Alienated and Despairing; Community Kitchens

Council of Christian Communions of Greater Cincinnati

42 Calhoun St., Cincinnati, OH 45219-1525 Tel. (513)559-3151 Fax —
E-mail: —
Website: —
Media Contact, Exec. Dir., Joellen W. Grady
Exec. Dir., Joellen W. Grady
Justice Chaplaincy, Assoc. Dir., Rev. Jack Marsh
Educ., Assoc., Sharon D. Jones
Pres., Rev. Randall Hyvonen
Major activities: Christian Unity & Interfaith Cooperation; Justice Chaplaincies; Police-Clergy Team; Adult and Juvenile Jail Chaplains; Religious Education

Greater Dayton Christian Connection

601 W. Riverview Ave., Dayton, OH 45406 Tel. (513)227-9485 Fax (513)227-9486
E-mail: —
Website: —
Media Contact, Exec. Dir., James S. Burton
Exec. Dir., James S. Burton
Jail Ministry, Dir., Nancy Haas
Reconciliation Ministry, Dir., James S. Burton
Pres., Sr. Alice Schottelkotte

Major activities: Communications: Service to Churches and Community; Race Relations Advocacy; Jail Chaplaincy; CROP Walk; The Gleaning Project; Saturday Meals for Seniors; Newsletter; Martin Luther King Activities; Workplace Reconnections

Interchurch Council of Greater Cleveland

2230 Euclid Ave., Cleveland, OH 44115 Tel. (216)621-5925 Fax (216)621-0588
E-mail: —
Website: —
Media Contact, Janice Giering
Exec. Dir., Dr. Dennis N. Paulson, Tel. (216)621-5925
Church & Society, Dir., Rev. Mylion Waite
Communications, Dir., Janice Giering, Karen Drasler
Chmn. of the Assembly, Rev. Jeremiah Pryce
Dir. Of Development, Lynn Paulin
Major activities: Church and Society; Communications; Hunger; Christian Education; Legislation; Faith and Order; Public Education; Interchurch News; Tutoring; Parent-Child First Teachers Program; Shelter for Homeless Women and Children; Radio & TV; Interracial Cooperation; Interfaith Cooperation; Adopt-A-School; Women of Hope; Leadership Development; Religious Education; Center for Peace & Reconciliation-Youth and the Courts; Support Services to Local Churches.

Mahoning Valley Association of Churches

25 W. Rayen Ave., Youngstown, OH 44503 Tel. (330)744-8946 Fax (330)774-0018
E-mail: —
Website: —
Media Contact, Exec. Dir., Elsie L. Dursi
Exec. Dir., Elsie L. Dursi
Pres., Rev. Connie Sassanella
Treas., Paul Fryman
Major activities: Communications; Christian Education; Ecumenism; Social Action; Advocacy

Metropolitan Area Church Council

760 E. Broad St., Columbus, OH 43205 Tel. (614)461-7103 Fax —
E-mail: —
Website: —
Media Contact, Exec. Dir., Rev. Burton Cantrell
Exec. Dir., Rev. Burton Cantrell
Chpsn. of Bd., Alvin Hadley
Sec./Treas., Lily Schlichter
Major activities: Newspaper; Liaison with Community organizations; Assembly; Week of Prayer for Christian Unity; Support for Ministerial Associations and Church Councils; Seminars for Church Leaders; Prayer Groups; CROP Walk; Social Concerns Hearings

Metropolitan Area Religious Coalition of Cincinnati

Ste. 1035, 617 Vine St., Cincinnati, OH 45202-2423 Tel. (513)721-4843 Fax (513)721-4891
E-mail: —
Website: —
Media Contact, Dir., Rev. Duane Holm
Dir., Rev. Duane Holm
Pres., Burton Perlman
Major activities: Children-At-Risk; Housing; Public Education; Local Social Policy Concerns; Local Social Policy Concerns; 1998: Welfare Reform; Judicatories' Statement on Race

Pike County Outreach Council

122 E. Second St., Waverly, OH 45690 Tel. (614)947-7151 Fax —
E-mail: —
Website: —
Dir., Judy Dixon
Major activities: Emergency Service Program; Self Help Groups; Homeless Shelter

Toledo Ecumenical Area Ministries

444 Floyd St., Toledo, OH 43620 Tel. (419)242-7401 Fax (419)242-7404
E-mail: —
Website: —
Media Contact, Admn., Nancy Lee Atkins
Metro-Toledo Churches United, Admn., Nancy Lee Atkins
Toledo Metropolitan Mission, Exec. Dir., Nancy Lee Atkins
Major activities: Ecumenical Relations; Interfaith Relations; Food Program; Housing Program; Social Action- Public Education; Health Care; Urban Ministry; Employment; Welfare Rights; Housing; Mental Retardation; Voter Registration/Education; Substance Abuse Treatment; Youth Leadership; Children At-risk; Elimination of Discrimination

Tuscarawas County Council for Church and Community

107 West High , Ste. B, New Philadelphia, OH 44663 Tel. (330)343-6012 Fax (330)343-9845
E-mail: —
Website: —
Media Contact, Barbara E. Lauer
Exec. Dir., Barbara E. Lauer
Pres., Zoe Ann Kelley, 201 E. 12th St., Dover, OH 44622
Treas., James Barnhouse, 120 N. Broadway, New Philadelphia, OH 44663
Major activities: Human Services; Health; Family Life; Child Abuse; Housing; Educational Programs; Emergency Assistance; Legislative Concerns; Juvenile Prevention Program; Character Formation;; Prevention Program for High Risk Children; Bimonthly newsletter The Pilot

West Side Ecumenical Ministry

5209 Detroit Ave, Cleveland, OH 44102 Tel. (216)651-2037 Fax (216)651-4145
E-mail: wsem@stratos.net
Website: —
Media Contact, Exec. Dir., Elving F. Otero
Exec. Dir., Elving F. Otero
Director of Operations, Adam Roth
Major activities: Emergency Food Centers; Senior Meals Programs; Youth Services; Advocacy, Empowerment Programs; Church Clusters; Employment Assistance Program; Head Start Centers; Theatre; Teen Centers

OKLAHOMA

*Oklahoma Conference of Churches

301 Northwest 36th St., Oklahoma City, OK 73118 Tel. (405)525-2928 Fax (405)525-2636
E-mail: okconfch@flash.net
Website: —
Media Contact, Deborah Canary-Marshall
Exec. Dir., The Rev. Dr. Rita K. Newton
Pres., The Rev. Dr. Gary Peluso
Treas., The Rev. Lura Cayton
Major activities: Christian Unity Issues; COCU Covenanting; Community Building Among Members; Rural Community Care; Ecumenical Decade with Women; Children's Advocacy; Day at the Legislature; Impact; Criminal Justice

Tulsa Metropolitan Ministry

221 S. Nogales, Tulsa, OK 74127 Tel. (918)582-3147 Fax (918)582-3159
E-mail: TMM@ionet.com
Website: http://www. TUMM.org
Media Contact, Sr. Sylvia Schmidt
Exec. Dir., Sr. Sylvia Schmidt, S.F.C.C.
Operations Dir., James Robinson
Day Center for the Homeless, Dir., Sandra Holden
Corrections Min. Coordinator, Rev. Mary McAnnally
Pres., Dr. James W. Johnson
Vice-Pres., Dr. Sandra Rana
Sec., Rev. John McLemore
Treas., Sara Jo Waggoner
Major activities: Corrections Ministry; Religious Understanding; Shelter for the Homeless; Women's Issues; U.N. Decade on Indigenous People; Legislative Issues; Interfaith Dialogue TV Series; Christian Issues; Justice and Peace Issues; Immigration Concerns; Communications; Task Force Against Racism; Metro. Comm. Building; Directory of Metro. Religious Community

OREGON

*Ecumenical Ministries of Oregon

0245 S.W. Bancroft St., Ste. B, Portland, OR 97201 Tel. (503)221-1054 Fax (503)223-7007
E-mail: emoor0245@aol.com
Website: —

Media Contact, Shannon Gustafson
Exec. Dir., David A. Leslie
Community Ministry, Dir., Janet Miller
Congregational Rel., Dir., Jack Kennedy
Finance and Administrative Services, Dir., Gary B. Logsdon
Public Policy, Dir., Ellen C. Lowe
Hopewell House, Colleen Lyman
Drug Educ. Proj., Misty Springer
Alcohol Polcy Initiative Program, Nigel Wrangham
Sponsors Organized to Assist Refugees, Penny Strauss
HIV Center, Rick Stoller
Shared Housing, Margaret Tassia
Patton Home, Ben Paroulek
Northeast Emergency Food Program, Drew Hudson
Russian Oregon Social Services, Yelena Sergeva
Intl. Learning Program, Jackie Sandquist
Pres., The Rev. Stephen Schneider
Major activities: Educational Ministries; Legislation; Urban Ministries; Refugees; Social Concerns; Jewish-Christian Relations; Farm\Rural Ministry; Alcohol\Drug Education; Welfare Advocacy; Faith & Order; Peace Ministries; IMPACT; Diversity Training; Communications; AIDS Ministry; HIV Center; Religious Education; Health & Human Ministries; Medical Clinic; Emergency Food

PENNSYLVANIA

*Pennsylvania Conference on Interchurch Cooperation

P.O. Box 2835, 223 North St., Harrisburg, PA 17105 Tel. (717)545-4761 Fax (717)238-1473
900 S. Arlington Ave., Harrisburg, PA 17109
E-mail: pcc@ezonline.com
Website: http://www.pachurches.org
Media Contact, Dr. Robert J. O'Hara
Co-Staff: Dr. Robert J. O'Hara, Jr., Kermit L. Lloyd (Interim)
Co-Chpsns.: Bishop Nicolas C. Datillo; Bishop Robert D. Rowley, Jr.
Major activities: Theological Consultation; Social Concerns; Inter-Church Planning; Conferences and Seminars; Disaster Response Preparedness

*The Pennsylvania Council of Churches

900 S. Arlington Ave., Ste. 100, Harrisburg, PA 17109-5089 Tel. (717)545-4761
E-mail: pcc@pachurches.org
Website: http://www.pachurches.org
Media Contact, Exec. Dir., Rev. Dr. Carl W. Gittings, Fax (717)545-4765
Exec. Dir., Rev. Dr. Carl W. Gittings
Public Policy, Dir., Rev. K. Joy Kaufmann
Coord. for Contract Chaplaincy, Rev. Charles R. Meile, Jr.

Coord. for Leisure Ministries, —
Coord. for Farmworker Ministries, Rev. Ray L. Kauffman
Coord. for Save Our Youth Program, Antoinette Hodge
Consultant for Trucker/Travel Ministries, —
Pres., Rev. Dr. Lyle J. Weible
Vice-Pres., Bishop A. Donald Main
Sec., Mrs. Nancy S. Ritter
Treas., Barry R. Herr
Bus. Mgr., Janet Gollick
Major activities: Institutional Ministry; Migrant Ministry; Truck Stop Chaplaincy; Social Ministry; Leisure Ministry; Inter-Church Planning and Dialogue; Conferences; Disaster Response; Trade Association Activities; Church Education; Ethnic Cooperation

Allegheny Valley Association of Churches

1333 Freeport Rd., Natrona Heights, PA 15065 Tel. (724)226-0606 Fax (724)226-3197
E-mail: —
Website: —
Media Contact, Exec. Dir., Luella H. Barrage
Exec. Dir., Luella H. Barrage
Pres., Rev. Dr. W. James Legge, 232 Tarentum-Culmerville Rd., Tarentum, PA 15084
Treas., Libby Grimm, 312 Butternut Ln., Tarentum, PA 15084
Major activities: Ecumenical Services; Dial-a-Devotion; CROP Walk for Hunger; Food Bank; Emergency Aid; Cross-on-the-Hill; AVAC Hospitality Network for Homeless Families; AVAC Volunteer Caregivers; Senior Citizen Housing

Christian Associates of Southwest Pennsylvania

204 37th St., Suite 201, Pittsburgh, PA 15201 Tel. (412)688-9070 Fax (412)688-9091
E-mail: casp1817@aol.com
Website: http://www.casp.org
Media Contact, Dir. of Communications, Bruce J. Randolph
Chair of Council, Bishop Donald Wuerl
Pres. Of the Board, Rev. Dr. Arnold Klukas
Dir. of Communications, Bruce J. Randolph
AIDS Interfaith Care Teams, Director, Patricia Zerega
Allegheny County Jail Chaplaincy, Director, Rev. Ulrich Klemm
Shuman Detention Center Chaplaincy, Director, Rev. Floyd Palmer
Cable TV Coord., Earl C. Hartman, Jr.
Administrative Assist., Nancy Raymond
Major activities: Television & Print ministry; AIDS Interfaith Care Teams; Jail & Youth Incarceration Chaplaincy Programs; Church and Community; Leadership Development; Theological Dialogue; Racism

Christian Churches United of the Tri-County Area

P.O. Box 60750, Harrisburg, PA 17106-0750 Tel. (717)230-9550 Fax (717)230-9554
E-mail: —
Website: —
Media Contact, Exec. Dir., Jaqueline P. Rucker
Exec. Dir., Jaqueline P. Rucker
Pres., Joe Fiedler
Treas., Dorothy Shaffner
Vice-Pres., Betty Ann Funk
Sec., Lenore Cameron, Esq.
HELP & LaCasa Ministries, Dir., Victoria Hess, PO Box 60750, Harrisburg, PA 17106-0750 Tel. (717)238-2851 Fax (717)238-1916
Major activities: Volunteer Ministries to Prisons; Aging; HELP (Housing, Rent, Food, Medication, Transportation, Home Heating, Clothing); La Casa de Amistad (The House of Friendship) Social Services; AIDS Outreach; Prison Chaplaincy; Lend-A-Hand (Disaster Rebuilding)

Christians United in Beaver County

1098 Third St., Beaver, PA 15009 Tel. (412)774-1446 Fax —
E-mail: —
Website: —
Media Contact, Exec. Sec., Lois L. Smith
Exec. Sec., Lois L. Smith
Chaplains: Rev. Bernard Tench; Erika Bruner; Rev. Anthony Massey; Rev. Frank Churchill; Jack Kirkpatrick
Pres., Rev. Anthony Catullo, 3393 Old Darlington Rd., Darlington, PA 16115
Treas., Ima Moldovon, 302 Lynn Dr., New Brighton, PA 15066
Major activities: Christian Education; Evangelism; Radio; Social Action; Church Women United; United Church Men; Ecumenism; Hospital, Detention Home and Jail Ministry

East End Cooperative Ministry

250 N. Highland Ave., Pittsburgh, PA 15206 Tel. (412)361-5549 Fax (412)361-0151
E-mail: —
Website: —
Media Contact, Nancy Paul
Exec. Dir., Myrna Zelenitz
Major activities: Food Pantry; Soup Kitchen; Men's Emergency Shelter; Drop-In Shelter for Homeless; Meals on Wheels; Casework and Supportive Services for Elderly; Information and Referral; Program for Children and Youth; Bridge Housing Program for Men and Women in Recovery and Their Children

Ecumenical Conference of Greater Altoona

1208 - 13th St., P.O. Box 305, Altoona, PA 16603 Tel. (814)942-0512 Fax —
E-mail: eilbeck@aol.com

Website: —
Media Contact, Exec. Dir., Eileen Becker
Exec. Dir., Eileen Becker
Major activities: Religious Education; Workshops; Ecumenical Activities; Religious Christmas Parade; Campus Ministry; Community Concerns; Peace Forum; Religious Education for Mentally Challenged; Inter-faith Committee; Prison Ministry

Greater Bethlehem Area Council of Churches

1021 Center St., P.O. Box 1245, Bethlehem, PA 18016-1245 Tel. (610)867-8671 Fax —
E-mail: —
Website: —
Media Contact, Exec. Dir., —
Exec. Dir., —
Pres., Richard Hurd
Treas., Robert Gerst, 900 Wedgewood Rd., Bethlehem, PA 18017
Major activities: Support Ministry; Institutional Ministry to Elderly and Infirm; Family Concerns; Scripture Center; Social Concerns; World Local Hunger Projects; Elderly Ministry; Ecumenical worship/cooperation; Mentoring - youth prisoners and other persons at risk.

Hanover Area Council of Churches

136 Carlisle St., Hanover, PA 17331-2406 Tel. (717)633-6353 Fax (717)633-1992
E-mail: nicknonick@aol.com
Website: http://www. netrax.net/~bouchord/hacc. htm
Exec. Dir., Faye C. Snyder
Major activities: Meals on Wheels, Provide a Lunch Program, Fresh Air Program, Clothing Bank, Hospital Chaplaincy Services; Congregational & Interfaith Relations, Public Ecumenical Programs and Services, State Park Chaplaincy Services & Children's Program; Compeer; Faith at Work; CROP Walk; Stolte Scholarship Fund; Community Needs

Inter-Church Ministries of Erie County

2216 Peach St., Erie, PA 16502 Tel. (814)454-2411 Fax —
E-mail: —
Website: —
Adjunct Staff: Aging Prog., Carolyn A. DiMattio Voucher Program, Mary Stewart
Pres., Rev. Msgr. William E. Biebel, 230 W. 10th St., Erie, PA 16501
Treas., Mrs. Dorothy Christoph, 3224 Cascade St., Erie, PA 16508
Major activities: Local Ecumenism; Ministry with Aging; Social Ministry; Continuing Education; N.W. Pa. Conf. of Bishops and Judicatory Execs.; Theological Dialogue; Coats for Kids; Voucher Program for Emergency Assistance

Lancaster County Council of Churches

447 E. King St., Lancaster, PA 17602 Tel. (717)291-2261 Fax (717)291-6403
E-mail: —
Website: —
Media Contact, Pres., Rev. John Smaligo
Pres., Rev. John Smaligo
Prescott House, Dir., Casey Jones
Asst. Admn., Kim Y. Wittel
Child Abuse, Dir., Louise Schiraldi
CONTACT, Dir., Lois Gascho
Service Ministry, Dir., Adela Dohner
Major activities: Social Ministry; Residential Ministry to Youthful Offenders; CONTACT; Advocacy; Child Abuse Prevention

Lebanon County Christian Ministries

818 Water St., P.O. Box 654, Lebanon, PA 17046 Tel. (717)274-2601 Fax —
E-mail: —
Website: —
Media Contact, Exec. Dir., Dale M. Miller
Exec. Dir., Dale M. Miller
Food & Clothing Bank Dir., Lillian Morales
H.O.P.E. Services, Dale M. Miller
Noon Meals Coord., Elaine Zapata
Major activities: H.O.P.E. (Helping Our People in Emergencies); Food & Clothing Bank; Free Meal Program; Commodity Distribution Program; Ecumenical Events; Chaplaincy and Support Services

Lehigh County Conference of Churches

534 Chew St., Allentown, PA 18102 Tel. (610)433-6421 Fax (610)439-8039
E-mail: LCCCED@aol.com
Website: —
Media Contact, Exec. Dir., Rev. William A. Seaman
Assoc. Dir., Marlene Merz
Pres., Dr. Pat Murray
1st Vice-Pres., Mr. Tony Muir
Sec., Rita Sparrow
Treas., David Schumacher
Major activities: Chaplaincy Program; Social Concerns and Action; Clergy Dialogues; Drop-In-Center for De-Institutionalized Adults; Ecumenical Soup Kitchen; Housing Advocacy Program; Pathways (Reference to Social Services); Street Contact; Linkage; Guardianship

Metropolitan Christian Council of Philadelphia

1501 Cherry St., Philadelphia, PA 19102-1429 Tel. (215)563-7854 Fax (215)563-6849
E-mail: rev_geiger@mccp.org
Website: http://www.mccp.org
Media Contact, Assoc. Communications, Nancy L. Nolde
Exec. Dir., Rev. C. Edward Geiger
Assoc. Communications, Nancy L. Nolde

Office Mgr., Joan G. Shipman
Pres., Rev. Janet K. Hess
First Vice-Pres., Rev. Steve B. Lawrence
Treas., A. Louis Denton, Esq.
Major activities: Congregational Clusters; Public Policy Advocacy; Communication; Interfaith Dialogue

North Hills Youth Ministry Counseling Center

802 McKnight Park Dr., Pittsburgh, PA 15237 Tel. (412)366-1300 Fax —
E-mail: NHYM@SGI.NET
Website: —
Media Contact, Exec. Dir., Rev. Ronald B. Barnes
Exec. Dir., Ronald B. Barnes
Major activities: Elementary, Junior and Senior High School Individual and Family Counseling; Elementary Age Youth Early Intervention Counseling; Educational Programming for Churches and Schools; Youth Advocacy; Parent Education; Marital Counseling

Northside Common Ministries

P.O. Box 99861, Pittsburgh, PA 15233 Tel. (412)323-1163 Fax (412)323-1749
E-mail: NCM@citynet.com
Website: —
Media Contact, Exec. Dir., Mark Stephen Bibro
Exec. Dir., Mark Stephen Bibro
Pres., Rev. Robert J. Wilde, MSW
Major activities: Pleasant Valley Shelter for Homeless Men; Advocacy around Hunger, Housing, Poverty, and Racial Issues; Community Food Pantry and Service Center; Supportive Housing

Northwest Interfaith Movement

6757 Greene St., Philadelphia, PA 19119 Tel. (215)843-5600 Fax (215)843-2755
E-mail: nim@libertynet.org
Website: —
Media Contact, Exec. Dir., Rev. Richard R. Fernandez
Exec. Dir., Rev. Richard R. Fernandez
Chpsn., Elaine Dushoff
Long Term Care Connection, Dir., Dollyne Wayman-Brody
Neighborhood Child Care Resource Prog., Dir., Amy Gendall
School Age Ministry, Dir., Brenda Rochester
Major activities: Resources amd Technical Assistance for Child Care Programs; Conflict Mediation and Support for Nursing and Boarding Home Residents; Development of After-School Programs; Training and Financial Support to Congregation Engaged in Community Ministry

Project of Easton, Inc.

330 Ferry St., Easton, PA 18042 Tel. (215)258-4361 Fax —
E-mail: —

Website: —
Pres., Dr. John H. Updegrove
Vice-Pres. Public Relations, Rev. Charles E. Staples
Vice-Pres. Operations, Don Follett
Sec., Rosemary Reese
Treas., Steve Barsony
Exec. Dir., Maryellen Shuman
Major activities: Food Bank; Adult Literacy Program; English as a Second Language; Children's Programs; Parents as Student Support; CROP Walk; Interfaith Council; Family Literacy; Emergency Assistance; Even Start Family Literacy

Reading Berks Conference of Churches
54 N. 8th St., Reading, PA 19601 Tel. (610)375-6108 Fax (610)375-6205
E-mail: —
Website: —
Media Contact, Exec. Dir., Rev. Calvin Kurtz
Exec. Dir., Rev. Calvin Kurtz
Pres., John Roland, Esq.
Treas., William Maslo
Major activities: Institutional Ministry; Social Action; Migrant Ministry; CWS; CROP Walk for Hunger; Emergency Assistance; Prison Chaplaincy; AIDS Hospice Development; Hospital Chaplaincy; Interchurch/Intercultural Services; Children & Youth Ministry

Reading Urban Ministry
134 N. Fifth St., Reading, PA 19601 Tel. (610)374-6917 Fax (610)371-9791
E-mail: —
Website: —
Media Contact, Beth Bitler
Exec. Dir., Beth Bitler
Pres., Edward Robertson
Vice-Pres., Sarah Walters
Sec., Jill Braun
Treas., Karen Good
Major activities: Youth Ministry Program; Family Action Support Team (Child Abuse Prevention)

South Hills Interfaith Ministries
1900 Sleepy Hollow Rd., Library, PA 15129 Tel. (412)854-9120 Fax (412)854-9123
E-mail: —
Website: —
Media Contact, Exec. Dir., Donald Guinn
Prog. Dir., Susan Simons
Psychological Services, Don Zandier
Family Assistance Coordinator, Sherry Kotz
Business Mgr., Jeff Walley
Volunteer Coordinator, Kristin Snodgrass
Major activities: Basic Human Needs; Community Organization and Development; Inter-Faith Cooperation; Personal Growth; At-Risk Youth Development; Women in Transition; Elderly Support

United Churches of Lycoming County
202 E. Third St., Williamsport, PA 17701 Tel. (717)322-1110 Fax —
Website: —
Media Contact, Exec. Dir., Gwen Nelson Bernstine
E-mail: gwen_bernstine.parti@ecunet.org
Exec. Dir., Gwen Nelson Bernstine
Ofc. Sec., Linda Winter
Pres., The Rev. Robert L. Driesen, 324 Howard St., S. Williamsport, PA 17701
Treas., Raymond Fisher, 145 Linden St., S. Williamsport, PA 17701
Shepherd of the Streets, Rev. Wilbur L. Scranton, III, 130 E. 3rd St., Williamsport, PA 17701
Ecumenism, Dir., Rev. Jan L. Elsasser, R.R. 2 , Box 105, Cogan Station, PA 17728
Educ. Ministries, Dir., Rev. Bruce Drucken-miller, 202 E. Third St., Williamsport, PA 17701
Institutional Ministry, Dir., Linda Leonard, 12 E. Water St., Hughesville, PA 17737
Radio-TV, Dir., Rev. Louis Gatti, 3200 Lycoming Creek Rd., Williamsport, PA 17701
Prison Ministry, Dir., Jane Russell, 1200 Almond St., Williamsport, PA 17701
Christian Social Concerns, Dir., Rev. Robert Wallace, 1359 Mansel Ave., Williamsport, PA 17701
Major activities: Ecumenism; Educational Ministries; Church Women United; Church World Service and CROP; Prison Ministry; Radio-TV; Nursing Homes; Fuel Bank; Food Pantry; Family Life; Shepherd of the Streets Urban Ministry; Peace Concerns; Housing Initiative; Interfaith Dialogue

Wilkinsburg Community Ministry
710 Mulberry St., Pittsburgh, PA 15221 Tel. (412)241-8072 Fax (412)241-8315
E-mail: —
Website: —
Media Contact, Dir., Rev. Vivian Lovingood
Dir., Rev. Vivian Lovingood
Pres. of Bd., Jack Peffer
Major activities: Hunger Ministry; After School Youth Programs; Summer Bible School; Teen-Moms Infant Care; Meals on Wheels; Tape Ministry

Wyoming Valley Council of Churches
35 S. Franklin St., Wilkes-Barre, PA 18701 Tel. (717)825-8543 Fax —
E-mail: —
Website: —
Media Contact, Exec. Dir., Susan Grine Harper
Exec. Dir., Susan Grine Harper
Ofc. Sec., Sandra Karrott
Pres., Dn. Sergei Kapral
Treas., H. Merritt Hughes
Major activities: Nursing Home Chaplaincy; Martin Luther King, Jr. Fuel Drive in

Association with Local Agencies; Hospital Referral Service; Choral Festival of Faith; Migrant Ministry; Ecumenical Pulpit Exchange, Int.; CROP Hunger Walk; Pastoral Care Ministries; Clergy Retreats and Seminars

York County Council of Churches
P.O. Box 1865, York, PA 17405-1865 Tel. (717)854-9504 Fax (717)843-5295
E-mail: yccc@juno.com
Website: —
Media Contact, Exec. Dir., Rev. Patrick B. Walker
Pres., Rev. Stephany Sechrist
Exec. Dir., Rev. Patrick B. Walker
Major activities: Educational Development; Spiritual Growth and Renewal; Worship and Witness; Congregational Resourcing; Outreach and Mission

RHODE ISLAND

*The Rhode Island State Council of Churches
734 Hope St., Providence, RI 02906 Tel. (401)861-1700 Fax (401)331-3080
E-mail: riscc734@aol.com
Website: —
Media Contact, Exec. Min., Rev. James C. Miller
Exec. Min., Rev. James C. Miller
Admn. Asst., Peggy MacNie
Pres., Rev. Quinton Ivy
Treas., George Weavill
Major activities: Urban Ministries; TV; Institutional Chaplaincy; Advocacy/Justice & Service; Legislative Liaison; Faith & Order; Leadership Development; Campus Ministries

SOUTH CAROLINA

*South Carolina Christian Action Council, Inc.
P.O. Drawer 3248, Columbia, SC 29230 Tel. (803)786-7115 Fax (803)786-7116
E-mail: sc.council@ecunet.org
Website: —
Media Contact, Exec. Min., Dr. L. Wayne Bryan
Exec. Min., Dr. L. Wayne Bryan
Pres., Rev. Dr. Lewis Galloway
Major activities: Advocacy and Ecumenism; Continuing Education; Interfaith Dialogue; Citizenship and Public Affairs; Publications

United Ministries
606 Pendleton St., Greenville, SC 29601 Tel. (864)232-6463 Fax (864)370-3518
E-mail: —
Website: —
Media Contact, Exec. Dir., Rev. Beth Templeton
Exec. Dir., Rev. Beth Templeton
Pres., Jordan Earle
Vice-Pres., Jim Freeman
Sec., Vic Greene
Treas., Robert Clanton

Major activities: Survival Programs (Emergency Assistance, Day Shelter for Homeless, Travelers Aid); Stabilization Program (Transitions, Adopt-A-House); Barrier Removal Programs (Employment Readiness); Magdalene Project (Women in Crisis); Life Skills (Educational Classes, Living Skills, Employment Skills)

SOUTH DAKOTA

*Association of Christian Churches
1320 S. Minnesota Ave., Ste. 210, Sioux Falls, SD 57105-0657 Tel. (605)334-1980 Fax (605)996-1766
E-mail: rwfisher@midco.net
Website: —
Media Contact, Pres., Rev. Richard Fisher, P.O. Box 460, Mitchell, SD 57301 Tel. (605)996-6552
Pres., Rev. Richard Fisher
Ofc. Mgr., Pat Willard
Major activities: Ecumenical Forums; Continuing Education for Clergy; Legislative Information; Resourcing Local Ecumenism; Native American Issues; Ecumenical Fields Ministries; Rural Economic Development

TENNESSEE

*Tennessee Association of Churches
103 Oak St., Ashland City, TN 37015 Tel. (615)792-4631 Fax —
E-mail: —
Website: —
Ecumenical Admn., —
Pres., Rev. Steve Mosley
Treas., Paul Milliken
Major activities: Faith and Order; Christian Unity; Social Concern Ministries; Governmental Concerns; Governor's Prayer Breakfast

Metropolitan Inter Faith Association (MIFA)
P.O. Box 3130, Memphis, TN 38173-0130 Tel. (901)527-0208 Fax (901)527-3202
E-mail: —
Website: —
Media Contact, Dir., Media Relations, Kim Gaskill
Exec. Dir., Allie Prescott
Major activities: Emergency Housing; Emergency Services (Rent, Utility, Food, Clothing Assistance); Home-Delivered Meals and Senior Support Services; Youth Services

Volunteer Ministry Center
103 South Gay St., Knoxville, TN 37902 Tel. (423)524-3926 Fax (423)524-7065
E-mail: —
Website: —
Media Contact, Exec. Dir., Angelia Moon, 103 South Gay St., Knoxville, TN 37902 Tel. (423)524-3926 Fax (423)524-7065

Exec. Dir., Angelia Moon
Pres., David Leech
Vice-Pres., John Moxham
Treas., Doug Thompson
Major activities: Homeless Program; Food Line; Crisis Referral Program; Subsidized Apartment Program; Counselling Program; Parenting Education for Single Parents

TEXAS

*Texas Conference of Churches

1033 La Posada, Ste. 225, Austin, TX 78752 Tel. (512)451-0991 Fax (512)451-5348
E-mail: tcc@prismnet.com
Website: —
Media Contact, Exec. Dir., Dr. Carol M. Worthing
Exec. Dir., Dr. Carol M. Worthing
Admin., Keitha Hatfield
Pres., Bishop Joe Delaney
Major activities: Faith & Order; Related Ecumenism; Christian-Jewish Relations; Church and Society Issues

Austin Metropolitan Ministries

2026 Guadalupe, Ste. 226, Austin, TX 78705 Tel. (512)472-7627 Fax (512)472-5274
E-mail: amm@prismnet.com
Website: —
Media Contact, Exec. Dir., Patrick Flood
Exec. Dir., Patrick Flood
Pres., Ronald W. Kessler
Treas., Fred I. Lewis
Program Director, David Davis
Admn., Carole Hatfield
Major activities: Broadcast Ministry; Older Adult Commission; Youth at Risk Mentoring; Interfaith Dialogues; Family Issues; Hispanic Older Adult Caregivers; Housing Rehabilitation; Homeless Issues; VISTA Volunteers; Hunger Issues; Refugee Resettlement

Border Association for Refugees from Central America (BARCA), Inc.

P.O. Box 715, Edinburg, TX 78540 Tel. (210)631-7447 Fax (210)687-9266
E-mail: —
Website: —
Media Contact, Exec. Dir. Ninfa Ochoa-Krueger
Exec. Dir, Ninfa Ochoa-Krueger
Refugee Children Services, Dir., Bertha de la Rosa
Major activities: Food, Shelter, Clothing to Newly Arrived Indigent Immigrants & Refugees; Medical and Other Emergency Aid; Special Services to Children; Speakers on Refugee and Immigrant Concerns for Church Groups; Orientation, Advocacy and Legal Services for Immigrants and Refugees

Corpus Christi Metro Ministries

1919 Leopard St., P.O. Box 4899, Corpus Christi, TX 78469-4899 Tel. (512)887-0151 Fax (512)887-7900
E-mail: edseeger@electrotex.com
Website: —
Media Contact, Exec. Dir., Rev. Edward B. Seeger
Exec. Dir., Rev. Edward B. Seeger
Admn. Dir., Ginger Flewelling-Leeds
Volunteer Dir., Ann Walters
Fin. Coord., Sue McCown
Loaves & Fishes Dir., Ray Gomez
Emergency Services Mgr., Dannette Valdez
Employment Dir., Larry Curtis
Adopt A Caseworker Dir., Jo Flindt
Health and Human Services, Dir., Ann Walters
Major activities: Free Cafeteria;Transitional Shelters; Job Readiness; Job Placement; Primary Health Care; Community Service Restitution; Emergency Clothing; Information and Referral; Case Management

East Dallas Cooperative Parish

P.O. Box 720305, Dallas, TX 75372-0305 Tel. (214)823-9149 Fax (214)823-2015
E-mail: edcp@swbell.net
Website: —
Media Contact, Larry Cox
Pres., Ford Keith
Sec., Norma Worrall
Major activities: Emergency Food, Clothing, Job Bank; Medical Clinic; Legal Clinic, Tutorial Education; Home Companion Service; Pre-School Education; Developmental Learning Center; Asian Ministry; Hispanic Ministry; Activity Center for Low Income Older Adults; Pastoral Counseling; English Language Ministry

Greater Dallas Community of Churches

2800 Swiss Ave., Dallas, TX 75204 Tel. (214)824-8680 Fax (214)824-8726
E-mail: gdcc@churchcommunity.org
Website: —
Media Contact, Exec. Dir., Larry James
Exec. Dir., Larry James
Assoc. Dirs.: The Rev. Holsey Hickman; John Stoesz
AmeriCorps/Building Blocks Dir., —
InnerCity Community College Min., Dir., —
Development Dir., Carole Rylander
Pres., Dr. William J. Carl, III
Treas., Robert Jones
Major activities: Interdenominational, Interfaith and Interracial Understanding and Joint Work; AmeriCorps/Building Blocks (Direct Service to Develop Inner City Children, Youth & Families); Summer Food & Reading; Community College Ministry; Hospital Chaplaincy; Hunger; Peacemaking; Public Policy; Social Justice; Faith & Life

Interfaith Ministries for Greater Houston

3217 Montrose Blvd., Houston, TX 77006 Tel. (713)522-3955 Fax (713)520-4663
E-mail: —
Website: —
Media Contact, Exec. Dir., Betty P. Taylor
Exec. Dir., Betty P. Taylor
Pres., Charles R. Erickson
Development, Dir., Sharon Ervine
Assoc. Exec. Dir., Larry Norton
Treas., Fort D. Flowers, Jr.
Sec., Darlene Alexander
Major activities: Community Concerns: Hunger; Older Adults; Families; Youth; Child Abuse; Refugee Services; Congregational Relations and Development; Social Service Programs: Refugee Services; Hunger Coalition; Youth Victim Witness; Family Connection; Meals on Wheels; Senior Health; RSVP; Foster Grandparents

North Dallas Shared Ministries

2530 Glenda Ln., #500, Dallas, TX 75229 Tel. (214)620-8696 Fax (214)620-0433
E-mail: —
Website: —
Media Contact, Exec. Dir., J. Dwayne Martin
Exec. Dir., J. Dwayne Martin
Pres., —
Major activities: Emergency Assistance; Job Counseling; ESL

Northside Inter-Church Agency (NICA)

1600 Circle Park Blvd., Fort Worth, TX 76106 Tel. (817)626-1102 Fax (817)626-9043
E-mail: —
Website: —
Media Contact, Exec. Dir., Judy Gutierrez
Exec. Dir., Judy Gutierrez
Major activities: Food; Clothing; Counseling; Information and Referral; Furniture and Household Items; Nutrition Education and Teen Program; Employment Services; Thankgiving Basket Program; "Last Resort" Christmas Program; Community Networking; Ecumenical Worship Services; Volunteer Training; Newsletter

San Antonio Community of Churches

1101 W. Woodlawn, San Antonio, TX 78201 Tel. (210)733-9159 Fax (210)733-5780
E-mail: —
Website: —
Media Contact, Exec. Dir., Dr. Kenneth Thompson
Exec. Dir., Dr. Kenneth Thompson
Pres., Fr. Jose De La Rosa
Major activities: Christian Education; Missions; Infant Formula and Medical Prescriptions for Children of Indigent Families; Continuing Education For Clergy and Laity; Media Resource Center; Social Issues; Aging Concerns; Youth Concerns; Family Concerns;

Sponsor annual CROP Walk for Hunger; Peace and Anti-Violence Initiatives

San Antonio Urban Ministries

535 Bandera Rd., San Antonio, TX 78228 Tel. —
Fax —
E-mail: —
Website: —
Media Contact, Sue Kelly
Exec. Dir., Sue Kelly
Pres., Rev. Leslie Ellison
Major activities: Homes for Discharged Mental Patients; After School Care for Latch Key Children; Christian Based Community Ministry

Southeast Area Churches (SEARCH)

P.O. Box 51256, Fort Worth, TX 76105 Tel. (817)531-2211 Fax —
E-mail: —
Website: —
Media Contact, Exec. Dir., Dorothy Anderson-Develrow
Dir., Dorothy Anderson-Develrow
Major activities: Emergency Assistance; Advocacy; Information and Referral; Community Worship; School Supplies; Direct Aid to Low Income and Elderly

Southside Area Ministries, Inc. (SAM)

305 W. Broadway, Fort Worth, TX 76104 Tel. (817)332-3778 Fax —
E-mail: —
Website: —
Media Contact, Linda Freeto
Exec. Dir., Linda Freeto
Major activities: Assisting Children for Whom English is a Second Language; Tutoring Grades K-5; Mentoring Grades 6-8; Programs for Senior Citizens

Tarrant Area Community of Churches

P.O. Box 11471, Fort Worth, TX 76110-0471 Tel. (817)922-9446 Fax (817)922-9291
E-mail: revkm@flash.net
Website: —
Pres., Dr. Toni Craven
Treas., Cindy Mulkey
Exec. Dir., Dr. Kenneth W. McIntosh
Major activities: Eldercare Program; Children's Sabbath Sponsorship; Week of Prayer for Christian Unity; CROP Walk for Hunger Relief; Community Issues Forums; Family Pathfinders

United Board of Missions

1701 Bluebonnet Ave., P.O. Box 3856, Port Arthur, TX 77643-3856 Tel. (409)982-9412 Fax (409)985-3668
E-mail: —
Website: —
Media Contact, Admn. Asst., Carolyn Schwarr, P.O.Box 3856, Port Arthur, TX 77643 Tel. (409)982-9412 Fax (409)985-3668

Exec. Dir., Clark Moore
Pres., Glenda McCoy
Major activities: Emergency Assistance (Food and Clothing, Rent and Utility, Medical, Dental, Transportation); Share a Toy at Christmas; Counseling; Back to School Clothing Assistance; Information and Referral; Hearing Aid Bank; Meals on Wheels; Super Pantry; Energy Conservation Programs; Job Bank Assistance to Local Residents Only

VERMONT

*Vermont Ecumenical Council and Bible Society
285 Maple St., Burlington, VT 05401 Tel. (802)864-7723 Fax —
E-mail: vecumen@together.net
Website: —
Media Contact, Admn. Asst., Betsy Wackernagel
Exec. Sec., Mr. Philip C. Kimball
Pres., Rev. Dr. Louis A. George
Vice-Pres., Most Rev. Kenneth A. Angell
Treas., Rev. E. Lon Schneider
Major activities: Christian Unity; Bible Distribution; Social Justice; Committee on Faith and Order; Committee on Peace, Justice and the Integrity of Creation

VIRGINIA

*Virginia Council of Churches, Inc.
1214 W. Graham Rd., Richmond, VA 23220-1409 Tel. (804)321-3300 Fax (804)329-5066
E-mail: vcc-net@aol.com
Website: http://www. vcc-net.org
Media Contact, Gen. Min., Rev. James F. McDonald
Gen. Min., Rev. James F. McDonald
Assoc. Gen. Min., Dr. Judith Fa Galde Bennett
Migrant Head Start, Dir., Richard D. Cagan
Refugee Resettlement, Dir., Rev. Richard D. Cline
Weekday Rel. Educ., Coord., Evelyn W. Simmons, P.O. Box 245, Clifton Forge, VA 24422
Campus Ministry Forum, Coord., Rev. Steve Darr, c/o Community College Ministries, 305 Washington St., N.W., Blacksburg, VA 24060-4745
Major activities: Faith and Order; Network Building & Coordination; Ecumenical Communications; Justice and Legislative Concerns; Educational Development; Rural Concerns; Refugee Resettlement; Migrant Ministries and Migrant Head Start; Disaster Coordination; Infant Mortality Prevention

Community Ministry of Northern Virginia
6020 Commack Ct., Springfield, VA 22152-1313
Tel. (703)352-3434 Fax (703)912-3516
E-mail: —

Website: —
Media Contact, Exec. Dir., John Wells, 10530 Rosehaven St. Ste. 350, Fairfax, VA 22030 Tel. (703)352-3434
Exec. Dir., John Wells
Newsletter Ed., John Wells
Chpsn., Phil True
Treas., Robert Gaudian
Major activities: Ecumenical Social Ministry; Elderly; Criminal Justice; Housing; Public Education

WASHINGTON

*Washington Association of Churches
419 Occidental Ave. S., Ste. 201, Seattle, WA 98104 Tel. (206)625-9790 Fax (206)625-9791
Website: —
Media Contact, John C. Boonstra
E-mail: boonstra@thewac.org
Exec. Min., Rev. John C. Boonstra
Public Policy Associate, Sara Fleming
Public Church Associate, Michael Ramos
Admn. Assoc., Bette Schneider
Native American Network, Shelley Means
Major activities: Faith and Order; Justice Advocacy; Confronting Poverty; Hunger Action; Legislation; Denominational Ecumenical Coordination; Theological Formation; Leadership Development; Refugee Advocacy; Racial Justice Advocacy; International Solidarity

Associated Ministries of Tacoma-Pierce County
1224 South "I" St., Tacoma, WA 98405-5021 Tel. (253)383-3056 Fax (253)383-2672
E-mail: associated.ministries@ecunet.org
Website: http://www. associatedministries.org
Media Contact, Exec. Dir., Rev. David T. Alger
Exec. Dir., Rev. David T. Alger, 4510 Defiance, Tacoma, WA 98407
Assoc. Dir., Janet Leng, 1809 N. Lexington, Tacoma, WA 98406
Dir. of Mental Health Chaplaincy, Father Paul Reitmann
Dir. of Anti-Poverty Resource Center, Marin Johnson
Dir. of Point Tacoma/Pierce Beautiful, Sallie Shawl
Dir. of Face of Hunger, Maureen Fife
Dir. of Hilltop Action Coalition, Jacquie Hacket
Pres., Rev. Richard Cook
Sec., Dorothy Diers
Treas., Dr. Judy Thompson
Vice-Pres., Rev. Richard Tietjen
Major activities: County-wide Hunger Walk; Hunger Awareness; Economic Justice; Religious Education; Shalom (Peacemaking) Resource Center; Social Service Program Advocacy; Communication and Networking of Churches; Housing; Paint Tacoma/Pierce Beautiful; Anti-Poverty Resource Center;

Mental Health Chaplaincy; Theological Dialogue; Welfare to Work Mentoring; Hilltop Action Coalition; ComPeer

Associated Ministries of Thurston County

P.O. Box 895, Olympia, WA 98507 Tel. (360)357-7224 Fax —
E-mail: AMofThurstonCo@juno.com
Website: —
Media Contact, Exec. Dir., Cheri Gonyaw
Exec. Dir., Cheri Gonyaw
Pres., George Hinkel
Treas., Bob McCoy
Major activities: Church Information and Referral; Interfaith Relations; Social and Health Concerns; Community Action

Center for the Prevention of Sexual and Domestic Violence

936 N. 34th St., Ste. 200, Seattle, WA 98103 Tel. (206)634-1903 Fax (206)634-0115
E-mail: cpsdv@cpsdv.org
Website: www.cpsdv.org
Media Contact, Exec. Dir., Rev. Dr. Marie M. Fortune, 936 N. 34th St., Ste. 200, Seattle, WA 98103 Tel. (206)634-1903 Fax (206)634-0115
Exec. Dir., Rev. Dr. Marie M. Fortune
Assoc. Dir., Rev. Kathryn J. Johnson
Program Staff: Jean Anton; Rev. Thelma B. Burgonio-Watson; Sandra Barone; Ellen Johanson; Rev. Aubra Love
Admn. Staff: Carolyn Eastman
Major activities: Prevention and Response Education; Clergy and Lay Training; Video and Print Resources; Bi-national Educational Ministry

Church Council of Greater Seattle

4759 15th Ave. NE, Seattle, WA 98105 Tel. (206)525-1213 Fax (206)525-1218
E-mail: CCGSea@aol.com
Website: —
Media Contact, Assoc. Dir., Development, Meredith E. Brown
Pres./Dir., Rev. Thomas H. Quigley
Assocociate Dir., Program, Alice M. Woldt
Assocociate Dir., Development, Meredith G. Brown
Admin. Asst., Mary Rolston
Emergency Feeding Prog., Dir., Arthur Lee
Friend-to-Friend, Dir., Marilyn Soderquist
Youth Chaplaincy Program, Dir., Rev. Vera Diggins
The Sharehouse, Dir., —
Homelessness Project, Dir., Nancy Dorman
Mission for Music & Healing, Dir., Esther "Little Dove" John
Sound Youth-Americorps, Dir., Rachel Allen
Interfaith Relations, Coord., Rev. Joyce Manson
Academy of Religious Broadcasting, Dir., Rev. J. Graley Taylor
Board President, Rev. Mary Moore

Board Treas., Steve Faust
Homestead Organizing Project, Dir., Bob Kubiniec
Commisson on Children, Youth & Families, Dir., Rachel Allen
Young Adult Living Project, Dir., Antonia Koening
Editors, The Source: Marge Lueders; Joan Reed
Seattle Youth Garden Works, Dir., Margaret Hauptman
SW King County Mental Health Ministry, Dir., Rev. Richard Lutz
Major activities: Children; Youth & Families; Hunger Relief; Global Peace and Justice; Housing and Homelessness; Pastoral Care; Services for the Aging; Public Witness; Interfaith and Ecumenical Relations

The Interfaith Assn. Of Snohomish County

2301 Hoyt, P.O. Box 12824, Everett, WA 98206 Tel. (206)252-6672 Fax —
E-mail: —
Website: —
Media Contact, Exec. Dir., Pam W. Estes, P.O. Box 12824, Everett, WA 98206 Tel. (206)252-6672
Exec. Dir., Pam W. Estes
Pres., Evie Stegath
Major activities: Housing and Shelter; Economic Justice; Hunger; Interfaith Worship and Collaboration

Northwest Harvest/E. M. M.

P.O. Box 12272, Seattle, WA 98102 Tel. (206)625-0755 Fax (206)625-7518
E-mail: nharvest@blarg.net
Website: http://www. northwestharvest.org
Media Contact, Comm. Affairs Dir., Ellen Hansen
Exec. Dir., Ruth M. Velozo
Chpsn., Robert Raphael
Major activities: Northwest Harvest (Statewide Hunger Response); Cherry Street Food Bank (Community Hunger Response); Northwest Infants Corner (Special Nutritional Products for Infants and Babies)

Spokane Council of Ecumenical Ministries

E. 245-13th Ave., Spokane, WA 99202 Tel. (509)624-5156 Fax —
E-mail: scem@tincan.org
Website: http://www. tincan.org/~scem
Media Contact, Editor & Comm. Dir., Mary Stamp, Tel. (509)535-1813
Exec. Dir., Rev. John Olson
Chair,The Rev. Jim Burford
Vice-Chair, Pat Copeland-Malone
Treas., Barbara Shaffer
Sec., Judy Butler
Vice-Chair, Barbara Schaffer
Major activities: Greater Spokane Coalition

262

Against Poverty; Camp PEACE: Multi-Cultural Human Relations- High School Youth Camp; Night Walk Ministry; Clergy Families in Crisis Project; *Fig Tree* Newspaper; Dir. of Churches & Community Agencies; Interfaith Thanksgiving Worship; Easter Sunrise Service; Friend to Friend Visitation with Nursing Home Patients; CROP Walk; Eastern Washington Legislative Conference; Inland Northwest Disaster Response; Ecumenical Sunday; Churches Against Racism

WEST VIRGINIA
*West Virginia Council of Churches
1608 Virginia St. E., Charleston, WV 25311 Tel. (304)344-3141 Fax (304)342-1506
Website: www.wvcc.org
Media Contact, Exec. Dir., The Rev. Nathan D. Wilson
E-mail: nathanwilson@wvcc.org
Pres., Dr. William B. Allen, Rt. 5, Box 167, Parkersburg, WV 26101
Vice-Pres., Bishop Clifton Ives
Sec., The Rev. Peggy Scharff
Treas., Patricia Trader, 326 Prudential Dr., Beckley, WV 25801-8870
Major activities: Leisure Ministry; Disaster Response; Faith and Order; Family Concerns; Inter-Faith Relations; Peace and Justice; Government Concerns; Support Sevices Network

Greater Fairmont Council of Churches
P.O. Box 108, Fairmont, WV 26554 Tel. (304)366-8126 Fax —
E-mail: —
Website: —
Media Contact, Exec. Sec., Nancy Hoffman
Exec. Sec., Nancy Hoffman
Major activities: Community Ecumenical Services; Youth and Adult Sports Leagues; CROP Walk Sponsor; Weekly Radio Broadcasts

The Greater Wheeling Council of Churches
1060 Chapline St., #110, Wheeling, WV 26003 Tel. (304)232-5315 Fax —
E-mail: —
Website: —
Media Contact, Exec. Dir., Kathy J. Burley
Exec. Dir., Kathy J. Burley
Hospital Notification Sec., Ruth Fletcher
Pres., Rev. Robert A. Dinges
Finance Chpn., P. Kim McCluskey
Major activities: Christian Education; Evangelism; Christian Heritage Week Celebration; Institutional Ministry; Regional Jail Chaplaincy; Church Women United; Volunteer Chaplaincy Care at OVMC Hospital; School of Religion; Hospital Notification; Hymn Sing in the Park; Anti-Gambling Crusade; Pentecost Celebration; Clergy Council; Easter Sunrise Service; Community Seder; Church Secretaries Fellowship; Natl. Day of Prayer Service; Videotape Library/Audiotape Library

WISCONSIN
*Wisconsin Council of Churches
750 Windsor St. Ste. 301, Sun Prairie, WI 53590-2149 Tel. (608)837-3108 Fax (608)837-3038
E-mail: wcc@ecunet.org
Website: —
Media Contact, Comm. Coord., Jan Johnson
Exec. Dir., Rev. Jerry Folk
Assoc. Dir., Bonnee Lauridsen Voss
Ofc. Mgr., Jan Johnson
Peace & Justice Ecumenical Partnership, Dir., Catherine Coy
Pres., Bishop Sharon Zimmerman Rader
Treas., Donald Cleven
Major activities: Social Witness; Migrant Ministry; Aging; Wisconsin Interfaith IMPACT; Institutional Chaplaincy; Peace and Justice; Faith and Order; Rural Concerns; American Indian Ministries Council; Park Ministry; State Women's Committee

Center for Community Concerns
1501 Villa St., Racine, WI 53403 Tel. (414)637-9176 Fax (414)637-9265
E-mail: ccc1501@miliserv.net
Website: —
Media Contact, Exec. Dir., Sr. Michelle Olley
Exec. Dir., Sr. Michelle Olley
Skillbank Coord., Eleanor Sorenson
RSVP (Retired Senior Volunteer Program), Chris Udell-Sorberg
Volunteer Today (55 and under), Karen Whyte
Major activities: Advocacy; Direct Services; Research; Community Consultant; Criminal Justice; Volunteerism; Senior Citizen Services

Christian Youth Council
1715-52nd St., Kenosha, WI 53140 Tel. (414)652-9543 Fax (414)652-4461
E-mail: —
Website: —
Media Contact, Exec. Dir., Steven L. Nelson
Exec. Dir., Steven L. Nelson
Sports Dir., Jerry Tappen
Outreach Dir., Linda Osborne
Accountant, Debbie Cutts
Class Director, Jill Cox
Pres. & Chmn. of Board, Lon Knoedler
Gang Prevention Dir., Sam Sauceda
Major activities: Leisure Time Ministry; Institutional Ministries; Ecumenical Committee; Social Concerns; Outreach Sports(with a Christian Philosophy)

Interfaith Conference of Greater Milwaukee

1442 N. Farwell Ave., Ste. 200, Milwaukee, WI
  53202 Tel. (414)276-9050 Fax (414)276-8442
E-mail: —
Website: —
Media Contact, Exec. Dir., Jack Murtaugh
Chpsn., Rabbi Isaac Serotta
First Vice-Chair, Archbishop Rembert G.
  Weakland
Second Vice-Chair, Rev. Charles Graves
Sec., Rev. Peter Nenner
Treas., Rev. Mary Ann Neevel
Exec. Dir., Jack Murtaugh
Poverty Issues, Program Coord., Marcus White
Consultant in Communications, Rev. Robert P.
  Seater
Development., Lisa Zeilenger
Major activities: Economic Issues; Racism;
  CROP Walk; Public Policy; Suburban and
  Urban Partnerships; TV Programming; Peace
  and International Issues Committee; Annual
  Membership Luncheon; Substance Abuse,
  Violence Prevention

Madison Urban Ministry

1127 University Ave., Madison, WI 53715 Tel.
  (608)256-0906 Fax (608)256-4387
E-mail: —
Website: —
Media Contact, Office/Program Mgr., Shirley
  Manion
Exec. Dir., Charles Pfeifer
Ofc./Program Mgr., Shirley Manion
Major activities: Community Projects; Dialogue/
  Forums; Affordable Housing Coalition; Youth
  & Violence Conference; Prayer at the Heart of
  Social Action; Safety Net; Safe Night; Social
  & Economic Justice

WYOMING

*Wyoming Church Coalition

P.O. Box 20812, Cheyenne, WY 82003-7017 Tel.
  (307)635-4251 Fax (307)778-9060
E-mail: Dan_Monson@ecunet.org
Website: —
Media Contact, Rev. Daniel E. Monson, 1032
  Melton St., Cheyenne, WY 82009 Tel.
  (307)635-4251
Dir., Rev. Daniel E. Monson
Assoc. Dir., Mary A. Monson
Chair, Chesie Lee
Penitentiary Chaplain, Rev. Lynn Schumacher,
  P.O. Box 400, Rawlins, WY 82301
Major activities: Death Penalty; Empowering the
  Poor and Oppressed; Peace and Justice; Prison
  Ministry; Malicious Harassment; Domestic
  Violence, Public Health Issues; Welfare
  Reform

Index of Select Programs for U.S. Regional and Local Ecumenical Bodies

For many years the Yearbook of American & Canadian Churches has published a directory of U.S. Ecumenical Bodies, each entry of which contains a brief description of the programs offered by each agency. Researchers, pastors, service organizations and theological seminaries often inquire about specific programs and which agencies carry out such programs. In the 1999 Yearbook of American & Canadian Churches, we have initiated an index listing agencies which provide programs in the areas which are most frequently the subject of inquiry to our offices: Interfaith Dialogue, Hunger/Food Programs, Youth Activities, Faith and Order, and Homelessness/Shelter Ministries. We trust that this chapter index will prove useful to readers as they seek information regarding these areas of program.

INTERFAITH DIALOGUE

ALABAMA
Interfaith Mission Service, Huntsville, AL

ALASKA
Alaska Christian Conference, Fairbanks, AK

ARIZONA
Arizona Ecumenical Council, Phoenix, AZ

CALIFORNIA
California Council of Churches/California Church Impact, Sacramento, CA
The Ecumenical Council of San Diego County, San Diego, CA
The Ecumenical Council of the Pasadena Area Churches, Pasadena, CA
Fresno Metro Ministry, Fresno, CA
Interfaith Council of Contra Costa County, Walnut Creek, CA
Interfaith Service Bureau, Sacramento, CA
Marin Interfaith Council, San Rafael, CA
Northern California Interreligious Conference, San Francisco, CA
San Fernando Valley Interfaith Council, Chatsworth, CA
South Coast Ecumenical Council, Long Beach, CA

COLORADO
Colorado Council of Churches, Denver, CO

CONNECTICUT
Christian Conference of Connecticut (CHRISCON), Hartford, CT
Center City Churches, Hartford, CT
Council of Churches and Synagogues of Southwestern Connecticut, Stamford, CT
Council of Churches of Greater Bridgeport, Inc., Bridgeport, CT

DELAWARE
The Christian Council of Delaware and Maryland's Eastern Shore, Baltimore, MD

DISTRICT OF COLUMBIA
The Council of Churches of Greater Washington, Washington, DC
InterFaith Conference of Metropolitan Washington, Washington, DC

GEORGIA
Georgia Christian Council, Macon, GA
Christian Council of Metropolitan Atlanta, Atlanta, GA

ILLINOIS
Churches United of the Quad City Area, Rock Island, IL
Greater Chicago Broadcast Ministries, Chicago, IL
The Hyde Park & Kenwood Interfaith Council, Chicago, IL
Oak Park-River Forest Community of Congregations, Oak Park, IL
Peoria Friendship House of Christian Service, Peoria, IL

INDIANA
Evansville Area Community of Churches, Inc., Evansville, IN
United Religious Community of St. Joseph County, South Bend, IN

IOWA
Des Moines Area Religious Council, Des Moines, IA

KENTUCKY
Highlands Community Ministries, Louisville, KY
Paducah Cooperative Ministry, Paducah, KY

LOUISIANA
Louisiana Interchurch Conference, Baton Rouge, LA

MAINE
Maine Council of Churches, Portland, ME

MASSACHUSETTS
The Cape Cod Council of Churches, Inc., Hyannis, MA
Council of Churches of Greater Springfield, Springfield, MA
Cooperative Metropolitan Ministries, Newton, MA
Inter-Church Council of Greater New Bedford, New Bedford, MA
Worcester County Ecumenical Council, Worcester, MA

MICHIGAN
Christian Communication Council of Metropolitan Detroit Churches, Detroit, MI
Grand Rapids Area Center for Ecumenism (GRACE), Grand Rapids, MI
Greater Flint Association of Christian Churches, Flint, MI
The Jackson County Interfaith Council, Clarklake, MI
Muskegon County Cooperating Churches, Muskegon, MI

265

MINNESOTA
Arrowhead Interfaith Council, Duluth, MN
Greater Minneapolis Council of Churches, Minneapolis, MN
The Joint Religious Legislative Coalition, Minneapolis, MN
Minnesota Council of Churches, Minneapolis, MN
Metropolitan Interfaith Council on Affordable Housing (MICAH), Minneapolis, MN
St. Paul Council of Churches, St. Paul, MN

MISSOURI
Council of Churches of the Ozarks, Springfield, MO
Interfaith Community Services, St. Joseph, MO

MONTANA
Montana Association of Churches, Billings, MT

NEBRASKA
Interchurch Ministries of Nebraska, Lincoln, NE
Lincoln Interfaith Council, Lincoln, NE

NEW HAMPSHIRE
New Hampshire Council of Churches, Concord, NH

NEW JERSEY
Metropolitan Ecumenical Ministry, Newark, NJ

NEW MEXICO
New Mexico Conference of Churches, Albuquerque, NM
Inter-Faith Council of Santa Fe, New Mexico, Santa Fe, NM

NEW YORK
Capital Area Council of Churches, Inc., Albany, NY
CAPITAL Region Ecumenical Organization (CREO), Scotia, NY
Chautauqua County Rural Ministry, Dunkirk, NY
Council of Churches of Chemung County, Inc., Elmira, NY
Council of Churches of the City of New York, New York, NY
Dutchess Interfaith Council, Inc., Poughkeepsie, NY
Genesee County Churches United, Inc., Batavia, NY
InterReligious Council of Central New York, Syracuse, NY
The Long Island Council of Churches, Hempstead, NY

OHIO
Ohio Council of Churches, Columbus, OH
Akron Area Association of Churches, Akron, OH
Greater Dayton Christian Connection, Dayton, OH
Toledo Ecumenical Area Ministries, Toledo, OH

OKLAHOMA
Tulsa Metropolitan Ministry, Tulsa, OK

OREGON
Ecumenical Ministries of Oregon, Portland, OR

PENNSYLVANIA
The Pennsylvania Council of Churches, Harrisburg, PA
Christian Churches United of the Tri-County Area, Harrisburg, PA
Ecumenical Conference of Greater Altoona, Altoona, PA
Inter-Church Ministries of Erie County, Erie, PA
Lancaster County Council of Churches, Lancaster, PA
Lehigh County Conference of Churches, Allentown, PA
Metropolitan Christian Council of Philadelphia, Philadelphia, PA
Reading Berks Conference of Churches, Reading, PA
South Hills Interfaith Ministries, Library, PA
York County Council of Churches, York, PA

RHODE ISLAND
The Rhode Island State Council of Churches, Providence, RI

SOUTH CAROLINA
South Carolina Christian Action Council, Inc., Columbia, SC

SOUTH DAKOTA
Association of Christian Churches, Sioux Falls, SD

TEXAS
Texas Conference of Churches, Austin, TX
Austin Metropolitan Ministries, Austin, TX
East Dallas Cooperative Parish, Dallas, TX
Greater Dallas Community of Churches, Dallas, TX
Interfaith Ministries for Greater Houston, Houston, TX

WASHINGTON
Washington Association of Churches, Seattle, WA
Associated Ministries of Tacoma-Pierce County, Tacoma, WA
Associated Ministries of Thurston County, Olympia, WA
Church council of Greater Seattle, Seattle, WA

WEST VIRGINIA
West Virginia Council of Churches, Charleston, WV

WYOMING
Wyoming Church Coalition, Cheyenne, WY

HUNGER/FOOD PROGRAMS
ALABAMA
Interfaith Mission Service, Huntsville, AL

ARIZONA
Arizona Ecumenical Council, Phoenix, AZ

ARKANSAS
Arkansas Interfaith Conference, Scott, AR

CALIFORNIA
California Council of Churches/California Church Impact, Sacramento, CA
The Ecumenical Council of San Diego County, San Diego, CA
The Ecumenical Council of the Pasadena Area Churches, Pasadena, CA
Fresno Metro Ministry, Fresno, CA
Northern California Interreligious Conference, San Francisco, CA
Pomona Inland Valley Council of Churches, Pomona, CA
San Fernando Valley Interfaith Council, Chatsworth, CA
South Coast Ecumenical Council, Long Beach, CA

CONNECTICUT
Center City Churches, Hartford, CT
Council of Churches and Synagogues of Southwestern Connecticut, Stamford, CT
New Britain Area Conference of Churches (NEWBRACC), New Britain, CT
Waterbury Area Council of Churches, Waterbury, CT

DISTRICT OF COLUMBIA
The Council of Churches of Greater Washington, Washington, DC
InterFaith Conference of Metropolitan Washington, Washington, DC

FLORIDA
Christian Services Center for Central Florida, Inc., Orlando, FL

GEORGIA
Georgia Christian Council, Macon, GA

ILLINOIS
Illinois Conference of Churches, Springfield, IL
Churches United of the Quad City Area, IL
Evanston Ecumenical Action Council, Evanston, IL
The Hyde Park & Kenwood Interfaith Council, IL
Oak Park-River Forest Community of Congregations, Oak Park, IL
Peoria Friendship House of Christian Service, Peoria, IL

INDIANA
Christian Ministries of Delaware County, Muncie, IN
Evansville Area Community of Churches, Inc., Evansville, IN
United Religious Community of St. Joseph County, South Bend, IN
West Central Neighborhood Ministry, Inc., Fort Wayne, IN

IOWA
Des Moines Area Religious Council, Des Moines, IA

KANSAS
Cross-Lines Cooperative Council, Kansas City, KS

KENTUCKY
Fern Creek/Highview United Ministries, Louisville, KY
Highlands Community Ministries, Louisville, KY
Paducah Cooperative Ministry, Paducah, KY
South Louisville Community Ministries, Louisville, KY

MARYLAND
Community Ministry of Montgomery County, Rockville, MD

MASSACHUSETTS
Attleboro Area Council of Churches, Inc., Attleboro, MA
The Cape Cod Council of Churches, Inc., Hyannis, MA
Council of Churches of Greater Springfield, Springfield, MA
Worcester County Ecumenical Council, Worcester, MA

MICHIGAN
ACCORD-Area Churches Together-Serving, Battle Creek, MI
Christian Communication Council of Metropolitan Detroit Churches, Detroit, MI
Grand Rapids Area Center for Ecumenism (GRACE), Grand Rapids, MI
The Jackson County Interfaith Council, Clarklake, MI
Muskegon County Cooperating Churches, Muskegon, MI

MINNESOTA
Arrowhead Interfaith Council, Duluth, MN
Greater Minneapolis Council of Churches, Minneapolis, MN
The Joint Religious Legislative Coalition, Minneapolis, MN
St. Paul Council of Churches, St. Paul, MN

MISSOURI
Council of Churches of the Ozarks, Springfield, MO
Interfaith Community Services, St. Joseph, MO

NEBRASKA
Interchurch Ministries of Nebraska, Lincoln, NE
Lincoln Interfaith Council, Lincoln, NE

NEW MEXICO
Inter-Faith Council of Santa Fe, New Mexico, Santa Fe, NM

NEW YORK
Capital Area Council of Churches, Inc., Albany, NY
Chautauqua County Rural Ministry, Dunkirk, NY
Concerned Ecumenical Ministry to the Upper West Side, Buffalo, NY
Council of Churches of Chemung County, Inc., Elmira, NY

Dutchess Interfaith Council, Inc., Poughkeepsie, NY

Genesee County Churches United, Inc., Batavia, NY

The Long Island Council of Churches, Hempstead, NY

Queens Federation of Churches, Richmond Hill, NY

Schenectady Inner City Ministry, Schenectady, NY

Southeast Ecumenical Ministry, Rochester, NY

Troy Area United Ministries, Troy, NY

NORTH CAROLINA

Greensboro Urban Ministry, Greensboro, NC

OHIO

Ohio Council of Churches, Columbus, OH

Greater Dayton Christian Connection, Dayton, OH

Toledo Ecumenical Area Ministries, Toledo, OH

West Side Ecumenical Ministry, Cleveland, OH

OREGON

Ecumenical Ministries of Oregon, Portland, OR

PENNSYLVANIA

Allegheny Valley Association of Churches, Natrona Heights, PA

Hanover Area Council of Churches, Hanover, PA

Inter-Church Ministries of Erie County, Erie, PA

Lancaster County Council of Churches, Lancaster, PA

Lebanon County Christian Ministries, Lebanon, PA

Lehigh County Conference of Churches, Allentown, PA

Northside Common Ministries, Pittsburgh, PA

Reading Berks Conference of Churches, Reading, PA

South Hills Interfaith Ministries, Library, PA

SOUTH CAROLINA

United Ministries, Greenville, SC

TEXAS

Corpus Christi Metro Ministries, Corpus Christi, TX

East Dallas Cooperative Parish, Dallas, TX

Greater Dallas Community of Churches, Dallas, TX

Interfaith Ministries for Greater Houston, Houston, TX

Northside Inter-Church Agency (NICA), Fort Worth, TX

Tarrant Area Community of Churches, Fort Worth, TX

WASHINGTON

Associated Ministries of Tacoma-Pierce County, Tacoma, WA

Associated Ministries of Thurston County, Olympia, WA

Church Council of Greater Seattle, Seattle, WA

Northwest Harvest/E.M.M., Seattle, WA

Spokane Council of Ecumenical Ministries, Spokane, WA

Washington Association of Churches, Seattle, WA

YOUTH ACTIVITIES

ARIZONA

Arizona Ecumenical Council, Phoenix, AZ

CALIFORNIA

The Ecumenical Council of San Diego County, San Diego, CA

Fresno Metro Ministry, Fresno, CA

Pomona Inland Valley Council of Churches, Pomona, CA

CONNECTICUT

Center City Churches, Hartford, CT

Council of Churches of Greater Bridgeport, Inc., Bridgeport, CT

New Britain Area Conference of Churches (NEWBRACC), New Britain, CT

DISTRICT OF COLUMBIA

The Council of Churches of Greater Washington, Washington, DC

InterFaith Conference of Metropolitan Washington, Washington, DC

GEORGIA

Georgia Christian Council, Macon, GA

Christian Council of Metropolitan Atlanta, Atlanta, GA

ILLINOIS

Greater Chicago Broadcast Ministries, Chicago, IL

Peoria Friendship House of Christian Service, Peoria, IL

INDIANA

Evansville Area Community of Churches, Inc., Evansville, IN

West Central Neighborhood Ministry, Inc., Fort Wayne, IN

KENTUCKY

Fern Creek/Highview United Ministries, Louisville, KY

Highlands Community Ministries, Louisville, KY

South Louisville Community Ministries, Louisville, KY

MASSACHUSETTS

Attleboro Area Council of Churches, Inc., Attleboro, MA

Greater Lawrence Council of Churches, Lawrence, MA

MICHIGAN

Grand Rapids Area Center for Ecumenism (GRACE), Grand Rapids, MI

MINNESOTA

Greater Minneapolis Council of Churches, Minneapolis, MN

St. Paul Council of Churches, St. Paul, MN

MISSOURI

Council of Churches of the Ozarks, Springfield, MO

Ecumenical Ministries, Fulton, MO

Interfaith Community Services, St. Joseph, MO

MONTANA

Montana Association of Churches, Billings, MT

NEBRASKA

Lincoln Interfaith Council, Lincoln, NE

NEW HAMPSHIRE

New Hampshire Council of Churches, Concord, NH

NEW JERSEY

Metropolitan Ecumenical Ministry, Newark, NJ

NEW YORK

Concerned Ecumenical Ministry to the Upper West Side, Buffalo, NY

Dutchess Interfaith Council, Inc., Poughkeepsie, NY

Genesee County Churches United, Inc., Batavia, NY

Rural Migrant Ministry, Poughkeepsie, NY

Schenectady Inner City Ministry, Schenectady, NY

OHIO

Ohio Council of Churches, Columbus, OH

Toledo Ecumenical Area Ministries, Toledo, OH

West Side Ecumenical Ministry, Cleveland, OH

OREGON

Ecumenical Ministries of Oregon, Portland, OR

PENNSYLVANIA

The Pennsylvania Council of Churches, Harrisburg, PA

Metropolitan Christian Council of Philadelphia, Philadelphia, PA

North Hills Youth Ministry Counseling Center, Pittsburgh, PA

Reading Berks Conference of Churches, Reading, PA

South Hills Interfaith Ministries, Library, PA

York County Council of Churches, York, PA

TEXAS

Austin Metropolitan Ministries, Austin, TX

East Dallas Cooperative Parish, Dallas, TX

Greater Dallas Community of Churches, Dallas, TX

Interfaith Ministries for Greater Houston, Houston, TX

Northside Inter-Church Agency (NICA), Fort Worth, TX

Tarrant Area Community of Churches, Fort Worth, TX

WASHINGTON

Church Council of Greater Seattle, Seattle, WA

Spokane Council of Ecumenical Ministries, Spokane, WA

FAITH AND ORDER

ALASKA

Alaska Christian Conference, Fairbanks, AK

ARIZONA

Arizona Ecumenical Council, Phoenix, AZ

CALIFORNIA

California Council of Churches/California Church Impact, Sacramento, CA

The Ecumenical Council of San Diego County, San Diego, CA

The Ecumenical Council of the Pasadena Area Churches, Pasadena, CA

Fresno Metro Ministry, Fresno, CA

Interfaith Council of Contra Costa County, Walnut Creek, CA

Marin Interfaith Council, San Rafael, CA

Northern California Interreligious Conference, San Francisco, CA

South Coast Ecumenical Council, Long Beach, CA

COLORADO

Colorado Council of Churches, Denver, CO

CONNECTICUT

Christian Conference of Connecticut (CHRISCON), Hartford, CT

Center City Churches, Hartford, CT

Council of Churches and Synagogues of Southwestern Connecticut, Stamford, CT

New Britain Area Conference of Churches (NEWBRACC), New Britain, CT

DELAWARE

The Christian Council of Delaware and Maryland's Eastern Shore, Baltimore, MD

DISTRICT OF COLUMBIA

The Council of Churches of Greater Washington, Washington, DC

GEORGIA

Georgia Christian Council, Macon, GA

Christian Council of Metropolitan Atlanta, Atlanta, GA

ILLINOIS

Illinois Conference of Churches, Springfield, IL

Churches United of the Quad City Area, Rock Island, IL

Evanston Ecumenical Action Council, Evanston, IL

INDIANA

Evansville Area Community of Churches, Inc., Evansville, IN

Indiana Partners for Christian Unity and Mission, Indianapolis, IN

United Religious Community of St. Joseph County, South Bend, IN

KANSAS

Kansas Ecumenical Ministries, Topeka, KS

KENTUCKY

Kentucky Council of Churches, Lexington, KY

Highlands Community Ministries, Louisville, KY

LOUISIANA
Louisiana Interchurch Conference, Baton Rouge, LA

MASSACHUSETTS
Council of Churches of Greater Springfield, Springfield, MA
Inter-Church Council of Greater New Bedford, New Bedford, MA
Massachusetts Commission on Christian Unity, Lowell, MA

MICHIGAN
Michigan Ecumenical Forum, Lansing, MI
Christian Communication Council of Metropolitan Detroit Churches, Detroit, MI
The Jackson County Interfaith Council, Clarklake, MI

MINNESOTA
Greater Minneapolis Council of Churches, Minneapolis, MN
Minnesota Council of Churches, Minneapolis, MN

MISSOURI
Ecumenical Ministries, Fulton, MO

MONTANA
Montana Association of Churches, Billings, MT

NEBRASKA
Lincoln Interfaith Council, Lincoln, NE

NEW HAMPSHIRE
New Hampshire Council of Churches, Concord, NH

NEW MEXICO
New Mexico Conference of Churches, Albuquerque, NM

NEW YORK
New York State Community of Churches, Inc. -A Household of Christians, Albany, NY
CAPITAL Region Ecumenical Organization (CREO), Scotia, NY
Council of Churches of the City of New York, New York, NY

NORTH DAKOTA
North Dakota Conference of Churches, Bismarck, ND

OHIO
Ohio Council of Churches, Columbus, OH
Akron Area Association of Churches, Akron, OH
Greater Dayton Christian Connection, Dayton, OH
Toledo Ecumenical Area Ministries, Toledo, OH

OKLAHOMA
Oklahoma Conference of Churches, Oklahoma City, OK
Tulsa Metropolitan Ministry, Tulsa, OK

OREGON
Ecumenical Ministries of Oregon, Portland, OR

PENNSYLVANIA
The Pennsylvania Council of Churches, Harrisburg, PA

Allegheny Valley Association of Churches, Natrona Heights, PA
Ecumenical Conference of Greater Altoona, Altoona, PA
Lancaster County Council of Churches, Lancaster, PA
Lehigh County Conference of Churches, Allentown, PA
Metropolitan Christian Council of Philadelphia, Philadelphia, PA
Reading Berks Conference of Churches, Reading, PA
York County Council of Churches, York, PA

RHODE ISLAND
The Rhode Island State Council of Churches, Providence, RI

SOUTH CAROLINA
South Carolina Christian Action Council, Inc., Columbia, SC

TEXAS
Texas Conference of Churches, Austin, TX
Greater Dallas Community of Churches, Dallas, TX
Interfaith Ministries for Greater Houston, Houston, TX

VERMONT
Vermont Ecumenical Council and Bible Society, Burlington, VT

VIRGINIA
Virginia Council of Churches, Richmond, VA

WASHINGTON
Associated Ministries of Tacoma-Pierce County, Tacoma, WA
Spokane Council of Ecumenical Ministries, Spokane, WA
Washington Association of Churches, Seattle, WA

WISCONSIN
Wisconsin Council of Churches, Sun Prairie, WI

HOMELESSNESS/SHELTER MINISTRIES

ARIZONA
Arizona Ecumenical Council, Phoenix, AZ

CALIFORNIA
The Ecumenical Council of San Diego County, San Diego, CA
The Ecumenical Council of the Pasadena Area Churches, Pasadena, CA
San Fernando Valley Interfaith Council, Chatsworth, CA
South Coast Ecumenical Council, Long Beach, CA

CONNECTICUT
Center City Churches, Hartford, CT
Christian Community Action, New Haven, CT
Council of Churches of Greater Bridgeport, Inc., Bridgeport, CT
Pomona Inland Valley Council of Churches, Pomona, CA

DISTRICT OF COLUMBIA
InterFaith Conference of Metropolitan Washington, Washington, DC

FLORIDA
Christian Services Center for Central Florida, Inc., Orlando, FL

GEORGIA
Christian Council of Metropolitan Atlanta, Atlanta, GA

ILLINOIS
Evanston Ecumenical Action Council, Evanston, IL
Oak Park-River Forest Community of Congregations, Oak Park, IL
Peoria Friendship House of Christian Service, Peoria, IL

INDIANA
Christian Ministries of Delaware County, Muncie, IN
United Religious Community of St. Joseph County, South Bend, IN

KANSAS
Cross-Lines Cooperative Council, Kansas City, KS

KENTUCKY
Paducah Cooperative Ministry, Paducah, KY

MARYLAND
Community Ministry of Montgomery County, Rockville, MD

MASSACHUSETTS
Council of Churches of Greater Springfield, Springfield, MA
Inter-Church Council of Greater New Bedford, New Bedford, MA

MICHIGAN
The Jackson County Interfaith Council, Clarklake, MI

MINNESOTA
Greater Minneapolis Council of Churches, Minneapolis, MN
Metropolitan Interfaith Council on Affordable Housing (MICAH), Minneapolis, MN
St. Paul Council of Churches, St. Paul, MN

MISSOURI
Ecumenical Ministries, Fulton, MO
Interfaith Community Services, St. Joseph, MO
The Joint Religious Legislative Coalition, Minneapolis, MN

NEBRASKA
Lincoln Interfaith Council, Lincoln, NE

NEW YORK
Capital Area Council of Churches, Inc., Albany, NY
Chautaugua County Rural Ministry, Dunkirk, NY
Council of Churches of Chemung County, Inc., Elmira, NY
Genesee County Churches United, Inc., Batavia, NY

Schenectady Inner City Ministry, Schenectady, NY
Troy Area United Ministries, Troy, NY

NORTH CAROLINA
Greensboro Urban Ministry, Greensboro, NC

OHIO
Toledo Ecumenical Area Ministries, Toledo, OH

OKLAHOMA
Tulsa Metropolitan Ministry, Tulsa, OK

OREGON
Ecumenical Ministries of Oregon, Portland, OR

PENNSYLVANIA
Allegheny Valley Association of Churches, Natrona Heights, PA
Christian Churches United of the Tri-County Area, Harrisburg, PA
Hanover Area Council of Churches, Hanover, PA
Inter-Church Ministries of Erie County, Erie, PA
Lehigh County Conference of Churches, Allentown, PA
Northside Common Ministries, Pittsburgh, PA
Reading Berks Conference of Churches, Reading, PA
York County Council of Churches, York, PA

SOUTH CAROLINA
United Ministries, Greenville, SC

TEXAS
Austin Metropolitan Ministries, Austin, TX
Corpus Christi Metro Ministries, Corpus Christi, TX

WASHINGTON
Associated Ministries of Tacoma-Pierce County, Tacoma, WA
Associated Ministries of Thurston County, Olympia, WA
Church Council of Greater Seattle, Seattle, WA
Spokane Council of Ecumenical Ministries, Spokane, WA
Washington Association of Churches, Seattle, WA

271

7. Canadian Regional and Local Ecumenical Bodies

Most of the Organizations listed below are councils of churches in which churches participate officially, whether at the parish or judicatory level. They operate at the city, metropolitan area, or county level. Parish clusters within urban areas are not included.

Canadian local ecumenical bodies operate without paid staff, with the exception of a few which have part-time staff. In most cases the name and address of the president or chairperson is listed. As these offices change from year to year, some of this information may be out of date by the time the Yearbook of American and Canadian Churches is published. Up-to-date information may be secured from the Canadian Council of Churches, 40 St. Clair Ave. E., Ste. 201, Toronto, ON M4T 1M9.

The following is a reprinted list of Canadian Regional and Local Ecumenical Bodies as updated for the 1998 Yearbook of American and Canadian Churches. In the past these organizations have not provided program descriptions, as have their counterparts in the United States. Working with the Canadian Council of Churches a new directory chapter will be developed for the 2000 Yearbook of American and Canadian Churches which will more fully represent the breath of ecumenical bodies throughout Canada and better express the Canadian ecumenical experience. If you have any information (contact names, numbers, etc.) please forward them to our office via e-mail at yearbook@ncccusa.org , via fax at 212/870-2817, via telephone at 212/870-2031, or through the mail addressed to Office of the Yearbook of American and Canadian Churches, 475 Riverside Dr., Rm. 812, New York, NY 10115. We would appreciate any information provided.

- The Editors

ALBERTA

Calgary Council of Churches
Stephen Kendall, Treas. 1009 - 15 Ave. SW, Calgary, Alberta T3R 0S5

Calgary Inter-Faith Community Association
Rev. V. Hennig, 7515 7th St.SW, Calgary, Alberta T2V 1G1

Calgary Inter-Faith SAWDAP
Mrs. Caroline Brown, #240-15 Ave. SW, Calgary, Alberta T2R 0P7

ATLANTIC PROVINCES

Atlantic Ecumenical Council of Churches
Pres., Rev. John E. Boyd, Box 637, 90 Victoria St., Amherst, Nova Scotia B4H 4B4

Pictou Council of Churches
Rev. D. J. Murphy, Sec., P.O. Box 70, Pictou, Nova Scotia B0K 1H0

BRITISH COLUMBIA

Canadian Ecumenical Action
Co-ordinator, 1410 West 12th Ave., Vancouver, British Columbia V6H 1M8

Greater Victoria Council of Churches
c/o Rev. Edwin Taylor, St. Alban's Church, 1468 Ryan St. at Balmont, Victoria, British Columbia V8R 2X1

Vancouver Council of Churches
Murray Moerman, 700 Kingsway, Vancouver, British Columbia V5V 3C1 Tel. (604)420-0761

MANITOBA

Association of Christian Churches in Manitoba
The Rev. Ted Chell, President, 484 Maryland St., Winnipeg, Manitoba R3G 1M5 Tel. (204)774-3143 or (204)775-3536

NEW BRUNSWICK

First Miramichi Inter-Church Council
Pres., Ellen Robinson, Doaktown, New Brunswick E0C 1G0

Moncton Area Council of Churches
Rev. Yvon Berrieau, Visitation Ministry, Grande Digue, New Brunswick E0A 1S0

UC Maritime Conference ICIF Com.
The Rev. Leslie Robinson, P.O. Box 174, Chipman, New Brunswick, E0E 1C0 Tel. (506)339-6626
E-mail: maronf@nbnet.nb.ca

NOVA SCOTIA

Amherst and Area Council of Churches
Mrs. Jean Miller, President, R.R.#3 1065 HWY 204, Amherst, Nova Scotia B4H 3Y1 Tel. (902)667-8107

272

Atlantic Ecumenical Council of Churches

The Rev. P.A. Sandy MacDonald, 4 Pinehill Road, Dartmouth, Nova Scotia B3A 2E6 Tel.(902)469-4480 or (902)466-6247

Bridgewater Inter-Church Council

Pres., Wilson Jones, 30 Parkdale Ave., Bridgewater, Nova Scotia B4V 1L8

Cornwallis District Inter-Church Council

Pres., Mr. Tom Regan, Centreville, R.R. #2, Kings County, Nova Scotia BOT 1JO

Halifax-Dartmouth Council of Churches

Mrs. Betty Short, 3 Virginia Avenue, Dartmouth, Nova Scotia B2W 2Z4

Industrial Cape Breton Council of Churches

Rev. Karen Ralph, 24 Huron Ave., Sydney Mines, Nova Scotia B1S 1V2

Kentville Council of Churches

Rev. Canon S.J.P. Davies, 325-325 Main St., Kentville, Nova Scotia B4N 1C5

Lunenburg Queens BA Association

Mrs. Nilda Chute, 56 Hillside Dr., R.R.#4, Bridgewater, Nova Scotia B4V 2W3

Mahone Bay Interchurch Council

Patricia Joudrey, R.R. #1., Blockhouse, Nova Scotia BOJ1EO

Queens County Association of Churches

Mr. Donald Burns, Box 537, Liverpool, Nova Scotia BOT 1K6

ONTARIO

Burlington Inter-Church Council

Mr. Fred Townsend, 425 Breckenwood, Burlington, Ontario L7L 2J6

Christian Council—Capital Area

Fr. Peter Shonenback, 1247 Kilborn Ave., Ottawa, Ontario K1H 6K9

Christian Leadership Council of Downtown Toronto

Ken Bhagan, Chair, 40 Homewood Ave, #509, Toronto, Ontario M4Y 2K2

Ecumenical Committee

Rev. William B. Kidd, 76 Eastern Ave., Sault Ste. Marie, Ontario P6A 4R2

Glengarry-Prescott-Russell Christian Council

Pres., Rev. G. Labrosse, St. Eugene's, Prescott, Ontario KOB 1PO

Hamilton & District Christian Churches Association

The Rev. Dr. John Johnston, 147 Chedoke Avenue, Hamilton, Ontario L8P 4P2 Tel. (905)529-6896, [O] (905)528-2730 Fax (509)521-2539

Ignace Council of Churches

Box 5, 205 Pine St., St. Ignace, Ontario P0T 1H0

Inter Church Council of Burlington

Michael Bittle, Box 62120 Burlington Mall R.P.O., Burlington, Ontario L7R 4K2 Tel. (905)526-1523 Fax(509)526-9056
E-Mail: mbittle@istar.ca
Website: http://home.istar.cal/mbittle/eo_schl.htm

Kitchener-Waterloo Council of Churches

Rev. Clarence Hauser, CR, 53 Allen St. E., Waterloo, Ontario N2J 1J3

London Inter-City Faith Team

David Carouthers, Chair, c/o United Church, 711 Colbourne St., London, Ontario N6A 3Z4

Massey Inter-Church Council

The Rev. Hope Jackson, Box 238, Massey, Ontario P0P 1P0 Tel. (705)865-2630

Ottawa Christian Council of the Capital Area

1247 Kilborn Ave., Ottawa, Ontario K1H 6K9

St. Catharines & Dist. Clergy Fellowship

Rev. Victor Munro, 663 Vince4 St., St. Catharines, Ontario L2M 3V8

Spadina-Bloor Interchurch Council

Rev. Frances Combes, Chair, c/o Bathurst St. United Church, 427 Bloor St. W, Toronto, Ontario M5S 1X7

Stratford & District Council of Churches

Rev. Ted Heinze, Chair, 202 Erie St., Stratford, Ontario N5A 2M8

Thorold Inter-Faith Council

1 Dunn St., St. Catharines, Ontario L2T 1P3

Thunder Bay Council of Churches

Rev. Richard Darling, 1800 Moodie St. E., Thunder Bay, Ontario P7E 4Z2

PRINCE EDWARD ISLAND

Atlantic Ecumenical Council

The Rev. Arthur Pendergast, Secretary, Immaculate Conception Church, St. Louis, Prince Edward Island C0B 1Z0 Tel. (902)963-2202 or (902)822-2622

273

Summerside Christian Council

Ms. A. Kathleen Miller, P.O. Box 1551, Summerside, Prince Edward Island C1N 4K4

QUEBEC

Canadian Centre for Ecumenism/Centre d'oecuménisme

Fr. Emmanuel Lapierre, 2065 Sherbrooke Street West, Montreal, Quebec H3H 1G6 Tel. (514)937-9176 Fax (514)937-2684

Christian Direction

The Rev. Glen Smith, #3602-465 St. Antoine St. W., Montreal, Quebec H2Z 1J1

The Ecumenical Group

c/o Mrs. C. Haten, 1185 Ste. Foy, St. Bruno, Quebec J3V 3C3

Hemmingford Ecumenical Committee

c/o Catherine Priest, Box 300, Hemmingford, Quebec J0L 1H0

Montréal Council of Churches

The Rev. Ralph Watson, 4995 Coronation Avenue, Montrèal, Quèbec H4V 2E1 Tel. (514)484-7196

Mtl. Association for the Blind Foundation

The Rev. Dr. John A. Simms, 7000 Sherbrooke St. W., Montreal, Quebec H4B 1R3 Tel. (514)489-8201

SASKATCHEWAN

Humboldt Clergy Council

Fr. Leo Hinz, OSB, Box 1989, Humboldt, Saskatchewan S0K 2A0

Melville Association of Churches

Attn., Catherine Gaw, Box 878, Melville, Saskatchewan S0A 2P0

Regina Council of Churches

The Rev. Bud Harper, 5 Robinson Crescent, Regina, Saskatchewan S4R 3R1 Tel. (306)545-3375

Saskatoon Centre for Ecumenism

Nicholas Jesson, 1006 Broadway, Saskatoon, Saskatchewas S7N 1B9 Tel. (306)553-1633 Fax (306)242-8916
E-Mail: sce@sfn.saskatoon.sk.ca

Saskatoon Council of Churches

Dr. Colin Clay, 812 Colony St., Saskatoon, Saskatchewan S7H 0S1

8. Theological Seminaries and Bible Colleges in the United States

The following list includes theological seminaries and departments in colleges and universities in which ministerial training is given. Many denominations have additional programs. The lists of Religious Bodies in the United States should be consulted for the address of denominational headquarters.

Inclusion in or exclusion from this list implies no judgment about the quality or accreditation of any institution. Those schools that are members (both accredited and affiliated) of the Association of Theological Schools are marked with a "*". Additional information about enrollment in ATS member schools can be found in the statistical section.

Each of the listings include: the institution name, denominational sponsor when appropriate, location, head, telephone and fax numbers when known and e-mail and website addresses when available.

Abilene Christian University, (Churches of Christ), ACU Station, Box 29100, Abilene, TX 79699. Royce Money, Ph.D. Tel. (915)674-2412. Fax (915)674-2958
E-mail: moneyr@nicanor.acu.edu
Website: http://www.acu.edu

Alaska Bible College, (Nondenominational), P.O. Box 289, Glennallen, AK 99588. Steven J. Hostetter. Tel. (907)822-3201. Fax (907) 822-5027
E-mail: info@akbible.edu
Website: http://www.akbible.edu

Alliance Theological Seminary,* (The Christian and Missionary Alliance), 350 N. Highland Ave., Nyack, NY 10960-1416. David L. Rambo. Tel. (914)353-2020. Fax (914)358-2651

American Baptist College, (National Baptist Convention, U.S.A., Inc.), 1800 Baptist World Center Dr., Nashville, TN 37207. Bernard Lafayette. Tel. (615)262-1369. Fax (615)226-7855

American Baptist Seminary of the West,* (American Baptist Churches in the U .S.A.), 2606 Dwight Way, Berkeley, CA 94704-3029. Dr. Keith A. Russell. Tel. (510)841-1905. Fax (510)841-2446

Anderson University School of Theology,* (Church of God (Anderson, Ind.), Anderson University, Anderson, IN 46012-3495. David Sebastian. Tel. (765)641-4032. Fax (765)641-3005

Andover Newton Theological School,* (American Baptist Churches in the U .S.A.; United Church of Christ), 210 Herrick Rd., Newton Centre, MA 02459. Benjamin Griffin. Tel. (617)964-1100. Fax (617)965-9756
E-mail: admissions@ants.edu
Website: http://www.ants.edu

The Anglican Theological Seminary International, (The Anglican Orthodox Church), President Robert J. Godfrey, 2558 Hickory Tree Rd., Winston-Salem, NC 27127-9145
Tel. (336)775-9866 Fax (336)775-9867

E-mail: AOCCranmer@aol.com
Website: http://www.netministries.org/churches/ ch01051

Appalachian Bible College, (Nondenominational), P.O. Box ABC, Bradley, WV 25818. Daniel L. Anderson. Tel. (304)877-6428. Fax (304)877-5082
E-mail: abc@appbibco.edu

Aquinas Institute of Theology,* (The Roman Catholic Church), 3642 Lindell Blvd., St. Louis, MO 63108. Charles E. Bouchard. Tel. (314)977-3882. Fax (314)977-7225

Arizona College of the Bible, (Interdenominational), 2045 W. Northern Ave., Phoenix, AZ 85021-5197. Douglas K. Winn. Tel. (602)995-2670. Fax (602)864-8183

Arlington Baptist College, (Baptist), 3001 W. Division, Arlington, TX 76012-3425. David Bryant. Tel. (817)461-8741. Fax (817)274-1138

Asbury Theological Seminary,* (Interdenominational), 204 N. Lexington Ave., Wilmore, KY 40390-1199. Maxie D. Dunnam. Tel. (606)858-3581
E-mail: First Name_Last Name@ats.wilmore. ky. us
Website: http://www.ats.wilmore.ky.us

Ashland Theological Seminary,* (Brethren Church (Ashland, Ohio)), 910 Center St., Ashland, OH 44805. Frederick J. Finks. Tel. (419)289-5161. Fax (419)289-5969

Assemblies of God Theological Seminary,* (Assemblies of God), 1445 Boonville Ave., Springfield, MO 65802. Del H. Tarr. Tel. (417)862-3344. Fax (417)862-3214

Associated Mennonite Biblical Seminary,* (Mennonite Church; General Conference Mennonite Church), 3003 Benham Ave., Elkhart, IN 46517-1999. J. Nelson Kraybill. Tel. (219)295-3726. Fax (219)295-0092
E-mail: nkraybill@ambs.edu
Website: http://www.ambs.edu

275

Athenaeum of Ohio,* (The Roman Catholic Church), 6616 Beechmont Ave., Cincinnati, OH 45230-2091. Robert J. Mooney. Tel. (513)231-2223. Fax (513)231-3254

Atlanta Christian College, (Christian Churches and Churches of Christ), 2605 Ben Hill Rd., East Point, GA 30344. R. Edwin Groover. Tel. (404)761-8861. Fax (404)669-2024

Austin Presbyterian Theological Seminary,* (Presbyterian Church (U.S.A.)), 100 E. 27th St., Austin, TX 78705. Robert M. Shelton. Tel. (512)472-6736. Fax (512)479-0738
Website: http://www.austinseminary.edu/

Azusa Pacific University,* (Interdenominational), 901 E. Alosta, P.O. Box APU, Azusa, CA 91702. Richard Felix. Tel. (818)969-3434. Fax (818)969-7180

Bangor Theological Seminary,* (United Church of Christ), 300 Union St., Bangor, ME 04401. President Ansley Coe Throckmorton. Tel. (207)942-6781. Fax (207)942-4914
E-mail: jwiebe@bts.edu
Website: http://www.bts.edu

Baptist Bible College, (Baptist Bible Fellowship International), 628 E. Kearney, Springfield, MO 65803. Leland Kennedy. Tel. (417)268-6060. Fax (417)268-6694

Baptist Bible College and Seminary, (Baptist), 538 Venard Rd., Clarks Summit, PA 18411. Milo Thompson. Tel. (717)586-2400. Fax (717)586-1753
E-mail: bbc@bbc.edu
Website: http://www.bbc.edu

Baptist Missionary Association Theological Seminary, (Baptist Missionary Association of America), 1530 E. Pine St., Jacksonville, TX 75766. Philip R. Bryan. Tel. (903)586-2501. Fax (903)586-0378
E-mail: prbryan@E-tex.com OR bmaisem@ flash. net
Website: http://www.geocities.com/Athens/Acropolis/3386

Baptist Theological Seminary at Richmond,* (Cooperative Baptist Fellowship), 3400 Brook Rd., Richmond, VA 23227. Thomas H. Graves. Tel. (804)355-8135. Fax (804)355-8182
E-mail: btsr@mindspring.com

Barclay College, (Interdenominational), P.O. Box 288, Haviland, KS 67059. Walter E. Moody. Tel. (316)862-5252. Fax (316)862-5403
E-mail: barclaycollege@havilandtalco.com

Bay Ridge Christian College, (Church of God (Anderson, Ind.)), P.O. Box 726, Kendleton, TX 77451. Charles Denniston. Tel. (409)532-3982. Fax (409)532-4352

Beeson Divinity School of Samford University, (Interdenominational), 800 Lakeshore Dr.,

Birmingham, AL 35229-2252. Timothy George. Tel. (205)870-2991. Fax (205)870-2260

Bethany College, (Assemblies of God), 800 Bethany Dr., Scotts Valley, CA 95066. Tom Duncan. Tel. (408)438-3800. Fax (408)438-4517

Bethany Lutheran Theological Seminary, (Evangelical Lutheran Synod), 6 Browns Ct., Mankato, MN 56001. G. R. Schmeling. Tel. (507)344-7354. Fax (507)344-7426
E-mail: gschmeli@blc.edu
Website: http://sem-09.blc.edu/default.html

Bethany Theological Seminary,* (Church of the Brethren), 615 National Rd. W., Richmond, IN 47374. Eugene F. Roop. Tel. (765)983-1800. Fax (765)983-1840
E-mail: roopge@earlham.edu

Bethel Theological Seminary,* (Baptist General Conference), 3949 Bethel Dr., St. Paul, MN 55112. George K. Brushaber. Tel. (651)638-6230. Fax (651)638-6008
E-mail: webmaster@bethel.edu
Website: http://www.bethel.edu

Beulah Heights Bible College, (The International Pentecostal Church of Christ), 892 Berne St. SE, Atlanta, GA 30316. Samuel R. Chand. Tel. (404)627-2681. Fax (404)627-0702
E-mail: b.h.b.c@beulah.org

Bible Church of Christ Theological Institute, (Nondenominational), 1358 Morris Ave., Bronx, NY 10456. Roy Bryant, Sr. Tel. (718)588-2285

Biblical Theological Seminary, (Interdenominational), 200 N. Main St., Hatfield, PA 19440. David G. Dunbar. Tel. (215)368-5000. Fax (215)368-7002

Boise Bible College, (Christian Churches and Churches of Christ), 8695 Marigold St., Boise, ID 83714. Charles A. Crane. Tel. (208)376-7731. Fax (208)376-7743
E-mail: boibible@micron.net
Website: http://netnow.micron.net/~boibible

Boston University (School of Theology),* (The United Methodist Church), 745 Commonwealth Ave., Boston, MA 02215. Robert C. Neville. Tel. (617)353-3050. Fax (617)353-3061
Website: http://web.bu.edu/

Brite Divinity School, Texas Christian University,* (Christian Church (Disciples of Christ)), TCU Box 298130, Ft. Worth, TX 76129. Leo G. Perdue. Tel. (817)921-7575. Fax (817)921-7305
E-mail: L.Perdue@tcu.edu
Website: http://www.brite.tcu.edu/brite/

Calvary Bible College and Theological Seminary, (Independent Fundamental Churches of America), 15800 Calvary Rd., Kansas City,

MO 64147-1341. James L. Anderson. Tel. (800)326-3960. Fax (816)331-4474

Calvin Theological Seminary,* (Christian Reformed Church in North America), 3233 Burton St. S.E., Grand Rapids, MI 49546.President James A. DeJong. Tel. (616)957-6036. Fax (616)957-8621
E-mail: kprg@calvin.edu
Website: http://www.calvin.edu/seminary

Candler School of Theology, Emory University,* (The United Methodist Church), 500 Kilgo Circle N.E., Emory Univ., Atlanta, GA 30322. R. Kevin LaGree. Tel. (404)727-6324. Fax (404)727-3182
E-mail: candler@emory.edu
Website: http://www.emory.edu/candler

Catholic Theological Union at Chicago,* (The Roman Catholic Church), 5401 S. Cornell Ave., Chicago, IL 60615-5698. Norman Bevan. Tel. (312)324-8000. Fax (312)324-8490

Catholic University of America,* (The Roman Catholic Church), 113 Caldwell Hall, Cardinal Sta., Washington, DC 20064. Rev. Raymond F. Collins, STD. Dean. Tel. (202)319-5683. Fax (202)319-4967
E-mail: cua-deansrs@cua.edu
Website: http://www.cua.edu/www/srs/

Central Baptist College, (Baptist Missionary Association of Arkansas), 1501 College Ave., Conway, AR 72032. Charles Attebery. Tel. (501)329-6872. Fax (501)329-2941

Central Baptist Theological Seminary,* (Baptist), 741 N. 31st St., Kansas City, KS 66102-3964. Thomas E. Clifton. Tel. (913)371-5313. Fax (913)371-8110
E-mail: central@cbts.edu
Website: http://www.cbts.edu

Central Baptist Theological Seminary in Indiana, (National Baptist Convention, U.S.A., Inc.), 1535 Dr. A. J. Brown Ave. N., Indianapolis, IN 46202. F. Benjamin Davis. Tel. (317)636-6622

Central Bible College, (Assemblies of God), 3000 N. Grant Ave., Springfield, MO 65803. H. Maurice Lednicky. Tel. (417)833-2551. Fax (417)833-5141

Central Christian College of the Bible, (Christian Churches and Churches of Christ), 911 E. Urbandale, Moberly, MO 65270. Lloyd M. Pelfrey. Tel. (816)263-3900. Fax (816)263-3936

Central Indian Bible College, (Assemblies of God), P.O. Box 550, Mobridge, SD 57601. Robert Koscak. Tel. (605)845-7801. Fax (605)845-7744

Chicago Theological Seminary,* (United Church of Christ), 5757 South University Ave., Chicago, IL 60637. Kenneth B. Smith. Tel. (773)752-5757. Fax (773)752-5925
E-mail: ksmith@chgosem.edu
Website: http://www.chgosem.edu

Christ the King Seminary,* (The Roman Catholic Church), 711 Knox Rd., P.O. Box 607, East Aurora, NY 14052. Richard W. Siepka. Tel. (716)652-8900. Fax (716)652-8903

Christ the Savior Seminary, (The American Carpatho-Russian Orthodox Greek Catholic Church), 225 Chandler Ave., Johnstown, PA 15906. Nicholas Smisko. Tel. (814)539-8086. Fax (814)536-4699

Christian Theological Seminary,* (Christian Church (Disciples of Christ)), 1000 W. 42nd St., Indianapolis, IN 46208. Dr. Edward L. Wheeler. Tel. (317)931-2305. Fax (317)923-1961

Church Divinity School of the Pacific,* (Episcopal Church), 2451 Ridge Rd., Berkeley, CA 94709. Donn F. Morgan. Tel. (510)204-0700. Fax (510)644-0712

Church of God Theological Seminary,* (Church of God (Cleveland, Tenn.)), P.O. Box 3330, Cleveland, TN 37320-3330. Cecil B. Knight. Tel. (423)478-1131. Fax (423)478-7711
E-mail: cogseminary@wingnet.com
Website: http://www.wingnet.net/~cogseminary

Cincinnati Bible College and Seminary, (Christian Churches and Churches of Christ), 2700 Glenway Ave., Cincinnati, OH 45204. David A. Grubbs. Tel. (513)244-8100. Fax (513)244-8140
E-mail: info@cincybible.edu
Website: http://www.cincybible.edu

Circleville Bible College, (Churches of Christ in Christian Union), P.O. Box 458, Circleville, OH 43113. John Conley. Tel. (614)474-8896. Fax (614)477-7755
E-mail: cbc@biblecollege.edu
Website: http://www.biblecollege.edu

Claremont School of Theology,* (The United Methodist Church), 1325 N. College Ave., Claremont, CA 91711. Robert W. Edgar. Tel. (800)626-7821. Fax (909)626-7062
E-mail: Kbronson@cst.edu
Website: http://www.cst.edu

Clear Creek Baptist Bible College, (Southern Baptist Convention), 300 Clear Creek Rd., Pineville, KY 40977. President Bill Whittaker. Tel. (606)337-3196. Fax (606)337-2372
E-mail: ccbbc@tcnet.net
Website: http://www.ccbbc.edu

Colegio Biblico Pentecostal de Puerto Rico, (Church of God (Cleveland, Tenn.)), P.O. Box 901, Saint Just, PR 00978. Luz M. Rivera. Tel. (787)761-0640. Fax (787)748-9228

277

Colgate Rochester/Bexley Hall/Crozer,* (American Baptist Churches in the USA, Episcopal Church), 1100 S. Goodman St., Rochester, NY 14620. James H. Evans. Tel. (716)271-1320. Fax (716)271-8013

Colorado Christian University, (Nondenominational), 180 S. Garrison St., Lakewood, CO 80226. Ronald R. Schmidt. Tel. (303)202-0100. Fax (303)274-7560

Columbia International University,* (Multidenominational), P.O. Box 3122, Columbia, SC 29230-3122. Johnny V. Miller. Tel. (803)754-4100. Fax (803)786-4209

Columbia Theological Seminary,* (Presbyterian Church (U.S.A.)), 701 Columbia Dr., P.O. Box 520, Decatur, GA 30031. Douglas Oldenburg. Tel. (404)378-8821. Fax (404)377-9696

Concordia Seminary,* (The Lutheran Church-Missouri Synod), 801 De Mun Ave., St. Louis, MO 63105. John F. Johnson. Tel. (314)505-7000. Fax (314)505-7001

Concordia Theological Seminary,* (The Lutheran Church-Missouri Synod), 6600 N. Clinton St., Ft. Wayne, IN 46825. Dean O. Wenthe. Tel. (219)452-2100. Fax (219)452-2121
E-mail: sem_relations@ctsfw.edu
Website: http://www.ctsfw.edu

Covenant Theological Seminary,* (Prebyterian Church in America), 12330 Conway Rd., St. Louis, MO 63141. Bryan Chapell. Tel. (314)434-4044. Fax (314)434-4819

Cranmer Seminary, (The Anglican Orthodox Church), P.O. Box 329, 323 Walnut St., Statesville, NC 28687. Robert J. Godfrey. Tel. (704)873-8365. Fax (704)873-8948
E-mail: AOCCranmer
Website: http://members.tripod.com/~Anglican Orthodox /index.html

Criswell Center for Biblical Studies, (Southern Baptist Convention), 4010 Gaston Ave., Dallas, TX 75246. Tel. (214)821-5433. Fax (214)818-1320

Crown College, (The Christian and Missionary Alliance), 6425 County Rd. 30, St. Bonifacius, MN 55375. Gary M. Benedict. Tel. (612)446-4100. Fax (612)446-4149
E-mail: crown@gw.crown.edu
Website: http://www.crown.edu

Cummins Theological Seminary, (Reformed Episcopal Church), 705 S. Main St., Summerville, SC 29483. James C. West. Tel. (803)873-3451. Fax (803)875-6200

Dallas Christian College, (Christian Churches and Churches of Christ), 2700 Christian Pkwy., Dallas, TX 75234. Keith Ray. Tel. (214)241-3371. Fax (214)241-8021

Dallas Theological Seminary,* (Interdenominational), 3909 Swiss Ave., Dallas, TX 75204. Charles R. Swindoll. Tel. (214)824-3094. Fax (214)841-3625

Denver Seminary,* (Conservative Baptist Association of America), Box 10,000, Denver, CO 80250-0100. Clyde B. McDowell, President. Tel. (303)761-2482. Fax (303)761-8060
E-mail: info@densem.edu
Website: http://www.gospelcom.net/densem/

Disciples Divinity House, University of Chicago, (Christian Church (Disciples of Christ)), 1156 E. 57th St., Chicago, IL 60637. Kristine A. Culp. Tel. (773)643-4411. Fax (773)643-4413

Dominican House of Studies,* (The Roman Catholic Church), 487 Michigan Ave. N.E., Washington, DC 20017-1585. Thomas McCreesh, O.P. Tel. (202)529-5300. Fax (202)636-4460

Dominican School of Philosophy and Theology,* (The Roman Catholic Church), 2401 Ridge Rd., Berkeley, CA 94709. Gregory Rocca. Tel. (510)849-2030. Fax (510)849-1372

Dominican Study Center of Bayamon Central Univ.,* (Roman Catholic), Apartado Postal 1968, Bayamon, PR 00960-1968. P. Felix Struik. Tel. (787)787-1826. Fax (787)798-2712

Drew University (Theological School),* (The United Methodist Church), 36 Madison Ave., Madison, NJ 07940-4010. Leonard I. Sweet. Tel. (201)408-3258. Fax (201)408-3808

Duke University (Divinity School),* (The United Methodist Church), Box 90968, Durham, NC 27708-0968. Dean L. Gregory Jones. Tel. (919)660-3400. Fax (919)660-3473

Earlham School of Religion,* (Interdenominational-Friends), 228 College Ave., Richmond, IN 47374. Dean Andrew P. Grannell. Tel. (800)432-1377. Fax (765)983-1688
E-mail: woodna@earlham.edu
Website: http://www.esr.earlham.edu/esr

East Coast Bible College, (Church of God (Cleveland, Tenn.)), 6900 Wilkinson Blvd., Charlotte, NC 28214. T. David Sustar. Tel. (704)394-2307. Fax (704)393-3689

Eastern Baptist Theological Seminary,* (American Baptist Churches in the U.S.A.), 6 Lancaster Ave., Wynnewood, PA 19096. Manfred T. Brauch. Tel. (800)220-EBTS. Fax (610)649-3834
Website: http://www.ebts.edu

Eastern Mennonite Seminary,* (Mennonite Church), Eastern Mennonite Seminary, Harrisonburg, VA 22802. George R. Brunk. Tel. (540)432-4260. Fax (540)432-4444 E-mail: info@emu.edu Website: http://www.emu.edu/units/sem/sem.htm

Eden Theological Seminary,* (United Church of Christ), 475 E. Lockwood Ave., St. Louis, MO 63119. President David M. Greenhaw. Tel. (314)961-3627. Fax (314)961-9063

Emmanuel School of Religion,* (Christian Churches and Churches of Christ), One Walker Dr., Johnson City, TN 37601. C. Robert Wetzel. Tel. (423)926-1186. Fax (423)926-6198 E-mail: emmanuel.johnson-city.tn.us Website: http://www.emmanuel.johnson-city.tn.us

Emmaus Bible College, (Christian Brethren (also known as Plymouth Brethren)), 2570 Asbury Rd., Dubuque, IA 52001. Daniel H. Smith. Tel. (319)588-8000. Fax (319)588-1216

Episcopal Divinity School,* (Episcopal Church), 99 Brattle St., Cambridge, MA 02138. Ben Matlock. Tel. (617)868-3450. Fax (617)864-5385 Website: http://www.episdivschool.org

Episcopal Theological Seminary of the Southwest,* (Episcopal Church), P.O. Box 2247, Austin, TX 78768-2247. Durstan R. McDonald. Tel. (512)472-4133. Fax (512)472-3098

Erskine Theological Seminary,* (Associate Reformed Presbyterian Church (General Synod)), Drawer 668, Due West, SC 29639. R. T. Ruble. Tel. (864)379-8885. Fax (864)379-2171 E-mail: ruble@erskine.edu

Eugene Bible College, (Open Bible Standard Churches, Inc.), 2155 Bailey Hill Rd., Eugene, OR 97405. Robert L. Whitlow. Tel. (503)485-1780. Fax (503)343-5801

Evangelical School of Theology,* (The Evangelical Congregational Church), 121 S. College St., Myerstown, PA 17067. Kirby N. Keller. Tel. (717)866-5775. Fax (717)866-4667

Faith Baptist Bible College and Theological Seminary, (General Association of Regular Baptist Churches), 1900 N.W. 4th St., Ankeny, IA 50021-2152. Richard W. Houg. Tel. (515)964-0601. Fax (515)964-1638

Faith Evangelical Lutheran Seminary, (Conservative Lutheran Association), 3504 N. Pearl St., Tacoma, WA 98407. R. H. Redal. Tel. (206)752-2020. Fax (206)759-1790

Florida Christian College, (Christian Churches and Churches of Christ), 1011 Bill Beck Blvd., Kissimmee, FL 34744. A. Wayne Lowen. Tel. (407)847-8966. Fax (407)847-3925 E-mail: fcc@fcc.edu

Franciscan School of Theology,* (The Roman Catholic Church), 1712 Euclid Ave., Berkeley, CA 94709. William M. Cieslak. Tel. (510)848-5232. Fax (510)549-9466

Free Will Baptist Bible College, (National Association of Free Will Baptists), 3606 West End Ave., Nashville, TN 37205. Tom Malone. Tel. (615)383-1340. Fax (615)269-6028 E-mail: president@fwbbc.edu Website: http://www.fwbcc.edu

Fuller Theological Seminary,* (Interdenominational), 135 N. Oakland Ave., Pasadena, CA 91182. Richard J. Mouw. Tel. (626)584-5200. Fax (626)795-8767

Garrett-Evangelical Theological Seminary,* (The United Methodist Church), 2121 Sheridan Rd., Evanston, IL 60201. Neal F. Fisher. Tel. (847)866-3900. Fax (847)866-3957 E-mail: seminary@nwu.edu Website: http://www.garrett.nwu.edu

General Theological Seminary, The,* (Episcopal Church), 175 Ninth Ave., New York, NY 10011-4977. G.P. Mellick Belshaw (Interim) Tel. (212)243-5150. Fax (212)727-3907

George Mercer, Jr. Memorial School of Theology, (Episcopal Church), 65 Fourth St., Garden City, NY 11530. Lloyd A. Lewis. Tel. (516)248-4800. Fax (516)248-4883

God's Bible School and College, (Nondenominational), 1810 Young St., Cincinnati, OH 45210. Michael Avery. Tel. (513)721-7944. Fax (513)721-3971 E-mail: GBS.po@juno.com Website: http://www.gbs.edu

Golden Gate Baptist Theological Seminary,* (Southern Baptist Convention), 201 Seminary Dr., Mill Valley, CA 94941-3197. William O. Crews. Tel. (415)380-1300. Fax (415)380-1302 E-mail: seminary@ggbts.edu Website: http://www.ggbts.edu/index.html

Gonzaga University,* (The Roman Catholic Church), Spokane, WA 99258-0001. Michael L. Cook. Tel. (509)328-4220. Fax (509)324-5718

Gordon-Conwell Theological Seminary,* (Interdenominational), 130 Essex St., South Hamilton, MA 01982. President Walter C. Kaiser, Jr. Tel. (978)468-7111. Fax (978)468-0137 E-mail: info@gcts.edu Website: http://www.gcts.edu

279

Grace Bible College, (Grace Gospel Fellowship), P.O. Box 910, Grand Rapids, MI 49509. Bruce Kemper. Tel. (616)538-2330. Fax (616)538-0599
E-mail: gbc@gbcol.edu
Website: http://www.gbcol.edu

Grace Theological Seminary, (Fellowship of Grace Brethren Churches), 200 Seminary Dr., Winona Lake, IN 46590. Ronald E. Manahan. Tel. (219)372-5100. Fax (219)372-5265
Website: http://www.grace.edu

Grace University, (Independent), 1311 South 9th St., Omaha, NE 68108. Neal F. McBride. Tel. (402)449-2809. Fax (402)341-9587

Graduate Theological Union,* (Inter-denominational), 2400 Ridge Rd., Berkeley, CA 94709. Glenn R. Bucher. Tel. (510)649-2410. Fax (510)649-1417
E-mail: maloney@gtu.edu
Website: http://www.gtu.edu

Great Lakes Christian College, (Christian Churches and Churches of Christ), 6211 W. Willow Hwy., Lansing, MI 48917. Jerry M. Paul. Tel. (517)321-0242. Fax (517)321-5902

Greenville College, (Free Methodist Church of North America), 315 E. College Ave., P.O. Box 159, Greenville, IL 62246. President Robert E. Smith. Tel. (618)664-2800. Fax (618)664-1748
E-mail: rsmith@Greenville.edu
Website: http://www.greenville.edu

Harding University Graduate School of Religion, (Churches of Christ), 1000 Cherry Rd., Memphis, TN 38117. Bill Flatt. Tel. (901)761-1352. Fax (901)761-1358

Hartford Seminary,* (Interdenominational), 77 Sherman St., Hartford, CT 06105. Barbara Brown Zikmund. Tel. (860)509-9502. Fax (860)509-9509
E-mail: hartsem@mail.hartsem.edu
Website: http://www.hartsem.edu

Harvard Divinity School,* (Nondenominational), 45 Francis Ave., Cambridge, MA 02138. Ronald F. Thiemann. Tel. (617)495-5761. Fax (617)495-9489
Website: http://www.divweb.harvard.edu

Hebrew Union College-Jewish Institute of Religion, (Jewish), 3101 Clifton Ave., Cincinnati, OH 45220. Sheldon Zimmerman. Tel. (513)221-1875. Fax (513)221-4652
E-mail: rabbiz@cn.huc.edu
Website: http://www.huc.edu

Hebrew Union College-Jewish Institute of Religion, (Jewish), 1 W. 4th St., New York, NY 10012. Sheldon Zimmerman. Tel. (212)674-5300. Fax (212)533-0129

Hebrew Union College-Jewish Institute of Religion, (Jewish), 3077 University, Los Angeles, CA 90007. Sheldon Zimmerman. Tel. (213)749-3424. Fax (213)747-6128

Hobe Sound Bible College, (Nondenominational), P.O. Box 1065, Hobe Sound, FL 33475. P. Daniel Stetler. Tel. (407)546-5534. Fax (407)545-1421

Holy Cross Greek Orthodox School of Theology,* (Greek Orthodox Archdiocese of America), 50 Goddard Ave., Brookline, MA 02146. Bishop Isaiah of Denver, President. Tel. (617)731-3500. Fax (617)232-7819
E-mail: admissions@hchc.edu
Website: http://www.hchc.edu

Holy Trinity Orthodox Seminary, (The Russian Orthodox Church Outside of Russia), P.O. Box 36, Jordanville, NY 13361. Archbishop Laurus Skurla. Tel. (315)858-0940. Fax (315)858-0505

Hood Theological Seminary, (African Methodist Episcopal Zion Church), 800 W. Thomas St., Salisbury, NC 28144. Albert J.D. Aymer. Tel. (704)638-5644. Fax (704)638-5736

Houston Graduate School of Theology, * (Friends), 1311 Holman, Ste. 200, Houston, TX 77004. Dr. David Robinson. Tel. (713)942-9505 Fax (713)942-9506

Howard University School of Divinity,* (Nondenominational), 1400 Shepherd St. N.E., Washington, DC 20017. Clarence G. Newsome. Tel. (202)806-0500. Fax (202)806-0711

Huntington College, Graduate School of Christian Ministries, (Church of the United Brethren in Christ), 2303 College Ave., Huntington, IN 46750. David D. Rahn. Tel. (219)356-6000. Fax (219)358-3700
E-mail: gscm@huntington.edu
Website: http://www.huntington.edu/academics/ gscm

Iliff School of Theology,* (The United Methodist Church), 2201 S. University Blvd., Denver, CO 80210. Donald E. Messer. Tel. (303)744-1287. Fax (303)744-3387

Immaculate Conception Seminary School of Theology,* (The Roman Catholic Church), 400 S. Orange Ave., South Orange, NJ 07079. John W. Flesey. Tel. (201)761-9575. Fax (201)761-9577

Indiana Wesleyan University, (The Wesleyan Church), 4201 S. Washington, Marion, IN 46953-4999. James Barnes. Tel. (765)674-6901. Fax (765)677-2499
E-mail: jbarnes@indwes.edu
Website: http://www.indwes.edu

Interdenominational Theological Center,* (Interdenominational), 700 Martin L. King, Jr.

Dr. S.W., Atlanta, GA 30314. Dr. Robert M. Franklin. Tel. (404)527-7702. Fax (404)527-7770
E-mail: rfranklin@itc.edu

International School of Theology, 24600 Arrowhead Springs Rd., San Bernardino, CA 92414-0001. Donald A. Weaver. Tel. (909)886-7876. Fax (909)882-8458

Jesuit School of Theology at Berkeley,* (The Roman Catholic Church), 1735 LeRoy Ave., Berkeley, CA 94709. T. Howland Sanks. Tel. (510)841-8804. Fax (510)841-8536

Jewish Theological Seminary of America, (Jewish), 3080 Broadway, New York, NY 10027-4649. Ismar Schorsch. Tel. (212)678-8000. Fax (212)678-8947
E-mail: webmaster@jtsa.edu
Website: http://www.jtsa.edu

John Wesley College, (Interdenominational), 2314 N. Centennial St., High Point, NC 27265. Brian C. Donley. Tel. (336)889-2262. Fax (336)889-2261

Johnson Bible College, (Christian Churches and Churches of Christ), 7900 Johnson Dr., Knoxville, TN 37998. David L. Eubanks. Tel. (423)573-4517. Fax (423)251-2336
E-mail: jbc@jbc.edu
Website: http://www.jbc.edu

Kansas City College and Bible School, (Church of God (Holiness)), 7401 Metcalf Ave., Overland Park, KS 66204. Gayle Woods. Tel. (913)722-0272. Fax (913)722-2135

Kenrick-Glennon Seminary,* (The Roman Catholic Church), 5200 Glennon Dr., St. Louis, MO 63119. Rev. Msgr. George Lucas. Tel. (314)644-0266. Fax (314)644-3079

Kentucky Christian College, (Christian Churches and Churches of Christ), 100 Academic Parkway, Grayson, KY 41143. Keith P. Keeran. Tel. (606)474-3246. Fax (606)474-3155

Kentucky Mountain Bible College, (Inter-denominational), Box 10, Vancleve, KY 41385. Philip Speas. Tel. (606)666-5000. Fax (606)666-7744

L.I.F.E. Bible College, (International Church of the Foursquare Gospel), 1100 Covina Blvd., San Dimas, CA 91773. Dick Scott. Tel. (909)599-5433. Fax (909)599-6690

La Sierra University, (Seventh-day Adventist Church), 4700 Pierce St., Riverside, CA 92515-8247. Lawrence T. Geraty. Tel. (909)785-2000. Fax (909)785-2901

Lancaster Bible College, (Nondenominational), 901 Eden Rd., Lancaster, PA 17601. Gilbert A. Peterson. Tel. (717)569-7071. Fax (717)560-8213
Website: http://www.lbc.edu

Lancaster Theological Sem. of the United Church of Christ,* (United Church of Christ), 555 W. James St., Lancaster, PA 17603-2897. Peter Schmiechen. Tel. (717)393-0654. Fax (717)393-0423
E-mail: dean@lts.org

Lexington Theological Seminary,* (Christian Church (Disciples of Christ)), 631 S. Limestone St., Lexington, KY 40508. Richard L. Harrison. Tel. (606)252-0361. Fax (606)281-6042

Liberty Baptist Theological Seminary,* (Independent Baptist), 1971 University Blvd., Lynchburg, VA 24502-2269. A. Pierre Guillermin. Tel. (804)582-2000. Fax (804)582-2304

Lincoln Christian College and Seminary,* (Christian Churches and Churches of Christ), 100 Campus View Dr., Lincoln, IL 62656. Phillip B. Zoeller. Tel. (217)732-3168. Fax (217)732-4078
E-mail: psnyder@lccs.edu
Website: http://www.lccs.edu

Logos Evangelical Seminary,* (Evangelical Formosan Church), 9358 Telstar Ave., El Monte, CA 91731. Felix Liu. Tel. (626)571-5110. Fax (626)571-5119
E-mail: logos@sprynet.com

Louisville Presbyterian Theological Seminary,* (Presbyterian Church (U.S.A.)), 1044 Alta Vista Rd., Louisville, KY 40205. John M. Mulder. Tel. (502)895-3411. Fax (502)895-1096

Loyola Univ. Chicago Institute of Pastoral Studies,* (The Roman Catholic Church), 6525 North Sheridan Rd., Chicago, IL 60626. Camilla Burns. Tel. (773)508-2320. Fax (773)508-2319

Luther Seminary,* (Evangelical Lutheran Church in America), 2481 Como Ave., St. Paul, MN 55108. President David L. Tiede. Tel. (651)641-3456. Fax (651)641-3425
E-mail: sbooms@luthersem.edu
Website: http://www.luthersem.edu/

Lutheran Bible Institute in California, (Intersynodical Lutheran), 5321 University Dr., Ste. H, Irvine, CA 92612-2938. Benjamin Johnson. Tel. (949)262-9222. Fax (949)262-0283

Lutheran Bible Institute of Seattle, (Inter-denominational/Lutheran), 4221 - 228th Ave. S.E., Issaquah, WA 98029-9299. James A. Bergquist. Tel. (425)392-0400. Fax (425)392-0404
E-mail: admissn@lbi.edu
Website: http://www.lbi.edu

Lutheran Brethren Seminary, (Church of the Lutheran Brethren of America), 815 W.

281

Vernon, Fergus Falls, MN 56537. John C. Kilde. Tel. (218)739-3375. Fax (218)739-3372

Lutheran School of Theology at Chicago,* (Evangelical Lutheran Church in America), 1100 E. 55th St., Chicago, IL 60615-5199. James Kenneth Echols. Tel. (773)256-0700. Fax (773)256-0782

Lutheran Theological Seminary,* (Evangelical Lutheran Church in America), 61 N.W. Confederate Ave., Gettysburg, PA 17325-1795. Darold H. Beekmann. Tel. (717)334-6286. Fax (717)334-3469
Website: http://www.ltsg.edu

Lutheran Theological Seminary at Philadelphia,* (Evangelical Lutheran Church in America), 7301 Germantown Ave., Philadelphia, PA 19119. Robert G. Hughes. Tel. (215)248-4616. Fax (215)248-4577
E-mail: mtairy@ltsp.edu
Website: http://www.ltsp.edu

Lutheran Theological Southern Seminary,* (Evangelical Lutheran Church in America), 4201 North Main St., Columbia, SC 29203. H. Frederick Reisz. Tel. (803)786-5150. Fax (803)786-6499
E-mail: Freisz@ltss.edu
Website: http://www.ltss.edu

Magnolia Bible College, (Churches of Christ), P.O. Box 1109, Kosciusko, MS 39090. Cecil May. Tel. (601)289-2896. Fax (601)289-1850

Manhattan Christian College, (Christian Churches and Churches of Christ), 1415 Anderson Ave., Manhattan, KS 66502. Kenneth Cable. Tel. (785)539-3571. Fax (785)539-0832
Website: http://www.mccks.edu

McCormick Theological Seminary,* (Presbyterian Church (U.S.A.)), 5555 S. Woodlawn Ave., Chicago, IL 60637. Cynthia M. Campbell. Tel. (773)947-6300. Fax (773)947-0376

Meadville/Lombard Theological School,* (Unitarian Universalist Association), 5701 S. Woodlawn Ave., Chicago, IL 60637. William Murry. Tel. (773)256-3000. Fax (773)256-3008

Memphis Theol. Sem. of the Cumberland Presbyterian Church,* (Cumberland Presbyterian Church), 168 E. Parkway S at Union, Memphis, TN 38104-4395. Larry A. Blakeburn. Tel. (901)458-8232. Fax (901)452-4051
E-mail: wa4mff@aol.com

Mennonite Brethren Biblical Seminary,* (General Conference of Mennonite Brethren Churches), 4824 E. Butler Ave. (at Chestnut Ave.), Fresno, CA 93727. President Henry J. Schmidt. Tel. (209)251-8628. Fax (209)251-7212

E-mail: mbseminary@aol.com
Website: http://www.fresno.edu/MBSeminary

Methodist Theological School in Ohio,* (The United Methodist Church), 3081 Columbus Pike, P.O. Box 8004, Delaware, OH 43015-8004. President Norman E. Dewire. Tel. (740)363-1146. Fax (740)362-3135
E-mail: pres@mtso.edu
Website: http://www.mtso.edu

Mid-America Bible College, (The Church of God), 3500 S.W. 119th St., Oklahoma City, OK 73170. Forrest R. Robinson. Tel. (405)691-3800. Fax (405)692-3165

Midwestern Baptist Theological Seminary,* (Southern Baptist Convention), 5001 N. Oak Trafficway, Kansas City, MO 64118. Mark Coppenger. Tel. (816)453-4600. Fax (816)455-3439

Minnesota Bible College, (Christian Churches and Churches of Christ), 920 Mayowood Rd. S.W., Rochester, MN 55902. Robert W. Cash. Tel. (507)288-4563. Fax (507)288-9046
E-mail: academic@mnbc.edu
Website: http://www.mnbc.edu

Moody Bible Institute, (Interdenominational), 820 N. La Salle Blvd., Chicago, IL 60610. Joseph M. Stowell. Tel. (312)329-4000. Fax (312)329-4109

Moravian Theological Seminary,* (Moravian Church in America (Unitas Fratrum)), 1200 Main St., Bethlehem, PA 18018. David A. Schattschneider. Tel. (610)861-1516. Fax (610)861-1569
E-mail: merge01@moravian.edu
Website: http://www.moravian.edu

Moreau Seminary (Congregation of Holy Cross), (The Roman Catholic Church), Moreau Seminary, Notre Dame, IN 46556. Richard Gribble, C.S.C. Tel. (219)631-7735. Fax (219)631-9233

Morehouse School of Religion, (Interdenominational Baptist), 645 Beckwith St. S.W., Atlanta, GA 30314. William T. Perkins. Tel. (404)527-7777. Fax (404)681-1005

Mount Angel Seminary,* (The Roman Catholic Church), St. Benedict, OR 97373. Patrick S. Brennan. Tel. (503)845-3951. Fax (503)845-3126

Mt. St. Mary's Seminary,* (The Roman Catholic Church), Emmitsburg, MD 21727-7797. Very Rev. Kevin C. Rhoades. Tel. (301)447-5295. Fax (301)447-5636
Website: http://www.msmary.edu

Mt. St. Mary's Seminary of the West, (The Roman Catholic Church), 6616 Beechmont Ave., Cincinnati, OH 45230. Gerald R. Haemmerle. Tel. (513)231-2223. Fax (513)231-3254

282

Multnomah Bible College and Biblical Seminary,* (Interdenominational), 8435 N.E. Glisan St., Portland, OR 97220. Dr. Daniel R. Lockwood. Tel. (503)255-0332. Fax (503)251-5351
Website: http://www.multnomah.edu

Mundelein Seminary of the Univ. of St. Mary-of-the-Lake,* (The Roman Catholic Church), 1000 E. Maple, Mundelein, IL 60060-1174. John Canary. Tel. (847)566-6401. Fax (847)566-7330

N.Y. City Full Gospel Theological Seminary, (Full Gospel Assembly), 6902 11th Ave., Brooklyn, NY 11228. Frank A. Garofalo. Tel. (908)302-9553. Fax (908)302-9553

Nashotah House (Theological Seminary),* (Episcopal Church), 2777 Mission Rd., Nashotah, WI 53058-9793. Gary W. Kriss. Tel. (414)646-3371. Fax (414)646-2215
E-mail: nashotah@nashotah.edu
Website: http://www.nashotah.edu

Nazarene Bible College, (Church of the Nazarene), 1111 Academy Park Loop, Colorado Springs, CO 80910-3717. Hiram Sanders. Tel. (719)596-5110. Fax (719)550-9437
E-mail: nbc@rmii.com
Website: http://www.members.aol.com/ nazbibleco

Nazarene Theological Seminary,* (Church of the Nazarene), 1700 E. Meyer Blvd., Kansas City, MO 64131. A. Gordon Wetmore. Tel. (816)333-6254. Fax (816)333-6271

Nebraska Christian College, (Christian Churches and Churches of Christ), 1800 Syracuse Ave., Norfolk, NE 68701. Ray D. Stites. Tel. (402)379-5000. Fax (402)391-5100

New Brunswick Theological Seminary,* (Reformed Church in America), 17 Seminary Pl., New Brunswick, NJ 08901-1107. President Norman J. Kansfield. Tel. (732)247-5241. Fax (732)249-5412
E-mail: rsh@nbts.edu
Website: http://www.nbts.edu

New Orleans Baptist Theological Seminary,* (Southern Baptist Convention), 3939 Gentilly Blvd., New Orleans, LA 70126. Charles S. Kelley. Tel. (504)282-4455. Fax (504)286-3623
E-mail: nobts@nobts.edu
Website: http://www.nobts.edu

New York Theological Seminary,* (Non-Denominational), 5 W. 29th St., 9th Fl., New York, NY 10001. M. William Howard. Tel. (212)532-4012. Fax (212)684-0757
Website: http://www.nyts.edu

North American Baptist Seminary,* (North American Baptist Conference), 1525 S. Grange Ave., Sioux Falls, SD 57105. Charles

M. Hiatt. Tel. (605)336-6588. Fax (605)335-9090
E-mail: train@nabs.edu
Website: http://www.nabs.edu

North Central Bible College, (Assemblies of God), 910 Elliot Ave. S., Minneapolis, MN 55404. Gordon L. Anderson. Tel. (612)332-3491. Fax (612)343-4778

North Park Theological Seminary,* (The Evangelical Covenant Church), 3225 W. Foster Ave., Chicago, IL 60625. John E. Phelan, President and Dean. Tel. (773)244-6214. Fax (773)244-6244
E-mail: jphelan@northpark.edu
Website: http://www.northpark.edu/cs

Northern Baptist Theological Seminary,* (American Baptist Churches in the U.S.A.), 660 E. Butterfield Rd., Lombard, IL 60148. Ian M. Chapman. Tel. (630)620-2100. Fax (630)620-2194

Northwest College, (Assemblies of God), 5520 108th Ave. N.E., P.O. Box 579, Kirkland, WA 98083-0579. Don H. Argue, Ed.D. Tel. (425)822-8266. Fax (425)827-0148
E-mail: mail@ncag.edu
Website: http://www.nwcollege.edu

Notre Dame Seminary,* (The Roman Catholic Church), 2901 S. Carrollton Ave., New Orleans, LA 70118-4391. Most Rev. Gregory M. Aymond, D.D. Tel. (504)866-7426. Fax (504)866-3119

Oak Hills Christian College, (Interdenominational), 1600 Oak Hills Rd. S.W., Bemidji, MN 56601. Tel. (218)751-8670. Fax (218)751-8825

Oblate College,* (The Roman Catholic Church), 391 Michigan Ave. N.E., Washington, DC 20017. Harry Winter. Tel. (202)529-6544. Fax (202)636-9444

Oblate School of Theology,* (The Roman Catholic Church), 285 Oblate Dr., San Antonio, TX 78216-6693. J. William Morell. Tel. (210)341-1366. Fax (210)341-4519

Oral Roberts University School of Theology and Missions,* (Interdenominational), 7777 S. Lewis Ave., Tulsa, OK 74171. Jerry Horner. Tel. (918)495-6096. Fax (918)495-6259
E-mail: jhorner@oru.edu
Website: http://www.oru.edu

Ozark Christian College, (Christian Churches and Churches of Christ), 1111 N. Main St., Joplin, MO 64801. President Dr. Ken Idleman. Tel. (417)624-2518. Fax (417)624-0090

Pacific Christian College, (Christian Churches and Churches of Christ), 2500 E. Nutwood Ave., Fullerton, CA 92831. President E. LeRoy Lawson. Tel. (714)879-3901. Fax (714)526-0231
E-mail: rlawson@pacificc.edu

283

Pacific Lutheran Theological Seminary,* (Evangelical Lutheran Church in America), 2770 Marin Ave., Berkeley, CA 94708. President Timothy F. Lull. Tel. (510)524-5264. Fax (510)524-2408
E-mail: president@plts.edu
Website: http://www.plts.edu

Pacific School of Religion,* (United Church of Christ), 1798 Scenic Ave., Berkeley, CA 94709. William McKinney. Tel. (510)848-0528. Fax (510)845-8948
E-mail: comm@psr.edu
Website: http://www.psr.edu

Payne Theological Seminary,* (African Methodist Episcopal Church), Box 474, 1230 Wilberforce-Clifton Rd., Wilberforce, OH 45384-0474. Obery Hendricks. Tel. (937)376-2946. Fax (937)376-3330
E-mail: dbalsbau@wu.wilberforce.edu

Pepperdine University, (Churches of Christ), Religion Division, Malibu, CA 90263. Rick R. Marrs. Tel. (310)456-4352. Fax (310)317-7271
E-mail: rmarrs@pepperdine.edu
Website: http://www.pepperdine.edu/seaver/religion/main.html

Perkins School of Theology (Southern Methodist University),* (The United Methodist Church), Kirby Hall, Dallas, TX 75275-0133. Robin W. Lovin. Tel. (214)768-2138. Fax (214)768-1042
E-mail: theoadms@smu.edu
Website: http://www.smu.edu/~theology

Philadelphia College of Bible, (Nondenominational), 200 Manor Ave., Langhorne, PA 19047-2990. W. Sherrill Babb. Tel. (215)752-5800. Fax (215)702-4341
E-mail: president@pcb.edu

Philadelphia Theological Seminary, (Reformed Episcopal Church), 7372 Henry Ave., Philadelphia, PA 19128-1401. Leonard W. Riches. Tel. (215)483-2480. Fax (215)483-2484
E-mail: info@ptsorec.edu
Website: http://www.ptsofrec.edu

Phillips Theological Seminary,* (Christian Church (Disciples of Christ)), 4242 S. Sheridan Rd., Tulsa, OK 74145. William Tabbernee. Tel. (918)610-8303. Fax (918)610-8404
E-mail: ptspres@fullnet.net
Website: http://www.ptsem.org

Piedmont Baptist College, (Baptist (Independent), 716 Franklin St., Winston-Salem, NC 27101. Howard L. Wilburn. Tel. (336)725-8344. Fax (336)725-5522
E-mail: admissions@pbc.edu
Website: http://www.pbc.edu

Pittsburgh Theological Seminary,* (Presbyterian Church (U.S.A.)), 616 N. Highland Ave., Pittsburgh, PA 15206. Carnegie Samuel Calian. Tel. (412)362-5610. Fax (412)363-3260

Point Loma Nazarene College, (Church of the Nazarene), 3900 Lomaland Dr., San Diego, CA 92106. Tel. (619)849-2200. Fax (619)849-7007
Website: http://www.ptloma.edu

Pontifical College Josephinum,* (The Roman Catholic Church), 7625 N. High St., Columbus, OH 43235. Thomas J. Olmsted. Tel. (614)885-5585. Fax (614)885-2307

Pope John XXIII National Seminary,* (The Roman Catholic Church), 558 South Ave., Weston, MA 02193. Francis D. Kelly. Tel. (617)899-5500. Fax (617)899-9057

Practical Bible College, (Independent Baptist), Box 601, Bible School Park, NY 13737. Dale E. Linebaugh. Tel. (607)729-1581. Fax (607)729-2962
E-mail: pbc@lakenet.org
Website: http://www.lakenet.org/~pbc

Presbyterian School of Christian Education,* (Presbyterian Church (U.S.A.)), 1205 Palmyra Ave., Richmond, VA 23227. Wayne G. Boulton. Tel. (804)359-5031. Fax (804)254-8060

Princeton Theological Seminary,* (Presbyterian Church (U.S.A.)), P.O. Box 821, Princeton, NJ 08542-0803. Thomas W. Gillespie. Tel. (609)921-8300. Fax (609)924-2973

Protestant Episcopal Theological Seminary in Virginia,* (Episcopal Church), 3737 Seminary Rd., Alexandria, VA 22304. Martha J. Horne. Tel. (703)370-6600. Fax (703)370-6234

Puget Sound Christian College, (Christian Churches and Churches of Christ), 410 Fourth Ave. N., Edmonds, WA 98020-3171. President R. Allan Dunbar. Tel. (425)775-8686. Fax (425)775-8688
E-mail: psccpres@ricochet.ent

Rabbi Isaac Elchanan Theological Seminary, (Jewish), 2540 Amsterdam Ave., New York, NY 10033. Dean Zevulun Charlop. Tel. (212)960-5344. Fax (212)960-0061

Reconstructionist Rabbinical College, (Jewish), Church Rd. and Greenwood Ave., Wyncote, PA 19095. David A. Teutsch. Tel. (215)576-0800. Fax (215)576-6143
E-mail: rrcinfo@rrc.edu

Reformed Bible College, (Interdenominational), 3333 East Beltline N.E., Grand Rapids, MI 49525. Nicholas Kroeze. Tel. (616)222-3000. Fax (616)222-3045

Reformed Presbyterian Theological Seminary,* (Reformed Presbyterian Church of North America), 7418 Penn Ave., Pittsburgh, PA 15208. Jerry F. O'Neill. Tel. (412)731-8690. Fax (412)731-4834
E-mail: rpseminary@aol.com

Reformed Theological Seminary,* (Nondenominational), 5422 Clinton Blvd., Jackson, MS 39209. Luder G. Whitlock. Tel. (601)922-4988. Fax (601)922-1153
E-mail: rts.Jackson@rts.edu
Website: http://www.rts.edu

Regent University School of Divinity,* (Interdenominational), 1000 Regent University Dr., Virginia Beach, VA 23464-9801. Terry Lindvall. Tel. (757)579-4010. Fax (757)579-4037
E-mail: uinssyn@regent.edu
Website: http://www.regent.edu

Roanoke Bible College, (Christian Churches and Churches of Christ), 714 First St., Elizabeth City, NC 27909. William A. Griffin. Tel. (919)338-5191. Fax (919)338-0801

SS. Cyril and Methodius Seminary, (The Roman Catholic Church), 3535 Indian Trail, Orchard Lake, MI 48324. Francis B. Koper. Tel. (810)683-0311. Fax (810)683-0402
E-mail: 103244.3555@compuserve.com OR deansoff@sscms.edu
Website: http://www.metronet.lib.mi.us/aml.html (Library)
Website: http://www.sscms.edu/deansoff (Seminary)

Sacred Heart Major Seminary,* (The Roman Catholic Church), 2701 Chicago Blvd., Detroit, MI 48206. Allen H. Vigneron. Tel. (313)883-8500. Fax (313)868-6440

Sacred Heart School of Theology,* (The Roman Catholic Church), P.O. Box 429, Hales Corners, WI 53130-0429. James D. Brackin, S.C.J. Tel. (414)425-8300. Fax (414)529-6999
E-mail: shst@msn.com
Website: http://www.execpc.com./~rakirsch/shst

Saint Bernard's Institute,* (The Roman Catholic Church), 1100 S. Goodman St., Rochester, NY 14620. Patricia A. Schoelles. Tel. (716)271-3657. Fax (716)271-2045

St. Charles Borromeo Seminary,* (The Roman Catholic Church), 100 East Wynnewood Rd., Wynnewood, PA 19096. James E. Molloy. Tel. (610)667-3394. Fax (610)667-7635

St. Francis Seminary,* (The Roman Catholic Church), 3257 S. Lake Dr., St. Francis, WI 53235. Very Rev. Andrew L. Nelson. Tel. (414)747-6400. Fax (414)747-6442

St. John's Seminary,* (The Roman Catholic Church), 127 Lake St., Brighton, MA 02135. Timothy Moran. Tel. (617)254-2610. Fax (617)787-2336

St. John's Seminary College,* (The Roman Catholic Church), 5118 Seminary Rd., Camarillo, CA 93012-2599. Edward Wm. Clark. Tel. (805)482-2755. Fax (805)987-5097

St. John's University, School of Theology Seminary,* (The Roman Catholic Church), Box 7288, Collegeville, MN 56321. Dale Launderville. Tel. (320)363-2100. Fax (320)363-2504

St. Joseph's Seminary,* (The Roman Catholic Church), 201 Seminary Ave., (Dunwoodie) Yonkers, NY 10704. Edwin F. O'Brien. Tel. (914)968-6200. Fax (914)968-7912

St. Louis Christian College, (Christian Churches and Churches of Christ), 1360 Grandview Dr., Florissant, MO 63033. Kenneth L. Beck. Tel. (314)837-6777. Fax (314)837-8291

St. Mary Seminary and Graduate School of Theology,* (The Roman Catholic Church), 28700 Euclid Ave., Wickliffe, OH 44092. Donald B. Cozzens. Tel. (216)943-7600. Fax (216)943-7577

St. Mary's Seminary, (The Roman Catholic Church), 9845 Memorial Dr., Houston, TX 77024-3498. Chester L. Borski. Tel. (713)686-4345. Fax (713)681-7550

St. Mary's Seminary and University,* (The Roman Catholic Church), 5400 Roland Ave., Baltimore, MD 21210. Robert F. Leavitt. Tel. (410)323-3200. Fax (410)323-3554

St. Meinrad School of Theology,* (The Roman Catholic Church), St. Meinrad, IN 47577. Mark O'Keefe. Tel. (812)357-6611. Fax (812)357-6964

St. Patrick's Seminary,* (The Roman Catholic Church), 320 Middlefield Rd., Menlo Park, CA 94025. Gerald D. Coleman. Tel. (415)325-5621. Fax (415)322-0997

Saint Paul School of Theology,* (The United Methodist Church), 5123 Truman Rd., Kansas City, MO 64127. Lovett H. Weems, Jr. Tel. (816)483-9600. Fax (816)483-9605
E-mail: spst@spst.edu
Website: http://www.spst.edu

St. Paul Seminary School of Divinity,* (The Roman Catholic Church), 2260 Summit Ave., St. Paul, MN 55105. Phillip J. Rask. Tel. (612)962-5050. Fax (612)962-5790

St. Tikhon's Orthodox Theological Seminary, (The Orthodox Church in America), Box 130, St. Tikhon's Rd., South Canaan, PA 18459-0121. Archbishop Herman. Tel. (717)937-4411. Fax (717)937-3100.
E-mail: stots@stots.edu (Admin.)
stotsfac@stots.edu (Faculty)
stotscat@stots.edu (Library)

Websites: http://www. stots.edu AND http://www. oca.org/OCA/pim/oca-stostots.html

St. Vincent Seminary,* (The Roman Catholic Church), 300 Fraser Purchase Rd., Latrobe, PA 15650-2690. Very Rev. Thomas Acklin, O.S.B. Tel. (724)537-4592. Fax (724)532-5052

St. Vincent de Paul Regional Seminary,* (The Roman Catholic Church), 10701 S. Military Trail, Boynton Beach, FL 33436-4899. Pablo A. Navarro. Tel. (561)732-4424. Fax (561)737-2205

St. Vladimir's Orthodox Theological Seminary,* (The Orthodox Church in America), 575 Scarsdale Rd., Crestwood, NY 10707. Thomas Hopko. Tel. (914)961-8313. Fax (914)961-4507
E-mail: thopko@svots.edu
Website: http://www.svots.edu

San Francisco Theological Seminary,* (Presbyterian Church (U.S.A.), 2 Kensington Rd., San Anselmo, CA 94960. Donald W. McCullough. Tel. (415)258-6500. Fax (415) 258-1608
E-mail: sftsinfo@sfts.edu
Website: http://www.sfts.edu

San Jose Christian College, (Christian Churches and Churches of Christ), 790 S. 12th St., P.O. Box 1090, San Jose, CA 95108. Bryce L. Jessup. Tel. (408)293-9058. Fax (408)293-7352

Savonarola Theological Seminary, (Polish National Catholic Church of America), 1031 Cedar Ave., Scranton, PA 18505. John F. Swantek. Tel. (717)343-0100

Seabury-Western Theological Seminary,* (Episcopal Church), 2122 Sheridan Rd., Evanston, IL 60201. James B. Lemler. Tel. (847)328-9300. Fax (847)328-9624
Website: http://www.swts.nwu.edu

Seattle University School of Theology and Ministry,* (The Roman Catholic Church and 10 Participating Denominations and Associations), 900 Broadway, Seattle, WA 98122. Dean Loretta Jancoski. Tel. (206)296-5330. Fax (206)296-5329
E-mail: jancoski@seattleu.edu

Seminario Evangelico de Puerto Rico,* (Interdenominational), 776 Ponce de LeÛn Ave., San Juan, PR 00925. Samuel Pag·n. Tel. (787)763-6700. Fax (787)751-0847

Seminary of the East (Conservative Baptist), (Conservative Baptist Association of America), 1605 N. Limekiln Pike, Dresher, PA 19025. Philip J. Baur. Tel. (215)641-4801. Fax (215)641-4804

Seminary of the Immaculate Conception,* (The Roman Catholic Church), 440 West Neck Rd., Huntington, NY 11743. Vincent F. Fullam. Tel. (516)423-0483. Fax (516)423-2346

Seventh Day Baptist School of Ministry, (Seventh Day Baptist General Conference, USA and Canada), 3120 Kennedy Rd., P.O. Box 1678, Janesville, WI 53547. Rodney Henry. Tel. (608)752-5055. Fax (608)752-7711

Seventh-day Adventist Theological Seminary,* (Seventh-day Adventist Church), Andrews University, Berrien Springs, MI 49104-1500. Werner Vyhmeister. Tel. (616)471-3537. Fax (616)471-6202
E-mail: seminary@andrews.edu
Website: http://www.andrews.edu/sem

Shaw Divinity School, (Baptist), P.O. Box 2090, Raleigh, NC 27602. Talbert O. Shaw. Tel. (919)832-1701. Fax (919)832-6082

Simpson College, (The Christian and Missionary Alliance), 2211 College View Dr., Redding, CA 96003. James M. Grant. Tel. (916)224-5600. Fax (916)224-5608

Southeastern Baptist College, (Baptist Missionary Association of America), 4229 Highway 15N, Laurel, MS 39440. Jentry W. Bond. Tel. (601)426-6346. Fax (601)426-6346

Southeastern Baptist Theological Seminary,* (Southern Baptist Convention), 222 N. Wingate, P.O. Box 1889, Wake Forest, NC 27588-1889. President Paige Patterson. Tel. (919)556-3101. Fax (919)556-0998
Website: http://www.sebts.edu

Southeastern Bible College, (Interdenominational), 3001 Highway 280 E., Birmingham, AL 35243. John D. Talley. Tel. (205)969-0880. Fax (205)970-9207

Southeastern College of the Assemblies of God, (Assemblies of God), 1000 Longfellow Blvd., Lakeland, FL 33801. James L. Hennesy. Tel. (941)667-5000. Fax (941)667-5200

Southern Baptist Theological Seminary,* (Southern Baptist Convention), 2825 Lexington Rd., Louisville, KY 40280. R. Albert Mohler. Tel. (502)897-4011. Fax (502)899-1770
E-mail: mohler@sbts.edu
Website: http://www.sbts.edu

Southern Christian University, (Churches of Christ), 1200 Taylor Rd., Montgomery, AL 36117-3553. President Dr. Rex A. Turner, Jr. Tel. (334)277-2277. Fax (334)271-0002
E-mail: scuniversity@mindspring.com
Website: http://www.southernchristian.edu

Southern Wesleyan University, (The Wesleyan Church), 907 Wesleyan Dr., P.O. Box 1020, Central, SC 29630-1020. President David J.

Spittal. Tel. (864)639-2453. Fax (864)639-0826
Website: http://www.swu.edu

Southwestern Assemblies of God University, (Assemblies of God), 1200 Sycamore St., Waxahachie, TX 75165. Delmer R. Guynes. Tel. (972)937-4010. Fax (972)923-0488

Southwestern Baptist Theological Seminary,* (Southern Baptist Convention), P.O. Box 22000, Fort Worth, TX 76122. Kenneth S. Hemphill. Tel. (817)923-1921. Fax (817)923-0610
Website: http://www.swbts.edu

Southwestern College, (Conservative Baptist Association of America), 2625 E. Cactus Rd., Phoenix, AZ 85032. Brent D. Garrison. Tel. (602)992-6101. Fax (602)404-2159

Starr King School for the Ministry,* (Unitarian Universalist Association), 2441 LeConte Ave., Berkeley, CA 94709. Rebecca Parker. Tel. (510)845-6232. Fax (510)845-6273

Swedenborg School of Religion, (The Swedenborgian Church), 48 Sargent St., Newton, MA 02458. Dr. Mary Kay Klein. Tel. (617)244-0504. Fax (617)558-0357
E-mail: maryk59988@aol.com

Talbot School of Theology,* (Nondenominational), 13800 Biola Ave., La Mirada, CA 90639. Dennis H. Dirks. Tel. (562)903-4816. Fax (562)903-4759
E-mail: biola.edu/biola/talbot/
Website: http://www.talbot.edu

Temple Baptist Seminary, (Independent Baptist), 1815 Union Ave., Chattanooga, TN 37404. Barkev Trachian. Tel. (423)493-4221. Fax (423)493-4471

Theological School of the Protestant Reformed Churches, (Protestant Reformed Churches in America), 4949 Ivanrest Ave., Grandville, MI 49418. Robert D. Decker. Tel. (616)531-1490. Fax (616)531-3033
E-mail: decker@prca.org

Toccoa Falls College, (The Christian and Missionary Alliance), P.O. Box 800777, Toccoa Falls, GA 30598. Paul L. Alford. Tel. (706)886-6831. Fax (706)282-6005
E-mail: president@toccoafalls.edu
Website: http://www.toccoafalls.edu

Trevecca Nazarene University, (Church of the Nazarene), 333 Murfreesboro Rd., Nashville, TN 37210. Millard Reed. Tel. (615)248-1200. Fax (615)248-7728

Trinity Bible College, (Assemblies of God), 50 S. 6th Ave., Ellendale, ND 58436. Howard Young. Tel. (701)349-3621. Fax (701)349-5443

Trinity College of Florida, (Nondenominational), 2430 Trinity Oaks Blvd., New Port Richey, FL 34655. Glenn C. Speed, Jr., President. Tel. (727)376-6911. Fax (727)376-0781
E-mail: trinity@gte.net

Trinity Episcopal School for Ministry,* (Episcopal Church), 311 Eleventh St., Ambridge, PA 15003. The Very Rev. Peter C. Moore, Dean and President. Tel. (412)266-3838. Fax (412)266-4617
E-mail: tinalockett@tesm.edu
Website: http://www.episcopalian.org

Trinity International University,* (The Evangelical Free Church of America), 2065 Half Day Rd., Deerfield, IL 60015. Gregory L. Waybright. Tel. (847)945-8800. Fax (847)317-8090
E-mail: tedsadm@tiu.edu
Website: http://www.tiu.edu

Trinity Lutheran Seminary,* (Evangelical Lutheran Church in America), 2199 E. Main St., Columbus, OH 43209-2334. Dennis A. Anderson. Tel. (614)235-4136. Fax (614)238-0263

Union Theological Seminary,* (Interdenominational), 3041 Broadway, New York, NY 10027. Holland L. Hendrix. Tel. (212)662-7100. Fax (212)280-1416

Union Theological Seminary in Virginia,* (Presbyterian Church (U.S.A.)), 3401 Brook Rd., Richmond, VA 23227. Louis B. Weeks. Tel. (804)355-0671. Fax (804)355-3919

United Theological Seminary,* (The United Methodist Church), 1810 Harvard Blvd., Dayton, OH 45406-4599. Michael G. Nickerson. Tel. (513)278-5817. Fax (513)278-1218
E-mail: utsadmis@united.edu
Website: http://www.united.edu

United Theological Seminary of the Twin Cities,* (United Church of Christ), 3000 Fifth St. N.W., New Brighton, MN 55112. Wilson Yates. Tel. (612)633-4311. Fax (612)633-4315
E-mail: general@unitedseminary-mn.org
Website: http://www.unitedseminary-mn.org

University of Chicago (Divinity School),* (Interdenominational), 1025 E. 58th St., Chicago, IL 60637. W. Clark Gilpin. Tel. (773)702-8221. Fax (773)702-6048
Website: http://www2.uchicago.edu/divinity

University of Dubuque Theological Seminary,* (Presbyterian Church (U.S.A.)), 2000 University Ave., Dubuque, IA 52001. Jeffrey Bullock. Tel. (319)589-3223. Fax (319)589-3682

287

University of Notre Dame, Dept. of Theology,* (The Roman Catholic Church), Notre Dame, IN 46556. Lawrence S. Cunningham. Tel. (219)631-7811. Fax (219)631-4268

University of St. Thomas School of Theology,* (The Roman Catholic Church), 9845 Memorial Dr., Houston, TX 77024. Louis T. Brusatti. Tel. (713)686-4345. Fax (713)683-8673

University of the South School of Theology,* (Episcopal Church), 335 Tennessee Ave., Sewanee, TN 37383-0001. Guy Fitch Lytle. Tel. (931)598-1288. Fax (931)598-1412 E-mail: glytle@seraphl.sewanee.edu Website: http://www.sewanee.edu

Valley Forge Christian College, (Assemblies of God), 1401 Charlestown Rd., Phoenixville, PA 19460. Earl Baldwin. Tel. (610)935-0450. Fax (610)935-9353

Vanderbilt University Divinity School,* (Interdenominational), Nashville, TN 37240. Joseph C. Hough, Jr. Tel. (615)322-2776. Fax (615)343-9957 E-mail: HoughJC@CTRVax.Vanderbilt.edu Website: http://www.vanderbilt.edu

Vennard College, (Interdenominational), Box 29, University Park, IA 52595. W. Edward Rickman. Tel. (515)673-8391. Fax (515)673-8365 E-mail: Vennard@kds:.net Website: http://www.kds:.net/VennardCollege/

Virginia Union University (School of Theology),* (American Baptist Churches in the U.S.A.), 1500 N. Lombardy St., Richmond, VA 23220. John W. Kinney. Tel. (804)257-5715. Fax (804)257-5785

Walla Walla College (School of Theology), (Seventh-day Adventist Church), 204 S. College Ave., College Place, WA 99324-1198. Ernie Bursie. Tel. (509)527-2194. Fax (509)527-2253 E-mail: burser@wwc.edu Website: http://www.wwc.edu

Wartburg Theological Seminary,* (Evangelical Lutheran Church in America), 333 Wartburg Pl., P.O. Box 5004, Dubuque, LA 52004-5004. Roger Fjeld. Tel. (319)589-0200. Fax (319)589-0333 E-mail: Roger_Fjeld.parti@ecunet.org

Washington Bible College/Capital Bible Seminary, (Nondenominational), 6511 Princess Garden Pkwy., Lanham, MD 20706. Homer Heater. Tel. (301)552-1400. Fax (301)552-2775

Washington Theological Consortium, (Nondenominational), 487 Michigan Ave. N.E., Washington, DC 20017. John W. Crossin, Exec. Dir. Tel. (202)832-2675. Fax (202)526-0818 E-mail: wtconsort@aol.com

Washington Theological Union,* (The Roman Catholic Church), 6896 Laurel St. N.W., Washington, DC 20012. Vincent D. Cushing. Tel. (202)726-8800. Fax (202)726-1716 Website: http://www.wtu.edu

Wesley Biblical Seminary,* (Interdenominational), P.O. Box 9938, Jackson, MS 39286-0938. Robert R. Lawrence. Tel. (601)957-1314. Fax (601)957-1314

Wesley Theological Seminary,* (The United Methodist Church), 4500 Massachusetts Ave. N.W., Washington, DC 20016-5690. G. Douglass Lewis, President. Tel. (800)882-4987. Fax (202)885-8600 E-mail: admiss@clark.net Website: http://www.WesleySem.org

Western Evangelical Seminary,* (Interdenominational), 12753 S.W. 68th Ave., Portland, OR 97223. Ed Stevens. Tel. (503)538-8383. Fax (503)598-4338

Western Seminary, (Conservative Baptist Association of America), 5511 S.E. Hawthorne Blvd., Portland, OR 97215. Ronald E. Hawkins. Tel. (503)233-8561. Fax (503)239-4216

Western Theological Seminary,* (Reformed Church in America), 101 E. 13th St., Holland, MI 49423. Dennis N. Voskuil. Tel. (616)392-8555. Fax (616)392-7717 Website: http://www.westernsem.org

Westminster Theological Seminary,* (Nondenominational), Chestnut Hill, P.O. Box 27009, Philadelphia, PA 19118. Samuel T. Logan. Tel. (215)887-5511. Fax (215)887-5404

Westminster Theological Seminary in California,* (Nondenominational), 1725 Bear Valley Pkwy., Escondido, CA 92027-4128. W. Robert Godfrey. Tel. (619)480-8474. Fax (619)480-0252

Weston Jesuit School of Theology,* (Roman Catholic), 3 Phillips Pl., Cambridge, MA 02138. Robert Manning. Tel. (617)492-1960. Fax (617)492-5833 E-mail: rmanning@wjst.edu

William Tyndale College, (Interdenominational), 35700 W. Twelve Mile Rd., Farmington Hills, MI 48331. James C. McHann. Tel. (810)553-7200. Fax (810)553-5963

Winebrenner Theological Seminary,* (Churches of God, General Conference), 701 E. Melrose Ave., P.O. Box 478, Findlay, OH 45839. David E. Draper, President. Tel. (419)422-4824. Fax (419)422-3999 E-mail: wtseminary@aol.com Website: http://www.winebrenner.edu

Wisconsin Lutheran Seminary, (Wisconsin Evangelical Lutheran Synod), 11831 N. Seminary Dr., 65W, Mequon, WI 53092. President David J. Valleskey. Tel. (414)257-8800. Fax (414)257-8810

Yale University Divinity School,* 409 Prospect St., New Haven, CT 06511. Richard J. Wood. Tel. (203)432-5303. Fax (203)432-5356

9. Theological Seminaries and Bible Colleges in Canada

The following list includes theological seminaries and departments in colleges and universities in which ministerial training is given. Many denominations have additional programs. The lists of Religious Bodies in Canada should be consulted for the address of denominational headquarters.

The list has been developed from direct correspondence with the institutions. Inclusion in or exclusion from this list implies no judgment about the quality or accreditation of any institution.

Each of the listings include: the institution name, denominational sponsor when appropriate, location, head, telephone and fax numbers when known and e-mail and website addresses when available.

Acadia Divinity College,* (United Baptist Convention of the Atlantic Provinces), Acadia University, Wolfville, NS B0P 1X0. Timothy R. Ashley. Tel. (902)542-2285. Fax (902)542-7527. E-mail: mashley@acadiau.ca
Website: http://ace.acadiau.ca/divcol

Alberta Bible College, (Christian Churches and Churches of Christ in Canada), 599 Northmount Dr. N.W., Calgary, AB T2K 3J6. Ronald A. Fraser. Tel. (403)282-2994. Fax (403)282-3084
E-mail: abbible@cadvision.com
Website: http://www.abc-ca.org

Arthur Turner Training School, (The Anglican Church of Canada), Anglican Center for Christian Studies, Diocese of the Arctic, Box 378, Pangnirtung, NT X0A 0R0. Principal, Roy Bowkett. Tel. (867)473-8375. Fax (867)473-8064

Associated Can. Theological Schools of Trinity Western Univ.,* (Baptist General Conference of Canada, Evangelical Free Church of Canada, The Fellowship of Evangelical Baptist Churches in Canada), 7600 Glover Rd., Langley, BC V3A 6H4. Guy S. Saffold. Tel. (604)888-6158. Fax (604)888-5729

Atlantic Baptist University, (United Baptist Convention of the Atlantic Provinces), Box 6004, Moncton, NB E1C 9L7. W. Ralph Richardson. Tel. (506)858-8970. Fax (506)858-9694

Atlantic School of Theology,* (Interdenominational), 640 Francklyn St., Halifax, NS B3H 3B5. Gordon Mac Dermid. Tel. (902)423-6801. Fax (902)492-4048

Baptist Leadership Training School, (Canadian Baptist Ministries), 4330 16th St. S.W., Calgary, AB T2T 4H9. Hugh Fraser. Tel. (403)243-3770. Fax (403)287-1930
E-mail: blts@imag.net
Website: http://www.yet.ca

Bethany Bible College-Canada, (The Wesleyan Church), 26 Western St., Sussex, NB E4E 1E6. President Dr. David S. Medders. Tel. (506)432-4400. Fax (506)432-4425

Bethany Bible Institute, (Canadian Conference of Mennonite Brethren Churches), Box 160, Hepburn, SK S0K 1Z0. Doug Berg. Tel. (306)947-2175. Fax (306)947-4229
E-mail: bethany@sk.sympatico.ca
Website: http://www.bethany.sk.ca

Briercrest Bible College, (Interdenominational), Enrollment Services, Briercrest Family of Schools, 510 College Dr., Caronport, SK S0H 0S0. Tel. (800)667-5199. Fax (306)756-3366
Website: http://www.briercrest.ca

Briercrest Biblical Seminary,* (Interdenominational), Enrollment Services, Briercrest Family of Schools, 510 College Dr., Caronport, SK S0H 0S0. Tel. (800)667-5199. Fax (306) 756-3366
Website: http://www.briercrest.ca

Canadian Bible College, (Christian and Missionary Alliance in Canada), 4400-4th Ave., Regina, SK S4T 0H8. Melvin P. Sylvester. Tel. (306)545-1515. Fax (306)545-0210

Canadian Lutheran Bible Institute, (Lutheran), 4837 52A St., Camrose, AB T4V 1W5. Norman C. Miller. Tel. (403)672-4454. Fax (403)672-4455
E-mail: clbi@cable-lynx.net

Canadian Nazarene College, (Church of the Nazarene Canada), 610, 833 4th Ave. SW, Calgary, AB T2P 3T5. Riley Coulter. Tel. (403)571-2550. Fax (403)571-2556
E-mail: cncoff@cnaz.ab.ca

Canadian Theological Seminary,* (Christian and Missionary Alliance in Canada), 4400-4th Ave., Regina, SK S4T 0H8. Melvin P. Sylvester. Tel. (306)545-1515. Fax (306)545-0210

Central Pentecostal College, University of Saskatchewan, (The Pentecostal Assemblies of Canada), 1303 Jackson Ave., Saskatoon, SK S7H 2M9. D. Munk. Tel. (306)374-6655. Fax (306)373-6968

Centre for Christian Studies, (The Anglican Church of Canada, The United Church of

290

Canada), 60 Maryland, Winnipeg, MB R36 1K7. Tel. (204)783-4490. Fax (204)786-3012 E-mail: centre@escape.ca

Church Army College of Evangelism, (The Anglican Church of Canada), 397 Brunswick Ave., Toronto, ON M5R 2Z2. Roy E. Dickson. Tel. (416)924-9279. Fax (416)924-2931

Collége Dominicain de Philosophie et de Théologie, (The Roman Catholic Church in Canada), 96 avenue Empress, Ottawa, ON K1R 7G3. Michel Gourgues. Tel. (613)233-5696. Fax (613)233-6064

College Biblique Québec, (The Pentecostal Assemblies of Canada), 740 Lebourgneuf, Ste. 100, Ancienne Lorette, QC G2J 1E2. William Raccah. Tel. (418)622-7552. Fax (418)622-1470

College of Emmanuel and St. Chad, (The Anglican Church of Canada), 1337 College Dr., Saskatoon, SK S7N 0W6. William Niels Christensen. Tel. (306)975-3753. Fax (306)934-2683 E-mail: christen@duke.usask.ca

Columbia Bible College, (Mennonite), 2940 Clearbrook Rd., Abbotsford, BC V2T 2Z8. Walter Unger. Tel. (604)853-3358. Fax (604)853-3063 E-mail: info@columbiabc.edu Website: http://www.columbiabc.edu

Concord College, (Mennonite Brethren Churches), 169 Riverton Ave., Winnipeg, MB R2L 2E5. Harry Olfert. Tel. (204)669-6583. Fax (204)663-2468

Concordia Lutheran Seminary,* (Lutheran Church-Canada), 7040 Ada Blvd., Edmonton, AB T5B 4E3. L. Dean Hempelmann. Tel. (403)474-1468. Fax (403)479-3067 E-mail: clsadmin@connect.ab.ca

Concordia Lutheran Theological Seminary,* (Lutheran Church-Canada), 470 Glenridge Ave., St. Catharines, ON L2T 4C3. Jonathan Grothe. Tel. (905)688-2362. Fax (905)688-9744

Covenant Bible College, (The Evangelical Covenant Church of Canada), Campuses: *CANADA:* 630 Westchester Rd., Strathmore, AB T1P 1H8. Neil R. Josephson. Tel. (403)934-6200. Fax (403)934-6220 E-mail: covbibco@cadvision.com Website: http://www.covenantbiblecollege.ab.ca *COLORADO:* 675 Southwood Ln., Windsor, CO 80550 Tel./Fax (970)686-6977 E-mail: 103354.2431@compuserve.com

Eastern Pentecostal Bible College, (The Pentecostal Assemblies of Canada), 780 Argyle St., Peterborough, ON K9H 5T2. Carl F. Verge. Tel. (705)748-9111. Fax (705)748-3931

Edmonton Baptist Seminary,* (North American Baptist Conference), 11525-23 Ave., Edmonton, AB T6J 4T3. Rev. Marvin Dewey. Tel. (403)436-9416. Fax (403)431-5200

Emmanuel Bible College, (The Evangelical Missionary Church of Canada), 100 Fergus Ave., Kitchener, ON N2A 2H2. Thomas E. Dow. Tel. (519)894-8900. Fax (519)894-5331 E-mail: dmin@ebcollege.on.ca Website: http://www.ebcollege.on.ca

Emmanuel College,* (The United Church of Canada), 75 Queens Park Crescent, Toronto, ON M5S 1K7. Roger C. Hutchinson. Tel. (416)585-4539. Fax (416)585-4516 E-mail: ec.office@utoronto.ca Website: http://vicu.utoronto.ca

Faculté De Théologie Évangélique, (Union d'Eglises Baptistes FranÁaises au Canada), 2285, Avenue Papineau, Montréal, QC H2K 4J5. Amar Djaballah. Tel. (514)526-6643. Fax (514)526-9269

Faith Alive Bible College, (Nondenominational), 637 University Dr., Saskatoon, SK S7N 0H8. David Pierce. Tel. (306)652-2230. Fax (306)665-1125

Full Gospel Bible Institute, (Apostolic Church of Pentecost of Canada Inc.), Box 579, Eston, SK S0L 1A0. Todd Atkinson. Tel. (306)962-3621. Fax (306)962-3810

Gardner College, A Centre for Christian Studies, (Church of God (Anderson, Ind.)), 4704 55th St., Camrose, AB T4V 2B6. John Alan Howard. Tel. (403)672-0171. Fax (403)672-6888 E-mail: gardnerc@cable-lynx.net Website: http://cable-lynx/~gardnerc

Grand Seminaire de Montréal,* (The Roman Catholic Church in Canada), 2065 Sherbrook Quest, Montréal, QC H3H 1G6. Louis-Paul Gauvreau. Tel. (514)935-1169. Fax (514)935-5497

Great Lakes Bible College, (Churches of Christ in Canada), 62 Hickory St. W., Waterloo, ON N2L 3J4. Dr. Geoffrey Ellis, Principal. Tel. (905)885-6330. Fax (905)563-0818 E-mail: info@glcc.vaxxine.com

Heritage Baptist College/Heritage Theological Seminary, (The Fellowship of Evangelical Baptist Churches in Canada), 175 Holiday Inn Dr., Cambridge, ON N3C 3T2. Marvin Brubacher. Tel. (519)651-2869. Fax (519)651-2870 E-mail: admin@heritage-theo.edu Website: http://www.heritage-theo.edu

Huron College,* (The Anglican Church of Canada), 1349 Western Rd., London, ON N6G 1H3. Dr. David Bevan, Principal. Tel. (519)438-7224. Fax (519)438-3938

Institut Biblique Beree, (The Pentecostal Assemblies of Canada), 1711 Henri-Bourassa Est, Montréal, QC H2C 1J5. André L. Gagnon. Tel. (514)385-4238. Fax (514)385-4238

Institut Biblique Laval, (Canadian Conference of Mennonite Brethren Churches), 1775, boul Édouard-Laurin, Ville Saint-Laurent, QC H4L 2B9. Jean ThÈorÍt. Tel. (514)331-0878. Fax (514)331-0879

Institute for Christian Studies, (Nondenominational), 229 College St., Toronto, ON M5T 1R4. Harry Fernhout. Tel. (416)979-2331. Fax (416)979-2332
E-mail: wcoffeybailey@icscanada.edu
Website: http://icscanada.edu

International Bible College, (Church of God (Cleveland, Tenn.)), 401 Trinity La., Moose Jaw, SK S6H 0E3. Alex Allan. Tel. (306)692-4041. Fax (306)692-7968

Joint Board of Theological Colleges,* (Interdenominational), 3473 University St., Montréal, QC H3A 2A8. Dr. John Simons. Tel. (514)849-8511. Fax (514)849-4113
E-mail: dio@colba.net
Website: http://www.mcgill.ca/religion/jbtc.htm

Key-Way-Tin Bible Institute, (Nondenominational), Box 540, Lac La Biche, AB T0A 2C0. Dir. Dave Petkau. Tel. (403)623-4565. Fax (403)623-1788

Knox College,* (Presbyterian Church of Canada), 59 St. George St., Toronto, ON M5S 2E6. Arthur Van Seters. Tel. (416)978-4500. Fax (416)971-2133
E-mail: knox.college@utoronto.ca
Website: http://www.utoronto.ca/knox

Living Faith Bible College, (Fellowship of Christian Assemblies (Canada)), Box 100, Caroline, AB T0M 0M0. Cliff A. Stalwick. Tel. (403)722-2225. Fax (403)722-2459
E-mail: livfaith@telusplanet.net
Website: http://www.telusplanet.net/public/liv faith. htm

Lutheran Theological Seminary,* (Evangelical Lutheran Church in Canada), 114 Seminary Crescent, Saskatoon, SK S7N 0X3. Faith Rohrbough. Tel. (306)966-7850. Fax (306) 966-7852
E-mail: rohrb@duke.usask.ca

Maritime Christian College, (Christian Churches and Churches of Christ in Canada), 503 University Ave., Charlottetown, PE C1A 7Z4. Merle W. Zimmerman. Tel. (902)628-8887. Fax (902)892-3959

McGill University Faculty of Religious Studies,* (Interdenominational), 3520 University St., Montréal, QC H3A 2A7. Donna R. Runnalls. Tel. (514)398-4121. Fax (514)398-6665

McMaster Divinity College,* (Baptist Convention of Ontario and Quebec), McMaster Divinity College, Hamilton, ON L8S 4K1. William H. Brackney. Tel. (905)525-9140 Ext 24401. Fax (905)577-4782
E-mail: divinity@mcmaster.ca
Website: http://www.mcmaster.ca/divinity

Millar College of the Bible, (Interdenominational), Box 25, Pambrun, SK S0N 1W0. A. Brian Atmore. Tel. (306)582-2033. Fax (306)582-2027

Montreal Diocesan Theological College,* (The Anglican Church of Canada), 3473 University St., Montreal, QC H3A 2A8. John Simons. Tel. (514)849-3004. Fax (514)849-4113

Mount Carmel Bible School, (Christian Brethren (also known as Plymouth Brethren)), 4725 106 Ave., Edmonton, AB T6A 1E7. Gordon King. Tel. (403)465-3015. Toll-free 1(800) 561-6443. Fax (403)466-2485
E-mail: carmel@worldgate.com

National Native Bible College, (Elim Fellowship of Evangelical Churches and Ministers), Box 478, Deseronto, ON K0K 1X0. Levi Samson Beardy. Tel. (613)396-2311. Fax (613)396-2314

Newman Theological College,* (The Roman Catholic Church in Canada), 15611 St. Albert Trail, Edmonton, AB T6V 1H3. Kevin J. Carr. Tel. (403)447-2993. Fax (403)447-2685
E-mail: admin@newman.edu
Website: http://www.newman.edu

Nipawin Bible Institute, (Interdenominational), Box 1986, Nipawin, SK S0E 1E0. Mark Leppington. Tel. (306)862-5095. Fax (306) 862-3651

Northwest Baptist Theological College and Seminary, (The Fellowship of Evangelical Baptist Churches in Canada), 22606 76A Ave., P.O. Box 790, Langley, BC V3A 8B8. Larry D. McCullough. Tel. (604)888-3310. Fax (604) 888-3354

Northwest Bible College, (The Pentecostal Assemblies of Canada), 11617-106 Ave., Edmonton, AB T5H 0S1. G. Johnson. Tel. (403)452-0808. Fax (403)452-5803
E-mail: northwest@oanet.com
Website: http://www.nwbc.ab.ca

Ontario Christian Seminary, (Christian Churches and Churches of Christ in Canada), P.O. Box 324, Stn. D; 260 High Park Ave., Toronto, ON M6P 3J9. James R. Cormode. Tel. (416)769-7115. Fax (416)769-7047

Pacific Life Bible College, (Interdenominational), 15100 66 A Ave., Surrey, BC V3S 2A6. Dennis L. Hixson. Tel. (604)597-9082. Fax (604)597-9090
E-mail: paclife@smartt.com

Parole de Vie Bethel/Word of Life Bethel, (Nondenominational), 1175 Chemin Woodward Hill, RR1, Lennoxville, QC J1M 2A2. Ken Beach. Tel. (819)823-8435. Fax (819)823-2468

Peace River Bible Institute, (Interdenominational), Box 99, Sexsmith, AB T0H 3C0. Reuben Kvill. Tel. (780)568-3962. Fax (780)568-4431 E-mail: prbi@telusplanet.net

Prairie Graduate School, (Interdenominational), 2540 S Ave. NW, Calgary, AB T2N 0T5. Rick Down (Interim President). Tel. (403)777-0150. Fax (403)270-2336

Providence College and Theological Seminary,* (Interdenominational), General Delivery, Otterburne, MB R0A 1G0. Larry J. McKinney. Tel. (204)433-7488. Fax (204)433-7158 E-mail: info@providence.mb.ca Website: http://www.providence.mb.ca

Queens College,* (The Anglican Church of Canada), 210 Prince Phillip Dr., St. Johns, NF A1B 3R6. Boyd Morgan. Tel. (709)753-0640. Fax (709)753-1214

Queen's Theological College,* (The United Church of Canada), Queen's Theological College, Kingston, ON K7L 3N6. Hallett E. Llewellyn. Tel. (613)545-2110. Fax (613)545-6879 E-mail: theology@post.queensu.ca Website: http://info.queensu.ca/theology/qtc home. html

Reformed Episcopal Theological College, (Reformed Episcopal Church of Canada), 320 Armstrong St., Box 2532, New Liskeard, ON P0J 1P0. Rt. Rev. Michael Fedechko. Tel. (705)647-4565 Fax (705)647-4565 E-mail: fed@nt.net

Regent College,* (Interdenominational), 5800 University Blvd., Vancouver, BC V6T 2E4. Walter C. Wright. Tel. (800)663-8664. Fax (604)224-3097 E-mail: regentcollege@compuserve.com Website: http://www.regent-college.edu

Regis College,* (The Roman Catholic Church in Canada), 15 St. Mary St., Toronto, ON M4Y 2R5. John Allan Loftus, S.J. Tel. (416)922-5474. Fax (416)922-2898 Website: http://www.utornonto.ca/regis

Rocky Mountain College: Centre for Biblical Studies, (The Evangelical Missionary Church of Canada), 4039 Brentwood Rd. NW, Calgary, AB T2L 1L1. Gordon Dirks. Tel. (403)284-5100. Fax (403)220-9567

Saint Paul University, Faculty of Theology, (The Roman Catholic Church in Canada), 223 Main St., Ottawa, ON K1S 1C4. James R. Pambrun. Tel. (613)236-1393. Fax (613)751-4016

Salvation Army College for Officer Training, (The Salvation Army in Canada), 2130 Bayview Ave., North York, ON M4N 3K6. Wayne N. Pritchett (Principal). Tel. (416)481-6131. Fax (416)481-6810; (416)481-2895 (Library)

St. Andrew's Theological College,* (The United Church of Canada), 1121 College Dr., Saskatoon, SK S7N 0W3. Charlotte Caron and Michael Bourgeois. Tel. (306)966-8970. Fax (306)966-8981

St. Augustine's Seminary of Toronto,* (The Roman Catholic Church in Canada), 2661 Kingston Rd., Scarborough, ON M1M 1M3. John A. Boissonneau. Tel. (416)261-7207. Fax (416)261-2529 Website: http://www. canxsys.com/staugust.htm

St. John's College, Univ. of Manitoba, Faculty of Theology, (The Anglican Church of Canada), 92 Dysart Rd., Winnipeg, MB R3T 2M5. B. Hudson McLean. Tel. (204)474-6852. Fax (204)261-1215

St. Peter's Seminary,* (The Roman Catholic Church in Canada), 1040 Waterloo St., London, ON N6A 3Y1. Thomas C. Collins. Tel. (519)432-1824. Fax (519)432-0964

St. Stephen's College, Grad. & Continuing Theological Educ.,* (The United Church of Canada), 8810 112th St., Edmonton, AB T6G 2J6. Christopher V. Levan. Tel. (403)439-7311. Fax (403)433-8875

Steinbach Bible College, (Mennonite), Box 1420, Steinbach, MB R0A 2A0. Stan Plett. Tel. (204)326-6451. Fax (204)326-6908 E-mail: pr@sbcollege.mb.ca Website: http://www.sbcollege.mb.ca

The Presbyterian College, Montreal, (Presbyterian Church in Canada), 3495 University St., Montreal, QC H3A 2A8. W. J. Klempa. Tel. (514)288-5256. Fax (514)398-6665

The Salvation Army William and Catherine Booth Bible College, (The Salvation Army in Canada), 447 Webb Pl., Winnipeg, MB R3B 2P2. Lloyd Hetherington. Tel. (204)947-6701. Fax (204)942-3856 E-mail: wcbc@cc.umanitoba.ca

Theol. College of the Canadian Reformed Churches, (Canadian and American Reformed Churches), 110 West 27th St., Hamilton, ON L9C 5A1. N. H. Gootjes. Tel. (416)575-3688. Fax (416)575-0799

Toronto Baptist Seminary and Bible College, (Association of Regular Baptist Churches (Canada)), 130 Gerrard St., E., Toronto, ON M5A 3T4. Andrew M. Fountain. Tel. (416)925-3263. Fax (416)925-8305 E-mail: tbs@tbs.edu Website: http://www.tbs.edu

293

Toronto School of Theology,* (Interdenominational), 47 Queens Park Crescent E., Toronto, ON M5S 2C3. Jean-Marc Laporte. Tel. (416)978-4039. Fax (416)978-7821 E-mail: registrar.tst@utoronto.ca Website: http://www.utoronto.ca/tst

Trinity College, Faculty of Divinity,* (The Anglican Church of Canada), 6 Hoskin Ave., Toronto, ON M5S 1H8. D. Wiebe. Tel. (416)978-7750. Fax (416)978-4949

Tyndale College and Seminary,* (Transdenominational), 25 Ballyconnor Ct., Toronto, ON M2M 4B3. Dr. Brian C. Stiller. Tel. (416)226-6380. Fax (416)226-6746 E-mail: info@tyndale-canada.edu Website: http://www.tyndale-canada.edu

United Theological College/Le Séminaire Uni, (The United Church of Canada), 3521 rue Université, Montréal, QC H3A 2A9. Pierre Goldberger. Tel. (514)849-2042. Fax (514) 398-6665

Université Laval, Faculé de théologie, (The Roman Catholic Church in Canada), Cité Universitaire Ste-Foy, Ste-Foy, QC G1K 7P4. René-Michael Roberge. Tel. (418)656-2131. Fax (418)656-3273

Université de Montréal, Faculté de théologie, (The Roman Catholic Church in Canada), C. P. 6128 Succ. Centre Ville, Montréal, QC H3C 3J7. Jean-Marc Charron. Tel. (514)343-7160. Fax (514)343-5738 E-mail: theologie@post.umontreal.ca Website: http://mistral.ere.umontreal.ca/davidrob/theo

Université de Sherbrooke, Faculté de theologié, (The Roman Catholic Church in Canada), 2500 boul. Université, Sherbrooke, QC J1K 2R1. Jean-François Malherbe. Tel. (819)821-7600. Fax (819)821-7677

University of St. Michael's College, Faculty of Theology,* (The Roman Catholic Church in Canada), 81 St. Mary St., Toronto, ON M5S 1J4. Dean Brian F. Hogan. Tel. (416)926-7140. Fax (416)926-7294 Website: http://www.utoronto.ca/stmikes/index.html

The University of Winnipeg, Faculty of Theology,* (The United Church of Canada), 515 Portage Ave., Winnipeg, MB R3B 2E9. Ray Whitehead. Tel. (204)786-9390. Fax (204)772-2584 E-mail: ray.whitehead@uwinnipeg.ca

Vancouver School of Theology,* (Interdenominational), 6000 Iona Dr., Vancouver, BC V6T 1L4. W. J. Phillips. Tel. (604)822-9031. Fax (604)822-9212

Waterloo Lutheran Seminary,* (Evangelical Lutheran Church in Canada), 75 University Ave. W., Waterloo, ON N2L 3C5. Richard C. Crossman. Tel. (519)884-1970. Fax (519)725-2434 Website: http://www.wlu.ca/~wwwsem/

Western Christian College, (Churches of Christ in Canada), Box 5000, 220 Whitmore Ave. W., Dauphin, MB R7N 2V5. John McMillan. Tel. (204)638-8801. Fax (204)638-7054

Western Pentecostal Bible College, (The Pentecostal Assemblies of Canada), Box 1700, Abbotsford, BC V2S 7E7. James G. Richards. Tel. (604)853-7491. Fax (604)853-8951 E-mail: wpbcr@uniserve.com

Winkler Bible Institute, (Canadian Conference of Mennonite Brethren Churches), 121 7 St. S., Winkler, MB R6W 2N4. Paul Kroeker. Tel. (204)325-4242. Fax (204)325-9028

Wycliffe College,* (The Anglican Church of Canada), 5 Hoskin Ave., Toronto, ON M5S 1H7. Rev. Dr. Alan L. Hayes. Tel. (416)946-3521. Fax (416)946-3545

10. Religious Periodicals in the United States

This list focuses on publications of the organizations listed in Chapter 3 of the Directories section, however, there are also some independent publications listed. Regional publications and newsletters are not included.

Perhaps the most inclusive list of religious periodicals published in the United States can be found in *Gale Directory of Publications and Broadcast Media* (Gale Research, Inc., P.O. Box 33477, Detroit, MI 48232-5477).

Each entry gives: the title of the periodical, frequency of publication, religious affiliation, editor's name, address, telephone and fax number when known and e-mail and website addresses when available. Frequency of publication is indicated in parenthesis following the title.

21st Century Christian, (m) Churches of Christ, M. Norvel Young and Prentice A. Meador, Jr., P.O. Box 40304, Nashville, TN 37204. Tel. (800)331-5991. Fax (615)385-5915

Action, (10/yr) Churches of Christ, Tex Williams, Box 9346, Austin, TX 78766. Tel. (512)345-8191. Fax (512)345-6634

Adra Today, (q) Seventh-day Adventist Church, Beth Schaefer, 12501 Old Columbia Pike, Silver Spring, MD 20904-6600. Tel. (301)680-6355. Fax (301)680-6370

Adult Lessons Quarterly, (q) Nondenominational, Braille and Cassette Only, Darcy Quigley, J. Milton Society for the Blind, 475 Riverside Dr., Rm. 455, New York, NY 10115-0122. Tel. (212)870-3335. Fax (212)870-3229 Website: http://www.jmsblind.org

Adult Quarterly, The, (q) Associate Reformed Presbyterian Church (General Synod), W. H. F. Kuykendall, Ph.D., P.O. 575, Due West, SC 29693. Tel. (864)232-8297

Advent Christian News, (m) Advent Christian Church, Keith D. Wheaton, P.O. Box 23152, Charlotte, NC 28227. Tel. (704)545-6161. Fax (704)573-0712

Advent Christian Witness, The, (m) Advent Christian Church, Keith D. Wheaton, P.O. Box 23152, Charlotte, NC 28227. Tel. (704)545-6161. Fax (704)573-0712

Adventist Review, (w) Seventh-day Adventist Church, W. G. Johnsson, 12501 Old Columbia Pike, Silver Spring, MD 20904-6600. Tel. (301)680-6560. Fax (301)680-6638

Advocate, The, (10/yr) Kay Collier-Slone, P.O. Box 610, Lexington, KY 40586-0610. Tel. (606)252-6527. Fax (606)231-9077

Again Magazine, (q) The Antiochian Orthodox Christian Archdiocese of North America, John W. Hardenbrook, P.O. Box 76, Ben Lomond, CA 95005-0076. Tel. (408)336-5118. Fax (408)336-8882

Agenda, (10/yr.) Church of the Brethren, Newsletter for Congregational Leadership, Howard Royer and Nevin Dulabaum, 1451 Dundee Ave., Elgin, IL 60120-1674. Tel. (847)742-5100

ALERT, (q) Universal Fellowship of Metropolitan Community Churches, A. Stephen Pieters, 8704 Santa Monica Blvd., 2nd Fl., West Hollywood, CA 90069. Tel. (310)360-8640. Fax (310)360-8680

Alive Now, (6/yr) The United Methodist Church, George Graham, P.O. Box 189, Nashville, TN 37202. Tel. (615)340-7218

Allegheny Wesleyan Methodist, The, (m) Allegheny Wesleyan Methodist Connection (Original Allegheny Conference), Michael Marshall, P.O. Box 357, Salem, OH 44460. Tel. (330)337-9376. Fax (330)337-9700

Alliance Life, (bi-w) The Christian and Missionary Alliance, P.O. Box 35000, Colorado Springs, CO 80935. Tel. (719)599-5999. Fax (719)593-8692

A.M.E. Christian Recorder, The, (bi-w) African Methodist Episcopal Church, Ricky Spain, Editor, 500 8th Ave. S., Suite 213, Nashville, TN 37203. Tel. (615)256-8548. Fax (615)244-1833

A.M.E. Review, (q) African Methodist Episcopal Church, Paulette Coleman, Ph.D., 500 Eighth Ave. S., Ste. 211, Nashville, TN 37203-4181. Tel. (615)256-7020. Fax (615) 256-7092. E-mail: Amervw@Aol.com

American Baptist Quarterly, (q) American Baptist Churches in the U.S.A., William R. Millar, P.O. Box 851, Valley Forge, PA 19482-0851. Tel. (610)768-2269

American Baptists In Mission, (6/yr) American Baptist Churches in the U.S.A., Richard W. Schramm, P.O. Box 851, Valley Forge, PA 19482-0851. Tel. (610)768-2077. Fax (610) 768-2320

American Bible Society Record, (6/yr) Nondenominational, Mike Maus, 1865 Broad-

US PERIODICALS

295

way, New York, NY 10023-7505. Tel. (212) 408-1419. Fax (212)408-1456

American Jewish History, (q) Jewish, Marc Lee Raphael, 2 Thornton Rd., Waltham, MA 02154. Tel. (617)891-8110. Fax (617)899-9208

Armenian Church, The, (m) Diocese of the Armenian Church of America, Michael A. Zeytoonian, 630 Second Ave., New York, NY 10016. Tel. (212)686-0710. Fax (212)779-3558

Associate Reformed Presbyterian, The, (m) Associate Reformed Presbyterian Church (General Synod), Ben Johnston, One Cleveland St., Greenville, SC 29601. Tel. (864)232-8297. Fax (864)271-3729

At Ease, (bi-m) Assemblies of God, Lemuel D. McElyea, 1445 Boonville Ave., Springfield, MO 65802. Tel. (417)862-2781. Fax (417) 863-7276

Attack, A Magazine for Christian Men, (q) National Association of Free Will Baptists, James E. Vallance, P.O. Box 5002, Antioch, TN 37011-5002. Tel. (615)731-4950 ext. 281. Fax (615)731-0771

Banner of Truth, The, (m) Netherlands Reformed Congregations, J. den Hoed, 824 18th Ave. S., Rock Valley, IA 51247. Tel. (712)476-2442

Banner, The, (w) Christian Reformed Church in North America, John A. Suk, 2850 Kalamazoo Ave. S.E., Grand Rapids, MI 49560. Tel. (616) 224-0732. Fax (616)224-0834

Baptist Bible Tribune, The, (m) Baptist Bible Fellowship International, Mike Randall, P.O. Box 309 HSJ, Springfield, MO 65801. Tel. (417)831-3996. Fax (417)831-1470

Baptist Bulletin, (m) General Association of Regular Baptist Churches, David M. Gower, Editor, 1300 N. Meacham Rd., Schaumburg, IL 60173-4806. Tel. (847)843-1600. Fax (847)843-3757
E-mail: baptistbulletin@garbc.org
Website: http://www.garbc.org

Baptist History and Heritage, (3/yr) Southern Baptist Historical Society, Slayden A. Yarbrough, Oklahoma Baptist University, 500 W. University, Box 61838, Shawnee, OK 74804-2590. Tel. (800)966-2278. Fax (405)878-2233

Baptist Leader, (q) American Baptist Churches in the U.S.A., Donald Ng, P.O. Box 851, Valley Forge, PA 19482-0851. Tel. (610)768-2143. Fax (610)768-2056

Baptist Peacemaker, (q) Baptist, Ken Sehested, P.O. Box 280, Lake Junaluska, NC 28745. Tel. (704)456-1881. Fax (704)456-1883

Baptist Peacemaker, (q) Nondenominational, Ken Sehested, P.O. Box 280, Lake Junaluska, NC 28745. Tel. (704)456-1881. Fax (704)456-1883

Baptist Progress, (q) Progressive National Baptist Convention, Inc., Archie Logan, 601 50th St. N.E., Washington, DC 20019. Tel. (202)396-0558. Fax (202)398-4998

Baptist Witness, (m) Primitive Baptists, Lasserre Bradley, Jr., Box 17037, Cincinnati, OH 45217. Tel. (513)821-7289. Fax (513)821-7303

Bible Advocate, The, (m) The Church of God (Seventh Day), Denver, Colo., Calvin Burrell, P.O. Box 33677, Denver, CO 80233. Tel. (303)452-7973. Fax (303)452-0657

Brethren Evangelist, The, (m) Brethren Church (Ashland, Ohio), Richard C. Winfield, 524 College Ave., Ashland, OH 44805. Tel. (419)289-1708. Fax (419)281-0450

Brethren Journal, (10/yr) Unity of the Brethren, Milton Maly, 6703 FM 2502, Brenham, TX 77833-9803. Tel. (409)830-8762

Bridegroom's Messenger, The, (bi-m) The International Pentecostal Church of Christ, Janice Boyce, 121 W. Hunters Tr., Elizabeth City, NC 27909. Tel. (919)338-3003. Fax (919)338-3003

Builder, (m) Mennonite, David R. Hiebert, 616 Walnut Ave., Scottdale, PA 15683. Tel. (724)887-3363 ext. 281. Fax (724)887-3111

Burning Bush, The, (bi-m) The Metropolitan Church Association, Inc., E. L. Adams, The Metropolitan Church Association, 323 Broad St., Lake Geneva, WI 53147. Tel. (414)248-6786

Calvary Messenger, The, (m) Beachy Amish Mennonite Churches, David Sommers, Rt. 2, Box 187-A, Abbeville, SC 29620. Tel. (814)662-2483

Campus Life, (9/yr) Nondenominational, Harold B. Smith, 465 Gunderson Dr., Carol Stream, IL 60188. Tel. (630)260-6200. Fax (630)260-0114

Capsule, (m) General Association of General Baptists, Jack Eberhardt, 100 Stinson Dr., Poplar Bluff, MO 63901. Tel. (573)785-7746. Fax (573)785-0564

Caring, (6/yr) Assemblies of God, Owen Wilkie, 1445 Boonville Ave., Springfield, MO 65802. Tel. (417)862-2781. Fax (417)862-4832

Cathedral Age, (q) Interdenominational, Craig W. Stapert, Mass. & Wisconsin Ave. N.W., Washington, DC 20016-5098. Tel. (202)537-5681. Fax (202)364-6600

Catholic Chronicle, (bi-w) The Roman Catholic Church, Patricia Lynn Morrison, 2130

Madison Ave., P.O. Box 1866, Toledo, OH 43603-1866. Tel. (419)243-4178. Fax (419)243-4235

Catholic Digest, (m) The Roman Catholic Church, Richard Reece, Editor, 2115 Summit Ave., St. Paul, MN 55105-1081. Tel. (612)962-6725. Fax (612)962-6755
E-mail: cdigest@stthomas.edu
Website: http://www.CatholicDigest.org

Catholic Herald, (w) The Roman Catholic Church, Ethel M. Gintoft, 3501 S. Lake Dr., St. Francis, WI 53235-0913. Tel. (414)769-3500. Fax (414)769-3468
E-mail: chn@execpc.com

Catholic Light, (bi-w) The Roman Catholic Church, Jerome M. Zufelt, 300 Wyoming Ave., Scranton, PA 18503. Tel. (717)346-8915. Fax (717)346-8917

Catholic Peace Voice, The, (q) The Roman Catholic Church, Dave Robinson, 532 W. 8th St., Erie, PA 16502. Tel. (814)453-4955. Fax (814)452-4784

Catholic Review, The, (w) The Roman Catholic Church, Daniel L. Medinger, P.O. Box 777, Baltimore, MD 21203. Tel. (410)625-8477. Fax (410)332-1069

Catholic Standard and Times, (w) The Roman Catholic Church, Paul S. Quinter, 222 N. 17th St., Philadelphia, PA 19103. Tel. (215)587-3660. Fax (215)587-3979

Catholic Transcript, The, (w) The Roman Catholic Church, Christopher M. Tiano, 785 Asylum Ave., Hartford, CT 06105-2886. Tel. (203)527-1175. Fax (203)947-6397

Catholic Universe Bulletin, (bi-w) The Roman Catholic Church, Dennis Sadowski, 1027 Superior Ave., Cleveland, OH 44114-2556. Tel. (216)696-6525 ext. 2010. Fax (216)696-6519

Catholic Worker, (7/yr) The Roman Catholic Church, Brian Harte, 36 E. First St., New York, NY 10003. Tel. (212)777-9617

CCAR Journal: A Reform Jewish Quarterly, (q) Jewish, Henry Bamberger, 192 Lexington Ave., New York, NY 10016. Tel. (212)684-4990. Fax (212)689-1649

Cela Biedrs, (10/yr) The Latvian Evangelical Lutheran Church in America, Velta Pelcis, 5808 W. Carmen Ave., Milwaukee, WI 53218-2051. Tel. (414)463-6613

Celebration: An Ecumenical Worship Resource, (m) Interdenominational, Patrick Marrin, P.O. Box 419493, Kansas City, MO 64141-6493. Tel. (816)531-0538. Fax (816)968-2280

Challenge, The, (q) The Bible Church of Christ, Inc., Alice M. Jones, 1358 Morris Ave., Bronx,

NY 10456. Tel. (718)588-2284. Fax (718)992-5597

Charisma, (m) Nondenominational, J. Lee Grady, 600 Rinehart Rd., Lake Mary, FL 32746. Tel. (407)333-0600. Fax (407)333-7133

Childlife, (q) Nondenominational, Terry Madison, P.O. Box 9716, Federal Way, WA 98063-9716. Tel. (206)815-2300. Fax (206)815-3445

Children's Friend, (q) Seventh-day Adventist Church, Richard Kaiser, P.O. Box 6097, Lincoln, NE 68506. Tel. (402)488-0981. Fax (402)488-7582

Christadelphian Advocate, (m) Christadelphians, Edward W. Farrar, 4 Mountain Park Ave., Hamilton, ON L9A 1A2. Tel. (905)383-1817 Fax (905)383-2705

Christadelphian Tidings, (m) Christadelphians, Donald H. Styles, 42076 Hartford Dr., Canton, MI 48187. Tel. (313)844-2426. Fax (313)844-8304

Christadelphian Watchman, (m) Christadelphians, George Booker, 2500 Berwyn Cir., Austin, TX 78745. Tel. (512)447-8882

Christian Baptist, The, (m) Primitive Baptists, S. T. Tolley, P.O. Box 68, Atwood, TN 38220. Tel. (901)662-7417

Christian Bible Teacher, (m) Churches of Christ, J. J. Turner, Box 1060, Abilene, TX 79604. Tel. (915)677-6262. Fax (915)677-1511

Christian Century, The, (37/yr) Nondenominational, James M. Wall, 407 S. Dearborn St., Chicago, IL 60605. Tel. (312)427-5380. Fax (312)427-1302

Christian Chronicle, The, (m) Churches of Christ, Bailey McBride, Box 11000, Oklahoma City, OK 73136-1100. Tel. (405)425-5070. Fax (405)425-5076

Christian Community, The, (8/yr) International Council of Community Churches, Dr. J. Ralph Shotwell, Interim Exec. Dir., 21116 Washington Pky., Frankfort, IL 60423. Tel. (815)464-5690. Fax (815)464-5692

Christian Education Counselor, (bi-m) Assemblies of God, Sylvia Lee, Sunday School Promotion and Training, 1445 Boonville Ave., Springfield, MO 65802-1894. Tel. (417)862-2781. Fax (417)862-0503

Christian Endeavor World, The, (q) Nondenominational, David G. Jackson, 3575 Valley Rd., P.O. Box 820, Liberty Corner, NJ 07938-0820. Tel. (908)604-9440. Fax (908)604-6075

Christian Index, The, (m) Christian Methodist Episcopal Church, Lawrence L. Reddick, III,

P.O. Box 665, Memphis, TN 38101-0665. Tel. (901)345-1173

Christian Leader, (m) U.S. Conference of Mennonite Brethren Churches, Editor, Box V, Hillsboro, KS 67063. Tel. (316)947-5543. Fax (316)947-3266

Christian Living, (8/yr) Mennonite Church, Levi Miller, 616 Walnut Ave., Scottdale, PA 15683. Tel. (412)887-8500. Fax (412)887-3111

Christian Ministry, The, (6/yr) Nondenominational, James M. Wall, 407 S. Dearborn St., Chicago, IL 60605. Tel. (312)427-5380. Fax (312)427-1302

Christian Monthly, (m) Apostolic Lutheran Church of America, Alvin Holmgren, 1327 9th Ave. N., Edmonds, WA 98020. Tel. (360)687-4416

Christian Outlook, (m) Pentecostal Assemblies of the World, Inc., Johnna E. Hampton, 3939 Meadows Dr., Indianapolis, IN 46205. Tel. (317)547-9541. Fax (317)543-0512

Christian Reader, The, (bi-m) Nondenominational, Bonne Steffen, 465 Gundersen Dr., Carol Stream, IL 60188. Tel. (630)260-6200. Fax (630)260-0114

Christian Record, (q) Seventh-day Adventist Church, Richard Kaiser, P.O. Box 6097, Lincoln, NE 68506. Tel. (402)488-0981. Fax (402)488-7582

Christian Science Journal, The, (m) Church of Christ, Scientist, William E. Moody, One Norway St., P-602, Boston, MA 02115. Tel. (617)450-2014. Fax (617)450-2707

Christian Science Monitor, The, (d & w) Church of Christ, Scientist, David T. Cook, One Norway St., Boston, MA 02115. Tel. (617)450-2000. Fax (617)450-7575

Christian Science Quarterly Bible Lessons, (q) Church of Christ, Scientist, Pamela Lishin Jones, One Norway St., P-980, Boston, MA 02115. Tel. (617)450-2000. Fax (617)450-2930

Christian Science Sentinel, (w) Church of Christ, Scientist, William E. Moody, One Norway St., P-602, Boston, MA 02115. Tel. (617)450-2000. Fax (617)450-2707

Christian Social Action, (m) The United Methodist Church, Lee Ranck, 100 Maryland Ave. N.E., Washington, DC 20002. Tel. (202)488-5621. Fax (202)488-1617

Christian Standard, (w) Christian Churches and Churches of Christ, Sam E. Stone, 8121 Hamilton Ave., Cincinnati, OH 45231. Tel. (513)931-4050. Fax (513)931-0950

Christian Woman, (bi-m) Churches of Christ, Sandra Humphrey, Box 150, Nashville, TN

37202. Tel. (615)254-8781. Fax (615)254-7411

Christianity & The Arts, (q) Non-denominational, Marci Whitney-Schenck, P.O. Box 118088, Chicago, IL 60611. Tel. (312)642-8606. Fax (312)266-7719

Church & Society Magazine, (bi-m) Presbyterian Church (U.S.A.), Kathy Lancaster, 100 Witherspoon St., Louisville, KY 40202-1396. Tel. (502)569-5810. Fax (502)569-8116

Church and State, (m) Independent, Journal of Religion and Politics, Joseph L. Conn, 1816 Jefferson Pl. N.W., Washington, DC 20036. Tel. (202)466-2587

Church Advocate, The, (q) Churches of God, General Conference, Evelyn J. Sloat, P.O. Box 926, 700 E. Melrose Ave., Findlay, OH 45839. Tel. (419)424-1961. Fax (419)424-3433 E-mail: ejs@brt.bright.net

Church Bytes, (6/yr) Nondenominational, Neil B. Houk, 304C Crossfield Dr., Versailles, KY 40383. Tel. (606)873-0550. Fax (606)879-0121

Church Herald, The, (11/yr) Reformed Church in America, Christina Van Eyl, 4500 60th St. S.E., Grand Rapids, MI 49512. Tel. (616)698-7071 Fax (616)698-6606

Church History, (q) Nondenominational, Elizabeth Clark, and Grant Wacker and Hans Willebr and Richard Heitzenrater,The Divinity School, Duke University, Box 90975, Durham, NC 27708-0971 5. Tel. (919)660-3436. Fax (919)660-3473

Church Messenger, The, (bi-m) James S. Dutko, 280 Clinton St., Binghamton, NY 13905. Tel. —

Church School Herald, (q) African Methodist Episcopal Zion Church, Mary A. Love, P.O. Box 32305, Charlotte, NC 28232-2305. Tel. (704)332-9873. Fax (704)333-1769

Church of God Evangel, (m) Church of God (Cleveland, Tenn.), Homer G. Rhea, P.O. Box 2250, Cleveland, TN 37320-2250. Tel. (423)478-7592. Fax (423)478-7521

Church of God Missions, (bi-m) Church of God (Anderson, Ind.), J. David Reames, Box 2337, Anderson, IN 46018-2337. Tel. (765)648-2128 .Fax (765)642-4279

Church of God Progress Journal, (bi-m) Church of God General Conference (Oregon, IL and Morrow, GA), David Krogh, Box 100,000, Morrow, GA 30260. Tel. (404)362-0052. Fax (404)362-9307

Churchman's Human Quest, The, Nondenominational, Edna Ruth Johnson, 1074 23rd Ave.

N., St. Petersburg, FL 33704. Tel. (813)894-0097

Churchwoman, (q) Interdenominational, Martha M. Cruz, 475 Riverside Dr., Ste. 500, New York, NY 10115. Tel. (212)870-2344. Fax (212)870-2338

Circuit Rider, (6/yr.) The United Methodist Church, Jill S. Reddig, 201 Eighth Ave. S., Nashville, TN 37202. Tel. (615)749-6334. Fax (615)749-6512

Clarion Herald, (bi-w) The Roman Catholic Church, Peter P. Finney, Jr., P. O. Box 53247, 1000 Howard Ave., Suite 400, New Orleans, LA 70153. Tel. (504)596-3035. Fax (504)596-3020

Clergy Journal, The, (10/yr) Nondenominational, Sharilyn A. Figuroa and Clyde Steckel, 6160 Carmen Ave. E., Inver Grove Heights, MN 55076-4422. Tel. (800)328-0200. Fax (612)457-4617

Club Connection, (q) Assemblies of God, Kerry Clarensau, 1445 Boonville Ave., Springfield, MO 65802-1894. Tel. (417)862-2781. Fax (417)862-0503

Co-Laborer, (bi-m) National Association of Free Will Baptists, Suzanne Franks, Women Nationally Active for Christ, P.O. Box 5002, Antioch, TN 37011-5002. Tel. (615)731-6812. Fax (615)731-0771
E-mail: Colaborer@nafwb.org

Collegiate Quarterly, (q) Seventh-day Adventist Church, Gary B. Swanson, 12501 Old Columbia Pike, Silver Spring, MD 20904. Tel. (301)680-6160. Fax (301)680-6155

Columbia, (m) The Roman Catholic Church, Richard McMunn, One Columbus Plaza, New Haven, CT 06510. Tel. (203)772-2130. Fax (203)777-0114

Commission, The, (12/yr) International Mission Board, Southern Baptist Convention, Mary Jane Welch, Box 6767, Richmond, VA 23230-0767. Tel. (804)219-1327. Fax (804)219-1410

Common Lot, (q) United Church of Christ, Martha J. Hunter, 700 Prospect Ave., Cleveland, OH 44115. Tel. (216)736-2150. Fax (216)736-2156

Commonweal, (bi-w) The Roman Catholic Church, Margaret O'Brien Steinfels, 475 Riverside Dr., Rm. 405, New York, NY 10115. Tel. (212)662-4200. Fax (212)662-4183

Communique, (m) National Baptist Convention of America, Inc., Robert Jeffrey, 1320 Pierre Ave., Shreveport, LA 71103. Tel. (318)221-3701. Fax (318)222-7512

Congregationalist, The, (5/yr) National Association of Congregational Christian

Churches, Joe Polhemus, 1105 Briarwood Rd., Mansfield, OH 44907. Tel. (419)756-5526. Fax (419)524-2621

Conqueror, (bi-m) United Pentecostal Church International, John F. Sills, 8855 Dunn Rd., Hazelwood, MO 63042. Tel. (314)837-7300. Fax (314)837-4503

Conservative Judaism, (q) Jewish, Amy Gottlieb, 3080 Broadway, New York, NY 10027. Tel. (212)678-8060. Fax (212)749-9166

Contact, (m) National Association of Free Will Baptists, Jack Williams, P.O. Box 5002, Antioch, TN 37011-5002. Tel. (615)731-6812. Fax (615)731-0771

Context, (22/yr) Nondenominational, Martin Marty, 205 W. Monroe St., Chicago, IL 60606-5013. Tel. (312)236-7782. Fax (312)236-8207

Cornerstone Connections, (q) Seventh-day Adventist Church, Gary B. Swanson, 12501 Old Columbia Pike, Silver Spring, MD 20904. Tel. (301)680-6160. Fax (301)680-6155

Courage in the Struggle for Justice and Peace, (q) United Church of Christ, Sandy Sorensen, 110 Maryland Ave. N.E., Ste. 207, Washington, DC 20002. Tel. (202)543-1517. Fax (202)543-5994

Covenant Companion, (m) The Evangelical Covenant Church, Donald L. Meyer, 5101 N. Francisco Ave., Chicago, IL 60625. Tel. (773)784-3000. Fax (773)784-4366
E-mail: Covcom@compuserve.com

Covenant Home Altar, (q) The Evangelical Covenant Church, Donald L. Meyer, 5101 N. Francisco Ave., Chicago, IL 60625. Tel. (773)784-3000. Fax (773)784-4366
E-mail: Covcom@compuserve.com

Covenant Quarterly, (q) The Evangelical Covenant Church, Wayne C. Weld, 3225 W. Foster Ave., Chicago, IL 60625-4895. Tel. (773)244-6230. Fax (773)244-6244

Covenanter Witness, The, (11/yr) Reformed Presbyterian Church of North America, Drew Gordon and Lynne Gordon, 7408 Penn Ave., Pittsburgh, PA 15208. Tel. (412)241-0436. Fax (412)731-8861

Credinta-The Faith, (q) The Romanian Orthodox Church in America, Vasile Vasilachi, 45-03 48th Ave., Woodside, Queens, NY 11377. Tel. (313)893-8390

Credo, (m) The Antiochian Orthodox Christian Archdiocese of North America, Charles Dinkler, P.O. Box 84, Stanton, NJ 08885-0084. Tel. (908)236-7890

Criterion, The, (w) The Roman Catholic Church, John F. Fink, P.O. Box 1717, 1400 N.

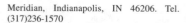

Meridian, Indianapolis, IN 46206. Tel. (317)236-1570

Cross Walk, (w) Church of the Nazarene, Jim Hampton, Word Action Publishing, 6401 The Paseo, Kansas City, MO 64131. Tel. (816)333-7000. Fax (816)333-4315

Cumberland Flag, The, (m) Cumberland Presbyterian Church in America, Robert Stanley Wood, 226 Church St., Huntsville, AL 35801. Tel. (205)536-7481. Fax (205)536-7482

Cumberland Presbyterian, The, (15/yr) Cumberland Presbyterian Church, M. Jacqueline De Berry Warren, 1978 Union Ave., Memphis, TN 38104. Tel. (901)276-4572. Fax (901)272-3913

Currents in Theology and Mission, (6/yr) Evangelical Lutheran Church in America, Ralph W. Klein, 1100 E. 55th St., Chicago, IL 60615. Tel. (773)256-0721. Fax (773)256-0782
E-mail: currents@lstc.edu

Decision, (12/yr) Nondenominational, Roger C. Palms, 1300 Harmon Pl., Minneapolis, MN 55403. Tel. (612)338-0500. Fax (612)335-1299

Disciple, The, (m) Christian Church (Disciples of Christ), Patricia R. Case, 130 E. Washington St., P.O. Box 1986, Indianapolis, IN 46206-1986. Tel. (317)635-3100. Fax (317)635-3700

Discovery, (q) Nondenominational, Braille Only, for Youth 8-18, Darcy Quigley, J. Milton Society for the Blind, 475 Riverside Dr., Rm. 455, New York, NY 10115-0122. Tel. (212)870-3335. Fax (212)870-3229
Website: http://www.jmsblind.org

Doors and Windows, (q) The Evangelical Congregational Church, Timothy Christman, 100 W. Park Ave., Myerstown, PA 17067.

Ecu-Link, (q) Interdenominational, Sarah Vilankulu, 475 Riverside Dr., Rm. 850, New York, NY 10115-0050. Tel. (212)870-2227. Fax (212)870-2030

Ecumenical Trends, (m) Nondenominational, Kevin McMorrow, P.O. Box 300, Garrison, NY 10524. Tel. (914)424-3671

El Aposento Alto, (6/yr) The United Methodist Church, Carmen Gaud, P.O. Box 189, Nashville, TN 37202. Tel. (615)340-7246. Fax (615)340-7006

El Intérprete, (6/yr) The United Methodist Church, P.O. Box 320, Nashville, TN 37202. Tel. (615)742-5115. Fax (615)742-5460

Eleventh Hour Messenger, (bi-m) Wesleyan Holiness Association of Churches, John

Brewer, R R 2, Box 9, Winchester, IN 47394. Tel. (317)584-3199

Elim Herald, (q) Elim Fellowship, Bernard J. Evans, 7245 College St., Lima, NY 14485. Tel. (716)582-2790. Fax (716)624-1229

EMC Today, (bi-m) Evangelical Mennonite Church, Donald W. Roth, 1420 Kerrway Ct., Fort Wayne, IN 46805. Tel. (219)423-3649. Fax (219)420-1905

Emphasis on Faith and Living, (bi-m) The Missionary Church, Robert Ransom, P.O. Box 9127, Ft. Wayne, IN 46899. Tel. (219)747-2027. Fax (219)747-5331

Enrichment: A Journal for Pentecostal Ministry, (q) Assemblies of God, Wayde I. Goodall, 1445 Boonville Ave., Springfield, MO 65802. Tel. (417)862-2781. Fax (417)862-0416

Ensign, The, (m) The Church of Jesus Christ of Latter-day Saints, Jay M. Todd, Managing Editor, 50 E. North Temple St., 23rd Fl., Salt Lake City, UT 84150-3224. Tel. (801)240-2950. Fax (801)240-5997

Epiphany Journal, (q) Interdenominational, Nun Macaria, 1516 N. Delaware, Indianapolis, IN 46202. Tel. (317)926-7468

Episcopal Life, (m) Episcopal Church, Jerrold F. Hames, 815 2nd Ave., New York, NY 10017-4503. Tel. (800)334-7626 ext. 5398. Fax (212)949-8059

Evangel, The, (10/yr) The American Association of Lutheran Churches, Charles D. Eidum, 10800 Lyndale Ave. S., #210, Minneapolis, MN 55420-5614. Tel. (612)884-7784. Fax (612)884-7894

Evangel, The, (q) The Evangelical Church Alliance, Derick Miller, 205 W. Broadway, Bradley, IL 60915. Tel. (815)937-0720. Fax (815)937-0001

Evangelical Advocate, The, (m) Churches of Christ in Christian Union, Ralph Hux, P.O. Box 30, Circleville, OH 43113. Tel. (740)474-8856. Fax (740)477-7766

Evangelical Beacon, (7/yr) The Evangelical Free Church of America, Carol Madison, 901 East 78th St., Minneapolis, MN 55420-1300. Tel. (612)854-1300. Fax (612)853-8488

Evangelical Challenge, The, (bi-m) The Evangelical Church, John F. Sills, Evangelical Church Missions, 7733 West River Rd., Minneapolis, MN 55444-2190. Tel. (612)561-0886. Fax (612)561-0774

Evangelical Visitor, (m) Brethren in Christ Church, Glen A. Pierce, P.O. Box 166, Nappanee, IN 46550. Tel. (219)773-3164. Fax (219)773-5934

Evangelism USA, (m) International Pentecostal Holiness Church, Dr. Ronald W. Carpenter,

Sr., P.O. Box 12609, Oklahoma City, OK 73157. Tel. (405)787-7110. Fax (405)789-3957

Evangelist, The, (w) The Roman Catholic Church, James Breig, 40 N. Main Ave., Albany, NY 12203. Tel. (518)453-6688. Fax (518)453-6793
E-mail: evannews@global2000.net
Website: http://www.evangelist.org

Explorations, (q) Nondenominational, Irvin J. Borowsky, 321 Chestnut St., 4th Fl., Philadelphia, PA 19106-2779. Tel. (215)925-2800. Fax (215)925-3800

Extension, (m) The Roman Catholic Church, Bradley Collins, 150 S. Wacker Dr. 20th Fl., Chicago, IL 60606. Tel. (312)236-7240. Fax (312)236-5276

Faith & Fellowship, (m) Church of the Lutheran Brethren of America, David Rinden, P.O. Box 655, Fergus Falls, MN 56538. Tel. (218)736-7357. Fax (218)736-2200

Faith and Truth, (m) Pentecostal Fire-Baptized Holiness Church, Edgar Vollratlt, 593 Harris-Lord Rd., Commerce, GA 30529. Tel. (706)335-5796

Faith-Life, (bi-m) Lutheran, Marcus Albrecht, 2107 N. Alexander St., Appleton, WI 54911. Tel. (920)733-1839. Fax (920)733-4834

Fellowship, (6/yr) Interfaith, Richard Deats, P.O. Box 271, Nyack, NY 10960-0271. Tel. (914)358-4601. Fax (914)358-1179

Fellowship Magazine, The, (6/yr) Assemblies of God International Fellowship (Independent/Not affiliated), T. A. Lanes, 5284 Eastgate Mall, San Diego, CA 92121. Tel. (619)677-9701. Fax (619)677-0038

Fellowship News, (m) Bible Fellowship Church, Carol Snyder, 2660 Allentown Rd., Quakertown, PA 18951.

Fellowship Tidings, (q) Full Gospel Fellowship of Churches and Ministers International, Chester P. Jenkins, 4325 W. Ledbetter Dr., Dallas, TX 75233. Tel. (214)339-1200. Fax (214)339-8790

Firm Foundation, (m) Churches of Christ, H. A. Dobbs, P.O. Box 690192, Houston, TX 77269-0192. Tel. (713)469-3102. Fax (713)469-7115

First Things: A Monthly Journal of Religion and Public, (m) Interdenominational, Richard J. Neuhaus, 156 Fifth Ave., Ste. 400, New York, NY 10010. Tel. (212)627-1985. Fax (212)627-2184

Flaming Sword, The, (m) Bible Holiness Church, Susan Davolt, 10th St. & College Ave., Independence, KS 67301. Tel. (316)331-2580. Fax (316)331-2580

For the Poor, (bi-m) Primitive Baptists, W. Hartsel Cayce, P.O. Box 38, Thornton, AR 71766. Tel. (501)352-3694

Foresee, (bi-m) Conservative Congregational Christian Conference, Walter F. Smith, 7582 Currell Blvd., #108, St. Paul, MN 55125. Tel. (612)739-1474. Fax (612)739-0750

Forum Letter, (m) Independent, Intra-Lutheran, Russell E. Saltzman, P.O. Box 638, Stover, MO 65078-0368. Tel. (573)377-2819
E-mail: Saltzman@midmo.net

Forward, (q) United Pentecostal Church International, J. L. Hall, 8855 Dunn Rd., Hazelwood, MO 63042. Tel. (314)837-7300. Fax (314)837-4503

Foursquare World Advance, (6/yr) International Church of the Foursquare Gospel, Ron Williams, P.O. Box 26902, 1910 W. Sunset Blvd., Ste. 200, Los Angeles, CA 90026-0176. Tel. (213)989-4220. Fax (213)989-4544

Free Methodist World Mission People, (6/yr) Free Methodist Church of North America, Dan Runyon, P.O. Box 535002, Indianapolis, IN 46253-5002. Tel. (317)244-3660. Fax (317)244-1247

Free Will Baptist Gem, (m) National Association of Free Will Baptists, Nathan Ruble, P.O. Box 991, Lebanon, MO 65536. Tel. (417)532-6537

Free Will Baptist, The, (m) Original Free Will Baptist Church, Tracy A. McCoy, P.O. Box 159, 811 N. Lee St., Ayden, NC 28513. Tel. (919)746-6128. Fax (919)746-9248

Free Will Bible College Bulletin, (6/yr) National Association of Free Will Baptists, Bert Tippett, 3606 West End Ave., Nashville, TN 37205. Tel. (615)383-1340. Fax (615)269-6028

Friend Magazine, (m) The Church of Jesus Christ of Latter-day Saints, Vivian Paulsen, 50 E. South Temple St., 23rd Fl., Salt Lake City, UT 84150. Tel. (801)240-2210. Fax (801)240-5997

Friends Bulletin, (10/yr) Religious Society of Friends (Unaffiliated Meetings), Anthony Manousos, 5238 Andalucia Court, Whittier, CA 90601. Tel. (310)699-5670

Friends Journal, (m) Friends General Conference, Vinton Deming, 1216 Arch St., 2A, Philadelphia, PA 19107-2835. Tel. (215)563-8629. Fax (215)568-1377
E-mail: Friendsjnl@aol.com

Friends Voice, The, (q) Evangelical Friends International-North America Region, Becky Towne, 2748 E. Pikes Peak Ave., Colorado Springs, CO 80909. Tel. (719)635-4011. Fax (719)632-5721

Front Line, Conservative Baptist Association of America, Al Russell, P.O. Box 66, Wheaton, IL 60189. Tel. (630)260-3800. Fax (630)653-5387 E-mail: Chapalruss@aol.com

Full Gospel Ministries Outreach Report, (q) Full Gospel Assemblies International, Simeon Strauser, P.O. Box 1230, Coatsville, PA 19320. Tel. (610)857-2357. Fax (610)857-3109

Gem, The, (w) Churches of God, General Conference, Evelyn J. Sloat, P.O. Box 926, Findlay, OH 45839. Tel. (419)424-1961. Fax (419)424-3433 E-mail: ejs@brt.bright.net

General Baptist Messenger, (m) General Association of General Baptists, Samuel S. Ramdial, 400 Stinson Dr., Poplar Bluff, MO 63901. Tel. (573)686-9051. Fax (573)686-5198

Gleaner, The, (m) Baptist Missionary Association of America, F. Donald Collins, P.O. Box 193920, Little Rock, AR 72219-3920. Tel. (501)455-4977. Fax (501)455-3636

Global Partners, (q) Baptist Bible Fellowship International, Loran McAlister, P.O. Box 191, Springfield, MO 65801. Tel. (417)862-5001. Fax (417)865-0794

God's Field, (bi-w) Polish National Catholic Church of America, Rt. Rev. Anthony M. Rysz, 1002 Pittston Ave., Scranton, PA 18505. Tel. (717)346-9131. Fax (717)346-2188

Gospel Advocate, (m) Churches of Christ, F. Furman Kearley, Box 150, Nashville, TN 37202. Tel. (615)254-8781. Fax (615)254-7411

Gospel Herald, (w) Mennonite Church, J. Lorne Peachey, 616 Walnut Ave., Scottdale, PA 15683. Tel. (412)887-8500. Fax (412)887-3111

Gospel Herald, The, (m) Church of God, Mountain Assembly, Inc., James Kilgore, P.O. Box 157, Jellico, TN 37762. Tel. (423)784-8260. Fax (423)784-3258

Gospel Light, The, (q) The Bible Church of Christ, Inc., Carol Crenshaw, 1358 Morris Ave., Bronx, NY 10456. Tel. (718)588-2284. Fax (718)992-5597

Gospel Messenger, The, (m) Congregational Holiness Church, Cullen L. Hicks, P.O. Box 643, Lincolnton, GA 30817. Tel. (706)359-4000

Gospel News, The, (m) The Church of Jesus Christ (Bickertonites), Donald Ross, 201 Royalbrooke Dr., Venetia, PA 15367. Tel. (412)348-6828 Fax (412)348-0919

Gospel Tidings, (bi-m) Fellowship of Evangelical Bible Churches, Robert L. Frey, 5800 S. 14th St., Omaha, NE 68107. Tel. (402)731-4780. Fax (402)731-1173

Gospel Truth, The, (m) Church of the Living God (Motto: Christian Workers for Fellowship), W. E. Crumes, 430 Forest Ave., Cincinnati, OH 45229. Tel. (513)569-5660. Fax (513)569-5661

Grow Magazine, (q) Church of the Nazarene, Neil B. Wiseman, 6401 The Paseo, Kansas City, MO 64131. Tel. (816)333-7000. Fax (816)361-5202

Guide, (w) Seventh-day Adventist Church, Timothy J. Lale, 55 W. Oak Ridge Dr., Hagerstown, MD 21740. Tel. (301)393-4037. Fax (301)393-4055 E-mail: guide@rhpa.org

Happy Harvester, The, (m) Church of God of Prophecy, Beth Anderson, P.O. Box 2910, Cleveland, TN 37320-2910. Tel. (423)559-5435. Fax (423)559-5444

Heart Beat, (m) The Evangelical Church, John F. Sills, 7733 West River Rd., Minneapolis, MN 55444. Tel. (612)561-0886. Fax (612)561-0774

Heartbeat, (bi-m) National Association of Free Will Baptists, Don Robirds, Foreign Missions Office, P.O. Box 5002, Antioch, TN 37011-5002. Tel. (615)731-6812. Fax (615)731-5345

Helping Hand, (bi-m) International Pentecostal Holiness Church, Doris Moore, P.O. Box 12609, Oklahoma City, OK 73157. Tel. (405)787-7110. Fax (405)789-3957

Herald of Christian Science, The, (m) Church of Christ, Scientist, William E. Moody, One Norway St., P-602, Boston, MA 02115. Tel. (617)450-2000. Fax (617)450-2707

Holiness Today, (m) Church of the Nazarene, 6401 The Paseo, Kansas City, MO 64131. Tel. (816)333-7000. Fax (816)333-1748

Heritage, (q) Assemblies of God, Wayne E. Warner, 1445 Boonville Ave., Springfield, MO 65802. Tel. (417)862-1447. Fax (417)862-8558

High Adventure, (q) Assemblies of God, Marshall Bruner, 1445 Boonville Ave., Springfield, MO 65802-1894. Tel. (417)862-2781. Fax (417)862-0416

Higher Way, (bi-m) Apostolic Faith Mission of Portland, Oregon, Dwight L. Baltzell, 6615 S.E. 52nd Ave., Portland, OR 97206. Tel. (503)777-1741. Fax (503)777-1743

Holiness Digest, (q) Nondenominational, Marlin Hotle, 263 Buffalo Rd., Clinton, TN 37716. Tel. (423)457-5978. Fax (423)463-7280

Holiness Union, The, (m) United Holy Church of America, Inc., Joseph T. Durham, 13102 Morningside Ln., Silver Spring, MD 20904. Tel. (301)989-9093. Fax (301)989-9202

302

Homelife, (6/yr) United Pentecostal Church International, Scott Graham, 8855 Dunn Rd., Hazelwood, MO 63042. Tel. (314)837-7300. Fax (314)837-4503

Homiletic and Pastoral Review, (m) The Roman Catholic Church, Kenneth Baker, 10 Audrey Pl., Fairfield, NJ 07004. Tel. (201)882-8700

Horizons, (7/yr) Presbyterian Church (U.S.A.), Marie Cross, Presbyterian Women, 100 Witherspoon St., Louisville, KY 40202-1396. Tel. (502)569-5367. Fax (502)569-8085

Horizons, (m) Christian Churches and Churches of Christ, Reggie Hundley, Box 13111, Knoxville, TN 37920-0111. Tel. (800)655-8524. Fax (423)577-9743

Image, (bi-m) Churches of Christ, Denny Boultinghouse, 3117 N. 7th St., West Monroe, LA 71291-2227. Tel. (318)396-4366

Insight, (w) Seventh-day Adventist Church, Lori L. Peckham, 55 W. Oak Ridge Dr., Hagerstown, MD 21740. Tel. (301)393-4038. Fax (301)393-4055 E-mail: insight@rhpa.org

Insight, (q) Advent Christian Church, Dawn Rutan, P.O. Box 23152, Charlotte, NC 28227. Tel. (704)545-6161. Fax (704)573-0712

Interlit, (q) Nondenominational, Susan Miller, 4050 Lee Vance View Dr., Colorado Springs, CO 80918. Tel. (719)536-0100. Fax (719)536-3266

International Bulletin of Missionary Research, (q) Nondenominational, Gerald H. Anderson, Overseas Ministries Study Ctr., 490 Prospect St., New Haven, CT 06511. Tel. (203)624-6672. Fax (203)865-2857

Interpretation, (q) Presbyterian Church (U.S.A.), Jack D. Kingsbury, 3401 Brook Rd., Richmond, VA 23227. Tel. (804)278-4296. Fax (804)278-4208

Interpreter, (8/yr) The United Methodist Church, M. Garlinda Burton, P.O. Box 320, Nashville, TN 37202-0320. Tel. (615)742-5107. Fax (615)742-5460

Islamic Horizons, (m) Muslims, Omer Bin Abdullah, P.O. Box 38, Plainfield, IN 46168. Tel. (317)839-8157. Fax (317)839-1840

Issachar File, (m) International Pentecostal Holiness Church, Shirley Spencer, P.O. Box 12609, Oklahoma City, OK 73157. Tel. (405)787-7110. Fax (405)789-3957

Jewish Action, (q) Jewish, Charlotte Friedland, 333 Seventh Ave., New York, NY 10001. Tel. (212)563-4000. Fax (212)613-8333

John Milton Magazine, (q) Nondenominational, Large Print, Darcy Quigley, J. Milton Society for the Blind, 475 Riverside Dr., Rm. 455, New York, NY 10115-0122. Tel. (212)870-3335. Fax (212)870-3229 Website: http://www.jmsblind.org

John Three Sixteen, (q) Bible Holiness Church, Mary Cunningham, 10th St. & College Ave., Independence, KS 67301. Tel. (316)331-2580. Fax (316)331-2580

Journal From the Radical Reformation, A, (q) Church of God General Conference (Oregon, IL and Morrow, GA), Kent Ross and Anthony Buzzard and Mark Mattison, Box 100,000, Morrow, GA 30260-7000. Tel. (404)362-0052. Fax (404)362-9307

Journal of Adventist Education, (5/yr) Seventh-day Adventist Church, Beverly Rumble, 12501 Old Columbia Pike, Silver Spring, MD 20904-6600. Tel. (301)680-5075. Fax (301)622-9627

Journal of Christian Education, (q) African Methodist Episcopal Church, Kenneth H. Hill, 500 Eighth Ave., S., Nashville, TN 37203. Tel. (615)242-1420. Fax (615)726-1866

Journal of Ecumenical Studies, (q) Interdenominational, Leonard Swidler, Temple Univ. (022-38), 1114 W. Berks St., Philadelphia, PA 19122-6090. Tel. (215)204-7714. Fax (215)204-4569

Journal of Pastoral Care, The, (q) Nondenominational, Orlo Strunk, Jr., 1068 Harbor Dr. S.W., Calabash, NC 28467. Tel. (910)579-5084. Fax (910)579-5084

Journal of Presbyterian History: Studies in Reformed History and Culture, (q) Presbyterian Church (U.S.A.), James H. Moorhead, 425 Lombard St., Philadelphia, PA 19147. Tel. (215)627-1852. Fax (215)627-0509

Journal of Theology, (q) Church of the Lutheran Confession, John Lau, Immanuel Lutheran College, 501 Grover Road, Eau Claire, WI 54701-7199. Tel. (715)832-9936. Fax (715)836-6634

Journal of the American Academy of Religion, (q) Nondenominational, Glenn Yocum, Whittier College, P.O. Box 634, Whittier, CA 90608-0634. Tel. (562)907-4200. Fax (562)907-4910

Joyful Noiseletter, The, (10/yr) Interdenominational, Cal Samra, P.O. Box 895, Portage, MI 49081-0895. Tel. (616)324-0990. Fax (616)324-3984

Judaism, (q) Jewish, Murray Baumgatter, 15 E. 84th St., New York, NY 10028-0458. Tel. (212)360-1586. Fax (212)249-3672

Keeping in Touch, (m) Universal Fellowship of Metropolitan Community Churches, Ravi Verma, 8704 Santa Monica Blvd., 2nd Fl., West Hollywood, CA 90069-4548. Tel. (310)360-8640. Fax (310)360-8680

Kindred Minds, (q) Sovereign Grace Baptists, Larry Scouten, P.O. Box 10, Wellsburg, NY 14894. Tel. (607)734-6985

Lantern, The, (bi-m) National Baptist Convention of America, Inc., Robert Jeffrey, 1320 Pierre Ave., Shreveport, LA 71103. Tel. (318)221-3701. Fax (318)222-7512

Leadership: A Practical Journal for Church Leaders, (q) Nondenominational, Kevin Miller, 465 Gundersen Dr., Carol Stream, IL 60188. Tel. (630)260-6200. Fax (630)260-0114

Leaves of Healing (q) Christian Catholic Church (Evangekical-Protestant), 2500 Dowie Memorial Dr., Zion, IL 60099. Tel. (847)746-1411. Fax (847)746-1452

Liahona, (m) The Church of Jesus Christ of Latter-day Saints, Marvin K. Gardner, 50 East North Temple St., Salt Lake City, UT 84150. Tel. (801)240-2490. Fax (801)240-4225

Liberty, (bi-m) Seventh-day Adventist Church, Clifford R. Goldstein, 12501 Old Columbia Pike, Silver Spring, MD 20904. Tel. (301)680-6691. Fax (301)680-6695

Lifeglow, (q) Seventh-day Adventist Church, Richard Kaiser, P.O. Box 6097, Lincoln, NE 68506. Tel. (402)488-0981. Fax (402)488-7582

Light and Life Magazine, (m) Free Methodist Church of North America, Douglas M. Newton, P.O. Box 535002, Indianapolis, IN 46253-5002. Tel. (317)244-3660. Fax (317)244-1247

Liguorian, (m) The Roman Catholic Church, Allan J. Weinert, C.SS.R., 1 Liguori Dr., Liguori, MO 63057. Tel. (314)464-2500. Fax (314)464-8449
E-mail: 104626.1547@compuserve.com

Listen, (m) Seventh-day Adventist Church, Lincoln E. Steed, 55 W. Oak Ridge Dr., Hagerstown, MD 21740. Tel. (301)791-7000. Fax (301)790-9734

Living Orthodoxy, (bi-m) The Russian Orthodox Church Outside of Russia, Fr. Gregory Williams, 1180 Orthodox Way, Liberty, TN 37095. Tel. (615)536-5239. Fax (615)536-5945

Long Island Catholic, The, (w) The Roman Catholic Church, Elizabeth O'Connor, P. O. Box 9009, 99 North Village Ave., Rockville Centre, NY 11571-9009. Tel. (516)594-1000. Fax (516)594-1092

Lookout, The, (w) Christian Churches and Churches of Christ, David Faust, 8121 Hamilton Ave., Cincinnati, OH 45231. Tel. (513)931-4050. Fax (513)931-0950

Lutheran, The, (m) Evangelical Lutheran Church in America, Edgar R. Trexler, 8765 W. Higgins Rd., Chicago, IL 60631-4183. Tel. (773)380-2540. Fax (773)380-2751
E-mail: lutheran@elca.org
Website/ Online Edition: http://www.thelutheran.org

Lutheran Ambassador, The, (16/yr) The Association of Free Lutheran Congregations, Craig Johnson, 86286 Pine Grove Rd., Eugene, OR 97402. Tel. (541)687-8643. Fax (541)683-849

Lutheran Educator, The, (q) Wisconsin Evangelical Lutheran Synod, John R. Isch, Martin Luther College, 1995 Luther Ct., New Ulm, MN 56073. Tel. (507)354-8221. Fax (507)354-8225

Lutheran Forum, (q) Interdenominational Lutheran, Ronald B. Bagnall, 207 Hillcrest Ave., Trenton, NJ 08618. Tel. (609)393-0417

Lutheran Layman, The, (m) The Lutheran Church-Missouri Synod, Gerald Perschbacher, 2185 Hampton Ave., St. Louis, MO 63139-2904. Tel. (314)951-4100. Fax (314)951-4295

Lutheran Parent, (bi-m) Wisconsin Evangelical Lutheran Synod, Kenneth J. Kremer, 1250 N. 113th St., Milwaukee, WI 53226-3284. Tel. (414)475-6600. Fax (414)475-7684

Lutheran Parent's Wellspring, (bi-m) Wisconsin Evangelical Lutheran Synod, Kenneth J. Kremer, 1250 N. 113th St., Milwaukee, WI 53226-3284. Tel. (414)475-6600. Fax (414)475-7684

Lutheran Partners, (6/yr) Evangelical Lutheran Church in America, Carl E. Linder, 8765 W. Higgins Rd., Chicago, IL 60631-4101. Tel. (773)380-2875. Fax (773)380-2829

Lutheran Sentinel, (m) Evangelical Lutheran Synod, Theodore Gullixson, 1451 Pearl Pl., Escondido, CA 92027. Tel. (619)745-0583. Fax (619)743-4440

Lutheran Spokesman, The, (m) Church of the Lutheran Confession, Paul Fleischer, 710 4th Ave. S.W., Sleepy Eye, MN 56085. Tel. (507)794-7793. Fax (507)794-3551
E-mail: pgflei@prairie.lakes.com

Lutheran Synod Quarterly, (q) Evangelical Lutheran Synod, G. R. Schmeling, Bethany Lutheran Theological Seminary, 6 Browns Ct., Mankato, MN 56001. Tel. (507)344-7855. Fax (507)344-7426

Lutheran Witness, The, (m) The Lutheran Church-Missouri Synod, David Mahsman, 1333 S. Kirkwood Rd., St. Louis, MO 63122-7295. Tel. (314)965-9917. Fax (314)965-3396

Lutheran Woman Today, (11/yr) Evangelical Lutheran Church in America, Sue Edison-Swift, 8765 W. Higgins Rd., Chicago, IL 60631-4101. Tel. (773)380-2743. Fax (773)380-2419

Magyar Egyhaz, (q) Hungarian Reformed Church in America, Stephen Szabo, 464 Forest Ave., Paramus, NJ 07652. Tel. (201)262-2338. Fax (914)359-2313

Maranatha, (q) Advent Christian Church, Robert Mayer, P.O. Box 23152, Charlotte, NC 28227. Tel. (704)545-6161. Fax (704)573-0712

Marriage Partnership, (q) Nondenominational, Ron R. Lee, 465 Gundersen Dr., Carol Stream, IL 60188. Tel. (630)260-6200. Fax (630)260-0114

Maryknoll, (11/yr) The Roman Catholic Church, Joseph R. Veneroso, Maryknoll Fathers and Brothers, P.O. Box 308, Maryknoll, NY 10545-0308. Tel. (914)941-7590. Fax (914)945-0670

Mennonite, The, (48/yr) Mennonite Church & The General Conference Mennonite Church, J. Lorne Peachey, Box 347, Newton, KS 67114. Tel. (800)790-2498 OR (316)283-5100. Fax (316)283-0454
E-mail: theMennonite@gcmc.org OR the Mennonite @mph.org
Website: http://www.mph.lm.com/themenno.html

Mature Years, (q) The United Methodist Church, Marvin W. Cropsey, 201 Eighth Ave. S, Nashville, TN 37202. Tel. (615)749-6292. Fax (615)749-6512
E-mail: mcropsey@umpublishing.org

Mennonite Historical Bulletin, (q) Mennonite Church, John E. Sharp, 1700 S. Main St., Goshen, IN 46526-4794. Tel. (219)535-7477. Fax (219)535-7293
E-mail: johnes@goshen.edu
Website: http://www.Goshen.edu/mcarchives

Mennonite Quarterly Review, (q) Mennonite Church, John D. Roth, 1700 S. Main St., Goshen, IN 46526. Tel. (219)535-7433. Fax (219)535-7438

Message, (bi-m) Seventh-day Adventist Church, Stephen P. Ruff, 55 West Oak Ridge Dr., Hagerstown, MD 21740. Tel. (301)393-4099. Fax (301)393-4103

Message of the Open Bible, (bi-m) Open Bible Standard Churches, Andrea Johnson, 2020 Bell Ave., Des Moines, IA 50315-1096. Tel. (515)288-6761. Fax (515)288-2510

Messenger, (11/yr) Church of the Brethren, Fletcher Farrar, 1451 Dundee Ave., Elgin, IL 60120. Tel. (847)742-5100. Fax (847)742-1407

Messenger, The, (m) The (Original) Church of God, Inc., Wayne Jolley and William Dale, P.O. Box 3086, Chattanooga, TN 37404-0086. Tel. (800)827-9234

Messenger, The, (m) The Swedenborgian Church, Patte LeVan, P.O. Box 985, Julian, CA 92036. Tel. (760)765-2915. Fax (760)765-0218

Messenger, The, (m) The Pentecostal Free Will Baptist Church, Inc., P.O. Box 1568, Dunn, NC 28335. Tel. (910)892-4161. Fax (910)892-6876

Messenger, The, The Bible Church of Christ, Inc., Gwendolyn Harris, 1358 Morris Ave., Bronx, NY 10456. Tel. (718)588-2284. Fax (718)992-5597

Messenger of Truth, (bi-w) Church of God in Christ, Mennonite, Gladwin Koehn, P.O. Box 230, Moundridge, KS 67107. Tel. (316)345-2532. Fax (316)345-2582

Methodist History, (q) The United Methodist Church, Charles Yrigoyen, Jr., P.O. Box 127, Madison, NJ 07940. Tel. (973)408-3189. Fax (973)408-3909

Mid-Stream: The Ecumenical Movement Today, (q) Christian Church (Disciples of Christ), Paul A. Crow, Jr., 130 E. Washington St., P.O. Box 1986, Indianapolis, IN 46206-1986. Tel. (317)635-3100. Fax (317)635-3700

Ministry, (m) Seventh-day Adventist Church, Willmore D. Eva, 12501 Old Columbia Pike, Silver Spring, MD 21029-6600. Tel. (301)680-6510. Fax (301)680-6502

Mission Grams, (bi-m) National Association of Free Will Baptists, Ida Lewis, Home Missions Office, P.O. Box 5002, Antioch, TN 37011-5002. Tel. (615)731-6812. Fax (615)731-7655

Mission Herald, (bi-m) National Baptist Convention, U.S.A., Inc., William J. Harvey, 701 S. 19th St., Philadelphia, PA 19146. Tel. (215)735-9853. Fax (215)735-1721

Mission, Adult, Youth, and Children's Editions, (q) Seventh-day Adventist Church, Charlotte Ishkanian, 12501 Old Columbia Pike, Silver Spring, MD 20904. Tel. (301)680-6167. Fax (301)680-6155

Missionary Magazine, The, (9/yr) Bertha O. Fordham, 800 Risley Ave., Pleasantville, NJ 08232-4250.

Missionary Messenger, The, (m) Christian Methodist Episcopal Church, Barbara E. Bouknight, P.O. Box 172, Flint, MI 48501-0172. Tel. (810)733-7076

Missionary Messenger, The, (6/yr) Cumberland Presbyterian Church, Carol Penn, 1978 Union Ave., Memphis, TN 38104. Tel. (901)276-4572. Fax (901)276-4578

Missionary Seer, (m) African Methodist Episcopal Zion Church, Kermit J. DeGraffenreidt, 475 Riverside Dr., Rm. 1935, New York, NY 10115. Tel. (212)870-2952 Fax (212)870-2808

Missionary Signal, The, (bi-m) Churches of God, General Conference, Kathy Rodabaugh,

P.O. Box 926, Findlay, OH 45839. Tel. (419)424-1961. Fax (419)424-3433

MissionsUSA, (bi-m) Southern Baptist Convention, Wayne Grinstead, 4200 North Point Pkwy., Alphretta, GA 30202-4174. Tel. (770)410-6251. Fax (770)410-6006

Monday Morning, (21/yr) Presbyterian Church (U.S.A.), Houston Hodges, 100 Witherspoon St., Louisville, KY 40202. Tel. (502)569-5502. Fax (502)569-8073

Moody Magazine, (6/yr) Nondenominational, Bruce Anderson, 820 N. LaSalle Blvd., Chicago, IL 60610. Tel. (312)329-2164. Fax (312)329-2149

Moravian, The, (10/yr) Moravian Church in America (Unitas Fratrum), Hermann I. Weinlick, 1021 Center St., P.O. Box 1245, Bethlehem, PA 18016. Tel. (610)867-0594. Fax (610)866-9223

Mother Church, The, (m)Western Diocese of the Armenian Church of North America, Fr. Sipan Mekhsian, Editor, 3325 N. Glenoaks Blvd., Burbank, CA 91504. Tel. (818)558-7474. Fax (818)558-6333

Mountain Movers, (m) Assemblies of God, John Maempa, 1445 Boonville Ave., Springfield, MO 65802. Tel. (417)862-2781. Fax (417)862-0085

Muslim World, The, (q) Muslim, Ibrahim Abu-Rabi and Jane I. Smith, Hartford Seminary, 77 Sherman St., Hartford, CT 06105. Tel. (860)509-9534. Fax (860)509-9539

NAE Leadership Alert, (bi-m) Interdenominational, David L. Melvin, 450 E. Gundersen Dr., Carol Stream, IL 60188. Tel. (630)665-0500. Fax (630)665-8575

NAE Washigton Insight, (m) Interdenominational, David L. Melvin, 450 E. Gundersen Dr., Carol Stream, IL 60188. Tel. (630)665-0500. Fax (630)665-8575

National Baptist Union Review, (m) Non-denominational, Willie Paul, 6717 Centennial Blvd., Nashville, TN 37209-1000. Tel. (615)350-8000. Fax (615)350-9018

National Catholic Reporter, (44/yr) The Roman Catholic Church, Michael J. Farrell, P.O. Box 419281, Kansas City, MO 64141. Tel. (816)531-0538. Fax (816)968-2280

National Christian Reporter, The, (w) Non-denominational, John A. Lovelace, P.O. Box 222198, Dallas, TX 75222. Tel. (214)630-6495. Fax (214)630-0079

National Spiritualist Summit, The, (m) National Spiritualist Association of Churches, Sandra Pfortmiller, 3521 W. Topeka Dr., Glendale, AZ 85308. Tel. (602)581-6686. Fax (602)581-5544

New Church Life, (m) General Church of the New Jerusalem, Donald L. Rose, Box 277, Bryn Athyn, PA 19009. Tel. (215)947-6225. Fax (215)938-1871

New Era, The, (m) The Church of Jesus Christ of Latter-day Saints, Richard Romney, 50 E. North Temple St., Salt Lake City, UT 84150. Tel. (801)240-2951. Fax (801)240-5997

New Horizons in the Orthodox Presbyterian Church, (11/yr) The Orthodox Presbyterian Church, Thomas E. Tyson, 607 N. Easton Rd., Bldg. E, P.O. Box P, Willow Grove, PA 19090-0920. Tel. (215)830-0900. Fax (215)830-0350

New Oxford Review, (11/yr) The Roman Catholic Church, 1069 Kains Ave., Berkeley, CA 94706. Tel. (510)526-5374. Fax (510)526-3492

New World Outlook, (bi-m) The Mission Magazine of the United Methodist Church, Alma Graham, Editor, 475 Riverside Dr., Rm. 1476, New York, NY 10115. Tel. (212)870-3765. Fax (212)870-3940
E-mail: nwo@gbgm-umc.org
Website: http://gbgm-umc.org/nwo

New World, The, (w) The Roman Catholic Church, Mary Claire Gart, 1144 W. Jackson Blvd., Chicago, IL 60607. Tel. (312)243-1300. Fax (312)243-1526

News of Interest , (m) Christian Brethren (also known as Plymouth Brethren), Naomi Bauman, P.O. Box 190, Wheaton, IL 60189 Tel. (630)653-6573. Fax (630)653-6595

News, The, (m) The Anglican Orthodox Church, Margaret D. Lane, Anglican Orthodox Church, P.O. Box 128, Statesville, NC 28687. Tel. (704)873-8365. Fax (704)873-8948

Newscope, (w) The United Methodist Church, J. Richard Peck, P.O. Box 801, Nashville, TN 37202. Tel. (615)749-6007. Fax (615)749-6061 E-mail: rpeck@umpublishing.org

North American Catholic, The, (m) North American Old Roman Catholic Church, Theodore J. Remalt, 4200 N. Kedvale Ave., Chicago, IL 60641. Tel. (312)685-0461. Fax (312)286-5783

North American Challenge, The, (m) Home Missions Division of The United Pentecostal Church International, Joseph Fiorino, 8855 Dunn Rd., Hazelwood, MO 63042-2299. Tel. (314)837-7300. Fax (314)837-5632

Northwestern Lutheran, (m) Wisconsin Evangelical Lutheran Synod, Gary Baumler, 2929 N. Mayfair Rd., Milwaukee, WI 53222. Tel. (414)256-3888. Fax (414)256-3899. Email: nl@sab.wels.net

Nuestra Parroquia, (m) The Roman Catholic Church, Carmen Aguinaco, 205 W. Monroe

St., Chicago, IL 60606-5013. Tel. (312)236-7782. Fax (312)236-8207

On Course, (q) Assemblies of God, Melinda Booze, 1445 Boonville Ave., Springfield, MO 65802-1894. Tel. (417)862-2781. Fax (417) 866-1146

On the Line, (bi-m) Denomination not Listed, Mary C. Meyer, 616 Walnut Ave., Scottdale, PA 15683. Tel. (412)887-8500. Fax (412)887-3111

One Church, (bi-m) Patriarchal Parishes of the Russian Orthodox Church in the U.S.A., Bishop Paul, 15 E. 97th St., New York, NY 10029. Tel. (212)831-6294. Fax (212)427-5003

Open Hands, (q) Interdenominational, Mary Jo Osterman, 3801 N. Keeler Ave., Chicago, IL 60641-3007. Tel. (312)736-5526. Fax (312) 736-5475

Orthodox America, (8/yr) The Russian Orthodox Church Outside of Russia, Mary Mansur, P.O. Box 383, Richfield Springs, NY 13439-0383. Tel. (978)448-5592

Orthodox Church, The, (m) The Orthodox Church in America, Leonid Kishkovsky, P.O. Box 675, Syosset, NY 11791. Tel. (516)922-0550. Fax (516)922-0954

Orthodox Family, (q) The Russian Orthodox Church Outside of Russia, George Johnson and Deborah Johnson, P.O. Box 45, Beltsville, MD 20705. Tel. (301)890-3552

Orthodox Life, (Bi-m) The Russian Orthodox Church Outside of Russia, Fr. Luke, Holy Trinity Monastery, P.O. Box 36, Jordanville, NY 13361-0036. Tel. (315)858-0940. Fax (315)858-0505

Orthodox Observer, The, (m) Greek Orthodox Archdiocese of America, Jim Golding, 8 E. 79th St., New York, NY 10021. Tel. (212)628-2590. Fax (212)570-4005

Orthodox Russia (Russian), (26/yr) The Russian Orthodox Church Outside of Russia, Archbishop Laurus, Holy Trinity Monastery, P.O. Box 36, Jordanville, NY 13361-0036. Tel. (315)858-0940. Fax (315)858-0505

Orthodox Voices, (q) The Russian Orthodox Church Outside of Russia, Thomas Webb and Ellen Webb, P.O. Box 23644, Lexington, KY 40523. Tel. (606)271-3877

Other Side, The, (bi-m) Interdenominational, Dee Dee Risher and Douglas Davidson, 300 W. Apsley St., Philadelphia, PA 19144-4221. Tel. (215)849-2178. Fax (215)849-3755
E-mail: editors@theotherside.org
Website: http://www.theotherside.org

Our Daily Bread, (m) The Swedenborgian Church, Lee Woofenden, P.O. Box 396,

Bridgewater, MA 02324 Tel. (508)946-1767. Fax (508)946-1757

Our Little Friend, (w) Seventh-day Adventist Church, Aileen Andres Sox, P.O. Box 5353, Nampa, ID 83653-5353. Tel. (208)465-2500. Fax (208)465-2531

Our Sunday Visitor, (w) The Roman Catholic Church, David Scott, 200 Noll Plaza, Huntington, IN 46750. Tel. (219)356-8400. Fax (219)356-8472

Outreach, (10/yr) Armenian Apostolic Church of America, Iris Papazian, 138 E. 39th St., New York, NY 10016. Tel. (212)689-7810. Fax (212)689-7168

Pastoral Life, (m) The Roman Catholic Church, Anthony Chenevey, Box 595, Canfield, OH 44406-0595. Tel. (330)533-5503. Fax (330)533-1076

Path of Orthodoxy, The, (m) Serbian Orthodox Church in the U.S.A. and Canada, Nedeljko Lunich, 300 Striker Ave., Joliet, IL 60436. Tel. (815)741-1023. Fax (815)741-1023

Pentecostal Evangel, (w) Assemblies of God, Hal Donaldson, 1445 Boonville Ave., Springfield, MO 65802-1894. Tel. (417)862-2781. Fax (417)862-0416

Pentecostal Herald, The, (m) United Pentecostal Church International, United Pentecostal Church of Canada, J. L. Hall, 8855 Dunn Rd., Hazelwood, MO 63042. Tel. (314)837-7300. Fax (314)837-4503

Pentecostal Leader, (q) The International Pentecostal Church of Christ, Clyde M. Hughes, Editor, P.O. Box 439, London, OH 43140. Tel. (614)852-4722. Fax (614)852-0348

Pentecostal Messenger, The, (m) Pentecostal Church of God, Aaron Wilson, P.O. Box 850, Joplin, MO 64802. Tel. (417)624-7050. Fax (417)624-7102

People's Mouthpiece, The, (q) Apostolic Overcoming Holy Church of God, Inc., Juanita R. Arrington, Ph.D., 1120 North 24th St., Birmingham, AL 35234. Tel. (205)324-2202

Perspectives, (10/yr) Reformed Church in America, Thomas A. Boogaart and Evelyn Diephouse, P.O. Box 470, Ada, MI 49301-0470. Tel. (616)285-8074. Fax (616)285-9828

Perspectives on Science & Christian Faith, (q) Nondenominational, J. W. Haas, Jr., P.O. Box 668, Ipswich, MA 01938. Tel. (508)356-5656. Fax (508)356-4375

Pillar Monthly, The, (12/yr) Pillar of Fire, Donald J. Wolfram and Mark Tomlin, P.O. Box 9045, Zarephath, NJ 08890. Tel. (908)356-0561

307

Pilot, The, (w) The Roman Catholic Church, Peter V. Conley, 49 Franklin St., Boston, MA 02110-1381. Tel. (617)482-4316. Fax (617)482-5647

Pockets, (11/yr) The United Methodist Church, Janet R. Knight, P.O. Box 189, Nashville, TN 37202. Tel. (615)340-7333. Fax (615)340-7006

Polka, (q) Polish National Catholic Church of America, Cecelia Lallo, 1127 Frieda St., Dickson City, PA 18519-1304. Tel. (717)489-4364 Fax (717)346-2188

Pravoslavnaya Rus, (Bi-w) The Russian Orthodox Church Outside of Russia, Andrei Psarev, Holy Trinity Monastery, P.O. Box 36, Jordanville, NY 13361-0036. Tel. (315)858-0940. Fax (315)858-0505

Pravoslavnaya Zhisn, (m) The Russian Orthodox Church Outside of Russia, Andrei Psarev, Holy Trinity Monastery, P.O. Box 36, Jordanville, NY 13361-0036. Tel. (315)858-0940. Fax (315)858-0505

Praying, (bi-m) Spirituality for Everyday Living, Rich Heffern, P.O. Box 419335, 115 E. Armour Blvd., Kansas City, MO 64141. Tel. (816)968-2258. Fax (816)968-2280

Preacher's Magazine, (q) Church of the Nazarene, Randal Denny, 10814 E. Broadway, Spokane, WA 99206. Tel. (509)226-3464. Fax (509)926-8740

Preacher, The, (bi-m) Baptist Bible Fellowship International, Mike Randall, P.O. Box 309 HSJ, Springfield, MO 65801. Tel. (417)831-3996. Fax (417)831-1470

Presbyterian News Service "News Briefs", (w) Presbyterian Church (U.S.A.), Jerry L. VanMarter, 100 Witherspoon St., Rm. 5418, Louisville, KY 40202. Tel. (502)569-5493. Fax (502)569-8073
E-mail: jerryv@ctr.pcusa.org

Presbyterian Outlook, (w) Presbyterian Church (U.S.A.), Robert H. Bullock, Jr., Box 85623, Richmond, VA 23285-5623. Tel. (804)359-8442. Fax (804)353-6369
E-mail: outlook.parti@pcusa.org
Website: http://www.pres-outlook.com

Presbyterians Today, (m) Presbyterian Church (U.S.A.), Catherine Cottingham and Eva Stimson, 100 Witherspoon St., Louisville, KY 40202-1396. Tel. (502)569-5637. Fax (502)569-8632

Primary Treasure, (w) Seventh-day Adventist Church, Aileen Andres Sox, P.O. Box 5353, Nampa, ID 83653-5353. Tel. (208)465-2500. Fax (208)465-2531

Primitive Baptist, The, (bi-m) Primitive Baptists, H. H. Cayce, P.O. Box 38, Thornton, AR 71766. Tel. (501)352-3694

Priority, (m) The Missionary Church, Ken Stucky, P.O. Box 9127, Ft. Wayne, IN 46899. Tel. (219)747-2027. Fax (219)747-5331

Providence Visitor, (w) The Roman Catholic Church, Michael Brown, 184 Broad St., Providence, RI 02903. Tel. (401)272-1010. Fax (401)421-8418

Purpose, (w) Mennonite Church, James E. Horsch, 616 Walnut Ave., Scottdale, PA 15683. Tel. (412)887-8500. Fax (412)887-3111

Pursuit, (q) The Evangelical Free Church of America, Carol Madison, 901 East 78th St., Minneapolis, MN 55420-1300. Tel. (612)853-1763. Fax (612)853-8488

Qala min M 'Dinkha (Voice from the East), (q) Apostolic Catholic Assyrian Church of the East, North American Dioceses, Shlemon Heseqial, Diocesan Offices, 7201 N. Ashland, Chicago, IL 60626. Tel. (773)465-4777. Fax (773)465-0776

Quaker Life, (10/yr) Friends United Meeting, Johan Maurer, 101 Quaker Hill Dr., Richmond, IN 47374-1980. Tel. (765)962-7573. Fax (765)966-1293
E-mail: Quakerlife@xc.org

Quarterly Review, (q) The United Methodist Church, Sharon Hels, Box 871, Nashville, TN 37202. Tel. (615)340-7334. Fax (615)340-7048

Quarterly Review, A.M.E. Zion, (q) African Methodist Episcopal Zion Church, James D. Armstrong, P.O. Box 33247, Charlotte, NC 28231. Tel. (704)334-0728. Fax (704)333-1769

Reconstructionism Today, (q) Jewish, Lawrence Bush, Church Rd. & Greenwood Ave., Wycote, PA 19095. Tel. (215)887-1988. Fax (215)887-5348

Reflections, (bi-m) United Pentecostal Church International, Melissa Anderson, 8855 Dunn Rd., Hazelwood, MO 63042. Tel. (918)371-2659. Fax (918)371-6320

Reformation Today, (bi-m) Sovereign Grace Baptists, Erroll Hulse, c/o Tom Lutz, 3743 Nichol Ave., Anderson, IN 46011-3008. Tel. (317)644-0994. Fax (317)644-0994

Reformed Herald, (m) Reformed Church in the United States, David Dawn, 1000 Evergreen Way, Rock Springs, WY 82901-4104. Tel. (307)362-5107

Reformed Worship, (q) Christian Reformed Church in North America, Emily Brink, 2850 Kalamazoo Ave. S.E., Grand Rapids, MI 49560-0001. Tel. (616)224-0785. Fax (616)224-0834

Rejoice!, (q) Mennonite Church, Rose Mary Stutzman, 616 Walnut Ave., Scottdale, PA 15683. Tel. (724)887-8500. Fax (724)887-3111

Rejoice!, (q) Mennonite & Mennonite Brethren Church, Philip Wiebe, 1218 Franklin St. N.W., Salem, OR 97304. Tel. (503)585-4458. Fax (503)585-4458

Religious Broadcasting, (10/yr) Nondenominational, Ron Kopczick, National Religious Broadcasters, 7839 Ashton Ave., Manassas, VA 20109-2883. Tel. (703)330-7000. Fax (703)330-6996

Report From The Capital, (24/yr) Baptist Joint Committee, Larry Chesser, 200 Maryland Ave. N.E., Washington, DC 20002-5724. Tel. (202)544-4226. Fax (202)544-2094

Reporter, (m) The Lutheran Church-Missouri Synod, David Mahsman, 1333 S. Kirkwood Rd., St. Louis, MO 63122-7295. Tel. (314)965-9917. Fax (314)965-3396

Rescue Herald, The, (q) American Rescue Workers, Rev. Colonel Robert N. Coles, 1209 Hamilton Blvd., Hagerstown, MD 21742. Tel. (301)797-0061. Fax (301)797-1480

Response, (m) The United Methodist Church, Dana Jones, 475 Riverside Dr., Rm. 1356, New York, NY 10115. Tel. (212)870-3755. Fax (212)870-3940

Restitution Herald, The, (bi-m) Church of God General Conference (Oregon, IL and Morrow, GA), Jeffrey Fletcher, Box 100,000, Morrow, GA 30260-7000. Tel. (504)543-0290. Fax (404)362-9307

Restoration Herald, (m) Christian Churches and Churches of Christ, H. Lee Mason, 5664 Cheviot Rd., Cincinnati, OH 45247-7071. Tel. (513)385-0461. Fax (513)385-0660

Restoration Quarterly, (q) Churches of Christ, James W. Thompson, Box 28227, Abilene, TX 79699-8227. Tel. (915)674-3781. Fax (915)674-3776

Restoration Witness, (bi-m) Reorganized Church of Jesus Christ of Latter Day Saints, Richard A. Brown, P.O. Box 1770, Independence, MO 64055. Tel. (816)252-5010. Fax (816)252-3976

Review for Religious, (bi-m) The Roman Catholic Church, David L. Fleming, S.J., 3601 Lindell Blvd., St. Louis, MO 63108. Tel. (314)977-7363. Fax (314)977-7362

Review of Religious Research, (q) Nondenominational, D. Paul Johnson, Texas Tech. Univ., Dept. of Sociology, Anthropology, & SW, Lubbock, TX 79409-1012. Tel. (806)742-2400. Fax (806)742-1088

Rocky Mountain Christian, (m) Churches of Christ, Ron L. Carter, P.O. Box 26620, Colorade Springs, CO 80936. Tel. (719)598-4197. Fax (719)528-1549

Sabbath Recorder, (m) Seventh Day Baptist General Conference, USA and Canada, Kevin J. Butler, 3120 Kennedy Rd., P.O. Box 1678, Janesville, WI 53547. Tel. (608)752-5055. Fax (608)752-7711

Sabbath School Leadership, (m) Seventh-day Adventist Church, Faith Crumbly, Review and Herald Publishing Assoc., 55 W. Oak Ridge Dr., Hagerstown, MD 21740. Tel. (301)393-4090. Fax (301)393-4055
E-mail: fcrumbly@rhpa.org
Website: http://www.rhpa.org

Saint Anthony Messenger, (m) The Roman Catholic Church, Norman Perry, 1615 Republic St., Cincinnati, OH 45210. Tel. (513)241-5616. Fax (513)241-0399

Saints Herald, (m) Reorganized Church of Jesus Christ of Latter Day Saints, James C. Cable, P.O. Box 1770, Independence, MO 64055-0770. Tel. (816)252-5010. Fax (816)252-3976

St. Willibrord Journal, (q) Christ Catholic Church, Charles E. Harrison, P.O. Box 271751, Houston, TX 77277-1751. Tel. (713) 622-5311

SBC Life, (10/yr) Southern Baptist Convention, Bill Merrell, 901 Commerce St., Nashville, TN 37203. Tel. (615)244-2355. Fax (615)742-8919

Schwenkfeldian, The, (q) The Schwenkfelder Church, Andrew C. Anders, 105 Seminary St., Pennsburg, PA 18073. Tel. (215)679-3103

Searching Together, (q) Sovereign Grace Believers, Jon Zens, Box 548, St. Croix Falls, WI 54024. Tel. (651)465-6516. Fax (651)465-5101

Secret Chamber, (q) African Methodist Episcopal Church, George L. Champion, Sr., 5728 Major Blvd., Orlando, FL 32819. Tel. (407)352-8797. Fax (407)352-6097

Secret Place, The, (q) American Baptist Churches in the U.S.A., Kathleen Hayes, Managing Editor, P.O. Box 851, Valley Forge, PA 19482-0851. Tel. (610)768-2240. Fax (610)768-2441

Seeds for the Parish, (bi-m) Evangelical Lutheran Church in America, Elizabeth Hunter, 8765 W. Higgins Rd., Chicago, IL 60631-4101. Tel. (773)380-2949. Fax (773)380-1465

Sharing, (q) Interdenominational Anabaptist, Judy Martin Godshalk, P.O. Box 438, Goshen, IN 46527. Tel. (219)533-9511. Fax (219)533-5264

Shiloh's Messenger of Wisdom, (m) Israelite House of David, William Robertson, P.O. Box 1067, Benton Harbor, MI 49023.

Shining Light, The, (bi-m) Church of God (Anderson, Ind.), Wilfred Jordan, Box 1235, Anderson, IN 46015. Tel. (317)644-1593

Signs of the Times, (m) Seventh-day Adventist Church, Marvin Moore, P.O. Box 5353, Nampa, ID 83653-5353. Tel. (208)465-2577. Fax (208)465-2531

Silver Lining, The, (m) Apostolic Christian Churches of America, Bruce Leman, R.R. 2, Box 50, Roanoke, IL 61561-9625. Tel. (309)923-7777. Fax (309)923-7359

Social Questions Bulletin, (bi-m) The United Methodist Church, George McClain, 76 Clinton Ave., Shalom House, Staten Island, NY 10301. Tel. (718)273-6372. Fax (718)273-6372

Sojourners, (6/yr) Nondenominational, Jim Wallis, 2401 15th St. N.W., Washington, DC 20009. Tel. (202)328-8842. Fax (202)328-8757
Website http://www.sojourners.com

Solia-The Herald, (m) The Romanian Orthodox Episcopate of America, Rev. Deacon David Oancea, P.O. Box 185, Grass Lake, MI 49240-0185. Tel. (517)522-3656. Fax (517)522-5907

Southern Methodist, The, (m) Southern Methodist Church, Thomas M. Owens, Sr., P.O. Box 39, Orangeburg, SC 29116-0039. Tel. (803)534-9853. Fax (803)535-3881

Spectrum, (bi-m) Conservative Baptist Association of America (CBAmerica), Mariel Kindl and Ed Mitchell, P.O. Box 66, Wheaton, IL 60189-0066. Tel. (630)260-3800. Fax (630)653-5387

Spirit, (q) Volunteers of America, Arthur Smith and Dennis N. Baker, 1321 Louisiana Ave., New Orleans, LA 70115. Tel. (504)897-1731

Spiritual Sword, The, (q) Churches of Christ, Alan E. Highers, 1511 Getwell Rd., Memphis, TN 38111. Tel. (901)743-0464. Fax (901)743-2197

Spotlight, (10/yr) National Spiritualist Association of Churches, Cosie Allen, 1418 Hall St., Grand Rapids, MI 49506. Tel. (616)241-2761. Fax (616)241-4703

Standard, The, (m) Baptist General Conference, Gary D. Marsh, 2002 S. Arlington Heights Rd., Arlington Heights, IL 60005. Tel. (847)228-0200. Fax (847)228-5376

Standard Bearer, The, (21/yr) Protestant Reformed Churches in America, David J. Engelsma, 4949 Ivanrest Ave., Grandville, MI 49418. Tel. (616)531-1490. Fax (616)531-3033. E-mail: engelsma@prca.org

Star of Zion, (bi-w) African Methodist Episcopal Zion Church, Morgan W. Tann, P.O.

Box 31005, Charlotte, NC 28231. Tel. (704)377-4329. Fax (704)377-2809

Stewardship USA, (q) Nondenominational, Raymond Barnett Knudsen II, P.O. Box 9, Bloomfield Hills, MI 48303-0009. Tel. (248)737-0895. Fax (248)737-0895

Story Friends, (w) Mennonite Church, Rose Mary Stutzman, 616 Walnut Ave., Scottdale, PA 15683. Tel. (724)887-8500. Fax (724)887-3111

Student, The, (m) Seventh-day Adventist Church, Richard Kaiser, P.O. Box 6097, Lincoln, NE 68506. Tel. (402)488-0981. Fax (402)488-7582

Sunday, (q) Interdenominational, Jack P. Lowndes, 2930 Flowers Rd. S., #16, Atlanta, GA 30341-5532. Tel. (770)936-5376. Fax (770)452-6582

Tablet, The, (w) The Roman Catholic Church, Ed Wilkinson, 653 Hicks St., Brooklyn, NY 11231. Tel. (718)858-3838. Fax (718)858-2112

Teacher Touch, (q) Nondenominational, Marlene LeFever, 4050 Lee Vance View, Colorado Springs, CO 80918. Tel. (800)708-5550. Fax (719)535-3202

Theology Digest, (q) The Roman Catholic Church, Bernhard A. Asen and Rosemary Jermann, 3634 Lindell Blvd., St. Louis, MO 63108-3395. Tel. (314)977-3410 Fax (314) 977-2947

Theology Today, (q) Nondenominational, Patrick D. Miller, P.O. Box 29, Princeton, NJ 08542. Tel. (609)497-7714. Fax (609)924-2973

These Days, (bi-m) Interdenominational, Kay Snodgrass, 100 Witherspoon St., Louisville, KY 40202-1396. Tel. (502)569-5080. Fax (502)569-5113

Tidings, The, (w) The Roman Catholic Church, Tod M. Tamberg, 3424 Wilshire Blvd., Los Angeles, CA 90010. Tel. (213)637-7360. Fax (213)637-6360

Timbrel: The Publication of Mennonite Women, Mennonite Church and the General Conference, Mennonite Church, Cathleen Hockman-Wert, 3445 Harris St., Eugene, OR 97405 Tel. (541)302-5929 E-mail: dhwert@oregon.uoregon.edu

Today's Christian Woman, (6/yr) Nondenominational, Ramona Cramer Tucker, 465 Gundersen Dr., Carol Stream, IL 60188. Tel. (630)260-6200. Fax (630)260-0114

Tomorrow Magazine, (q) American Baptist Churches in the U.S.A., Sara E. Hopkins, 475 Riverside Dr., Rm. 1700, New York, NY 10115-0049. Tel. (800)986-6222. Fax (800)986-6782

Tover of St. Cassian, The, (bi-annual) Apostolic Episcopal Church- Order of Corporate Reunion, Rt. Rev. Francis C. Spataro D.D., Editor, 80-46 234th St., Queens, NY 11427 Tel. (718)740-4134

Tradition: A Journal of Orthodox Jewish Thought, (q) Emanuel Feldman, Rabbinical Council of America, 305 Seventh Ave., New York, NY 10001. Tel. (212)807-7888. Fax (212)727-8452

Truth, (bi-m) Grace Gospel Fellowship, Roger G. Anderson and Sherry Macy, 2125 Martindale S.W., Grand Rapids, MI 49509. Tel. (616)247-1999. Fax (616)241-2542

Truth Magazine, (bi-w) Churches of Christ, Mike Willis, Box 9670, Bowling Green, KY 42102. Tel. (800)428-0121.

U.S. Catholic, (m) The Roman Catholic Church, Rev. Mark J. Brummel, Editor, 205 W. Monroe St., Chicago, IL 60606. Tel. (312)236-7782. Fax (312)236-8207

Ubique, (q) The Liberal Catholic Church-Province of the United States of America, Joseph Tisch, P.O. Box 1117, Melbourne, FL 32902. Tel. (407)254-0499

Ukrainian Orthodox Herald, Ukrainian Orthodox Church of America (Ecumenical Patriarchate), Anthony Ugolnik, P.O. Box 774, Allentown, PA 18105.

United Church News, (10/yr) United Church of Christ, W. Evan Golder, 700 Prospect Ave., Cleveland, OH 44115. Tel. (216)736-2218. Fax (216)736-2223

United Methodist Reporter, (52/yr) The United Methodist Church, Ronald P. Patterson, P.O. Box 660275, Dallas, TX 75266-0275. Tel. (214)630-6495. Fax (214)630-0079

United Methodist Review, (26/yr) The United Methodist Church, John A. Lovelace, P.O. Box 660275, Dallas, TX 75266-0275. Tel. (214)630-6495. Fax (214)630-0079

Upper Room, The, (6/yr) The United Methodist Church, Janice Grana, P.O. Box 189, Nashville, TN 37202. Tel. (615)340-7200. Fax (615)340-7006

Upreach, (bi-m) Churches of Christ, Randy Becton, Box 2001, Abilene, TX 79604. Tel. (915)698-4370. Fax (915)691-5736

Vibrant Life, (bi-m) Seventh-day Adventist Church, Larry Becker, 55 W. Oak Ridge Dr., Hagerstown, MD 21740. Tel. (301)393-4019. Fax (301)393-4055

Victory (Youth Magazine), (m) Church of God of Prophecy, Dewayne Hamby, P.O. Box 2910, Cleveland, TN 37320-2910. Tel. (423)559-5207. Fax (423)559-5202

Vida Radiante, (q) Seventh-day Adventist Church, Richard Kaiser, P.O. Box 6097, Lincoln, NE 68506. Tel. (402)488-0981. Fax (402)488-7582

Vindicator, The, (m) Old German Baptist Brethren, Keith Skiles, 701 St. Rt. 571, Union City, OH 45390. Tel. (937)968-3877

Vista, (bi-m) Christian Church of North America, General Council, Gregory Miheli, 1294 Rutledge Rd., Transfer, PA 16154. Tel. (412)962-3501. Fax (412)962-1766

Voice ! (q) General Association of General Baptists, Gene Koker, 100 Stinson Dr., Poplar Bluff, MO 63901. Tel. (573)785-7746. Fax (573) 785-0564

Voice, The, (6/yr) IFCA International, Richard I. Gregory, P.O. Box 810, Grandville, MI 49468-0810. Tel. (616)531-1840. Fax (616)531-1814

Voice, The, (q) The Bible Church of Christ, Inc., Montrose Bushrod, 1358 Morris Ave., Bronx, NY 10456. Tel. (718)588-2284. Fax (718)992-5597

War Cry, The, (bi-w) The Salvation Army, Marlene Chase, 615 Slaters Ln., Alexandria, VA 22313. Tel. (703)684-5500. Fax (703)684-5539

Wave, The, (q) General Association of General Baptists, Sandra Trivitt, 100 Stinson Dr., Poplar Bluff, MO 63901. Tel. (573)785-7746. Fax (573)785-0564

Weavings: A Journal of the Christian Spiritual Life, (6/yr) The United Methodist Church, John S. Mogabgab, P.O. Box 189, Nashville, TN 37202-0189. Tel. (615)340-7254. Fax (615)340-7006

Wesleyan Advocate, The, (11/yr) The Wesleyan Church, Norman G. Wilson, P.O. Box 50434, Indianapolis, IN 46250-0434. Tel. (317)570-5204. Fax (317)570-5260

Wesleyan Woman, (q) The Wesleyan Church, Martha Blackburn, P.O. Box 50434, Indianapolis, IN 46250. Tel. (317)570-5164. Fax (317)570-5280

Wesleyan World, (q) The Wesleyan Church, Wayne Derr, P.O. Box 50434, Indianapolis, IN 46250. Tel. (317)570-5172. Fax (317)570-5256
E-mail: wwm@iquest.net

White Wing Messenger, The, (bi-w) Church of God of Prophecy, Virginia E. Chatham, P.O. Box 3000, Cleveland, TN 37320-3000. Tel. (423) 559-5413. Fax (423)559-5444

Whole Truth, (m) The Church Of God In Christ, Larry Britton, P.O. Box 2017, Memphis, TN 38101. Tel. (901)578-3841. Fax (901)527-6807

311

Wineskins, (bi-m) Churches of Christ, Mike Cope and Rubel Shelly, Box 129004, Nashville, TN 37212-9004. Tel. (615)373-5004. Fax (615)373-5006

Winner, The, (9/yr.) Nondenominational, Lincoln Sterd, The Health Connection, P.O. Box 859, Hagerstown, MD 21741. Tel. (301)790-9735. Fax (301)790-9734

Wisconsin Lutheran Quarterly, (q) Wisconsin Evangelical Lutheran Synod, John F. Brug, 11831 N. Seminary Dr., Mequon, WI 53092. Tel. (414)257-8839. Fax (414)257-8810

With: The Magazine for Radical Christian Youth, (8/yr) Interdenominational, Carol Duerksen, P.O. Box 347, Newton, KS 67114. Tel. (316)283-5100. Fax (316)283-0454

Witness, The, (10/yr) Jeanie Wylie-Kellermannand and Julie A. Wortman, 7000 Michigan Ave., Detroit, MI 48210. Tel (313)841-1967 Fax (313) 841-1956

Woman's Pulpit, The, (q) Nondenominational, LaVonne Althouse, 6210 Loretto Ave., Philadelphia, PA 19111. Tel. (215)743-4528

Woman's Touch, (bi-m) Assemblies of God, Lillian Sparks, 1445 Boonville Ave., Springfield, MO 65802-1894. Tel. (417)862-2781. Fax (417)862-0503

Women's Missionary Magazine, (9/yr) African Methodist Episcopal Church, Bettye J. Allen, 1901 E. 169th Place, S. Holland, IL 60473. Tel. (708)895-0703. Fax (708)895-0706

Word and Work, (11/yr) Churches of Christ, Alex Wilson, 2518 Portland Ave., Louisville, KY 40212. Tel. (502)897-2831

Word, The, (10/yr) The Antiochian Orthodox Christian Archdiocese of North America, George S. Corey, 52 78th St., Brooklyn, NY 11209. Tel. (718)748-7940. Fax (718)855-3608

Worker, The, (q) Progressive National Baptist Convention, Inc., Mattie A. Robinson, 601 50th St. N.E., Washington, DC 20019 Tel. (202)398-5343

World Harvest Today, (q) United Pentecostal Church International, J. S. Leaman, 8855 Dunn Rd., Hazelwood, MO 63042. Tel. (314)837-7300. Fax (314)837-2387

World Mission, (m) Church of the Nazarene, R. Franklin Cook, World Mission Division, 6401 The Paseo, Kansas City, MO 64131. Tel. (816)333-7000. Fax (816)333-1748

World Parish: Intl. Organ of the World Meth. Council, (s-m) Interdenominational Methodist, Joe Hale, P.O. Box 518, Lake Junaluska, NC 28745. Tel. (704)456-9432. Fax (704)456-9433

World Vision, (bi-m) Open Bible Standard Churches, Inc., Paul V. Canfield, 2020 Bell Ave., Des Moines, IA 50315-1096. Tel. (515)288-6761. Fax (515)288-2510

World Vision Today, (bi-m) Nondenominational, P.O. Box 9716, Federal Way, WA 98063-9716. Tel. (206)815-2300. Fax (206)815-3445

Worldorama, (m) International Pentecostal Holiness Church, Donald Duncan, P.O. Box 12609, Oklahoma City, OK 73157. Tel. (405)787-7110. Fax (405)787-7729

Worship, (6/yr) The Roman Catholic Church, R. Kevin Seasoltz, St. John's Abbey, Collegeville, MN 56321. Tel. (612)363-3883. Fax (612)363-2504

Worship Arts, (6/yr) Nondenominational, David A. Wiltse, P.O. Box 6247, Grand Rapids, MI 49516-6247. Tel. (616)459-4503. Fax (616)459-1051

Young & Alive, (q) Seventh-day Adventist Church, Richard Kaiser, P.O. Box 6097, Lincoln, NE 68506. Tel. (402)488-0981. Fax (402)488-7582

Youth Ministry Accent, (q) Seventh-day Adventist Church, David S.F. Wong, 12501 Old Columbia Pike, Silver Spring, MD 20904-6600. Tel. (301)680-6180. Fax (301)680-6155

Zion's Advocate, (m) Church of Christ, Mike McGhee, 18907 E. 6th St. N, Independence, MO 64056. Tel. (816)796-6255

Zion's Herald, (m) United Zion Church, Kathy Long, 5095 School Creek Ln., Annville, PA 17003. Tel. (717)867-1201

11. Religious Periodicals in Canada

The religious periodicals below constitute a basic core of important journals and periodicals circulated in Canada. The list does not include all publications prepared by religious bodies. The listing of religious bodies in Canada includes the titles of publications found in this list. The information contained in parenthesis following the title indicates the frequency of publication.

Each entry gives: the title of the periodical, frequency of publication, religious affiliation, editor's name, address, telephone and fax number when known and e-mail and website addresses when available.

Again, (q) The Antiochian Orthodox Christian Archdiocese of North America, John W. Hardenbrook. Conciliar Press, P.O. Box 75, Ben Lomond, CA 95005-0076. Tel. (800)967-7377

Anglican Journal, (10/yr) The Anglican Church of Canada, David Harris, 600 Jarvis St., Toronto, ON M4Y 2J6. Tel. (416)924-9199. Fax (416)921-4452 (Editorial); Fax (416)925-8811 (advertising & circulation) E-mail: editor@national.anglican.ca

Anglican, The, (10/yr) The Anglican Church of Canada, Stuart Mann, 135 Adelaide St. E., Toronto, ON M5C 1L8. Tel. (416)363-6021. Fax (416)363-7678

Armenian Evangelical Church, (q) Armenian Evangelical Church, Yessayi Sarmazian, 2600-14th Ave., Markham, ON, L3R 3X1. Tel. (905)305-8144. Fax (905)305-8125

Aujourd hui Credo, (10/yr) The United Church of Canada, Comite de Redaction, 1332 Victoria, Greenfield Park, QC J4V 1L8. Tel. (450)466-7733. Fax (450)466-2664 E-mail: copermit@sympatico.ca Website: http://www.egliseunie.org

B.C. Fellowship Baptist, (m) The Fellowship of Evangelical Baptist Churches in Canada, Bruce Christensen, Box 800, Langley, BC V3A 8C9. Tel. (604)888-3616. Fax (604)888-3601

BGC Canada News, (4/yr) Baptist General Conference of Canada, Abe Funk, 4306 97th St. N.W., Edmonton, AB T6E 5R9. Tel. (403)438-9127. Fax (403)435-2478

Banner, The, (w) Christian Reformed Church in North America, John A. Suk, 2850 Kalamazoo Ave. S.E., Grand Rapids, MI 49560. Tel. (616)224-0791. Fax (616)224-0834

The Baptist Horizon, (m) Canadian Convention of Southern Baptists, Nancy McGough, P.O. Box 300, Cochrane, AB T0L 0W0. Tel. (403)932-5688. Fax (403)932-4937 E-mail: office@ccsb.ca

Blackboard Bulletin, (10/yr) Old Order Amish Church, Delbert Farmwald, Rt. 4, Aylmer, ON N5H 2R3.

Budget, The, (w) Old Order Amish Church, George R. Smith, P.O. Box 249, Sugarcreek, OH 44681. Tel. (330)852-4634. Fax (330)852-4421

CLBI-Cross Roads, (bi-m) Lutheran, Felicitas Ackermann, 4837-52A St., Camrose, AB T4V 1W5. Tel. (403)672-4454. Fax (403)672-4455 E-mail: clbipbad@cable-lynx.net

Cahiers de Spiritualite Ignatienne, (q) The Roman Catholic Church in Canada, Jean-Guy Saint-Arnaud, Centre de Spiritualite Manrse, 2370 Rue Nicolas-Pinel, Ste-Foy, QC G1V 4L6. Tel. (418)653-6353. Fax (418)653-1208

Canada Lutheran, (9/yr) Evangelical Lutheran Church in Canada, Kenn Ward, 302-393 Portage Ave., Winnipeg, MB R2B 3H6. Tel. (204)984-9170. Fax (204)984-9185 E-Mail: canaluth@elcic.ca

Canada Update, (q) The Church of God of Prophecy in Canada, Adrian L. Varlack, P.O. Box 457, Brampton, ON L6V 2L4. Tel. (905)843-2379. Fax (905)843-3990

Canadian Adventist Messenger, (12/yr) Seventh-day Adventist Church in Canada, Shelley Nolan, 1148 King St. E., Oshawa, ON L1H 1H8. Tel. (905)433-0011. Fax (905)433-0982

Canadian Baptist, The, (10/yr) Baptist Convention of Ontario and Quebec, Larry Matthews, 195 The West Mall, Ste. 414, Etobicoke, ON M9C 5K1. Tel. (416)622-8600. Fax (416)622-0780

Canadian Disciple, (4/yr) Christian Church (Disciples of Christ) in Canada, Stanley Litke, 255 Midvalley Dr. S.E., Calgary, AB T2X 1K8. Tel. (403)256-3280. Fax (403)254-6178

Canadian Friend, The, (bi-m) Canadian Yearly Meeting of the Religious Society of Friends, Anne Marie Zilliacus, 218 Third Ave., Ottawa, ON K1S 2K3. Tel. (613)567-8628. Fax (613)567-1078

Canadian Jewish News, (50/yr) Jewish, Mordecai Ben-Dat, 1500 Don Mills Rd., Ste. 205, North York, ON M3B 3K4. Tel. (416)391-1836. Fax (416)391-0829

Canadian Jewish Outlook, (8/yr) Jewish, Henry M. Rosenthal, 6184 Ash St., #3,

Vancouver, BC V5Z 3G9. Tel. (604)324-5101. Fax (604)325-2470

Canadian Lutheran, (9/yr) Lutheran Church Canada, Ian Adnams, 3074 Portage Ave., Winnipeg, MB R3K 0Y2. Tel. (204)895-3433. Fax (204)897-4319

Canadian Mennonite, (bi-w) Conference of Mennonites in Canada, Ron Rempel, 312 Marsland Dr., Waterloo, ON N2J 3Z1. Tel. (519)884-3810. Fax (519)884-3331

Canadian Orthodox Messenger, (q) Orthodox Church in America (Canada Section), Rhoda Zion, P.O. Box 179, Spencerville, ON K0E 1X0. Tel. (613)925-5226. Fax (613)925-1521

Catalyst, The, (8/yr) Nondenominational, Andrew Brouwer, 229 College St., #311, Toronto, ON M5T 1R4. Tel. (416)979-2443. Fax (416)979-2458

Catholic Register, The, (w) The Roman Catholic Church in Canada, Joseph Sinasac, 1155 Yonge St., Ste. 401, Toronto, ON M4T 1W2. Tel. (416)934-3410. Fax (416)934-3409

Catholic Times (Montreal), The, (10/yr) The Roman Catholic Church in Canada, Eric Durocher, 2005 Saint Marc St., Montreal, QC H3H 2G8. Tel. (514)937-2301. Fax (514)937-3051

Channels, (q) Presbyterian Church in Canada, J. H. (Hans) Kouwenberg, 5800 University Blvd., Vancouver, BC V6T 2E4. Tel. (604)224-3245. Fax (604)224-3097

Chinese Herald, (q) Canadian Conference of Mennonite Brethren Churches, Keynes Kan, 2622 Saint Johns St., Port Moody, BC V3H 2B6. Tel. (604)939-8281. Fax (604)939-8201

Christian Contender, The, (m) Mennonite Church (Canada), James Baer, Box 584, McBride, BC V0J 2E0. Tel. (604)569-3302. Fax (604)569-3256

Christian Courier, (w) Nondenominational, Bert Witvoet, 261 Martindale Rd., Unit 4, St. Catharines, ON L2W 1A1. Tel. (905)682-8311. Fax (905)682-8313

Church in Canada, Richard Riccioli, Station F, Box 535, Toronto, ON M4Y 2L8. Tel. (416)690-5611. Fax (416)690-3320

Church of God Beacon, (q) Church of God (Cleveland, Tenn.), Canute Blake, P.O. Box 2036, Brampton Commercial Service Center, Brampton, ON L6T 3T0. Tel. (905)793-2213. Fax (905)793-9173

Clarion: The Canadian Reformed Magazine, (bi-w) Canadian and American Reformed Churches, C. Van Dam, One Beghin Ave., Winnipeg, MB R2J 3X5. Tel. (204)663-9000. Fax (204)663-9202

College News & Updates, (6/yr) Church of God (Anderson, Ind.), John Alan Howard, 4704 - 55 St., Camrose, AB T4V 2B6. Tel. (403)672-0171. Fax (403)672-6888

Communications Bi-Monthly, (6/yr) Congregational Christian Churches in Canada, Don Bernard, 5 Townsville Ct., Brantford, ON N3S 7H8. Tel. (519)751-0421. Fax (519)751-0852

Communicator, The, (3/yr) The Roman Catholic Church in Canada, P. Giroux, P.O. Box 142, Tantallon, NS B0J3J0. Tel. (902)826-7236. Fax (902)826-7236

Companion Magazine, (m) The Roman Catholic Church in Canada, Friar Phillip Kelly, O.F.M. Conv., Editor, Conventual Franciscan Centre, 695 Coxwell Ave., Ste. 600, Toronto, ON M4C 5R6. Tel. (416)690-5611. Fax (416)690-3320

Connexions, (4/yr) Interdenominational, Ulli Diemer, P.O. Box 158, Stn. D, Toronto, ON M6P 3J8. Tel. (416)537-3949
Website: http://www.connexions.org

Covenant Messenger, The, (6/yr) The Evangelical Covenant Church of Canada, 2791 Pembina Hwy., Winnipeg, MB R3T 2H5 Tel. (204)269-3437 Fax (204)269-3584

Die Botschaft, (w) Old Order Amish Church, James Weaver, Brookshire Publishing, Inc., 200 Hazel St., Lancaster, PA 17603. Tel. (717)392-1321. Fax (717)392-2078

Discover the Bible, (w) The Roman Catholic Church in Canada, Guy Lajoie, P.O. Box 2400, London, ON N6A 4G3. Tel. (519)439-7211. Fax (519)439-0207

EMMC Recorder, (m) Evangelical Mennonite Mission Conference, Jack Heppner, Box 52059 Niakwa P.O., Winnipeg, MB R2M 5P9. Tel. (204)253-7929. Fax (204)256-7384

Ecumenism/Oecumenisme, (q) Interdenominational, 2065 Sherbrooke St. W, Montreal, QC H3H 1G6. Tel. (514)937-9176. Fax (514)937-2684

Edge, The, (10/yr) The Salvation Army in Canada, Pamela Richardson, 2 Overlea Blvd., Toronto, ON M4H 1P4. Tel. (416)422-6114. Fax (416)422-6120
E-mail: edge@sallynet.org

Eesti Kirik, (q) The Estonian Evangelical Lutheran Church, Edgar Heinsoo, 383 Jarvis St., Toronto, ON M5B 2C7. Tel. (416)925-5465. Fax (416)925-5688

En Avant!, (24/yr) The Salvation Army in Canada, Betty Lessard, 2050 Rue Stanley, Bureau 602, Montreal, QB H3A 3G3. Tel. (514)288-2848. Fax (514)849-7600

Ensign, The, (m) The Church of Jesus Christ of Latter-day Saints, Jay M. Todd., 50 E. North

Temple St., 23rd Fl., Salt Lake City, UT 84150. Tel. (801)240-2950. Fax (801)240-5997

Esprit, (q) Evangelical Lutheran Church in Canada, Gayle Johannesson, 302-393 Portage Ave., Winnipeg, MB R3B 3H6. Tel. (204)984-9160. Fax (204)984-9162

Evangel: The Good News of Jesus Christ, (4/yr) Canadian and American Reformed Churches, D. Moes, 21804 52nd Ave., Langley, BC V3A 4R1. Tel. (604)576-2124. Fax (604)576-2101

Evangelical Baptist, The, (5/yr.) The Fellowship of Evangelical Baptist Churches in Canada, Terry D. Cuthbert, 679 Southgate Dr., Guelph, ON N1G 4S2. Tel. (519)821-4830. Fax (519)821-9829
E-mail: president@fellowship.ca

Expression, (q) Canadian Conference of Mennonite Brethren Churches, Burton Buller, 225 Riverton Ave., Winnipeg, MB R2L 0N1. Tel. (204)667-9576. Fax (204)669-6079

Faith and Fellowship, (m) Church of the Lutheran Brethren, David Rinden, P.O. Box 655, Fergus Falls, MN 56538. Tel. (218)736-7357. Fax (218)736-2200

Faith and Friends, (m) The Salvation Army in Canada, Sharon Stinka, 2 Overlea Blvd., Toronto, ON M4H 1P4. Tel. (416)425-2111. Fax (416)422-6120
E-mail: faithandfriends@salleynet.org

Faith Today, (bi-m) Interdenominational, Marianne Meed-Ward, M.I.P. Box 3745, Markham, ON L3R 0Y4. Tel. (905)479-5885. Fax (905)479-4742
E-mail: ft@efc-canada.com

Family Life, (11/yr) Old Order Amish Church, Joseph Stoll and David Luthy, Rt. 4, Aylmer, ON N5H 2R3.

Fellowship Magazine, (4/yr) The United Church of Canada, Gail Reid, Box 237, Barrie, ON L4M 4T3. Tel. (705)737-0114. Fax (705)726-7160

Free Methodist Herald, The, (bi-m) Free Methodist Church in Canada, Donna Elford, 3719-44 St. S.W., Calgary, AB T3E 3S1. Tel. (403)246-6838. Fax (403)686-3787

Glad Tidings, (6/yr) Presbyterian Church in Canada, L. June Stevenson, Women's Missionary Society, 50 Wynford Dr., North York, ON M3C 1J7. Tel. (800)619-7301 OR (416)441-1111. Fax (416)441-2825
E-mail: jsterens@presbyterian.ca

Global Village Voice, (q) The Roman Catholic Church in Canada, Jack J. Panozzo, 420-10 Saint Mary St., Toronto, ON M4Y 1P9. Tel. (416)922-1592. Fax (416)922-0957

Good Tidings, (10/yr) Pentecostal Assemblies of Newfoundland, Rev. A. E. Batstone, 57 Thorburn Rd., P.O. Box 8895, Sta. A, St. John's, NF A1B 3T2. Tel. (709)753-6314. Fax (709)753-4945
E-mail: paon@paon.nf.ca

Gospel Contact, The, (4/yr) Church of God, Editorial Committee, 4717 56th St., Camrose, AB T4V 2C4. Tel. (780)672-0772. Fax (780)672-6888
E-mail: wcdncog@cable-lynx.net
Website: http://www.cable-lynx.net/~wcdncog

Gospel Herald, (m) Churches of Christ in Canada, Wayne Turner and Eugene C. Perry, 4904 King St., Beamsville, ON L0R 1B6. Tel. (905)563-7503. Fax (905)563-7503
E-mail: eperry9953@aol.com OR wpgwayne@aol.com

Gospel Standard, The, (m) Nondenominational, Perry F. Rockwood, Box 1660, Halifax, NS B3J 3A1. Tel. (902)423-5540

Gospel Tidings, (m) Independent Holiness Church, R. E. Votary, 1564 John Quinn Rd., Greely, ON K4P 1J9. Tel. (613)821-2237. Fax (613)821-4663

The Grape Vine, (12/yr) The Church of Our Lord (Reformed Episcopal Church in Canada), Rev. Dr. Rod Ellis, Rector, Barbara Brennan, Editor, 626 Blanshard St., Victoria, BC, V8W 3G6. Tel. (250)383-8915 Fax. (250) 383-8916
E-mail: bbrennan@islandnet.com

Hallelujah, (bi-m) The Bible Holiness Movement, Wesley H. Wakefield, Box 223, Postal Station A, Vancouver, BC V6C 2M3. Tel. (250)498-3895

Handmaiden, (q) The Antiochian Orthodox Christian Archdiocese of North America, Katherine Hyde, Conciliar Press, P.O. Box 76, Ben Lomond, CA 95005-0076. Tel. (800)967-7377

Herold der Wahreit, Old Order Amish Church, Cephas Kauffman, 1829 110th St., Kalona, IA 52247.

Horizons, (bi-m) The Salvation Army in Canada, Frederick Ash, 2 Overlea Blvd., Toronto, ON M4H 1P4. Tel. (416)425-6118. Fax (416)422-6120

IdeaBank, (q) Canadian Conference of Mennonite Brethren Churches, David Wiebe, Christian Ed. Office, 3-169 Riverton Ave., Winnipeg, MB R2L 2E5. Tel. (204)669-6575. Fax (204)654-1865

InfoMission, (11/yr) Canadian Baptist Ministries, Donna Lee Pancorvo, 7185 Millcreek Dr., Mississauga, ON L5N 5R4. Tel. (905)821-3533. Fax (905)826-3441
E-mail: dlpancorvo@cbmin.org
Website: http://www.cbmin.org

315

In Holy Array, (9/yr) Canadian and American Reformed Churches, N. Gunnink, Canadian Ref. Young Peoples Societies, 17655-48 Ave., Surrey, BC V4P 1M5. Tel. (604)574-6227

Insight*Insound*In Touch, Interdenominational, David Brinton, 40 St. Clair Ave. E., Ste. 202, Toronto, ON M4T 1M9. Tel. (416)960-3953

Intercom, (bi-m) The Fellowship of Evangelical Baptist Churches in Canada, Terry D. Cuthbert, 679 Southgate Dr., Guelph, ON N1G 4S2. Tel. (519)821-4830. Fax (519)821-9829 E-mail: president@fellowship.com

ISKRA, (22/yr) Union of Spiritual Communities of Christ, Interim Editorial Collective, Box 760, Grand Forks, BC V0H 1H0. Tel. (604)442-8252 Fax. (604)442-3433

Jewish Standard, (semi-m) Jewish, Julius Hayman, 77 Mowat Ave., Ste. 016, Toronto, ON M6K 3E3. Tel. (416)537-2696. Fax (416)789-3872

Journal of Psychology and Judaism, (q) Jewish, Reuven P. Bulka, 1747 Featherston Dr., Ottawa, ON K1H 6P4. Tel. (613)731-9119. Fax (613)521-0067

L'eglise Canadienne, (11/yr) The Roman Catholic Church in Canada, Pierre Chouinard, C.P. 990, Outremont, QC H2V 4S7. Tel. (514)278-3020. Fax (514)278-3030

Lien, Le, (11/yr) Canadian Conference of Mennonite Brethren Churches, Annie Brosseau, 1775 Edouard-Laurin, St. Laurent, QC H4L 2B9. Tel. (514)331-0878. Fax (514)331-0879

Liturgie, Foi et Culture (Bulletin Natl. de Liturgie), (4/yr) The Roman Catholic Church in Canada, Service des Editions de la CECC, Service des Editions, Office National de Liturgie, 3530 Rue Adam, Montreal, QC H1W 1Y8. Tel. (514)522-4930. Fax (514)522-1557

Mandate, (4/yr) The United Church of Canada, Rebekah Chevalier, Div. of Communication, 3250 Bloor St. W., Ste. 300, Etobicoke, ON M8X 2Y4. Tel. (416)231-5931. Fax (416)232-6004 E-mail: rchevali@uccan.org

Mantle, The, (m) Independent Assemblies of God International (Canada), Philip Rassmussen, P.O. Box 2130, Laguna Hills, CA 92654-9901. Tele National de Liturgie, 3530 Rue Adam, Montreal, QC H1W 1Y8. Tel. (514)522-4930. Fax (514)522-1557

Mandate, (4/yr) The United Church of Canada, Rebekah Chevalier, Div. of Communication, 3250 Bloor St. W., Etobicoke, ON M8X 2Y4. Tel. (416)231-5931. Fax (416)232-6004

Mantle, The, (m) Independent Assemblies of God International (Canada), Philip

Rassmussen, P.O. Box 2130, Laguna Hills, CA 92654-9901.

Mennonite Historian, (q) Canadian Conference of Mennonite Brethren Churches, Conference of Mennonites in Canada, Abe Dueck, and Ken Reddig, Ctr. for Menn. Brethren Studies, 169 Riverton Ave., Winnipeg, MB R2L 2E5. Tel. (204)669-6575. Fax (204)654-1865

Mennonitische Post, Die, (bi-m) Interdenominational Mennonite, Abe Warkentin, Box 1120, 383 Main St., Steinbach, MB R0A 2A0. Tel. (204)326-6790. Fax (204)326-6302

Mennonitische Rundschau, (m) Canadian Conference of Mennonite Brethren Churches, Lorina Marsch, 3-169 Riverton Ave., Winnipeg, MB R2L 2E5. Tel. (204)669-6575. Fax (204)654-1865

Messenger (of the Sacred Heart), (m) The Roman Catholic Church in Canada, F. J. Power, Apostleship of Prayer, 661 Greenwood Ave., Toronto, ON M4J 4B3. Tel. (416)466-1195

Messenger of Truth, (bi-w) Church of God in Christ (Mennonite), Gladwin Koehn, P.O. Box 230, Moundridge, KS 67107. Tel. (316)345-2532. Fax (316)345-2582

Messenger, The, (22/yr.) Evangelical Mennonite Conference, Terry M. Smith, P.O. Box 1268, Steinbach, MB R0A 2A0. Tel. (204)326-6401. Fax (204)326-1613 E-mail: emconf@mts.net

Messenger, The, (6/yr) Church of God in Eastern Canada (Anderson, Ind.), 65 Albacore Crescent, Scarborough, ON M2H 2L2. Tel. (416)431-9800

Messenger, The, (q) The Reformed Episcopal Church of Canada, Rt. Rev. Michael Fedechko, 320 Armstrong St., New Liskeard, ON P0J 1P0.

Missions Today, Pontifical Mission Societeies (English Canada), Natl. Dir., Sis. Leona Spencer, C.S.J., Editor, R.Wolak, O.M.I., 3329 Danforth Ave., Scarborough, ON M1L 4T3. Tel. (416)699-7077. Fax (416)699-9019 E-mail: missions@eda.net Website: http://www.eda.net/~missions

Monitor, The, (m) The Roman Catholic Church in Canada, Patrick J. Kennedy, P.O. Box 986, St. John's, NF A1C 5M3. Tel. (709)739-6553. Fax (709)739-6458

Multiply, Presbyterian Church in America (Canadian Section), Fred Marsh, 1852 Century Pl., Ste. 205, Atlanta, GA 30345. Tel. (404)320-3330. Fax (404)982-9108

N.A.B. Today, (6/yr) North American Baptist Conference, Marilyn Schaer, 1 S. 210 Summit Ave., Oakbrook Terrace, IL 60181. Tel. (630)495-2000. Fax (630)495-3301

National Bulletin on Liturgy, (4/yr) The Roman Catholic Church in Canada, Zita Maier, 90 Parent Ave., Ottawa, ON K1N 7B1. Tel. (613)241-9461. Fax (613)241-8117

New Church Canadian, (q) General Church of the New Jerusalem, T. J. Kerr and Erica Wyncoll, 152 Collingwood St., Kingston, ON K7L 3X5. Tel. (613)544-6176. Fax (416)239-4935

New Freeman, The, (w) The Roman Catholic Church in Canada, Bill Donovan, One Bayard Dr., Saint John, NB E2L 3L5. Tel. (506)653-6806. Fax (506)653-6812

News of Québec, Christian Brethren (also known as Plymouth Brethren), P.O. Box 1054, Sherbrooke, QC J1H 5L3 Tel. —

NEXUS, (9/yr) Conference of Mennonites in Canada, Roma Quapp, 600 Shaftesbury Blvd., Winnipeg, MB R3P 0M4. Tel. (204)888-6781. Fax (204)831-5675

Orthodox Way, (m) Greek Orthodox Metropolis of Toronto (Canada), Orthodox Way Committee, 86 Overlea Blvd., 4th Fl., Toronto, ON M4H 1C6. Tel. (416)429-5757. Fax (416)429-4588.
E-mail: gocanada@total.net.ca
Website: http://www.gocanada.org

Passport, (q) Interdenominational, Dwight Friesen, Briercrest Family of Schools, 510 College Dr., Caronport, SK S0H 0S0. Tel. (306)756-3200. Fax (306)756-3366
Website: http://www.briercrest.ca

Pentecostal Testimony, (m) The Pentecostal Assemblies of Canada, Richard P. Hiebert, 6745 Century Ave., Mississauga, ON L5N 6P7. Tel. (905)542-7400. Fax (905)542-7313

Pioneer, The, (bi-m) Reformed Church in America, Tom Torrance, Reformed Church Center, RR #4, Cambridge, ON N1R 5S5. Tel. (519)622-1777. Fax (519)622-1993

PMC: The Practice of Ministry in Canada, (4-5/yr) Interdenominational, Jim Taylor, 10162 Newene Rd., Winfield, BC V4V 1R2. Tel. (250)766-2778. Fax (250)766-2736

Pourastan, (bi-m) Armenian Holy Apostolic Church—Canadian Diocese, N. Ouzounian, 615 Stuart Ave., Outremont, QC H2V 3H2. Tel. (514)279-3066. Fax (514)276-9960

Presence, (8/yr) The Roman Catholic Church in Canada, Jean-Claude Breton, Peres Dominicains, 2715 chemin de la Cote St. Catherine, Montreal, QC H3T 1B6. Tel. (514)739-9797. Fax (514)739-1664

Prairie Messenger, (w) The Roman Catholic Church in Canada, Andrew M. Britz, O.S.B., Box 190, Muenster, SK S0K 2Y0. Tel. (306)682-1772. Fax (306)682-5285

Presbyterian Message, The, (10/yr) Presbyterian Church in Canada, Janice Carter, Kouchibouguac, NB E0A 2A0. Tel. (506)876-4379
E-mail: mjcarter@nb.sympatico.ca

Presbyterian Record, (11/yr) Presbyterian Church in Canada, John Congram, 50 Wynford Dr., North York, ON M3C 1J7. Tel. (416)441-1111. Fax (416)441-2825

Pulse, The, (4/yr) Evangelical Free Church of Canada, Rick Penner, E.F.C.C., Box 56109, Valley Ctr. P.O., Langley, BC V3A 8B3. Tel. (604)888-8668. Fax (604)888-3108
E-mail: efcc@twu.ca
Website: http://www.twu.ca/efcc/efcc.htm

Quaker Concern, (q) Canadian Yearly Meeting of the Religious Society of Friends, Peter Chapman, 60 Lowther Ave., Toronto, ON M5R 1C7. Tel. (416)920-5213. Fax (416)920-5214

Reformed Perspective: A Magazine for the Christian Fam., (m) Canadian and American Reformed Churches, Allard Gunnink, 34 Parkwater Crescent, Winnipeg, MB R2C 4W7. Tel. (204)224-9206. Fax (204)669-7013

Relations, (m) The Roman Catholic Church in Canada, Carolyn Sharp, 25 Ouest Jarry, Montreal, QC H2P 1S6. Tel. (514)387-2541. Fax (514)387-0206

RESCUE, (bi-m) International Union of Gospel Missions, Phillip Rydman, 1045 Swift, N. Kansas City, MO 64116. Tel. (816)471-8020. Fax (816)471-3718
E-mail: iugm@iugm.org
Website: http://www.iugm.org

Resource: The National Leadership Magazine, (5/yr) The Pentecostal Assemblies of Canada, Michael P. Horban, 6745 Century Ave., Mississauga, ON L5N 6P7. Tel. (905)542-7400. Fax (905)542-7313

Revival Fellowship News, (q) Interdenominational, Harold Lutzer, Canadian Revival Fellowship, Box 584, Regina, SK S4P 3A3. Tel. (306)522-3685. Fax (306)522-3686

SR: Studies in Religion: Sciences religieuses, (q) Nondenominational, Willi Braun, Bishop's University, Lennoxville, QB J1M 1Z7. Tel. (819)822-9600 ext.2377 Fax (819)822-9661

St. Luke Magazine, (m) Christ Catholic Church International, Donald W. Mullan, 5165 Palmer Ave., Niagara Falls, ON L2E 6S8. Tel. (905)354-2329. Fax (905)354-9934

Saints Herald, (m) Reorganized Church of Jesus Christ of Latter Day Saints, James Cable, The Herald Publishing House, P.O. Box 1770, Independence, MO 64055-0770. Tel. (816) 252-5010. Fax (816)252-3976

Sally Ann, (10/yr) The Salvation Army in Canada, Shirley Pavey, 2 Overlea Blvd., Toronto, ON M4H 1P4. Tel. (416)422-6113. Fax (416)422-6120

Scarboro Missions, (9/yr) The Roman Catholic Church in Canada, G. Curry, S.F.M., 2685 Kingston Rd., Scarborough, ON M1M 1M4. Tel. (416)261-7135. Fax (416)261-0820

Servant Magazine, (4/yr) Interdenominational, Phil Callaway, Prairie Bible Institute, Box 4000, Three Hills, AB T0M 2N0. Tel. (403)443-5511 Fax (403)443-5540

Shantyman, The, (bi-m) Nondenominational, Arthur C. Dixon, 2476 Argentia Rd., Ste. 213, Mississauga, ON L5N 6M1. Tel. (905)821-6310 Fax (905)821-6311

Sister Triangle, (q) Churches of Christ in Canada, Marge Roberts, PO 948, Dauphin, MB R7N 3J5. Tel. (204)638-8156 Fax (204)638-6025

Solia-The Herald, (m) The Romainian Orthodox Episcopate of America (Jackson, MI), Rev. Deacon David Oancea, PO Box 185, Grass Lake, MI 49240-0185. Tel. (517)522-3656 Fax (517)522-5907

Stocnik, (4/yr) Serbian Orthodox Church in the U.S.A. and Canada, Father Tomic, 7470 McNiven Rd., RR3, Campbellville, ON L0P 1B0. Tel. (905)878-0043 Fax (905)878-1909

Topic, (m) The Anglican Church of Canada, Lorie Chortyk, 580-401 W. Georgia St., Vancouver, BC V6B 5A1. Tel. (604)684-6306. Fax (604)684-7017

Trait d'Union, Le, (4-5/yr) Union d'Eglises Baptistes Francaises au Canada, Fritz Obas, 2285 Ave. Papineau, Montreal, QC H2K 4J5. Tel. (514)526-6643. Fax (514)526-9269

United Church Observer, (m) The United Church of Canada, Muriel Duncan, 478 Huron St., Toronto, ON M5R 2R3. Tel. (416)960-8500. Fax (416)960-8477

VIP Communique, Foursquare Gospel Church of Canada, Timothy J. Peterson, 8459-160th St., Ste. 100, Surrey, BC V3S 3T9. Tel. (604)543-8414. Fax (604)543-8417

Vie Chrétienne, La, (m) Presbyterian Church in Canada, Jean Porret, P.O. Box 272, Suzz. Rosemont, MontrÇal, QC H1X 3B8. Tel. (514)737-4168

Vie des Communautés religieuses, La, (5/yr) The Roman Catholic Church in Canada, André Bellefeuille, 251 St-Jean-Baptiste, Nicolet, QC J3T 1X9. Tel. (819)293-8736. Fax (819)293-2419

Vie Liturgique, (8/yr) The Roman Catholic Church in Canada, Novalis, 6255 Rue

Hutchison, Bureau 103, Montreal, QC H2V 4C7. Tel. (514)278-3020. Fax (514)278-3030

Visnyk: The Herald, (m) Ukrainian Orthodox Church of Canada, Ihor Kutash and Marusia Zurek, 9 St. John's Ave., Winnipeg, MB R2W 1G8. Tel. (204)586-3093. Fax (204)582-5241

Voce Evangelica/Evangel Voice, (bi-m) The Italian Pentecostal Church of Canada, Joseph Manafo and Daniel Ippolito, 384 Sunnyside Ave., Toronto, ON M6R 2S1. Tel. (416)766-6692. Fax (416)766-8014

War Cry, The, (m) The Salvation Army in Canada, Sharon Stinka, 2 Overlea Blvd., Toronto, ON M4H 1P4. Tel. (416)425-2111. Fax (416)422-6120 E-mail: warcry@salleynet.org

Word Alive, (4/yr) Nondenominational, Dwayne Janke, Wycliffe Bible Translators of Canada, Inc., 4316 10 St. N.E., Calgary, AB T2E 6K3. Tel. (403)250-5411. Fax (403)250-2623

Word, The, (10/yr) The Antiochian Orthodox Christian Archdiocese of North America, John P. Abdallah, 1777 Quigg Dr., Pittsburgh, PA 15241-2071. Tel. (201)871-1355. Fax (201) 871-7954

World: Journal of Unitarian Universalist Assoc., (bi-m) Unitarian, Tom Stites, 25 Beacon St., Boston, MA 02108. Tel. (617)742-2100. Fax (617)367-3237

Young Companion, (11/yr) Old Order Amish Church, Joseph Stoll and Christian Stoll, Rt. 4, Aylmer, ON N5H 2R3.

Young Soldier, The, (24/yr) The Salvation Army in Canada, Sharon Stinka, 2 Overlea Blvd., Toronto, ON M4H 1P4. Tel. (416)422-6114. Fax (416)422-6120

12. Church Archives and Historical Records Collections

American and Canadian history is interwoven with the social and cultural experience of religious life and thought. Most repositories of primary research materials in North America will include some documentation on religion and church communities. This directory is not intended to replace standard bibliographic guides to those resources. The intent is to give a new researcher entry to major archival holdings of religious collections and to programs of national scope. The repositories listed herein will not only provide information on materials in their custody, but also reference to significant regional and local church archives, as well as specialized collections such as those of religious orders, educational and charitable organizations, and personal papers. In the interest of space, no attempt has been made to list the plethora of research libraries of North America. Standard directories that serve this purpose are available in most public libraries. This directory has been thoroughly re-edited to include updated entries and contact information. Future editions will include updates to the bibliographic guides and source books. For that purpose the editor requests recommendations of current works. Please contact: Assistant Editor, Yearbook of American and Canadian Churches, 475 Riverside Dr., Rm. 812, New York, NY 10115 Tel. (212)870-2031 Fax (212)870-2817 E-mail: yearbook@ncc-cusa.org

Repositories marked with an asterisk (*) are designated by their denomination as the official archives. The reference departments at these archives will assist researchers in locating primary material of geographic or subject focus.

Mark J. Duffy, C.A.
The Archives of the Episcopal Church, U.S.A.

IN THE UNITED STATES

Adventist

Aurora University, Charles B. Phillips Library, 347 S. Gladstone, Aurora, IL 60506, Curator: Dr. David T. Arthur, Tel. (630) 844-5437, Fax (630) 844-3848, E-mail: jhuggins@aurora.edu

Archival materials on the Millerite/Early Adventist movement (1830-1860); also denominational archives relating to Advent Christian Church, Life and Advent Union, and, to a lesser extent, Evangelical Adventists and Age-to-Come Adventists.

Adventist Heritage Center, James White Library, Andrews University, Berrien Springs, MI 49104, Curator: Jim Ford, Tel. (616) 471-3274, Fax (616) 471-6166, E-mail: ahc@andrews.edu, Website: http://www.andrews.edu/library/collections/departments/ahc.html

Large collection of Seventh-day Adventist material.

Department of Archives and Special Collections/ Ellen G. White Estate Branch Office, Loma Linda University Library, Loma Linda, CA 92350, Chairman/Director: Elder Merlin D. Burt, Tel. (909) 824-4942, Fax (909) 824-4188

Photographs, sound and video recordings, personal papers, and library pertaining to the Seventh-day Adventist Church.

Ellen G. White Estate, Inc., 12501 Old Columbia Pike, Silver Spring, MD 20904, Archivist: Tim Poirier, Tel. (301) 680-6540, Fax (301) 680-6559, Website: http://www.whiteestate.org

Records include letters and manuscripts (1840s to 1915), pamphlets and publications and the White papers.

*General Conference of Seventh-day Adventists: Archives and Statistics, 12501 Old Columbia Pike, Silver Spring, MD 20904-6600, Assistant Director: Bert Haloviak, Tel. (301) 680-5022, Fax (301) 680-6090

Repository of the records created at the world administrative center of the Seventh-day Adventist Church, including the period from the 1860s to the present.

Assemblies of God

*Flower Pentecostal Heritage Center, 1445 Boonville Ave., Springfield, MO 65802, Director: Wayne Warner, Tel. (417) 862-1447x4400, Fax (417) 862-6203, E-mail: archives@ag.org

Official repository for materials related to the Assemblies of God, as well as materials related to the early Pentecostal movement in general.

Baptist

American Baptist-Samuel Colgate Historical Library, 1106 S Goodman St., Rochester, NY 14620-2532, Director: Dana Martin, Tel. (716) 473-1740, Fax (716) 473-1740 [Call first], E-mail: abhs@crds.edu, Website: http://www.crds.edu/abhs.html

Manuscript holdings include collections of

319

Baptist ministers, missionaries, and scholars, and some records of Baptist churches, associations, and national and international bodies.

*American Baptists Archives Center, P.O. Box 851, Valley Forge, PA 19482-0851, Archivist: Betty Layton, Tel. (610) 768-2374, Fax (610) 768-2266

Repository for the non-current records of the national boards and administrative organizations of American Baptist churches in the USA. Collections include mission files, publications, correspondence, official minutes and annual reports.

Andover Newton Theological School, Franklin Trask Library, 159 Herrick Rd., Newton Centre, MA 02159, Associate Director: Diana Yount, Tel. (617) 964-1100x252, Fax (617) 965-9756, E-mail: dyount@ants.edu, Website: http://www.ants.edu

The collections document Baptist, Congregational and United Church history, including personal papers relating to national denominational work and foreign missions, with emphasis on New England Church history.

Primitive Baptist Library of Carthage, Illinois, 416 Main St., Carthage, IL 62321, Director of Library: Elder Robert Webb, Tel. (217) 357-3723, Fax (217) 357-3723, E-mail: bwebb9@juno.com, Website: http://www.carthage.lib.il.us/community/churches/primbap/pbl.html

Collects the records of congregations and associations.

*Seventh-day Baptist Historical Society, 3120 Kennedy Rd., P.O. Box 1678, Janesville, WI 53547, Historian: Rev. Don A. Sanford, Tel. (608) 752-5055, Fax (608) 752-7711, E-mail: sdbhist@inwave.com, Website: http://www.seventhdaybaptist.org

Serves as a depository for records of Seventh-day Baptists, Sabbath and Sabbath-keeping Baptists since the mid-seventeenth century.

*Southern Baptists Historical Library & Archives, 901 Commerce St., Suite 400, Nashville, TN 37203-3630, Director and Archivist: Bill Sumners, Tel. (615) 244-0344, Fax (615) 782-4821, E-mail: bsumners@edge.net, Website: http://www.sbhla.org

Central depository of the Southern Baptist Convention. Materials include official records of denominational agencies; personal papers of denominational leaders; records of related Baptist organizations; and annual proceedings of national and regional bodies.

Brethren in Christ

*Archives of the Brethren in Christ Church, Messiah College, Grantham, PA 17027-9990, Archivist: Dr. E. Morris Sider, Tel. (717) 691-6048, Fax (717) 691-6042

Records of general church boards and agencies, regional conferences, congregations and personal papers of church leaders.

Church of the Brethren

*Brethren Historical Library and Archives, 1451 Dundee Ave., Elgin IL 60120, Librarian/Archivist: Kenneth M. Shaffer, Jr., Tel. (847) 742-5100, Fax (847) 742-6103, E-mail: kshaffer_gb@brethren.org

Archival materials dating from the 19th Century relating to the cultural, socio-economic, theological, genealogical, and institutional history of the Church of the Brethren.

Churches of God, General Conference

*Winebrenner Theological Seminary, 701 East Melrose Ave., Findlay, OH 45804, Director of Library Services: Dr. Gene Crutsinger, Tel. (419) 422-4824, Fax (419) 422-3999, E-mail: wtslib@aol.com

Archival materials of the Churches of God, General Conference including local conference journals.

Churches of Christ

Center for Restoration Studies, Abilene Christian University, 1700 Judge Ely Blvd., P.O. Box 29208, Abilene, TX 79699-8177, Special Services Librarian: Erma Jean Loveland, Tel. (915) 674-2538, Fax (915) 674-2202, E-mail: loveland@nicanor.acu.edu, Website: http://www.acu.edu/academics/library

Archival materials connected with the Stone-Campbell Movement. The chief focus is on the Church of Christ in the twentieth century.

Emmanuel School of Religion Library, One Walker Drive, Johnson City, TN 37601-9438, Director: Thomas E. Stokes, Tel. (423) 926-1186, Fax (423) 926-6198, E-mail: library@esr.edu, Website: http://www.esr.edu

Materials related to the Stone-Campbell/Restoration Movement tradition. Collection includes items from the Christian Church and Churches of Christ, the a cappella Churches of Christ, and the Christian Church (Disciples of Christ).

Disciples of Christ

*Disciples of Christ Historical Society, 1101 19th Ave. South, Nashville, TN 37212, Director of Library and Archives: David McWhirter, Tel. (615) 327-1444, Fax (615) 327-1445, E-mail: dishistsoc@aol.com, Website: http://www.users.aol.com/dishistsoc.index.html

Collects documents of the Stone-Campbell Movement.

Christian Theological Seminary Library, 1000 W. 42nd St., P.O. Box 88267, Indianapolis, IN 46208, Reference Librarian: Laura Isenthal, Tel. (317) 924-1331, Website: http://www.cts.edu

Archival materials dealing with the Disciples of Christ and related movements.

Episcopal

*Archives of the Episcopal Church, P.O. Box 2247, Austin, TX 78768-2247, Archivist: Mark J. Duffy, Tel. (512) 472-6816, Fax (512) 480-0437, E-mail: Research@Episcopal Archives.org, Website: http://www.Episcopal Archives.org

Repository for the official records of the national Church, its corporate bodies and affiliated agencies, personal papers, and some diocesan archives. Contact the Archives for reference to diocesan and parochial church records.

General Theological Seminary, Saint Mark's Library, 175 Ninth Ave., New York, NY 10011, Director of Special Collections: Isaac Gewirtz, Tel. (212) 243-5150, Fax (212) 924-6304, E-mail: gewirtz@gts.edu, Website: http://www.gts.edu

Manuscript collections of early Episcopal bishops and organizations.

Evangelical Congregation Church

*Archives of the Evangelical Congregational Church, Evangelical School of Theology, Rostad Library, 121 S. College St., Myerstown, PA 17067, Archivist: Terry M. Heisey, Tel. (717) 866-5775, Fax (717) 866-4667, E-mail: theisey@evangelical.edu, Website: http://www.evangelical.edu

Repository of records of the administrative units of the denomination, affiliated organizations, and closed churches. Also collected are records of local congregations and materials related to the United Evangelical Church and the Evangelical Association.

Evangelical and Reformed

*Evangelical and Reformed Historical Society, Lancaster Theological Seminary, 555 W. James St., Lancaster, PA 17603, Archivist: Richard R. Berg, Tel. (717) 290-8711, E-mail: erhs@lts.org

Manuscripts and transcriptions of early German Reformed Church, pastoral records and minutes of synods and classes, as well as records of the Evangelical and Reformed Church (1934-1957).

Friends

Friends' Historical Library of Swarthmore, Swarthmore College, 500 College Ave., Swarthmore, PA 19081-1399, Curator: Mary Ellen Chijioke, Tel. (610) 328-8496, E-mail: friends@swarthmore.edu, Website: http://www.swarthmore.edu/library/friends/

Official depository for the records of the Philadelphia, Baltimore, and New York Yearly Meetings. Comprehensive collection of originals and copies of other Quaker meeting archives.

The Quaker Collection, Haverford College, Haverford, PA 19041-1392, Quaker Bibliographer: Elizabeth Potts-Brown, Tel.

(610) 896-1161, Fax (610) 896-1102, E-mail: ebrown@haverford.edu, Website: http://www.haverford.edu/library/sc

Repository for material relating to the Society of Friends, especially to that segment of the Society known from 1827 to the mid-20th century as "Orthodox."

Jewish

American Jewish Historical Society, Friedman Memorial Library, 2 Thornton Rd., Waltham, MA 02453, Director: Dr. Michael Feldberg, Tel. (781) 891-8110, Fax (781) 899-9208

Archival repository of the Jewish people in America, including significant religious contributions to American life.

Jacob Rader Marcus Center of the American Jewish Archives, 3101 Clifton Ave., Cincinnati, OH 45220, Chief Archivist: Kevin Proffitt, Tel. (513) 221-1875, Fax (513) 221-7812, E-mail: aja@cn.huc.edu, Website: http://www.huc.edu/aja

Materials documenting the Jewish experience in the Western Hemisphere with emphasis on the Reform movement. Included in the collection are congregational and organizational records, personal papers of rabbis and secular leaders, and genealogical materials.

Latter-day Saints

Family History Library, 35 North West Temple, Salt Lake City, UT 84150, Tel. (801) 240-2331, Fax (801) 240-5551, E-mail: fhl@ldschurch.org

Primarily microfilmed vital, church, probate, land, census, and military records including local church registers.

*Historical Department, Archives Division, Church of Jesus Christ of the Latter-day Saints, 50 E. North Temple, Salt Lake City, UT 84150-3800, Archives Division Director: Steven R. Sorensen, Tel. (801) 240-2272, Fax (801) 240-1845

Repository of official records of church departments, missions, congregations, and associated organizations. Includes personal papers of church leaders and members.

Lutheran

*Archives of the Evangelical Lutheran Church in America, 8765 West Higgins Rd., Chicago, IL 50531-4198, Archivist: Elizabeth Wittman, Tel. (773) 380-2818, Fax (773) 380-2977, E-mail: archives@elca.org, Website: http://www.elca.org

Official repository for the churchwide offices of the denomination and its predecessors. For further information on synod and regional archives, contact the Chicago archives or check the ELCA World Wide Web site. For ELCA college and seminary archives, contact those institutions directly, or consult the ELCA Archives.

*Concordia Historical Institute, Dept. of Archives and History, Lutheran Church-Missouri Synod, 801 De Mun Ave., St. Louis, MO 63105-3199, Director: Rev. Daniel Preus, Tel. (314) 505-7900, Fax (314) 505-7901, E-mail: chi@chi.lcms.org, Website: http://www.chi.lcms.org

Official repository of The Lutheran Church-Missouri Synod. Collects synodical and congregational records, personal papers and records of Lutheran agencies.

Mennonite

*Archives of the Mennonite Church, 1700 South Main, Goshen, IN 46526, Directory: John E. Sharp, Tel. (219) 535-7477, Fax (219) 535-7293, E-mail: johnes@goshen.edu, Website: http://www.goshen.edu/mcarchives

Repository of the official organizational records of the Mennonite Church and personal papers of leaders and members.

*Mennonite Library and Archives, Bethel College, P. O. Drawer A, North Newton, KS 67117-9998, Archivist: John Thiesen, Tel. (316) 284-5304, E-mail: mla@bethelks.edu, Website: http://www.bethelks.edu

Official repository for the General Conference Mennonite Church and several other organizations related to the General Conference.

*Center for Mennonite-Brethren Studies, 1717 S. Chestnut, Fresno, CA 93702, Archivist: Kevin Enns-Rempel, Tel. (209) 453-2225, Fax (209) 453-2124, E-mail: kennsrem@fresno.edu, Website: http://www.fresno.edu/affiliation/cmbs

Official repository for the General Conference of Mennonite Brethren churches.

Methodist

B. L. Fisher Library, Asbury Theological Seminary, 204 N. Lexington Ave., Wilmore, KY 40390, Archivist and Special Collections Librarian: Bill Kostlevy, Tel. (606) 858-3581, Fax (606) 858-2350, E-mail: bill_kostlevy@ats.wilmore.ky.us

Documents the Holiness Movement and evangelical currents in the United Methodist Church. Holdings include records of related associations, camp meetings, personal papers, and periodicals.

*Heritage Hall at Livingstone College, 701 W. Monroe St., Salisbury, NC 28144, Director: Dr. Phyllis H. Galloway, Tel. (704) 638-5664

Records of the African Methodist Episcopal Zion Church.

*Office of the Historiographer of the African Methodist Episcopal Church, P.O. Box 301, Williamstown, MA 02167, Historiographer: Dr. Dennis C. Dickerson, Tel. (413) 597-2484, Fax (413) 597-3673, E-mail: dennis.c.dickerson@williams.edu

General and annual conference minutes; reports of various departments such as missions and publications; and congregational histories and other local materials. The materials are housed in the office of the historiographer and other designated locations.

*General Commission on Archives and History, The United Methodist Church, P. O. Box 127, Madison, NJ 07940, Archivist/Records Administrator: Dr. L. Dale Patterson, Tel. (973) 408-3189, Fax (973) 408-3909, E-mail: gcah@gcah.org, Website: http://www.gcah.org

Collects administrative and episcopal records, and personal papers of missionaries and leaders. Holds limited genealogical information on ordained ministers. Will direct researchers to local and regional collections of congregational records and information on United Methodism and its predecessors.

Center for Evangelical United Brethren Heritage, United Theological Seminary, 1810 Harvard Blvd., Dayton, OH 45406-4599, Director: Dr. James D. Nelson, Tel. (937) 278-5817x214, Fax (937) 275-5701, E-mail: nels039@ibm.net, Website: http://www.united.edu

Documents predecessor bodies of the United Methodist Church including Church of the United Brethren in Christ, Evangelical Association, United Evangelical Church, Evangelical United Brethren Church, Evangelical Congregational Church, and Evangelical Church of North America.

Moravian

Archives of the Moravian Church, Northern Province, 41 W. Locust St., Bethlehem, PA 18018, Archivist: Vernon H. Nelson, Tel. (610) 866-3255, Fax (610) 866-9210

Records of the Northern Province of the Moravian Church in America, including affiliated provinces in the Eastern West Indies, Nicaragua, Honduras, Labrador, and Alaska.

Moravian Archives, Southern Province, 4 East Bank St., Winston-Salem, NC 27101, Archivist: Dr. C. Daniel Crews, Tel. (336) 722-1742

Repository of the records of the Moravian Church, Southern Province, its congregations, and its members.

*Nazarene Archives, Church of the Nazarene, 6401 The Paseo, Kansas City, MO 64131, Archives Manager: Stan Ingersol, Tel. (816) 333-7000x2437, Fax (816) 361-4983, E-mail: singersol@nazarene.org, Website: http://www.nazarene.org/hoo/archives.html

Focus is on denominational archives, including those of leaders, agencies, and study commissions. The Archives also collect materials on districts, congregations, church-related colleges and seminaries around the world.

Pentecostal

David du Plessis Archives, Fuller Theological Seminary, 135 North Oakland, Pasadena, CA

91182, Archivist: Kate McGin, Tel. (626) 584-5311, Fax (626) 584-5644, E-mail: kmcgin@fuller.edu

Collects interdenominational Pentecostal records specializing in international leaders.

*International Pentecostal Holiness Church Archives and Research Center, P. O. Box 12609, Oklahoma City, OK 73157, Director: Dr. Harold Hunter, Tel. (405) 787-7110, Fax (405) 789-3957, E-mail: archives@iphc.org, Website: http://www.pctii.org/arc/archives.html

Official repository for records produced by the international headquarters, conferences, and influential leaders.

*Hal Bernard Dixon Jr. Pentecostal Research Center, 260 11th St. NE, Cleveland, TN 37311, Director: David G. Roebuck, Tel. (423) 614-8576, Fax (423) 614-8555, E-mail: dixon_research@leeuniversity.edu, Website: http://www.leeuniversity.edu/library/dixon/html

Official repository of the Pentecostal Church of God. Also collects other Pentecostal and Charismatic materials.

United Pentecostal Church International Historical Center, 8855 Dunn Rd., Hazelwood, MO 63042, Chair, Historical Committee: Rev. J. L. Hall, Tel. (314) 837-7300, Fax (314) 837-4503, E-mail: upcimain@aol.com

Collects a variety of Pentecostal archives, primarily the United Pentecostal (Oneness) Branch.

Polish National Catholic

*Polish National Catholic Church Commission on History and Archives, 1031 Cedar Ave., Scranton, PA 18505, Chair: Dr. Joseph Wieczerzak, Tel. (717) 343-0100

Documents pertaining to the Church's national office, parishes, Prime Bishop, leaders, and organizations.

Presbyterian

*Department of History and Records Management Services, Presbyterian Church (USA),

Headquarters Office, 425 Lombard St., Philadelphia, PA 19147-1516, Manager: Marjorie N. Sly, Tel. (215) 627-1852, Fax (215) 627-0509, E-mail: preshist@shrsys.hslc.org, Website: http://www.libertynet.org/pacscl/phs

Southern Regional Office, P. O. Box 849, Montreat, NC 28757, Deputy Director: Michelle A. Francis, Tel. (828) 669-7061, Fax (828) 669-5369, E-mail: pcusadoh@montreat.edu

Collects the official records of the Church's national offices and agencies, synods, presbyteries, and some local congregations. The Department also houses records of the Church's predecessor denominations and personal papers of prominent Presbyterians. The Southern Regional Office holds records of the predecessor Presbyterian Church in the US and congregational records.

*Historical Foundation of the Cumberland Presbyterian Church, 1978 Union Ave., Memphis, TN 38104, Archivist: Susan Knight Gore, Tel. (901) 276-8602, Fax (901) 272-3913, E-mail: skg@cumberland.org, Website: http://www.cumberland.org/hfcpc

Princeton Theological Seminary Libraries, Library Place and Mercer Street, P. O. Box 111, Princeton, NJ 08542-0803, Librarian for Archives and Special Collections: William O. Harris, Tel. (609) 497-7950, Fax (609) 497-1826

Documents the history of American Presbyterianism, including an extensive collection of congregational histories and missionary reports.

Reformed

*Reformed Church Archives, 21 Seminary Place, New Brunswick, NJ 08901-1159, Archivist: Russell Gasero, Tel. (732) 246-1779, Fax (732) 249-5412, E-mail: rgasero@aol.com, Website: http://www.rca.org

Official repository for denominational records including congregations, classes, synods, missions, and national offices.

Evangelical and Reformed Historical Society, Lancaster Theological Seminary, 555 W. James St., Lancaster, PA 17603, Archivist: Richard R. Berg, Tel. (717) 290-8711, E-mail: erhs@lts.org

Materials on the early German Reformed Church and pastoral records and minutes of synods and classes, as well as records of the Evangelical and Reformed Church (1934-1957).

*Heritage House, Calvin College, 3201 Burton St. S.E., Grand Rapids, MI 49546, Curator of Archives: Dr. Richard H. Harms, Tel. (616) 957-6313, Fax (616) 957-6470, E-mail: rharms@calvin.edu, Website: http://www.calvin.edu

Repository of the official records of the Christian Reformed Church in North America, including classes, congregations, and denominational agencies and committees.

Roman Catholic

U.S. Catholic Documentary Heritage Project. For holdings information on various dioceses and religious orders, consult: http://www.uschs.com

Catholic University of America (Mullen Library), 5 Mullen, Washington, DC 20064, Archivist: Timothy Meagher, Tel. (202) 319-5065, Fax (202) 319-6554, E-mail: meagher@cua.edu

Marquette University, Department of Special

CHURCH ARCHIVES

Collections and Archives, P. O. Box 3141, Milwaukee, WI 93201-3141, Department Head: Charles Elston, Tel. (414) 288-7256, Fax (414) 288-6709, E-mail: charles.elston @marquette.edu, Website: http://www.marquette.edu/library/collections/archives/index.html

Collection strengths are in the areas of Catholic social action, American missions and missionaries, and other work with Native Americans and African Americans.

University of Notre Dame Archives, 607 Hesburgh Library, Notre Dame, IN 46556, Curator of Manuscripts: William Kevin Cawley, Tel. (219) 631-6448, Fax (219) 631-7980, E-mail: archives.1@nd.edu, Website: http://www.nd.edu/~archives

Papers of bishops and prominent Catholics and records of Catholic organizations. Includes parish histories, but few parish records.

Salvation Army

*Salvation Army Archives and Research Center, 615 Slaters Lane, Alexandria, VA 22313, Archivist: Susan Mitchem, Tel. (703) 684-5500, Fax (703) 299-5552

Holds the documents of Salvation Army history, personalities, and events in the United States from 1880.

Swedenborgian

*Bryn Athyn College of the New Church, Swedenborg Library, 2815 Huntingdon Pike, P.O. Box 278-68, Bryn Athyn, PA 19009, Carroll C. Odhner, Tel. (215) 938-2547, Fax (215) 938-2637, E-mail: ccodhner@newchurch.edu

Unitarian Universalist

*Andover-Harvard Theological Library, Harvard Divinity School, 45 Francis Ave., Cambridge, MA 02138, Curator: Timothy Driscoll, Tel. (617) 496-5153, Fax (617) 496-4111, E-mail: timothy_driscoll@harvard.edu, Website: http://www.divweb.harvard.edu/library

Institutional archives of the Unitarian Universalist Association (including some congregational records) and the Unitarian Universalist Service Committee. The library also houses numerous personal manuscript collections of Unitarian ministers and church leaders.

Meadville/Lombard Theological School Library, 5701 S. Woodlawn Ave., Chicago, IL 60637, Library Director and Professor: Neil W. Gerdes, Tel. (773) 256-3000, Fax (773) 256-3008, E-mail: ngerdes@meadville.edu

Repository for materials relating to Unitarian Universalism in particular and liberal religion in general. Includes personal papers and church records from many UU churches in the Midwestern USA.

United Church of Christ

*United Church of Christ Archives, 700 Prospect Ave., Cleveland, OH 44115, Archivist: Ng. George Hing, Tel. (216) 736-3285, Fax (216) 736-2120, E-mail: hingg@ucc.org

Records created in the national setting of the Church since its founding in 1957, including the General Synod, Executive Council, officers, instrumentalities, and bodies created by and/or related to the General Synod.

Andover Newton Theological School, Franklin Trask Library, 159 Herrick Rd., Newton Centre, MA 02159, Associate Director for Special Collections: Diana Yount, Tel. (617) 964-1100x252, Fax (617) 965-9756, E-mail: dyount@ants.edu, Website: http://www.ants.edu

Collections document Baptists, Congregational, and UCC history. Some personal papers relating to national denominational work and foreign missionary activity; majority of collections relate to New England history.

Archives of the Evangelical Synod of North America, Eden Theological Seminary, Luhr Library, 475 E. Lockwood Ave., Webster Groves, MO 63119-3192, Archivist: Clifton W. Kerr, Tel. (314) 961-3627x348, E-mail: ckerr@eden.edu

Archival records include organization records, personal papers and immigration records.

Congregational Library, 14 Beacon St., Boston, MA 02108, Archivist: Virginia A. Hunt, Tel. (617) 523-0470, Fax (617) 523-0491, E-mail: vhunt@14beacon.org, Website: http://www.14beacon.org

Documentation on the Congregational, Congregational Christian, Christian, and United Church of Christ throughout the world, including local church records, associations, charitable organizations, and papers of clergy, missionaries and others.

Elon College Library, P. O. Box 187, Elon College, NC 27244, Archivist/Technical Services Librarian: Connie L. Keller, Tel. (336) 538-6545, Fax (336) 538-6547, E-mail: keller@numen.elon.edu

Collection of membership records and other archival material on the predecessor churches of the UCC: Christian Church and the Southern Conference of the Christian Church; also maintains records of churches that no longer exist.

Interdenominational

American Bible Society Library, 1865 Broadway, New York, NY 10023-9980, Director: Mary Jane Ballou, Tel. (212) 408-1495, Fax (212) 408-1526, E-mail: mballou@americanbible.org, Website: http://www.americanbible.org

Billy Graham Center Archives, Wheaton

College, 500 College Ave., Wheaton, Il 60187-5593, Director of Archives: Robert Shuster, Tel. (630) 752-5910, Fax (630) 752-5916, E-mail: bgcarc@wheaton.edu, Website: http://www.wheaton.edu/bgc/archives.archhpl.html

National Council of Churches of Christ Archives, Department of History and Records Management Services, Presbyterian Church (USA), 425 Lombard St., Philadelphia, PA 19147-1516, Manager: Marjorie N. Sly, Tel. (215) 627-1852, Fax (215) 627-0509, E-mail: preshist@shrsys.hslc.org, Website: http://www.libertynet.org/pacscl/phs/

Graduate Theological Union Archives, 2400 Ridge Road, Berkeley, CA 94709, Archivist: Lucinda Glenn Rand, Tel. (510) 649-2507, Fax (510) 649-2508, E-mail: LGlenn@gtu.edu, Website: http://www.gtu. edu/library/archives. html

Holy Spirit Research Center, Oral Roberts University Library, P.O. Box 2187, 7777 S. Lewis, Tulsa OK 74171, Director: Jim Zigler, Tel. (918) 495-6898, Fax (918) 495-6033, E-mail: hsrc@oru.edu

Schomburg Center for Research in Black Culture, 515 Malcolm X Blvd., New York, NY 10037, Manuscripts, Archives, and Rare Books Division, Tel. (212) 491-2200, Fax (212) 491-6760, Website: http://www.nypl.org

Union Theological Seminary, Burke Library, 3041 Broadway, New York, NY 10027, Archivist and Head of Special Collections: Claire McCurdy, Tel. (212) 280-1502, Fax (212) 280-1456, E-mail: awt@uts.columbia. edu, Website: http://www.uts.columbia.edu

University of Chicago, Regenstein Library, 1100 E 57th St., Chicago, IL 60537-1502, Curtis Bochanyin, Tel. (312) 702-8740

Yale Divinity School Library, 409 Prospect St., New Haven, CT 06511, Research Services Librarian: Martha Smalley, Tel. (203) 432-6374, Fax (203) 432-3906, E-mail: divinity.library@yale.edu, Website: http://www.Library.yale.edu.div

STANDARD GUIDES TO CHURCH ARCHIVES

William Henry Allison, *Inventory of Unpublished Material for American Religious History in Protestant Church Archives and other Depositories*, (Washington, DC, Carnegie Institution of Washington, 1910) 254 pp.

John Graves Barrow, *A Bibliography of Bibliographies in Religion*, (Ann Arbor, Mich., 1955), pp. 185-198

Edmund L. Binsfield, "Church Archives in the United States and Canada: A Bibliography," in *American Archivist*, V.21, No. 3 (July 1958) pp. 311-332, 219 entries.

Nelson R. Burr, "Sources for the Study of American Church History in the Library of Congress," 1953. 13 pp. Reprinted from *Church History*, Vol. XXII, No. 3 (Sept. 1953).

Canadian Archival Resources on the Internet: University of Saskatchewan Archives, Web Site maintained by Cheryl Avery and Steve Billington at http://www.usask.ca/archives/menu.html

Mable Deutrick, "Supplement to Church Archives in the United States and Canada, a Bibliography," (Washington, DC, 1964).

Andrea Hinding, ed., *Women's History Sources: A guide to Archives and Manuscript Collections in the U.S.*, (New York, Bowker, 1979) 2 vols.

Kay Kirkham, *A Survey of American Church Records, for the Period Before The Civil War, East of the Mississippi River*, (Salt Lake City, 1959-60) 2 vols. Includes the depositories and bibliographies.

Peter G. Mode, *Source Book and Bibliographical Guide for American Church History*, (Menasha, Wisc., George Banta Publishing Co., 1921) 735 pp.

Society of American Archivists, American Archivist, 1936/37 (continuing). Has articles on church records and depositories.

A.R. Suelflow, *A Preliminary Guide to Church Records Repositories*, (Society of American Archivists, Church Archives Committee, 1969) Lists more than 500 historical-archival depositories with denominational and religious history in America.

U.S. National Historical Publications and Records Commission, *Directory of Archives and Manuscript Repositories in the United States*, (Washington, D.C., 1988).

United States, Library of Congress, Division of Manuscripts, *Manuscripts in Public and Private Collections in the United States*, (Washington, DC, 1924).

U.S. Library of Congress, Washington, DC: *The National Union Catalog of Manuscript Collections*, Serially published from 1959 to 1993 (1959-1993).Contains many entries for collections of church archives. Researchers may consult the cumulative paper indexes or use the NUCMC home page to access the RLIN database of archives and manuscripts collections at http:/lcweb.loc.gov/coll/nucmc/nucmc.html

IN CANADA

Anglican

*General Synod Archives, 600 Jarvis St. Toronto, ON M4Y 2J6, Archivist: Terry Thompson, Tel. (416) 924-9199 x 279, Fax (416) 968-7983, E-mail: archives@national. anglican.ca, Website: http://www.anglican.ca

Collects the permanent records of the General Synod, its committees and its employees. The Archives has a national scope and provides referral services on local Church records.

Baptist

*Atlantic Baptist Historical Collection of the Acadia University Archives, Vaughan Memorial Library, Wolfville, NS BOP 1XO, Archivist: Patricia Townsend, Tel. (902) 585-1412, E-mail: patricia.townsend@acadiau.ca

Collection of denominational newspapers, mission materials, Atlantic Baptist Church records and microfilm collections on the Protestant Reformation.

Canadian Baptist Archives, McMaster Divinity College, Hamilton, ON L8S 4K1, Director: Dr. Kenneth R. Morgan, Tel. (905) 525-9140, Fax (905) 577-4782, E-mail: morgankr@ mcmaster.ca

Friends

Canadian Yearly Meeting Archives, Pickering College, 16945 Bayview Avenue, New Market, ON L3Y 4X2, Yearly Meeting Archivist: Jane Zavitz-Bond, Tel. (905) 895-1700, Fax (905) 895-9076

Holds the extant records for Quakers in Canada beginning with Adolphus in 1798 to the present, including the records of the Canadian Friends Service Committee.

Jewish

Canadian Jewish Congress National Archives, 1590 Avenue Docteur Penfield, Montreal, Que. H3G 1C5, Director of Archives: Janice Rosen, Tel. (514) 931-7531, Fax (514) 931-0548, E-mail: archives@cjc.ca, Website: http://www.cjc.ca/htm

Collects documentation on all aspects of social, political and cultural history of the Jewish presence in Quebec and Canada.

Lutheran

*Archives of the Evangelical Lutheran Church in Canada, 302-393 Portage Ave., Winnepeg, MB R3B 3H6, National Secretary/Archivist: Robert H. Granke, Tel. (204) 984-9150, Fax (204) 984-9185, E-mail: rhgranke@elcic.ca, Website: http://www.elcic.com

Official repository for the ELCIC and its predecessor bodies, the Evangelical Lutheran Church of Canada and the Evangelical Lutheran Church of America-Canada Section.

Lutheran Historical Institute, 7100 Ada Blvd., Edmonton, Alberta T5B 4E4, Archivist: Karen Baron, Tel. (403) 474-8156, Fax (403) 477-9829, E-mail: abclcc@connect.ab.ca

Mennonite

*Archives of the Conference of Mennonites in Canada, 600 Shaftesbury Blvd., Winnipeg, MB R3P OM4, Director: Kenneth W. Reddig, Tel. (204) 888-6781, Fax (204) 831-5675, E-mail: kreddig@confmenno.ca, Website: http://www.mbnet.mb.ca/~mhc/

Institutional records and personal papers of leaders within the Mennonite Community. Holdings include the records of the Conference, various Church boards and agencies.

*Center for Mennonite Brethren Studies, 1-169 Riverton Ave., Winnepeg, MB R2L 2E5, Director: Dr. Abe Dueck, Tel. (204) 559-6575, Fax (204) 654-1865, E-mail: adueck@conmb-conf.ca

Institutional records of the boards and agencies of the Mennonite Brethren Church in Canada with some holdings pertaining to other parts of North America. Also personal papers of leaders.

Pentecostal

*Pentecostal Assemblies of Canada, 6745 Century Ave., Mississauga, ON L5N 6P7, Director of Archives: Douglas Rudd, Tel. (905) 542-7400, Fax (905) 542-7313, E-mail: admin@paoc.org

Repository of archival records created by the Pentecostal Assemblies of Canada.

Presbyterian

*Presbyterian Church in Canada Archives and Records, 50 Wynford Drive, North York, ON M3C 1J7, Archivist/Records Administrator: Kim M. Arnold, Tel. (416) 441-1111x310, Fax (416) 441-2825, E-mail: karnold@presbyterian.ca, Website: http://www.presbyterian.ca

Records of the Presbyterian Church in Canada, its officials, ministers, congregations and organizations.

Roman Catholic

Research Center in Religious History in Canada, St. Paul University, 223 Main St., Ottawa, ON K1S 1C4, Tel. (613) 237-0580

Holds guides to many Canadian Catholic archives.

Salvation Army

George Scott Railton Heritage Centre, 2130 Bayview Ave., Toronto, ON M4N 3K6, Director: Major Paul Murray, Tel. (416) 481-4441, Fax (416) 481-6096, E-mail: fpmurray@sallynet.org

Records include publications and comprehensive financial, personnel, social welfare and immigration records.

United Church of Canada

*United Church of Canada Central Archives, Victoria University, 73 Queens Park Crescent, Toronto, ON M5S 1K7, Chief Archivist: Jean Dryden, Tel. (416) 585-4563, E-mail: uccvu.archives@utoronto.ca, Website: http://www.vicu.utoronto.ca/archives/archives.htm

Records of the United Church and its antecedent denominations and local and regional records of the United Church in Ontario. Call or view the web page for information on other regional archives.

Interdenominational

Canadian Council of Churches Archives, on deposit in National Archives of Canada, 395 Wellington, Ottawa,ON K1A 0N3, Tel. Research Services Division: (613) 992-3884; Genealogical assistance: (613) 996-7458, E-mail: reference@archives.ca, Website: http://www.archives.ca

National Archives of Canada, 395 Wellington, Ottawa, ON K1A 0N3, Tel. Research Services Division: (613) 992-3884; Genealogical assistance: (613) 996-7458, E-mail: reference@archives.ca, Website: http://www.archives.ca

Records of interdenominational and ecumenical organizations, missionary societies, denominational churches, parish registers and papers of prominent clergy.

CHURCH ARCHIVES

III

STATISTICAL SECTION

Guide to Statistical Tables

Since there are no religious questions in the U.S. Census, the *Yearbook of American & Canadian Churches* is as near an "official" record of denominational statistics as is available.

Because the data represents the most complete annual compilation of church statistics, there is a temptation to expect more than is reasonable. These tables provide the answers to very simple and straightforward questions. Officials in church bodies were asked: "How many members does your organization spend?" Each respondent interprets the questions according to the policies of the organization.

Caution should, therefore, be exercised when comparing statistics across denominational lines, comparing statistics from one year to another and adding together statistics from different denominations.

Some particular methodological issues and therefore cautions in interpretation include the following considerations:

1. Definitions of membership, clergy, and other important characteristics differ from denomination to denomination. In this section, full or confirmed membership refers to those with full communicant status. Inclusive membership refers to those who are full communicants or confirmed members plus other members baptized, non-confirmed or non-communicant. Each denomination determines the age at which a young person is considered a member. Denominations also vary in their approaches to statistics. For some, very careful counts are made of members. Other groups only make estimates.

2. Each year the data is collected with the same questions. While most denominations have consistent reporting practices from one year to the next, any change in practices is not noted in the tables. Church mergers and splits can also influence the statistics when they are compared over a number of years. Denominations have different reporting schedules and some do not report on a regular basis. Only data that has been reported within the last ten years is included.

3. The two problems listed above make adding figures from different denominations problematic. However, an additional complication is that individuals may be included more than once. For example, a person who attends the Church of God in Christ on Wednesday evening and an AME service on Sunday morning will likely be included in both counts.

329

Canadian Current Membership Statistics

Religious Body	Year Reporting	Number of Churches Reporting	Full Communicant or Confirmed Members	Inclusive Membership	Number of Pastors Serving Parishes	Total Number of Clergy	Number of Sunday or Sabbath Schools	Total Enrollment
The Anglican Church of Canada	1996	2,957	736,699	739,699	1,622	3,368	1,827	66,756
Antiochian Orthodox Christian Archdiocese of North America	1996	215	350,000	350,000	400	445	200	
Apostolic Christian Church (Nazarene)	1985	14		830	49	49		
Apostolic Church in Canada	1992	14	1,200	1,600	14	19	14	350
Apostolic Church of Pentecost of Canada, Inc.	1997	153	22,300	22,300	310	447		
Armenian Holy Apostolic Church—Canadian Diocese	1996	10	75,000	75,000	8	9	10	4,650
Associated Gospel Churches	1992	126	9,284	9,284	118	239		
Association of Regular Baptist Churches (Canada)	1994	12			8	11		
Baptist Convention of Ontario and Quebec	1997	386*	32,000*	57,800*	408	734		
Baptist General Conference of Canada	1987	70		60,066	80	84		
Baptist Union of Western Canada	1994	161	20,006	20,006	181	273	137	7,961
United Baptist Convention of the Atlantic Provinces	1997	550	63,787	63,787	302	496	353	
Bible Holiness Church	1996	18	459	758	12	14	18	

Canadian Current Membership Statistics (continued)

Religious Body	Year Reporting	Number of Churches Reporting	Full Communicant or Confirmed Members	Inclusive Membership	Number of Pastors Serving Parishes	Total Number of Clergy	Number of Sunday or Sabbath Schools	Total Enrollment
The Bible Holiness Movement	1996	18	459	758	12	14	18	
Brethren in Christ Church, Canadian Conference	1997	42	3,219	3,219	22	41	42	1,934
British Columbia Baptist Conference	1995	24	2,427	2,427	40	50	19	1,247
Canadian and American Reformed Churches	1997	48	7,801	14,722	43	60		
Canadian Baptist Ministries	1996	1,133	129,055	129,055				
Canadian Conference of Mennonite Brethren Churches	1997	208	31,477	31,733	343	385	170	22,199
Canadian Convention of Southern Baptists	1997	130	8,228	8,228	111	133	120	7,872
Canadian Yearly Meeting of the Religious Society of Friends	1995	22	1,125	1,893	0	0	30	
Central Canada Baptist Conference, The	1993	36			50	51		
Christian and Missionary Alliance in Canada	1995	376	31,719	87,197	1,054	1,211	376	36,860
Christian Brethren (Plymouth Brethren)	1997	600		50,000		250	550	
Christian Church (Disciples of Christ) in Canada	1997	30	2,053	3,285	22	46	15	291

331

Canadian Current Membership Statistics (*continued*)

Religious Body	Year Reporting	Number of Churches Reporting	Full Communicant or Confirmed Members	Inclusive Membership	Number of Pastors Serving Parishes	Total Number of Clergy	Number of Sunday or Sabbath Schools	Total Enrollment
Christian Reformed Church in North America	1997	246	48,139	81,023	207	300		
Church of God (Anderson, Ind.)	1997	50	3,723	3,723	62	89	42	1,761
Church of God (Cleveland, Tenn.)	1995	115	8,908	8,908	58	97	94	4,864
Church of God in Christ (Mennonite)	1997	46	3,946	3,946	144	144	46	
Church of God of Prophecy in Canada	1995	40	3,107	3,107	98	100	37	
Church of Jesus Christ of Latter-day Saints in Canada	1992	391	130,000	130,000			391	
Church of the Lutheran Brethren	1997	10	343	559	10	11	8	473
Church of the Nazarene Canada	1997	165	11,963	11,963	137	276	149	15,588
Churches of Christ in Canada	1997	140	8,000	8,000				
Conference of Mennonites in Canada	1995	223	35,995	35,995	281	464		
Congregational Christian Churches in Canada	1997	96	4,302	4,302		230		
Coptic Orthodox Church in Canada	1992	12			20		17	
The Estonian Evangelical Lutheran Church	1997	11	5,089	5,089	10	13	3	106
The Evangelical Covenant Church of Canada	1997	22	1,290	1,290	15	25	21	1,763

Canadian Current Membership Statistics *(continued)*

Religious Body	Year Reporting	Number of Churches Reporting	Full Communicant or Confirmed Members	Inclusive Membership	Number of Pastors Serving Parishes	Total Number of Clergy	Number of Sunday or Sabbath Schools	Total Enrollment
Evangelical Free Church of Canada	1996	133	7,169	22,528				
Evangelical Lutheran Church in Canada	1995	650	141,921	198,751	455	855	443	22,773
Evangelical Mennonite Conference of Canada	1996	53	6,508	6,508	89	105	50	4,254
Evanglical Mennonite Mission Conference	1997	44	4,633	4,633	75	201		
Evangelical Missionary Church of Canada	1993	145	9,923	12,217	172	367	125	7,465
Fellowship of Evangelical Baptist Churches in Canada	1995	506	72,288					7,475
Foursquare Gospel Church of Canada	1996	54	3,063	3,063	66	103		1,258
Free Methodist Church in Canada	1996	129	5,360	5,360	158	271		
Free Will Baptists	1998	10	347		3	4	8	
Greek Orthodox Diocese of Toronto (Canada)	1997	76	350,000	350,000	58	71	76	
Independent Assemblies of God International (Canada)	1997	214			265	508		
Independent Holiness Church	1994	5		150	4	10	4	118

333

Canadian Current Membership Statistics *(continued)*

Religious Body	Year Reporting	Number of Churches Reporting	Full Communicant or Confirmed Members	Inclusive Membership	Number of Pastors Serving Parishes	Total Number of Clergy	Number of Sunday or Sabbath Schools	Total Enrollment
Jehovah's Witness	1997	1,388	113,763	113,763				
Latvian Evangelical Lutheran Church in America	1995	17	4,162	4,647	11	13	4	104
Lutheran Church—Canada	1994	329	58,316	79,844	251	373	291	13,259
Mennonite Church (Canada)	1996	117	8,172	8,172	177	291	173	21,827
Moravian Church in America, Canadian District	1997	9	1,272	1,770	6	11	9	612
North American Baptist Conference	1997	123	17,557	17,557	125	199	123	
Old Catholic Church of Canada	1996	3	40	40	4	5		
Old Order Amish Church	1992	930						
Open Bible Faith Fellowship of Canada, The	1987	4		1,000	5	6		
Orthodox Church in America (Canada Section)	1993	606	1,000,000	1,000,000	740		502	
Patriarchal Parishes of the Russian Orthodox Church in Canada	1997	23	800	1,500	3	4	3	34
Pentecostal Assemblies of Canada	1995	1,100		218,782	1,758	1,758	753	65,928
Pentecostal Assemblies of Newfoundland	1997	140	14,715	29,361	189	301	121	10,272

Canadian Current Membership Statistics (continued)

Religious Body	Year Reporting	Number of Churches Reporting	Full Communicant or Confirmed Members	Inclusive Membership	Number of Pastors Serving Parishes	Total Number of Clergy	Number of Sunday or Sabbath Schools	Total Enrollment
Presbyterian Church in America (Canadian Section)	1997	16	701	1,140	20	27		457
The Presbyterian Church in Canada	1997	1,012	143,784	211,812		1,245		
Reformed Church in Canada	1995	41	4,000	6,490	33	71	37	1,841
The Reformed Episcopal Church of Canada	1997	8	600	750	8	11	3	36
Reinland Mennonite Church	1995	6	877	1,816	10	13	5	347
Reorganized Church of Jesus Christ of Latter Day Saints	1995	75	11,264	11,264	1,020	1,020		
The Roman Catholic Church in Canada/Canadian Conference of Catholic Bishops	1997	5,716	12,498,605*	12,498,605*		110,760		
The Romanian Orthodox Episcopate of America (Jackson, MI)	1997	19	900		13	14	12	
Salvation Army in Canada	1995	370	31,256	95,763	760	2,008	410	23,120
Seventh-day Adventist Church in Canada	1997	336	46,962	46,962	172	282	381	29,507
Swedenborgians	1994	3	347	1,085	6	6	3	185

Canadian Current Membership Statistics (continued)

Religious Body	Year Reporting	Number of Churches Reporting	Full Communicant or Confirmed Members	Inclusive Membership	Number of Pastors Serving Parishes	Total Number of Clergy	Number of Sunday or Sabbath Schools	Total Enrollment
Syrian Orthodox Church of Antioch (Archdiocese of the United States and Canada)	1995	5	2,500	2,500	3	4		
Ukrainian Orthodox Church of Canada	1988	258		120,000	75	91		
United Brethren Church in Canada	1992	9	835	835	5	12	9	447
The United Church of Canada	1997	3,820	701,968	1,649,754	2,048	2,223	3,125	88,426
United Pentecostal Church in Canada	1997	199				340*		
Universal Fellowship of Metropolitan Community Churches	1992	12	50	1,500	8	9	1	36
The Wesleyan Church of Canada	1997	82	5,166	5,374	85	171	64	19,296
Wisconsin Evangelical Lutheran Synod	1995	16	958	1,361	16	16	16	350

United States Current Membership Statistics

Religious Body	Year Reporting	Number of Churches Reporting	Full Communicant or Confirmed Members	Inclusive Membership	Number of Pastors Serving Parishes	Total Number of Clergy	Number of Sunday or Sabbath Schools	Total Enrollment
Advent Christian Church	1997	311	17,154	26,819	300	500	315	15,041
African Methodist Episcopal Church	1991	8,000		3,500,000				
African Methodist Episcopal Zion Church	1998	3,098	1,035,963	1,252,369	2,572	2,767	1,672	67,320
Albanian Orthodox Diocese of America	1996	2	1,995	1,995	1	2	2	121
Allegheny Wesleyan Methodist Connection (Original Allegheny Conference)	1997	115	1,849	2,013	86	188	114	6,113
The American Association of Lutheran Churches	1997	90	14,231	18,704	100	144	85	4,641
American Baptist Association	1986	1,705		250,000	1,740	1,760		
American Baptist Churches in the USA	1997	5,830		4,145	7,846			
The American Carpatho-Russian Orthodox Greek Catholic Church	1997	79	12,998	12,998	83	101	76	
American Catholic Church	1997	100		25,000	80	100		
American Rescue Workers	1996	15	3,000	10,000	50	56	10	325
Antiochian Orthodox Christian Diocese of North America	1995	16	50,000	50,000	100	110	1,000	
Apostolic Christian Church (Nazarene)	1993	63	3,723	3,723	217	234	55	

United States Current Membership Statistics (continued)

Religious Body	Year Reporting	Number of Churches Reporting	Full Communicant or Confirmed Members	Inclusive Membership	Number of Pastors Serving Parishes	Total Number of Clergy	Number of Sunday or Sabbath Schools	Total Enrollment
Apostolic Christian Church of America	1997	89	12,538	12,538			89	6,480
Apostolic Episcopal Church	1997	250	14,000	14,000	250	300	50	
Apostolic Faith Mission Church of God	1997	18	8,100	10,450	24	41	26	4,280
Apostolic Faith Mission of Portland, Oregon	1997	115	1,849	2,013	86	188	114	6,113
Apostolic Lutheran Church of America	1997	60				62		
Apostolic Orthodox Catholic Church	1997	19		1,154	19	24		
Apostolic Overcoming Holy Catholic Church of God, Inc.	1997	146	12,871	12,871	358	378	146	
Armenian Apostolic Church of America	1997	28	100,000	200,000	22	28		1,103
Assemblies of God	1997	11,920	1,419,717	2,494,574	18,221	32,367	11,376	1,393,214
Associated Reformed Presbyterian Church (General Synod)	1997	238	34,344	40,060	194	325	206	17,078
The Association of Free Lutheran Congregations	1997	243	24,488	32,659	140	209	213	6,345
Baptist Bible Fellowship International	1997	4,500	1,200,000	1,200,000		7,500	4,500	
Baptist General Conference	1997	879	134,795	134,795			145,347	

United States Current Membership Statistics (continued)

Religious Body	Year Reporting	Number of Churches Reporting	Full Communicant or Confirmed Members	Inclusive Membership	Number of Pastors Serving Parishes	Total Number of Clergy	Number of Sunday or Sabbath Schools	Total Enrollment
Baptist Missionary Association of America	1997	1,342	234,334	234,334	1,500	2,700		91,347
Beachy Amish Mennonite Churches	1997	114	7,853	7,853	381	381		
Berean Fundamental Church	1997	51		8,000				
Bible Church of Christ	1993	6	4,150	6,850	11	52	6	
Bible Fellowship Church	1995	58	7,132	7,132	63	121	58	
Brethren Church (Ashland, Ohio)	1997	117	13,856	13,856	86	186	108	6433*
Brethren in Christ	1996	199	18,424	18,424	133	318	199	13,000
Christ Catholic Church	1996	7	1,205	2,728	7	8	2	23
The Christian and Missionary Alliance	1997	1,964	146,513	328,078	1,654	2,498	1,627	212,809
Christian Brethren (Plymouth Brethren)	1997	1,150		100,000		500	1,000	
Christian Catholic Church (Evangelical-Protestant)	1995	7	1,221	1,697	7	8	2	
Christian Church (Disciples of Christ)	1997	3,818	568,921	879,436	3,419	7,266	3,576	198,457
Christian Churches of North America, General Council	1996	350	31,558	31,558	261	498	350	23,814
Christian Churches and Churches of Christ	1988	5,579		1,071,616	5,525			

339

United States Current Membership Statistics (continued)

Religious Body	Year Reporting	Number of Churches Reporting	Full Communicant or Confirmed Members	Inclusive Membership	Number of Pastors Serving Parishes	Total Number of Clergy	Number of Sunday or Sabbath Schools	Total Enrollment
The Christian Congregation, Inc.	1997	1,438	115,881	115,881	1,436	1,438	1,294	40,243
Christian Methodist Episcopal Church	1983	2,340	718,922	718,922				
Christian Reformed Church in North America	1997	723	133,463	196,464	642	1,189		
Church of Christ (Holiness) U.S.A.	1997	166	10,243	10,243	210	223	159	11,230
Church of Christ, Scientist		2,200						
Church of God (Anderson, Ind.)	1997	2,347	229,302	229,302	2,920	4,123		
Church of God by Faith, Inc.	1991	145	6,819	8,235	155	170		13,000
Church of God (Cleveland, Tenn.)	1995	6,060	753,230	753,230	3,121	5,556	5,354	407,445
Church of God General Conference (Oregon, IL and Morrow, GA)	1997	90	3,877	5,040	65	80	86	2,585
Church of God in Christ	1991	15,300	5,499,875	5,499,875	28,988	33,593		
Church of God in Christ, International								
Church of God in Christ, Mennonite	1997	102	11,551	11,551	418	420	102	
Church of God of the Mountain Assembly, Inc.	1994	118	6,140	6,140				
Church of God of Prophecy	1997	1,908	76,531	76,531	2,000	2,049	1,880	81,608

United States Current Membership Statistics (continued)

Religious Body	Year Reporting	Number of Churches Reporting	Full Communicant or Confirmed Members	Inclusive Membership	Number of Pastors Serving Parishes	Total Number of Clergy	Number of Sunday or Sabbath Schools	Total Enrollment
The Church of God (Seventh Day) Denver, Colo.	1997	175	7,000	10,000	94	123	175	
Church of Illumination	1996	3	300	1,200	8	15	2	216
Church of Jesus Christ (Bickertonites)	1989	63		2,707	183	262		
The Church of Jesus Christ of Latter-day Saints	1997	10,811	4,417,700	4,923,100	32,433	36,418	10,811	3,963,700
Church of the Brethren	1997	1,095	141,400	141,400	827	1,945	858	43,577
Church of the Living God (Motto: Christian Workers for Fellowship)	1985	170		4,200	170			
Church of the Lutheran Brethren of America	1997	117	8232	13,530	136	233	105	9,674
Church of the Lutheran Confession	1997	74	6,510	8,768	58	85	74	1,391
Church of the Nazarene	1997	5,118	615,632	619,576	4,581	9,907	4,850	816,375
Church of the United Brethren in Christ	1997	2280	23,585	23,585	315	449	228	12,837
Churches of Christ	1997	14,400	1,400,000	1,800,000	14,000	15,850	12,000	1,400,000
Church Christ in Christian Union	1998	226	9,858	9,858	318	540	188	11,629
Churches of God, General Conference (CGGC)	1997	342	31,557	31,557	247	431	342	22,688

United States Current Membership Statistics (*continued*)

Religious Body	Year Reporting	Number of Churches Reporting	Full Communicant or Confirmed Members	Inclusive Membership	Number of Pastors Serving Parishes	Total Number of Clergy	Number of Sunday or Sabbath Schools	Total Enrollment
Congregational Holiness Church	1993	190		2,468			190	
Conservative Baptist Association of America	1992	1,084	200,000	200,000				
Conservative Congregational Christian Conference	1997	227	38,956	38,956	282	517	189	13,930
Conservative Lutheran Association	1997	6	862	1,338	9	22	5	185
Coptic Orthodox Church	1992	85	180,000	180,000	65	68	85	
Cumberland Presbyterian Church	1997	771	88,068	88,068	634	822		38,851
Cumberland Presbyterian Church in America	1996	152	15,142	15,142	141	156	152	9,465
Diocese of America, Armenian Church	1991	72	14,000	414,000	49	70		
Elim Fellowship	1997	90			600	814		
The Estonian Evangelical Lutheran Church	1997	21	3,508	15,142	10	12		
The Evangelical Church	1997	134	12,430	12,430	132	234		
The Evangelical Congregational Church	1997	148	22,957	22,957	99	184	148	13,173
The Evangelical Covenant Church	1997	622	93,414	93,414	565	1,110	540	88,924

United States Current Membership Statistics *(continued)*

Religious Body	Year Reporting	Number of Churches Reporting	Full Communicant or Confirmed Members	Inclusive Membership	Number of Pastors Serving Parishes	Total Number of Clergy	Number of Sunday or Sabbath Schools	Total Enrollment
The Evangelical Free Church of America	1995	1,224	124,499	242,619	1,936	2,436		
Evangelical Friends International—North American Region	1995	92	8,666	8,666		185	90	7,226
Evangelical Lutheran Church in America	1997	10,889	3,844,169	5,185,055	9,695	17,510	8,658	940,048
Evangelical Lutheran Synod	1997	136	16,444	22,089	96	166	125	3,601
Evanglical Mennonite Church	1998	31	4,348	4,646	69	103	31	4,216
Evangelical Methodist Church	1997	123	8,615	8,615	105	215	120	6,547
Evangelical Presbyterian Church	1997	186	53,100	57,502	247	419	180	37,287
Fellowship of Evangelical Bible Churches	1996	37	4,039	4,039	44	106	29	2,693
Fellowship of Fundamental Bible Churches	1994	23	1,343	1,343	35	42	23	1,276
Fellowship of Grace Brethren Churches	1997	260	30,371	30,371		564		
Free Methodist Church of North America	1997	1,029	66,829	72,834		1,956	915	89,317
Friends General Conference	1997	620	32,000	32,000				
Friends United Meeting	1997	620	32,000	32,000	242	360	409	
Full Gospel Assemblies International	1995	44	3,960	3,960	290	290	44	

343

United States Current Membership Statistics *(continued)*

Religious Body	Year Reporting	Number of Churches Reporting	Full Communicant or Confirmed Members	Inclusive Membership	Number of Pastors Serving Parishes	Total Number of Clergy	Number of Sunday or Sabbath Schools	Total Enrollment
Full Gospel Fellowship of Churches and Ministers International	1995	650	195,000	195,000	725			215,000
Fundamental Methodist Church, Inc.	1993	12	682	787	17	22	12	454
General Assembly of the Korean Presbyterian Church in America	1992	203	21,788	26,988	326	382		
General Association of General Baptists	1997	790	72,326	72,326	1,085	1,228	832	37,906
General Association of Regular Baptist Churches	1996	1,440		115,950				
General Church of the New Jerusalem	1997	34	3,049	5,424	27	57		
General Conference Mennonite Brethren Churches	1996	368	50,915	82,130	590			34,668
Grace Gospel Fellowship	1992	128		60,000	160	196	128	
Greek Orthodox Diocese of America	1998	523		1,954,500	596	806	500	
Hungarian Reformed Church in America	1989	27		9,780	29	32		
Hutterian Brethren	1997	428	36,000	42,800	500	575	50	8,900
Independent Fundamental Churches of America	1995	670	69,857	69,857				64,779
Hungarian Reformed Church in America	1989	27		9,780	29	32		

United States Current Membership Statistics *(continued)*

Religious Body	Year Reporting	Number of Churches Reporting	Full Communicant or Confirmed Members	Inclusive Membership	Number of Pastors Serving Parishes	Total Number of Clergy	Number of Sunday or Sabbath Schools	Total Enrollment
Full Gospel Fellowship of Churches and Ministers International	1995	650	195,000	195,000	725			215,000
Fundamental Methodist Church, Inc.	1993	12	682	787	17	22	12	454
General Assembly of the Korean Presbyterian Church in America	1992	203	21,788	26,988	326	382		
General Association of General Baptists	1997	790	70,562	70,562	1,085	1,228	832	37,906
General Association of Regular Baptist Churches	1996	1,440		115,950				
General Church of the New Jerusalem	1997	34	3,049	5,424	27	57		
General Conference Mennonite Brethren Churches	1996	368	50,915	82,130	590			34,668
Grace Gospel Fellowship	1992	128		60,000	160	196	128	
Greek Orthodox Diocese of America	1998	523		1,954,500	596	806	500	
Hungarian Reformed Church in America	1989	27		9,780	29	32		
Hutterian Brethren	1997	428	36,000	42,800	500	575	50	8,900
Independent Fundamental Churches of America	1995	670	69,857	69,857				64,779
International Church of the Foursquare Gospel	1997	1,832	231,522	231,522	2,421	5,163*		59,630*

United States Current Membership Statistics (*continued*)

Religious Body	Year Reporting	Number of Churches Reporting	Full Communicant or Confirmed Members	Inclusive Membership	Number of Pastors Serving Parishes	Total Number of Clergy	Number of Sunday or Sabbath Schools	Total Enrollment
International Council of Community Churches	1995	517	250,000	250,000	491	501		
The International Pentecostal Church of Christ	1997	70	2,494	5,311	77	163	68	3,867
International Pentecostal Holiness Church	1997	1,681	170,382	170,382	1,472	1,915		93,685
Jehovah's Witnesses	1997	10,883	974,719	974,719	0	0	0	0
The Latvian Evangelical Lutheran Church in America	1996	74	15,200	16,900	56	84		
The Liberal Catholic Church—Province of the U.S.A.	1996	16	6,500	6,500	54	54		
The Lutheran Church—Missouri Synod	1997	6,215	1,951,391	2,603,036	5,276	8,672	5,739	606,408
The Malankara Mar Thoma Syrian Church, The Diocese of North America and Europe	1997	65	30,000	30,000	33	38	50	3,950
Mennonite Church	1996	1,004	90,959	90,959	1,525	2,817	1,495	139,859
Mennonite Church, The General Conference	1997	264	34,731	34,731	338	687	264	12,838
The Missionary Church	1997	333	31,197	47,550	427	720		29,928
Moravian Church in America (Unitas Fratrum), North Province	1997	260	30,371	30,371		564		
National Association of Congregational Christian Churches	1998	435	68,510	68,510	534	668		

United States Current Membership Statistics *(continued)*

Religious Body	Year Reporting	Number of Churches Reporting	Full Communicant or Confirmed Members	Inclusive Membership	Number of Pastors Serving Parishes	Total Number of Clergy	Number of Sunday or Sabbath Schools	Total Enrollment
National Association of Free Will Baptists	1997	2,320	210,305	210,305	2,800	2,900	2,494	132,859
National Baptist Convention of America, Inc.	1987	2,500		3,500,000	8,000			
National Baptist Convention, USA, Inc.	1992	33,000	8,200,000	8,200,000	32,832	32,832		
National Missionary Baptist Convention of America, Inc.	1992			2,500,000				
National Organization of the New Apostolic Church of North America	1993	554	41,863	41,863	983	1,096	554	2,764
National Spiritualist Association of Churches	1997	130	3,530	3,530	99	134	44	
Netherlands Reformed Congregations	1997	23	4,218	8,753	7	8	20	2,600
North American Baptist Conference	1997	268	43,850	43,850	276	422	268	
Old German Baptist Brethren	1997	57	5,832	5,832	253			
Old Order Amish Church	1993	898	80,820	80,820	3,592	3,617	55	
Open Bible Standard Churches, Inc.	1997	374				1,057		
Orthodox Church in America	1995	600	1,000,000	2,000,000	650	792	450	
The Orthodox Presbyterian Church	1997	198	15,072	21,765	376	341	11,475	

United States Current Membership Statistics *(continued)*

Religious Body	Year Reporting	Number of Churches Reporting	Full Communicant or Confirmed Members	Inclusive Membership	Number of Pastors Serving Parishes	Total Number of Clergy	Number of Sunday or Sabbath Schools	Total Enrollment
Patriarchal Parishes of the Russial Orthodox Church in the U.S.A.	1985	38		9,780	37	45		
Pentecostal Assemblies of the World, Inc.	1997	1,600	1,000,000	1,000,000				
Pentecostal Church of God	1996	1,230	45,200	111,900	1,818		1,230	70,100
Pentecostal Fire-Baptized Holiness Church	1996	27	223	223		28	25	400
Pentecostal Free Will Baptist Church, Inc.	1996	157	16,000	16,000	157	250		
Presbyterian Church in America	1997	1,340	224,154	279,549	1,642	2,665		116,720
Presbyterian Church (U.S.A.)	1997	11,295	2,609,191	3,610,753	9,385	20,858	9,317	1,065,388
Primitive Advent Christian Church	1993	10	345	345	11	11	10	292
Primitive Methodist Church in the U.S.A.	1997	78	4,917	6,588	70	106	78	3,583
Progressive National Baptist Convention, Inc.	1995	2,000	2,500,000	2,500,000				
Protestant Reformed Churches in America	1997	27	3,615	6,494	52	39	23	
Reformed Church in America	1997	949	185,074	305,476	905	1,888	895	107,457
Reformed Church in the United States	1997	38	3,169	4,246	32	42	35	922
Reformed Episcopal Church	1995	102	6,084	6,084	125	160		

United States Current Membership Statistics *(continued)*

Religious Body	Year Reporting	Number of Churches Reporting	Full Communicant or Confirmed Members	Inclusive Membership	Number of Pastors Serving Parishes	Total Number of Clergy	Number of Sunday or Sabbath Schools	Total Enrollment
Reformed Mennonite Church	1993	10	331	346	20	20		
Reformed Presbyterian Church of North America	1997	86	4,363	6,105	70	137	78	3,373
Religious Society of Friends (Conservative)	1994	1,200		104,000				
Reorganized Church of Jesus Christ of Latter Day Saints	1997	1,237	248,450	248,523		19,188		
The Roman Catholic Church	1996	22,728		61,207,914		49,071		4,208,295*
The Romanian Orthodox Episcopate of North America	1996	37	65,000	65,000	37	81	30	1,800
The Russian Orthodox Church Outside of Russia	1994	177				319	319	
The Salvation Army	1995	1,264	139,781	453,150	3,645	5,242	1,261	110,890
The Schwenkfelder Church	1995	5	2,524	2,524	8	9	5	701
Separate Baptists in Christ	1992	100	8,000	8,000	95	140	100	
Serbian Orthodox Church in the U.S.A. and Canada	1986	68		67,000	60	82		
Seventh-day Adventist Church	1997	4,348	825,654	825,654	2,401	4,912	4,648	455,745

United States Current Membership Statistics *(continued)*

Religious Body	Year Reporting	Number of Churches Reporting	Full Communicant or Confirmed Members	Inclusive Membership	Number of Pastors Serving Parishes	Total Number of Clergy	Number of Sunday or Sabbath Schools	Total Enrollment
Seventh Day Baptist General Conference	1995	80	4,800		46	74		
Southern Baptist Convention	1997	40,887	15,891,514	15,891,514	57,300	80,274	36,417	8,140,107
Southern Methodist Church	1997	122	7,992	7,992	112	151	118	6,075
Sovereign Grace Baptists	1997	300	3,000	3,000	400	400	300	
The Swedenborgian Church	1997	37	1,521	2,029	33	53		
Syrian Orthodox Church of Antioch	1997	21	32,500	32,500	14	20		
True Orthodox Church of Greece (SOMC), American Exarchate	1993	9	1,080	1,080	18	19		
Ukranian Orthodox Church of America (Ecumenical Patriarachate)	1986	27		5,000	36	37		
United Christian Church	1996	11	334	430	8	10	11	647
United Church of Christ	1997	6,061	1,438,181	1,438,181	4,379	10,296		358,651
The United Methodist Church	1996	36,170	8,496,047	8,496,047	19,580^	39,061^	33,659	3,705,863
United Pentecostal Chuirch International	1995	3,790			7,903			
United Zion Church	1993	13	852	852	13	23	13	618
Unity of the Brethren	1993	27	2,550	3,090	29	38	23	1,434

United States Current Membership Statistics *(continued)*

Religious Body	Year Reporting	Number of Churches Reporting	Full Communicant or Confirmed Members	Inclusive Membership	Number of Pastors Serving Parishes	Total Number of Clergy	Number of Sunday or Sabbath Schools	Total Enrollment
University Fellowship of Metropolitan Community Churches	1996	285		46,000	316			
The Wesleyan Church	1997	1,578	111,771	119,107	1,524	3,143	1,503	334,691
Wisconsin Evangelical Lutheran Synod	1997	1,240	315,355	411,295	1,222	1,648	1,197	45,667

Membership Statistics for the National Council of the Churches of Christ in the U.S.A.

Religious Body	Year Reporting	Number of Churches Reporting	Inclusive Membership	Number of Pastors Serving Parishes
African Methodist Episcopal Church	1991	8,000	3,500,000	
African Methodist Episcopal Zion Church	1997	3,098	1,252,369	2,571
American Baptist Churches in the U.S.A.	1997	5,830	1,503,267*	4,145
Antiochian Orthodox Christian Diocese of North America	1995	16	50,000	100
Armenian Apostolic Church	1997	28	200,000	22
Christian Church (Disciples of Christ)	1997	3,818	879,436	3,419
Christian Methodist Episcopal Church	1983	2,340	718,922	
Church of the Brethren	1997	1,095	141,400	827
Coptic Orthodox Church	1992	85	180,000	65
Episcopal Church	1996	7,390	2,364,559	8,131
Evangelical Lutheran Church in America	1997	10,889	5,185,055	9,695
Friends United Meeting^	1997	501	41,614	242
Greek Orthodox Archdiocese of North America and South America	1997	523	1,954,500	596
Hungarian Reformed Church in America	1989	27	9,780	29
International Council of Community Churches	1995	517	250,000	491
Korean Presbyterian Church in America	1992	203	26,988	326
The Malankara Mar Thoma Syrian Church, Diocese of North America and Europe	1997	65	30,000	33
Moravian Church in America, Northern Province	1997	94	21,108	95
Moravian Church in America, Southern Province	1991	56	21,513	63

National Council of Churches Current Membership Statistics *(continued)*

Religious Body	Year Reporting	Number of Churches Reporting	Inclusive Membership	Number of Pastors Serving Parishes
National Baptist Convention of America, Inc.	1987	2,500	3,500,000	8,000
National Baptist Convention, USA, Inc.	1992	33,000	8,200,000	32,832
National Missionary Baptist Convention of America	1992	2,500,000		
Orthodox Church in America	1995	600	2,000,000	650
Polish National Catholic Church of America	1960	162		
Presbyterian Church (U.S.A.)	1997	11,295	3,610,753	9,385
Progressive National Baptist Convention, Inc.	1995	2,000	2,500,000	
Reformed Church in America	1997	949	305,476	905
Russian Orthodox Church in the USA, Patriarchal Parishes	1985	38		
Serbian Orthodox Church in the U.S.A. and Canada	1986	68	67,000	60
The Swedenborgian Church	1997	37	2,096	33
Syrian Orthodox Church of Antioch	1997	17	32,500	14
Ukranian Orthodox Church of America (Ecumenical Patriarchate)	1986	27	5,000	36
United Church of Christ	1997	6,061	1,438,181	4,379
The United Methodist Church	1997	36,170*	8,496,047*	19,580

Selected Statistics of Church

Religious Body	Year	Full or Confirmed Members	Inclusive Members	TOTAL CONTRIBUTIONS		
				Total Contributions	Per Capita Full or Confirmed Members	Per Capita Inclusive Members
The Antiochian Orthodox Christian Archdiocese of North America	1996	50,000	50,000	$3,475,000	$69.50	$69.50
The Bible Holiness Movement	1996	459	758	$226,816	$494.15	$299.23
Brethren in Christ Church, Canadian Conference	1997	3,219	3,219	$4,916,548	$1,527.35	$1,527.35
United Baptist Convention of the Atlantic Provinces	1997	63,787	63,787	$33,207,092	$520.59	$520.59
Christian and Missionary Alliance in Canada	1995	31,719	87,197	$76,658,338	$2,416.80	$879.14
Christian Church (Disciples of Christ) in Canada	1997	2,053	3,285	$1,353,560	$659.31	$412.04
Church of God (Anderson Ind.)	1997	3,723	3,723	$595,579	$159.97	$159.97
Church of the Lutheran Brethren	1997	343	559	$574,316	$1,674.39	$1,027.40
Church of the Nazarene Canada	1997	11,963	11,963	$8,343,404	$697.43	$697.43
The Evangelical Covenant Church of Canada	1997	1,290	1,290	$7,690,321	$5,961.49	$5,961.49
Evangelical Lutheran Church in Canada	1995	141,921	198,751	$54,609,875	$384.79	$274.77
Foursquare Gospel Church of Canada	1996	3,063	3,063	$4,376,923	$1,428.97	$1,428.97
Free Methodist Church in Canada	1996	5,360	5,360	$3,177,707	$592.86	$592.86
The Latvian Evangelical Lutheran Church in America	1995	4,162	4,647	$2,201,332	$288.64	$258.52
Lutheran Church—Canada	1994	58,316	79,844	$26,046,000	$446.64	$326.21
Mennonite Church—Canada	1996	8,172	8,172	$12,924,965	$1,581.62	$1,581.62
Moravian Church in America, Canadian District	1997	1,272	1,770	$1,142,954	$898.55	$645.74
North American Baptist Conference	1997	17,557	17,557	$24,308,553	$1,384.55	$1,384.55
Patriarchal Parishes of the Russian Orthodox Church in Canada	1997	800	1,500	$317,000	$396.25	$211.33
Pentecostal Assemblies of Newfoundland	1997	14,715	29,361	$3,143,197	$213.60	$107.05
Presbyterian Church in America (Canadian Section)	1997	701	1,140	$1,708,607	$2,437.39	$1,498.78
The Presbyterian Church in Canada	1997	145,328	211,075	$85,326,113	$587.13	$404.25
Reformed Church in Canada	1995	4,000	6,490	$5,155,531	$1,288.88	$794.38
The Reformed Episcopal Church of Canada	1997	600	750	$125,000	$208.33	$166.67
Seventh-day Adventist in Canada	1997	46,962	46,962	$57,546,475	$1,225.38	$1,225.38
The United Church of Canada	1997	701,968	1,649,754	$291,308,150	$414.99	$176.58
The Wesleyan Church of Canada	1997	5,166	5,374	$10,193,278	$1,973.15	$1,896.78
Wisconsin Evangelical Lutheran Synod	1995	958	1,361	$830,695	$867.11	$610.36

Finances—Canadian Churches

CONGREGATIONAL FINANCES			BENEVOLENCES			
Total Congregation Contributions	Per Capita Full or Confirmed Members	Per Capita Inclusive Members	Total Benevolences	Per Capita Full or Confirmed Members	Per Capita Inclusive Members	Benevolences as a Percentage
$1,385,000	$27.70	$27.70	$2,090,000	$41.80	$41.80	60%
$27,946	$60.99	$36.87	$199,866	$435.44	$263.68	$44%
$3,598,458	$1,117.88	$1,117.88	$1,318,090	$409.47	$409.47	27%
$30,065,091	$471.34	$471.34	$3,142,001	$49.26	$49.26	9%
$62,505,203	$1,970.59	$716.83	$14,153,135	$446.20	$162.31	18%
$1,237,213	$602.64	$376.62	$116.347	$56.67	$35.42	9%
$263,957	$70.90	$70.90	$331,622	$89.07	$89.07	56%
$471,997	$1,376.08	$844.36	$102,319	$298.31	$183.04	18%
$6,769,849	$565.90	$565.90	$1,573,555	$131.54	$131.54	19%
$2,096,979	$1,625.57	$1,625.57	$5,503,342	$4,335.92	$4,335.92	73%
$47,826,658	$336.99	$240.64	$6,783,217	$47.80	$34.13	12%
$4,428,451	$1,387.02	$1,387.02	$128,472	$41.94	$41.94	3%
$925,703	$172.71	$172.71	$2,252,004	$420.15	$420.15	71%
$1,014,766	$243.82	$218.37	$186,566	#44.83	$40.15	16%
$21,405,000	$367.05	$268.09	$4,641,000	$79.58	$58.13	18%
$9,310,612	$1,139.33	$1,139.33	$3,614,353	$442.28	$442.28	28%
$1,011,578	$795.27	$571.51	$131,376	$103.28	$74.22	11%
$18,715,211	$1,065.97	$1,065.97	$5,593,342	$318.58	$318.58	23%
$110,000*	$137.50*	$73.33*	$207,000	$258.75	$138.00	65%
$1,835,046	$124.71	$62.50	$1,308,151	$88.90	$44.55	42%
$1,486,362	$2,120.35	$1,303.83	$222,245	$317.04	$194.95	13%
$73,507,501	$505.80	$348.25	$11,818,612	$81.32	$55.99	14%
$4,286,394	$1,071.60	$660.46	$869,137	$217.28	$133.92	17%
$120,000	$200.00	$160.00	$5,500	$9.17	$7.33	4%
$18,473,256	$393.37	$393.37	$39,073,219	$832.02	$832.02	68%
$251,284,999	$357.97	$152.32	$40,023,151	$57.02	$24.26	14%
$8,755,161	$1,694.77	$1,629.17	$1,438,117	$278.38	$267.61	14%
$741,206	$773.70	$544.60	$89,490	$93.41	$65.75	11%

Selected Statistics of Church

Religious Body	Year	Full or Confirmed Members	Inclusive Members	TOTAL CONTRIBUTIONS		
				Total Contributions	Per Capita Full or Confirmed Members	Per Capita Inclusive Members
African Methodist Episcopal Zion Church	1998	1,035,963	1,252,369	$76,997,130	$74.32	$61.48
Albanian Orthodox Diocese of America	1996	1,995	1,995	$171,900	$86.17	$86.17
Allegheny Wesleyan Methodist Connection (Original Allegheny Conference)	1997	1,849	2,013	$4,690,138	$2,536.58	$2,329.92
American Baptist Churches in the U.S.A.	1996	1,503,267	1,503,267	$407,344,795	$270.97	$270.97
Apostolic Faith Mission Church of God	1997	8,100	10,450	$560,000	$69.14	$53.59
Associate Reformed Presbyterian Church (General Synod)	1997	34,344	40,060	$31,848,213	$927.33	$795.01
Baptist General Conference	1997	134,795	134,795	$22,784,518	$169.03	$169.03
Brethren in Christ Church	1996	18,424	18,424	$21,641,025	$1,174.61	$1,174.61
The Christian and Missionary Alliance	1997	146,153	328,078	$249,484,961	$1,707.01	$760.44
Christian Church (Disciples of Christ)	1997	568,921	879,436	$424,473,173	$746.10	$482.67
Christian Church of North America, General Council	1996	31,558	31,558	$20,783,896	$658.59	$658.59
Church of Christ (Holiness) U.S.A.	1997	10,243	10,243	$7,332,546	$715.86	$715.86
Church of God (Anderson, Ind.)	1997	229,302	229,302	$223,492,670	$974.67	$974.67
Church of God General Conference (Oregon, IL and Morrow, GA.)	1997	3,877	5,040	$3,502,584	$903.43	$694.96
Church of the Brethren	1997	141,400	141,400	$77,644,344	$549.11	$549.11
Church of the Lutheran Brethren of America	1997	8,232	13,530	$11,300,212	$1,372.71	$835.20
Church of the Lutheran Confession	1997	6,510	8,768	$4,472,340	$687.00	$510.08
Church of the Nazarene	1997	615,632	619,576	$532,896,902	$865.61	$860.10
Church of the United Brethren in Christ	1997	23,585	23,585	$27,184,899	$1,152.64	$1,152.64
Churches of Christ	1997	1,400,000	1,800,000	$1,445,000,000	$1,032.14	$802.78
Churches of God, General Conference (CGGC)	1997	31,557	31,557	$21,192,337	$671.56	$671.56
Conservative Congregational Christian Conference	1997	38,956	38,956	$33,371,999	$856.66	$856.66
Cumberland Presbyterian Church	1997	88,068	88,068	$39,960,964	$453.75	$453.75
Cumberland Presbyterian Church in America	1996	88,066	88,066	$37,529,737	$426.15	$426.15
Episcopal Church	1996	1,593,413	2,364,559	$1,812,882,445	$1,137.74	$766.69
The Evangelical Church	1997	12,430	12,430	$13,885,472	$1,117.09	$1,117.09
The Evangelical Congregational Church	1997	22,957	22,957	$19,119,453	$832.84	$832.84

Finances—United States Churches

CONGREGATIONAL FINANCES			BENEVOLENCES			
Total Congregation Contributions	Per Capita Full or Confirmed Members	Per Capita Inclusive Members	Total Benevolences	Per Capita Full or Confirmed Members	Per Capita Inclusive Members	Benevolences as a Percentage
$74,280,000	$71.70	#59.31	$2,717,130	$2.62	$2.17	4%
$164,600	$82.51	$82.51	$7,300	$3.66	$3.66	4%
$3,646,644	$1,972.22	$1,811.55	$1,043,494	$564.36	$518.38	22%
$351,362,401	$233.73	$233.73	$55,982,394	$37.24	$37.24	14%
$276,000	$34.07	$26.41	$284,000	$35.06	$27.18	51%
$27,931,115	$813.27	$697.23	$3,917,098	$114.05	$97.78	12%
	$0.00	$0.00	$22,784,518	$169.03	$169.03	100%
$16,892,154	$916.86	$916.86	$4,748,871	$257.75	$257.75	22%
$206,461,968	$1,412.64	$629.31	$43,022,993	$294.37	$131.14	17%
$381,463,761	$670.50	$433.76	$43,009,412	$75.60	$48.91	10%
$17,136,919	$543.03	$543.03	$3,646,977	$115.56	$115.56	18%
$6,990,146	$682.43	$682.43	$342,400	$33.43	$33.43	5%
$194,438,623	$847.96	$847.96	$29,054,047	$126.71	$126.71	13%
$2,987,337	$770.53	$592.73	$515,247	$132.90	$102.23	15%
$60,923,817	$430.86	$430.86	$16,720,527	$118.25	$118.25	22%
$9,459,182	$1,149.07	$699.13	$1,841,030	$223.64	$136.07	16%
$3,821,360	$587.00	$435.83	$650,980	$100.00	$74.24	15%
$433,821,461	$704.68	$700.19	$99,085,440	$160.93	$159.91	19%
$23,770,417	$1,007.86	$1,007.86	$3,414,482	$144.77	$144.77	13%
$1,414,000,000	$1,010.00	$785.56	$31,000,000	$22.14	$17.22	2%
$17,204,995	$545.20	$545.20	$3,987,342	$126.35	$126.35	19%
$28,204,355	$724.01	$724.01	$5,167,644	$132.65	$132.65	15 %
$34,375,614	$390.33	$390.33	$5,585,350	$63.42	$63.42	14%
$34,921,064	$396.53	$396.53	$5,487,460	$62.31	$62.31	15%
$1,559,950,226	$979.00	$659.72	$252,932,219	$158.74	$106.97	14% '
$11,351,934	$913.27	$913.27	$2,533,538	$203.82	$203.82	28%
$15,658,454	$682.08	$682.08	$3,460,999	$150.76	$150.76	18%

Selected Statistics of Church

Religious Body	Year	Full or Confirmed Members	Inclusive Members	TOTAL CONTRIBUTIONS		
				Total Contributions	Per Capita Full or Confirmed Members	Per Capita Inclusive Members
The Evangelical Covenant Church	1997	93,414	93,414	$148,105,585	$1,585.48	$1,585.48
Evangelical Lutheran Church in America	1997	3,844,169	5,185,055	$1,932,921,574	$502.82	$372.79
Evangelical Lutheran Synod	1997	16,444	22,098	$10,087,522	$613.45	$456.49
Evangelical Mennonite Church	1998	4,348	4,646	$9,057,328	$2,083.10	$1,949.49
Free Methodist Church of North America	1997	66,829	72,834	$90,948,790	$1,360.92	$1,248.71
General Association of General Baptists	1997	72,326	72,326	$29,874,795	$413.06	$413.06
General Conference of Mennonite Brethren Churches	1996	50,915	82,130	$65,983,528	$1,295.95	$803.40
The International Pentecostal Church of Christ	1997	2,494	5,311	$5,319,133	$2,132.77	$1,001.53
The Latvian Evangelical Lutheran Church in America	1996	15,200	16,900	$6,791,000	$446.78	$401.83
The Lutheran Church—Missouri Synod	1997	1,951,391	2,603,036	$998,449,172	$511.66	$383.57
Mennonite Church	1996	90,959	90,959	$104,481,914	$1,148.67	$1,148.67
Mennonite Church, The General Conference	1997	34,731	34,731	$21,205,665	$610.57	$610.57
The Missionary Church	1997	31,197	47,550	$50,854,462	$1,630.11	$1,069.49
Moravian Church in America (Unitas Fratrum), Northern Province	1997	21,108	27,181	$13,704,238	$649.24	$504.18
National Association of Free Will Baptists	1997	210,305	210,305	$81,700,000	$388.48	$388.48
North American Baptist Conference	1997	43,850	43,850	$45,387,274	$1,035.06	$1,035.06
The Orthodox Presbyterian Church	1997	15,072	21,765	$24,057,749	$1,596.19	$1,105.34
Presbyterian Church in America	1997	224,154	279,549	$374,861,599	$1,672.34	$1,340.95
Presbyterian Church (U.S.A.)	1997	2,609,191	3,610,753	$2,409,546,564	$923.48	$667.33
Primitive Methodist Church in the U.S.A.	1997	4,917	6,588	$3,913,068	$795.82	$593.97
Reformed Church in America	1997	185,074	305,476	$185,226,508	$1,000.82	$606.35
Reformed Church in the United States	1997	3,169	4,246	$2,768,134	$873.50	$651.94
Reformed Presbyterian Church of North America	1997	4,363	6,105	$6,446,899	$1,477.63	$1,056.00
Reorganized Church of Jesus Christ of Latter Day Saints	1997	248,450	248,523	$30,601,085	$123.53	$123.49
Seventh-day Adventist Church	1997	825,654	825,654	$802,224,678	$971.62	$971.62
Southern Baptist Convention	1997	15,891,514	15,891,514	$7,029,110,046	$442.32	$442.32
United Church of Christ	1997	1,438,181	1,438,181	$721,356,966	$501.58	$501.58
The United Methodist Church	1996	8,496,047	8,496,047	$3,744,602,223	$440.76	$440.76

Finances—United States Churches (*continued*)

CONGREGATIONAL FINANCES			BENEVOLENCES			
Total Congregation Contributions	Per Capita Full or Confirmed Members	Per Capita Inclusive Members	Total Benevolences	Per Capita Full or Confirmed Members	Per Capita Inclusive Members	Benevolences as a Percentage
$127,642,950	$1,366.42	$1,366.42	$20,462,435	$219.05	$219.05	14%
$1,731,806,133	$450.50	$334.00	$201,115,441	$52.32	$38.79	10%
$8,937,103	$543.49	$404.43	$1,150,419	$69.96	$52.06	11%
$7,017,588	$1,613,98	$1,510.46	$2,039,740	$469.12	$439.03	23%
$78,687,325	$1,177.44	$1,080.37	$12,261,465	$183.48	$168.35	13%
$28,093,944	$388.43	$388.43	$1,780,851	$24.62	$24.62	6%
$50,832,814	$998.39	$618.93	$15,018,667	$194.98	$182.86	23%
$2,472,409	$991.34	$465.53	$2,846,724	$1,141.43	$536.01	54%
$2,652,000	$174.47	$156.92	$4,139,000	$272.30	$244.91	61%
$887,928,255	$455.02	$341.11	$110,520,917	$56.64	$42.46	11%
$76,669,365	$842.90	$842.90	$27,812,549	$305.77	$305.77	27%
$14,690,904	$$422.99	$422.99	$6,514,761	$187.58	$187.58	31%
$42,915.770	$1,375.64	$902.54	$7,938,692	$254.47	$166.95	16%
$12,555,760	$594.83	$461.93	$1,148,478	$54.41	$42.25	8%
$66,900,000	$318.11	$318.11	$14,800,000	$70.37	$70.37	18%
$37,401,175	$852.93	$852.93	$7,986,099	$182.12	$182.12	18%
$20,090,259	$1,332.95	$923.05	$3,967,490	$263.24	$182.29	16%
$304,848,405	$1,360.00	$1,090.50	$70,013,194	$312.34	$250.45	19%
$2,064,789,378	$791.35	$571.84	$344,757,186	$132.13	$95.48	14%
$3,529,806	$717.88	$535.79	$383,262	$77.95	$58.18	10%
$149,935,171	$810.14	$490.82	$35,291,337	$190.69	$115.53	19%
$2,194,612	$692.53	$516.87	$573,522	$180.98	$135.07	21%
$5,792,856	$1,327.72	$948.87	$654,043	$149.91	$107.13	10%
$15,921,761	$64.,08	$64.07	$14,769,324	$59.45	$59.43	48%
$249,591,109	$302.30	$302.30	$552,633,569	$669.33	$669.33	69%
$6,098,933,137	$383.79	$383.79	$930,176,909	$58.53	$58.53	13%
$651,176,773	$452.78	$452.78	$70,180,193	$48.80	$48.80	10%
$3,135,982,182	$369.11	$369.11	$608,710,041	$71.65	$71.65	16%

Selected Statistics of Church

Religious Body	Year	Full or Confirmed Members	Inclusive Members	TOTAL CONTRIBUTIONS		
				Total Contributions	Per Capita Full or Confirmed Members	Per Capita Inclusive Members
Unity of the Brethren	1996	2,543	3,230	$208,181	$81.86	$64.45
The Wesleyan Church	1997	111,771	119,107	$175,811,302	$1,572.96	$1,476.08
Wisconsin Evangelical Lutheran Synod	1997	315,355	411,295	$216,578,830	$686.78	$526.58

Summary Statitistics

Nation	Number Reporting	Full or Confirmed Members	Inclusive Members	TOTAL CONTRIBUTIONS		
				Total Contributions	Per Capita Full or Confirmed Members	Per Capita Inclusive Members
United States	58	44,724,732	49,980,841	$29,913,914,465	$557.05	$498.47
Canada	28	1,328,619	2,497,351	$719,652,634	$541.65	$288.17

Finances—United States Churches (continued)

CONGREGATIONAL FINANCES			BENEVOLENCES			
Total Congregation Contributions	Per Capita Full or Confirmed Members	Per Capita Inclusive Members	Total Benevolences	Per Capita Full or Confirmed Members	Per Capita Inclusive Members	Benevolences as a Percentage
$161,307	$63.43	$49.94	$46,874	$18.43	$14.51	23%
$148,273,193	$1,326.58	$1,244.87	$27,539,109	$246.38	$231.20	16%
$164,256,655	$520.86	$399.36	$52,322,175	$165.92	$127.21	24%

# of Church Finances

CONGREGATIONAL FINANCES			BENEVOLENCES			
Total Congregation Contributions	Per Capita Full or Confirmed Members	Per Capita Inclusive Members	Total Belevolences	Per Capita Full or Confirmed Members	Per Capita Inclusive Members	Benevolences as a Percentage of Total Contributions
$21,124,174,647	$472.32	$422.65	$3,792,486,358	$84.80	$75.88	15%
$572,628,391	$431.00	$229.29	$146,915,739	$110.58	$58.83	20%

Trends in Seminary Enrollment

Data Provided by The Association
of Theological Schools (ATS)
In the United States and Canada

Table 1: ATS total student enrollment figures include the number of individuals enrolled in degree programs as well as persons enrolled in non-degree programs of study. Growth in total enrollment is a function of both increased enrollment in the seminaries and the increased number of schools admitted to ATS membership. The number of students studying at ATS institutions has remained relatively stable, increasing only 3.13% since 1993.

Table 1 Number of Member Schools from 1988 to 1997

Year	Number of Schools	Total Enrollment	Canada Head Count	FTE	United States Head Count	FTE	By Membership Accredited	Non-Accredited
1988	207	55,746	3,995	2,679	51,751	34,827	51,863	4,063
1989	205	56,178	4,142	2,679	52,036	35,013	52,949	3,229
1990	211	59,003	4,053	2,636	54,950	37,590	54,052	4,951
1991	211	59,897	4,648	2,631	55,249	36,456	55,028	4,869
1992	220	63,484	4,897	2,999	58,587	39,554	57,784	5,700
1993	219	63,429	5,040	3,150	58,389	39,506	57,823	6,606
1994	226	65,089	5,241	3,212	59,848	40,293	60,490	4,599
1995	224	64,480	5,203	3,267	59,277	39,834	59,813	4,667
1996	233	65,697	5,568	3,304	60,129	40,170	60,587	5,110
1997	229	65,416	5,544	3,225	69,872	40,077	61,553	3,863

Table 2: ATS computes enrollment both by the total number of individual students (Head Count) and the equivalent of full-time students (FTE). If all students were enrolled full-time, the Head Count number and the full-time equivalency number would be the same. The FTE is calculated by dividing the total number of credits required for the degree by the number of semesters prescribed for degree duration to determine the average academic load. The total of credit hours taken by all students in a given degree program in a semester is then divided by the average academic load. During the last five years, full time equivalent enrollment as a percentage of head count enrollment has decreased slightly, which indicates a rise in the number of part-time students.

Table 2 Head County and FTE for all Member Schools 1988 to 1997

Year	Head Count	% Change	FTE	% Change	FTE % of Head Count
1988	55,746	-0.04	37,506	-2.15	67.3%
1989	56,178	0.77	37,681	0.47	67.1%
1990	59,003	5.03	40,226	6.75	68.2%
1991	659,897	1.52	39,987	-2.83	65.3%
1992	63,484	5.99	42,553	8.87	67.0%
1993	63,429	0.09	42,656	0.24	67.2%
1994	65,089	2.62	43,505	1.99	66.8%
1995	64,480	-0.94	43,101	-0.93	66.8%
1996	65,697	1.89	43,475	0.87	66.2%
1997	65,416	-0.43	43,302	0.40	66.2%

Table 3: ATA member schools offer a variety of degree programs, as reflected in Table 3. Table 3 displays enrollment by categories of degree programs. The Master of Divinity (M.Div.) degree is the normative degree to prepare persons for ordained ministry and for general pastoral and religious leadership responsibilities in congregations. Enrollment in the M.Div. degree has increased slightly (3.7%) from 1993 to 1997. The largest enrollment increase, over the same five-year period, has been in the Master of Arts in a variety of specialized ministry areas (25.76%). This is followed by an increase of 25.85% in the Master of Pastoral Studies degree program. The number of students enrolled in Advanced Theological Research programs has increased over the past five years, largely due to rising Ph.D./Th.D. enrollment, which is up 9.73% since 1993, and an increase in the number of institutions within the Association that grant these advanced degrees.

Table 3 Total Enrollment By Degree Categories
(New categories based on new accreditation standards (adopted 1996)

Year	Basic Ministerial Leadership (M.Div.)	(Non-M.Div.)	General Theological Studies	Advanced Ministerial Leadership	Advanced Theological Research	Others
1987	26,977	5,025	5,175	6,590	4,062	7,516
1988	26,581	5,131	5,423	6,511	4,203	7,897
1989	25,954	5,080	5,485	7,004	4,186	8,469
1990	25,615	5,284	6,144	7,417	5,046	9,497
1991	25,710	5,805	6,105	7,598	5,044	9,635
1992	26,956	5,812	6,872	7,961	5,036	10,847
1993	27,264	6,536	7,131	8,302	5,157	9,039
1994	27,240	6,891	7,229	7,841	5,330	10,558
1995	27,497	6,964	7,211	8,233	5,302	9,273
1996	28,035	7,474	7,157	8,375	5,499	9,157
1997	28,283	7,463	7,048	8,250	5,391	8,981

Table 4: In 1997, women constituted 33.1% of the total enrollment in all ATS schools. When ATS first began gathering enrollment data by gender in 1972, women represented 10.2% of enrollment. Only once in the past 25 years has the number of women students decreased from one year to the next, that being in 1993, with a 0.65% decrease. In 1997, women constituted 29% of the total Master of Divinity enrollment.

Table 4 Women Student Head Count Enrollment 1988 to 1997

Year	Number of Students	% Annual Increase	% of Total Enrollment
1988	16,326	0.00	29.29%
1989	16,525	1.20	29.42%
1990	17,498	5.56	29.66%
1991	18,188	3.79	30.37%
1992	19,856	8.40	31.28%
1993	19,727	-0.65	31.10%
1994	20,564	4.07	31.59%
1995	20,795	1.12	32.25%
1996	21,523	3.50	32.76%
1997	21,652	0.60	33.10%

Table 5, 6, 7: Enrollment of racial/ethnic minority students in ATS schools has grown from 6.3% of total enroll-ment in 1977 to 19.1% of total enrollment in 1997. Between 1993 and 1997, the number of African American stu-dents has increased by 11.08%; Hispanic students by 7.32%; and Pacific/Asian American students by 25.39%. Tables 5, 6, and 7 show the number of African American, Hispanic and Pacific/Asian American students enrolled by year. The Asian student population was the only group that had an increase in all degree programs for both men and women. The only race or ethnic group that experienced an overall decrease was the White enrollment, down 2.8% over five years, mostly due to a 6.06% decrease in White men students. The percentage of racial/ethnic minority students in ATS schools continues to be smaller than the percentage of racial/ethnic minority persons in the North American population as a whole.

Table 5 African American Student Head Count Enrollment 1988 to 1997

Year	Number of Students	% Annual Increase	% of Total Enrollment
1988	3,660	8.72	6.57%
1989	3,925	6.75	6.99%
1990	4,265	7.97	7.23%
1991	4,658	8.44	7.78%
1992	5,558	16.19	8.75%
1993	5,223	-6.41	8.23%
1994	5,526	5.48	8.49%
1995	5,698	3.11	8.84%
1996	5,550	-2.60	8.45%
1997	5,802	4.54	8.87%

Table 6 Hispanic Student Head Count Enrollment 1988 to 1997

Year	Number of Students	% Annual Increase	% of Total Enrollment
1988	1,415	1.13	2.54%
1989	1,485	4.71	2.64%
1990	1,912	22.33	3.24%
1991	1,626	-17.59	2.71%
1992	1,689	3.73	2.66%
1993	1,790	5.64	2.82%
1994	1,799	0.50	2.76%
1995	1,817	1.00	2.82%
1996	1,792	-1.38	2.73%
1997	1,921	7.20	2.94%

Table 7 Pacific/Asian American Student Head Count Enrollment 1988 to 1997

Year	Number of Students	% Annual Increase	% of Total Enrollment
1988	1,963	13.75	3.06%
1989	2,062	4.80	3.67%
1990	2,437	15.39	4.13%
1991	2,649	8.00	4.42%
1992	3,142	15.69	4.95%
1993	3,631	13.47	5.72%
1994	3,876	6.32	5.95%
1995	4,245	9.52	6.58%
1996	4,496	5.91	6.84%
1997	4,553	1.27	6.96%

IV

A CALENDAR FOR CHURCH USE

1999–2002

This Calendar presents for a four-year period the major days of religious observances for Christians, Jews, Baha'is, and Muslims; and, within the Christian community, major dates observed by Roman Catholic, Orthodox, Episcopal, and Lutheran churches. Within each of these communions many other days of observance, such as saints' days, exist, but only those regarded as major are listed. Dates of interest to many Protestant communions are also included.

In the Orthodox dates, immovable observances are listed in accordance with the Gregorian calendar. Movable dates (those depending on the date of Easter) often will differ from Western days, since Paschal (Easter) in the Orthodox communions does not always fall on the same day as in the Western churches. For Orthodox churches that use the old Julian calendar, observances are held thirteen days later than listed here.

For Jews and Muslims, who follow differing lunar calendars, the dates of major observances are translated into Gregorian dates. Since the actual beginning of a new month in the Islamic calendar is determined by the appearance of the new moon, the corresponding dates given here on the Gregorian calendar may vary slightly. Following the lunar calendar, Muslim dates fall eleven days earlier each year on the Gregorian calendar, thus the month of Ramadan for 1998 actually begins in 1997.

(Note: "RC" stands for Roman Catholic, "O" for Orthodox, "E" for Episcopal, "L" for Lutheran, "ECU" for Ecumenical, "M" for Muslim)

Event	1999	2000	2001	2002
New Year's Day (RC-Solemnity of Mary: O-Circumcision of Jesus Christ; E-Feast of Holy Name; L-Name of Jesus)	Jan 01	Jan 01	Jan 01	Jan 01
Epiphany (Armenian Christmas)	Jan 06	Jan 06	Jan 06	Jan 06
Feast Day of St. John the Baptist (Armenian)	Jan 13	Jan 13	Jan 13	Jan 13
First Sunday After Epiphany (Feast of the Baptism of Our Lord)	Jan 10	Jan 09	Jan 07	Jan 13
Week of Prayer for Christian Unity (ECU)	Jan 18 to Jan 25	Jan 18 to Jan 25	Jan 18 to Jan 25	Jan 18 to Jan 25
Ecumenical Sunday (ECU)	Jan 24	Jan 23	Jan 21	Jan 20
Week of Prayer for Christian Unity, Canada (ECU)	Jan 18 to Jan 25	Jan 24 to Jan 31	Jan 22 to Jan 29	Jan 21 to Jan 28
First Day of the Month of Ramadan (M)	Dec 09	Nov 28	Nov 17	Nov 6
Presentation of Jesus in the Temple (O-The Meeting of Our Lord and Savior Jesus Christ)	Feb 02	Feb 02	Feb 02	Feb 02
Brotherhood Week (Interfaith)	Feb 21 to Feb 27	Feb 20 to Feb 26	Feb 18 to Feb 24	Feb 17 to Feb 23
Eid al- Fitr (M) (Festival of the End of Ramadan, celebrated on the first day of the month of Shawwal)	Jan. 19	Jan 08	Dec 27	Dec. 17
Ash Wednesday (Western Churches)	Feb 17	Mar 08	Feb 28	Feb 13
Easter Lent Begins (Eastern Orthodox)	Feb 22	Mar 13	Feb 26	Mar 18
World Day of Prayer (ECU)	Mar 05	Mar 03	Mar 04	Mar 01
Fasting Season begins (Baha'i, 19 days)	Mar 02	Mar 02	Mar 02	Mar 02
Purim (Jewish)	Mar 02	Mar 21	Mar 09	Feb 26
Joseph, Husband of Mary (RC, E, L)	Mar 19	Mar 19	Mar 19	Mar 19
Feast of Naw-Ruz (Baha'i New Year)	Mar 21	Mar 21	Mar 21	Mar 21
The Annunciation (O) (L-Apr 01; RC, E-Apr 08)	Mar 25	Mar 25	Mar 25	Mar 25

365

Event	1999	2000	2001	2002
Holy Week (Western Churches)	Mar 28 to Apr 03	Apr 16 to Apr 22	Apr 08 to Apr 15	Mar 24 to Mar 31
First Day of the Month of Muharram (M) (Beginning of Muslim Liturgical Year)	Apr 17	Apr 06	Mar 26	Mar 15
Holy Thursday (Western Churches)	Apr 01	Apr 20	Apr 12	Mar 28
First Day of Passover (Jewish, 8 days)	Apr 01	Apr 20	Apr 08	Apr 03
Good Friday (Friday of the Passion of Our Lord (Western Churches)	Apr 02	Apr 21	Apr 13	Mar 29
Easter (Western Churches)	Apr 04	Apr 23	Apr 15	Mar 31
Palm Sunday (O)	Apr 04	Apr 23	Apr 08	Apr 28
Holy Week (O)	Apr 05 to Apr 09	Apr 24 to Apr 28	Apr 08 to Apr 15	Apr 28 to May 05
Holy Thursday (O)	Apr 08	Apr 2	Apr 12	May 02
Holy (Good) Friday, Burial of Jesus Christ (O)	Apr 09	Apr 28	Apr 13	May 03
Paschal (Orthodox Easter)	Apr 11	Apr 30	Apr 15	May 05
Feast of Ridvan (Baha'i) (Declaration of Baha'u'llah)	Apr 21 to May 02	Apr 21 to May 02	Apr 21 to May 02	Apr 21 to May 02
Eid al-Adha (M) (festival of Sacrifice at time of annual Pilgrimage to Mecca)	Mar 28	Mar 16	Mar 6	Feb 23
National Day of Prayer	May 06	May 04	May 03	May 02
May Fellowship Day (ECU)	May 07	May 05	May 04	May 03
Rural Life Sunday (ECU)	May 09	May 14	May 13	May 12
Ascension Day (Eastern Churches)	May 13	Jun 01	May 24	May 09
Ascension Day (O)	May 20	Jun 08	May 24	Jun 13
Declaration of the Bab (Baha'i)	May 23	May 23	May 23	May 23
First Day of Shavuout (Jewish, 2 days)	May 21	Jun 09	May 28	May 17
Pentecost (Whitsunday) (Western Churches)	May 23	Jun 11	Jun 03	May 19
Ascension of Baha'u'llah (Baha'i')	May 29	May 29	May 29	May 29
Visitation of the Blessed Virgin Mary (RC, E, L)	May 31	May 31	May 31	May 31
Pentecost (O)	May 30	Jun 18	Jun 03	Jun 23
Holy Trinity (RC, E, L)	May 30	Jun 18	Jun 10	May 26
Corpus Christi (RC)	Jun 06	Jun 25	Jun 17	June 02
Sacred Heart of Jesus (RC)	Jun 11	Jun 30	Jun 22	June 07
Nativity of St. John the Baptist (RC, E, L)	Jun 24	Jun 24	Jun 24	June 24
Saint Peter and Saint Paul, Apostles of Christ (O)	Jun 29	Jun 29	Jun 29	Jun 29
Feast Day of the Twelve Apostles of Christ (O)	Jun 30	Jun 30	Jun 30	Jun 30
Martyrdom of the Bab (Baha'i)	Jun 09	Jun 09	Jun 09	Jun 09
Mawlid an-Nabi (M) (Anniversary of Prophet Muhammed's Birthday)	Jun 26	Jun 15	Jun 04	May 24
Transfiguration of the Lord (RC, O, E)	Aug 06	Aug 06	Aug 06	Aug 06
Feast of the Blessed Virgin Mary (E) (RC-Assumption of Blessed Mary the Virgin; O-Falling Asleep (Domition) of the Blessed Virgin)	Aug 15	Aug 15	Aug 15	Aug 15
The Birth of the Blessed Virgin (RC, O)	Sep 08	Sep 08	Sep 08	Sep 08
Holy Cross Day (O' Adoration of the Holy Cross; RC-Triumph of the Cross)	Sep 14	Sep 14	Sep 14	Sep 14
First Day of Rosh Hashanah (Jewish, 2 days)	Sep 11	Sep 30	Sep 18	Sep 07
Yom Kippur (Jewish)	Sep 20	Oct 09	Sep 27	Sep 16
First Day of Sukkot (Jewish, 7 days)	Sep 25	Oct 14	Oct 02	Sep 21
World Communion Sunday (ECU)	Oct 03	Oct 01	Oct 07	Oct 06
Laity Sunday (ECU)	Oct 10	Oct 08	Oct 14	Oct 13
Thanksgiving Day (Canada)	Oct 11	Oct 09	Oct 08	Oct 14
Shemini Atzeret (Jewish)	Oct 02	Oct 21	Oct 09	Oct 28
Simhat Torah (Jewish)	Oct 03	Oct 22	Oct 10	Oct 29
Birth of the Bab (Baha'i)	Oct 20	Oct 20	Oct 20	Oct 20
Reformation Sunday (L)	Oct 31	Oct 29	Oct 28	Oct 27
Reformation Day (L)	Oct 31	Oct 31	Oct 31	Oct. 31
All Saints Day (RC, E, L)	Nov 01	Nov 01	Nov 01	Nov 01
World Community Day (ECU)	Nov 05	Nov 03	Nov 02	Nov 01

Event	1999	2000	2001	2002
Birth of Baha'u'llah (Baha'i)	Nov 12	Nov 12	Nov 12	Nov 12
Bible Sunday (ECU)	Nov 21	Nov 09	Nov 18	Nov 17
Presentation of the Blessed Virgin Mary in the Temple (also Presentation of the Theotokos) (O)	Nov 21	Nov 21	Nov 21	Nov 21
Last Sunday After Pentecost (RC, L-Feast of Christ the King)	Nov 21	Nov 19	Nov 25	Nov 24
Thanksgiving Sunday (U.S.)	Nov 21	Nov 19	Nov 25	Nov 24
The Day of the Covenant (Baha'i	Nov 26	Nov 26	Nov 26	Nov 26
Thanksgiving Day (U.S.)	Nov 25	Nov 23	Nov 22	Nov 28
Ascension of 'Abdu'l-Baha (Baha'i)	Nov 28	Nov 28	Nov 28	Nov 28
Feast Day of St. Andrew the Apostle (RC, O, E, L)	Nov 30	Nov 30	Nov 30	Nov 30
First Sunday of Advent	Nov 28	Dec 03	Dec 02	Dec 01
First Day of Hanukkah (Jewish, 8 days)	Dec 04	Dec 22	Dec 10	Nov 30
Immaculate Conception of the Blessed Virgin May (RC)	Dec 08	Dec 08	Dec 08	Dec 08
Fourth Sunday of Advent (Sunday before Christmas)	Dec 19	Dec 24	Dec 23	Dec 22
Christmas (Except Armenian)	Dec 25	Dec 25	Dec 25	Dec 25

CALENDAR

367

V

INDEXES

Organizations

INDEX

INDEX

373

374

Individuals

INDEX

381

382

INDEX

INDEX

383

390

INDEX

391

393

INDEX

INDEX

399

INDEX

400

401

404

INDEX

405

INDEX

INDEX

407

95649

280.5
Y3
1999

NO TE LO TOMES DE FORMA PERSONAL